Concise Readings
in Philosophy

CONCISE READINGS IN PHILOSOPHY

William H. Halverson
THE OHIO STATE UNIVERSITY

Random House New York

First Edition

987654321

Library of Congress Cataloging in Publication Data

Main entry under title:

Concise readings in philosophy.

  Includes index.
  1. Philosophy—Addresses, essays, lectures.
I. Halverson, William H.
B21.C79   190   80-23084
ISBN 0-394-32551-6

Manufactured in the United States of America

To the memory of George Finger Thomas,
1899–1977, under whose patient tutelage I
first learned to appreciate the primary sources

Preface

The original concept for this anthology was developed several years ago, but for various reasons it was not brought to fruition until now. According to that concept, *Concise Readings in Philosophy* was to be planned in strict accordance with the following criteria:

1. The problems treated shall include all those most frequently covered in introductory "problems of philosophy" courses at colleges and universities.
2. The readings selected for each problem shall provide a balanced treatment of that problem. Every major position on each problem shall be represented by a competent advocate of that position.
3. The most historically important treatments of each problem shall be included—for example, Kant on a priori knowledge, Hume on induction, Aquinas on the existence of God, Augustine and Leibniz on the problem of evil, and so on.
4. So far as possible, all the major figures in Western philosophy shall be represented by at least one selection.
5. Each individual selection shall meet three important tests: (1) *readability* —it must be capable of being understood by beginning students in philosophy; (2) *effectiveness in advocating the position in question*—no position shall be allowed to suffer merely as a result of being poorly represented; and (3) *brevity*—it shall waste no words in stating the case for the position being presented.

In carrying out the above plan, I have made as few compromises as possible. I have not knowingly compromised with respect to readability, effectiveness, or brevity. But, in order not to do so, I have, in some cases, been obliged to omit a philosopher whom I would like to have included in favor of another whose writing more adequately fit my criteria. I have not hesitated to edit out passages that appear to obscure rather than to elucidate the position in question. In all such cases, the omission is indicated by the usual elliptical dots.

Concise Readings in Philosophy is intended for use either as a supplementary text—that is, a companion volume of primary reading materials—or as the sole text in an introductory course. The sequence of topics follows that of my book *A Concise Introduction to Philosophy,* Fourth Edition, but the anthology would serve equally well as a companion volume in courses using any other text that employs a systematic approach to the problems of philosophy.

In order to facilitate the use of *Concise Readings in Philosophy* as an independent text, I have written introductions for each of the fourteen sections into which the book is divided. In these introductions, I attempt to state clearly the problem of each section and to identify the principal alternatives available with respect to that problem. Each reading is also preceded by a biographical note on the author and a brief introductory summary that is intended to assist the reader in "placing" the selection in relation to the problem being discussed.

Concise Readings in Philosophy could not have come into being without the help and cooperation of many people to whom I express my sincere thanks. Dr. David Mellick spent countless hours helping me identify readings appropriate for inclusion in this volume, and I am grateful for his help. The original publishers of the materials reprinted here were uniformly cooperative in granting permission to reprint; appropriate acknowledgments appear elsewhere in this volume. I wish also to express my thanks to David Nichols for the translation of the passages from Nietzsche, to Carol Halverson for the translations of Pascal and Sartre and for extensive research assistance, to Susan Mahler for typing the first draft, to Doris Coon for coordinating the typing of several later versions of the manuscript, and to Marolyn Halverson for coordinating the transcription of the anthologized materials and assembling the final manuscript. All these people, as well as the Random House readers and editors whose identities are unknown to me, have played a sufficiently large role in the creation of this volume to warrant a certain possessiveness toward the finished product.

Finally, as I write these words, I am remembering my late teacher and friend, Dr. George F. Thomas, who, in his classes at Princeton many years ago, enriched my understanding of many of the philosophers represented in this anthology. His acquaintance with the writings of Western philosophers was both broad and deep, and I would have cherished his counsel in the preparation of this volume. Lacking that, I nonetheless acknowledge my lasting debt to him, and dedicate this book to his memory with the hope that he would have approved of most, if not all, of the choices that I have made.

W. H. H.
Columbus, Ohio
October 1980

Contents

Contents

Concise Readings
in Philosophy

PART I

A Prologue to Philosophy

Philosophy, it has been said, begins in wonder. One is born at a particular time and in a particular place, and one is taught as a child to think, speak, and act in ways that are acceptable to people who are living at that time and in that place. We grow up thinking that all good and decent and right-thinking people must think and speak and act as we do—or, what is even more likely, we simply presuppose these things without consciously thinking them. We take them for granted.

But if we are lucky there comes a magic moment when we ask, "Is it really so?" That is the moment of wonder. That is the moment when, for us, philosophy is born.

It is a marvelous question. It can be asked about anything that is put forward as the truth, whether in science, religion, politics, ethics, or just plain common sense. And when it is asked, it deserves an honest answer.

It can also be an unpopular question. Some people feel strongly about certain things that they hold to be true and do not want even to entertain the possibility that they might be wrong. The flat-earth mentality, whether it be exhibited in defense of truth or of falsehood, is the principal enemy of philosophy because it attempts to stifle that wonder in the absence of which philosophy cannot survive.

About half of what we call philosophy revolves around this question, "Is it really so?" This half constitutes what is called the *critical* task of philosophy.

There is a second moment of wonder that inspires all philosophy, and that is the moment in which the question is asked, "How does it all hang together?" Happily, as one asks the critical question again and again, one sometimes concludes that certain truth claims do, indeed, appear to stand

1

up under close scrutiny. "Yes," we may say, "it really is so: People *are* morally responsible for their actions under such-and-such conditions," or perhaps, "Yes, it really is so: Every event *does* have a cause." But if we have our wits about us we may then go on to ask, "Now if every event has a cause, including my decision to act in such-and-such a way, how can I be responsible for that decision and the action that follows from it? How do these two things hang together?"

The attempt to figure out "how things hang together" constitutes what is called the *constructive* task of philosophy. Its ultimate goal is to construct an all-inclusive picture of reality in which every element of our knowledge, and every dimension of our experience, finds its proper place.

Philosophers—which is to say, people whose lives are dominated by the sense of wonder—have been at this dual task for many years. And even as they have been inspired by their sense of wonder, so have they nourished that same sense among those who came after them. They have asked many more questions than they have been able to answer, but that is to be expected: wonder knows no bounds; it is never assuaged. Indeed, the unanswered questions left behind by the philosophers of the past—from Socrates, Plato, and Aristotle to all those who followed—are important parts of the priceless legacy that they have given us.

1

PLATO (427–347 B.C.)

The Apology of Socrates

So far as anyone knows, Socrates (469–399 B.C.) wrote nothing that has been preserved. Everything known about him and his thought has been learned from others, notably Plato. But in the dialogues of Plato, we often *feel* as if we are reading the

From Plato, *Apology of Socrates,* in *Dialogues of Plato,* trans. Benjamin Jowett (New York: Colonial Press, 1900), pp. 11–36.

words of Socrates because he is so often the main character, and a consistent personality shines through, with a ring of authenticity. It is impossible to know how many of the ideas attributed to Socrates in the Socratic dialogues really are his. Plato does not tell us, and there is little else available to help us decide.

The *Apology,* in any case, is almost certainly a reasonably faithful account of Socrates' actual words as he attempted to defend himself before the Athenian Court. The year is 399 B.C. Socrates, already an old man of seventy, has been haled into court on charges of impiety and corruption of youth. As the *Apology* begins, Socrates' accusers have just completed their case, and now it is his turn to speak. He speaks —eloquently, wittily, sometimes sarcastically—but to no avail. In the end, he is found guilty and is condemned to die.

The trial and execution of Socrates made him into a kind of secular saint, a martyr to the cause of philosophy. The spirit of Socrates—questioning, probing, cross-examining, being concerned only for truth and virtue, refusing to barter his principles for his life, tenaciously following the argument wherever it might lead, courageously accepting death at the hands of his enemies—hovers over Western philosophy like a mystical presence. He epitomizes the earnest questioning of received truths, the "Is it really so?" that lies at the heart of all philosophy. He never ceased to wonder. On the day of his execution, he wondered about, and discussed at great length with his friends, the question, Is the soul immortal?

The *Apology* should be read, then, not for the details of the arguments it contains, but for the picture it presents of a noted philosopher pursuing the critical philosophical task. Let Socrates be a symbol of the critical, questioning side of philosophy, and let the reigning orthodoxy of ancient Athens—defended with such devastating consequences by Socrates' accusers—be a symbol of the received truths of any age toward which philosophy may turn its questioning gaze. Then, you may understand how it is that the *Apology* has served as a continuing source of inspiration to philosophers for over two thousand years.

How you have felt, O men of Athens, at hearing the speeches of my accusers, I cannot tell; but I know that their persuasive words almost made me forget who I was, such was the effect of them; and yet they have hardly spoken a word of truth. But many as their falsehoods were, there was one of them which quite amazed me: I mean when they told you to be upon your guard, and not to let yourself be deceived by the force of my eloquence. They ought to have been ashamed of saying this, because they were sure to be detected as soon as I opened my lips and displayed my deficiency; they certainly did appear to be most shameless in saying this, unless by the force of eloquence they mean the force of truth; for then I do indeed admit that I am eloquent. But in how different a way from theirs! Well, as I was saying, they have hardly uttered a word, or not more than a word, of truth; but you shall hear from me the whole truth: not, however, delivered after their manner, in a set oration duly ornamented with words and phrases. No, indeed! but I shall use the words and arguments which occur to me at the moment; for I am certain that this is right, and that at my time of life I ought not to be appearing before you, O men of Athens, in the character of a juvenile orator: let no one expect this of me. And I must beg of you to grant me one favor, which is this—if you hear me using the same words in my defence which I have been in the habit of using, and which most of you may have heard in the *agora,* and at the tables of the money-changers, or anywhere else, I would ask you not to be surprised at this, and not to interrupt me. For I am more than seventy years of age, and this is the first time that I have ever appeared in a court of law, and I am quite a stranger to the ways of the place; and therefore I would have you regard me as if I were really a stranger, whom you would excuse if he spoke in his native tongue, and after the fashion of his country: that I think is not an unfair request. Never mind the manner, which may or may not be good; but think only of the justice of my cause, and give heed to that: let the judge decide justly and the speaker speak truly.

And first, I have to reply to the older charges and to my first accusers, and then I will go on to the later ones. For I have had many accusers, who accused me of old, and their false charges have continued during many years: and I am more afraid of them than of Anytus and his associates, who are dangerous, too, in their own way. But far more dangerous are these, who began when you were children, and took possession of your minds with their falsehoods, telling of one Socrates, a wise man, who speculated about the heaven above, and searched into the earth beneath, and made the worse appear the better cause. These are the accusers whom I dread; for they are the circulators of this rumor, and their hearers are too apt to fancy that speculators of this sort do not believe in the gods. And they are many, and their charges against me are of ancient date, and they made them in days when you were impressible—in childhood, or perhaps in youth—and the cause when heard went by default, for there was none to answer. And hardest of all, their names I do not know and cannot tell; unless in the chance case of a comic poet. But the main body of these slanderers who from envy and malice have wrought upon you—and there are some of them who are convinced themselves, and impart their convictions to others— all these, I say, are most difficult to deal with; for I cannot have them up here, and examine them, and therefore I must simply fight with shadows in my own defence, and examine when there is no one who answers. I will ask you then to assume with me, as I was saying, that my opponents are of two kinds—one recent, the other ancient; and I hope that you will see the propriety of my answering the latter first, for these accusations you heard long before the others, and much oftener.

Well, then, I will make my defence, and I will endeavor in the short time which is allowed to do away with this evil opinion of me which you have held for such a long time; and I hope that I may succeed, if this be well for you and me, and that my words may find favor with you. But I know that to accomplish this is not easy—I quite see the nature of the task. Let the event be as God wills: in obedience to the law I make my defence.

I will begin at the beginning, and ask what the accusation is which has given rise to this slander of me, and which has encouraged Meletus to proceed against me. What do the slanderers say? They shall be my prosecutors, and I will sum up their words in an affidavit: "Socrates is an evildoer, and a curious person, who searches into things under the earth and in heaven, and he makes the worse appear the better cause; and he teaches the aforesaid doctrines to others." That is the nature of the accusation, and that is what you have seen yourselves in the comedy of Aristophanes, who has introduced a man whom he calls Socrates, going about and saying that he can walk in the air, and talking a deal of nonsense concerning matters of which I do not pretend to know either much or little—not that I mean to say anything disparaging of anyone who is a student of natural philosophy. I should be very sorry if Meletus could lay that to my charge. But the simple truth is, O Athenians, that I have nothing to do with these studies. Very many of those here present are witnesses to the truth of this, and to them I appeal. Speak then, you who have heard me, and tell your neighbors whether any of you have ever known me hold forth in few words or in many upon matters of this sort. . . . You hear their answer. And from what they say of this you will be able to judge of the truth of the rest.

As little foundation is there for the report that I am a teacher, and take money; that is no more true than the other. Although, if a man is able to teach, I honor him for being paid. There is Gorgias of Leontium, and Prodicus of Ceos, and Hippias of Elis, who go the round of the cities, and are able to persuade the young men to leave their own citizens, by whom they might be taught for nothing, and come to them, whom they not only pay, but are thankful if they may be allowed to pay them. There is actually a Parian philosopher residing in Athens, of whom I have heard; and I came to hear of him in this way: I met a man who has spent a world of money on the Sophists, Callias the son of Hipponicus, and knowing that he had sons, I asked him: "Callias," I said, "if your two sons were foals or calves, there would be no difficulty in finding someone to put over them; we should hire a trainer of horses or a farmer probably who would improve and perfect them in their own proper virtue and excellence; but as they are human beings, whom are you thinking of placing over them? Is there anyone who understands human and political virtue? You must have thought about this as you have sons; is there anyone?" "There is," he said. "Who is he?" said I, "and of what country? and what does he charge?" "Evenus the Parian," he replied; "he is the man, and his charge is five minæ." Happy is Evenus, I said to myself, if he really has this wisdom, and teaches at such a modest charge. Had I the same, I should have been very proud and conceited; but the truth is that I have no knowledge of the kind, O Athenians.

I dare say that someone will ask the question, "Why is this, Socrates, and what is the origin of these accusations of you: for there must have been something strange which you have been doing? All this great fame and talk about you would never have arisen if you had been like other men: tell us, then, why this is, as we should be sorry to judge hastily of you." Now I regard this as a fair challenge, and I will endeavor to explain to you the origin of this name of "wise," and of this evil fame. Please to attend them. And although some of you may think that I am joking, I declare that I will tell you the entire truth. Men of Athens, this reputation of mine has come of a certain sort of wisdom which I possess. If you ask me what kind of wisdom, I reply, such wisdom as is attainable by man, for to that extent I am inclined to believe that I am wise; whereas the persons of whom I was speaking have a superhuman wisdom, which I may fail to describe, because I have it not myself; and he who says that I have, speaks falsely, and is taking away my character. And here, O men of Athens, I must beg you not to interrupt me, even if I seem to say something extravagant. For the word which I will speak is not mine. I will refer you to a witness who is worthy of credit, and will tell you about my wisdom—whether I have any, and of what sort—and that witness shall be the god of Delphi. You must have known Chærephon; he was early a friend of mine, and also a friend of yours, for he shared in the exile of the people, and returned with you. Well, Chærephon, as you know, was very impetuous in all his doings, and he went to Delphi and boldly asked the oracle to tell him whether—as I was saying, I must beg you not to interrupt—he asked the oracle to tell him whether there was anyone wiser than I was, and the Pythian prophetess answered that there was no man wiser. Chærephon is dead himself, but his brother, who is in court, will confirm the truth of this story.

Why do I mention this? Because I am going to explain to you why I have such an evil name. When I heard the answer, I said to myself, What can the god mean? and what is the interpretation of this riddle? for I know that I have no wisdom, small or great. What can he mean when he says that I am the wisest of men? And yet he is a god and cannot lie; that would be against his nature. After a long consideration, I at last thought of a method of trying the question. I reflected that if I could only find a man wiser than myself, then I might go to the god with a refutation in my hand. I should say to him, "Here is a man who is wiser than I am; but you said that I was the wisest." Accordingly I went to one who had the reputation of wisdom, and observed to him —his name I need not mention; he was a politician whom I selected for examination—and the result was as follows: When I began to talk with him, I could not help thinking that he was not really wise, although he was thought wise by many, and wiser still by himself; and I went and tried to explain to him that he thought himself wise, but was not really wise; and the consequence was that he hated me, and his enmity was shared by several who were present and heard me. So I left him, saying to myself, as I went away: Well, although I do not suppose that either of us knows anything really beautiful and good, I am better off than he is—for he knows nothing, and thinks that he knows.

I neither know nor think that I know. In this latter particular, then, I seem to have slightly the advantage of him. Then I went to another, who had still higher philosophical pretensions, and my conclusion was exactly the same. I made another enemy of him, and of many others besides him.

After this I went to one man after another, being not unconscious of the enmity which I provoked, and I lamented and feared this: but necessity was laid upon me—the word of God, I thought, ought to be considered first. And I said to myself, Go I must to all who appear to know, and find out the meaning of the oracle. And I swear to you, Athenians, by the dog I swear!—for I must tell you the truth—the result of my mission was just this: I found that the men most in repute were all but the most foolish; and that some inferior men were really wiser and better. I will tell you the tale of my wanderings and of the "Herculean" labors, as I may call them, which I endured only to find at last the oracle irrefutable. When I left the politicians, I went to the poets; tragic, dithyrambic, and all sorts. And there, I said to myself, you will be detected; now you will find out that you are more ignorant than they are. Accordingly, I took them some of the most elaborate passages in their own writings, and asked what was the meaning of them—thinking that they would teach me something. Will you believe me? I am almost ashamed to speak of this, but still I must say that there is hardly a person present who would not have talked better about their poetry than they did themselves. That showed me in an instant that not by wisdom do poets write poetry, but by a sort of genius and inspiration; they are like diviners or soothsayers who also say many fine things, but do not understand the meaning of them. And the poets appeared to me to be much in the same case; and I further observed that upon the strength of their poetry they believed themselves to be the wisest of men in other things in which they were not wise. So I departed, conceiving myself to be superior to them for the same reason that I was superior to the politicians.

At last I went to the artisans, for I was conscious that I knew nothing at all, as I may say, and I was sure that they knew many fine things; and in this I was not mistaken, for they did know many things of which I was ignorant, and in this they certainly were wiser than I was. But I observed that even the good artisans fell into the same error as the poets; because they were good workmen they thought that they also knew all sorts of high matters, and this defect in them overshadowed their wisdom—therefore I asked myself on behalf of the oracle, whether I would like to be as I was, neither having their knowledge nor their ignorance, or like them in both; and I made answer to myself and the oracle that I was better off as I was.

This investigation has led to my having many enemies of the worst and most dangerous kind, and has given occasion also to many calumnies. And I am called wise, for my hearers always imagine that I myself possess the wisdom which I find wanting in others: but the truth is, O men of Athens, that God only is wise; and in this oracle he means to say that the wisdom of men is little or nothing; he is not speaking of Socrates, he is only using my name as an illustration, as if he said, He, O men, is the wisest, who, like Socrates, knows that his wisdom is in truth worth nothing. And so I go my way, obedient to the god, and make inquisition into the wisdom of anyone, whether citizen or stranger, who appears to be wise; and if he is not wise, then in vindication of the oracle I show him that he is not wise; and this occupation quite absorbs me, and I have no time to give either to any public matter of interest or to any concern of my own, but I am in utter poverty by reason of my devotion to the god.

There is another thing:—young men of the richer classes, who have not much to do, come about me of their own accord; they like to hear the pretenders examined, and they often imitate me, and examine others themselves; there are plenty of persons, as they soon enough discover, who think that they know something, but really know little or nothing: and then those who are examined by them instead of being angry with themselves are angry with me: This confounded Socrates, they say; this villainous misleader of youth!—and then if somebody asks them, Why, what evil does he practice or teach? they do not know, and cannot tell; but in order that they may not appear to be at a loss, they repeat the readymade charges which are used against all philosophers about teaching things up in the clouds and under the earth, and having no gods, and making the worse appear the better cause; for they do not like to confess that their pretence of knowledge has been detected—which is the truth: and as they are numerous and ambitious and energetic, and are all in battle array and have persuasive tongues, they have filled your ears with their loud and inveterate calumnies. And this is the reason why my three accusers, Meletus and Anytus and Lycon, have set upon me: Meletus, who has a quarrel with me on behalf of the poets; Anytus, on behalf of the craftsmen; Lycon, on behalf of the rhetoricians: and as I said at the beginning, I cannot expect to get rid of this mass of calumny all in a moment. And this, O men of Athens, is the truth and the whole truth; I have concealed nothing, I have dissembled nothing. And yet I know that this plainness of speech makes them hate me, and what is their hatred but a proof that I am speaking the truth?—this is the occasion and reason of their slander of me, as you will find out either in this or in any future inquiry.

I have said enough in my defence against the first class of my accusers; I turn to the second class, who are headed by Meletus, that good and patriotic man, as he calls himself. And now I will try to defend myself against them: these new accusers must also have their affidavit read. What do they say? Something of this sort: That Socrates is a doer of evil, and corrupter of the youth, and he does not believe in the gods of the State, and has other new divinities of his own. That is the sort of charge; and now let us examine the particular counts. He says that I am a doer of evil, who corrupts the youth; but I say, O men of Athens, that Meletus is a doer of evil, and the evil is that he makes a joke of a serious matter, and is too ready at bringing other men to trial from a pretended zeal and interest about matters in which he really never had the smallest interest. And the truth of this I will endeavor to prove.

Come hither, Meletus, and let me ask a question of you. You think a great deal about the improvement of youth?

Yes, I do.

Tell the judges, then, who is their improver; for you must know, as you have taken the pains to discover their corrupter, and are citing and accusing me before them. Speak, then, and tell the judges who their improver is. Observe, Meletus, that you are silent, and have nothing to say. But is not this rather disgraceful, and a very considerable proof of what I was saying, that you have no interest in the matter? Speak up, friend, and tell us who their improver is.

The laws.

But that, my good sir, is not my meaning. I want to know who the person is, who, in the first place, knows the laws.

The judges, Socrates, who are present in court.

What do you mean to say, Meletus, that they are able to instruct and improve youth?

Certainly they are.

What, all of them, or some only and not others?

All of them.

By the goddess Here, that is good news! There are plenty of improvers, then. And what do you say of the audience—do they improve them?

Yes, they do.

And the Senators?

Yes, the Senators improve them.

But perhaps the ecclesiasts corrupt them?—or do they too improve them?

They improve them.

Then every Athenian improves and elevates them; all with the exception of myself; and I alone am their corrupter? Is that what you affirm?

That is what I stoutly affirm.

I am very unfortunate if that is true. But suppose I ask you a question: Would you say that this also holds true in the case of horses? Does one man do them harm and all the world good? Is not the exact opposite of this true? One man is able to do them good, or at least not many; the trainer of horses, that is to say, does them good, and others who have to do with them rather injure them? Is not that true, Meletus, of horses, or any other animals? Yes, certainly. Whether you and Anytus say yes or no, that is no matter. Happy indeed would be the condition of youth if they had one corrupter only, and all the rest of the world were their improvers. And you, Meletus, have sufficiently shown that you never had a thought about the young: your carelessness is seen in your not caring about the matters spoken of in this very indictment.

And now, Meletus, I must ask you another question: Which is better, to live among bad citizens, or among good ones? Answer, friend, I say; for that is a question which may be easily answered. Do not the good do their neighbors good, and the bad do them evil?

Certainly.

And is there anyone who would rather be injured than benefited by those who live with him? Answer, my good friend; the law requires you to answer —does anyone like to be injured?

Certainly not.

And when you accuse me of corrupting and deteriorating the youth, do you allege that I corrupt them intentionally or unintentionally?

Intentionally, I say.

But you have just admitted that the good do their neighbors good, and the evil do them evil. Now is that a truth which your superior wisdom has recognized thus early in life, and am I, at my age, in such darkness and ignorance as not to know that if a man with whom I have to live is corrupted by me, I am very likely to be harmed by him, and yet I corrupt him, and intentionally, too? That is what you are saying, and of that you will never persuade me or any other human being. But either I do not corrupt them, or I corrupt them unintentionally, so that on either view of the case you lie. If my offense is unintentional, the law has no cognizance of unintentional offenses: you ought to have taken me privately, and warned and admonished me; for if I had been better advised, I should have left off doing what I only did unintentionally—no doubt I should; whereas you hated to converse with me or teach me, but you indicted me in this court, which is a place, not of instruction, but of punishment.

I have shown, Athenians, as I was saying, that Meletus has no care at all, great or small, about the matter. But still I should like to know, Meletus, in what I am affirmed to corrupt the young. I suppose you mean, as I infer from your indictment, that I teach them not to acknowledge the gods which the State acknowledges, but some other new divinities or spiritual agencies in their stead. These are the lessons which corrupt the youth, as you say.

Yes, that I say emphatically.

Then, by the gods, Meletus, of whom we are speaking, tell me and the court, in somewhat plainer terms, what you mean! for I do not as yet understand whether you affirm that I teach others to acknowledge some gods, and there-fore do believe in gods and am not an entire atheist—this you do not lay to my charge; but only that they are not the same gods which the city recognizes —the charge is that they are different gods. Or, do you mean to say that I am an atheist simply, and a teacher of atheism?

I mean the latter—that you are a complete atheist.

That is an extraordinary statement, Meletus. Why do you say that? Do you mean that I do not believe in the god-head of the sun or moon, which is the common creed of all men?

I assure you, judges, that he does not believe in them; for he says that the sun is stone, and the moon earth.

Friend Meletus, you think that you are accusing Anaxagoras: and you have but a bad opinion of the judges, if you fancy them ignorant to such a degree as not to know that those doctrines are found in the books of Anaxagoras the Clazomenian, who is full of them. And these are the doctrines which the youth are said to learn of Socrates, when there are not unfrequently exhibitions of them at the theatre[1] (price of admission one drachma at the most); and they might cheaply purchase them, and laugh at Socrates if he pretends to father such eccentricities. And so, Meletus, you really think that I do not believe in any god?

I swear by Zeus that you believe absolutely in none at all.

You are a liar, Meletus, not believed even by yourself. For I cannot help thinking, O men of Athens, that Meletus is reckless and impudent, and that he has written this indictment in a spirit of mere wantonness and youthful bravado. Has he not compounded a riddle, thinking to try me? He said to himself: I shall see whether this wise Socrates will discover my ingenious contradiction, or whether I shall be able to deceive him and the rest of them. For he certainly does appear to me to contradict himself in the indictment as much as if he said that Socrates is guilty of not believing in the gods, and yet of believing in them—but this surely is a piece of fun.

I should like you, O men of Athens, to join me in examining what I conceive to be his inconsistency; and do you, Meletus, answer. And I must remind you that you are not to interrupt me if I speak in my accustomed manner.

Did ever man, Meletus, believe in the existence of human things, and not of human beings? ... I wish, men of Athens, that he would answer, and not be always trying to get up an interruption. Did ever any man believe in horsemanship, and not in horses? or in flute-playing, and not in flute-players? No, my friend; I will answer to you and to the court, as you refuse to answer for yourself. There is no man who ever did. But now please to answer the next question: Can a man believe in spiritual and divine agencies, and not in spirits or demigods?

He cannot.

I am glad that I have extracted that answer, by the assistance of the court; nevertheless you swear in the indictment that I teach and believe in divine or spiritual agencies (new or old, no matter for that); at any rate, I believe in spiritual agencies, as you say and swear in the affidavit; but if I believe in divine beings, I must believe in spirits or demigods; is not that true? Yes, that is true, for I may assume that your silence gives assent to that. Now what are spirits or demigods? are they not either gods or the sons of gods? Is that true?

Yes, that is true.

But this is just the ingenious riddle of which I was speaking: the demigods or spirits are gods, and you say first that I don't believe in gods, and then again

[1]Probably an allusion to Aristophanes, who caricatured, and to Euripides, who borrowed, the notions of Anaxagoras, as well as to other dramatic poets.

that I do believe in gods; that is, if I believe in demigods. For if the demigods are the illegitimate sons of gods, whether by the Nymphs or by any other mothers, as is thought, that, as all men will allow, necessarily implies the existence of their parents. You might as well affirm the existence of mules, and deny that of horses and asses. Such nonsense, Meletus, could only have been intended by you as a trial of me. You have put this into the indictment because you had nothing real of which to accuse me. But no one who has a particle of understanding will ever be convinced by you that the same man can believe in divine and superhuman things, and yet not believe that there are gods and demigods and heroes.

I have said enough in answer to the charge of Meletus: any elaborate defence is unnecessary; but as I was saying before, I certainly have many enemies, and this is what will be my destruction if I am destroyed; of that I am certain; not Meletus, nor yet Anytus, but the envy and detraction of the world, which has been the death of many good men, and will probably be the death of many more; there is no danger of my being the last of them.

Someone will say: And are you not ashamed, Socrates, of a course of life which is likely to bring you to an untimely end? To him I may fairly answer: There you are mistaken: a man who is good for anything ought not to calculate the chance of living or dying; he ought only to consider whether in doing anything he is doing right or wrong—acting the part of a good man or of a bad. Whereas, according to your view, the heroes who fell at Troy were not good for much, and the son of Thetis above all, who altogether despised danger in comparison with disgrace; and when his goddess mother said to him, in his eagerness to slay Hector, that if he avenged his companion Patroclus, and slew Hector, he would die himself—"Fate," as she said, "waits upon you next after Hector"; he, hearing this, utterly despised danger and death, and instead of fearing them, feared rather to live in dishonor, and not to avenge his friend. "Let me die next," he replies, "and be avenged of my enemy, rather than abide here by the beaked ships, a scorn and a burden of the earth." Had Achilles any thought of death and danger? For wherever a man's place is, whether the place which he has chosen or that in which he has been placed by a commander, there he ought to remain in the hour of danger; he should not think of death or of anything, but of disgrace. And this, O men of Athens, is a true saying.

Strange, indeed, would be my conduct, O men of Athens, if I who, when I was ordered by the generals whom you chose to command me at Potidæa and Amphipolis and Delium, remained where they placed me, like any other man, facing death—if, I say, now, when, as I conceive and imagine, God orders me to fulfil the philosopher's mission of searching into myself and other men, I were to desert my post through fear of death, or any other fear; that would indeed be strange, and I might justly be arraigned in court for denying the existence of the gods, if I disobeyed the oracle because I was afraid of death: then I should be fancying that I was wise when I was not wise. For this fear of death is indeed the pretence of wisdom, and not real wisdom, being the appearance of knowing the unknown; since no one knows whether death, which they in their fear apprehend to be the greatest evil, may not be the greatest good. Is there not here conceit of knowledge, which is a disgraceful sort of ignorance? And this is the point in which, as I think, I am superior to men in general, and in which I might perhaps fancy myself wiser than other men—that whereas I know but little of the world below, I do not suppose that I know: but I do know that injustice and disobedience to a better, whether God or man, is evil and dishonorable, and I will never fear or avoid a possible good rather than a certain evil. And therefore if you let me go now, and reject the counsels of Anytus, who said that if I were not put to death I ought not to have been prosecuted, and that if I escape now, your sons will all be utterly ruined by listening to my words—if you say to me, Socrates, this time we will not mind Anytus, and will let you off, but upon one condition, that you are not to inquire and speculate in this way any more, and that if you are caught doing this again you shall die—if this was the condition on which you let me go, I should reply: Men of Athens, I honor and love you; but I shall obey God rather than you, and while I have life and strength I shall never cease from the practice and teaching of philosophy, exhorting anyone whom I meet after my manner, and convincing him, saying: O my friend, why do you, who are a citizen of the great and mighty and wise city of Athens, care so much about laying up the greatest amount of money and honor and reputation, and so little about wisdom and truth and the greatest improvement of the soul; which you never regard or heed at all? Are you not ashamed of this? And if the person with whom I am arguing says: Yes, but I do care; I do not depart or let him go at once; I interrogate and examine and cross-examine him, and if I think that he has no virtue, but only says that he has, I reproach him with undervaluing the greater, and overvaluing the less. And this I should say to everyone whom I meet, young and old, citizen and alien, but especially to the citizens, inasmuch as they are my brethren. For this is the command of God, as I would have you know; and I believe that to this day no greater good has ever happened in the State than my service to the God. For I do nothing but go about persuading you all, old and young alike, not to take thought for your persons and your properties, but first and chiefly to care about the greatest improvement of the soul. I tell you that virtue is not given by money, but that from virtue come money and every other good of man, public as well as private. This is my teaching, and if this is the doctrine which corrupts the youth, my influence is ruinous indeed. But if anyone says that this is not my teaching, he is speaking an untruth. Wherefore, O men of Athens, I say to you, do as Anytus bids or not as Anytus bids, and either acquit me or not; but whatever you do, know that I shall never alter my ways, not even if I have to die many times.

Men of Athens, do not interrupt, but hear me; there was an agreement between us that you should hear me out. And I think that what I am going

to say will do you good: for I have something more to say, at which you may
be inclined to cry out; but I beg that you will not do this. I would have you
know that, if you kill such a one as I am, you will injure yourselves more than
you will injure me. Meletus and Anytus will not injure me: they cannot; for
it is not in the nature of things that a bad man should injure a better than
himself. I do not deny that he may, perhaps, kill him, or drive him into exile,
or deprive him of civil rights, and he may imagine, and others may imagine,
that he is doing him a great injury: but in that I do not agree with him; for
the evil of doing as Anytus is doing—of unjustly taking away another man's
life—is greater far. And now, Athenians, I am not going to argue for my own
sake, as you may think, but for yours, that you may not sin against the God,
or lightly reject his boon by condemning me. For if you kill me you will not
easily find another like me, who, if I may use such a ludicrous figure of speech,
am a sort of gadfly given to the State by the God; and the State is like a great
and noble steed who is tardy in his motions owing to his very size, and requires
to be stirred into life. I am that gadfly which God has given the State, and all
day long and in all places am always fastening upon you, arousing and persuading and reproaching you. And as you will not easily find another like me, I
would advise you to spare me. I dare say that you may feel irritated at being
suddenly awakened when you are caught napping; and you may think that if
you were to strike me dead, as Anytus advises, which you easily might, then
you would sleep on for the remainder of your lives, unless God in his care of
you gives you another gadfly. And that I am given to you by God is proved
by this: that if I had been like other men, I should not have neglected all my
own concerns, or patiently seen the neglect of them during all these years, and
have been doing yours, coming to you individually, like a father or elder
brother, exhorting you to regard virtue; this, I say, would not be like human
nature. And had I gained anything, or if my exhortations had been paid, there
would have been some sense in that: but now, as you will perceive, not even
the impudence of my accusers dares to say that I have ever exacted or sought
pay of anyone; they have no witness of that. And I have a witness of the truth
of what I say; my poverty is a sufficient witness.

Someone may wonder why I go about in private, giving advice and busying
myself with the concerns of others, but do not venture to come forward in
public and advise the State. I will tell you the reason of this. You have often
heard me speak of an oracle or sign which comes to me, and is the divinity
which Meletus ridicules in the indictment. This sign I have had ever since I
was a child. The sign is a voice which comes to me and always forbids me to
do something which I am going to do, but never commands me to do anything,
and this is what stands in the way of my being a politician. And rightly, as
I think. For I am certain, O men of Athens, that if I had engaged in politics,
I should have perished long ago, and done no good either to you or to myself.
And don't be offended at my telling you the truth: for the truth is that no man
who goes to war with you or any other multitude, honestly struggling against

the commission of unrighteousness and wrong in the State, will save his life; he who will really fight for the right, if he would live even for a little while, must have a private station and not a public one.

I can give you as proofs of this, not words only, but deeds, which you value more than words. Let me tell you a passage of my own life, which will prove to you that I should never have yielded to injustice from any fear of death, and that if I had not yielded I should have died at once. I will tell you a story—tasteless, perhaps, and commonplace, but nevertheless true. The only office of State which I ever held, O men of Athens, was that of Senator; the tribe Antiochis, which is my tribe, had the presidency at the trial of the generals who had not taken up the bodies of the slain after the battle of Arginusæ; and you proposed to try them all together, which was illegal, as you all thought afterwards; but at the time I was the only one of the Prytanes who was opposed to the illegality, and I gave my vote against you; and when the orators threatened to impeach and arrest me, and have me taken away, and you called and shouted, I made up my mind that I would run the risk, having law and justice with me, rather than take part in your injustice because I feared imprisonment and death. This happened in the days of the democracy. But when the oligarchy of the Thirty was in power, they sent for me and four others into the rotunda, and bade us bring Leon the Salaminian from Salamis, as they wanted to execute him. This was a specimen of the sort of commands which they were always giving with the view of implicating as many as possible in their crimes; and then I showed, not in words only, but in deed, that, if I may be allowed to use such an expression, I cared not a straw for death, and that my only fear was the fear of doing an unrighteous or unholy thing. For the strong arm of that oppressive power did not frighten me into doing wrong; and when we came out of the rotunda the other four went to Salamis and fetched Leon, but I went quietly home. For which I might have lost my life, had not the power of the Thirty shortly afterwards come to an end. And to this many will witness.

Now do you really imagine that I could have survived all these years, if I had led a public life, supposing that like a good man I had always supported the right and had made justice, as I ought, the first thing? No, indeed, men of Athens, neither I nor any other. But I have been always the same in all my actions, public as well as private, and never have I yielded any base compliance to those who are slanderously termed my disciples, or to any other. For the truth is that I have no regular disciples: but if anyone likes to come and hear me while I am pursuing my mission, whether he be young or old, he may freely come. Nor do I converse with those who pay only, and not with those who do not pay; but anyone, whether he be rich or poor, may ask and answer me and listen to my words; and whether he turns out to be a bad man or a good one, that cannot be justly laid to my charge, as I never taught him anything. And if anyone says that he has ever learned or heard anything from me in private which all the world has not heard, I should like you to know that he is speaking an untruth.

But I shall be asked, Why do people delight in continually conversing with you? I have told you already, Athenians, the whole truth about this: they like to hear the cross-examination of the pretenders to wisdom; there is amusement in this. And this is a duty which the God has imposed upon me, as I am assured by oracles, visions, and in every sort of way in which the will of divine power was ever signified to anyone. This is true, O Athenians; or, if not true, would be soon refuted. For if I am really corrupting the youth, and have corrupted some of them already, those of them who have grown up and have become sensible that I gave them bad advice in the days of their youth should come forward as accusers and take their revenge; and if they do not like to come themselves, some of their relatives, fathers, brothers, or other kinsmen, should say what evil their families suffered at my hands. Now is their time. Many of them I see in the court. There is Crito, who is of the same age and of the same *deme* with myself; and there is Critobulus his son, whom I also see. Then again there is Lysanias of Sphettus, who is the father of Æschines—he is present; and also there is Antiphon of Cephisus, who is the father of Epigenes; and there are the brothers of several who have associated with me. There is Nicostratus the son of Theosdotides, and the brother of Theodotus (now Theodotus himself is dead, and therefore he, at any rate, will not seek to stop him); and there is Paralus the son of Demodocus, who had a brother Theages; and Adeimantus the son of Ariston whose brother Plato is present; and Æantodorus, who is the brother of Apollodorus, whom I also see. I might mention a great many others, any of whom Meletus should have produced as witnesses in the course of his speech; and let him still produce them, if he has forgotten; I will make way for him. And let him say, if he has any testimony of the sort which he can produce. Nay, Athenians, the very opposite is the truth. For all these are ready to witness on behalf of the corrupter, of the destroyer of their kindred, as Meletus and Anytus call me; not the corrupted youth only—there might have been a motive for that—but their uncorrupted elder relatives. Why should they too support me with their testimony? Why, indeed, except for the sake of truth and justice, and because they know that I am speaking the truth, and that Meletus is lying.

Well, Athenians, this and the like of this is nearly all the defence which I have to offer. Yet a word more. Perhaps there may be someone who is offended at me, when he calls to mind how he himself, on a similar or even a less serious occasion, had recourse to prayers and supplications with many tears, and how he produced his children in court, which was a moving spectacle, together with a posse of his relations and friends; whereas I, who am probably in danger of my life, will do none of these things. Perhaps this may come into his mind, and he may be set against me, and vote in anger because he is displeased at this. Now if there be such a person among you, which I am far from affirming, I may fairly reply to him: My friend, I am a man, and like other men, a creature of flesh and blood, and not of wood or stone, as Homer says; and I have a family, yes, and sons, O Athenians, three in number, one of whom is growing up, and the two others are still young; and yet I will not bring any of them hither in order to petition you for an acquittal. And why not? Not from any self-will or disregard of you. Whether I am or am not afraid of death is another question, of which I will not now speak. But my reason simply is that I feel such conduct to be discreditable to myself, and you, and the whole State. One who has reached my years, and who has a name for wisdom, whether deserved or not, ought not to debase himself. At any rate, the world has decided that Socrates is in some way superior to other men. And if those among you who are said to be superior in wisdom and courage, and any other virtue, demean themselves in this way, how shameful is their conduct! I have seen men of reputation, when they have been condemned, behaving in the strangest manner: they seemed to fancy that they were going to suffer something dreadful if they died, and that they could be immortal if you only allowed them to live; and I think that they were a dishonor to the State, and that any stranger coming in would say of them that the most eminent men of Athens, to whom the Athenians themselves give honor and command, are no better than women. And I say that these things ought not to be done by those of us who are of reputation; and if they are done, you ought not to permit them; you ought rather to show that you are more inclined to condemn, not the man who is quiet, but the man who gets up a doleful scene, and makes the city ridiculous.

But, setting aside the question of dishonor, there seems to be something wrong in petitioning a judge, and thus procuring an acquittal instead of informing and convincing him. For his duty is, not to make a present of justice, but to give judgment; and he has sworn that he will judge according to the laws, and not according to his own good pleasure; and neither he nor we should get into the habit of perjuring ourselves—there can be no piety in that. Do not then require me to do what I consider dishonorable and impious and wrong, especially now, when I am being tried for impiety on the indictment of Meletus. For if, O men of Athens, by force of persuasion and entreaty, I could overpower your oaths, then I should be teaching you to believe that there are no gods, and convict myself, in my own defence, of not believing in them. But that is not the case; for I do believe that there are gods, and in a far higher sense than that in which any of my accusers believe in them. And to you and to God I commit my cause, to be determined by you as is best for you and me.[2]

There are many reasons why I am not grieved, O men of Athens, at the vote of condemnation. I expected this, and am only surprised that the votes are so nearly equal; for I had thought that the majority against me would have been far larger; but now, had thirty votes gone over to the other side, I should have been acquitted. And I may say that I have escaped Meletus. And I may say more; for without the assistance of Anytus and Lycon, he would not have had a fifth part of the votes, as the law requires, in which case he would have incurred a fine of a thousand drachmæ, as is evident.

[2]At this point a vote is taken and Socrates is found guilty [Ed.].

And so he proposes death as the penalty. And what shall I propose on my part, O men of Athens? Clearly that which is my due. And what is that which I ought to pay or to receive? What shall be done to the man who has never had the wit to be idle during his whole life; but has been careless of what the many care about—wealth and family interests, and military offices, and speaking in the assembly, and magistracies, and plots, and parties. Reflecting that I was really too honest a man to follow in this way and live, I did not go where I could do no good to you or to myself; but where I could do the greatest good privately to everyone of you, thither I went, and sought to persuade every man among you that he must look to himself, and seek virtue and wisdom before he looks to his private interests, and look to the State before he looks to the interests of the State; and that this should be the order which he observes in all his actions. What shall be done to such a one? Doubtless some good thing, O men of Athens, if he has his reward; and the good should be of a kind suitable to him. What would be a reward suitable to a poor man who is your benefactor, who desires leisure that he may instruct you? There can be no more fitting reward than maintenance in the Prytaneum, O men of Athens, a reward which he deserves far more than the citizen who has won the prize at Olympia in the horse or chariot race, whether the chariots were drawn by two horses or by many. For I am in want, and he has enough; and he only gives you the appearance of happiness, and I give you the reality. And if I am to estimate the penalty justly, I say that maintenance in the Prytaneum is the just return.

Perhaps you may think that I am braving you in saying this, as in what I said before about the tears and prayers. But that is not the case. I speak rather because I am convinced that I never intentionally wronged anyone, although I cannot convince you of that—for we have had a short conversation only; but if there were a law at Athens, such as there is in other cities, that a capital cause should not be decided in one day, then I believe that I should have convinced you; but now the time is too short. I cannot in a moment refute great slanders; and, as I am convinced that I never wronged another, I will assuredly not wrong myself. I will not say of myself that I deserve any evil, or propose any penalty. Why should I? Because I am afraid of the penalty of death which Meletus proposes? When I do not know whether death is a good or an evil, why should I propose a penalty which would certainly be an evil? Shall I say imprisonment? And why should I live in prison, and be the slave of the magistrates of the year—of the Eleven? Or shall the penalty be a fine, and imprisonment until the fine is paid? There is the same objection. I should have to lie in prison, for money I have none, and cannot pay. And if I say exile (and this may possibly be the penalty which you will affix), I must indeed be blinded by the love of life if I were to consider that when you, who are my own citizens, cannot endure my discourses and words, and have found them so grievous and odious that you would fain have done with them, others are likely to endure me. No, indeed, men of Athens, that is not very likely. And what a life should I lead, at my age, wandering from city to city, living in everchanging exile, and always being driven out! For I am quite sure that into whatever place I go, as here so also there, the young men will come to me; and if I drive them away, their elders will drive me out at their desire: and if I let them come, their fathers and friends will drive me out for their sakes.

Someone will say: Yes, Socrates, but cannot you hold your tongue, and then you may go into a foreign city, and no one will interfere with you? Now I have great difficulty in making you understand my answer to this. For if I tell you that this would be a disobedience to a divine command, and therefore that I cannot hold my tongue, you will not believe that I am serious; and if I say again that the greatest good of man is daily to converse about virtue, and all that concerning which you hear me examining myself and others, and that the life which is unexamined is not worth living—that you are still less likely to believe. And yet what I say is true, although a thing of which it is hard for me to persuade you. Moreover, I am not accustomed to think that I deserve any punishment. Had I money I might have proposed to give you what I had, and have been none the worse. But you see that I have none, and can only ask you to proportion the fine to my means. However, I think that I could afford a mina, and therefore I propose that penalty: Plato, Crito, Critobulus, and Apollodorus, my friends here, bid me say thirty minæ, and they will be the sureties. Well, then, say thirty minæ, let that be the penalty; for that they will be ample security to you.

Not much time will be gained, O Athenians, in return for the evil name which you will get from the detractors of the city, who will say that you killed Socrates, a wise man; for they will call me wise even although I am not wise when they want to reproach you. If you had waited a little while, your desire would have been fulfilled in the course of nature. For I am far advanced in years, as you may perceive, and not far from death. I am speaking now only to those of you who have condemned me to death. And I have another thing to say to them: You think that I was convicted through deficiency of words —I mean, that if I had thought fit to leave nothing undone, nothing unsaid, I might have gained an acquittal. Not so; the deficiency which led to my conviction was not of words—certainly not. But I had not the boldness or impudence or inclination to address you as you would have liked me to address you, weeping and wailing and lamenting, and saying and doing many things which you have been accustomed to hear from others, and which, as I say, are unworthy of me. But I thought that I ought not to do anything common or mean in the hour of danger: nor do I now repent of the manner of my defence, and I would rather die having spoken after my manner, than speak in your manner and live. For neither in war nor yet at law ought any man to use every way of escaping death. For often in battle there is no doubt that if a man will throw away his arms, and fall on his knees before his pursuers, he may escape death; and in other dangers there are other ways of escaping death, if a man is willing to say and do anything. The difficulty, my friends, is not in avoiding death, but in avoiding unrighteousness; for that runs faster than death. I am old and move slowly, and the slower runner has overtaken me, and my accusers are keen and quick, and the faster runner, who is unrighteousness, has overtaken them. And now I depart hence condemned by you to suffer the penalty of death, and they, too, go their ways condemned by the truth to suffer the penalty of villainy and wrong; and I must abide by my award—let them abide by theirs. I suppose that these things may be regarded as fated—and I think that they are well.

And now, O men who have condemned me, I would fain prophesy to you; for I am about to die, and that is the hour in which men are gifted with prophetic power. And I prophesy to you who are my murderers, that immediately after my death punishment far heavier than you have inflicted on me will surely await you. Me you have killed because you wanted to escape the accuser, and not to give an account of your lives. But that will not be as you suppose: far otherwise. For I say that there will be more accusers of you than there are now; accusers whom hitherto I have restrained: and as they are younger they will be more severe with you, and you will be more offended at them. For if you think that by killing men you can avoid the accuser censuring your lives, you are mistaken; that is not a way of escape which is either possible or honorable; the easiest and the noblest way is not to be crushing others, but to be improving yourselves. This is the prophecy which I utter before my departure, to the judges who have condemned me.

Friends, who would have acquitted me, I would like also to talk with you about this thing which has happened, while the magistrates are busy, and before I go to the place at which I must die. Stay then awhile, for we may as well talk with one another while there is time. You are my friends, and I should like to show you the meaning of this event which has happened to me. O my judges—for you I may truly call judges—I should like to tell you of a wonderful circumstance. Hitherto the familiar oracle within me has constantly been in the habit of opposing me even about trifles, if I was going to make a slip or error about anything; and now as you see there has come upon me that which may be thought, and is generally believed to be, the last and worst evil. But the oracle made no sign of opposition, either as I was leaving my house and going out in the morning, or when I was going up into this court, or while I was speaking, at anything which I was going to say; and yet I have often been stopped in the middle of a speech; but now in nothing I either said or did touching this matter has the oracle opposed me. What do I take to be the explanation of this? I will tell you. I regard this as a proof that what has happened to me is a good, and that those of us who think that death is an evil are in error. This is a great proof to me of what I am saying, for the customary sign would surely have opposed me had I been going to evil and not to good.

Let us reflect in another way, and we shall see that there is great reason to hope that death is a good, for one of two things: either death is a state of nothingness and utter unconsciousness, or, as men say, there is a change and migration of the soul from this world to another. Now if you suppose that there is no consciousness, but a sleep like the sleep of him who is undisturbed even by the sight of dreams, death will be an unspeakable gain. For if a person were to select the night in which his sleep was undisturbed even by dreams, and were to compare with this the other days and nights of his life, and then were to tell us how many days and nights he had passed in the course of his life better and more pleasantly than this one, I think that any man, I will not say a private man, but even the great king, will not find many such days or nights, when compared with the others. Now if death is like this, I say that to die is gain; for eternity is then only a single night. But if death is the journey to another place, and there, as men say, all the dead are, what good, O my friends and judges, can be greater than this? If indeed when the pilgrim arrives in the world below, he is delivered from the professors of justice in this world, and finds the true judges who are said to give judgment there, Minos and Rhadamanthus and Æacus and Triptolemus, and other sons of God who were righteous in their own life, that pilgrimage will be worth making. What would not a man give if he might converse with Orpheus and Musæus and Hesiod and Homer? Nay, if this be true, let me die again and again. I, too, shall have a wonderful interest in a place where I can converse with Palamedes, and Ajax the son of Telamon, and other heroes of old, who have suffered death through an unjust judgment; and there will be no small pleasure, as I think, in comparing my own sufferings with theirs. Above all, I shall be able to continue my search into true and false knowledge; as in this world, so also in that; I shall find out who is wise, and who pretends to be wise, and is not. What would not a man give, O judges, to be able to examine the leader of the great Trojan expedition; or Odysseus or Sisyphus, or numberless others, men and women too! What infinite delight would there be in conversing with them and asking them questions! For in that world they do not put a man to death for this; certainly not. For besides being happier in that world than in this, they will be immortal, if what is said is true.

Wherefore, O judges, be of good cheer about death, and know this of a truth —that no evil can happen to a good man, either in life or after death. He and his are not neglected by the gods; nor has my own approaching end happened by mere chance. But I see clearly that to die and be released was better for me; and therefore the oracle gave no sign. For which reason, also, I am not angry with my accusers, or my condemners; they have done me no harm, although neither of them meant to do me any good; and for this I may gently blame them.

Still I have a favor to ask of them. When my sons are grown up, I would ask you, O my friends, to punish them; and I would have you trouble them, as I have troubled you, if they seem to care about riches, or anything, more than about virtue; or if they pretend to be something when they are really nothing—then reprove them, as I have reproved you, for not caring about that for which they ought to care, and thinking that they are something when they are really nothing. And if you do this, I and my sons will have received justice at your hands.

The hour of departure has arrived, and we go our ways—I to die, and you to live. Which is better God only knows.

For Further Reading

Ayer, A. J. *Philosophy and Language.* New York: Oxford University Press, 1960.

Hahn, Lewis E. "Philosophy as Comprehensive Vision," *Philosophy and Phenomenological Research,* 22 (1961), 1–25.

Hamblin, Charles L. *Fallacies.* London: Methuen, 1970.

Iribadjakov, N. "Philosophy and Antiphilosophy," *Philosophy and Phenomenological Research,* 35 (1974–1975), 181–200. A Marxist account of the task of philosophy and its relation to the sciences.

Jaspers, Karl. *Way to Wisdom,* trans. by Ralph Manheim. New Haven, Conn.: Yale University Press, 1951 (paperbound). See especially Chaps. 1–3.

Körner, Stephen. *What Is Philosophy? One Philosopher's Answer.* Baltimore, Md.: Penguin Books, 1969.

Krikorian, Yervant H. (ed.). *Naturalism and the Human Spirit.* New York: Columbia University Press, 1944. See especially Chap. 15, "The Nature of Naturalism," by John Herman Randall, Jr.

Loewenberg, Jacob. *Reason and the Nature of Things.* LaSalle, Ill.: Open Court Publishing Co., 1959.

Merleau-Ponty, Maurice. *In Praise of Philosophy,* trans. by John Wild and James M. Edie. Evanston, Ill.: Northwestern University Press, 1963. See especially pp. 33–64.

Nagel, Ernest. *Logic Without Metaphysics.* New York: Free Press, 1956. See Part I, Chap. I, "Naturalism Reconsidered."

Newell, R. W. *The Concept of Philosophy.* London: Methuen, 1967.

Parsons, H. L. "The Philosopher and Mankind's Struggle for Value," *Philosophy and Phenomenological Research,* 36 (1975), 246–252. Attempts to relate the philosophical enterprise to some fundamental forms of human experience.

Passmore, John. *Philosophical Reasoning.* London: Gerald Duckworth, 1969 (paperbound). An examination of some common forms of philosophical argument.

Russell, Bertrand. *The Problems of Philosophy.* New York: Oxford University Press, 1959. See especially Chap. 15, "The Value of Philosophy."

Ryle, G. "Systematically Misleading Expressions," in Antony Flew (ed.). *Essays on Logic and Language,* First Series. New York: Philosophical Library, 1951.

Sheldon, W. H. "Critique of Naturalism," *The Journal of Philosophy,* 42 (1945), 253–270.

Smart, J. J. C. *Philosophy and Scientific Realism.* New York: Humanities Press, 1963. See especially Chap. 1, "The Province of Philosophy."

Supek, Ivan. "The Task of Philosophy Today," *Philosophy and Phenomenological Research,* 24 (1963), 117–124.

Waismann, Friedrich. "How I See Philosophy," in H. D. Lewis (ed.). *Contemporary British Philosophy,* Third Series. New York: Macmillan, 1956.

White, Morton. *Toward Reunion in Philosophy.* Cambridge, Mass.: Harvard University Press, 1956.

Wisdom, J. O. *Philosophy and Its Place in Our Culture.* New York: Gordon and Breach Science Publishers, 1975. An interesting characterization of the philosophical enterprise by an influential contemporary philosopher.

PART II

Rationalists and Empiricists

Presumably, almost everyone knows that we have some knowledge of the world "out there," the world in which we live. We know, for example, many particular truths: the name of the street on which we live, the color of our eyes, the number of people in our immediate family, and so on. We also know a number of general truths: that grass is green, that unsupported objects fall, that fire burns. Scientific knowledge consists entirely of general truths about the world "out there."

Let us call these two kinds of truths—that is, particular and general truths about the world—*empirical* truths. An empirical truth is a true empirical statement. The essential feature of an empirical statement is that it is about some matter of fact: its truth depends on the facts being what they are. Since my eyes happen to be blue, the statement "My eyes are blue" (when uttered by me) is an empirical truth (a true empirical statement). The statement "My eyes are brown" (when uttered by me) would be an empirical falsehood (a false empirical statement).

Now consider further that some propositions (statements) appear to be *self-evidently true*. The statement "All circles are round," for example, appears to be such a statement. There is, we might say, a logical connection between "being a circle" and "being round." Once we understand this connection we feel absolutely certain that the proposition is true, that if anything is a circle, then it must be round. The statement, we may say, is *necessarily* true.

Self-evidence is not the same as obviousness. If we imagine two people standing on opposite sides of what they both believe to be a stone, it may be obvious to them that "there is a stone between us," but the statement "There is a stone between us" is, nonetheless, not self-evidently true. Indeed, they may be totally mistaken: the object between them may, for example, be a stump that looks like a stone. But even if they are not mistaken, the statement "There is a stone between us," though obviously true to both of them, is not self-evident. Self-evidence implies necessity, the quality of "it could not be otherwise." If a proposition is self-evidently true, an exception to that which it affirms is inconceivable —as in the example about the circles. In the case of self-evident truths, to affirm that all xs are ys is to affirm that all xs *must* be ys: it is to affirm a necessary connection between the subject and the predicate of the statement.

The question that interests us here is whether there are any truths about the world (empirical truths) that are self-evidently true. Those who affirm that there are some such truths are called *rationalists.* Those who deny that such truths exist are called *empiricists.*

Bear in mind that the question is not whether there are any empirical truths that are obviously true: everyone agrees that there are. The question is whether there are any such truths—truths about the world— that are self-evidently true, necessarily true, true in such a way that an exception is inconceivable. To answer this question one way is to be a rationalist; to answer it the other way is to be an empiricist.

Consider once again the statement, "All circles are round." It seems clear to most people that this is a self-evident truth, a necessary truth. Let us assume for the moment that it is. The crucial question then becomes: Is it also an empirical truth, a truth about the world? If you know that all circles are round, do you know something about the world or merely something about the meanings of the terms "circle" and "round"? If the former, and if this is indeed a self-evident truth, then rationalism is correct: there is at least one empirical truth that is self-evidently true. If we conclude that this is not an example of such a truth, then we must look at other examples that may be offered of truths that are said to be both empirical (about the world) and self-evident. If every such example that may be put forward turns out, upon closer inspection, to be either not self-evident or not empirical, then empiricism is correct: we have no knowledge about the world that is self-evidently, necessarily, incontro-vertibly true.

Obviously, we either do or do not have some such knowledge about the world. Thus, either rationalism is correct (if we do) or empiricism is correct (if we don't). *Which* is correct is the issue that is being debated in this section.

2

PLATO (427–347 B.C.)

On Knowing Geometrical Truths

It has been said that since the fourth century B.C. the whole of Western philosophy consists of a series of footnotes to Plato. This is, perhaps, an exaggeration, but it is not an exaggeration to say that Plato is the most influential philosopher of all time. The ideas set forth in his *Dialogues* have made their mark on numerous fields of human thought and endeavor—theology, ethics, aesthetics, political science, and virtually every branch of philosophy.

Plato was a rationalist. Indeed, he believed that the *only* real knowledge we have is our direct knowledge of eternal and unchanging truths. According to Plato, we are only confused by the impressions that we receive through the senses. Sensory perceptions, in his view, are only shadows or copies of the things that are "really real." The best we can hope for from sense experience is that it will *remind* us of ("put us in mind of") the eternal and unchanging realities.

In this selection from the *Meno*, Plato attempts to demonstrate that an unlearned slave boy is capable of directly grasping the geometrical truth that the square on the diagonal of a right triangle is equal to the sum of the squares on the sides. Socrates begins by asking a series of questions. Step by step, the boy proceeds from ignorance to knowledge and ends up *knowing* this simple geometrical truth.

Is this an example of a self-evident truth? That is the question that you should try to answer as you read the dialogue. If the slave boy ends up knowing this truth on the authority of Socrates then it is not such a truth. If he ends up knowing it "directly," then, perhaps, it is. And if it is a self-evident truth, then the next question that one must ask is whether this knowledge constitutes knowledge of the world. Plato thought it did. You may or may not agree with him.

MEN. Yes, Socrates; but what do you mean by saying that we do not learn, and that what we call learning is only a process of recollection? Can you teach me that?

From Plato, *Meno*, in *The Dialogues of Plato*, trans. Benjamin Jowett. (Boston: Aldine Publishing Co., 1911), pp. 11–55.

soc. I told you, Meno, that you were a rogue, and now you ask whether I can teach you, when I am saying that there is no teaching, but only recollection; and thus you imagine that you will involve me in a contradiction.

MEN. Indeed, Socrates, I protest that I had no such intention. I only asked the question from habit; but if you can prove to me that what you say is true, I wish that you would.

soc. That is no easy matter, but I will try to please you to the utmost of my power. Suppose that you call one of your numerous attendants, that I may demonstrate on him.

MEN. Certainly. Come hither, boy.

soc. He is Greek, and speaks Greek, does he not?

MEN. Yes; he was born in the house.

soc. Attend now to the questions which I ask him, and observe whether he learns of me or only remembers.

MEN. I will.

soc. Tell me, boy, do you know that a figure like this is a square?

BOY. I do.

soc. And you know that a square figure has these four lines equal?

BOY. Certainly.

soc. And these lines which I have drawn through the middle of the square are also equal?

BOY. Yes.

soc. A square may be of any size?

BOY. Certainly.

soc. And if one side of the figure be of two feet, and the other side be of two feet, how much will the whole be? Let me explain: if in one direction the space was of two feet, and in the other direction of one foot, the whole would be of two feet taken once?

BOY. Yes.

soc. But since this side is also of two feet, there are twice two feet?

BOY. There are.

soc. Then the square is of twice two feet?

BOY. Yes.

soc. And how many are twice two feet? count and tell me.

BOY. Four, Socrates.

soc. And might there not be another square twice as large as this, and having like this the lines equal?

BOY. Yes.

soc. And of how many feet will that be?

BOY. Of eight feet.

soc. And now try and tell me the length of the line which forms the side of that double square: this is two feet—what will that be?

BOY. Clearly, Socrates, that will be double.

soc. Do you observe, Meno, that I am not teaching the boy anything, but only asking him questions; and now he fancies that he knows how long a line is necessary in order to produce a figure of eight square feet; does he not?

MEN. Yes.

SOC. And does he really know?

MEN. Certainly not.

SOC. He only guesses that because the square is double, the line is double.

MEN. True.

SOC. Observe him while he recalls the steps in regular order. *(To the Boy.)* Tell me, boy, do you assert that a double space comes from a double line? Remember that I am not speaking of an oblong, but of a square, and of a square twice the size of this one—that is to say of eight feet; and I want to know whether you still say that a double square comes from a double line?

BOY. Yes.

SOC. But does not this line become doubled if we add another such line here?

BOY. Certainly.

SOC. And four such lines will make a space containing eight feet?

BOY. Yes.

SOC. Let us describe such a figure: is not that what you would say is the figure of eight feet?

BOY. Yes.

SOC. And are there not these four divisions in the figure, each of which is equal to the figure of four feet?

BOY. True.

SOC. And is not that four times four?

BOY. Certainly.

SOC. And four times is not double.

BOY. No, indeed.

SOC. But how much?

BOY. Four times as much.

SOC. Therefore the double line, boy, has formed a space, not twice, but four times as much.

BOY. True.

SOC. And four times four are sixteen—are they not?

BOY. Yes.

SOC. What line would give you a space of eight feet, as this gives one of sixteen feet;—do you see?

BOY. Yes.

SOC. And the space of four feet is made from this half line?

BOY. Yes.

SOC. Good; and is not a space of eight feet twice the size of this, and half the size of the other?

BOY. Certainly.

SOC. Such a space, then, will be made out of a line greater than this one, and less than that one?

BOY. Yes; that is what I think.

SOC. Very good; I like to hear you say what you think. And now tell me, is not this a line of two feet and that of four?

BOY. Yes.

SOC. Then the line which forms the side of eight feet ought to be more than this line of two feet, and less than the other of four feet?

BOY. It ought.

SOC. Try and see if you can tell me how much it will be.

BOY. Three feet.

SOC. Then if we add a half to this line of two, that will be the line of three. Here are two and there is one; and on the other side, here are two also and there is one: and that makes the figure of which you speak?

BOY. Yes.

SOC. But if there are three feet this way and three feet that way, the whole space will be three times three feet?

BOY. That is evident.

SOC. And how much are three times three feet?

BOY. Nine.

SOC. And how much is the double of four?

BOY. Eight.

SOC. Then the figure of eight is not made out of a line of three?

BOY. No.

SOC. But from what line?—tell me exactly; and if you would rather not reckon, try and show me the line.

BOY. Indeed, Socrates, I do not know.

SOC. Do you see, Meno, what advances he has made in his power of recollection? He did not know at first, and he does not know now, what is the side of a figure of eight feet: but then he thought that he knew, and answered confidently as if he knew, and had no difficulty; but now he has a difficulty, and neither knows nor fancies that he knows.

MEN. True.

SOC. Is he not better off in knowing his ignorance?

MEN. I think that he is.

SOC. If we have made him doubt, and given him the "torpedo's shock," have we done him any harm?

MEN. I think not.

SOC. We have certainly done something that may assist him in finding out the truth of the matter; and now he will wish to remedy his ignorance, but then he would have been ready to tell all the world that the double space should have a double side.

MEN. True.

SOC. But do you suppose that he would ever have inquired or learned what he fancied that he knew and did not know, until he had fallen into perplexity under the idea that he did not know, and had desired to know?

MEN. I think not, Socrates.

SOC. Then he was the better for the torpedo's touch?

MEN. I think that he was.

SOC. Mark now the farther development. I shall only ask him, and not teach him, and he shall share the inquiry with me: and do you watch and see if you find me telling or explaining anything to him, instead of eliciting his opinion. Tell me, boy, is not this a square of four feet which I have drawn?

BOY. Yes.

SOC. And now I add another square equal to the former one?

BOY. Yes.

SOC. And a third, which is equal to either of them?

BOY. Yes.

SOC. Suppose that we fill up the vacant corner.

BOY. Very good.

SOC. Here, then, there are four equal spaces?

BOY. Yes.

SOC. And how many times is this space larger than this?

BOY. Four times.

SOC. But it ought to have been twice only, as you will remember.

BOY. True.

SOC. And does not this line, reaching from corner to corner, bisect each of these spaces?

BOY. Yes.

SOC. And are there not here four equal lines which contain this space?

BOY. There are.

SOC. Look and see how much this space is.

BOY. I do not understand.

SOC. Has not each interior line cut off half of the four spaces?

BOY. Yes.

SOC. And how many such spaces are there in this division?

BOY. Four.

SOC. And how many in this?

BOY. Two.

SOC. And four is how many times two?

BOY. Twice.

SOC. And this space is of how many feet?

BOY. Of eight feet.

SOC. And from what line do you get this figure?

BOY. From this.

SOC. That is, from the line which extends from corner to corner?

BOY. Yes.

SOC. And that is the line which the learned call the diagonal. And if this is the proper name, then you, Meno's slave, are prepared to affirm that the double space is the square of the diagonal?

BOY. Certainly, Socrates.

SOC. What do you say of him, Meno? Were not all these answers given out of his own head?

MEN. Yes, they were all his own.

SOC. And yet, as we were just now saying, he did not know?

MEN. True.

SOC. And yet he had those notions in him?

MEN. Yes.

SOC. Then he who does not know still has true notions of that which he does not know?

MEN. He has.

SOC. And at present these notions are just wakening up in him, as in a dream; but if he were frequently asked the same questions, in different forms, he would know as well as any one at last?

MEN. I dare say.

SOC. Without any one teaching him he will recover his knowledge for himself, if he is only asked questions?

MEN. Yes.

SOC. And this spontaneous recovery in him is recollection?

MEN. True.

SOC. And this knowledge which he now has must he not either have acquired or always possessed?

MEN. Yes.

SOC. But if he always possessed this knowledge he would always have known; or if he has acquired the knowledge, he could not have acquired it in this life, unless he has been taught geometry; for he may be made to do the same with all geometry and every other branch of knowledge. Now, has any one ever taught him? You must know that, if, as you say, he was born and bred in your house.

MEN. And I am certain that no one ever did teach him.

SOC. And yet has he not the knowledge?

MEN. That, Socrates, is most certain.

SOC. But if he did not acquire this knowledge in this life, then clearly he must have had and learned it at some other time?

MEN. That is evident.

SOC. And that must have been the time when he was not a man?

MEN. Yes.

SOC. And if there have been always true thoughts in him, both at the time when he was and was not a man, which only need to be awakened into knowledge by putting questions to him, his soul must have always possessed this knowledge, for he always either was or was not a man?

MEN. That is clear.

SOC. And if the truth of all things always existed in the soul, then the soul is immortal. Wherefore be of good cheer, and try to recollect what you do not know, or rather do not remember.

MEN. I feel, somehow, that I like what you are saying.

SOC. And I, Meno, like what I am saying. Some things I have said of which I am not altogether confident. But that we shall be better and braver and less helpless if we think that we ought to inquire, than we should have been if we indulged in the idle fancy that there was no knowing and no use in searching after what we know not;—that is a theme upon which I am ready to fight, in word and deed, to the utmost of my power.

3

DAVID HUME (1711–1776)

Relations of Ideas and Matters of Fact

The figure of the great Scottish philospher David Hume towers over modern British and American philosophy in somewhat the same way that the figure of Plato looms large over the whole of Western philosophy. A native of Edinburgh, Hume studied law as a young man, but devoted the greater part of his life to historical and philosophical research and writing. His most important philosophical works are *A Treatise on Human Nature* (1739–1740), *An Inquiry Concerning Human Understanding* (1748), *An Inquiry Concerning the Principles of Morals* (1751), and *Dialogues Concerning Natural Religion* (1779). He also wrote a monumental *History of England* (1754–1762) and several volumes of essays.

Notwithstanding this prodigious output, success did not come easily to Hume. He reported that his first book "fell deadborn from the press," and many of those that followed fared no better during Hume's lifetime. Only later did it become clear that Hume was one of the most original thinkers of the modern era, and his influence on subsequent philosophical thought has been and continues to be enormous.

Hume believed that all our knowledge of empirical truths arises out of experience. He was, in other words, an empiricist. What Hume calls "relations of ideas" are, he

From David Hume, *An Inquiry Concerning Human Understanding,* Section IV, Part I, in *The Philosophical Works of David Hume,* Volume IV (London: Adam Black, William Tait, & Charles Tait, 1826), pp. 32–40.

says, demonstrably (self-evidently) true, but they are not empirical. What he calls
"matters of fact" are empirical, but are not demonstrably (self-evidently) true.

In the following selection, Hume tries to show that we cannot establish any truths
about the world merely by thinking about them, for "all the laws of nature, and all
the operations of bodies, without exception, are known only by experience. . . ."

All the objects of human reason or inquiry may naturally be divided into two
kinds, to wit, *Relations of Ideas,* and *Matters of Fact.* Of the first kind are the
sciences of Geometry, Algebra, and Arithmetic, and, in short, every affirmation which is either intuitively or demonstratively certain. *That the square of
the hypotenuse is equal to the square of the two sides,* is a proposition which
expresses a relation between these figures. *That three times five is equal to the
half of thirty,* expresses a relation between these numbers. Propositions of this
kind are discoverable by the mere operation of thought, without dependence
on what is anywhere existent in the universe. Though there never were a circle
or triangle in nature, the truths demonstrated by Euclid would forever retain
their certainty and evidence.

Matters of fact, which are the second objects of human reason, are not
ascertained in the same manner; nor is our evidence of their truth, however
great, of a like nature with the foregoing. The contrary of every matter of fact
is still possible, because it can never imply a contradiction, and is conceived
by the mind with the same facility and distinctness, as if ever so conformable
to reality. *That the sun will not rise to-morrow,* is no less intelligible a proposition, and implies no more contradiction, than the affirmation, *that it will rise.*
We should in vain, therefore, attempt to demonstrate its falsehood. Were it
demonstratively false, it would imply a contradiction, and could never be
distinctly conceived by the mind.

It may therefore be a subject worthy of curiosity, to inquire what is the
nature of that evidence, which assures us of any real existence and matter of
fact, beyond the present testimony of our senses, or the records of our memory.
This part of philosophy, it is observable, had been little cultivated either by
the ancients or moderns; and therefore our doubts and errors, in the prosecu-
tion of so important an inquiry, may be the more excusable, while we march
through such difficult paths without any guide or direction. They may even
prove useful, by exciting curiosity, and destroying that implicit faith and
security which is the bane of all reasoning and free inquiry. The discovery of
defects in the common philosophy, if any such there be, will not, I presume,
be a discouragement, but rather an incitement, as is usual, to attempt something more full and satisfactory than has yet been proposed to the public.

All reasonings concerning matter of fact seem to be founded on the relation
of *Cause and Effect.* By means of that relation alone we can go beyond the
evidence of our memory and senses. If you were to ask a man why he believes

any matter of fact which is absent, for instance, that his friend is in the country or in France, he would give you a reason, and this reason would be some other fact: as a letter received from him, or the knowledge of his former resolutions and promises. A man, finding a watch or any other machine in a desert island, would conclude that there had once been men in that island. All our reasonings concerning fact are of the same nature. And here it is constantly supposed, that there is a connection between the present fact and that which is inferred from it. Were there nothing to bind them together, the inference would be entirely precarious. The hearing of an articulate voice and rational discourse in the dark, assures us of the presence of some person: Why? because these are the effects of the human make and fabric, and closely connected with it. If we anatomize all the other reasonings of this nature, we shall find, that they are founded on the relation of cause and effect, and that this relation is either near or remote, direct or collateral. Heat and light are collateral effects of fire, and the one effect may justly be inferred from the other.

If we would satisfy ourselves, therefore, concerning the nature of that evidence which assures us of matters of fact, we must inquire how we arrive at the knowledge of cause and effect.

I shall venture to affirm, as a general proposition which admits of no exception, that the knowledge of this relation is not, in any instance, attained by reasonings *a priori;* but arises entirely from experience, when we find, that any particular objects are constantly conjoined with each other. Let an object be presented to a man of ever so strong natural reason and abilities; if that object be entirely new to him, he will not be able, by the most accurate examination of its sensible qualities, to discover any of its causes or effects. Adam, though his rational faculties be supposed, at the very first, entirely perfect, could not have inferred from the fluidity and transparency of water, that it would suffocate him; or from the light and warmth of fire that it would consume him. No object ever discovers, by the qualities which appear to the senses, either the causes which produced it, or the effects which will arise from it; nor can our reason, unassisted by experience, ever draw any inference concerning real existence and matter of fact.

This proposition, *that causes and effects are discoverable, not by reason, but by experience,* will readily be admitted with regard to such objects as we remember to have once been altogether unknown to us; since we must be conscious of the utter inability which we then lay under of foretelling what would arise from them. Present two smooth pieces of marble to a man who has no tincture of natural philosophy; he will never discover that they will adhere together in such a manner as to require great force to separate them in a direct line, while they make so small a resistance to a lateral pressure. Such events as bear little analogy to the common course of nature, are also readily confessed to be known only by experience; nor does any man imagine that the explosion of gunpowder, or the attraction of a loadstone, could ever be discovered by arguments *a priori.* In like manner, when an effect is supposed to depend upon an intricate machinery or secret structure of parts, we make no difficulty in attributing all our knowledge of it to experience. Who will assert that he can give the ultimate reason, why milk or bread is proper nourishment for a man, not for a lion or tiger?

But the same truth may not appear at first sight to have the same evidence with regard to events, which have become familiar to us from our first appearance in the world, which bear a close analogy to the whole course of nature, and which are supposed to depend on the simple qualities of objects, without any secret structure of parts. We are apt to imagine, that we could discover these effects by the mere operation of our reason without experience. We fancy, that were we brought on a sudden into this world, we could at first have inferred, that one billiard-ball would communicate motion to another upon impulse; and that we needed not to have waited for the event, in order to pronounce with certainty concerning it. Such is the influence of custom, that where it is strongest, it not only covers our natural ignorance, but even conceals itself, and seems not to take place, merely because it is found in the highest degree.

But to convince us, that all the laws of nature, and all the operations of bodies, without exception, are known only by experience, the following reflections may perhaps suffice. Were any object presented to us, and were we required to pronounce concerning the effect which will result from it, without consulting past observation; after what manner, I beseech you, must the mind proceed in this operation? It must invent or imagine some event which it ascribes to the object as its effect; and it is plain that this invention must be entirely arbitrary. The mind can never possibly find the effect in the supposed cause, by the most accurate scrutiny and examination. For the effect is totally different from the cause, and consequently can never be discovered in it. Motion in the second billiard-ball is a quite distinct event from motion in the first; nor is there anything in the one to suggest the smallest hint of the other. A stone or piece of metal raised into the air, and left without any support, immediately falls: But to consider the matter *a priori,* is there anything we discover in this situation which can beget the idea of a downward, rather than an upward, or any other motion, in the stone or metal?

And as the first imagination or invention of a particular effect, in all natural operations, is arbitrary, where we consult not experience; so must we also esteem the supposed tie or connexion between the cause and effect which binds them together, and renders it impossible, that any other effect could result from the operation of that cause. When I see, for instance, a billiard-ball moving in a straight line towards another; even suppose motion in the second ball should by accident be suggested to me as the result of their contact or impulse; may I not conceive that a hundred different events might as well follow from that cause? May not both these balls remain at absolute rest? May not the first ball return in a straight line, or leap off from the second in any line or direction? All these suppositions are consistent and conceivable. Why then should we give the preference to one, which is no more consistent or conceivable than the rest? All our reasonings *a priori* will never be able to show us any foundation for this preference.

In a word, then, every effect is a distinct event from its cause. It could not, therefore, be discovered in the cause; and the first invention or conception of it, *a priori,* must be entirely arbitrary. And even after it is suggested, the conjunction of it with the cause must appear equally arbitrary; since there are always many other effects, which, to reason, must seem fully as consistent and natural. In vain, therefore, should we pretend to determine any single event, or infer any cause or effect, without the assistance of observation and experience.

Hence we may discover the reason, why no philosopher, who is rational and modest, has ever pretended to assign the ultimate cause of any natural operation, or to show distinctly the action of that power, which produces any single effect in the universe. It is confessed, that the utmost effort of human reason is, to reduce the principles productive of natural phenomena to a greater simplicity, and to resolve the many particular effects into a few general causes, by means of reasonings from analogy, experience, and observation. But as to the causes of these general causes, we should in vain attempt their discovery; nor shall we ever be able to satisfy ourselves by any particular explication of them. These ultimate springs and principles are totally shut up from human curiosity and inquiry. Elasticity, gravity, cohesion of parts, communication of motion by impulse; these are probably the ultimate causes and principles which we shall ever discover in nature; and we may esteem ourselves sufficiently happy, if, by accurate inquiry and reasoning, we can trace up the particular phenomona to, or near to, these general principles. The most perfect philosophy of the natural kind only staves off our ignorance a little longer; as perhaps the most perfect philosophy of the moral or metaphysical kind serves only to discover larger portions of it. Thus the observation of human blindness and weakness is the result of all philosophy, and meets us, at every turn, in spite of our endeavours to elude or avoid it.

Nor is geometry, when taken into the assistance of natural philosophy, ever able to remedy this defect, or lead us into the knowledge of ultimate causes, by all that accuracy of reasoning for which it is so justly celebrated. Every part of mixed mathematics proceeds upon the supposition, that certain laws are established by Nature in her operations; and abstract reasonings are employed, either to assist experience in the discovery of these laws, or to determine their influence in particular instances, where it depends upon any precise degree of distance and quantity. Thus, it is a law of motion, discovered by experience, that the moment or force of any body in motion, is in the compound ratio or proportion of its solid contents and its velocity: and consequently, that a small force may remove the greatest obstacle, or raise the greatest weight, if by any contrivance or machinery we can increase the velocity of that force, so as to make it an overmatch for its antagonist. Geometry assists us in the application of this law, by giving us the just dimensions of all the parts and figures which can enter into any species of machine; but still the discovery of the law itself is owing merely to experience; and all the abstract reasonings in the world could never lead us one step towards the knowledge of it. When we reason *a priori*, and consider merely any object or cause, as it appears to the mind, independent of all observation, it never could suggest to us the notion of any distinct object, such as its effect; much less show us the inseparable and inviolable connection between them. A man must be very sagacious who could discover by reasoning, that crystal is the effect of heat, and ice of cold, without being previously acquainted with the operation of these qualities.

4

IMMANUEL KANT (1724–1804)

Analytic and Synthetic Truths

Kant lived nearly his entire life in the German city of Königsberg, the city in which he was born. At the University of Königsberg he studied mathematics, physics, philosophy, and theology, and he spent most of his adult life as a teacher at that same university. His teaching responsibilities covered an incredibly broad range of fields: mathematics, physics, geography, anthropology, ethics, natural theology, logic, and metaphysics. His most important philosophical work, *Critique of Pure Reason*, was published in 1781 when Kant was already fifty-seven years of age. This book proved to be only the beginning of an astonishing authorship, however, as it was followed by *Prolegomena to Any Future Metaphysics* (1783), *Foundations of the Metaphysics of Morals* (1785), *Metaphysical First Principles of Natural Science* (1786), a second and substantially revised edition of the first *Critique* (1787), *Critique of Practical Reason* (1788), *Critique of Judgment* (1790), *Religion Within the Limits of Reason Alone* (1793), *Perpetual Peace* (1795), *Metaphysics of Morals* (1797), and *Thoughts*

From Immanuel Kant, *Prolegomena to Any Future Metaphysics*, Preamble, Section 2, in *Kant's Prolegomena and Metaphysical Foundations of Natural Science*, trans. E. Ban (London: George Bell & Sons, 1891), pp. 12–16.

on *Pedagogy* (1803). He made important contributions to many areas of philosophical study, and every philosopher since Kant has had to take account of his philosophy.

Although Kant remained a rationalist of sorts to the end of his life, he credited David Hume with having "awakened" him from his "dogmatic slumbers" and setting his thought moving in a new direction. Indeed, he acknowledges that he found the teachings of Hume extremely unsettling, for they seemed to undermine the whole of human knowledge, including mathematics and the natural sciences. Thus, a major part of the task that Kant set for himself was to show how it is possible to have an absolutely certain knowledge about space (in geometry) and nature (in natural science).

Kant uses the term *a priori* to describe a way of knowing that is not dependent on the facts of experience. A truth that is known directly, merely by attending to it and thinking about it, is known a priori. All knowledge of "analytical truths" (what Hume had called "relations of ideas") is a priori. But, according to Kant, the important question is whether we have any a priori knowledge of "synthetical" truths (Hume's "matters of fact"). Kant thinks we do, and in the selection that follows attempts to show that the truths of mathematics and, in particular, geometrical truths, are a priori in nature.

A. OF THE DISTINCTION BETWEEN SYNTHETIC AND ANALYTIC JUDGMENTS GENERALLY*

Metaphysical knowledge must contain simply judgments *a priori,* so much is demanded by the speciality of its sources. But judgments, let them have what origin they may, or let them even as regards logical form be constituted as they may, possess a distinction according to their content, by virtue of which they are either simply *explanatory* and contribute nothing to the content of a cognition, or they are *extensive,* and enlarge the given cognition; the first may be termed *analytic,* and the second *synthetic* judgments.

Analytic judgments say nothing in the predicate, but what was already cogitated in the conception of the subject, though perhaps not so clearly, or with the same degree of consciousness. When I say, all bodies are extended, I do not thereby enlarge my conception of a body in the least, but simply analyse it, inasmuch as extension, although not expressly stated, was already cogitated in that conception; the judgment is, in other words, analytic. On the other hand, the proposition, some bodies are heavy, contains something in the predicate which was not already cogitated in the general conception of a body; it enlarges, that is to say, my knowledge, in so far as it adds something to my conception; and must therefore be termed a synthetic judgment.

*Kant's expression "erkenntniss" I have variously translated "knowledge" and "cognition," according to circumstances and the usages of the English language (Tr.).

B. THE COMMON PRINCIPLE OF ALL ANALYTIC JUDGMENTS IS THE PRINCIPLE OF CONTRADICTION

All analytic judgments are based entirely on the principle of contradiction, and are by their nature cognitions *a priori,* whether the conceptions serving as their matter be empirical or not. For inasmuch as the predicate of an affirmative analytic judgment is previously cogitated in the conception of the subject, it cannot without contradiction be denied of it; in the same way, its contrary, in a negative analytic judgment, must necessarily be denied of the subject, likewise in accordance with the principle of contradiction. It is thus with the propositions—every body is extended; no body is unextended (simple). For this reason all analytic propositions are judgments *a priori,* although their conceptions may be empirical. Let us take as an instance the proposition, gold is a yellow metal. Now, to know this, I require no further experience beyond my conception of gold, which contains the propositions that this body is yellow and a metal; for this constitutes precisely my conception, and therefore I have only to dissect it, without needing to look around for anything elsewhere.

C. SYNTHETIC JUDGMENTS DEMAND A PRINCIPLE OTHER THAN THAT OF CONTRADICTION

There are synthetic judgments *a posteriori* whose origin is empirical; but there are also others of an *a priori* certainty, that spring from the Understanding and the Reason. But both are alike in this, that they can never have their source solely in the axiom of analysis, viz., the principle of contradiction; they require an altogether different principle, notwithstanding that whatever principle they may be deduced from, they must always *conform to the principle of contradiction,* for nothing can be opposed to this principle, although not everything can be deduced from it. I will first of all bring synthetic judgments under certain classes.

(1) *Judgments of experience* are always synthetic. It would be absurd to found an analytic judgment on experience, as it is unnecessary to go beyond my own conception in order to construct the judgment, and therefore the confirmation of experience is unnecessary to it. That a body is extended is a proposition possessing *a priori* certainty, and no judgment of experience. For before I go to experience I have all the conditions of my judgment already present in the conception, out of which I simply draw the predicate in accordance with the principle of contradiction, and thereby at the same time the *necessity* of the judgment may be known, a point which experience could never teach me.

(2) *Mathematical judgments* are in their entirety synthetic. This truth seems hitherto to have altogether escaped the analysts of human Reason; indeed, to be directly opposed to all their suppositions, although it is indisputa-

bly certain and very important in its consequences. For, because it was found that the conclusions of mathematicians all proceed according to the principle of contradiction (which the nature of every apodictic certainty demands), it was concluded that the axioms were also known through the principle of contradiction, which was a great error; for though a synthetic proposition can be viewed in the light of the above principle, it can only be so by presupposing another synthetic proposition from which it is derived, but never by itself.

It must be first of all remarked that essentially mathematical propositions are always *a priori,* and never empirical, because they involve necessity, which cannot be inferred from experience. Should any one be unwilling to admit this, I will limit my assertion to *pure mathematics,* the very conception of which itself brings with it the fact that it contains nothing empirical, but simply pure knowledge *a priori.*

At first sight, one might be disposed to think the proposition $7 + 5 = 12$ merely analytic, resulting from the conception of a sum of seven and five, according to the principle of contradiction. But more closely considered it will be found that the conception of the sum of 7 and 5 comprises nothing beyond the union of two numbers in a single one, and that therein nothing whatever is cogitated as to what this single number is, that comprehends both the others. The conception of twelve is by no means already cogitated, when I think merely of the union of seven and five, and I may dissect my conception of such a possible sum as long as I please, without discovering therein the number twelve. One must leave these conceptions, and call to one's aid an intuition corresponding to one or other of them, as for instance one's five fingers (or, like Segner in his Arithmetic, five points), and so gradually add the units of the five given in intuition to the conception of the seven. One's conception is therefore really enlarged by the proposition $7 + 5 = 12$; to the first a new one being added, that was in nowise cogitated in the former; in other words, arithmetical propositions are always synthetic, a truth which is more apparent when we take rather larger numbers, for we must then be clearly convinced, that turn and twist our conceptions as we may, without calling intuition to our aid, we shall never find the sum required, by the mere dissection of them.

Just as little is any axiom of pure geometry analytic. That a *straight* line is the shortest between two points, is a synthetic proposition. For my conception of *straight,* has no reference to size, but only to quality. The conception of the "shortest" therefore is quite additional, and cannot be drawn from any analysis of the conception of a straight line. Intuition must therefore again be taken to our aid, by means of which alone the synthesis is possible.

Certain other axioms, postulated by geometricians, are indeed really analytic and rest on the principle of contradiction, but they only serve, like identical propositions, as links in the chain of method, and not themselves as principles; as for instance $a = a$, the whole is equal to itself, or $(a + b) > a$, i.e., the whole is greater than its part. But even these, although they are contained in mere conceptions, are only admitted in mathematics because they can be presented in intuition. What produces the common belief that the predicate of such apodictic judgments lies already in our conception, and that the judgment is therefore analytic, is merely the ambiguity of expression. We *ought*, namely, to cogitate a certain predicate to a given conception, and this necessity adheres even to the conceptions themselves. But the question is not what we *ought* to, but what we actually *do,* although obscurely, cogitate in them; this shows us that the predicate of those conceptions is dependent indeed necessarily, though not immediately (but by means of an added intuition), upon its subject.

5

CLARENCE IRVING LEWIS (1883 – 1964)

The A Priori and the Empirical

C. I. Lewis, for many years a professor of philosophy at Harvard University, is best known for his contributions to the development of logic, epistemology, and value theory. His writings include two books on symbolic logic, an epistemological study called *An Analysis of Knowledge and Valuation,* and a wide-ranging work entitled *Mind and the World Order* (from which the following selection is taken).

Lewis argues that, in all knowledge of empirical truths, there are a priori elements as well as elements that are not a priori. His general thesis is that (a) conceptual systems are a priori, (b) the applicability of such systems to actual experience is a matter of trial and error, and (c) our choice of one conceptual system over another depends primarily on its usefulness. This, to be sure, is empiricism, since it follows that no empirical truths are self-evidently true (known a priori, to use Kant's terminology). But it is a form of empiricism that gives considerably more credence to the role of a priori conceptual systems than many empiricists would allow.

From C. I. Lewis, "The A Priori and the Empirical," in *Mind and the World Order* (New York: Dover, 1956), pp. 293–308. Reprinted by permission of the publisher.

Now I believe it should be obvious, no matter what theory of knowledge is held, that there is only one ground on which the necessary connection of X and Y, such that all X's will certainly be Y's can be known; that is, that if we find that the concept Y is inapplicable to any particular, then the concept X will be retracted as likewise inapplicable. If we know with certainty in advance that all men are mortal, we know it because if we discover any being not to be subject to the accident of death, then, however like a man he may appear, we shall refuse to recognize him as human. We can know that the sum of the angles of a triangle must be 180 degrees only if in case we find this not so in a particular instance, we shall retract the concept "Euclidean triangle" as inapplicable to the thing in question. Whenever this is so, the subject concept implies or includes the predicate concept and the proposition is a priori because the judgment is analytic.

If the problem of empirical knowledge is supposed to be "How can we be assured that objects met with in experience and identified as X's will never turn out not to be Y's?" then, again, I believe it should be clear on any theory of knowledge that we can never have such assurance, especially if it is remembered that there is no a priori certainty that perception in any particular case is not illusory or subject to the accident of mistaken identification. That is to say, it should always have been clear, if we remember that "experience" as we are confronted with it includes the non-veridical, that the application of concepts in naming and recognizing objects, itself implies characters of the object which are not now presented but wait upon further experience to be revealed.

Remembering this, it will be evident that the only kind of a priori knowledge of the empirical for which there is room in a consistent theory is that kind which consists in knowing the empirical eventualities, implicit in the application of our subject-concept, which are indispensable to the *correctness* of such application. We do not need any limitation of possible experience to be assured of this. If a thing is not an X unless further experience will corroborate a certain Y-character of it, then, let experience be what it will, all X's must be Y's. It is true that this leaves *all* empirical knowledge—except the hypothetical—subject to the tests of later experience, in the sense that such future experience may invalidate our identification and naming of objects. But my point is that no theory ever presented can do more, unless we can be absolutely certain of our recognitions of objects in momentary experience. Such certainty of momentary identification is something which no theory has ever claimed explicitly, though *most* theories have, as a matter of fact, proceeded *as if* it were possible.

Take, for example, geometrical knowledge. Kant claimed a *synthetic* ground of our knowledge of the necessary connection between "the triangular" and "figures having interior angles which sum up to 180 degrees." This synthetic ground was supplied by the limitation of possible human experience to the Euclidean space-form. But did Kant suppose that this limitation of possible experience enabled us to glance at a plot of ground and say with a priori certainty that the sum of its angles was exactly 180 degrees? If not, could one claim—accepting Kant's theory—that this a priori limitation of experience in any fashion assured to our knowledge of this particular plot of ground (or of any other particular) a certainty which future experience might not trench upon? There can be no doubt that the answer must be negative. What, then, as regards our knowledge of the empirical, is the supposed advantage of this synthetic element supplied by the limitation of possible experience? Absolutely all that it assures us, about any empirically given object, is that, *if* it be truly triangular, then the sum of its angles will be 180 degrees; and whether this condition is satisfied in any particular case, it leaves subject to the test of future and more exact determination.

One may further inquire: If we can never, in a momentary apprehension of anything, be absolutely certain that it is a real Euclidean triangle, *how* are we to know that the class of objects actually identifiable as triangles have this further property of the sum of their angles, unless by the fact that if they do not have it, then we shall retract the ascription of real triangularity as inapplicable to them? We now see this plot of ground: it looks triangular. In this momentary experience, there is absolutely no way in which we can tell that it is not. Suppose we proceed to measure its angles with a theodolite, and find that the sum is 181 degrees. Does the Kantian, or any other, theory deny this possibility? If not, then the only ground on which we can know that what is actually identifiable as triangle will have the further property in question is, in the last analysis, some ground which will lead to the repudiation as "not-triangular" of that which fails, in further experience, to give the required measure of its interior angles, even though, as presented at a certain moment, it was indistinguishable from a real triangle.

Let us take one step further. If a good Kantian must still grant, in the interests of veracity, that the generalization "All figures which are momentarily indistinguishable from the triangular have angles which sum up to 180 degrees" would be false, then how can it be claimed with plausibility that experience of a world in which the laws of Euclid do not hold would be impossible to human beings? If in *one* case we can see as triangular a figure the measure of whose angles exceeds 180 degrees, in what sense would it be impossible that this should be *universally* true? How would a form of intuition prevent us from seeing just as we now do a space whose properties would be Riemannian?

Is it not fairly obvious that the real question about the applicability of Euclid to our space is not the question of what we can imagine or could conceivably experience; but is the question whether the character of experience in general is such that the procedure by which the failure of any spatial object to verify the Euclidean properties is put down to mistaken apprehension is one which gets on better (*i.e.,* better serves our interests of reducing experience to order and securing control) than would any general revision of our whole system of geometrical conceptions?

The situation in which we find ourselves as a result of modern developments in geometry is in accord with this conception of a priori knowledge and its relation to the empirical. As modern mathematics discovers, the concept "triangle" (and the other basic concepts of geometry) include a logically sufficient ground for *all* the properties of triangles, without any synthetic element which is supposed to limit experience. To be sure, this means entire separation of the question of abstract geometrical truth from the truth of experience. This last becomes a question of empirical generalization—or more accurately, it is the complex question: Which of the alternative systems of geometrical concepts will best succeed in its application to experience; it being remembered that what such application requires is that any geometrical concept will be retracted as inapplicable when experience fails to verify the essential geometrical properties—*i. e.,* that all *divergence* of experience from our chosen geometry is to be explained on other grounds, or relegated to the status of mistaken apprehension?

From this point of view, the development of the conceptual system in the abstract is a priori; the question of the applicability of one of its constituent concepts to any single particular is a matter of probability; and the question of application *in general* is the question of the *choice* of an abstract conceptual system, determined by pragmatic considerations.

We find that there is much more in the abstract concepts than Kant thought —that as a fact the whole geometrical system can be drawn from them by purely logical analysis; and we find that in any case the application to *particulars* is no better than probable. Under these circumstances, it is extremely dubious what advantage would accrue if we *could* find a ground for a priori truth which was synthetic and consisted in some limitation of the possibilities of intuition. And we find the supposition that there *is* limitation and that we can know it, vitiated by the fact that we most certainly *could* have an experience in which Euclidean-appearing things should, upon further examination, turn out to have non-Euclidean properties. The *only* question about a priori truth in application which is left to be determined is the question what shall be accepted as the empirical *criteria* of triangularity, straightness, and so on. This is at once the question *what* kinds of sequences in experience are to be regarded as ground for attributing mistake to *previous identifications* of spatial characters in things, and the question *what* abstract system shall be our choice for application to experience in general. The chosen system becomes criterion of the veridical in experience, that is, its concepts become *criteria of reality* of a certain sort. It is this question of the choice of conceptual systems for the interpretation of experience which, on the view here presented, is a matter of pragmatic choice, whether that choice be made deliberately, or unconsciously and without recognition of its real grounds.

If, now, the reader will generalize from this illustration in terms of the geometrical, he will have before him the distinguishing characteristics of the present theory of the relation between a priori truth and the content of experience. While other concepts than the mathematical do not usually have their consequences so systematically worked out, nevertheless all concepts give rise to an a priori truth which is purely analytic and independent of any application to experience. Such analytic consequences of a single concept, in isolation, will be relatively meager and relatively trivial. But how complex, far-reaching, and important the analytic consequences may be when three or four such abstract concepts are conjoined, modern systems of mathematics serve to illustrate. That which *any* such concept denotes is always something which, in terms of experience, must have a temporal spread. What is required to determine its applicability, is some orderly sequence in experience, or some set of such. At any given moment, such applicability is verifiable only approximately or in degree. It is thus that the application of the concept to experience may be secured without loss of its a priori character: its logical consequences, which time alone can verify, become *criteria of its applicability.* Later experience which does not accord will lead to the retraction of the concept as inapplicable to the particular to which it was assigned by previous interpretation. Thus the logical requisites a priori of the concept become, in its application to experience, the criteria of reality of a certain sort. The application a priori of Euclidean geometry to nature means, for example, that whatever apprehended particular turns out, in the course of experience, not to have the properties logically implied by the concept "Euclidean triangle" will be condemned as *not a real triangle,* however much it may have looked like one.

Up to this point, there has been no consideration of the last of the five distinct kinds of apprehension or knowledge mentioned at the beginning of the chapter, *i. e.,* empirical generalizations, ordinarily so-called. We have found that a certain kind of empirical generalization enters into the judgment of truth about empirical particulars. But these are not of the type ordinarily called "generalizations" since the subject of them is the presentation itself; they are usually not expressed at all and are indeed, as we found, difficult to express in language without including reference beyond themselves to objective and enduring things. Customarily what is meant by "empirical generalization" is a universal proposition the subject of which denotes a class of *objects.* It is distinguished from the a priori in application by the fact that the connection between subject and predicate is not necessary but contingent. A simple illustration may be here of service. The proposition "All swans are birds" is a priori because if any creature originally designated as a "swan" should be discovered to lack some distinguishing character of birds, the name "swan" would be withdrawn. The applicability of the predicate term is logically requisite to the applicability of the subject. But the proposition "All swans are white" is an empirical generalization because white color is not included as essential in the denotation assigned to "swan." The former proposition can not be falsified by any possible experience because its truth has a purely logical warrant; it represents the implication of a concept. But the latter proposition has no such logical warrant and *may* be falsified by experience; black creatures having all the essential properties of swans may be discovered. It is to be noted that any universal proposition asserts the nonexistence of some class of things: that all swans are birds requires that there be no non-bird swans; that all swans are white, asserts that the class of swans of different color is a class which has no members. But the proposition which is a priori does *not* assert any limitation of experience; it asserts only that whatever lacks some essential property, *X*, is not to be classified under some concept, *A*. That all swans must be birds, does not legislate out of existence any possible creature. The empirical generalization, however, *does* require for its truth a limitation of nature and of experience: that all swans are white, excludes certain conceivable creatures from existence. It is thus that the a priori proposition is assured with certainty in advance, while the empirical generalization requires for its theoretical certitude a verification which extends to all reality.

The empirical generalization is forever at the mercy of future experience, and hence probable only, while the a priori proposition is forever certain. But as the above example points out, this does not represent any greater assurance about the content of future experience, or of nature, in the one case than in the other; it represents only an intention of interpretation or classification which maintains a connection between two concepts regardless of experience in the one case but not in the other. Since the a priori in general is definitive and analytic, not synthetic, the case is the same for all a priori propositions.

This particular example is trivial because the classification "swan" is not a very comprehensive one; its systematic interconnection with other classes and categories is relatively slight and unimportant. But more impressive examples can be given to illustrate the same point—that the a priori does not dictate to nature but concerns our interpretation of empirical facts. For example, the law of gravitation is a posteriori because, if it fails of verification, we shall still not abandon the concept "mass," or any of the other terms, but only the relation between them stated by the law. By contrast, geometry is a priori because if the sum of the angles of what is identified as a Euclidean triangle turn out to be other than 180°, we shall condemn the experience as "mistake"; and if a sufficient number of such attempted verifications have, without exception, the same result, we shall abandon the Euclidean character of our space but not the meaning of "Euclidean triangle." I should suppose that the probability of Newton's laws and of those theorems of celestial mechanics which are purely geometrical is of the same order of magnitude. Certainly there is nothing in the a priori character of geometry to give us any superior assurance that experience will conform to it. In so far as certain principles operate as criteria of reality and apparent exception to them condemns the experience as illusory, the a priori may seem to have another significance. But this is only because *"nature" is itself a category*—the very fundamental and important category of the physical: what is extruded from it is still an absolutely given and un-get-overable fact of experience, requiring to be dealt with in some other way if we are to understand it at all. It is, in fact, easy to exaggerate the cleavage between the physical and the merely mental or psychological, such as the illusory, as one may observe by a serious consideration of the question whether mirages and mirror-images belong to nature or are merely mental.

The facts which I should like here to emphasize are mainly two. In the first place, that no substantive conception, determined a priori, is able to confine particular experiences within its conceptual embrace with absolute assurance; that all identifications of objects and all *material* truth about future experience remains probable only. The supposition that any theory may secure for the a priori a different significance than this, is a delusion. The impossibility of it will become apparent if we remember two things: that experience includes dream, illusion, and mistake as much as "the physical"; and that no theory, even on its own showing, can attribute an a priori certainty which is not hypothetical to predications about the particular presented thing. In the second place, I would emphasize the fact that the whole body of our conceptual interpretations form a sort of hierarchy or pyramid with the most comprehensive, such as those of logic, at the top, and the least general, such as "swans," etc., at the bottom; that with this complex system of interrelated concepts, we approach particular experiences and attempt to fit them, somewhere and somehow, into its preformed patterns. Persistent failure leads to readjustment; the applicability of certain concepts to experiences of some particular sort is abandoned, and some other conceptual pattern is brought forward for application. The higher up a concept stands in our pyramid, the more reluctant we are to disturb it, because the more radical and far-reaching the results will be if we abandon the application of it in some particular fashion. The decision that there are no such creatures as have been defined as "swans," would be unimportant. The conclusion that there are no such things as Euclidean triangles, would be immensely disturbing. And if we should be forced to realize that nothing in experience possesses any stability—that our principle, "Nothing can both be and not be," was merely a verbalism, applying to nothing more than momentarily—that dénouement would rock our world to its foundations.

On the one hand, every concept, however unimportant, gives rise to a formal truth exhibiting its structure, which it is beyond experience to invalidate and which in its own little way is a criterion of reality. The concept "swan" determines what is, and what is not, a real *swan;* though what is not a swan is, perhaps, some other kind of bird. And on the other hand, *no* concept or principle, however basic, can be *guaranteed* to bring lucidity and comprehension by being applied to particular experiences in a predetermined way. Even the laws of logic prescribe only what is real *thing,* or properly determined *event,* and do not prevent those evanescent appearances and puzzling transitions of experience which it baffles us to understand. On the one side, there is the Platonic heaven of our concepts, with the beautiful clarity of their patterned interrelations, and their absolute truth. On the other side there is the chaos of given experience. The bringing of these two together is a matter of trial and error; is that empirical and material truth which is never more than probable, and is subject to continual revision in the process of our learning. That kind of revision which means the abandonment of certain concepts as not truly applicable to certain areas of experience is more fundamental and important than the mere giving up of empirical generalizations previously held. But it is only a deeper-lying phase of that process which the progress of our understanding may necessitate.

The truth of the a priori is formal only; but we cannot capture the truth of experience if we have no net to catch it in—that is its immense importance. But so far as the validity of all material truth depends upon the predictability of particular experience, the problem of our knowledge of it is that of the validity of our probability-judgments. That there may be no such valid knowledge because "there are no necessary connections of matters of fact," represents a problem which is still to be met.

For Further Reading

Aune, Bruce. *Rationalism, Empiricism, and Pragmatism.* New York: Random House, 1970 (paperbound).

Blanshard, Brand. *The Nature of Thought,* Vol. 1. New York: Humanities Press, 1939, Chaps. 28–30.

————. *Reason and Analysis.* LaSalle, Ill.: Open Court Publishing Co., 1962, Chaps. 6 and 10.

Cassirer, Ernst. *The Problem of Knowledge,* trans. by W. H. Woglom and C. W. Hendel. New Haven, Conn.: Yale University Press, 1950, Chaps. 1–4.

Hamlyn, D. W. *The Theory of Knowledge.* Garden City, N.Y.: Doubleday, 1970 (paperbound).

Harris, James F., and Richard H. Stevens (eds.). *Analyticity.* New York: Quadrangle Books, 1970.

Leibniz, G. W. *New Essays Concerning Human Understanding.* Many editions. See especially Book I and Book IV, Chaps. 1–9.

Monsat, Stanley (ed.). *The Analytic-Synthetic Distinction.* Belmont, Calif.: Wadsworth, 1971. Both classical and contemporary selections.

Morick, H. (ed.). *Challenges to Empiricism.* Belmont, Calif.: Wadsworth, 1972. Contemporary papers.

Pap, Arthur. "Are All Necessary Propositions Analytic?" *The Philosophical Review,* 58 (1949), 229–320.

Pears, David. *What Is Knowledge?* New York: Harper & Row, 1971.

Quine, W. van Orman. *From a Logical Point of View,* 2nd. ed., rev. New York: Harper & Row, 1961 (paperbound). See especially "Two Dogmas of Empiricism."

Reichenbach, Hans. *The Rise of Scientific Philosophy.* Berkeley and Los Angeles: University of California Press, 1958 (paperbound).

Russell, Bertrand. *Introduction to Mathematical Philosophy.* New York: Humanities Press, 1960, Chaps. 1, 2, 13, and 14.

Ryle, G., K. Popper, and C. Lewy. "Why Are the Calculuses of Logic and Mathematics Applicable to Reality?" *Proceedings of the Aristotelian Society,* Supplementary 20 (1946), 20–60.

Sleigh, R. C., Jr. (ed.). *Necessary Truth.* Englewood Cliffs, N.J.: Prentice-Hall, 1972.

Sumner, L. W., and John Woods (eds.). *Necessary Truth: A Book of Readings.* New York: Random House, 1969.

PART III

The Problem of Induction

If we assume that our senses do not usually deceive us, it is easy to understand how we know such everyday truths as the color of our eyes, the name of the city in which we live, or the shape of some object that is at this moment within our field of vision. We know these things by sense experience: we have looked at ourselves in the mirror, we have seen the name of our city displayed in countless places, we are at this moment seeing the object that is before us. If *any* knowledge about the world is relatively secure, it would seem to be just such knowledge.

Most of our supposed knowledge of the world, however, goes beyond the immediate facts of sense experience. Strictly speaking, our senses only tell us what appears to be the case in a particular place or at a particular moment in time. Even the statement, "My eyes are blue," goes beyond what I can absolutely assert on the basis of sense experience. All that my experience entitles me to assert is that each and every time that I have looked in the mirror I have observed a pair of blue eyes peering back at me. I confidently expect that the next time I look in the mirror I will again see a pair of blue eyes, but I cannot claim to know this on the basis of experience.

How, then, do I know this—or do I not know it? How do I know *anything* about the world except the particular facts that I happen to have observed? How do I know that unsupported heavier-than-air objects fall toward the earth, that the sun always rises in the East, that crows are black, that birds migrate? I have observed a few instances of each of these generalizations, but the generalizations go far beyond what I have observed: they concern *all* the fallings of unsupported heavier-than-air objects; *all* the risings of the sun; *all* past, present, and future migrating birds. How can I claim to know these things? How can I infer from the few facts that I have observed to the infinitely greater number of facts that I have not observed?

It helps a bit, perhaps, to supplement our own experience with that of others. "Millions of people have observed tens of millions of crows," it may be said, "and all those crows have been black. Therefore, it seems safe to conclude that *all* crows are black." Well, perhaps. But have any of those millions of observers seen any *future* crows? They have not. Their observations warrant only the assertion that all the crows observed *in the past* have been black. How, then, can we use this as evidence that future crows will also be black? How can we reason from the observed to the unobserved, from some to all, from the past to the future, from here to everywhere? This is the problem of induction.

Philosophers concerned with the problem of induction fall into three main groups: rationalists, empiricists, and skeptics. Rationalists argue that inductive reasoning presupposes a knowledge of some principle that is not a product of inductive reasoning but is self-evident (known a priori). Empiricists who seek to justify induction in a way consistent with empiricism usually attempt to show either that the inductive process is not dependent on any such principle or, alternatively, that the principle itself is a product of inductive reasoning. Finally, skeptics argue that induction cannot be shown to be reasonable in any of these ways. Some skeptics conclude from this that all empirical generalizations (including all scientific assertions) are, in principle, doubtful, while others hold that induction is not, in fact, the method by which such generalizations are established.

6

ARISTOTLE (384–322 B.C.)

Induction

Aristotle's influence on Western philosophy has been enormous, rivaling that of his great teacher Plato. While his thought is inherently more practical and "this-worldly" than is that of Plato, his interests are equally broad. In fact, for many years his writings were regarded as gospel in such diverse fields as logic, physics, biology, cosmology, ethics, political science, rhetoric, aesthetics, and metaphysics.

Aristotle's most important contribution to logic was the identification and analysis of the several types of *syllogism*. A syllogism is an argument consisting of a major premise, a minor premise, and a conclusion (for example, "All men are mortal, Socrates is a man, therefore Socrates is mortal"). In a syllogism, the conclusion is "deduced" from the premises. If a syllogism contains no logical errors (called *fallacies*), the conclusion must be true if the premises are true. Such a syllogism is said to be *valid*.

Since in syllogistic reasoning the truth of the conclusion is derived from the premises, the question that inevitably arises is, How is the truth of the premises established? In this selection, Aristotle attempts to answer that particular question.

. . .

As regards syllogism and demonstration, the definition of, and the conditions required to produce each of them, are now clear, and with that also the definition of, and the conditions required to produce, demonstrative knowledge, since it is the same as demonstration. As to the basic premises, how they become known and what is the developed state of knowledge of them is made clear by raising some preliminary problems.

We have already said[1] that scientific knowledge through demonstration is

From Aristotle, "Analytica Posteriora," Book II, Section 19, translated by G. R. G. Mure, from *The Oxford Translation of Aristotle,* edited by W. D. Ross, vol. 1, 1928. Reprinted by permission of Oxford University Press.

[1]i, ch. 2.

impossible unless a man knows the primary immediate premises. But there are questions which might be raised in respect of the apprehension of these immediate premises: one might not only ask whether it is of the same kind as the apprehension of the conclusions, but also whether there is or is not scientific knowledge of both; or scientific knowledge of the latter, and of the former a different kind of knowledge; and, further, whether the developed states of knowledge are not innate but come to be in us, or are innate but at first unnoticed. Now it is strange if we possess them from birth; for it means that we possess apprehensions more accurate than demonstration and fail to notice them. If on the other hand we acquire them and do not previously possess them, how could we apprehend and learn without a basis of pre-existent knowledge? For that is impossible, as we used to find [2] in the case of demonstration. So it emerges that neither can we possess them from birth, nor can they come to be in us if we are without knowledge of them to the extent of having no such developed state at all. Therefore we must possess a capacity of some sort, but not such as to rank higher in accuracy than these developed states. And this at least is an obvious characteristic of all animals, for they possess a congenital discriminative capacity which is called sense-perception. But though sense-perception is innate in all animals, in some the sense-impression comes to persist, in others it does not. So animals in which this persistence does not come to be have either no knowledge at all outside the act of perceiving, or no knowledge of objects of which no impression persists; animals in which it does come into being have perception and can continue to retain the sense-impression in the soul: and when such persistence is frequently repeated a further distinction at once arises between those which out of the persistence of such sense-impressions develop a power of systematizing them and those which do not. So out of sense-perception comes to be what we call memory, and out of frequently repeated memories of the same thing develops experience; for a number of memories constitute a single experience. [3] From experience again—i.e. from the universal now stabilized in its entirety within the soul, the one beside the many which is a single identity within them all—originate the skill of the craftsman and the knowledge of the man of science, skill in the sphere of coming to be and science in the sphere of being.

We conclude that these states of knowledge are neither innate in a determinate form, nor developed from other higher states of knowledge, but from sense-perception. It is like a rout in battle stopped by first one man making a stand and then another, until the original formation has been restored. The soul is so constituted as to be capable of this process.

Let us now restate the account given already, though with insufficient clearness. When one of a number of logically indiscriminable particulars has made a stand, the earliest universal is present in the soul: for though the act of

[2] i, ch. I.
[3] Cf. *Met.* A 980[a] 28. *Met.* A I should be compared with this chapter.

sense-perception is of the particular, its content is universal—is man, for example, not the man Callias. A fresh stand is made among these rudimentary universals, and the process does not cease until the indivisible concepts, the true universals, are established: e.g. such and such a species of animal is a step towards the genus animal, which by the same process is a step towards a further generalization.

Thus it is clear that we must get to know the primary premises by induction; for the method by which even sense-perception implants the universal is inductive. Now of the thinking states by which we grasp truth, some are unfailingly true, others admit of error—opinion, for instance, and calculation, whereas scientific knowing and intuition are always true: further, no other kind of thought except intuition is more accurate than scientific knowledge, whereas primary premises are more knowable than demonstrations, and all scientific knowledge is discursive. From these considerations it follows that there will be no scientific knowledge of the primary premises, and since except intuition nothing can be truer than scientific knowledge, it will be intuition that apprehends the primary premises—a result which also follows from the fact that demonstration cannot be the originative source of demonstration, nor, consequently, scientific knowledge of scientific knowledge. If, therefore, it is the only other kind of true thinking except scientific knowing, intuition will be the originative source of scientific knowledge. And the originative source of science grasps the original basic premise, while science as a whole is similarly related as originative source to the whole body of fact.

7

DAVID HUME (1711–1776)

Induction Is Not Reasoning

Here David Hume attempts to answer the question, How do we ascend from particular facts of experience to generalizations that go beyond those facts? In short, how does induction work? His answer is that induction does not work. The conclusions that appear to be established by induction are not "founded on reasoning or any process of the understanding." The position that Hume takes is called inductive skepticism. It has never been more lucidly or convincingly stated than in the selection that follows, which is the immediate sequel to the previous excerpt from Hume (see pp. 31–36). (See p. 31 for a brief biographical note on Hume.)

But we have not yet attained any tolerable satisfaction with regard to the question first proposed. Each solution still gives rise to a new question as difficult as the foregoing, and leads us on to farther inquiries. When it is asked, *What is the nature of all our reasonings concerning matter of fact?* the proper answer seems to be, That they are founded on the relation of cause and effect. When again it is asked, *What is the foundation of all our reasonings and conclusions concerning that relation?* it may be replied in one word, EXPERIENCE. But if we still carry on our sifting humour, and ask, *What is the foundation of all conclusions from experience?* this implies a new question, which may be of more difficult solution and explication. Philosophers that give themselves airs of superior wisdom and sufficiency, have a hard task when they encounter persons of inquisitive dispositions, who push them from every corner to which they retreat, and who are sure at last to bring them to some dangerous dilemma. The best expedient to prevent this confusion, is to be modest in our pretensions, and even to discover the difficulty ourselves before it is objected to us. By this means we may make a kind of merit of our very ignorance.

From David Hume, *An Inquiry Concerning Human Understanding*, Section IV, Part II, in *The Philosophical Works of David Hume*, Volume IV (London: Adam Black, William Tait, & Charles Tait, 1826), pp. 40–48.

I shall content myself in this section with an easy task, and shall pretend only to give a negative answer to the question here proposed. I say then, that even after we have experience of the operations of cause and effect, our conclusions from that experience are *not* founded on reasoning, or any process of the understanding. This answer we must endeavour both to explain and to defend.

It must certainly be allowed, that nature has kept us at a great distance from all her secrets, and has afforded us only the knowledge of a few superficial qualities of objects; while she conceals from us those powers and principles on which the influence of these objects entirely depends. Our senses inform us of the colour, weight, and consistence of bread; but neither sense nor reason can ever inform us of those qualities which fit it for the nourishment and support of the human body. Sight or feeling conveys an idea of the actual motion of bodies, but as to that wonderful force or power which would carry on a moving body forever in a continued change of place, and which bodies never lose but by communicating it to others; of this we cannot form the most distant conception. But notwithstanding this ignorance of natural powers[1] and principles, we always presume when we see like sensible qualities, that they have like secret powers, and expect that effects similar to those which we have experienced will follow from them. If a body of like colour and consistence with that bread which we have formerly eaten, be presented to us, we make no scruple of repeating the expcriment, and foresee, with certainty, like nourishment and support. Now, this is a process of the mind or thought, of which I would willingly know the foundation. It is allowed on all hands, that there is no known connection between the sensible qualities and the secret powers; and consequently, that the mind is not led to form such a conclusion concerning their constant and regular conjunction, by anything which it knows of their nature. As to past *Experience,* it can be allowed to give *direct* and *certain* information of those precise objects only, and that precise period of time which fell under its cognizance: But why this experience should be extended to future times, and to other objects, which, for aught we know, may be only in appearance similar, this is the main question on which I would insist. The bread which I formerly ate nourished me; that is, a body of such sensible qualities was, at that time, endued with such secret powers: But does it follow, that other bread must also nourish me at another time, and that like sensible qualities must always be attended with the like secret powers? The consequence seems nowise necessary. At least, it must be acknowledged, that there is here a consequence drawn by the mind, that there is a certain step taken, a process of thought, and an inference which wants to be explained. These two propositions are far from being the same: *I have found that such an object has always been attended with such an effect,* and *I foresee, that other objects which are in appearance similar, will be attended with similar effects.* I shall allow,

[1]The word Power is here used in a loose and popular sense. The more accurate explication of it would give additional evidence to this argument. See Sect. vii.

if you please, that the one proposition may justly be inferred from the other:
I know, in fact, that it always is inferred. But if you insist that the inference
is made by a chain of reasoning, I desire you to produce that reasoning. The
connection between these propositions is not intuitive. There is required a
medium, which may enable the mind to draw such an inference, if indeed it
be drawn by reasoning and argument. What that medium is, I must confess
passes my comprehension; and it is incumbent on those to produce it who
assert that it really exists, and is the original of all our conclusions concerning
matter of fact.

This negative argument must certainly, in process of time, become altogether convincing, if many penetrating and able philosophers shall turn their
inquiries this way; and no one be ever able to discover any connecting proposition or intermediate step which supports the understanding in this conclusion.
But as the question is yet new, every reader may not trust so far to his own
penetration as to conclude, because an argument escapes his inquiry, that
therefore it does not really exist. For this reason, it may be requisite to venture
upon a more difficult task; and, enumerating all the branches of human knowledge, endeavour to show, that none of them can afford such an argument.

All reasonings may be divided into two kinds, namely, demonstrative reasoning, or that concerning relations of ideas; and moral reasoning, or that
concerning matter of fact and existence. That there are no demonstrative
arguments in the case, seems evident, since it implies no contradiction, that
the course of nature may change, and that an object, seemingly like those
which we have experienced, may be attended with different or contrary effects.
May I not clearly and distinctly conceive, that a body, falling from the clouds,
and which in all other respects resembles snow, has yet the taste of salt or
feeling of fire? Is there any more intelligible proposition than to affirm, that
all the trees will flourish in December and January, and will decay in May and
June? Now, whatever is intelligible, and can be distinctly conceived, implies
no contradiction, and can never be proved false by any demonstrative argument or abstract reasoning *a priori.*

If we be, therefore, engaged by arguments to put trust in past experience,
and make it the standard of our future judgment, these arguments must be
probable only, or such as regard matter of fact and real existence, according
to the division above mentioned. But that there is no argument of this kind,
must appear, if our explication of that species of reasoning be admitted as solid
and satisfactory. We have said that all arguments concerning existence are
founded on the relation of cause and effect; that our knowledge of that relation
is derived entirely from experience; and that all our experimental conclusions
proceed upon the supposition, that the future will be conformable to the past.
To endeavour, therefore, the proof of this last supposition by probable arguments, or arguments regarding existence, must be evidently going in a circle,
and taking that for granted which is the very point in question.

In reality, all arguments from experience are founded on the similarity which we discover among natural objects, and by which we are induced to expect effects similar to those which we have found to follow from such objects. And though none but a fool or madman will ever pretend to dispute the authority of experience, or to reject that great guide of human life, it may surely be allowed a philosopher to have so much curiosity at least as to examine the principle of human nature which gives this mighty authority to experience, and makes us draw advantage from that similarity which nature has placed among different objects. From causes which appear similar, we expect similar effects. This is the sum of all our experimental conclusions. Now it seems evident, that if this conclusion were formed by reason, it would be as perfect at first, and upon one instance, as after ever so long a course of experience: but the case is far otherwise. Nothing so like as eggs; yet no one, on account of this appearing similarity, expects the same taste and relish in all of them. It is only after a long course of uniform experiments in any kind, that we attain a firm reliance and security with regard to a particular event. Now, where is that process of reasoning, which, from one instance, draws a conclusion so different from that which it infers from a hundred instances that are nowise different from that single one? This question I propose, as much for the sake of information, as with an intention of raising difficulties. I cannot find, I cannot imagine, any such reasoning. But I keep my mind still open to instruction, if any one will vouchsafe to bestow it on me.

Should it be said, that, from a number of uniform experiments, we *infer* a connection between the sensible qualities and the secret powers, this, I must confess, seems the same difficulty, couched in different terms. The question still occurs, On what process of argument is this *inference* founded? Where is the medium, the interposing ideas, which join propositions so very wide of each other? It is confessed, that the colour, consistence, and other sensible qualities of bread, appear not of themselves to have any connection with the secret powers of nourishment and support: For otherwise we could infer these secret powers from the first appearance of these sensible qualities, without the aid of experience, contrary to the sentiment of all philosophers, and contrary to plain matter of fact. Here then is our natural state of ignorance with regard to the powers and influence of all objects. How is this remedied by experience? It only shows us a number of uniform effects resulting from certain objects, and teaches us that those particular objects, at that particular time, were endowed with such powers and forces. When a new object, endowed with similar sensible qualities, is produced, we expect similar powers and forces, and look for a like effect. From a body of like colour and consistence with bread, we expect like nourishment and support. But this surely is a step or progress of the mind which wants to be explained. When a man says, *I have found, in all past instances, such sensible qualities, conjoined with such secret powers;* and when he says, *similar sensible qualities will always be conjoined with similar secret powers;* he is not guilty of a tautology, nor are these propositions in any respect the same. You say that the one proposition is an inference from the other: But you must confess that the inference is not intuitive, neither is it demonstrative. Of what nature is it then? To say it is experimental, is begging the question. For all inferences from experience suppose, as their foundation, that the future will resemble the past, and that similar powers will be conjoined with similar sensible qualities. If there be any suspicion that the course of nature may change, and that the past may be no rule for the future, all experience becomes useless, and can give rise to no inference or conclusion. It is impossible, therefore, that any arguments from experience can prove this resemblance of the past to the future: since all these arguments are founded on the supposition of that resemblance. Let the course of things be allowed hitherto ever so regular, that alone, without some new argument or inference, proves not that for the future it will continue so. In vain do you pretend to have learned the nature of bodies from your past experience. Their secret nature, and consequently all their effects and influence, may change, without any change in their sensible qualities. This happens sometimes, and with regard to some objects: Why may it not happen always, and with regard to all objects? What logic, what process of argument, secures you against this supposition? My practice, you say, refutes my doubts. But you mistake the purport of my question. As an agent, I am quite satisfied in the point; but as a philosopher, who has some share of curiosity, I will not say skepticism, I want to learn the foundation of this inference. No reading, no inquiry, has yet been able to remove my difficulty, or give me satisfaction in a matter of such importance. Can I do better than propose the difficulty to the public, even though, perhaps, I have small hopes of obtaining a solution? We shall at least, by this means, be sensible of our ignorance, if we do not augment our knowledge.

I must confess, that a man is guilty of unpardonable arrogance, who concludes, because an argument has escaped his own investigation, that therefore it does not really exist. I must also confess, that though all the learned, for several ages, should have employed themselves in fruitless search upon any subject, it may still, perhaps, be rash to conclude positively, that the subject must therefore pass all human comprehension. Even though we examine all the sources of our knowledge, and conclude them unfit for such a subject, there may still remain a suspicion, that the enumeration is not complete, or the examination not accurate. But with regard to the present subject, there are some considerations which seem to remove all this accusation of arrogance or suspicion of mistake.

It is certain, that the most ignorant and stupid peasants, nay infants, nay even brute beasts, improve by experience, and learn the qualities of natural objects, by observing the effects which result from them. When a child has felt the sensation of pain from touching the flame of a candle, he will be careful not to put his hand near any candle, but will expect a similar effect from a cause which is similar in its sensible qualities and appearance. If you assert, therefore, that the understanding of the child is led into this conclusion by any process of argument or ratiocination, I may justly require you to produce that argument; nor have you any pretence to refuse so equitable a demand. You cannot say that the argument is abstruse, and may possibly escape your inquiry, since you confess that it is obvious to the capacity of a mere infant. If you hesitate, therefore, a moment, or if, after reflection, you produce an intricate or profound argument, you, in a manner, give up the question, and confess, that it is not reasoning which engages us to suppose the past resembling the future, and to expect similar effects from causes which are to appearance similar. This is the proposition which I intended to enforce in the present section. If I be right, I pretend not to have made any mighty discovery. And if I be wrong, I must acknowledge myself to be indeed a very backward scholar, since I cannot now discover an argument which, it seems, was perfectly familiar to me long before I was out of my cradle.

8

BERTRAND RUSSELL (1872–1970)

On Induction

Bertrand Russell is probably as well known for his advocacy of unpopular causes as he is for his contributions to philosophy, especially to mathematical logic. Among the causes that he championed were pacifism (for which he served a prison sentence and lost his position as a faculty member at Cambridge University), civil liberties, the free-trade movement, new methods of education, rights for women, and free love. He was imprisoned a second time, in 1962, for his activities in the movement to ban all nuclear weapons. He was also an early opponent of American intervention in Vietnam.

Despite his frequent involvement in public controversies, Russell authored over

From *The Problems of Philosophy*, Chapter VI, by Bertrand Russell, published by Oxford University Press (1912). Reprinted by permission of Oxford University Press.

forty books dealing with a wide range of philosophical concerns. *Problems of Philosophy,* first published in 1912, presents Russell's views on various central problems of philosophy.

With respect to the problem of induction, Russell may be called a rationalist. Hume had said, "if you insist that in induction the inference is made by a chain of reasoning, I desire you to produce that reasoning" (see above, p. 56). Russell takes up that challenge. He attempts to show that inductive reasoning depends upon a *principle of induction* that we must either accept on the basis of its "intrinsic evidence" or else "forgo all justification of our expectations about the future." It is clear that Russell chooses the former alternative in preference to Humean skepticism.

In almost all our previous discussions we have been concerned in the attempt to get clear as to our data in the way of knowledge of existence. What things are there in the universe whose existence is known to us owing to our being acquainted with them? So far, our answer has been that we are acquainted with our sense-data, and, probably, with ourselves. These we know to exist. And past sense-data which are remembered are known to have existed in the past. This knowledge supplies our data.

But if we are to be able to draw inferences from these data—if we are to know of the existence of matter, of other people, of the past before our individual memory begins, or of the future, we must know general principles of some kind by means of which such inferences can be drawn. It must be known to us that the existence of some one sort of thing, *A,* is a sign of the existence of some other sort of thing, *B,* either at the same time as *A* or at some earlier or later time, as, for example, thunder is a sign of the earlier existence of lightning. If this were not known to us, we could never extend our knowledge beyond the sphere of our private experience; and this sphere, as we have seen, is exceedingly limited. The question we have now to consider is whether such an extension is possible, and if so, how it is effected.

Let us take as an illustration a matter about which none of us, in fact, feel the slightest doubt. We are all convinced that the sun will rise to-morrow. Why? Is this belief a mere blind outcome of past experience, or can it be justified as a reasonable belief? It is not easy to find a test by which to judge whether a belief of this kind is reasonable or not, but we can at least ascertain what sort of general beliefs would suffice, if true, to justify the judgement that the sun will rise to-morrow, and the many other similar judgements upon which our actions are based.

It is obvious that if we are asked why we believe that the sun will rise to-morrow, we shall naturally answer, 'Because it always has risen every day'. We have a firm belief that it will rise in the future, because it has risen in the past. If we are challenged as to why we believe that it will continue to rise as heretofore, we may appeal to the laws of motion: the earth, we shall say, is a freely rotating body, and such bodies do not cease to rotate unless something interferes from outside, and there is nothing outside to interfere with the earth between now and to-morrow. Of course it might be doubted whether we are quite certain that there is nothing outside to interfere, but this is not the interesting doubt. The interesting doubt is as to whether the laws of motion will remain in operation until to-morrow. If this doubt is raised, we find ourselves in the same position as when the doubt about the sunrise was first raised.

The *only* reason for believing that the laws of motion will remain in operation is that they have operated hitherto, so far as our knowledge of the past enables us to judge. It is true that we have a greater body of evidence from the past in favour of the laws of motion than we have in favour of the sunrise, because the sunrise is merely a particular case of fulfilment of the laws of motion, and there are countless other particular cases. But the real question is: Do *any* number of cases of a law being fulfilled in the past afford evidence that it will be fulfilled in the future? If not, it becomes plain that we have no ground whatever for expecting the sun to rise to-morrow, or for expecting the bread we shall eat at our next meal not to poison us, or for any of the other scarcely conscious expectations that control our daily lives. It is to be observed that all such expectations are only *probable*; thus we have not to seek for a proof that they *must* be fulfilled, but only for some reason in favour of the view that they are *likely* to be fulfilled.

Now in dealing with this question we must, to begin with, make an important distinction, without which we should soon become involved in hopeless confusions. Experience has shown us that, hitherto, the frequent repetition of some uniform succession or coexistence has been a *cause* of our expecting the same succession or coexistence on the next occasion. Food that has a certain appearance generally has a certain taste, and it is a severe shock to our expectations when the familiar appearance is found to be associated with an unusual taste. Things which we see become associated, by habit, with certain tactile sensations which we expect if we touch them; one of the horrors of a ghost (in many ghost-stories) is that it fails to give us any sensations of touch. Uneducated people who go abroad for the first time are so surprised as to be incredulous when they find their native language not understood.

And this kind of association is not confined to men; in animals also it is very strong. A horse which has been often driven along a certain road resists the attempt to drive him in a different direction. Domestic animals expect food when they see the person who usually feeds them. We know that all these rather crude expectations of uniformity are liable to be misleading. The man who has fed the chicken every day throughout its life at last wrings its neck instead, showing that more refined views as to the uniformity of nature would have been useful to the chicken.

But in spite of the misleadingness of such expectations, they nevertheless exist. The mere fact that something has happened a certain number of times causes animals and men to expect that it will happen again. Thus our instincts certainly cause us to believe that the sun will rise to-morrow, but we may be in no better a position than the chicken which unexpectedly has its neck wrung. We have therefore to distinguish the fact that past uniformities *cause* expectations as to the future, from the question whether there is any reasonable ground for giving weight to such expectations after the question of their validity has been raised.

The problem we have to discuss is whether there is any reason for believing in what is called 'the uniformity of nature'. The belief in the uniformity of nature is the belief that everything that has happened or will happen is an instance of some general law to which there are *no* exceptions. The crude expectations which we have been considering are all subject to exceptions, and therefore liable to disappoint those who entertain them. But science habitually assumes, at least as a working hypothesis, that general rules which have exceptions can be replaced by general rules which have no exceptions. 'Unsupported bodies in air fall' is a general rule to which balloons and aeroplanes are exceptions. But the laws of motion and the law of gravitation, which account for the fact that most bodies fall, also account for the fact that balloons and aeroplanes can rise; thus the laws of motion and the law of gravitation are not subject to these exceptions.

The belief that the sun will rise to-morrow might be falsified if the earth came suddenly into contact with a large body which destroyed its rotation; but the laws of motion and the law of gravitation would not be infringed by such an event. The business of science is to find uniformities, such as the laws of motion and the law of gravitation, to which, so far as our experience extends, there are no exceptions. In this search science has been remarkably successful, and it may be conceded that such uniformities have held hitherto. This brings us back to the question: Have we any reason, assuming that they have always held in the past, to suppose that they will hold in the future?

It has been argued that we have reason to know that the future will resemble the past, because what was the future has constantly become the past, and has always been found to resemble the past, so that we really have experience of the future, namely of times which were formerly future, which we may call past futures. But such an argument really begs the very question at issue. We have experience of past futures, but not of future futures, and the question is: Will future futures resemble past futures? This question is not to be answered by an argument which starts from past futures alone. We have therefore still to seek for some principle which shall enable us to know that the future will follow the same laws as the past.

The reference to the future in this question is not essential. The same question arises when we apply the laws that work in our experience to past things of which we have no experience—as, for example, in geology, or in theories as to the origin of the Solar System. The question we really have to ask is: 'When two things have been found to be often associated, and no instance is known of the one occurring without the other, does the occurrence of one of the two, in a fresh instance, give any good ground for expecting the other?' On our answer to this question must depend the validity of the whole of our expectations as to the future, the whole of the results obtained by induction, and in fact practically all the beliefs upon which our daily life is based.

It must be conceded, to begin with, that the fact that two things have been found often together and never apart does not, by itself, suffice to *prove* demonstratively that they will be found together in the next case we examine. The most we can hope is that the oftener things are found together, the more probable it becomes that they will be found together another time, and that, if they have been found together often enough, the probability will amount *almost* to certainty. It can never quite reach certainty, because we know that in spite of frequent repetitions there sometimes is a failure at the last, as in the case of the chicken whose neck is wrung. Thus probability is all we ought to seek.

It might be urged, as against the view we are advocating, that we know all natural phenomena to be subject to the reign of law, and that sometimes, on the basis of observation, we can see that only one law can possibly fit the facts of the case. Now to this view there are two answers. The first is that, even if *some* law which has no exceptions applies to our case, we can never, in practice, be sure that we have discovered that law and not one to which there are exceptions. The second is that the reign of law would seem to be itself only probable, and that our belief that it will hold in the future, or in unexamined cases in the past, is itself based upon the very principle we are examining.

The principle we are examining may be called the *principle of induction,* and its two parts may be stated as follows:

(*a*) When a thing of a certain sort *A* has been found to be associated with a thing of a certain other sort *B,* and has never been found dissociated from a thing of the sort *B,* the greater the number of cases in which *A* and *B* have been associated, the greater is the probability that they will be associated in a fresh case in which one of them is known to be present;

(*b*) Under the same circumstances, a sufficient number of cases of association will make the probability of a fresh association nearly a certainty, and will make it approach certainty without limit.

As just stated, the principle applies only to the verification of our expectation in a single fresh instance. But we want also to know that there is a probability in favour of the general law that things of the sort *A* are *always* associated with things of the sort *B,* provided a sufficient number of cases of association are known, and no cases of failure of association are known. The probability of the general law is obviously less than the probability of the particular case, since if the general law is true, the particular case must also be true, whereas the particular case may be true without the general law being true. Nevertheless the probability of the general law is increased by repetitions, just as the probability of the particular case is. We may therefore repeat the two parts of our principle as regards the general law, thus:

(*a*) The greater the number of cases in which a thing of the sort *A* has been found associated with a thing of the sort *B,* the more probable it is (if no cases of failure of association are known) that *A* is always associated with *B;*

(*b*) Under the same circumstances, a sufficient number of cases of the association of *A* with *B* will make it nearly certain that *A* is always associated with *B,* and will make this general law approach certainty without limit.

It should be noted that probability is always relative to certain data. In our case, the data are merely the known cases of coexistence of *A* and *B*. There may be other data, which *might* be taken into account, which would gravely alter the probability. For example, a man who had seen a great many white swans might argue, by our principle, that on the data it was *probable* that all swans were white, and this might be a perfectly sound argument. The argument is not disproved by the fact that some swans are black, because a thing may very well happen in spite of the fact that some data render it improbable. In the case of the swans, a man might know that colour is a very variable characteristic in many species of animals, and that, therefore, an induction as to colour is peculiarly liable to error. But this knowledge would be a fresh datum, by no means proving that the probability relatively to our previous data had been wrongly estimated. The fact, therefore, that things often fail to fulfil our expectations is no evidence that our expectations will not *probably* be fulfilled in a given case or a given class of cases. Thus our inductive principle is at any rate not capable of being *disproved* by an appeal to experience.

The inductive principle, however, is equally incapable of being *proved* by an appeal to experience. Experience might conceivably confirm the inductive principle as regards the cases that have been already examined; but as regards unexamined cases, it is the inductive principle alone that can justify any inference from what has been examined to what has not been examined. All arguments which, on the basis of experience, argue as to the future or the unexperienced parts of the past or present, assume the inductive principle; hence we can never use experience to prove the inductive principle without begging the question. Thus we must either accept the inductive principle on the ground of its intrinsic evidence, or forgo all justification of our expectations about the future. If the principle is unsound, we have no reason to expect the sun to rise to-morrow, to expect bread to be more nourishing than a stone, or to expect that if we throw ourselves off the roof we shall fall. When we see what looks like our best friend approaching us, we shall have no reason to suppose that his body is not inhabited by the mind of our worst enemy or of some total stranger. All our conduct is based upon associations which have worked in the past, and which we therefore regard as likely to work in the future; and this likelihood is dependent for its validity upon the inductive principle.

The general principles of science, such as the belief in the reign of law, and the belief that every event must have a cause, are as completely dependent upon the inductive principle as are the beliefs of daily life. All such general principles are believed because mankind have found innumerable instances of their truth and no instances of their falsehood. But this affords no evidence for their truth in the future, unless the inductive principle is assumed.

Thus all knowledge which, on a basis of experience tells us something about what is not experienced, is based upon a belief which experience can neither confirm nor confute, yet which, at least in its more concrete applications, appears to be as firmly rooted in us as many of the facts of experience. . . .

9

JOHN HOSPERS (1918– ———)

The Justification of Probability Statements

John Hospers is a contemporary American philosopher who has taught at Columbia University, the University of Minnesota, and the University of California at Los Angeles. Currently, he is professor of philosophy at Brooklyn College. The author of numerous books and articles, he is best known for his contributions to ethics and aesthetics.

Hospers is an empiricist. In the following selection, he attempts to show that if "evidence" is clearly defined, then the repeated occurrence of certain kinds of past events *is* evidence for their probable occurrence in the future.

Thus far we have been content to say that, while we cannot *know* that tomorrow water will boil, the sun will rise, and so forth, we have considerable *evidence* that these things will happen, and that the statements asserting that they will happen are, although not certain, at least extremely *probable.* At this point, however, a much more radical kind of question is sometimes raised: how

From John Hospers, *An Introduction to Philosophical Analysis,* © 1953, pp. 171–177. Reprinted by permission of Prentice-Hall, Inc., Englewood Cliffs, New Jersey.

does the fact that something has happened in the past constitute *any evidence whatever* that it will continue so in the future? What if someone said, "Very well—it's always happened that way in the past; so what? What has that to do with the future?"

Here is one comment we should consider first, lest it confuse the issue later: "You can't be so general about it—the occurrence of some regularities, or uniformities, in the past *is* evidence for their continuance in the future, but not so for others." Bertrand Russell uses the example of the chicken that has gone to its roost every night for several months in the belief that it will be secure there, perhaps because it has been secure there on past nights. But finally one night its owner comes into the henhouse and wrings its neck. If the chicken assumed that because it had been undisturbed in the past it would continue to be undisturbed in the future, it was mistaken. Some beliefs of this kind become *less* probable rather than more so with repetition: when you are eighty years old it's less probable that you will live till morning than it was when you were twenty, although the number of instances backing up the generalization is far greater at eighty. Whether the generalization is made more probable or less probable by the addition of repeated instances depends on the evidence we have for *other* generalizations relevant to the situation. We believe that the sun will rise tomorrow more confidently than we believe the eighty-year-old will live till morning because we know some statistics about the incidence of deaths and also some physiological laws about the human body, and we also know some things about the solar system, the earth's rotation on its axis, laws of planetary motion, principles of acceleration and momentum, and some of the other things that would have to be different if the sun were *not* to rise tomorrow. We have arrived at other generalizations about the behavior of nature besides the repeated rising of the sun; and these others all contribute, and add probability, to the statement about the continued rising of the sun. It is different with the case of the chicken, for our other generalizations—rather vague ones about the habits of chickens and farmers and the chicken market —do *not* lead to the belief that the past security of the chicken in any way guarantees its subsequent security. And the same with the example about the octogenarian: if the mere fact that he had lived so many days made it probable that he would live to see every next day that dawned, you would arrive at the conclusion that he would live forever! The mere repetition of days of life is subordinate to wider generalizations about the human constitution, which make it, every day that he lives, *less* probable that he will live to see the next day."

Both common sense and science would accept this view of the reasons for believing in continued uniformity in the case of the sun rising but not in the other cases. The same logical problem remains, however. It does not help to fortify the generalization about the sun's continued rising by appealing to *other* generalizations which are in precisely the same predicament that it is. How do we know that these other laws which are invoked to support the generalization

about the sun will continue to hold? Being laws, they too involve the future,
and therefore are as fallible as the generalization they are invoked to support.
If the past affords us no evidence that the sun will rise in the future, how can
it afford us evidence that the Law of Gravitation will continue to hold true,
and that all the other laws that are used to support it will do the same? How,
then, has our situation improved? It seems not to have improved at all.

One might suggest the easy way out, that of proving a law deductively. Thus:

> What has always occurred regularly in the past will continue to
> occur regularly in the future.
> The sun's rising has occurred regularly in the past.

> Therefore, The sun's rising will continue to occur regularly in the future.

Here we have proved our conclusion deductively. The trouble is, of course, . . .
that you cannot prove the *truth* of a conclusion by valid deduction from
premises; the premises must themselves be true. And if we do not know that
our present conclusion is true, because it involves the future, how can we know
that the major premise (the first line) is true, since it too involves the future?
It is, in fact, a bigger generalization than is the conclusion. This is clearly no
way out: if you want to deduce a conclusion which makes some reference to
the future, there must be some reference to the future in one or more of the
premises from which that conclusion is deduced. In that case the same skeptical questionings that can be made about the conclusion can be equally made
about that premise (or those premises). The question has merely shifted; it has
not been resolved.

The general principle, the one that covers all cases, that is usually invoked
as a major premise in arguments of this type is the *Principle of Uniformity of
Nature.* It is not always formulated in the same way, but it comes to this: "If
Nature has always been uniform in the past (generalizations have held good),
then Nature will continue to be uniform in the future." Some particular
uniformity in the past will then be stated in the minor premise, and the
continuance of that uniformity in the future will be deduced in the conclusion.
From the Principle of Uniformity of Nature, then, we can deduce the desired
conclusion. But how does one establish the Principle of Uniformity of Nature?
From what true premises can *it* be deduced? "Well, the Principle of Uniformity of Nature has been true of the past; therefore the Principle of Uniformity
of Nature will continue to be true of the future." But this conclusion does not
logically follow. It does not follow unless we add another premise:

> What has held true of the past will hold true of the future.
> The Principle of Uniformity of Nature has held true of the past.

> Therefore, The Principle of Uniformity of Nature will hold true of the future.

And thus we are back in the same situation: how are we going to prove *this*
major premise?

Or we could put the problem this way. "In the past, our predictions about
the continued uniformity of nature have turned out to be true; in other words,
our past predictions of the future have been verified. Thus we have considerable evidence that nature will continue to be uniform. After all, it's not as if
we had never observed our predictions turning out right." "But that's not the
question. I grant that our past predictions have been verified by the facts. In
other words, our past predictions about the then-future were verified when that
future was no longer future but became past. Now I'm not asking about past
futures; I'm asking about future futures! What have the past futures to do with
it? The fact that past futures turned out to be so-and-so doesn't prove that
future futures will turn out to be so-and-so. If you assume that because past
futures were so-and-so therefore the future futures will be so-and-so also, you
are again assuming the very point to be proved!"

In other words, every time we try to prove the Principle of Uniformity of
Nature we assume the principle in the very process of the proof. We cannot
prove the principle by means of itself; and yet without doing this we cannot
prove it at all. . . . No statement about nature being uniform in the past will
prove that nature will be uniform in the future unless we assume that the fact
of uniformity in the past proves future uniformity. Yet clearly it does not; from
"The uniformity of nature has held in the past" we cannot deduce "The
uniformity of nature will hold in the future."

If deduction fails us, how about induction? Induction, as we have seen, is
not a method of proof, but only a method of estimating the probability of a
conclusion; and it is the very basis of induction itself that is being questioned
here. What we are examining is our very right to use inductive procedure in
making generalizations. We cannot, therefore, justify this inductive procedure
on the basis of inductive reasoning.

Our question, then, still remains: Can the uniformities of the past and the
present render uniformities in the future any more probable? Does the fact that
the past has turned out a certain way render even probable the statement that
the future will turn out that way too?

There is much more agreement on the nature of the problem than on the
solution of it. Unfortunately most attempted solutions become too technical
to be discussed here. Nevertheless, two comments can be given which may
alleviate the pressure of the problem:

1. If someone seriously says that the way things have occurred in the past
affords *no* evidence whatever about the future, we can ask him what he means
when he uses the word "evidence." A million times in the past when I have
let go of a book or a stone it has fallen; never once has it risen into the air.
This, and all the other things I know about the behavior of material objects,
lead me to believe that it will fall when I let go of it this time. Is there really
no evidence either way as to what the stone will do next time? To say this is
to abandon all prediction and all science, and, more important here, *all meaning for the word "evidence."* For if the fact that it has fallen a million times

is *not* evidence, what *would* be? If you so use the word "evidence" that *nothing* that ever happened could be evidence, what would you mean by the word "evidence"? Would it not just be a meaningless noise? (You could not even say, "There is *no* evidence that *X* will happen," for that sentence contains the word "evidence," which must be given a meaning before it can meaningfully be used.)

The same point could be made regarding the word "probable." If the fact that the stone has always fallen and never risen, together with all the other things we have observed about stones and other material objects, does not even render more *probable* the statement that the stone will fall the next time, what in the world *could* make it so? And if nothing could, then what meaning can be attached by the speaker to the world "probable," or for that matter the word "improbable"? Remember that it would be just as meaningless to say "It is *im*probable that *X* will occur" as it would be to say "It is probable that *X* will occur"—for if the word "probable" has been deprived of all possible application to the universe, its opposite, which acquires meaning only by contrast with it, suffers precisely the same fate.

2. If the question is still asked, "How are we going to prove the Principle of Uniformity of Nature which is required to establish our inductions?" the answer is of course that we cannot. It cannot be proved by means of itself, and it cannot be proved without itself. As we have already seen, to prove (deductively) a conclusion involving the future we must have a proposition involving the future in the premises. In other words—as in the case of the principles of logic—we cannot give a *logical* justification for the Principle of Uniformity of Nature; we cannot give a logical basis for the very principle which is itself the logical basis for the deduction of laws.

It would seem, then, that to demand a logical basis for the principle is as unreasonable as to demand it in the case of the principles of logic themselves. Yet the principle is needed if our inductive conclusions (laws) are to be proved, since they involve the future. Laws are the basis of our predictions. "Why do you think that stone will fall?" "All unsupported bodies fall." If this last statement did not involve the future, it could not be employed to predict anything about the future, which it clearly *is* being employed to do.

What, then, can we do under the circumstances? As in the case of the principles of logic, . . . we can give a pragmatic justification for our *adoption* of these principles. In the case of the principles of logic it was the impossibility of any coherent discourse without the use of them; in the present case the situation is not quite so radical: it is the fruitlessness of any scientific procedure without the adoption of the Principle of Uniformity of Nature, which alone enables us to make inferences from past and present to future. We cannot prove that the principle which enables us to do this is true, but *if* we want to attempt any predictions at all—and as human beings we must all do this if we want to stay alive (do we not refrain from going to the street via the fifth-floor window because we are convinced that the uniformity of behavior of freely falling bodies will continue?)—then the laws of nature are the only sound basis for such prediction. It is these or nothing. We cannot prove deductively that these laws are true, for we cannot prove that the uniformities will hold in the future, and this is what every law implicitly asserts; but *if* nature is uniform, and *if* there is an order of nature which extends into the future, then the inductive method is the way in which to gain knowledge of this order. We want successful prediction; we cannot prove that our predictions, however well they may have worked out in the past, will be successful in the next instance; but if successful prediction is to be possible at all, it will be so only by means of these laws. This is our pragmatic basis, our practical justification, for asserting these laws, in spite of the fact that we cannot prove that the laws are true, or can prove them only by using an unprovable principle as a premise.

There is, to be sure, another way out of the situation: we can assert that the Principle of Uniformity of Nature is a synthetic necessary statement, something which *necessarily* holds of the universe. But here again, of course, there are difficulties: what entitles us to say that the principle is necessary? How do we know this, if we know it? To many it would seem that this way of resolving the Gordian knot is not by unraveling it but by cutting it with a knife.

10

KARL POPPER (1902– ————)

The Myth of Induction*

Karl Popper studied mathematics, physics, and philosophy at the university in his native city of Vienna. He was closely associated with a group of philosophers who called themselves "logical empiricists," the so-called Vienna Circle, although he was

*The title is mine, not Popper's. Some section headings and footnotes have been deleted.
Excerpted from Karl Popper, *The Logic of Scientific Discovery,* Chapter I, Sections 1–3 (New York: Basic Books, 1959). Reprinted by permission of the author and the Hutchinson Publishing Group Limited, London.

not a member of the group and disagreed with many of their principal doctrines. For several years, he was a lecturer at Canterbury University College in New Zealand, then he moved to the London School of Economics where, in 1949, he became professor of logic and scientific method. His principal writings include *The Logic of Scientific Discovery* (1935), *The Open Society and Its Enemies* (1945), *The Poverty of Historicism* (1957), and *Conjectures and Refutations* (1963).

Popper, like Hume, believes that the problem of induction is insoluble. Therefore, with respect to induction, he is a skeptic. However, Popper disagrees with Hume, and with nearly everyone else who has written on the problem, in holding that the insolubility of the problem has no serious consequences. According to Popper, induction is not, in fact, the method by which general empirical truths are established. Rather, such truths are established by a method that Popper calls "the deductive method of testing." In later writings, he refers to the method as "conjecture and refutation." Thus, Popper's answer to Hume is not to set forth, as Hume demanded, the reasoning by which inductive inferences are made, but rather to show that no such reasoning is required.

A scientist, whether theorist or experimenter, puts forward statements, or systems of statements, and tests them step by step. In the field of the empirical sciences, more particularly, he constructs hypotheses, or systems of theories, and tests them against experience by observation and experiment.

I suggest that it is the task of the logic of scientific discovery, or the logic of knowledge, to give a logical analysis of this procedure; that is, to analyse the method of the empirical sciences.

But what are these 'methods of the empirical sciences'? And what do we call 'empirical science'?

According to a widely accepted view, ... the empirical sciences can be characterized by the fact that they use *'inductive methods'*, as they are called. According to this view, the logic of scientific discovery would be identical with inductive logic, *i.e.* with the logical analysis of these inductive methods.

It is usual to call an inference 'inductive' if it passes from *singular statements* (sometimes also called 'particular' statements), such as accounts of the results of observations or experiments, to *universal statements,* such as hypotheses or theories.

Now it is far from obvious, from a logical point of view, that we are justified in inferring universal statements from singular ones, no matter how numerous; for any conclusion drawn in this way may always turn out to be false: no matter how many instances of white swans we may have observed, this does not justify the conclusion that *all* swans are white.

The question whether inductive inferences are justified, or under what conditions, is known as *the problem of induction.*

The problem of induction may also be formulated as the question of how to establish the truth of universal statements which are based on experience, such as the hypotheses and theoretical systems of the empirical sciences. For many people believe that the truth of these universal statements is *'known by experience'*; yet it is clear that an account of an experience—of an observation or the result of an experiment—can in the first place be only a singular statement and not a universal one. Accordingly, people who say of a universal statement that we know its truth from experience usually mean that the truth of this universal statement can somehow be reduced to the truth of singular ones, and that these singular ones are known by experience to be true; which amounts to saying that the universal statement is based on inductive inference. Thus to ask whether there are natural laws known to be true appears to be only another way of asking whether inductive inferences are logically justified.

Yet if we want to find a way of justifying inductive inferences, we must first of all try to establish a *principle of induction*. A principle of induction would be a statement with the help of which we could put inductive inferences into a logically acceptable form. In the eyes of the upholders of inductive logic, a principle of induction is of supreme importance for scientific method: ' . . . this principle', says Reichenbach, 'determines the truth of scientific theories. To eliminate it from science would mean nothing less than to deprive science of the power to decide the truth or falsity of its theories. Without it, clearly, science would no longer have the right to distinguish its theories from the fanciful and arbitrary creations of the poet's mind.'

Now this principle of induction cannot be a purely logical truth like a tautology or an analytic statement. Indeed, if there were such a thing as a purely logical principle of induction, there would be no problem of induction; for in this case, all inductive inferences would have to be regarded as purely logical or tautological transformations, just like inferences in deductive logic. Thus the principle of induction must be a synthetic statement; that is, a statement whose negation is not self-contradictory but logically possible. So the question arises why such a principle should be accepted at all, and how we can justify its acceptance on rational grounds.

1. THE PROBLEM OF INDUCTION

Some who believe in inductive logic are anxious to point out, with Reichenbach, that 'the principle of induction is unreservedly accepted by the whole of science and that no man can seriously doubt this principle in everyday life either'. Yet even supposing this were the case—for after all, 'the whole of science' might err— I should still contend that a principle of induction is superfluous, and that it must lead to logical inconsistencies.

That inconsistencies may easily arise in connection with the principle of induction should have been clear from the work of Hume; also, that they can be avoided, if at all, only with difficulty. For the principle of induction must be a universal statement in its turn. Thus if we try to regard its truth as known from experience, then the very same problems which occasioned its introduction will arise all over again. To justify it, we should have to employ inductive inferences; and to justify these we should have to assume an inductive principle of a higher order; and so on. Thus the attempt to base the principle of induction on experience breaks down, since it must lead to an infinite regress.

Kant tried to force his way out of this difficulty by taking the principle of induction (which he formulated as the 'principle of universal causation') to be *'a priori* valid'. But I do not think that his ingenious attempt to provide an *a priori* justification for synthetic statements was successful.

My own view is that the various difficulties of inductive logic here sketched are insurmountable. So also, I fear, are those inherent in the doctrine, so widely current today, that inductive inference, although not 'strictly valid', *can attain some degree of 'reliability' or of 'probability'.* According to this doctrine, inductive inferences are 'probable inferences'. 'We have described', says Reichenbach, 'the principle of induction as the means whereby science decides upon truth. To be more exact, we should say that it serves to decide upon probability. For it is not given to science to reach either truth or falsity . . . but scientific statements can only attain continuous degrees of probability whose unattainable upper and lower limits are truth and falsity'.

At this stage I can disregard the fact that the believers in inductive logic entertain an idea of probability that I shall later reject as highly unsuitable for their own purposes. . . . I can do so because the difficulties mentioned are not even touched by an appeal to probability. For if a certain degree of probability is to be assigned to statements based on inductive inference, then this will have to be justified by invoking a new principle of induction, appropriately modified. And this new principle in its turn will have to be justified, and so on. Nothing is gained, moreover, if the principle of induction, in its turn, is taken not as 'true' but only as 'probable.' In short, like every other form of inductive logic, the logic of probable inference, or 'probability logic', leads either to an infinite regress, or to the doctrine of *apriorism.*

The theory to be developed in the following pages stands directly opposed to all attempts to operate with the ideas of inductive logic. It might be described as the theory of *the deductive method of testing,* or as the view that a hypothesis can only be empirically *tested*—and only *after* it has been advanced.

Before I can elaborate this view (which might be called 'deductivism', in contrast to 'inductivism') I must first make clear the distinction between the *psychology of knowledge* which deals with empirical facts, and the *logic of knowledge* which is concerned only with logical relations. For the belief in inductive logic is largely due to a confusion of psychological problems with epistemological ones. It may be worth noticing, by the way, that this confusion spells trouble not only for the logic of knowledge but for its psychology as well.

2. ELIMINATION OF PSYCHOLOGISM

I said above that the work of the scientist consists in putting forward and
testing theories.

The initial stage, the act of conceiving or inventing a theory, seems to me
neither to call for logical analysis nor to be susceptible of it. The question how
it happens that a new idea occurs to a man—whether it is a musical theme,
a dramatic conflict, or a scientific theory—may be of great interest to empirical
psychology; but it is irrelevant to the logical analysis of scientific knowledge.
This latter is concerned not with *questions of fact* (Kant's *quid facti?*), but only
with questions of *justification or validity* (Kant's *quid juris?*). Its questions are
of the following kind. Can a statement be justified? And if so, how? Is it
testable? Is it logically dependent on certain other statements? Or does it
perhaps contradict them? In order that a statement may be logically examined
in this way, it must already have been presented to us. Someone must have
formulated it, and submitted it to logical examination.

Accordingly I shall distinguish sharply between the process of conceiving
a new idea, and the methods and results of examining it logically. As to the
task of the logic of knowledge—in contradistinction to the psychology of
knowledge—I shall proceed on the assumption that it consists solely in investi-
gating the methods employed in those systematic tests to which every new idea
must be subjected if it is to be seriously entertained.

Some might object that it would be more to the purpose to regard it as the
business of epistemology to produce what has been called a *'rational reconstruction'* of the steps that have led the scientist to a discovery—to the finding
of some new truth. But the question is: what, precisely, do we want to reconstruct? If it is the processes involved in the stimulation and release of an
inspiration which are to be reconstructed, then I should refuse to take it as the
task of the logic of knowledge. Such processes are the concern of empirical
psychology but hardly of logic. It is another matter if we want to reconstruct
rationally the *subsequent tests* whereby the inspiration may be discovered to
be a discovery, or become known to be knowledge. In so far as the scientist
critically judges, alters, or rejects his own inspiration we may, if we like, regard
the methodological analysis undertaken here as a kind of 'rational reconstruction' of the corresponding thought-processes. But this reconstruction would
not describe these processes as they actually happen: it can give only a logical
skeleton of the procedure of testing. Still, this is perhaps all that is meant by
those who speak of a 'rational reconstruction' of the ways in which we gain
knowledge.

It so happens that my arguments in this book are quite independent of this
problem. However, my view of the matter, for what it is worth, is that there
is no such thing as a logical method of having new ideas, or a logical reconstruction of this process. My view may be expressed by saying that every

discovery contains 'an irrational element', or 'a creative intuition', in Bergson's sense. In a similar way Einstein speaks of ' . . . the search for those highly universal . . . laws from which a picture of the world can be obtained by pure deduction. There is no logical path', he says, 'leading to these . . . laws. They can only be reached by intuition, based upon something like an intellectural love ('*Einfühlung*') of the objects of experience'.

According to the view that will be put forward here, the method of critically testing theories, and selecting them according to the results of tests, always proceeds on the following lines. From a new idea, put up tentatively, and not yet justified in any way—an anticipation, a hypothesis, a theoretical system, or what you will—conclusions are drawn by means of logical deduction. These conclusions are then compared with one another and with other relevant statements, so as to find what logical relations (such as equivalence, derivability, compatiblity, or incompatibility) exist between them.

We may if we like distinguish four different lines along which the testing of a theory could be carried out. First there is the logical comparison of the conclusions among themselves, by which the internal consistency of the system is tested. Secondly, there is the investigation of the logical form of the theory, with the object of determining whether it has the character of an empirical or scientific theory, or whether it is, for example, tautological. Thirdly, there is the comparison with other theories, chiefly with the aim of determining whether the theory would constitute a scientific advance should it survive our various tests. And finally, there is the testing of the theory by way of empirical applications of the conclusions which can be derived from it.

The purpose of this last kind of test is to find out how far the new consequences of the theory—whatever may be new in what it asserts—stand up to the demands of practice, whether raised by purely scientific experiments, or by practical technological applications. Here too the procedure of testing turns out to be deductive. With the help of other statements, previously accepted, certain singular statements—which we may call 'predictions'—are deduced from the theory; especially predictions that are easily testable or applicable. From among these statements, those are selected which are not derivable from the current theory, and more especially those which the current theory contradicts. Next we seek a decision as regards these (and other) derived statements by comparing them with the results of practical applications and experiments. If this decision is positive, that is, if the singular conclusions turn out to be acceptable, or *verified,* then the theory has, for the time being, passed its test: we have found no reason to discard it. But if the decision is negative, or in other words, if the conclusions have been *falsified,* then their falsification also falsifies the theory from which they were logically deduced.

It should be noticed that a positive decision can only temporarily support the theory, for subsequent negative decisions may always overthrow it. So long as a theory withstands detailed and severe tests and is not superseded by another theory in the course of scientific progress, we may say that it has 'proved its mettle' or that it is *'corroborated'*.

Nothing resembling inductive logic appears in the procedure here outlined. I never assume that we can argue from the truth of singular statements to the truth of theories. I never assume that by force of 'verified' conclusions, theories can be established as 'true', or even as merely 'probable'.

For Further Reading

Black, Max. *Problems of Analysis.* Ithaca, N.Y.: Cornell University Press, 1954, Chaps. 10–12.

Feigl, Herbert. "The Logical Character of the Principle of Induction," in H. Feigl and W. Sellars (eds.). *Readings in Philosophical Analysis.* New York: Appleton-Century-Crofts, 1949.

James, William. *Pragmatism and Other Essays.* Cleveland, Ohio: World Publishing Co., 1965. See Lecture VI, "Pragmatism's Conception of Truth."

Mill, John Stuart. *A System of Logic.* Toronto: University of Toronto Press, 1966. See especially Book III, Chaps. 1–5.

Nagel, Ernest. *Logic Without Metaphysics.* New York: Free Press, 1956. See Part II, Chap. 7. "The Ground of Induction."

Popper, Karl. *Conjectures and Refutations.* New York: Basic Books, 1963. See especially pp. 33–59.

Russell, Bertrand. *Human Knowledge.* New York: Simon and Schuster, 1962 (paperbound). See Part VI, "Postulates of Scientific Inference."

Salmon, W. C. "Russell on Scientific Inference," in G. Nakhnikian (ed.), *Bertrand Russell's Philosophy.* London: Duckworth, 1974.

Strawson, P. F. *Introduction to Logical Theory.* New York: Wiley, 1952, Chap. 9.

Wright, Georg Henrik von. *Treatise on Induction and Probability.* Paterson, N.J.: Littlefield, Adams, 1960 (paperbound).

PART IV

Realists and Phenomenalists

If there is anything in the ordinary person's view of things that is considered beyond question, it is, perhaps, the belief that the physical world exists, whether or not it is perceived by any individual. There are real roses, and they are red. There are real stones, and they are hard. Real objects are at rest or in motion, real organisms are growing and dying, real events are occurring continuously in this real world.

Let us assume, for the moment, that the ordinary person is right about this. Still we may ask, Is the world *exactly as it appears to us,* or is it different? Do our senses show us what the world is really like, or does the world appear the way it does because our senses perceive the world in a particular way?

Let us consider color. What is it that is colored when we see a rainbow? Nothing, we are told: the *appearance* of color results from the refraction of light as the rays of the sun pass through a natural prism formed by droplets of water. Let us accept that explanation. But what about this blue suit, this red car, this yellow daffodil? Are they colored? Well, not exactly. According to physics, it is more accurate to say that these objects are constructed in such a way, and our faculty of vision is constituted in such a way, that when light from the sun reflects from the objects into our retina *we see* blue, or red, or yellow. The objects are not really blue or red or yellow, any more than the droplets of water are the various colors of the rainbow. Color is a part of the way *we perceive* objects; it is not a quality of the objects themselves.

But if we accept that conclusion where will we draw the line? If the world as it appears to us is *somewhat* different from the world as it really is, how do we know that it is not *radically* different? Indeed, how can we know that there *is* a world apart from our perception of it? If color is merely a modification of our faculty of perception, may not shape, size, texture, solidity, sound, motion, and all other qualities also be merely modifications of perception? May it not be the case that the whole material world is constituted by our faculty of perception—that the very existence of the material world (like that of color) depends on its being perceived?

The philosophical problem, then, concerns the ontological status of the physical world. Does this world depend to some extent on a perceiver for its existence, and if so to what extent?

The ordinary person's view is called *common-sense realism* or *direct realism* (and sometimes, by its critics, *naïve realism*). It is the view that the world really is substantially as we perceive it to be, that its existence depends in no way on a perceiver. The antithesis of this view—that the physical world consists entirely of the perceptions of some perceiver or perceivers—is called *phenomenalism* (also *subjective idealism*). The other possibility with respect to this problem is to hold that the world as we perceive it is to some extent dependent on our faculty of perception and to some extent independent of our perceptions. This view is called *critical realism*.

11

JOHN LOCKE (1632–1706)

The World as We Perceive It and as It Really Is

Although John Locke was trained as a physician, he spent most of his life as a man of letters. He was deeply involved in the political affairs of his time and wrote several treatises that profoundly influenced Thomas Jefferson and other leaders of the Ameri-

From John Locke, *An Essay Concerning Human Understanding,* Volume I, Book II, Chapter VIII, Sections 7–24, and Volume II, Book IV, Chapter XI, Sections 1–9 (Oxford: Oxford University Press, 1894), pp. 168–180, 325–335.

can Revolution of 1776. He can justifiably be called the father of modern British philosophy and modern American philosophy as well, inasmuch as American philosophy in recent years has derived much of its inspiration from Great Britain.

Locke's argument in the selection that follows turns on the distinction between *qualities* (which are in the objects that we perceive) and *ideas* (which are in the mind of the perceiver). According to Locke, the process of perception is one wherein objects cause certain ideas to occur in the mind of the perceiver. Using this terminology we may then ask: Are these ideas *like* the qualities that inspired them, or are they not? Are they exact copies, imperfect copies, or radically different from the qualities that cause them to occur? The selection that follows is Locke's attempt to answer this question. His answer is such that he may be termed a critical realist with respect to the problem of the ontological status of the physical world.

.   .   .

7. To discover the nature of our *ideas* the better, and to discourse of them intelligibly, it will be convenient to distinguish them *as they are ideas or perceptions in our minds;* and *as they are modifications of matter in the bodies that cause such perceptions in us:* that so we may not think (as perhaps usually is done) that they are exactly the images and resemblances of something inherent in the subject; most of those of sensation being in the mind no more the likeness of something existing without us, than the names that stand for them are the likeness of our ideas, which yet upon hearing they are apt to excite in us.

8. Whatsoever the mind perceives *in itself,* or is the immediate object of perception, thought, or understanding, that I call *idea;* and the power to produce any idea in our mind, I call *quality* of the subject wherein that power is. Thus a snowball having the power to produce in us the ideas of white, cold, and round,—the power to produce those ideas in us, as they are in the snowball, I call qualities; and as they are sensations or perceptions in our understandings, I call them ideas; which *ideas*, if I speak of sometimes as in the things themselves, I would be understood to mean those qualities in the objects which produce them in us.

9. Qualities thus considered in bodies are,

First, such as are utterly inseparable from the body, in what state soever it be; and such as in all the alterations and changes it suffers, all the force can be used upon it, it constantly keeps; and such as sense constantly finds in every particle of matter which has bulk enough to be perceived; and the mind finds inseparable from every particle of matter, though less than to make itself singly be perceived by our senses: v.g. Take a grain of wheat, divide it into two parts; each part has still solidity, extension, figure, and mobility: divide it again, and it retains still the same qualities; and so divide it on, till the parts become insensible; they must retain still each of them all those qualities. For division (which is all that a mill, or pestle, or any other body, does upon another, in reducing it to insensible parts) can never take away either solidity, extension, figure, or mobility from any body, but only makes two or more distinct separate masses of matter, of that which was but one before; all which distinct masses, reckoned as so many distinct bodies, after division, make a certain number.

These I call *original* or *primary qualities* of body, which I think we may observe to produce simple ideas in us, viz. solidity, extension, figure, motion or rest, and number.

10. *Secondly,* such qualities which in truth are nothing in the objects themselves but powers to produce various sensations in us by their primary qualities, i.e. by the bulk, figure, texture, and motion of their insensible parts, as colours, sounds, tastes, &c. These I call *secondary qualities.* To these might be added a *third* sort, which are allowed to be barely powers; though they are as much real qualities in the subject as those which I, to comply with the common way of speaking, call qualities, but for distinction, secondary qualities. For the power in fire to produce a new colour, or consistency, in *wax* or *clay,* —by its primary qualities, is as much a quality in fire, as the power it has to produce in *me* a new idea or sensation of warmth or burning, which I felt not before,—by the same primary qualities, viz. the bulk, texture, and motion of its insensible parts.

11. The next thing to be considered is, how bodies produce ideas in us; and that is manifestly by impulse, the only way which we can conceive bodies to operate in.

12. If then external objects be not united to our minds when they produce ideas therein; and yet we perceive these *original* qualities in such of them as singly fall under our senses, it is evident that some motion must be thence continued by our nerves, or animal spirits, by some parts of our bodies, to the brains or the seat of sensation, there to produce in our minds the particular ideas we have of them. And since the extension, figure, number, and motion of bodies of an observable bigness, may be perceived at a distance by the sight, it is evident some singly imperceptible bodies must come from them to the eyes, and thereby convey to the brain some motion; which produces these ideas which we have of them in us.

13. After the same manner that the ideas of these original qualities are produced in us, we may conceive that the ideas of *secondary* qualities are also produced, viz. by the operation of insensible particles on our senses. For, it being manifest that there are bodies and good store of bodies, each whereof are so small, that we cannot by any of our senses discover either their bulk, figure, or motion,—as is evident in the particles of the air and water, and others extremely smaller than those; perhaps as much smaller than the particles of air and water, as the particles of air and water are smaller than peas or hail-stones;—let us suppose at present that the different motions and figures, bulk and number, of such particles, affecting the several organs of our senses,

produce in us those different sensations which we have from the colours and smells of bodies; v.g. that a violet, by the impulse of such insensible particles of matter, of peculiar figures and bulks, and in different degrees and modifications of their motions, causes the ideas of the blue colour, and sweet scent of that flower to be produced in our minds. It being no more impossible to conceive that God should annex such ideas to such motions, with which they have no similitude, than that he should annex the idea of pain to the motion of a piece of steel dividing our flesh with which that idea hath no resemblance.

14. What I have said concerning colours and smells may be understood also of tastes and sounds, and other the like sensible qualities; which, whatever reality we by mistake attribute to them, are in truth nothing in the objects themselves, but powers to produce various sensations in us; and depend on those primary qualities, viz. bulk, figure, texture, and motion of parts as I have said.

15. From whence I think it easy to draw this observation,—that the ideas of primary qualities of bodies are resemblances of them, and their patterns do really exist in the bodies themselves, but the ideas produced in us by these secondary qualities have no resemblance of them at all. There is nothing like our ideas, existing in the bodies themselves. They are, in the bodies we denominate from them, only a power to produce those sensations in us: and what is sweet, blue, or warm in idea, is but the certain bulk, figure, and motion of the insensible parts, in the bodies themselves, which we call so.

16. Flame is denominated hot and light; snow, white and cold; and manna, white and sweet, from the ideas they produce in us. Which qualities are commonly thought to be the same in those bodies that those ideas are in us, the one the perfect resemblance of the other, as they are in a mirror, and it would by most men be judged very extravagant if one should say otherwise. And yet he that will consider that the same fire that, at one distance produces in us the sensation of warmth, does, at a nearer approach, produce in us the far different sensation of pain, ought to bethink himself what reason he has to say—that this idea of warmth, which was produced in him by the fire, is *actually in the fire*; and his idea of pain, which the same fire produced in him the same way, is *not* in the fire. Why are whiteness and coldness in snow, and pain not, when it produces the one and the other idea in us; and can do neither, but by the bulk, figure, number, and motion of its solid parts?

17. The particular bulk, number, figure, and motion of the parts of fire or snow are really in them,—whether any one's senses perceive them or no: and therefore they may be called *real* qualities, because they really exist in those bodies. But light, heat, whiteness, or coldness, are no more really in them than sickness or pain is in manna. Take away the sensation of them; let not the eyes see light or colours, nor the ears hear sounds; let the palate not taste, nor the nose smell, and all colours, tastes, odours, and sounds, *as they are such particular ideas,* vanish and cease, and are reduced to their causes, i.e. bulk, figure, and motion of parts.

18. A piece of manna of a sensible bulk is able to produce in us the idea of

a round or square figure; and by being removed from one place to another, the idea of motion. This idea of motion represents it as it really is in manna moving: a circle or square are the same, whether in idea or existence, in the mind or in the manna. And this, both motion and figure, are really in the manna, whether we take notice of them or no: this everybody is ready to agree to. Besides, manna, by the bulk, figure, texture, and motion of its parts, has a power to produce the sensations of sickness, and sometimes of acute pains or gripings in us. That these ideas of sickness and pain are *not* in the manna, but effects of its operations on us, and are nowhere when we feel them not; this also every one readily agrees to. And yet men are hardly to be brought to think that sweetness and whiteness are not really in manna; which are but the effects of the operations of manna, by the motion, size and figure of its particles, on the eyes and palate: as the pain and sickness caused by manna are confessedly nothing but the effects of its operations on the stomach and guts, by the size, motion, and figure of its insensible parts, (for by nothing else can a body operate, as has been proved): as if it could not operate on the eyes and palate, and thereby produce in the mind particular distinct ideas, which in itself it has not, as well as we allow it can operate on the guts and stomach, and thereby produce distinct ideas, which in itself it has not. These ideas, being all effects of the operations of manna on several parts of our bodies, by the size, figure, number and motion of its parts;—why those produced by the eyes and palate should rather be thought to be really in the manna, than those produced by the stomach and guts; or why the pain and sickness, ideas that are the effect of manna, should be thought to be nowhere when they are not felt; and yet the sweetness and whiteness, effects of the same manna on other parts of the body, by ways equally as unknown, should be thought to exist in the manna, when they are not seen or tasted, would need some reason to explain.

19. Let us consider the red and white colours in porphyry. Hinder light from striking on it, and its colours vanish; it no longer produces any such ideas in us: upon the return of light it produces these appearances on us again. Can any one think any real alterations are made in the porphyry by the presence or absence of light; and that those ideas of whiteness and redness are really in porphyry in the light, when it is plain *it has no colour in the dark?* It has, indeed, such a configuration of particles, both night and day, as are apt, by the rays of light rebounding from some parts of that hard stone, to produce in us the idea of redness, and from others the idea of whiteness; but whiteness or redness are not in it at any time, but such a texture that hath the power to produce such a sensation in us.

20. Pound an almond, and the clear white colour will be altered into a dirty one, and the sweet taste into an oily one. What real alteration can the beating of the pestle make in any body, but an alteration of the texture of it?

21. Ideas being thus distinguished and understood, we may be able to give an account how the same water, at the same time, may produce the idea of cold by one hand and of heat by the other: whereas it is impossible that the

same water, if those ideas were really in it, should at the same time be both
hot and cold. For, if we imagine *warmth,* as it is in our hands, to be nothing
but a certain sort and degree of motion in the minute particles of our nerves
or animal spirits, we may understand how it is possible that the same water
may, at the same time, produce the sensations of heat in one hand and cold
in the other; which yet *figure* never does, that never producing the idea of a
square by one hand which has produced the idea of a globe by another. But
if the sensation of heat and cold be nothing but the increase or diminution of
the motion of the minute parts of our bodies, caused by the corpuscles of any
other body, it is easy to be understood, that if that motion be greater in one
hand than in the other; if a body be applied to the two hands, which has in
its minute particles a greater motion than in those of one of the hands, and
a less than in those of the other, it will increase the motion of the one hand
and lessen it in the other; and so cause the different sensations of heat and cold
that depend thereon.

·   ·   ·

23. The qualities, then, that are in bodies, rightly considered, are of three
sorts:—

First, The bulk, figure, number, situation, and motion or rest of their solid
parts. Those are in them, whether we perceive them or not; and when they are
of that size that we can discover them, we have by these an idea of the thing
as it is in itself; as is plain in artificial things. These I call *primary qualities.*

Secondly, The power that is in any body, by reason of its insensible primary
qualities, to operate after a peculiar manner on any of our senses, and thereby
produce in *us* the different ideas of several colours, sounds, smells, tastes, &c.
These are usually called *sensible qualities.*

Thirdly, The power that is in any body, by reason of the particular constitution of its primary qualities, to make such a change in the bulk, figure, texture,
and motion of *another body,* as to make it operate on our senses differently
from what it did before. Thus the sun has a power to make wax white, and
fire to make lead fluid. These are usually called *powers.*

The first of these, as has been said, I think may be properly called real,
original, or primary qualities; because they are in the things themselves,
whether they are perceived or not: and upon their different modifications it is
that the secondary qualities depend.

The other two are only powers to act differently upon other things: which
powers result from the different modifications of those primary qualities.

24. But, though the two latter sorts of qualities are powers barely, and nothing
but powers, relating to several other bodies, and resulting from the different
modifications of the original qualities, yet they are generally otherwise thought
of. For the *second* sort, viz. the powers to produce several ideas in us, by our

senses, are looked upon as real qualities in the things thus affecting us: but the *third* sort are called and esteemed barely powers. v.g. The idea of heat or light, which we receive by our eyes, or touch, from the sun, are commonly thought real qualities existing in the sun, and something more than mere powers in it. But when we consider the sun in reference to wax, which it melts or blanches, we look on the whiteness and softness produced in the wax, not as qualities in the sun, but effects produced by powers in it. Whereas, if rightly considered, these qualities of light and warmth, which are perceptions in me when I am warmed or enlightened by the sun, are no otherwise in the sun, than the changes made in the wax, when it is blanched or melted, are in the sun. They are all of them equally *powers in the sun, depending on its primary qualities*; whereby it is able, in the one case, so to alter the bulk, figure, texture, or motion of some of the insensible parts of my eyes or hands, as thereby to produce in me the idea of light or heat; and in the other, it is able so to alter the bulk, figure, texture, or motion of the insensible parts of the wax, as to make them fit to produce in me the distinct ideas of white and fluid.

.   .   .

1. The knowledge of our own being we have by intuition. The existence of a God, reason clearly makes known to us, as has been shown.

The knowledge of the existence of *any other thing* we can have only by *sensation*: for there being no necessary connexion of real existence with any *idea* a man hath in his memory; nor of any other existence but that of God with the existence of any particular man: no particular man can know the existence of any other being, but only when, by actual operating upon him, it makes itself perceived by him. For, the having the idea of anything in our mind, no more proves the existence of that thing, than the picture of a man evidences his being in the world, or the visions of a dream make thereby a true history.

2. It is therefore the *actual receiving* of ideas from without that gives us notice of the existence of other things, and makes us know, that something doth exist at that time without us, which causes that idea in us; though perhaps we neither know nor consider how it does it. For it takes not from the certainty of our senses, and the ideas we receive by them, that we know not the manner wherein they are produced: v.g. whilst I write this, I have, by the paper affecting my eyes, that idea produced in my mind, which, whatever object causes, I call *white*; by which I know that that quality or accident (i.e. whose appearance before my eyes always causes that idea) doth really exist, and hath a being without me. And of this, the greatest assurance I can possibly have, and to which my faculties can attain, is the testimony of my eyes, which are the proper and sole judges of this thing; whose testimony I have reason to rely on as so certain, that I can no more doubt, whilst I write this, that I see white and black, and that something really exists that causes that sensation in me,

than that I write or move my hand; which is a certainty as great as human nature is capable of, concerning the existence of anything, but a man's self alone, and of God.

3. The notice we have by our senses of the existing of things without us, though it be not altogether so certain as our intuitive knowledge, or the deductions of our reason employed about the clear abstract ideas of our own minds; yet it is an assurance that deserves the name of *knowledge*. If we persuade ourselves that our faculties act and inform us right concerning the existence of those objects that affect them, it cannot pass for an ill-grounded confidence: for I think nobody can, in earnest, be so skeptical as to be uncertain of the existence of those things which he sees and feels. At least, he that can doubt so far, (whatever he may have with his own thoughts,) will never have any controversy with me; since he can never be sure I say anything contrary to his own opinion. As to myself, I think God has given me assurance enough of the existence of things without me: since, by their different application, I can produce in myself both pleasure and pain, which is one great concernment of my present state. This is certain: the confidence that our faculties do not herein deceive us, is the greatest assurance we are capable of concerning the existence of material beings. For we cannot act anything but by our faculties; nor talk of knowledge itself, but by the help of those faculties which are fitted to apprehend even what knowledge is.

But besides the assurance we have from our senses themselves, that they do not err in the information they give us of the existence of things without us, when they are affected by them, we are further confirmed in this assurance by other concurrent reasons:—

4. I. It is plain those perceptions are produced in us by exterior causes affecting our senses: because those that want the *organs* of any sense, never can have the ideas belonging to that sense produced in their minds. This is too evident to be doubted: and therefore we cannot but be assured that they come in by the organs of that sense, and no other way. The organs themselves, it is plain, do not produce them: for then the eyes of a man in the dark would produce colours, and his nose smell roses in the winter: but we see nobody gets the relish of a pineapple, till he goes to the Indies, where it is, and tastes it.

5. II. Because sometimes I find that *I cannot avoid the having those ideas produced in my mind.* For though, when my eyes are shut, or windows fast, I can at pleasure recall to my mind the ideas of light, or the sun, which former sensations had lodged in my memory; so I can at pleasure lay by *that* idea, and take into my view that of the smell of a rose, or taste of sugar. But, if I turn my eyes at noon towards the sun, I cannot avoid the ideas which the light or sun then produces in me. So that there is a manifest difference between the ideas laid up in my memory, (over which, if they were there only, I should have constantly the same power to dispose of them, and lay them by at pleasure,) and those which force themselves upon me, and I cannot avoid having. And therefore it must needs be some exterior cause, and the brisk acting of some

objects without me, whose efficacy I cannot resist, that produces those ideas in my mind, whether I will or no. Besides, there is nobody who doth not perceive the difference in himself between contemplating the sun, as he hath the idea of it in his memory, and actually looking upon it: of which two, his perception is so distinct, that few of his ideas are more distinguishable one from another. And therefore he hath certain knowledge that they are not *both* memory, or the actions of his mind, and fancies only within him; but that actual seeing hath a cause without.

6. III. Add to this, that many of those ideas are *produced in us with pain,* which afterwards we remember without the least offence. Thus, the pain of heat or cold, when the idea of it is revived in our minds, gives us no disturbance; which, when felt, was very troublesome; and is again, when actually repeated: which is occasioned by the disorder the external object causes in our bodies when applied to them: and we remember the pains of hunger, thirst, or the headache, without any pain at all; which would either never disturb us, or else constantly do it, as often as we thought of it, were there nothing more but ideas floating in our minds, and appearances entertaining our fancies, without the real existence of things affecting us from abroad. The same may be said of *pleasure,* accompanying several actual sensations. And though mathematical demonstration depends not upon sense, yet the examining them by diagrams gives great credit to the evidence of our sight, and seems to give it a certainty approaching to that of demonstration itself. For, it would be very strange, that a man should allow it for an undeniable truth, that two angles of a figure, which he measures by lines and angles of a diagram, should be bigger one than the other, and yet doubt of the existence of those lines and angles, which by looking on he makes use of to measure that by.

7. IV. Our *senses* in many cases *bear witness to the truth of each other's report,* concerning the existence of sensible things without us. He that *sees* a fire, may, if he doubt whether it be anything more than a bare fancy, *feel* it too; and be convinced, by putting his hand in it. Which certainly could never be put into such exquisite pain by a bare idea or phantom, unless that the pain be a fancy too: which yet he cannot, when the burn is well, by raising the idea of it, bring upon himself again.

Thus I see, whilst I write this, I can change the appearance of the paper; and by designing the letters, tell *beforehand* what new idea it shall exhibit the very next moment, by barely drawing my pen over it: which will neither appear (let me fancy as much as I will) if my hands stand still; or though I move my pen, if my eyes be shut: nor, when those characters are once made on the paper, can I choose afterwards but see them as they are; that is, have the ideas of such letters as I have made. Whence it is manifest, that they are not barely the sport and play of my own imagination, when I find that the characters that were made at the pleasure of my own thoughts, do not obey them; nor yet cease to be, whenever I shall fancy it, but continue to affect my senses constantly and regularly, according to the figures I made them. To which if we will add, that the sight of those shall, from another man, draw such sounds as I beforehand design they shall stand for, there will be little reason left to doubt that those words I write do really exist without me, when they cause a long series of regular sounds to affect my ears, which could not be the effect of my imagination, nor could my memory retain them in that order.

8. But yet, if after all this any one will be so skeptical as to distrust his senses, and to affirm that all we see and hear, feel and taste, think and do, during our whole being, is but the series and deluding appearances of a long dream, whereof there is no reality; and therefore will question the existence of all things, or our knowledge of anything: I must desire him to consider, that, if all be a dream, then he doth but dream that he makes the question, and so it is not much matter that a waking man should answer him. But yet, if he pleases, he may dream that I make him this answer, That the certainty of things existing in *rerum natura* when we have the testimony of our senses for it is not only as great as our frame can attain to, but as our condition needs. For, our faculties being suited not to the full extent of being, nor to a perfect, clear, comprehensive knowledge of things free from all doubt and scruple; but to the preservation of us, in whom they are; and accommodated to the use of life: they serve to our purpose well enough, if they will but give us certain notice of those things, which are convenient or inconvenient to us. For he that sees a candle burning, and hath experimented the force of its flame by putting his finger in it, will little doubt that this is something existing without him, which does him harm, and puts him to great pain: which is assurance enough, when no man requires greater certainty to govern his actions by than what is as certain as his actions themselves. And if our dreamer pleases to try whether the glowing heat of a glass furnace be barely a wandering imagination in a drowsy man's fancy, by putting his hand into it, he may perhaps be wakened into a certainty greater than he could wish, that it is something more than bare imagination. So that this evidence is as great as we can desire, being as certain to us as our pleasure or pain, i.e. happiness or misery; beyond which we have no concernment, either of knowing or being. Such an assurance of the existence of things without us is sufficient to direct us in the attaining the good and avoiding the evil which is caused by them, which is the important concernment we have of being made acquainted with them.

9. In fine, then, when our senses do actually convey into our understandings any idea, we cannot but be satisfied that there doth something *at that time* really exist without us, which doth affect our senses, and by them give notice of itself to our apprehensive faculties, and actually produce that idea which we then perceive: and we cannot so far distrust their testimony, as to doubt that such *collections* of simple ideas as we have observed by our senses to be united together, do really exist together. But this knowledge extends as far as the present testimony of our senses, employed about particular objects that do then affect them, and no further. For if I saw such a collection of simple ideas as is wont to be called *man,* existing together one minute since, and am now

alone, I cannot be certain that the same man exists now, since there is no *necessary connexion* of his existence a minute since with his existence now: by a thousand ways he may cease to be, since I had the testimony of my senses for his existence. And if I cannot be certain that the man I saw last to-day is now in being, I can less be certain that he is so who hath been longer removed from my senses, and I have not seen since yesterday, or since the last year: and much less can I be certain of the existence of men that I never saw. And, therefore, though it be highly probable that millions of men do now exist, yet, whilst I am alone, writing this, I have not that certainty of it which we strictly call knowledge; though the great likelihood of it puts me past doubt, and it be reasonable for me to do several things upon the confidence that there are men (and men also of my acquaintance, with whom I have to do) now in the world: but this is but probability, not knowledge.

12

GEORGE BERKELEY (1685–1753)

To Be Is to Be Perceived

Berkeley (pronounced BARK-lee) was an Irishman, a sometime lecturer in Greek and theology at Trinity College, Dublin, and, for the last two decades of his life, a Bishop in the Church of England. He once dreamed of establishing a university in Bermuda for American students, and actually spent three years in Rhode Island in an unsuccessful attempt to raise money for that project. Berkeley's "immaterialism," as his philosophy came to be called, had a strong influence on many churchmen and educators both in Great Britain and in the British colonies of North America.

The *Treatise Concerning the Principles of Human Knowledge* was written when Berkeley was still in his twenties, and it established his reputation as the first modern philosopher to set forth what is now called the phenomenalist view concerning the existence of material objects. Berkeley's thesis, to use his own famous words, is "that

From George Berkeley, *A Treatise Concerning the Principles of Human Knowledge,* Sections I–XX, in *The Works of George Berkeley, D. D.,* Volume I (London: B. F. Dove, 1820), pp. 23–33.

all the choir of heaven and furniture of the earth, in a word all those bodies which compose the mighty frame of the world, have not any subsistence without a mind, that their being is to be perceived. . . . " Minds and their ideas are the only things that really exist. Physical objects, therefore, according to Berkeley, exist only as ideas in the mind of some perceiver.

I. It is evident to any one who takes a survey of the objects of human knowledge, that they are either ideas actually imprinted on the senses, or else such as are perceived by attending to the passions and operations of the mind, or lastly, ideas formed by help of memory and imagination, either compounding, dividing, or barely representing, those originally perceived in the aforesaid ways. By sight I have the ideas of light and colours with their several degrees and variations. By touch I perceive, for example, hard and soft, heat and cold, motion and resistance, and of all these more and less either as to quantity or degree. Smelling furnishes me with odours, the palate with tastes, and hearing conveys sounds to the mind in all their variety of tone and composition. And as several of these are observed to accompany each other, they come to be marked by one name, and so to be reputed as one thing. Thus, for example, a certain colour, taste, smell, figure, and consistence, having been observed to go together, are accounted one distinct thing, signified by the name *apple*. Other collections of ideas constitute a stone, a tree, a book, and the like sensible things; which, as they are pleasing or disagreeable, excite the passions of love, hatred, joy, grief, and so forth.

II. But besides all that endless variety of ideas or objects of knowledge, there is likewise something which knows or perceives them, and exercises divers operations; as willing, imagining, remembering about them. This perceiving active being is what I call *mind, spirit, soul,* or *myself.* By which words I do not denote any one of my ideas, but a thing entirely distinct from them, wherein they exist, or, which is the same thing, whereby they are perceived; for the existence of an idea consists in being perceived.

III. That neither our thoughts, nor passions, nor ideas formed by the imagination, exist without the mind, is what every body will allow. And it seems no less evident that the various sensations or ideas imprinted on the sense, however blended or combined together (that is, whatever objects they compose), cannot exist otherwise than in a mind perceiving them. I think an intuitive knowledge may be obtained of this, by any one that shall attend to what is meant by the term *exist,* when applied to sensible things. The table I write on, I say, exists, that is, I see and feel it; and if I were out of my study I should say it existed, meaning thereby that if I was in my study I might perceive it, or that some other spirit actually does perceive it. There was an odour, that is, it was smelled; there was a sound, that is to say, it was heard; a colour or figure, and it was perceived by sight or touch. This is all that I can understand by these and the like expressions. For as to what is said of the absolute existence of unthinking things without any relation to their being perceived, that seems perfectly unintelligible. Their *esse* is *percipi,* nor is it possible they should have any existence out of the minds or thinking things which perceive them.

IV. It is indeed an opinion strangely prevailing amongst men, that houses, mountains, rivers, and in a word all sensible objects, have an existence natural or real distinct from their being perceived by the understanding. But with how great an assurance and acquiescence soever this principle may be entertained in the world; yet whoever shall find in his heart to call it in question, may, if I mistake not, perceive it to involve a manifest contradiction. For what are the forementioned objects but the things we perceive by sense, and what do we perceive besides our own ideas or sensations; and is it not plainly repugnant that any one of these or any combination of them should exist unperceived?

V. If we thoroughly examine this tenet, it will, perhaps, be found at bottom to depend on the doctrine of *abstract ideas.* For can there be a nicer strain of abstraction, than to distinguish the existence of sensible objects from their being perceived, so as to conceive them existing unperceived? Light and colours, heat and cold, extension and figures, in a word the things we see and feel, what are they but so many sensations, notions, ideas or impressions on the sense; and is it possible to separate, even in thought, any of these from perception? For my part I might as easily divide a thing from itself. I may indeed divide in my thoughts or conceive apart from each other those things which, perhaps, I never perceived by sense so divided. Thus I imagine the trunk of a human body without the limbs, or conceive the smell of a rose without thinking on the rose itself. So far I will not deny I can abstract, if that may properly be called *abstraction* which extends only to the conceiving separately such objects as it is possible may really exist or be actually perceived asunder. But my conceiving or imagining power does not extend beyond the possibility of real existence or perception. Hence as it is impossible for me to see or feel anything without an actual sensation of that thing, so is it impossible for me to conceive in my thoughts any sensible thing or object distinct from the sensation or perception of it.

VI. Some truths there are so near and obvious to the mind, that a man need only open his eyes to see them. Such I take this important one to be, to wit, that all the choir of heaven and furniture of the earth, in a word all those bodies which compose the mighty frame of the world, have not any subsistence without a mind, that their being is to be perceived or known; that consequently so long as they are not actually perceived by me, or do not exist in my mind or that of any other created spirit, they must either have no existence at all, or else subsist in the mind of some eternal spirit: it being perfectly unintelligible, and involving all the absurdity of abstraction, to attribute to any single part of them an existence independent of a spirit. To be convinced of which, the reader need only reflect and try to separate in his own thoughts the being of a sensible thing from its being perceived.

VII. From what has been said, it follows, there is not any other substance than *spirit,* or that which perceives. But for the fuller proof of this point, let it be considered, the sensible qualities are colour, figure, motion, smell, taste, and such like, that is, the ideas perceived by sense. Now for an idea to exist in an unperceiving thing, is a manifest contradiction; for to have an idea is all one as to perceive: that therefore wherein colour, figure, and the like qualities exist, must perceive them; hence it is clear there can be no unthinking substance or *substratum* of those ideas.

VIII. But, say you, though the ideas themselves do not exist without the mind, yet there may be things like them whereof they are copies or resemblances, which things exist without the mind, in an unthinking substance. I answer, an idea can be like nothing but an idea; a colour or figure can be like nothing but another colour or figure. If we look but ever so little into our thoughts, we shall find it impossible for us to conceive a likeness except only between our ideas. Again, I ask whether those supposed originals or external things, of which our ideas are the pictures or representations, be themselves perceivable or not? if they are, then they are ideas, and we have gained our point; but if you say they are not, I appeal to any one whether it be sense, to assert a colour is like something which is invisible; hard or soft, like something which is intangible; and so of the rest.

IX. Some there are who make a distinction betwixt *primary* and *secondary* qualities: by the former, they mean extension, figure, motion, rest, solidity or impenetrability, and number: by the latter they denote all other sensible qualities, as colours, sounds, tastes, and so forth. The ideas we have of these they acknowledge not to be the resemblances of any thing existing without the mind or unperceived; but they will have our ideas of the primary qualities to be patterns or images of things which exist without the mind, in an unthinking substance which they call *matter*. By matter therefore we are to understand an inert, senseless substance, in which extension, figure, and motion, do actually subsist. But it is evident from what we have already shewn, that extension, figure and motion are only ideas existing in the mind, and that an idea can be like nothing but another idea, and that consequently neither they nor their archetypes can exist in an unperceiving substance. Hence it is plain, that the very notion of what is called *matter* or *corporeal substance,* involves a contradiction in it.

X. They who assert that figure, motion, and the rest of the primary or original qualities, do exist without the mind, in unthinking substances, do at the same time acknowledge that colours, sounds, heat, cold, and suchlike secondary qualities, do not, which they tell us are sensations existing in the mind alone, that depend on and are occasioned by the different size, texture, and motion, of the minute particles of matter. This they take for an undoubted truth, which they can demonstrate beyond all exception. Now if it be certain, that those original qualities are inseparably united with the other sensible qualities, and not, even in thought, capable of being abstracted from them, it plainly follows, that they exist only in the mind. But I desire any one to reflect and try, whether he can, by any abstraction of thought, conceive the extension and motion of a body, without all other sensibles qualities. For my own part, I see evidently that it is not in my power to frame an idea of a body extended and moved, but I must withal give it some colour or other sensible quality which is acknowledged to exist only in the mind. In short, extension, figure, and motion, abstracted from all other qualities, are inconceivable. Where therefore the other sensible qualities are, there must these be also, to wit, in the mind, and no where else.

XI. Again, *great* and *small, swift* and *slow,* are allowed to exist no where without the mind, being entirely relative, and changing as the frame or position of the organs of sense varies. The extension therefore which exists without the mind, is neither great nor small, the motion neither swift nor slow, that is, they are nothing at all. But, say you, they are extension in general, and motion in general: thus we see how much the tenet of extended, moveable substances existing without the mind, depends on that strange doctrine of *abstract ideas.* And here I cannot but remark, how nearly the vague and indeterminate description of matter or corporeal substance, which the modern philosophers are run into by their own principles, resembles that antiquated and so-much-ridiculed notion of *materia prima,* to be met with in Aristotle and his followers. Without extension solidity cannot be conceived. Since therefore it has been shewn that extension exists not in an unthinking substance, the same must also be true of solidity.

XII. That number is entirely the creature of the mind, even though the other qualities be allowed to exist without, will be evident to whoever considers, that the same thing bears a different denomination of number, as the mind views it with different respects. Thus, the same extension is one or three or thirty-six, according as the mind considers it with reference to a yard, a foot, or an inch. Number is so visibly relative, and dependent on men's understanding, that it is strange to think how any one should give it an absolute existence without the mind. We say one book, one page, one line; all these are equally units, though some contain several of the others. And in each instance it is plain, the unit relates to some particular combination of ideas arbitrarily put together by the mind.

XIII. Unity I know some will have to be a simple or uncompounded idea, accompanying all other ideas into the mind. That I have any such idea answering the word *unity,* I do not find; and if I had, methinks I could not miss finding it; on the contrary it should be the most familiar to my understanding, since it is said to accompany all other ideas, and to be perceived by all the ways of sensation and reflection. To say no more, it is an *abstract idea.*

XIV. I shall farther add, that after the same manner as modern philosophers prove certain sensible qualities to have no existence in matter, or without the mind, the same thing may be likewise proved of all other sensible qualities whatsoever. Thus, for instance, it is said that heat and cold are affections only of the mind, and not at all patterns of real beings existing in the corporeal substances which excite them, for that the same body which appears cold to one hand seems warm to another. Now why may we not as well argue that figure and extension are not patterns or resemblances of qualities existing in matter, because to the same eye at different stations, or eyes of a different texture at the same station, they appear various, and cannot therefore be the images of any thing settled and determinate without the mind? Again, it is proved that sweetness is not really in the sapid thing, because the thing remaining unaltered the sweetness is changed into bitter, as in case of a fever or otherwise vitiated palate. Is it not as reasonable to say, that motion is not without the mind, since if the succession of ideas in the mind becomes swifter, the motion, it is acknowledged, shall appear slower, without any alteration in any external object.

XV. In short, let any one consider those arguments, which are thought manifestly to prove that colours and tastes exist only in the mind, and he shall find they may with equal force, be brought to prove the same thing of extension, figure, and motion. Though it must be confessed this method of arguing doth not so much prove that there is no extension or colour in an outward object, as that we do not know by sense which is the true extension or colour of the object. But the arguments foregoing plainly shew it to be impossible that any colour or extension at all, or other sensible quality whatsoever, should exist in an unthinking subject without the mind, or in the truth, that there should be any such thing as an outward object.

XVI. But let us examine a little the received opinion. It is said, extension is a mode or accident of matter, and that matter is the *substratum* that supports it. Now I desire that you would explain what is meant by matter's *supporting* extension: say you, I have no idea of matter, and therefore cannot explain it. I answer, though you have no positive, yet if you have any meaning at all, you must at least have a relative idea of matter: though you know not what it is, yet you must be supposed to know what relation it bears to accidents, and what is meant by its supporting them. It is evident *support* cannot here be taken in its usual or literal sense, as when we say that pillars support a building: in what sense therefore must it be taken?

XVII. If we inquire into what the most accurate philosophers declare themselves to mean by *material substance*, we shall find them acknowledge, they have no other meaning annexed to those sounds, but the idea of being in general, together with the relative notion of its supporting accidents. The general idea of being appeareth to be the most abstract and incomprehensible of all other; and as for its supporting accidents, this, as we have just now observed, cannot be understood in the common sense of those words; it must therefore be taken in some other sense, but what that is they do not explain. So that when I consider the two parts or branches which make the signification of the words *material substance,* I am convinced there is no distinct meaning annexed to them. But why should we trouble ourselves any farther, in discussing this material *substratum* or support of figure and motion, and other sensible qualities? Does it not suppose they have an existence without the mind? And is not this a direct repugnancy and altogether inconceivable?

XVIII. But though it were possible that solid, figured, moveable substances may exist without the mind, corresponding to the ideas we have of bodies, yet how is it possible for us to know this? Either we must know it by sense, or by reason. As for our senses, by them we have the knowledge only of our sensations, ideas, or those things that are immediately perceived by sense, call them what you will: but they do not inform us that things exist without the mind, or unperceived, like to those which are perceived. This the materialists themselves acknowledge. It remains therefore that if we have any knowledge at all of external things, it must be by reason, inferring their existence from what is immediately perceived by sense. But what reason can induce us to believe the existence of bodies without the mind from what we perceive, since the very patrons of matter themselves do not pretend there is any necessary connexion betwixt them and our ideas? I say it is granted on all hands (and what happens in dreams, frenzies, and the like, puts it beyond dispute), that it is possible we might be affected with all the ideas we have now, though no bodies existed without resembling them. Hence it is evident the supposition of external bodies is not necessary for the producing our ideas: since it is granted they are produced sometimes, and might possibly be produced always, in the same order we see them in at present, without their concurrence.

XIX. But though we might possibly have all our sensations without them, yet perhaps it may be thought easier to conceive and explain the manner of their production, by supposing external bodies in their likeness rather than otherwise; and so it might be at least probable there are such things as bodies that excite their ideas in our minds. But neither can this be said; for though we give the materialists their external bodies, they by their own confession are never the nearer knowing how our ideas are produced: since they own themselves unable to comprehend in what manner body can act upon spirit, or how it is possible it should imprint any idea in the mind. Hence it is evident the production of ideas or sensations in our minds can be no reason why we should suppose matter or corporeal substances, since that is acknowledged to remain equally inexplicable with or without this supposition. If therefore it were possible for bodies to exist without the mind, yet to hold they do so must needs be a very precarious opinion; since it is to suppose, without any reason at all, that God has created innumerable beings that are entirely useless, and serve to no manner of purpose.

XX. In short, if there were external bodies, it is impossible we should ever come to know it; and if there were not, we might have the very same reasons to think there were that we have now. Suppose, what no one can deny possible, an intelligence, without the help of external bodies, to be affected with the same train of sensations or ideas that you are, imprinted in the same order, and with like vividness in his mind. I ask whether that intelligence hath not all the reason to believe the existence of corporeal substances, represented by his ideas, and exciting them in his mind, that you can possibly have for believing the same thing? Of this there can be no question; which one consideration is enough to make any reasonable person suspect the strength of whatever arguments he may think himself to have, for the existence of bodies without the mind. . . .

13

JOHN STUART MILL (1806–1873)

Matter as a Permanent Possibility of Sensation

John Stuart Mill was groomed from early childhood by his father, James Mill, to be a spokesman for *utilitarianism,* a philosophical theory developed and championed by the elder Mill's friend Jeremy Bentham. The younger Mill, after weathering a serious personal and intellectual crisis at age twenty, did, in fact, become that spokesman, and, in so doing, he put his own stamp on utilitarianism with such finality that today he is regarded as its principal representative.

Mill's philosophical interests were not, however, limited to the ethical concerns of utilitarianism. He wrote voluminously, and his writings include important contributions to logic, epistemology, political theory, philosophy of religion, and psychology, as well as ethics.

Mill's view of the ontological status of physical objects may properly be regarded as a modification of Berkeley's. The view that "to be is to be perceived" appears to imply that whenever a thing is not being perceived by some mind it must cease to

From John Stuart Mill, *An Examination of Sir William Hamilton's Philosophy,* 5th ed., Chapter XI (London: Longman's, Green, Reader, & Dyer, 1878), pp. 225–239.

exist—a consequence that even Berkeley considered so preposterous that he found it necessary to "rescue" permanence by asserting that the world is continually perceived by God. Mill, who had serious doubts about the existence of God, took a different tack. He argues that matter is a "permanent possibility of sensation." To say that things exist when we are not actually perceiving them is to say that we *could* perceive them if we put ourselves in the proper circumstances. Thus, for Mill, physical objects have an uninterrupted existence as *possible* perceptions regardless of whether those possibilities are actualized in the mind of a perceiver.

What is it we mean, or what is it which leads us to say, that the objects we perceive are external to us, and not a part of our own thoughts? We mean, that there is concerned in our perceptions something which exists when we are not thinking of it; which existed before we had ever thought of it, and would exist if we were annihilated; and further, that there exist things which we never saw, touched, or otherwise perceived, and things which never have been perceived by man. This idea of something which is distinguished from our fleeting impressions by what, in Kantian language, is called Perdurability; something which is fixed and the same, while our impressions vary; something which exists whether we are aware of it or not, and which is always square (or of some other given figure) whether it appears to us square or round—constitutes altogether our idea of external substance. Whoever can assign an origin to this complex conception, has accounted for what we mean by the belief in matter. Now all this, according to the Psychological Theory, is but the form impressed by the known laws of association, upon the conception or notion, obtained by experience, of Contingent Sensations; by which are meant, sensations that are not in our present consciousness, and individually never were in our consciousness at all, but which in virtue of the laws to which we have learnt by experience that our sensations are subject, we know that we should have felt under given supposable circumstances, and under these same circumstances, might still feel.

I see a piece of white paper on a table. I go into another room. If the phænomenon always followed me, or if, when it did not follow me, I believed it to disappear *è rerum natura,* I should not believe it to be an external object. I should consider it as a phantom—a mere affection of my senses: I should not believe that there had been any Body there. But, though I have ceased to see it, I am persuaded that the paper is still there. I no longer have the sensations which it gave me; but I believe that when I again place myself in the circumstances in which I had those sensations, that is, when I go again into the room, I shall again have them; and further, that there has been no intervening moment at which this would not have been the case. Owing to this property of my mind, my conception of the world at any given instant consists, in only a small proportion, of present sensations. Of these I may at the time have none at all, and they are in any case a most insignificant portion of the whole which I apprehend. The conception I form of the world existing at any moment, comprises, along with the sensations I am feeling, a countless variety of possibilities of sensation: namely, the whole of those which past observation tells me that I could, under any supposable circumstances, experience at this moment, together with an indefinite and illimitable multitude of others which though I do not know that I could, yet it is possible that I might, experience in circumstances not known to me. These various possibilities are the important thing to me in the world. My present sensations are generally of little importance, and are moreover fugitive: the possibilities, on the contrary, are permanent, which is the character that mainly distinguishes our idea of Substance or Matter from our notion of sensation. These possibilities, which are conditional certainties, need a special name to distinguish them from mere vague possibilities, which experience gives no warrant for reckoning upon. Now, as soon as a distinguishing name is given, though it be only to the same thing regarded in a different aspect, one of the most familiar experiences of our mental nature teaches us, that the different name comes to be considered as the name of a different thing.

There is another important peculiarity of these certified or guaranteed possibilities of sensation; namely, that they have reference, not to single sensations, but to sensations joined together in groups. When we think of anything as a material substance, or body, we either have had, or we think that on some given supposition we should have, not some *one* sensation, but a great and even an indefinite number and variety of sensations, generally belonging to different senses, but so linked together, that the presence of one announces the possible presence at the very same instant of any or all of the rest. In our mind, therefore, not only is this particular Possibility of sensation invested with the quality of permanence when we are not actually feeling any of the sensations at all; but when we are feeling some of them, the remaining sensations of the group are conceived by us in the form of Present Possibilities, which might be realized at the very moment. And as this happens in turn to all of them, the group as a whole presents itself to the mind as permanent, in contrast not solely with the temporariness of my bodily presence, but also with the temporary character of each of the sensations composing the group; in other words, as a kind of permanent substratum, under a set of passing experiences or manifestations: which is another leading character of our idea of substance or matter, as distinguished from sensation.

Let us now take into consideration another of the general characters of our experience, namely, that in addition to fixed groups, we also recognise a fixed Order in our sensations; an Order of succession, which, when ascertained by observation, gives rise to the ideas of Cause and Effect, according to what I hold to be the true theory of that relation, and is on any theory the source of all our knowledge of what causes produce what effects. Now, of what nature is this fixed order among our sensations? It is a constancy of antecedence and sequence. But the constant antecedence and sequence do not generally exist between one actual sensation and another. Very few such sequences are presented to us by experience. In almost all the constant sequences which occur in Nature, the antecedence and consequence do not obtain between sensations, but between the groups we have been speaking about, of which a very small portion is actual sensation, the greater part being permanent possibilities of sensation, evidenced to us by a small and variable number of sensations actually present. Hence, our ideas of causation, power, activity, do not become connected in thought with our sensations as *actual* at all, save in the few physiological cases where these figure by themselves as the antecedents in some uniform sequence. Those ideas become connected, not with sensations, but with groups of possibilities of sensation. The sensations conceived do not, to our habitual thoughts, present themselves as sensations actually experienced, inasmuch as not only any one or any number of them may be supposed absent, but none of them need be present. We find that the modifications which are taking place more or less regularly in our possibilities of sensation, are mostly quite independent of our consciousness, and of our presence or absence. Whether we are asleep or awake the fire goes out, and puts an end to one particular possibility of warmth and light. Whether we are present or absent the corn ripens, and brings a new possibility of food. Hence we speedily learn to think of Nature as made up solely of these groups of possibilities, and the active force in Nature as manifested in the modification of some of these by others. The sensations, though the original foundation of the whole, come to be looked upon as a sort of accident depending on us, and the possibilities as much more real than the actual sensations, nay, as the very realities of which these are only the representations, appearances, or effects. When this state of mind has been arrived at, then, and from that time forward, we are never conscious of a present sensation without instantaneously referring it to some one of the groups of possibilities into which a sensation of that particular description enters; and if we do not yet know to what group to refer it, we at least feel an irresistible conviction that it must belong to some group or other; *i.e.* that its presence proves the existence, here and now, of a great number and variety of possibilities of sensation, without which it would not have been. The whole set of sensations as possible, form a permanent background to any one or more of them that are, at a given moment, actual; and the possibilities are conceived as standing to the actual sensations in the relation of a cause to its effects, or of canvas to the figures painted on it, or of a root to the trunk, leaves, and flowers, or of a substratum to that which is spread over it, or, in transcendental language, of Matter to Form.

When this point has been reached, the Permanent Possibilities in question have assumed such unlikeness of aspect, and such difference of apparent relation to us, from any sensations, that it would be contrary to all we know of the constitution of human nature that they should not be conceived as, and believed to be, at least as different from sensations as sensations are from one another. Their groundwork in sensation is forgotten, and they are supposed to be something intrinsically distinct from it. We can withdraw ourselves from any of our (external) sensations, or we can be withdrawn from them by some other agency. But though the sensations cease, the possibilities remain in existence; they are independent of our will, our presence, and everything which belongs to us. We find, too, that they belong as much to other human or sentient beings as to ourselves. We find other people grounding their expectations and conduct upon the same permanent possibilities on which we ground ours. But we do not find them experiencing the same actual sensations. Other people do not have our sensations exactly when and as we have them: but they have our possibilities of sensation; whatever indicates a present possibility of sensations to ourselves, indicates a present possibility of similar sensations to them, except so far as their organs of sensation may vary from the type of ours. This puts the final seal to our conception of the groups of possibilities as the fundamental reality in Nature. The permanent possibilities are common to us and to our fellow-creatures; the actual sensations are not. That which other people become aware of when, and on the same grounds, as I do, seems more real to me than that which they do not know of unless I tell them. The world of Possible Sensations succeeding one another according to laws, is as much in other beings as it is in me; it has therefore an existence outside me; it is an External World.

Matter, then, may be defined, a Permanent Possibility of Sensation. If I am asked, whether I believe in matter, I ask whether the questioner accepts this definition of it. If he does, I believe in matter: and so do all Berkeleians. In any other sense than this, I do not. But I affirm with confidence, that this conception of Matter includes the whole meaning attached to it by the common world, apart from philosophical, and sometimes from theological, theories. The reliance of mankind on the real existence of visible and tangible objects, means reliance on the reality and permanence of Possibilities of visual and tactual sensations, when no such sensations are actually experienced.

Perhaps it may be objected, that the very possibility of framing such a notion of matter as Sir W. Hamilton's—the capacity in the human mind of imagining an external world which is anything more than what the Psychological Theory makes it—amounts to a disproof of the theory. If (it may be said) we had no revelation in consciousness, of a world which is not in some way or other identified with sensation, we should be unable to have the notion of such a world. If the only ideas we had of external objects were ideas of our sensations, supplemented by an acquired notion of permanent possibilities of sensation, we must (it is thought) be incapable of conceiving, and therefore still more incapable of fancying that we perceive, things which are not sensations at all. It being evident however that some philosophers believe this, and it being maintainable that the mass of mankind do so, the existence of a perdurable basis of sensations, distinct from sensations themselves, is proved, it might be said, by the possibility of believing it.

Let me first restate what I apprehend the belief to be. We believe that we perceive a something closely related to all our sensations, but different from those which we are feeling at any particular minute; and distinguished from sensations altogether, by being permanent and always the same, while these are fugitive, variable, and alternately displace one another. But these attributes of the object of perception are properties belonging to all the possibilities of sensation which experience guarantees. The belief in such permanent possibilities seems to me to include all that is essential or characteristic in the belief in substance. I believe that Calcutta exists, though I do not perceive it, and that it would still exist if every percipient inhabitant were suddenly to leave the place, or be struck dead. But when I analyse the belief, all I find in it is, that were these events to take place, the Permanent Possibility of Sensation which I call Calcutta would still remain; that if I were suddenly transported to the banks of the Hoogly, I should still have the sensations which, if now present, would lead me to affirm that Calcutta exists here and now. We may infer, therefore, that both philosophers and the world at large, when they think of matter, conceive it really as a Permanent Possibility of Sensation. But the majority of philosophers fancy that it is something more; and the world at large, though they have really, as I conceive, nothing in their minds but a Permanent Possibility of Sensation, would, if asked the question, undoubtedly agree with the philosophers: and though this is sufficiently explained by the tendency of the human mind to infer difference of things from difference of names, I acknowledge the obligation of showing how it can be possible to believe in an existence transcending all possibilities of sensation, unless on the hypothesis that such an existence actually is, and that we actually perceive it.

The explanation, however, is not difficult. It is an admitted fact, that we are capable of all conceptions which can be formed by generalizing from the observed laws of our sensations. Whatever relation we find to exist between any one of our sensations and something different from *it,* that same relation we have no difficulty in conceiving to exist between the sum of all our sensations and something different from *them.* The differences which our consciousness recognises between one sensation and another, give us the general notion of difference, and inseparably associate with every sensation we have, the feeling of its being different from other things: and when once this association has been formed, we can no longer conceive anything, without being able, and even being compelled, to form also the conception of something different from it. This familiarity with the idea of something different from *each* thing we know, makes it natural and easy to form the notion of something different from *all* things that we know, collectively as well as individually. It is true we can form no conception of what such a thing can be; our notion of it is merely negative; but the idea of a substance, apart from its relation to the impressions which we conceive it as making on our senses, *is* a merely negative one. There is thus no psychological obstacle to our forming the notion of a something which is neither a sensation nor a possibility of sensation, even if our consciousness does not testify to it; and nothing is more likely than that the Permanent Possibilities of Sensation, to which our consciousness does testify, should be confounded in our minds with this imaginary conception. All experience attests the strength of the tendency to mistake mental abstractions, even negative ones, for substantive realities; and the Permanent Possibilities of Sensation which experience guarantees, are so extremely unlike in many of their properties to actual sensations, that since we are capable of imagining something which transcends sensation, there is a great natural probability that we should suppose these to be it.

But this natural probability is converted into certainty, when we take into consideration that universal law of our experience which is termed the law of Causation, and which makes us mentally connect with the beginning of everything, some antecedent condition, or Cause. The case of Causation is one of the most marked of all the cases in which we extend to the sum total of our consciousness, a notion derived from its parts. It is a striking example of our power to conceive, and our tendency to believe, that a relation which subsists between every individual item of our experience and some other item, subsists also between our experience as a whole, and something not within the sphere of experience. By this extension to the sum of all our experiences, of the internal relations obtaining between its several parts, we are led to consider sensation itself—the aggregate whole of our sensations—as deriving its origin from antecedent existences transcending sensation. That we should do this, is a consequence of the particular character of the uniform sequences, which experience discloses to us among our sensations. As already remarked, the constant antecedent of a sensation is seldom another sensation, or set of sensations, actually felt. It is much oftener the existence of a group of possibilities, not necessarily including any actual sensations, except such as are required to show that the possibilities are really present. Nor are actual sensations indispensable even for this purpose; for the presence of the object (which is nothing more than the immediate presence of the possibilities) may be made known to us by the very sensation which we refer to it as its effect. Thus, the real antecedent of an effect—the only antecedent which, being invariable and unconditional, we consider to be the cause—may be, not any sensation really felt, but solely the presence, at that or the immediately preceding moment, of a group of possibilities of sensation. Hence it is not with sensations as actually experienced, but with their Permanent Possibilities, that the idea of Cause comes to be identified: and we, by one and the same process, acquire the habit of regarding Sensation in general, like all our individual sensations, as an Effect, and also that of conceiving as the causes of most of our individual sensations, not other sensations, but general possibilities of sensation. If all these considerations put together do not completely explain and account for our conceiving these Possibilities as a class of independent and substantive entities, I know not what psychological analysis can be conclusive.

It may perhaps be said, that the preceding theory gives, indeed, some account of the idea of Permanent Existence which forms part of our conception of matter, but gives no explanation of our believing these permanent objects to be external, or out of ourselves. I apprehend, on the contrary, that the very idea of anything out of ourselves is derived solely from the knowledge experience gives us of the Permanent Possibilities. Our sensations we carry with us wherever we go, and they never exist where we are not; but when we change our place we do not carry away with us the Permanent Possibilities of Sensation: they remain until we return, or arise and cease under conditions with which our presence has in general nothing to do. And more than all—they are, and will be after we have ceased to feel, Permanent Possibilities of Sensation to other beings than ourselves. Thus our actual sensations and the Permanent Possibilities of Sensation, stand out in obtrusive contrast to one another: and when the idea of Cause has been acquired, and extended by generalization from the parts of our experience to its aggregate whole, nothing can be more natural than that the Permanent Possibilities should be classed by us as existences generically distinct from our sensations, but of which our sensations are the effect.

The same theory which accounts for our ascribing to an aggregate of possibilities of sensation, a permanent existence which our sensations themselves do not possess, and consequently a greater reality than belongs to our sensations, also explains our attributing greater objectivity to the Primary Qualities of bodies than to the Secondary. For the sensations which correspond to what are called the Primary Qualities (as soon at least as we come to apprehend them by two senses, the eye as well as the touch) are always present when any part of the group is so. But colours, tastes, smells, and the like, being, in comparison, fugacious, are not, in the same degree, conceived as being always there, even when nobody is present to perceive them. The sensations answering to the Secondary Qualities are only occasional, those to the Primary, constant. The Secondary, moreover, vary with different persons, and with the temporary sensibility of our organs; the Primary, when perceived at all, are, as far as we know, the same to all persons and at all times.

14

WINSTON H. F. BARNES (1909– ———)

The Myth of Sense-Data*

Educated at Oxford University, Winston Barnes has held teaching positions at four universities in the British Isles—Liverpool, Durham, Edinburgh, and Manchester. His writings include *The Philosophical Predicament* (1950) and a number of articles in philosophical journals.

It will be recalled that Locke made a distinction between *qualities* in things and *ideas* caused by those qualities in the mind of the perceiver. The ideas that Locke held to be similar to the qualities causing them he called ideas of primary qualities (such as shape, size, solidity), and those that he held to be dissimilar, he called ideas of secondary qualities (such as color, odor, taste). Using Locke's terminology, Berkeley's theory, then, could be described as the view that *ideas* really exist, but *qualities* do not (at any rate, we cannot know that they exist), and Mill's theory is a further refinement of the same view.

There is an obvious awkwardness, however, in Locke's terminology, because the common-sense meaning of the term "idea" is what we have in our mind when we are *thinking* about something, not when we are *perceiving* it. Later writers, therefore, have preferred the term *sense datum* (plural *sense data*) to denote what Locke called "ideas." Accordingly, modern phenomenalists may be said to be advocating the theory that the immediate objects of perception are sense data, that the physical world consists of sense data, and that we have no basis for asserting that there is anything "out there" causing us to have these sense data. Modern phenomenalism, then, is the Berkeley-Mill theory expressed in new terms.

Barnes argues that phenomenalism is an erroneous theory that has come about because of the error of regarding sense data as the immediate objects of perception. The objects of perception, he argues, are real tables and chairs, not sense data that may or may not resemble real tables and chairs. The puzzles about sense data as the immediate objects of perception can be solved, he thinks, in a way that is more congenial to the common-sense view. The first part of this essay, then, is a critique

*Parts of the original paper and some footnotes have been eliminated.

From Winston H. F. Barnes, "The Myth of Sense Data," *Proceedings of the Aristotelian Society,* 45. (1944–1945), pp. 89–117. © 1945 The Aristotelian Society. Reprinted by courtesy of the Editor of The Aristotelian Society.

of phenomenalism. In the concluding paragraphs, Barnes attempts to establish his own view, which is a form of direct realism.

Our knowledge of the physical world is subject to many doubts and uncertainties but we commonly see no reason to doubt certain facts. We all agree, when we are out of the study, that we sometimes see tables and chairs, hear bells and clocks, taste liquids, smell cheeses, and feel the woollen vests that we wear next to our skin in winter. To put the matter generally, we agree that we perceive physical objects, physical objects being such things as tables, chairs and cheeses, and perceiving being a generic word which comprehends the specific activities of seeing, hearing, tasting, smelling, and feeling. These activities are invariably directed upon an object or objects; and this fact distinguishes them from other activities of ours—if that be the right word—such as feeling pained or feeling tired, which go on entirely within ourselves. We take it for granted that by means of the former activities we become aware of the existence, and acquainted with the qualities, of physical objects, and we further regard the kind of acquaintance which we acquire in this way as a basis for the far reaching and systematic knowledge of the physical world as a whole, which is embodied in the natural sciences.

Let us call experiences such as seeing a table, hearing a bell, etc., perceptual experiences; and the statements which assert the existence of such experiences perceptual statements. Many philosophers have cast doubt upon the claims made by such perceptual statements. They have produced arguments to show that we never perceive physical objects, and that we are in fact subject to a constant delusion on this score. As these arguments are by no means easily refuted and are such as any intelligent person interested in the matter will sooner or later come to think of, they are well worth considering. Moreover, certain modern philosophers claim to show by these arguments not only that we do not perceive physical objects but that what we do perceive is a different sort of thing altogether, which they call a sense-datum. They are obliged to invent a new term for it because no one had previously noticed that there were such things. This theory is obviously important because it not only claims to settle the doubts which we cannot help feeling when we reflect on our perceptual experience, but it makes the astonishing claim that we have all failed to notice a quite peculiar kind of entity, or at least have constantly made mistakes about its nature. I hope to show that the sense-datum theory is beset by internal difficulties; that it is not necessitated by the doubts we have about our perceptual experience; and finally that the doubts which are caused in us by a little reflection are allayed by further reflection.

The arguments which philosophers such as Professors Russell, Broad and Price use to demonstrate that we perceive not physical objects but sense-data, are many and various, and no good purpose would be served by stating them all, even if that were possible. Undoubtedly, however, these arguments do cause us to doubt whether we are acquainted with physical objects when we think we are; and, these doubts demand to be resolved in one way or another. If there is such a thing as a problem of perception, it must consist in reviewing the doubts which arise in our minds in this way. I shall select for brief statement three typical arguments so as to make clear the difficulties which are thought to justify the negative conclusion that we do not perceive physical objects and the positive conclusion that we perceive sense-data. There are two *caveats* to be registered. First, in compressing the arguments into a small compass I cannot hope to do full justice to the arguments, many and various, used by the sense-datum philosophers. I must leave it to the reader to decide whether I represent their general line of argument correctly or not. More than this I cannot hope to do; nor do I think more is necessary. Secondly, I should not be in the least surprised to be told that I already have misrepresented some of these philosophers by stating as one of their contentions that we do not perceive physical objects. Some of them would maintain that in some peculiar, or Pickwickian sense, to use Professor Moore's term, we do perceive physical objects. However, as, on their view, we do not perceive physical objects in the sense in which we think we perceive them, and we do perceive sense-data in precisely this sense, the misrepresentation is purely verbal and should mislead no one.

I now proceed to state the three arguments. They are all taken from visual experience, and they all pose in one way or another what we may call the "appearance-reality" problem of perception.

(1) A penny appears circular to an observer directly above it, but elliptical to an observer a few paces away. It cannot *be* both elliptical and circular at one and the same time. There is no good reason for supposing that the penny reveals its real shape to an observer in one position rather than to an observer in any other position. The elliptical appearance and the circular appearance cannot be identified with the penny or any parts of it, but they are entities of some kind. It is things of this sort which are called sense-data.

(2) The stick which looks straight in the air looks angularly bent when in water. There are good reasons for thinking that no such change of shape takes place in the stick. Yet there *is* something straight in the one case and something bent in the other, and there is no good reason for supposing either is less or more of an existent than the other. The straight-stick appearance and the bent-stick appearance are sense-data.

(3) There may seem to be things in a place when in fact there are no such things there, as illustrated by the mirages which appear in the desert and the highly coloured rodents which appear to habitual drunkards. Not unrelated to this type of experience is the one in which we see double. If an eyeball is pressed by the forefinger while one is looking at a candle flame, two flames are seen. Although it would be possible to say that one of the flames is the actual object and the other is something else, to be called a sense-datum, it seems even

more evident here than in the previous instances that there is no good reason for distinguishing between the two in this way.

In all these cases there is a suggestion that what we see in certain cases cannot be a physical object or the surface of a physical object, but is some kind of non-physical entity. It is non-physical entities of this kind which are called sense-data. The argument goes even further by urging that, if in some cases we see non-material things, it is possible and indeed likely, that we do so in all cases. This plausible suggestion is accepted by certain sense-datum theorists such as Professor Broad and is extended to cover all forms of perceiving. With the acceptance of this suggestion we reach the basic position taken by one form of the sense-datum theory, viz., we perceive only sense-data, and consequently have no direct acquaintance through our senses with physical objects.

It is clear that, on this view, the term sense-datum has as part of its connotation, the not being a physical body. As everything I experience is a sense-datum, the sense-experience of a table, for example, differs not at all, in itself, from an hallucination or an illusion. These latter again seem to differ only in degree from the images we have while we are day dreaming, or those we have while dreaming in the proper sense, or again from the after-images, or as they are more properly called, the after-sensations which sometimes follow our visual sensations. All these appearances would be regarded by certain philosophers as in principle of the same kind. This position is paradoxical to common-sense which regards perceptual experience as giving first-hand acquaintance with physical objects, and hallucinations and illusions as failing precisely in this respect. The common-sense ground for the distinction however is removed by the sense-datum theorist, and if in fact he does believe in physical objects, he has to substitute a new ground of a far more subtle and elaborate nature. In some cases he may prefer to get along altogether without physical objects, and may even urge that if we once give up the common-sense ground of distinction as untenable there is no other ground for believing in them. Such questions as these, however, are domestic problems of sense-datum theorists and need not detain us, as we are intent on coming to grips with the basis of the theory itself. It is important to note, however, that once the sense-datum theory is developed in the form stated above, it follows that, even if physical objects exist, they are never present in perceptual experience; and it becomes an open question whether they have any existence at all.

· · ·

I quoted earlier three typical arguments for the existence of sensa. I now wish to examine carefully a single argument which embodies the principle of these and other similar arguments. No one will deny, I think, that a situation may exist in which the following three propositions are true:

(i) I see the rose.

(ii) The rose appears pink to me.
(iii) The rose is red.

The belief in sensa is reached by arguing, not unplausibly, that since what I am seeing appears pink, there exists something which *is* pink; and since the rose is red, not pink, it cannot be the rose which is pink; therefore what I am seeing is something other than the rose. Whereupon the term sensum is invented and given as a name to this existent and others like it. And so we reach the conclusion:

(iv) I see a pink sensum.

The argument is fallacious. *That something appears pink to me is not a valid reason for concluding either that that thing is pink or that there is some other thing which is pink.* From the fact that a think *looks* pink I can sometimes with the help of certain other propositions infer that it *is* pink or that it *is* red; I may also, with the help of certain other propositions, be able to infer that something in some other place is pink, e.g., the electric light bulb which is illuminating the rose. But I cannot infer, as is proposed, *merely from the three facts that I am seeing something, that it looks pink and that it is red, that there is a pink something where the thing appears pink to me.*

This, when we examine it, is the foundation stone on which the great edifice of the sensum theory has been raised. Is it surprising that the upper storeys present doubts and perplexities? But there is worse to come. Not only is the argument fallacious but the conclusion contradicts one of the premises, viz., (i) I see a rose. It does so because, in order that the conclusion should seem at all plausible, it has been assumed that, if I were to see a rose which actually possessed a red colour, I should see it as red, i.e., it would necessarily appear red to me. This again is an assumption in contradiction with propositions (ii) and (iii) taken together. As soon as this self-induced contradiction is discovered by the sensum theorists, repair work is put in hand on one or other of alternative lines: (*a*) It is accepted that I do not see the rose, and an account is given of the relation in which I *do* stand to the rose and which has been mistaken for seeing. A little reflection, of course, soon convinces those who go this way that, if this is true, it is not only roses that are born to blush unseen, but the whole world of material things. In this way sensa become an impenetrable barrier barring for ever our acquaintance through the senses with the world of material things. This is strong meat for any but really metaphysical natures, and fortunately for the sensum theory there is another way of making the necessary repairs. (*b*) The alternative procedure is something like this: It is certain that I do see the rose. I have convinced myself, however, by argument that one thing I undoubtedly see, in a plain unvarnished use of the word *see,* is a pink rose-figured sensum. Hence the sense in which I see the rose must be different, *i.e.,* "seeing" is systematically ambiguous and what exactly is meant by seeing the rose needs to be elucidated. Seeing a rose and seeing a pink rose-figured sensum are then distinguished as quite different ways of seeing and it is convenient to refer to seeing a sensum as "directly seeing," and seeing a rose as "seeing." The analysis of seeing the rose can then be made in terms of directly seeing a certain sort of sensum and at the same time having perceptual assurance that ... etc., the complete analysis varying from one philosopher to another.

There is another way in which an attempt may be made to justify the conclusion of the argument we have condemned as fallacious. I have argued that from the fact that something which is red appears pink, it does not follow that a pink sensum exists. It may be said that the existence of a pink sensum, while not following from the premises, is justified by a direct appeal to our sense experience. "I see it, therefore it is." The argument can be stated as follows: "I certainly see a pink something and to say that there is nothing pink is to say that I have no reason for believing in what I see now; and if I cannot believe in what I see now, how can I believe in what I see on any occasion, or any one else in what he sees on any occasion? If you deny the existence of this pink patch, you deny the existence altogether of the world revealed by the senses." The answer to this objection is simple, if we reflect, viz., "You never can believe in what you see on any occasion, it always may mislead you as to what the thing is. If you wish to state only that something appears to be so and so, this can safely be done. But this is not a statement about something made on the basis of a piece of evidence, it is a statement of the piece of evidence itself, which you already have before you without clothing it in words." Modes of appearance are clues to the nature of what exists, not existents. I submit that it is improper to ask whether the pink mode of appearing, which is how the rose appears to me, exists. You may ask whether the rose exists and whether it is red or pink; and in answering this question account must be taken of how it appears under different conditions and to different people. Although modes of appearance are not existents, they are the material and the only material on which thinking can operate to discover the nature of existing things; and it is an epistemological ideal that if we were to discover completely the nature of existing things, there would be nothing left in the modes of appearance which would not entirely harmonise with our system of knowledge and find its explanation there.

.   .   .

I now propose to state briefly, the lines of an alternative account to the sensum theory. The account is quite simple and is implicit in the foregoing discussion. I can claim no great originality for it as it is substantially the theory put forward by Prof. Dawes Hicks [1] and called by Prof. Broad the Multiple Relation Theory of Appearance. I can claim only that I arrived at it by a

[1] In his "Critical Realism."

somewhat different line of thought and for that reason my statement of it may have some interest. I propose to call it simply the theory of appearing. I hope to show that it is the theory implicit in common sense and that it can be defended against the more obvious objections.

We saw that the sensum theory was led into difficulties by concluding from the propositions (i) I see the rose, (ii) The rose appears pink to me, and (iii) The rose is red, to a proposition (iv) I see a pink sensum. To attain consistency it was necessary to distinguish between the meaning which the word *see* has in proposition (i) and that which it has in proposition (iv). It is obvious, however, when we reflect, that propositions such as (i) must be incomplete versions of propositions such as (ii), *e.g.*, "I see the rose as pink" is the expanded form of the proposition (i), which says the same thing as proposition (ii), but begins with me and proceeds to the rose, instead of beginning with the rose and proceeding to me. It is evident, further, if this is so, that *see* must have the same sense but in the reverse direction, as *appears.*

The account I put forward, then, is that objects themselves appear to us in sense-perception; that they in general appear in sense-perception to have those qualities which they in fact have; that where they appear to have qualities which they do not in fact have, these instances are more properly regarded as their failing in differing degrees to appear to have the properties they do have, such failure being accounted for by the conditions under which they are perceived. We must be quite bold at this point and admit at once that on this account of the matter a thing can possess a certain quality and at the same time appear to some one to possess another quality, which it could not actually possess in conjunction with the former quality. Let us be quite clear about what we are saying. When I see a circular penny as elliptical I am seeing the circular surface of the penny, not some elliptical substitute. This circular surface, it is true, appears elliptical to me, but that fact has no tendency to show that I am not directly aware of the circular surface. Aeneas was none the less in the presence of his mother Venus though she concealed from him the full glory of her godhead.

It is clear that, on this theory, perception has a much closer resemblance to thinking than would be allowed by the sensum theorists. For (i) it may have a content more or less false to the real, as thought may; and (ii) this content does not exist independent of the act of perceiving any more than the content of a false proposition. The chief objection to this contention is stated by Prof. Broad as follows: "It is very hard to understand how we could seem to ourselves to *see* the property of bentness exhibited in a concrete instance, if in fact *nothing* was present to our minds that possessed that property."[2] I can see no great difficulty in this, and we have seen how the attempt to escape from the imagined difficulty leads to difficulties. Fourteen years later Prof. Broad himself was not so sure for he says: "Now one may admit that a certain

[2]"Scientific Thought," p. 241.

particular might seem to have a characteristic which differs from and is incompatible with the characteristic which it does have. But I find it almost incredible that one particular extended patch should seem to be two particular extended patches at a distance apart from each other."[3] Prof. Price finds the same difficulty, for he says: "It is not really sense to say 'To me the candle appears double' . . . 'double' is not really a predicate at all."[4]

Seven years have passed since Prof. Broad wrote the latter of his two quoted statements so it may be that he now finds the assertion more credible. I certainly find nothing incredible in it. No doubt it is impossible for one candle to *be* two candles but there seems no reason why it should not appear to be any number of things. Finally, hallucinations and delusions need present no insuperable difficulties. There appeared to Lady Macbeth to be a dagger but there was no dagger in fact. Something appeared to be a dagger, and there are certainly problems concerning exactly what it is in such circumstances that appears to be possessed of qualities which it does not possess. It is easy of course to object that an illusory dagger is not just nothing. The answer is neither "Yes, it is" nor "No, it isn't," but "An illusory dagger is a misleading expression if used to describe an element in the situation." It is misleading also in some degree to say that there exists "a dagger-like appearance," though we need not be misled by such a use of the word *appearance* if we are careful. Strictly speaking, however, there are no such things as appearances. To suppose that there are would be like supposing that because Mr. X put in an appearance, there must have been something over and above Mr. X which he was kind enough to put in. "Mr. X appeared": that is the proper mode of expression if we are to avoid difficulties.

.   .   .

There is another point about our account of the matter. It allows that it is *possible* for certain people at certain times to become acquainted through perception with things as they are, not merely as they appear to be. This can be seen best as follows. The word *sense-datum* was substituted for the word *appearance* to emphasise that there is an indubitable element in sense experience, in contrast with the use of the term *appearance* by philosophers who denied the existence of any such given, and who used the contrast between appearance and reality to grind a metaphysical axe of their own. But, as was pointed out by Prof. Moore, the term was often used with the connotation "not a physical reality." If this connotation is accepted, it follows that, however extensive our acquaintance with sense-data, we are no whit nearer to becoming acquainted with physical objects, and it is even difficult to see how we can know *about* these latter. This is the "great barrier" objection to the theory as

[3]"Mind and Its Place in Nature," p. 188.
[4]"Perception,"pp. 62–3.

held by Prof. Broad and his followers. Even for those who avoid putting into the term sense-datum this unwarrantable connotation the term is apt to give rise to unnecessary difficulties. For example, Mr. Wisdom, more careful than most philosophers not to be misled by the term, writes: "I should agree that it is unplausible to say that, although when I see a thing in bad light my corresponding sense-datum is not identical with the observed surface of the thing, nevertheless, when the light changes, the corresponding sense-datum which I then obtain is identical with the observed surface, I cannot say why I find this unplausible, but I do. I find such a discontinuity, such a popping in and out of the material world on so slight a provocation, most objectionable."[5] If we are content to talk in terms of appearance or, better still, of things appearing, we shall not have pseudo-problems of this kind. We need have no heart-burning about the following statement: "Although when I see a thing in bad light the surface does not appear to me in every respect as it really is, nevertheless, when the light is adequate, it does." The reason we are now talking better sense is that the language of appearance permits us to maintain (a) that a thing can not only appear what it is not, but what it is: (b) that a thing's appearing what it is not is best understood as a deviation from its appearing what it is. A terminology which purports to be neutral and yet makes these propositions sound absurd has prejudged the issue in a most unfortunate manner.[6]

On the theory outlined it is easy to explain how we can come to know about material objects for in all our perception we are perceiving material objects even though we are not always completely successful in perceiving them exactly as they are. On the sensum theory, as we have seen, it is difficult to explain why knowledge of sensa should contribute towards knowledge of material things; how we could ever have been led to the belief in material things; and, still less, how we could justify the belief.

Finally, the account of the matter I have given is, I think, remarkably close to common sense. As Prof. Broad claims that this type of theory departs as widely from common sense as the sensum theory, this claim needs to be defended. He argues that, as commonly used, a statement such as "I see a table" involves the unexpressed theory that there is a situation involving two constituents, myself and the table, related by a relation of seeing, a relation which proceeds from me to the table. This theory, ascribed to common sense, Prof. Broad calls naïve realism. Now it is only plausible to maintain that this theory is held by the ordinary man if carefully selected perceptual statements concerning objects at close range are considered. If we regard the whole range of perceptual situations the common sense belief is quite different. This belief

[5]"Problems of Mind and Matter," p. 156.
[6]In fairness to Mr. Wisdom it must be pointed out that immediately after making the statement quoted, he goes on to say something which, if I understand it rightly, is very like what I have said except that (a) he calls that which appears a sense-datum and (b) identifies it with an object's surface.

involves that in perceptual situations objects reveal more or less of their nature to us; and common sense would find no difficulty in admitting that there are cases where very little of the nature of the object of perception is revealed. For example, statements of the following type are a commonplace: "I can just see something, but I cannot make out what it is," "I think I can see something there but I cannot be sure," "It looks like a house, but it may be just an outcrop of rock." Instances could be multiplied indefinitely. Common sense would not scruple to admit that objects do not always have the qualities which they seem to have when seen, heard, tasted, touched or smelt. It accepts without flinching that the hills which look purple in the distance are really green. It is indeed a platitude enshrined in proverbial literature that "things are seldom what they seem."

I draw attention to these elementary facts, in the first place, to point out that the only naïveté about naïve realism is that philosophers should have thought the ordinary man believed it. More important, however, is that these facts show the common sense view not to involve belief in a simple two-termed relation between me and the things I perceive, in which no possibility of illusion can arise, but a relation in which there is the possibility of the object's nature being revealed to a greater or less degree. It is true, of course, that the plain man no less than the philosopher sometimes puts as the object of *see* not the material thing but the *how it appears* as when, looking into the distance, one says "I can see a purple haze; it may be mountains or cloud." No violence is done to his language if it is rewritten "I see something as purple and hazy" or "There is something which appears purple and hazy." It is the lack of sufficient information to establish the nature of the object appearing which leads to the varying form of statement. . . .

For Further Reading

Adams, E. M. "The Nature of the Sense-Datum Theory," *Mind,* 67 (1958), 216–226.

Alexander, Peter. "Curley on Locke and Boyle," *Philosophical Review,* 83 (1974), 229–237.

Armstrong, D. M. *Perception and the Physical World.* New York: Humanities Press, 1961.

Austin, J. L. *Sense and Sensibilia.* London: Oxford University Press, 1962 (paperbound).

Ayer, A. J. *The Foundations of Empirical Knowledge.* New York: St. Martin's Press, 1958, Chaps. 1, 2, and 5 (paperbound).

—————. *The Problem of Knowledge.* New York: St. Martin's Press, 1956, Chap. 3.

Bergmann, Gustav. *Logic and Reality.* Madison: University of Wisconsin Press, 1964, Chap. 14.

Chisholm, R. M. "The Problem of Empiricism," *The Journal of Philosophy,* 45 (1948), 512–517.

Cornman, J. W. *Perception, Common Sense and Science.* New Haven, Conn.: Yale University Press, 1975. A recent, important defense of direct realism.

Curley, E. M. "Locke, Boyle and the Distinction Between Primary and Secondary Qualities," *Philosophical Review,* 81 (1972), 438–464.

Dewey, John. *Essays in Experimental Logic.* New York: Dover, 1960 (paperbound), pp. 1–74, 250–302.

Dretske, Fred I. *Seeing and Knowing.* Chicago: University of Chicago Press, 1969.

Eddington, A. S. *The Nature of the Physical World.* Ann Arbor: University of Michigan Press, 1958 (paperbound).

Ewing, A. C. *The Fundamental Questions of Philosophy.* New York: Macmillan, 1951, Chap. 4.

Garnett, A. C. *The Perceptual Process.* London: G. Allen & Unwin, 1965. Short, highly readable, critical realist view.

Gibson, James J. *The Senses Considered as Perceptual Systems.* London: G. Allen & Unwin, 1968.

Hinton, J. M. *Experiences: An Inquiry into Some Ambiguities.* New York: Oxford University Press, 1973.

Jackson, F. *Perception: A Representative Theory.* New York: Cambridge University Press, 1977. A critical realist account.

Joske, W. D. *Material Objects.* New York: Macmillan, 1967.

Lewis, C. I. *An Analysis of Knowledge and Valuation.* LaSalle, Ill.: Open Court Publishing Co., 1947, Chap. 7 (paperbound).

Locke, D. *Perception and Our Knowledge of the External World.* London: G. Allen & Unwin, 1967.

Mandelbaum, M. *Philosophy, Science, and Sense Perception.* Baltimore, Md.: Johns Hopkins Press, 1964. Defends critical realism.

Mundle, C. W. K. *Perception: Facts and Theories.* New York: Oxford University Press, 1971 (paperbound).

Pitcher, George. *A Theory of Perception.* Princeton, N.J.: Princeton University Press, 1971.

Price, H. H. "The Argument from Illusion," in H. D. Lewis (ed.). *Contemporary British Philosophy,* Third Series. New York: Macmillan, 1956, pp. 391–400.

——————. *Perception,* 2nd ed. New York: Dover, 1950.

Rogers, G. A. J. "The Veil of Perception," *Mind,* 84 (1975), 210–224. Attempts to combine a causal theory of perception with a form of direct realism.

Russell, Bertrand. *Human Knowledge.* New York: Simon and Schuster, 1962 (paperbound). See Part III, "Science and Perception."

——————. *The Problems of Philosophy.* New York: Oxford University Press, 1959, Chaps. 1–4 (paperbound).

Warnock, G. J. *Berkeley.* Baltimore, Md.: Penguin Books, 1969 (paperbound).

PART V

The Existence of God

The Danish philosopher Sören Kierkegaard once observed that "Generally speaking, it is a difficult matter to prove that anything exists; and what is still worse for the intrepid souls who undertake the venture, the difficulty is such that fame scarcely awaits those who concern themselves with it."[1] Notwithstanding the alleged difficulty, however, many philosophers have believed it possible to prove the existence of God—that is, to prove that the proposition "God exists" is true—and have published their attempted proofs for all to see. It is with these attempted proofs that we shall be concerned in this section.

What, exactly, does it mean to affirm that God exists? Does it mean, for example, that someplace in the universe—perhaps beyond the reach of our most powerful telescopes—there exists an infinitely good, wise, and powerful being who created the world and everything in it, and who continues to care for it continually? Is that what theists are affirming when they affirm that God exists? No, not exactly. Most theists would object to the idea that God exists "someplace in the universe" (but not elsewhere). For God is not conceived as one being among many, a being who exists here but not there, at this time but not that. Rather, He is conceived as the cause or ground of everything that exists. He is beyond the categories of space and time, which is why He is said to be omnipresent and eternal. He transcends space and time. Yet, He is the ground of being of everything that exists in space and time. Moreover, He is worthy of human worship. That, roughly, is the concept.

[1]Sören Kierkegaard, *Philosophical Fragments,* trans. David F. Swenson (Princeton, N.J.: Princeton University Press, 1936), p. 31.

The first concept—that there is an infinitely good, wise, and powerful being who exists in some far-off corner of the universe—is reasonably clear, but it is not what theists mean when they affirm that God exists. The second concept—that there is a reality that transcends space and time and is worthy of human worship—is reasonably close to what theists have in mind when they affirm the existence of God, but it is distressingly unclear. This contrast illustrates one of the major problems that one must contend with in trying to understand and assess the arguments for the existence of God: it is difficult, if not impossible, to render the concept "God" sufficiently clear to enable one to understand what is to be proved without making the concept simply ludicrous. Nobody, after all, is interested in a Grand Old Man who lives on some remote and unseen planet—even if his name happens to be Jehovah. If God is not important, then it does not matter whether He exists. If His existence matters, then it must be because He is somehow involved in our life and our world. He must make some kind of difference here and now. People tend to be interested in the question of God's existence for reasons other than mere speculative curiosity.

At least five types of arguments have been put forward to prove the existence of God. These are:

1. The *ontological* argument, which attempts to show that the proposition "God exists" is necessarily true, that the denial of the assertion involves a logical contradiction.
2. The *cosmological* argument, which attempts to show that the existence of the physical universe presupposes, implies, or points to the existence of God.
3. The *teleological* argument, which attempts to prove that God exists because there is order in the universe.
4. The *moral* argument, which uses certain facts of moral experience to conclude that God exists.
5. The *argument from religious experience,* which affirms that some people know of the existence of God in the same way that they know of the existence of mountains in Colorado: by direct experience.

Three of these five types are represented in the readings that follow, namely, the ontological, the cosmological, and the teleological arguments. The readings also include a famous essay by the Christian philosopher Blaise Pascal in which he argues that even in the absence of a convincing proof of the existence of God it is reasonable to wager that God exists. In the final selection, Sigmund Freud attempts to answer the question, "Since the existence of God is evidently not supported by evidence, why is it that so many people believe that the proposition 'God exists' is true?"

15

ANSELM OF CANTERBURY (1033–1109)

The Ontological Argument

St. Anselm of Canterbury is one of a small number of philosopher-theologians of note who appeared during the long interval of time between St. Augustine (354–430) and St. Thomas Aquinas (1225–1274). Like his predecessor, Anselm held that the role of reason in relation to faith is to understand that which one already believes. As an orthodox Christian, Anselm, of course, believed in the existence of God quite apart from any proofs. As an apologist for Christianity, however (and, perhaps, as a believer seeking to understand), he desired a *proof* of the existence of God—a proof so simple that it could be understood by anyone, and so cogent that whoever understood it could not fail to be convinced by it. He believed he had found such a proof in what has come to be called the "ontological argument."

Anselm's argument is an attempt to show that the proposition "God exists" is *necessarily true,* just as the proposition "All circles are round" is necessarily true. To say that the proposition "God exists" is necessarily true, is to say that to deny it— to say, like the fool of Psalm 14, that there is no God—is to utter a contradiction. The very *idea* of a circle is such that the proposition "Some circles are not round" is self-contradictory. The very *idea* of God is such that the proposition "God does not exist" is self-contradictory. If one understands by the term "God" "that, than which nothing greater can be conceived," then, says Anselm, it is clear that only a fool could say that such a being does not exist—for such a being existing in concept only, and not in reality, would not be "that, than which nothing greater can be conceived."

Here is Anselm's famous argument.

CHAPTER II

Truly there is a God, although the fool hath said in his heart, There is no God.

From Anselm of Canterbury, *Proslogion,* Chapters II–IV, in *Proslogium; Monologium; An Appendix in Behalf of the Fool,* trans. Sidney Norton Deane (Chicago: Open Court Publishing, 1903), pp. 7–10.

And so, Lord, do thou, who dost give understanding to faith, give me, so far as thou knowest it to be profitable, to understand that thou art as we believe; and that thou art that which we believe. And, indeed, we believe that thou art a being than which nothing greater can be conceived. Or is there no such nature, since the fool hath said in his heart, there is no God? (Psalms xiv. 1). But, at any rate, this very fool, when he hears of this being of which I speak —a being than which nothing greater can be conceived—understands what he hears and what he understands is in his understanding; although he does not understand it to exist.

For, it is one thing for an object to be in the understanding, and another to understand that the object exists. When a painter first conceives of what he will afterwards perform, he has it in his understanding, but he does not yet understand it to be, because he has not yet performed it. But after he has made the painting, he both has it in his understanding, and he understands that it exists, because he has made it.

Hence, even the fool is convinced that something exists in the understanding, at least, than which nothing greater can be conceived. For, when he hears of this, he understands it. And whatever is understood, exists in the understanding. And assuredly that, than which nothing greater can be conceived, cannot exist in the understanding alone. For, suppose it exists in the understanding alone: then it can be conceived to exist in reality; which is greater.

Therefore, if that, than which nothing greater can be conceived, exists in the understanding alone, the very being, than which nothing greater can be conceived, is one, than which a greater can be conceived. But obviously this is impossible. Hence, there is no doubt that there exists a being, than which nothing greater can be conceived, and it exists both in the understanding and in reality.

CHAPTER III

God cannot be conceived not to exist.—God is that, than which nothing greater can be conceived.—That which can be conceived not to exist is not God.

And it assuredly exists so truly, that it cannot be conceived not to exist. For, it is possible to conceive of a being which cannot be conceived not to exist; and this is greater than one which can be conceived not to exist. Hence, if that, than which nothing greater can be conceived, can be conceived not to exist, it is not that, than which nothing greater can be conceived. But this is an irreconcilable contradiction. There is, then, so truly a being than which nothing greater can be conceived to exist, that it cannot even be conceived not to exist; and this being thou art, O Lord, our God.

So truly, therefore, dost thou exist, O Lord, my God, that thou canst not be conceived not to exist; and rightly. For, if a mind could conceive of a being better than thee, the creature would rise above the Creator; and this is most absurd. And, indeed, whatever else there is, except thee alone, can be conceived not to exist. To thee alone, therefore, it belongs to exist more truly than all other beings, and hence in a higher degree than all others. For, whatever else exists does not exist so truly, and hence in a less degree it belongs to it to exist. Why, then, has the fool said in his heart, there is no God (Psalms xiv. 1), since it is so evident, to a rational mind, that thou dost exist in the highest degree of all? Why, except that he is dull and a fool?

CHAPTER IV

How the fool has said in his heart what cannot be conceived.—A thing may be conceived in two ways: (1) when the word signifying it is conceived; (2) when the thing itself is understood. As far as the word goes, God can be conceived not to exist; in reality he cannot.

But how has the fool said in his heart what he could not conceive; or how is it that he could not conceive what he said in his heart? since it is the same to say in the heart, and to conceive.

But, if really, nay, since really, he both conceived, because he said in his heart; and did not say in his heart, because he could not conceive; there is more than one way in which a thing is said in the heart or conceived. For, in one sense, an object is conceived, when the word signifying it is conceived; and in another, when the very entity, which the object is, is understood.

In the former sense, then, God can be conceived not to exist; but in the latter, not at all. For no one who understands what fire and water are can conceive fire to be water, in accordance with the nature of the facts themselves, although this is possible according to the words. So, then, no one who understands what God is can conceive that God does not exist; although he says these words in his heart, either without any or with some foreign, signification. For, God is that than which a greater cannot be conceived. And he who thoroughly understands this, assuredly understands that this being so truly exists, that not even in concept can it be non-existent. Therefore, he who understands that God so exists, cannot conceive that he does not exist.

16

GAUNILON OF MARMOUTIER (11th Century)

In Behalf of the Fool

Gaunilon's sole claim to fame is that he wrote a critique of Anselm's ontological argument that is nearly as famous as is the argument. Almost nothing is known of Gaunilon except that he was a contemporary of St. Anselm and a monk at Marmoutier in France.

Gaunilon shared Anselm's belief in the existence of God, but he did not think that Anselm's argument succeeded in *proving* the existence of God. Since Anselm had been rather hard on the fool "who hath said in his heart, There is no God" (Psalm 14), Gaunilon entitled his reply "In Behalf of the Fool."

Gaunilon argues that (1) the mere fact that one can conceive of something does not prove that that thing exists, as is evident from the fact that we can conceive of all sorts of unreal objects, (2) even though one hears the term "God," this does not mean that the person has a clear concept of the term, (3) from the hypothetical assertion, "*If a being is that than which none greater can be conceived, then it must exist in reality,*" one cannot pass to the assertion "This being exists in reality" without a further proof, and (4) if the argument were sound, it should be possible, by parallel arguments, to prove the existence of other things—for example an "island which is more excellent than all lands."

... This being is said to be in my understanding already, only because I understand what is said. Now could it not with equal justice be said that I have in my understanding all manner of unreal objects, having absolutely no existence in themselves, because I understand these things if one speaks of them, whatever they may be?

Unless indeed it is shown that this being is of such a character that it cannot be held in concept like all unreal objects, or objects whose existence is uncertain: and hence I am not able to conceive of it when I hear of it, or to hold

From Gaunilon of Marmoutier, *An Appendix in Behalf of the Fool,* in *Proslogium; Monologium; An Appendix in Behalf of the Fool,* trans. Sidney Norton Deane (Chicago: Open Court Publishing, 1903), pp. 145–153.

it in concept; but I must understand it and have it in my understanding; because, it seems, I cannot conceive of it in any other way than by understanding it, that is, by comprehending in my knowledge its existence in reality.

But if this is the case, in the first place there will be no distinction between what has precedence in time—namely, the having of an object in the understanding—and what is subsequent in time—namely, the understanding that an object exists; as in the example of the picture, which exists first in the mind of the painter, and afterwards in his work.

Moreover, the following assertion can hardly be accepted: that this being, when it is spoken of and heard of, cannot be conceived not to exist in the way in which even God can be conceived not to exist. For if this is impossible, what was the object of this argument against one who doubts or denies the existence of such a being?

.   .   .

Let us notice also the point touched on above, with regard to this being which is greater than all which can be conceived, and which, it is said, can be none other than God himself. I, so far as actual knowledge of the object, either from its specific or general character, is concerned, am as little able to conceive of this being when I hear of it, or to have it in my understanding, as I am to conceive of or understand God himself: whom, indeed, for this very reason I can conceive not to exist. For I do not know that reality itself which God is, nor can I form a conjecture of that reality from some other like reality. For you yourself assert that that reality is such that there can be nothing else like it.

For, suppose that I should hear something said of a man absolutely unknown to me, of whose very existence I was unaware. Through that special or general knowledge by which I know what man is, or what men are, I could conceive of him also, according to the reality itself, which man is. And yet it would be possible, if the person who told me of him deceived me, that the man himself, of whom I conceived, did not exist; since that reality according to which I conceived of him, though a no less indisputable fact, was not that man, but any man.

Hence, I am not able, in the way which I should have this unreal being in concept or in understanding, to have that being of which you speak in concept or in understanding, when I hear the word *God* or the words, *a being greater than all other beings.* For I can conceive of the man according to a fact that is real and familiar to me: but of God, or a being greater than all others, I could not conceive at all, except merely according to the word. And an object can hardly or never be conceived according to the word alone.

For when it is so conceived, it is not so much the word itself (which is, indeed, a real thing—that is, the sound of the letters and syllables) as the signification of the word, when heard, that is conceived. But it is not conceived as by one who knows what is generally signified by the word; by whom, that is, it is conceived according to a reality and in true conception alone. It is conceived as by a man who does not know the object, and conceives of it only in accordance with the movement of his mind produced by hearing the word, the mind attempting to image for itself the signification of the word that is heard. And it would be surprising if in the reality of fact it could ever attain to this.

Thus, it appears, and in no other way, this being is also in my understanding, when I hear and understand a person who says that there is a being greater than all conceivable beings. So much for the assertion that this supreme nature already is in my understanding.

But that this being must exist, not only in the understanding but also in reality, is thus proved to me:

If it did not so exist, whatever exists in reality would be greater than it. And so the being which has been already proved to exist in my understanding, will not be greater than all other beings.

I still answer: if it should be said that a being which cannot be even conceived in terms of any fact, is in the understanding, I do not deny that this being is, accordingly, in my understanding. But since through this fact it can in no wise attain to real existence also, I do not yet concede to it that existence at all, until some certain proof of it shall be given.

For he who says that this being exists, because otherwise the being which is greater than all will not be greater than all, does not attend strictly enough to what he is saying. For I do not yet say, no, I even deny or doubt that this being is greater than any real object. Nor do I concede to it any other existence than this (if it should be called existence) which it has when the mind, according to a word merely heard, tries to form the image of an object absolutely unknown to it.

How, then, is the veritable existence of that being proved to me from the assumption, by hypothesis, that it is greater than all other beings? For I should still deny this, or doubt your demonstration of it, to this extent, that I should not admit that this being is in my understanding and concept even in the way in which many objects whose real existence is uncertain and doubtful, are in my understanding and concept. For it should be proved first that this being itself really exists somewhere; and then, from the fact that it is greater than all, we shall not hesitate to infer that it also subsists in itself.

For example: it is said that somewhere in the ocean is an island, which, because of the difficulty, or rather the impossibility, of discovering what does not exist, is called the lost island. And they say that this island has an inestimable wealth of all manner of riches and delicacies in greater abundance than is told of the Islands of the Blest; and that having no owner or inhabitant, it is more excellent than all other countries, which are inhabited by mankind, in the abundance with which it is stored.

Now if some one should tell me that there is such an island, I should easily understand his words, in which there is no difficulty. But suppose that he went on to say, as if by a logical inference: "You can no longer doubt that this island which is more excellent than all lands exists somewhere, since you have no doubt that it is in your understanding. And since it is more excellent not to be in the understanding alone, but to exist both in the understanding and in reality, for this reason it must exist. For if it does not exist, any land which really exists will be more excellent than it; and so the island already understood by you to be more excellent will not be more excellent."

If a man should try to prove to me by such reasoning that this island truly exists, and that its existence should no longer be doubted, either I should believe that he was jesting, or I know not which I ought to regard as the greater fool: myself, supposing that I should allow this proof; or him, if he should suppose that he had established with any certainty the existence of this island. For he ought to show first that the hypothetical excellence of this island exists as a real and indubitable fact, and in no wise as any unreal object, or one whose existence is uncertain, in my understanding. . . .

17

ANSELM OF CANTERBURY (1033–1109)

Reply to Gaunilon

Notwithstanding Gaunilon's critique, Anselm remained convinced that his argument was sound, and he attempted to defend it in a later writing known as *Anselm's Apologetic.* The reader must decide whether Anselm successfully refutes Gaunilon's arguments.

It was a fool against whom the argument of my Proslogium was directed. Seeing, however, that the author of these objections is by no means a fool, and

From Anselm of Canterbury, *Anselm's Apologetic,* in *Anselm,* trans. Sidney Norton Deane (Chicago: Open Court Publishing, 1910), pp. 153–159.

is a Catholic, speaking in behalf of the fool, I think it sufficient that I answer the Catholic.

You say—whosoever you may be, who say that a fool is capable of making these statements—that a being than which a greater cannot be conceived is not in the understanding in any other sense than that in which a being that is altogether inconceivable in terms of reality, is in the understanding. You say that the inference that this being exists in reality, from the fact that it is in the understanding, is no more just than the inference that a lost island most certainly exists, from the fact that when it is described the hearer does not doubt that it is in his understanding.

But I say: if a being than which a greater is inconceivable is not understood or conceived, and is not in the understanding or in concept, certainly either God is not a being than which a greater is inconceivable, or else he is not understood or conceived, and is not in the understanding or in concept. But I call on your faith and conscience to attest that this is most false. Hence, that than which a greater cannot be conceived is truly understood and conceived, and is in the understanding and in concept. Therefore either the grounds on which you try to controvert me are not true, or else the inference which you think to base logically on those grounds is not justified.

But you hold, moreover, that supposing that a being than which a greater cannot be conceived is understood, it does not follow that this being is in the understanding; nor, if it is in the understanding, does it therefore exist in reality.

In answer to this, I maintain positively: if that being can be even conceived to be, it must exist in reality. For that than which a greater is inconceivable cannot be conceived except as without beginning. But whatever can be conceived to exist, and does not exist, can be conceived to exist through a beginning. Hence what can be conceived to exist, but does not exist, is not the being than which a greater cannot be conceived. Therefore, if such a being can be conceived to exist, necessarily it does exist.

Furthermore: if it can be conceived at all, it must exist. For no one who denies or doubts the existence of a being than which a greater is inconceivable, denies or doubts that if it did exist, its non-existence, either in reality or in the understanding, would be impossible. For otherwise it would not be a being than which a greater cannot be conceived. But as to whatever can be conceived, but does not exist—if there were such a being, its non-existence, either in reality or in the understanding, would be possible. Therefore if a being than which a greater is inconceivable can be even conceived, it cannot be nonexistent.

·   ·   ·

But, you say, it is as if one should suppose an island in the ocean, which surpasses all lands in its fertility, and which, because of the difficulty, or rather the impossibility, of discovering that which does not exist, is called a lost island; and should say that there can be no doubt that this island truly exists in reality, for this reason, that one who hears it described easily understands what he hears.

Now I promise confidently that if any man shall devise anything existing either in reality or in concept alone (except that than which a greater cannot be conceived) to which he can adapt the sequence of my reasoning, I will discover that thing, and will give him his lost island, not to be lost again.

But it now appears that this being than which a greater is inconceivable cannot be conceived not to be, because it exists on so assured a ground of truth; for otherwise it would not exist at all.

Hence, if any one says that he conceives this being not to exist, I say that at the time when he conceives of this either he conceives of a being than which a greater is inconceivable, or he does not conceive at all. If he does not conceive, he does not conceive of the non-existence of that of which he does not conceive. But if he does conceive, he certainly conceives of a being which cannot be even conceived not to exist. For if it could be conceived not to exist, it could be conceived to have a beginning and an end. But this is impossible.

He, then, who conceives of this being conceives of a being which cannot be even conceived not to exist; but he who conceives of this being does not conceive that it does not exist; else he conceives what is inconceivable. The non-existence, then, of that than which a greater cannot be conceived is inconceivable. . . .

18

THOMAS AQUINAS (1225–1274)

The Five Ways

St. Thomas Aquinas was, without doubt, the greatest of the medieval philosopher-theologians. Moreover, he attempted the monumental task of reconciling Augustinian Christianity with the teachings of Aristotle, whose scientific and metaphysical writings

From Thomas Aquinas, *Summa Theologica,* Part I, Question II, Article 3, trans. the Fathers of the English Dominican Province (New York: Benziger Brothers, 1911), pp. 24–27.

were largely unknown in Christian Europe. Born to a noble family (his father was Count of Aquino in Italy), he studied at Naples, Cologne, and Paris. From 1256 to the end of his life, he was a professor of theology. A rigorously systematic thinker and writer, St. Thomas wrote two great treatises in which he attempted to "sum up" his teachings: the *Summa Contra Gentiles* (written about 1260) and the *Summa Theologica* (written about 1265–1272). The selection that follows is from the latter.

St. Thomas rejects the ontological argument. He argues that we must make a distinction between (1) that which is self-evident in itself but not to us, and (2) that which is self-evident in itself and to us. The proposition "God exists" is self-evident in itself, says Aquinas, for (as he will later show) God is his own existence, but it is not self-evident to us because we do not know the essence of God. Thus, for us, the existence of God must be proven in some other manner. That other manner is to argue from the effect to the cause, from the creation to the Creator.

Here, and throughout the *Summa Theologica,* St. Thomas' exposition consists of five parts: (1) a statement of the question that he is going to discuss, (2) objections that have been or might be raised against the position that he is going to take, (3) an argument or quotation supporting the opposite view, (4) a statement of his own position, and (5) replies to each of the objections previously raised. The writing is extremely compact and should be read slowly and with great care.

THIRD ARTICLE.

Whether God Exists?

We proceed thus to the Third Article:—

Objection 1. It seems that God does not exist; because if one of two contraries be infinite, the other would be altogether destroyed. But the word "God" means that He is infinite goodness. If, therefore, God existed, there would be no evil discoverable; but there is evil in the world. Therefore God does not exist.

Obj. 2. Further, it is superfluous to suppose that what can be accounted for by a few principles has been produced by many. But it seems that everything that appears in the world can be accounted for by other principles, supposing God did not exist. For all natural things can be reduced to one principle, which is nature: and all things that happen intentionally can be reduced to one principle, which is human reason, or will. Therefore there is no need to suppose God's existence.

On the contrary, It is said in the person of God: *I am Who am* (Exod. iii. 14).

I answer that, The existence of God can be proved in five ways.

The first and more manifest way is the argument from motion. It is certain and evident to our senses that some things are in motion. Whatever is in motion is moved by another, for nothing can be in motion except it have a potentiality for that towards which it is being moved; whereas a thing moves inasmuch as it is in act. By "motion" we mean nothing else than the reduction of something from a state of potentiality into a state of actuality. Nothing, however, can be reduced from a state of potentiality into a state of actuality, unless by something already in a state of actuality. Thus that which is actually hot, as fire, makes wood, which is potentially hot, to be actually hot, and thereby moves and changes it. It is not possible that the same thing should be at once in a state of actuality and potentiality from the same point of view, but only from different points of view. What is actually hot cannot simultaneously be only potentially hot; still, it is simultaneously potentially cold. It is therefore impossible that from the same point of view and in the same way anything should be both moved and mover, or that it should move itself. Therefore, whatever is in motion must be put in motion by another. If that by which it is put in motion be itself put in motion, then this also must needs be put in motion by another, and that by another again. This cannot go on to infinity, because then there would be no first mover, and consequently, no other mover —seeing that subsequent movers only move inasmuch as they are put in motion by the first mover; as the staff only moves because it is put in motion by the hand. Therefore it is necessary to arrive at a First Mover, put in motion by no other; and this everyone understands to be God.

The second way is from the formality of efficient causation. In the world of sense we find there is an order of efficient causation. There is no case known (neither is it, indeed, possible) in which a thing is found to be the efficient cause of itself; for so it would be prior to itself, which is impossible. In efficient causes it is not possible to go on to infinity, because in all efficient causes following in order, the first is the cause of the intermediate cause, and the intermediate is the cause of the ultimate cause, whether the intermediate cause be several, or one only. To take away the cause is to take away the effect. Therefore, if there be no first cause among efficient causes, there will be no ultimate cause, nor any intermediate. If in efficient causes it is possible to go on to infinity, there will be no first efficient cause, neither will there be an ultimate effect, nor any intermediate efficient causes; all of which is plainly false. Therefore it is necessary to put forward a First Efficient Cause, to which everyone gives the name of God.

The third way is taken from possibility and necessity, and runs thus. We find in nature things that could either exist or not exist, since they are found to be generated, and then to corrupt; and, consequently, then can exist, and then not exist. It is impossible for these always to exist, for that which can one day cease to exist must at some time have not existed. Therefore, if everything could cease to exist, then at one time there could have been nothing in existence. If this were true, even now there would be nothing in existence, because that which does not exist only begins to exist by something already existing. Therefore, if at one time nothing was in existence, it would have been impossible for anything to have begun to exist; and thus even now nothing would be in existence—which is absurd. Therefore, not all beings are merely possible, but there must exist something the existence of which is necessary. Every necessary thing either has its necessity caused by another, or not. It is impossible to go on to infinity in necessary things which have their necessity caused by another, as has been already proved in regard to efficient causes. Therefore we cannot but postulate the existence of some being having of itself its own necessity, and not receiving it from another, but rather causing in others their necessity. This all men speak of as God.

The fourth way is taken from the gradation to be found in things. Among beings there are some more and some less good, true, noble, and the like. But "more" and "less" are predicated of different things, according as they resemble in their different ways something which is in the degree of "most," as a thing is said to be hotter according as it more nearly resembles that which is hottest; so that there is something which is truest, something best, something noblest, and, consequently, something which is uttermost being; for the truer things are, the more truly they exist. What is most complete in any genus is the cause of all in that genus; as fire, which is the most complete form of heat, is the cause whereby all things are made hot. Therefore there must also be something which is to all beings the cause of their being, goodness, and every other perfection; and this we call God.

The fifth way is taken from the governance of the world; for we see that things which lack intelligence, such as natural bodies, act for some purpose, which fact is evident from their acting always, or nearly always, in the same way, so as to obtain the best result. Hence it is plain that not fortuitously, but designedly, do they achieve their purpose. Whatever lacks intelligence cannot fulfil some purpose, unless it be directed by some being endowed with intelligence and knowledge; as the arrow is shot to its mark by the archer. Therefore some intelligent being exists by whom all natural things are ordained towards a definite purpose; and this being we call God.

Reply Obj. 1. As Augustine says: *Since God is wholly good, He would not allow any evil to exist in His works, unless His omnipotence and goodness were such as to bring good even out of evil.* This is part of the infinite goodness of God, that He should allow evil to exist, and out of it produce good.

Reply Obj. 2. Since Nature works out its determinate end under the direction of a higher agent, whatever is done by nature must needs be traced back to God, as to its first cause. So also whatever is done designedly must also be traced back to some higher cause other than human reason or will, for these can suffer change and are defective; whereas things capable of motion and of defect must be traced back to an immovable and self-necessary first principle.

19

DAVID HUME (1711–1776)

The Teleological Argument

David Hume's *Dialogues Concerning Natural Religion* were completed sometime prior to 1761, but they were not published until 1779, three years after his death. The participants in the dialogue are: Demea, a representative of orthodox rationalism; Cleanthes, a somewhat more sophisticated philosophical theist; and Philo, a shrewd and brilliant skeptic. In the selection that follows, the subject of their discussion is the teleological argument, which is stated in summary form by Cleanthes in the opening paragraph. This argument, after a brief outburst by Demea, is then subjected to a searching critique by Philo. One can safely assume that it is Philo who speaks for Hume. (See p. 31 for a biographical note on David Hume.)

... Not to lose any time in circumlocutions, said CLEANTHES, addressing himself to DEMEA, much less in replying to the pious declamations of PHILO; I shall briefly explain how I conceive this matter. Look round the world: contemplate the whole and every part of it: You will find it to be nothing but one great machine, subdivided into an infinite number of lesser machines, which again admit of subdivisions, to a degree beyond what human senses and faculties can trace and explain. All these various machines, and even their most minute parts, are adjusted to each other with an accuracy, which ravishes into admiration all men, who have ever contemplated them. The curious adapting of means to ends, throughout all nature, resembles exactly, though it much exceeds, the productions of human contrivance; of human design, thought, wisdom, and intelligence. Since therefore the effects resemble each other, we are led to infer, by all the rules of analogy, that the causes also resemble; and that the Author of Nature is somewhat similar to the mind of man; though possessed of much larger faculties, proportioned to the grandeur of the work, which he has executed. By this argument *a posteriori,* and by this argument

From David Hume, *Dialogues Concerning Natural Religion,* Part II (London: William Blackwood & Sons, 1907; first published in 1779), pp. 26–48.

alone, do we prove at once the existence of a Deity, and his similarity to human mind and intelligence.

I shall be so free, CLEANTHES, said DEMEA, as to tell you, that from the beginning, I could not approve of your conclusion concerning the similarity of the Deity to men; still less can I approve of the mediums, by which you endeavour to establish it. What! No demonstration of the Being of a God! No abstract arguments! No proofs *a priori!* Are these, which have hitherto been so much insisted on by philosophers, all fallacy, all sophism? Can we reach no farther in this subject than experience and probability? I will not say, that this is betraying the cause of a deity: But surely, by this affected candour, you give advantage to Atheists, which they never could obtain, by the mere dint of argument and reasoning.

What I chiefly scruple in this subject, said PHILO, is not so much, that all religious arguments are by CLEANTHES reduced to experience, as that they appear not to be even the most certain and irrefragable of that inferior kind. That a stone will fall, that fire will burn, that the earth has solidarity, we have observed a thousand and a thousand times; and when any new instance of this nature is presented, we draw without hesitation the accustomed inference. The exact similarity of the cases gives us a perfect assurance of a similar event; and a stronger evidence is never desired nor sought after. But wherever you depart, in the least, from the similarity of the cases, you diminish proportionably the evidence; and may at last bring it to a very weak *analogy,* which is confessedly liable to error and uncertainty. After having experienced the circulation of the blood in human creatures, we make no doubt that it takes place in Titius and Mævius: but from its circulation in frogs and fishes, it is only a presumption, though a strong one, from analogy, that it takes place in men and other animals. The analogical reasoning is much weaker, when we infer the circulation of the sap in vegetables from our experience, that the blood circulates in animals; and those, who hastily followed that imperfect analogy, are found, by more accurate experiments, to have been mistaken.

If we see a house, CLEANTHES, we conclude, with the greatest certainty, that it had an architect or builder; because this is precisely that species of effect, which we have experienced to proceed from that species of cause. But surely you will not affirm, that the universe bears such a resemblance to a house, that we can with the same certainty infer a similar cause, or that the analogy is here entire and perfect. The dissimilitude is so striking, that the utmost you can here pretend to is a guess, a conjecture, a presumption concerning a similar cause; and how that pretension will be received in the world, I leave you to consider.

.   .   .

Were a man to abstract from every thing which he knows or has seen, he would be altogether incapable, merely from his own ideas, to determine what kind of scene the universe must be, or to give the preference to one state or situation of things above another. For as nothing which he clearly conceives, could be esteemed impossible or implying a contradiction, every chimera of his fancy would be upon an equal footing; nor could he assign any just reason, why he adheres to one idea or system, and rejects the others, which are equally possible.

Again; after he opens his eyes, and contemplates the world, as it really is, it would be impossible for him, at first, to assign the cause of any one event; much less, of the whole of things or of the universe. He might set his Fancy a rambling; and she might bring him in an infinite variety of reports and representations. These would all be possible; but being all equally possible, he would never, of himself, give a satisfactory account for his preferring one of them to the rest. Experience alone can point out to him the true cause of any phenomenon.

Now, according to this method of reasoning, DEMEA, it follows (and is, indeed, tacitly allowed by CLEANTHES himself) that order, arrangement, or the adjustment of final causes is not, of itself, any proof of design; but only so far as it has been experienced to proceed from that principle. For aught we can know *a priori,* matter may contain the source or spring of order originally, within itself, as well as mind does; and there is no more difficulty in conceiving, that the several elements, from an internal unknown cause, may fall into the most exquisite arrangement, than to conceive that their ideas, in the great, universal mind, from a like internal, unknown cause, fall into that arrangement. The equal possibility of both these suppositions is allowed. But by experience we find (according to CLEANTHES), that there is a difference between them. Throw several pieces of steel together, without shape or form; they will never arrange themselves so as to compose a watch: Stone, and mortar, and wood, without an architect, never erect a house. But the ideas in a human mind, we see, by an unknown, inexplicable œconomy, arrange themselves so as to form the plan of a watch or house. Experience, therefore, proves, that there is an original principle of order in mind, not in matter. From similar effects we infer similar causes. The adjustment of means to ends is alike in the universe, as in a machine of human contrivance. The causes, therefore, must be resembling.

.   .   .

That all inferences, CLEANTHES, concerning fact, are founded on experience, and that all experimental reasonings are founded on the supposition, that similar causes prove similar effects, and similar effects similar causes; I shall not, at present, much dispute with you. But observe, I entreat you, with what extreme caution all just reasoners proceed in the transferring of experiments to similar cases. Unless the cases be exactly similar, they repose no perfect confidence in applying their past observation to any particular phenomenon. Every alteration of circumstances occasions a doubt concerning the event; and it requires new experiments to prove certainly, that the new circumstances are of no moment or importance. A change in bulk, situation, arrangement, age, disposition of the air, or surrounding bodies; any of these particulars may be attended with the most unexpected consequences: And unless the objects be quite familiar to us, it is the highest temerity to expect with assurance, after any of these changes, an event similar to that which before fell under our observation. The slow and deliberate steps of philosophers, here, if any where, are distinguished from the precipitate march of the vulgar, who, hurried on by the smallest similitudes, are incapable of all discernment or consideration.

But can you think, CLEANTHES, that your usual phlegm and philosophy have been preserved in so wide a step as you have taken, when you compared to the universe, houses, ships, furniture, machines; and from their similarity in some circumstances inferred a similarity in their causes? Thought, design, intelligence, such as we discover in men and other animals, is no more than one of the springs and principles of the universe, as well as heat or cold, attraction or repulsion, and a hundred others, which fall under daily observation. It is an active cause, by which some particular parts of nature, we find, produce alterations on other parts. But can a conclusion, with any propriety, be transferred from parts to the whole? Does not the great disproportion bar all comparison and inference? From observing the growth of a hair, can we learn any thing concerning the generation of a man? Would the manner of a leaf's blowing, even though perfectly known, afford us any instruction concerning the vegetation of a tree?

But allowing that we were to take the *operations* of one part of nature upon another for the foundation of our judgment concerning the *origin* of the whole (which never can be admitted), yet why select so minute, so weak, so bounded a principle as the reason and design of animals is found to be upon this planet? What peculiar privilege has this little agitation of the brain which we call *thought,* that we must thus make it the model of the whole universe? Our partiality in our own favour does indeed present it on all occasions; but sound philosophy ought carefully to guard against so natural an illusion.

So far from admitting, continued PHILO, that the operations of a part can afford us any just conclusion concerning the origin of the whole, I will not allow any one part to form a rule for another part, if the latter be very remote from the former. Is there any reasonable ground to conclude, that the inhabitants of other planets possess thought, intelligence, reason, or any thing similar to these faculties in men? When Nature has so extremely diversified her manner of operation in this small globe; can we imagine, that she incessantly copies herself throughout so immense a universe? And if thought, as we may well suppose, be confined merely to his narrow corner, and has even there so limited a sphere of action; with what propriety can we assign it for the original cause of all things? The narrow views of a peasant, who makes his domestic œconomy the rule for the government of kingdoms, is in comparison a pardonable sophism.

But were we ever so much assured, that a thought and reason, resembling the human, were to be found throughout the whole universe, and were its activity elsewhere vastly greater and more commanding than it appears in this globe; yet I cannot see, why the operations of a world, constituted, arranged, adjusted, can with any propriety be extended to a world, which is in its embryo-state, and is advancing towards that constitution and arrangement. By observation, we know somewhat of the œconomy, action, and nourishment of a finished animal; but we must transfer with great caution that observation to the growth of a fœtus in the womb, and still more, to the formation of an animalcule in the loins of its male parent. Nature, we find, even from our limited experience, possesses an infinite number of springs and principles, which incessantly discover themselves on every change of her position and situation. And what new and unknown principles would actuate her in so new and unknown a situation as that of the formation of a universe, we cannot, without the utmost temerity, pretend to determine.

A very small part of this great system, during a very short time, is very imperfectly discovered to us: and do we thence pronounce decisively concerning the origin of the whole?

Admirable conclusion! Stone, wood, brick, iron, brass, have not, at this time, in this minute globe of earth, an order of arrangement without human art and contrivance: therefore the universe could not originally attain its order and arrangement, without something similar to human art. But is a part of nature a rule for another part very wide of the former? Is it a rule for the whole? Is a very small part a rule for the universe? Is nature in one situation, a certain rule for nature in another situation, vastly different from the former?

And can you blame me, CLEANTHES, if I here imitate the prudent reserve of SIMONIDES, who, according to the noted story, being asked by HIERO, *What God was?* desired a day to think of it, and then two days more; and after that manner continually prolonged the term, without ever bringing in his definition or description? Could you even blame me, if I had answered at first *that I did not know,* and was sensible that this subject lay vastly beyond the reach of my faculties? You might cry out skeptic and rallier as much as you pleased: but having found, in so many other subjects, much more familiar, the imperfections and even contradictions of human reason, I never should expect any success from its feeble conjectures, in a subject, so sublime, and so remote from the sphere of our observation. When two *species* of objects have always been observed to be conjoined together, I can *infer*, by custom, the existence of one wherever I *see* the existence of the other: and this I call an argument from experience. But how this argument can have place, where the objects, as in the present case, are single, individual, without parallel, or specific resemblance, may be difficult to explain. And will any man tell me with a serious countenance, that an orderly universe must arise from some thought and art, like the human; because we have experience of it? To ascertain this reasoning, it were requisite, that we had experience of the origin of worlds; and it is not sufficient, surely, that we have seen ships and cities arise from human art and contrivance . . .

20

BLAISE PASCAL (1623–1662)

The Wager

Blaise Pascal was a man of many interests. A brilliant mathematician and experimental scientist, he did original and important work in solid geometry (conic sections), atmospheric science (barometric pressure), hydraulics (Pascal's Law), and statistics (probability theory). He was also an inventor and entrepreneur: he invented the mechanical calculator and established the world's first taxi system (in Paris).

Throughout his short life, Pascal had a deep interest in religious and philosophical questions. He read and thought a great deal but wrote little: a collection of "thoughts" on various matters (*Pensées*) and a series of polemical letters (*The Provincial Letters*) are about all that we have from his hand. They are, however, enough to secure his place in history.

According to Pascal, the chief difficulty concerning the existence of God is that there is not enough evidence to make a decision one way or the other. He wrote:

"If I saw nothing [in nature] which revealed a Divinity, I would come to a negative conclusion; if I saw everywhere the signs of a Creator, I would remain peacefully in faith. But, seeing too much to deny and too little to be sure, I am in a state to be pitied; wherefore I have a hundred times wished that if a God maintains nature, she should testify to Him unequivocally, and that, if the signs she gives are deceptive, she should suppress them altogether; that she should say everything or nothing, that I might see which course I ought to follow."[1]

What, then, ought we to do? Pascal's answer is that, since we cannot decide the question on the basis of the evidence, we have no choice but to wager—to quite literally bet our lives—either that God exists or that God does not exist. According to Pascal, once we recognize that this is the basis on which we must decide the question, it is clear that the reasonable course is to wager that He exists.

Let us now speak of natural lights. If there is a God, He is infinitely incomprehensible since, having neither parts nor limits, He bears no resemblance to us.

From Blaise Pascal, *Pensées*, Fragment 233 (Brunschrieg numbering system), translated for this volume by Carol Halverson.

[1] *Pensées*, Fragment 229.

We are thus incapable of understanding either what He is or if He is. This being the case, who dares to undertake to resolve this question? Not we, who bear no resemblance to Him.

Who will blame the Christians, then, for being unable to give a reason for their belief, knowing they profess a religion for which they cannot give a reason? They declare in expounding it to the world that it is a folly; and then you complain that they do not prove it! If they proved it, they would not keep their word. It is in lacking proof that they do not lack sense. "Yes, but while that excuses those who offer it as such, and releases them from the blame of bringing it forth without reason, it does not excuse those who receive it."

Let us then examine this point and say: "God is, or He is not." But to which side do we lean? Reason can determine nothing here. There is an infinite chaos which separates us. A game is being played at the extremity of this infinite distance, where either heads or tails will turn up: what will you wager? Through reason you can do neither one nor the other; through reason you cannot defend either of the two.

Do not blame then the error of those who have made a choice, since you know nothing about it! "No, but I blame them for having made, not this choice, but a choice. For again, he who chooses heads and he who chooses the other are similarly at fault, they are both mistaken. The appropriate position is not to wager at all."

Yes, but one must wager. It is not voluntary; you are obligated. Which will you choose then? Let us see. Since one must choose, let us see which interests you the least. You have two things to lose, the true and the good; and two things to risk, your reason and your will, your knowledge and your happiness; and your nature has two things to avoid, error and misery. Your reason is no more offended, since choice is necessary, by choosing either one or the other. Thus one point is settled. But your happiness? Let us weigh the gain and the loss in choosing heads, in wagering that God is. Let us consider these two cases: if you win, you win everything; if you lose, you lose nothing. Wager then that He is, without hesitation!

"That is admirable. Yes, one must wager. But perhaps I wager too much." Let us see. Since there is an equal chance of winning and losing, if you had only to gain two lives for one, you might still wager. But if you had three to gain, you would have to play (since you are obligated to play); and you would be imprudent, when you are forced to play, not to risk your life in order to gain three in a game where there is an equal chance of losing and winning. But there is an eternity of life and happiness. And, that being the case, if there were an infinity of chances, only one of which was for you, you would still be correct to wager one to gain two; and you would be acting senselessly, being obliged to play, by refusing to play one life against three in a game where, of an infinity of chances, no more than one was for you, if there were an infinity of an infinitely happy life to gain. But here there *is* an infinity of an infinitely happy life to gain, a chance to gain against a finite number of chances to lose, and that which you stake is finite. That decides everything; wherever the infinite is, and where there is not an infinity of chances to lose against those to win, there is no longer reason to hesitate; one must give all. And thus, when one is forced to play, one must renounce reason to preserve his life, rather than risk it for the infinite gain just as likely to occur as the loss of nothingness.

For it is useless to say that it is uncertain if one will gain and it is certain that one risks, and that the infinite distance between the *certainty* of what is risked and the *uncertainty* of what may be gained equals the finite good which one stakes certainly against the infinity which is uncertain. This is not the case. Every player risks with certainty to gain with uncertainty; nevertheless, he certainly risks the finite to gain uncertainly the finite, without transgressing against reason. There is not an infinity of distance between this certainty of what is risked and the uncertainty of gain; this is false. There is, in truth, infinity between the certainty of winning and the certainty of losing. But the uncertainty of winning is proportionate to the certainty of what is risked, according to the proportion of chances for gain and loss. Hence it follows that, if there are as many chances on one side as on the other, the proper course is to play equal against equal; and thus the certainty of what is risked is equal to the uncertainty of gain: so much at fault is the notion that they are infinitely distant. Therefore, our proposition is of infinite force, since there is the finite to risk in a game where there are equal chances to win and to lose, and the infinite to gain. This is demonstrative, and if men are capable of some kind of truth, this is one. . . .

21

SIGMUND FREUD (1856–1939)

Theism Is an Illusion

Although Sigmund Freud is best known as the founder of psychoanalysis, in his later years his thoughts turned increasingly toward issues that lie far beyond the boundaries of psychology and neuropathology. Freud was well aware that the principles underlying psychoanalysis had profound implications for our understanding of human beings and their institutions, and he spent the last dozen or so years of his life attempting to spell out some of those implications. The major writings growing out of this effort were *The Future of an Illusion* (1927), *Civilization and Its Discontents* (1929), and *Moses and Monotheism* (1939).

Freud held that all religious beliefs result from the need of human beings to defend themselves against the terrors of nature. In a certain sense, he argues, these beliefs *humanize* nature, make it into something that we know how to deal with. These "religious fairy tales"—beliefs in God, or gods, or a soul, or life after death—are not supported by evidence; yet people cling to them with great tenacity. What is the reason for this? "We must ask where the inner force of religious doctrines lies," he writes, "and to what it is that they owe their efficacy, independent as it is of recognition by reason." In the selection that follows, Freud attempts to answer such questions.

I think we have prepared the way sufficiently for an answer to both these questions. It will be found if we turn our attention to the psychical origin of religious ideas. These, which are given out as teachings, are not precipitates of experience or end-results of thinking: they are illusions, fulfilments of the oldest, strongest and most urgent wishes of mankind. The secret of their strength lies in the strength of those wishes. As we already know, the terrifying impression of helplessness in childhood aroused the need for protection—for protection through love—which was provided by the father; and the recognition that this helplessness lasts throughout life made it necessary to cling to the existence of a father, but this time a more powerful one. Thus the benevolent rule of a divine Providence allays our fear of the dangers of life; the establishment of a moral world-order ensures the fulfilment of the demands of justice, which have so often remained unfulfilled in human civilization; and the prolongation of earthly existence in a future life provides the local and temporal framework in which these wish-fulfilments shall take place. Answers to the riddles that tempt the curiosity of man, such as how the universe began or what the relation is between body and mind, are developed in conformity with the underlying assumptions of this system. It is an enormous relief to the individual psyche if the conflicts of its childhood arising from the father-complex—conflicts which it has never wholly overcome—are removed from it and brought to a solution which is universally accepted.

When I say that these things are all illusions, I must define the meaning of the word. An illusion is not the same thing as an error; nor is it necessarily an error. Aristotle's belief that vermin are developed out of dung (a belief to

which ignorant people still cling) was an error; so was the belief of a former
generation of doctors that *tabes dorsalis* is the result of sexual excess. It would
be incorrect to call these errors illusions. On the other hand, it was an illusion
of Columbus's that he had discovered a new sea-route to the Indies. The part
played by his wish in this error is very clear. One may describe as an illusion
the assertion made by certain nationalists that the Indo-Germanic race is the
only one capable of civilization; or the belief, which was only destroyed by
psycho-analysis, that children are creatures without sexuality. What is characteristic of illusions is that they are derived from human wishes. In this respect
they come near to psychiatric delusions. But they differ from them, too, apart
from the more complicated structure of delusions. In the case of delusions, we
emphasize as essential their being in contradiction with reality. Illusions need
not necessarily be false—that is to say, unrealizable or in contradiction to
reality. For instance, a middle-class girl may have the illusion that a prince will
come and marry her. This is possible; and a few such cases have occurred. That
the Messiah will come and found a golden age is much less likely. Whether
one classifies this belief as an illusion or as something analogous to a delusion
will depend on one's personal attitude. Examples of illusions which have
proved true are not easy to find, but the illusion of the alchemists that all metals
can be turned into gold might be one of them. The wish to have a great deal
of gold, as much gold as possible, has, it is true, been a good deal damped by
our present-day knowledge of the determinants of wealth, but chemistry no
longer regards the transmutation of metals into gold as impossible. Thus we
call a belief an illusion when a wish-fulfilment is a prominent factor in its
motivation, and in doing so we disregard its relations to reality, just as the
illusion itself sets no store by verification.

Having thus taken our bearings, let us return once more to the question of
religious doctrines. We can now repeat that all of them are illusions and
insusceptible of proof. No one can be compelled to think them true, to believe
in them. Some of them are so improbable, so incompatible with everything we
have laboriously discovered about the reality of the world, that we may compare them—if we pay proper regard to the psychological differences—to delusions. Of the reality value of most of them we cannot judge; just as they cannot
be proved, so they cannot be refuted. We still know too little to make a critical
approach to them. The riddles of the universe reveal themselves only slowly
to our investigation; there are many questions to which science to-day can give
no answer. But scientific work is the only road which can lead us to a knowledge of reality outside ourselves. It is once again merely an illusion to expect
anything from intuition and introspection; they can give us nothing but particulars about our own mental life, which are hard to interpret, never any information about the questions which religious doctrine finds it so easy to answer.
It would be insolent to let one's own arbitrary will step into the breach and,
according to one's personal estimate, declare this or that part of the religious

system to be less or more acceptable. Such questions are too momentous for that; they might be called too sacred.

At this point one must expect to meet with an objection. 'Well then, if even obdurate skeptics admit that the assertions of religion cannot be refuted by reason, why should I not believe in them, since they have so much on their side—tradition, the agreement of mankind, and all the consolations they offer?' Why not, indeed? Just as no one can be forced to believe, so no one can be forced to disbelieve. But do not let us be satisfied with deceiving ourselves that arguments like these take us along the road of correct thinking. If ever there was a case of a lame excuse we have it here. Ignorance is ignorance; no right to believe anything can be derived from it. In other matters no sensible person will behave so irresponsibly or rest content with such feeble grounds for his opinions and for the line he takes. It is only in the highest and most sacred things that he allows himself to do so. In reality these are only attempts at pretending to oneself or to other people that one is still firmly attached to religion, when one has long since cut oneself loose from it. Where questions of religion are concerned, people are guilty of every possible sort of dishonesty and intellectual misdemeanour. Philosophers stretch the meaning of words until they retain scarcely anything of their original sense. They give the name of 'God' to some vague abstraction which they have created for themselves; having done so they can pose before all the world as deists, as believers in God, and they can even boast that they have recognized a higher, purer concept of God, notwithstanding that their God is now nothing more than an insubstantial shadow and no longer the mighty personality of religious doctrines. Critics persist in describing as 'deeply religious' anyone who admits to a sense of man's insignificance or impotence in the face of the universe, although what constitutes the essence of the religious attitude is not this feeling but only the next step after it, the reaction to it which seeks a remedy for it. The man who goes no further, but humbly acquiesces in the small part which human beings play in the great world—such a man is, on the contrary, irreligious in the truest sense of the word.

To assess the truth-value of religious doctrines does not lie within the scope of the present enquiry. It is enough for us that we have recognized them as being, in their psychological nature, illusions. But we do not have to conceal the fact that this discovery also strongly influences our attitude to the question which must appear to many to be the most important of all. We know approximately at what periods and by what kind of men religious doctrines were created. If in addition we discover the motives which led to this, our attitude to the problem of religion will undergo a marked displacement. We shall tell ourselves that it would be very nice if there were a God who created the world and was a benevolent Providence, and if there were a moral order in the universe and an after-life; but it is a very striking fact that all this is exactly as we are bound to wish it to be. And it would be more remarkable still if our wretched, ignorant and downtrodden ancestors had succeeded in solving all these difficult riddles of the universe.

For Further Reading

Alston, William P. "The Ontological Argument Revisited," *The Philosophical Review,* 69 (1960), 454–474.

Bowker, John. *The Sense of God: Sociological, Anthropological, and Psychological Approaches to the Origin of the Sense of God.* Oxford: Clarendon Press, 1973.

Brown, Patterson. "St. Thomas' Doctrine of Necessary Being," *The Philosophical Review,* 73 (1964), 76–90.

Devine, P. E. "Does St. Anselm Beg the Question?" *Philosophy,* 50 (1975), 271–281. Argues that St. Anselm does not beg the question.

Ducasse, C. J. *A Philosophical Scrutiny of Religion.* New York: Ronald Press, 1953.

Ebersole, Frank B. "Whether Existence Is a Predicate," *The Journal of Philosophy,* 60 (1963), 509–524.

Ewing, A. C. *The Fundamental Questions of Philosophy.* New York: Macmillan, 1951, Chap. 11.

————. *Value and Reality, The Philosophical Case for Theism.* London: G. Allen & Unwin, 1973. Argues for the possibility of an intuitive knowledge of the existence of God.

Flew, Antony. *God and Philosophy.* London: Hutchinson, 1966. Detailed critique of arguments for theism.

Harris, E. E. *Revelation Through Reason.* London: G. Allen & Unwin, 1959.

Harrison, C. "Totalities and the Logic of First Cause Arguments," *Philosophy and Phenomenological Research,* 35 (1974–1975), 1–19.

Hartshorne, Charles. *Anselm's Discovery: Re-examination of the Ontological Proof of God's Existence.* LaSalle, Ill.: Open Court Publishing Co., 1966.

————. *The Logic of Perfection and Other Essays in Neoclassical Metaphysics.* LaSalle, Ill.: Open Court Publishing Co., 1962.

————, and W. L. Reese. *Philosophers Speak of God.* Chicago: University of Chicago Press, 1963 (paperbound).

Hawkins, D. J. B. *The Essentials of Theism.* London: Sheed and Ward, 1949.

Hick, John. "God as Necessary Being," *The Journal of Philosophy,* 57 (1960), 725–734.

Hurlbutt, Robert H. *Hume, Newton and the Design Argument.* Lincoln: University of Nebraska Press, 1966.

Jack, Henry. "A Recent Attempt to Prove God's Existence," *Philosophy and Phenomenological Research,* 25 (1965), 575–579.

Kant, Immanuel. *Critique of Pure Reason,* trans. by Norman Kemp Smith. New York: St. Martin's Press, 1965 (paperbound). See section entitled "The Ideal of Pure Reason."

Kenny, Anthony. *The Five Ways: St. Thomas Aquinas' Proofs of God's Existence.* London: Routledge and Kegan Paul, 1969. Detailed analysis by a competent and sympathetic critic.

Leslie, J. "Efforts to Explain All Existence," *Mind,* 87 (1978), 181–194. An inconclusive examination of some alternative ways of "explaining all existence."

————. "God and Scientific Verifiability," *Philosophy,* 53 (1978), 71–79. A defense of the teleological argument against some common criticisms of that argument.

Lewis, H. D. *Our Experience of God.* London: G. Allen & Unwin; New York: Macmillan, 1959.

McIntyre, John. *St. Anselm and His Critics.* Edinburgh, Scot.: Oliver and Boyd, 1954.

Malcolm, Norman. "Anselm's Ontological Arguments," *The Philosophical Review,* 69 (1960), 41–62.

Martin, C. B. *Religious Belief.* Ithaca, N.Y.: Cornell University Press, 1959.

Mascall, E. L. *Existence and Analogy.* London: Longmans, Green, 1949.

Mavrodes, George I. (ed.). *The Rationality of Belief in God.* Englewood Cliffs, N.J.: Prentice-Hall, 1970.

Mill, John Stuart. *Three Essays on Religion.* New York: Henry Holt, 1874.

Paley, William. *Evidences of the Existence and Attributes of the Deity.* Many editions. Originally published in 1802.

Plantinga, A. *God and Other Minds.* Ithaca, N.Y.: Cornell University Press, 1967. A study of the rational justification of belief in God.

————. (ed.). *The Ontological Argument from St. Anselm to Contemporary Philosophers.* Garden City, N.Y.: Doubleday, 1965 (paperbound).

Reichenbach, B. R. *The Cosmological Argument: A Reassessment.* Springfield, Ill.: Charles C Thomas, 1972. Sympathetic to this type of argument.

Rowe, W. L. *The Cosmological Argument.* Princeton, N.J.: Princeton University Press, 1975. A detailed analysis of the argument and a defense of the argument against some common criticisms.

Shepherd, J. J. *Experience, Inference and God.* London: Macmillan, 1975. Defends a type of cosmological argument.

Shrader, K. S. "A Critique of Freud's Philosophy of Religion," *Philosophy Today,* 19 (1975), 213–227. An analysis of what the author calls the "Linus-Blanket Theory" of religious belief.

Smart, Ninian. *Philosophers and Religious Truth.* New York: Macmillan, 1970 (paperbound).

————. *Reasons and Faiths.* New York: Humanities Press, 1958.

Smith, J. E. *The Analogy of Experience.* New York: Harper & Row, 1973.

Taylor, R. *With Heart and Mind.* New York: St. Martin's Press, 1973.

Tillich, Paul. *Systematic Theology,* Vol. 1. Chicago: University of Chicago Press, 1951, pp. 204–235.

Torrance, Thomas F. *God and Rationality.* New York: Oxford University Press, 1971.

PART VI

The Problem of Evil

If God exists, and if He is infinitely good, wise, and powerful, and if this world is His creation, then it is indeed surprising that there is evil in the world. Evil cannot be the result of God's willing it to exist, for He is infinitely good. It cannot be the result of God's miscalculation, for He is infinitely wise. And it cannot be the result of His having done His best with a problem that exceeds His capacity, for He is infinite in power. Why, then—if God is all that He is said to be—is there evil in the world? This, in brief, is the problem of evil.

Note that this problem arises only on the supposition that the world is created by an infinitely good, wise, and powerful God who presumably wills what is best for the world. Clearly, this is a problem for theists. It is not a problem for anyone who denies the infinite goodness, wisdom, or power of God, and it goes without saying that it is not a problem for anyone who denies the existence of God.

It might seem that the problem is easily solved merely by the suppositions that (1) there is a demonic force (such as Satan) at work in the universe who tempts human beings to sin, and (2) evil results from humanity's free choice of the demonic over good. According to this view, evil is the result of humanity's rebellion against God; responsibility for the occurrence of evil in the world rests not with God but with humanity.

Upon reflection, however, it is clear that this explanation is not adequate to absolve God of responsibility for evil in the world. Where did this demonic force come from? Did God will it to exist? If so, He is not good. Did it come into being contrary to His will? Then, He must be lacking in wisdom (it outsmarted Him) or power (it overpowered Him). And if people, given the choice, have a propensity to choose evil instead of good, who made them that way? And is the maker of human beings, then, not ultimately responsible for their wrongdoing? Finally, how can humanity's wrongful choice possibly account for such *natural* evils (as opposed to *moral* evils) as plagues, floods, earthquakes, droughts, and animal suffering? These things seem to be integral parts of the natural order of things. How can they be attributed to anyone other than the creator of the natural order (if He exists)?

It seems clear, therefore, that if God is to be absolved of responsibility for evil in the world, it is necessary for the theist to argue that, notwithstanding the evil that is undeniably in it, this is the best of all possible worlds. If it can be plausibly maintained that the evil that is in the world is a necessary condition for the achievement of some very great good, then the fact of evil may not count decisively against belief in a God who is infinitely good, wise, and powerful. The challenge to the theist is to make this account plausible. The challenge to the critic of theism is to show that all attempts to explain evil in this way are ultimately unsuccessful.

22

AUGUSTINE OF HIPPO (354–430)

God and Evil

Not since St. Paul has there been so powerful an influence on Christian thought as St. Augustine, Bishop of Hippo. The son of a pagan father and a Christian mother, the young Augustine wrestled with doubt and uncertainty for many years before becoming, at thirty-two years of age, a convert to orthodox Christianity. Upon being converted, St. Augustine reports, "all the gloom of doubt vanished away." Augustine went on to become the principal spokesman for Catholic Christianity. In a long series of treatises, he worked out the details of a vast theological-philosophical system that attempts to sum up not only the teachings of the Christian scriptures and of the Church fathers but the best of classical learning as well.

From Augustine of Hippo, *Confessions,* Book VII, Chapters V and XII–XVI, trans. E. B. Pusey (New York: Columbian Co., 1891), pp. 171–173, 189–191.

Augustine was extremely vexed by the problem of evil, and he diligently sought for a solution that would satisfy the requirements of orthodox theism as well as meet the demands of his own restless and inquiring mind. The solution that he eventually adopted owes as much to Plotinus, a third-century A.D. disciple of Plato, as it does to traditional Christian thought. That solution contains Augustine's answers to the following questions: What, exactly, is evil? How did this evil come to be?

[V.] 7. And I sought, "whence is evil," and sought in an evil way; and saw not the evil in my very search. I set now before the sight of my spirit, the whole creation, whatsoever we can see therein, (as sea, earth, air, stars, trees, mortal creatures;) yea, and whatever in it we do not see, as the firmament of heaven, all angels moreover and all the spiritual inhabitants thereof. But these very beings, as though they were bodies, did my fancy dispose in place, and I made one great mass of Thy creation, distinguished as to the kinds of bodies; some, real bodies, some, what myself had feigned for spirits. And this mass I made huge, not as it was (which I could not know), but as I thought convenient, yet every way finite. But Thee, O Lord, I imagined on every part environing and penetrating it, though every way infinite: as if there were a sea, everywhere, and on every side, through unmeasured space, one only boundless sea, and it contained within it some sponge, huge, but bounded; that sponge must needs, in all its parts, be filled from that unmeasurable sea: so conceived I Thy creation, itself finite, full of Thee, the Infinite, and I said, Behold God, and behold what God hath created; and God is good, yea, most mightily and incomparably better than all these: but yet He, the Good, created them good; and see how He environeth and fulfills them. Where is evil then, and whence, and how crept it in hither? What is its root, and what its seed? Or hath it no being? Why then fear we and avoid what is not? Or if we fear it idly, then is that very fear evil, whereby the soul is thus idly goaded and racked. Yea, and so much a greater evil, as we have nothing to fear, and yet do fear. Therefore either is that evil which we fear, or else evil is, that we fear. Whence is it then? seeing God, the good, hath created all these things good. He indeed, the greater and chiefest Good, hath created these lesser goods; still both Creator and created, all are good. Whence is evil? Or, was there some evil matter of which He made, and formed, and ordered it, yet left something in it, which He did not convert into good? Why so then? Had He no might to turn and change the whole, so that no evil should remain in it, seeing He is All-mighty? Lastly, why would He make anything at all of it, and not rather by the same Allmightiness cause it not to be at all? Or, could it then be, against His will? Or if it were from eternity, why suffered He it so to be for infinite spaces of times past, and was pleased so long after to make something out of it? Or if He were suddenly pleased now to effect somewhat, this rather should the Allmighty have effected, that this evil matter should not be, and He alone be, the whole, true, sovereign, and infinite Good. Or if it was not good that He who was good, should not also frame and create something that were good, then, that evil matter being taken away and brought to nothing, He might form good matter, whereof to create all things. For He should not be Allmighty, if He might not create something good without the aid of that matter which Himself had not created. These thoughts I revolved in my miserable heart, overcharged with most gnawing cares, lest I should die ere I had found the truth; yet was the faith of Thy Christ our Lord and Saviour professed in the Church Catholic, firmly fixed in my heart, in many points, indeed, as yet unformed, and fluctuating from the rule of doctrine; yet did not my mind utterly leave it, but rather daily took in more and more of it.

.   .   .

[XII.] 18. And it was manifested unto me, that those things be good, which yet are corrupted; which neither were they sovereignly good, nor unless they were good, could be corrupted: for if sovereignly good, they were incorruptible, if not good at all, there were nothing in them to be corrupted. For corruption injures, but unless it diminished goodness, it could not injure. Either then corruption injures not, which cannot be; or which is most certain, all which is corrupted is deprived of good. But if they be deprived of all good, they shall cease to be. For if they shall be, and can now no longer be corrupted, they shall be better than before, because they shall abide incorruptibly. And what more monstrous, than to affirm things to become better by losing all their good? Therefore, if they shall be deprived of all good, they shall no longer be. So long therefore as they are, they are good: therefore whatsoever is, is good. That evil then which I sought, whence it is, is not any substance: for were it a substance, it should be good. For either it should be an incorruptible substance, and so a chief good: or a corruptible substance; which unless it were good, could not be corrupted. I perceived therefore, and it was manifested to me, that Thou madest all things good, nor is there any substance at all, which Thou madest not; and for that Thou madest not all things equal, therefore are all things; because each is good, and altogether very good, because our God *made all things very good.*

[XIII.] 19. And to Thee is nothing whatsoever evil; yea, not only to Thee, but also to Thy creation as a whole, because there is nothing without, which may break in, and corrupt that order which Thou hast appointed it. But in the parts thereof some things, because unharmonizing with other some, are accounted evil: whereas those very things harmonize with others, and are good: and in themselves are good. And all these things which harmonize not together, do yet with the inferior part, which we call Earth, having its own cloudy and windy sky harmonizing with it. Far be it then that I should say,

"These things should not be:" for should I see naught but these, I should indeed long for the better; but still must even for these alone praise Thee; for that Thou art to be *praised,* do show *from the earth, dragons, and all deeps, fire, hail, snow, ice, and stormy wind, which fulfill Thy word; mountains, and all hills, fruitful trees, and all cedars; beasts, and all cattle, creeping things, and flying fowls; kings of the earth, and all people, princes, and all judges of the earth: young men and maidens, old men and young, praise Thy Name.* But when, from heaven, these *praise Thee, praise Thee, our God, in the heights, all Thy angels, all Thy hosts, sun and moon, all the stars and light, the Heaven of heavens, and the waters that be above the heavens, praise Thy Name* (Ps. 148, 1–12); I did not now long for things better because I conceived of all: and with a sounder judgment I apprehended that the things above were better than these below, but all together better than those above by themselves.

[XIV.] 20. There is no soundness in them, whom aught of Thy creation displeaseth: as neither in me, when much which Thou has made, displeased me. And because my soul durst not be displeased at my God, it would fain not account that Thine, which displeased it. Hence it had gone into the opinion of two substances, and had no rest, but talked idly. And returning thence, it had made to itself a God, through infinite measures of all space; and thought it to be Thee, and placed it in its heart: and had again become the temple of its own idol, to Thee abominable. But after Thou hadst soothed my head, unknown to me, and closed *mine eyes that they should not behold vanity* (Ps. 119, 37), I ceased somewhat of my former self, and my phrenzy was lulled to sleep; and I awoke in Thee, and saw Thee infinite, but in another way, and this sight was not derived from the flesh.

[XV.] 21. And I looked back on other things; and I saw that they owed their being to Thee, and were all bounded in Thee: but in a different way; not as being in space; but because Thou containest all things in Thine hand in Thy Truth; and all things are true so far as they be; nor is there any falsehood, unless when that is thought to be, which is not. And I saw that all things did harmonize, not with their places only, but with their seasons. And that Thou, who only art Eternal, didst not begin to work after innumerable spaces of times spent; for that all spaces of times, both which have passed, and which shall pass, neither go nor come, but through Thee, working, and abiding.

[XVI.] 22. And I perceived and found it nothing strange, that bread which is pleasant to a healthy palate, is loathsome to one distempered: and to sore eyes light is offensive, which to the sound is delightful. And Thy righteousness displeaseth the wicked; much more the viper and reptiles, which Thou hast created good, fitting in with the inferior portions of Thy Creation, with which the very wicked also fit in; and that the more, by how much they be unlike Thee; but with the superior creatures, by how much they become more like to Thee. And I inquired what iniquity was, and found it to be no substance, but the perversion of the will, turned aside from Thee, O God the Supreme, toward these lower things, and *casting out his bowels,* and puffed up outwardly.

23

BENEDICT SPINOZA (1632–1677)

Good and Evil

Reared in the Jewish faith, Benedict Spinoza was banned from the Jewish community at the age of twenty-four because of his unorthodox views. Throughout much of his life, he was vilified as an atheist and free thinker whose writings ought to be suppressed. Nonetheless, he pursued his central convictions and published a series of treatises that, in time, established his reputation as one of the most brilliant minds of the seventeenth century. His most famous work, in which all his thoughts are woven together into a single pattern, is *Ethics,* completed in 1673.

Like St. Augustine, Spinoza approaches the problem of evil by attempting first to understand what evil is. He concludes that evil is simply a relationship perceived by the human mind between that which is less perfect and that which is more perfect. What exists in nature is an immense variety of finite beings—"everything which can be conceived by an infinite intellect"—and each of these beings acts according to its created nature. When some part of nature—a hurricane, an animal, a microbe, another human being—acts in ways that are displeasing or harmful to others, that is *called* evil, although in reality it is not so. All that exists in reality is finite beings acting according to their several natures, and each of them is good in its own way.

In order to explain briefly what good and evil are in themselves, we shall begin thus:

Some things are in our understanding and not in Nature, and so they are also only our own creation, and their purpose is to understand things distinctly: among these we include all relations, which have reference to different things, and these we call *Entia Rationis* [things of reason]. Now the question is, whether good and evil belong to the *Entia Rationis* or the *Entia Realia* [real things]. But since good and evil are only relations, it is beyond doubt that they must be placed among the *Entia Rationis;* for we never say that something is

From Benedict Spinoza, *Short Treatise on God, Man, and His Well-Being,* First Part, Chapter X (London: Adam and Charles Black, 1910), pp. 59–60; and *Ethics: Demonstrated in Geometrical Order,* Part I, Appendix, trans. W. White (New York: Macmillan, 1883), pp. 43–46.

good except with reference to something else which is not so good, or is not so useful to us as some other thing. Thus we say that a man is bad, only in comparison with one who is better, or also that an apple is bad, in comparison with another which is good or better.

All this could not possibly be said, if that which is better or good, in comparison with which it [the bad] is so called, did not exist.

Therefore, when we say that something is good, we only mean that it conforms well to the general Idea which we have of such things. But, as we have already said before, the things must agree with their particular Ideas, whose essence must be a perfect essence, and not with the general Ideas, since in that case they would not exist.

As to confirming what we have just said, the thing is clear to us; but still, to conclude our remarks, we will add yet the following proofs:

All things which are in Nature, are either things or actions. Now good and evil are neither things nor actions. Therefore good and evil do not exist in Nature.

For, if good and evil are things or actions, then they must have their definitions. But good and evil (as, for example, the goodness of Peter and the wickedness of Judas) have no definitions apart from the essence of Judas or Peter, because this alone exists in Nature, and they cannot be defined without their essence. Therefore, as above—it follows that good and evil are not things or actions which exist in Nature.

.   .   .

After man has persuaded himself that all things which exist are made for him, he must in everything adjudge that to be of the greatest importance which is most useful to him, and he must esteem that to be of surpassing worth by which he is most beneficially affected. In this way he is compelled to form those notions by which he explains nature; such, for instance, as *good, evil, order, confusion, heat, cold, beauty,* and *deformity,* &c.; and because he supposes himself to be free, notions like those of *praise* and *blame, sin* and *merit,* have arisen. These latter I shall hereafter explain when I have treated of human nature; the former I will here briefly unfold.

It is to be observed that man has given the name *good* to everything which leads to health and the worship of God; on the contrary, everything which does not lead thereto he calls *evil.* But because those who do not understand nature affirm nothing about things themselves, but only imagine them, and take the imagination to be understanding, they therefore, ignorant of things and their nature, firmly believe an *order* to be in things; for when things are so placed that, if they are represented to us through the senses, we can easily imagine them, and consequently easily remember them, we call them well arranged; but if they are not placed so that we can imagine and remember them, we call them badly arranged or *confused.* Moreover, since those things are more especially pleasing to us which we can easily imagine, men therefore prefer order to confusion, as if order were something in nature apart from our own imagination; and they say that God has created everything in order, and in this manner they ignorantly attribute imagination to God, unless they mean perhaps that God, out of consideration for the human imagination, has disposed things in the manner in which they can most easily be imagined. No hesitation either seems to be caused by the fact that an infinite number of things are discovered which far surpass our imagination, and very many which confound it through its weakness. But enough of this. The other notions which I have mentioned are nothing but modes in which the imagination is affected in different ways, and nevertheless they are regarded by the ignorant as being specially attributes of things, because, as we have remarked, men consider all things as made for themselves, and call the nature of a thing good, evil, sound, putrid, or corrupt, just as they are affected by it. For example, if the motion by which the nerves are affected by means of objects represented to the eye conduces to well-being, the objects by which it is caused are called *beautiful;* while those exciting a contrary motion are called *deformed.* Those things, too, which stimulate the senses through the nostrils are called sweet-smelling or stinking; those which act through the taste are called sweet or bitter, full-flavoured or insipid; those which act through the touch, hard or soft, heavy or light; those, lastly, which act through the ears are said to make a noise, sound, or harmony, the last having caused men to lose their senses to such a degree that they have believed that God even is delighted with it. Indeed, philosophers may be found who have persuaded themselves that the celestial motions beget a harmony. All these things sufficiently show that every one judges things by the constitution of his brain, or rather accepts the affections of his imagination in the place of things. It is not, therefore, to be wondered at, as we may observe in passing, that all those controversies which we see have arisen amongst men so that at last skepticism has been the result. For although human bodies agree in many things, they differ in more, and therefore that which to one person is good will appear to another evil, that which to one is well arranged to another is confused, that which pleases one will displease another, and so on in other cases which I pass by both because we cannot notice them at length here, and because they are within the experience of every one. For every one has heard the expressions: So many heads, so many ways of thinking; Every one is satisfied with his own way of thinking; Differences of brains are not less common than differences of taste;—all which maxims show that men decide upon matters according to the constitution of their brains, and imagine rather than understand things. If men understood things, they would, as mathematics prove, at least be all alike convinced if they were not all alike attracted. We see, therefore, that all those methods by which the common people are in the habit of explaining nature are only different sorts of imaginations, and do not reveal the nature of anything in itself, but only the constitution of the imagination; and because they have names as if they were entities existing apart from the imagination, I call them entities not of the reason but of the imagination. All argument, therefore, urged against us based upon such notions can be easily refuted. Many people, for instance, are accustomed to argue thus:—If all things have followed from the necessity of the most perfect nature of God, how is it that so many imperfections have arisen in nature—corruption, for instance, of things till they stink; deformity, exciting disgust; confusion, evil, crime, &c.? But, as I have just observed, all this is easily answered. For the perfection of things is to be judged by their nature and power alone; nor are they more or less perfect because they delight or offend the human senses, or because they are beneficial or prejudicial to human nature. But to those who ask why God has not created all men in such a manner that they might be controlled by the dictates of reason alone, I give but this answer: Because to Him material was not wanting for the creation of everything, from the highest down to the very lowest grade of perfection; or, to speak more properly, because the laws of His nature were so ample that they sufficed for the production of everything which can be conceived by an infinite intellect. . . .

24

GOTTFRIED WILHELM LEIBNIZ (1646–1716)

God Created the Best of All Possible Worlds

Gottfried Leibniz was one of the intellectual giants who gave the seventeenth century its reputation as "the century of genius." A versatile scholar, he was interested in such diverse areas as law, mathematics, natural science, history, theology, political theory, and philosophy. He shared with Isaac Newton the distinction of having developed the theory of differential and integral calculus.

Leibniz' *Theodicy,* published in 1710, is a famous and closely reasoned effort to solve the problem of evil. Leibniz attempts to demonstrate that this world, notwith-

From Gottfried Wilhelm Leibniz, *Theodicy,* "Abridgement of the Argument Reduced to Syllogistic Form, in *The Philosophical Works of Leibniz* (New Haven, Conn.: Tuttle, Morehouse & Taylor Co., 1908), pp. 284–285.

standing its imperfections, is the best of all possible worlds—a thesis that Voltaire was to attack with undisguised scorn in *Candide*. The excerpt that follows summarizes the principal line of argument of the *Theodicy*.

Some intelligent persons have desired that this supplement be made [to the Theodicy], and I have the more readily yielded to their wishes as in this way I have an opportunity to again remove certain difficulties and to make some observations which were not sufficiently emphasized in the work itself.

I. *Objection.* Whoever does not choose the best is lacking in power, or in knowledge, or in goodness.

God did not choose the best in creating this world.

Therefore, God has been lacking in power, or in knowledge, or in goodness.

Answer. I deny the minor, that is, the second premise of this syllogism; and our opponent proves it by this

Prosyllogism. Whoever makes things in which there is evil, which could have been made without any evil, or the making of which could have been omitted, does not choose the best.

God has made a world in which there is evil; a world, I say, which could have been made without any evil, or the making of which could have been omitted altogether.

Therefore, God has not chosen the best.

Answer. I grant the minor of this prosyllogism; for it must be confessed that there is evil in this world which God has made, and that it was possible to make a world without evil, or even not to create a world at all, for its creation has depended on the free will of God; but I deny the major, that is, the first of the two premises of the prosyllogism, and I might content myself with simply demanding its proof; but in order to make the matter clearer, I have wished to justify this denial by showing that the best plan is not always that which seeks to avoid evil, since it may happen that *the evil be accompanied by a greater good.* For example, a general of an army will prefer a great victory with a slight wound to a condition without wound and without victory. We have proved this more fully in the large work by making it clear, by instances taken from mathematics and elsewhere, that an imperfection in the part may be required for a greater perfection in the whole. In this I have followed the opinion of St. Augustine, who has said a hundred times, that God has permitted evil in order to bring about good, that is, a greater good; and that of Thomas Aquinas (in libr. II. sent. dist. 32, qu. I, art. 1), that the permitting of evil tends to the good of the universe. I have shown that the ancients called Adam's fall *felix culpa*, a happy sin, because it had been retrieved with immense advantage by the incarnation of the Son of God, who has given to the universe something nobler than anything that ever would have been among creatures except for it. And in order to a clearer understanding, I have added, following many good authors, that it was in accordance with order and the general good that God allowed to certain creatures the opportunity of exercising their liberty, even when he foresaw that they would turn to evil, but which he could so well rectify; because it was not fitting that, in order to hinder sin, God should always act in an extraordinary manner. To overthrow this objection, therefore, it is sufficient to show that a world with evil might be better than a world without evil; but I have gone even farther, in the work, and have even proved that this universe must be in reality better than every other possible universe.

25

DAVID HUME (1711–1776)

The Unsolved Problem of Evil

David Hume is, perhaps, less scornful of Leibniz's view than is Voltaire, but he is no less decisive in his rejection of the proposition that this is the best of all possible worlds. Demea, Cleanthes, and Philo—the participants in Hume's *Dialogues Concerning Natural Religion*—diligently seek a solution to the problem, but it is clear that in Hume's view there *is* no solution to the problem. "Epicurus' old questions are yet unanswered," Philo cries out in a famous passage. "Is [God] willing to prevent evil, but not able? then is he impotent. Is he able, but not willing? then is he malevolent. Is he both able and willing? Whence then is evil?" Nothing that Demea or Cleanthes say can shake the firmness of this reasoning. Nonetheless, their efforts to do so deserve a careful reading. (See p. 31 for a biographical note on Hume.)

As to authorities, replied DEMEA, you need not seek them. Look round this library of CLEANTHES. I shall venture to affirm, that, except authors of particular sciences, such as chemistry or botany, who have no occasion to treat of human life, there scarce is one of those innumerable writers, from whom the

From David Hume, *Dialogues Concerning Natural Religion,* Book X (London: William Blackwood & Sons , 1907), pp. 123–141.

sense of human misery has not, in some passage or other, extorted a complaint and confession of it. At least, the chance is entirely on that side; and no one author has ever, so far as I can recollect, been so extravagant as to deny it.

There you must excuse me, said PHILO: LEIBNITZ has denied it; and is perhaps the first,[1] who ventured upon so bold and paradoxical an opinion; at least, the first, who made it essential to his philosophical system.

And by being the first, replied DEMEA, might he not have been sensible of his error? For is this a subject, in which philosophers can propose to make discoveries, especially in so late an age? And can any man hope by a simple denial (for the subject scarcely admits of reasoning) to bear down the united testimony of mankind, founded on sense and consciousness?

And why should man, added he, pretend to an exemption from the lot of all other animals? The whole earth, believe me, PHILO, is cursed and polluted. A perpetual war is kindled amongst all living creatures. Necessity, hunger, want, stimulate the strong and courageous: Fear, anxiety, terror, agitate the weak and infirm. The first entrance into life gives anguish to the new-born infant and to its wretched parent: Weakness, impotence, distress attend each stage of that life: and 'tis at last finished in agony and horror.

Observe too, says PHILO, the curious artifices of Nature, in order to embitter the life of every living being. The stronger prey upon the weaker, and keep them in perpetual terror and anxiety. The weaker too, in their turn, often prey upon the stronger, and vex and molest them without relaxation. Consider that innumerable race of insects, which either are bred on the body of each animal, or flying about infix their stings in him. These insects have others still less than themselves, which torment them. And thus on each hand, before and behind, above and below, every animal is surrounded with enemies, which incessantly seek his misery and destruction.

Man alone, said DEMEA, seems to be, in part, an exception to this rule. For by combination in society, he can easily master lions, tigers, and bears, whose greater strength and agility naturally enable them to prey upon him.

On the contrary, it is here chiefly, cried PHILO, that the uniform and equal maxims of Nature are most apparent. Man, it is true, can, by combination, surmount all his *real* enemies, and become master of the whole animal creation: but does he not immediately raise up to himself *imaginary* enemies, the dæmons of his fancy, who haunt him with superstitious terrors, and blast every enjoyment of life? His pleasure, as he imagines, becomes, in their eyes, a crime: his food and repose give them umbrage and offence: his very sleep and dreams furnish new materials to anxious fear: and even death, his refuge from every other ill, presents only the dread of endless and innumerable woes. Nor does the wolf molest more the timid flock, than superstition does the anxious breast of wretched mortals.

[1]That sentiment had been maintained by Dr. King and some few others, before LEIBNITZ, though by none of so great fame as that GERMAN philosopher.

Besides, consider, DEMEA: this very society, by which we surmount those wild beasts, our natural enemies; what new enemies does it not raise to us? What woe and misery does it not occasion? Man is the greatest enemy of man. Oppression, injustice, contempt, contumely, violence, sedition, war, calumny, treachery, fraud; by these they mutually torment each other: and they would soon dissolve that society which they had formed, were it not for the dread of still greater ills, which must attend their separation.

But though these external insults, said DEMEA, from animals, from men, from all the elements, which assault us, form a frightful catalogue of woes, they are nothing in comparison of those, which arise within ourselves, from the distempered condition of our mind and body. How many lie under the lingering torment of diseases? Hear the pathetic enumeration of the great poet.

> Intestine stone and ulcer, colic-pangs,
> Demoniac frenzy, moping melancholy,
> And moon-struck madness, pining atrophy,
> Marasmus and wide-wasting pestilence.
> Dire was the tossing, deep the groans: DESPAIR
> Tended the sick, busiest from couch to couch.
> And over them triumphant DEATH his dart
> Shook, but delay'd to strike, tho' oft invok'd
> With vows, as their chief good and final hope.[2]

The disorders of the mind, continued DEMEA, though more secret, are not perhaps less dismal and vexatious. Remorse, shame, anguish, rage, disappointment, anxiety, fear, dejection, despair; who has ever passed through life without cruel inroads from these tormentors? How many have scarcely ever felt any better sensations? Labour and poverty, so abhorred by every one, are the certain lot of the far greater number; and those few privileged persons, who enjoy ease and opulence, never reach contentment or true felicity. All the goods of life united would not make a very happy man: but all the ills united would make a wretch indeed; and any one of them almost (and who can be free from every one), nay often the absence of one good (and who can possess all), is sufficient to render life ineligible.

Were a stranger to drop, on a sudden, into this world, I would show him, as a specimen of its ills, an hospital full of diseases, a prison crowded with malefactors and debtors, a field of battle strewed with carcasses, a fleet floundering in the ocean, a nation languishing under tyranny, famine, or pestilence. To turn the gay side of life to him, and give him a notion of its pleasures; whither should I conduct him? to a ball, to an opera, to court? He might justly think, that I was only showing him a diversity of distress and sorrow.

There is no evading such striking instances, said PHILO, but by apologies, which still farther aggravate the charge. Why have all men, I ask, in all ages, complained incessantly of the miseries of life? . . . They have no just reason,

[2]Milton: Paradise Lost, XI.

says one: these complaints proceed only from their discontented, repining, anxious disposition. . . . And can there possibly, I reply, be a more certain foundation of misery, than such a wretched temper?

But if they were really as unhappy as they pretend, says my antagonist, why do they remain in life? . . .

Not satisfied with life, afraid of death.

This is the secret chain, say I, that holds us. We are terrified, not bribed to the continuance of our existence.

It is only a false delicacy, he may insist, which a few refined spirits indulge, and which has spread these complaints among the whole race of mankind. . . . And what is this delicacy, I ask, which you blame? Is it any thing but a greater sensibility to all the pleasures and pains of life? and if the man of a delicate, refined temper, by being so much more alive than the rest of the world, is only so much more unhappy; what judgment must we form in general of human life?

Let men remain at rest, says our adversary; and they will be easy. They are willing artificers of their own misery. . . . No! reply I; an anxious languor follows their repose: disappointment, vexation, trouble, their activity and ambition.

I can observe something like what you mention in some others, replied CLEANTHES: but I confess, I feel little or nothing of it in myself, and hope that it is not so common as you represent it.

If you feel not human misery yourself, cried DEMEA, I congratulate you on so happy a singularity. Others, seemingly the most prosperous, have not been ashamed to vent their complaints in the most melancholy strains. Let us attend to the great, the fortunate Emperor, CHARLES V., when, tired with human grandeur, he resigned all his extensive dominions into the hands of his son. In the last harangue, which he made on that memorable occasion, he publicly avowed, *that the greatest prosperities which he had ever enjoyed, had been mixed with so many adversities, that he might truly say he had never enjoyed any satisfaction or contentment.* But did the retired life, in which he sought for shelter, afford him any greater happiness? If we may credit his son's account, his repentance commenced the very day of his resignation.

CICERO'S fortune, from small beginnings, rose to the greatest lustre and renown; yet what pathetic complaints of the ills of life do his familiar letters, as well as philosophical discourses, contain? And suitably to his own experience, he introduces CATO, the great, the fortunate CATO, protesting in his old age, that, had he a new life in his offer, he would reject the present.

Ask yourself, ask any of your acquaintance, whether they would live over again the last ten or twenty years of their lives. No! but the next twenty, they say, will be better:

> And from the dregs of life, hope to receive
> What the first sprightly running could not give.[3]

Thus at last they find (such is the greatness of human misery; it reconciles even contradictions) that they complain, at once, of the shortness of life, and of its vanity and sorrow.

And is it possible, CLEANTHES, said PHILO, that after all these reflections, and infinitely more, which might be suggested, you can still persevere in your Anthropomorphism, and assert the moral attributes of the Deity, his justice, benevolence, mercy, and rectitude, to be of the same nature with these virtues in human creatures? His power we allow infinite: whatever he wills is executed: but neither man nor any other animal is happy: therefore he does not will their happiness. His wisdom is infinite: he is never mistaken in choosing the means to any end: but the course of nature tends not to human or animal felicity: therefore it is not established for that purpose. Through the whole compass of human knowledge, there are no inferences more certain and infallible than these. In what respect, then, do his benevolence and mercy resemble the benevolence and mercy of men?

EPICURUS'S old questions are yet unanswered.

Is he willing to prevent evil, but not able? then is he impotent. Is he able, but not willing? then is he malevolent. Is he both able and willing? whence then is evil?

You ascribe, CLEANTHES, (and I believe justly) a purpose and intention to Nature. But what, I beseech you, is the object of that curious artifice and machinery, which she has displayed in all animals? The preservation alone of individuals and propagation of the species. It seems enough for her purpose, if such a rank be barely upheld in the universe, without any care or concern for the happiness of the members that compose it. No resource for this purpose: no machinery, in order merely to give pleasure or ease: no fund of pure joy and contentment: no indulgence without some want or necessity accompanying it. At least, the few phenomena of this nature are overbalanced by opposite phenomena of still greater importance.

Our sense of music, harmony, and indeed beauty of all kinds, gives satisfaction, without being absolutely necessary to the preservation and propagation of the species. But what racking pains, on the other hand, arise from gouts, gravels, megrims, tooth-aches, rheumatisms; where the injury to the animal-machinery is either small or incurable? Mirth, laughter, play, frolic, seem gratuitous satisfactions, which have no farther tendency: spleen, melancholy, discontent, superstition, are pains of the same nature. How then does the divine benevolence display itself, in the sense of you Anthropomorphites? None but we Mystics, as you were pleased to call us, can account for this strange mixture of phenomena, by deriving it from attributes, infinitely perfect, but incomprehensible.

[3]Dryden: Aurungzebe, Act IV., sc. i.

And have you at last, said CLEANTHES smiling, betrayed your intentions, PHILO? Your long agreement with DEMEA did indeed a little surprise me; but I find you were all the while erecting a concealed battery against me. And I must confess, that you have now fallen upon a subject, worthy of your noble spirit of opposition and controversy. If you can make out the present point, and prove mankind tó be unhappy or corrupted, there is an end at once of all religion. For to what purpose establish the natural attributes of the Deity, while the moral are still doubtful and uncertain?

You take umbrage very easily, replied DEMEA, at opinions the most innocent, and the most generally received even amongst the religious and devout themselves: and nothing can be more surprising than to find a topic like this, concerning the wickedness and misery of man, charged with no less than Atheism and profaneness. Have not all pious divines and preachers, who have indulged their rhetoric on so fertile a subject; have they not easily, I say, given a solution of any difficulties, which may attend it? This world is but a point in comparison of the universe; this life but a moment in comparison of eternity. The present evil phenomena, therefore, are rectified in other regions, and in some future period of existence. And the eyes of men, being then opened to larger views of things, see the whole connection of general laws; and trace, with adoration, the benevolence and rectitude of the Deity, through all the mazes and intricacies of his providence.

No! replied CLEANTHES, No! These arbitrary suppositions can never be admitted, contrary to matter of fact, visible and uncontroverted. Whence can any cause be known but from its known effects? Whence can any hypothesis be proved but from the apparent phenomena? To establish one hypothesis upon another, is building entirely in the air; and the utmost we ever attain, by these conjectures and fictions, is to ascertain the bare possibility of our opinion; but never can we, upon such terms, establish its reality.

The only method of supporting divine benevolence (and it is what I willingly embrace) is to deny absolutely the misery and wickedness of man. Your representations are exaggerated: Your melancholy views mostly fictitious: Your inferences contrary to fact and experience. Health is more common than sickness: Pleasure than pain: Happiness than misery. And for one vexation, which we meet with, we attain, upon computation, a hundred enjoyments.

Admitting your position, replied PHILO, which yet is extremely doubtful, you must, at the same time, allow, that, if pain be less frequent than pleasure, it is infinitely more violent and durable. One hour of it is often able to outweigh a day, a week, a month of our common insipid enjoyments: And how many days, weeks, and months are passed by several in the most acute torments? Pleasure, scarcely in one instance, is ever able to reach ecstasy and rapture: And in no one instance can it continue for any time at its highest pitch and altitude. The spirits evaporate; the nerves relax; the fabric is disordered; and the enjoyment quickly degenerates into fatigue and uneasiness. But pain often, good God, how often! rises to torture and agony; and the longer it continues, it becomes still more genuine agony and torture. Patience is exhausted; courage languishes; melancholy seizes us; and nothing terminates our misery but the removal of its cause, or another event, which is the sole cure of all evil, but which from our natural folly, we regard with still greater horror and consternation.

But not to insist upon these topics, continued PHILO, though must obvious, certain, and important; I must use the freedom to admonish you, CLEANTHES, that you have put this controversy upon a most dangerous issue, and are unawares introducing a total Skepticism, into the most essential articles of natural and revealed theology. What! no method of fixing a just foundation for religion, unless we allow the happiness of human life, and maintain a continued existence even in this world, with all our present pains, infirmities, vexations, and follies, to be eligible and desirable? But this is contrary to every one's feeling and experience: It is contrary to an authority so established as nothing can subvert: No decisive proofs can ever be produced against this authority; nor is it possible for you to compute, estimate, and compare all the pains and all the pleasures in the lives of all men and of all animals: And thus by your resting the whole system of religion on a point, which, from its very nature, must for ever be uncertain, you tacitly confess, that that system is equally uncertain.

But allowing you, what never will be believed; at least, what you never possibly can prove, that animal, or at least, human happiness, in this life, exceeds its misery; you have yet done nothing: For this is not, by any means, what we expect from infinite power, infinite wisdom, and infinite goodness. Why is there any misery at all in the world? Not by chance surely. From some cause then. Is it from the intention of the Deity? But he is perfectly benevolent. Is it contrary to his intention? But he is almighty. Nothing can shake the solidity of this reasoning, so short, so clear, so decisive; except we assert, that these subjects exceed all human capacity, and that our common measures of truth and falsehood are not applicable to them: a topic, which I have all along insisted on, but which you have, from the beginning, rejected with scorn and indignation.

26

FYODOR MIKHAILOVICH DOSTOIEVSKY
(1821–1881)

The Suffering of Children

Fyodor Dostoievsky was one of the literary giants of the nineteenth century. Born in Moscow, he survived a death sentence (reprieved at the last moment), was exiled to Siberia, and served four years of compulsory military service. He finally was permitted to retire to St. Petersburg (now Leningrad) to pursue his literary career. His writings include *Poor Folk* (1846), *Memoirs from the House of the Dead* (1862), *Notes from Underground* (1864), *Crime and Punishment* (1866), *The Idiot* (1868), *The Possessed* (1872), and *The Brothers Karamazov* (1880).

Dostoievsky was preoccupied with the problem of evil, returning to it again and again in his novels. In the selection that follows, Ivan and Alyosha—two of the four brothers in the novel—are discussing the suffering of children. Ivan, the "intellectual" brother, argues that no good that might conceivably result from the suffering of innocent children could possibly justify that suffering. Indeed, he argues, the suffering of even one innocent child is too high a price to pay for any good that it might create. Alyosha, the pious mystic, reluctantly agrees.

". . . There was in those days a general of aristocratic connections, the owner of great estates, one of those men—somewhat exceptional, I believe, even then —who, retiring from the service into a life of leisure, are convinced that they've earned absolute power over the lives of their subjects. There were such men then. So our general, settled on his property of two thousand souls, lives in pomp, and domineers over his poor neighbors as though they were dependents and buffoons. He has kennels of hundreds of hounds and nearly a hundred dog-boys—all mounted, and in uniform. One day a serf-boy, a little child of eight, threw a stone in play and hurt the paw of the general's favorite hound. 'Why is my favorite dog lame?' He is told that the boy threw a stone that hurt the dog's paw. 'So you did it.' The general looked the child up and down. 'Take him.' He was taken—taken from his mother and kept shut up all night. Early

From Fyodor Dostoievsky, *The Brothers Karamazov,* trans. C. Garnett (New York: Grosset & Dunlap, 1900), pp. 266–269.

that morning the general comes out on horseback, with the hounds, his dependents, dog-boys, and huntsmen, all mounted around him in full hunting parade. The servants are summoned for their edification, and in front of them all stands the mother of the child. The child is brought from the lock-up. It's a gloomy, cold, foggy autumn day, a capital day for hunting. The general orders the child to be undressed; the child is stripped naked. He shivers, numb with terror, not daring to cry. . . . 'Make him run,' commands the general. 'Run! run!' shout the dog-boys. The boy runs. . . . 'At him!' yells the general, and he sets the whole pack of hounds on the child. The hounds catch him, and tear him to pieces before his mother's eyes! . . . I believe the general was afterwards declared incapable of administering his estates. Well—what did he deserve? To be shot? To be shot for the satisfaction of our moral feelings? Speak, Alyosha!"

"To be shot," murmured Alyosha, lifting his eyes to Ivan with a pale, twisted smile.

"Bravo!" cried Ivan, delighted. "If even you say so . . . You're a pretty monk! So there is a little devil sitting in your heart, Alyosha Karamazov!"

"What I said was absurd, but—"

"That's just the point, that 'but'!" cried Ivan. "Let me tell you, novice, that the absurd is only too necessary on earth. The world stands on absurdities, and perhaps nothing would have come to pass in it without them. We know what we know!"

"What do you know?"

"I understand nothing," Ivan went on, as though in delirium. "I don't want to understand anything now. I want to stick to the fact. I made up my mind long ago not to understand. If I try to understand anything, I shall be false to the fact, and I have determined to stick to the fact."

"Why are you trying me?" Alyosha cried, with sudden distress. "Will you say what you mean at last?"

"Of course, I will; that's what I've been leading up to. You are dear to me, I don't want to let you go, and I won't give you up to your Zossima."

Ivan for a minute was silent, his face became all at once very sad.

"Listen! I took the case of children only to make my case clearer. Of the other tears of humanity with which the earth is soaked from its crust to its center, I will say nothing. I have narrowed my subject on purpose. I am a bug, and I recognize in all humility that I cannot understand why the world is arranged as it is. Men are themselves to blame, I suppose; they were given paradise, they wanted freedom, and stole fire from heaven, though they knew they would become unhappy, so there is no need to pity them. With my pitiful, earthly, Euclidian understanding, all I know is that there is suffering and that there are none guilty; that cause follows effect, simply and directly; that everything flows and finds its level—but that's only Euclidian nonsense, I know that, and I can't consent to live by it! What comfort is it to me that there

are none guilty and that cause follows effect simply and directly, and that I
know it?—I must have justice, or I will destroy myself. And not justice in some
remote infinite time and space, but here on earth, and that I could see myself.
I have believed in it. I want to see it, and if I am dead by then, let me rise again,
for if it all happens without me, it will be too unfair. Surely I haven't suffered,
simply that I, my crimes and my sufferings, may manure the soil of the future
harmony for somebody else. I want to see with my own eyes the hind lie down
with the lion and the victim rise up and embrace his murderer. I want to be
there when every one suddenly understands what it has all been for. All the
religions of the world are built on this longing, and I am a believer. But then
there are the children, and what am I to do about them? That's a question I
can't answer. For the hundredth time I repeat, there are numbers of questions,
but I've only taken the children, because in their case what I mean is so
unanswerably clear. Listen! If all must suffer to pay for the eternal harmony,
what have children to do with it, tell me please? It's beyond all comprehension
why they should suffer, and why they should pay for the harmony. Why should
they, too, furnish material to enrich the soil for the harmony of the future? I
understand solidarity in sin among men. I understand solidarity in retribution,
too; but there can be no such solidarity with children. And if it is really true
that they must share responsibility for all their fathers' crimes, such a truth
is not of this world and is beyond my comprehension. Some jester will say,
perhaps, that the child would have grown up and have sinned, but you see he
didn't grow up, he was torn to pieces by the dogs, at eight years old. Oh,
Alyosha, I am not blaspheming! I understand, of course, what an upheaval of
the universe it will be, when everything in heaven and earth blends in one
hymn of praise and everything that lives and has lived cries aloud: 'Thou art
just, O Lord, for Thy ways are revealed.' When the mother embraces the fiend
who threw her child to the dogs, and all three cry aloud with tears, 'Thou art
just, O Lord!' then, of course, the crown of knowledge will be reached and all
will be made clear. But what pulls me up here is that I can't accept that
harmony. And while I am on earth, I make haste to take my own measures.
You see, Alyosha, perhaps it really may happen that if I live to that moment,
or rise again to see it, I, too, perhaps, may cry aloud with the rest, looking at
the mother embracing the child's torturer, 'Thou art just, O Lord!' but I don't
want to cry aloud then. While there is still time, I hasten to protect myself,
and so I renounce the higher harmony altogether. It's not worth the tears of
that one tortured child who beat itself on the breast with its little fist and
prayed in its stinking outhouse, with its unexpiated tears to 'dear, kind God'!
It's not worth it, because those tears are unatoned for. They must be atoned
for, or there can be no harmony. But how? How are you going to atone for
them? Is it possible? By their being avenged? But what do I care for avenging
them? What do I care for a hell for oppressors? What good can hell do, since
those children have already been tortured? And what becomes of harmony, if

there is hell? I want to forgive. I want to embrace. I don't want more suffering. And if the sufferings of children go to swell the sum of sufferings which was necessary to pay for truth, then I protest that the truth is not worth such a price. I don't want the mother to embrace the oppressor who threw her son to the dogs! She dare not forgive him! Let her forgive him for herself, if she will, let her forgive the torturer for the immeasurable suffering of her mother's heart. But the sufferings of her tortured child she has no right to forgive; she dare not forgive the torturer, even if the child were to forgive him! And if that is so, if they dare not forgive, what becomes of harmony? Is there in the whole world a being who would have the right to forgive and could forgive? I don't want harmony. From love for humanity I don't want it. I would rather be left with the unavenged suffering. I would rather remain with my unavenged suffering and unsatisfied indignation, *even if I were wrong.* Besides, too high a price is asked for harmony; it's beyond our means to pay so much to enter on it. And so I hasten to give back my entrance ticket, and if I am an honest man I am bound to give it back as soon as possible. And that I am doing. It's not God that I don't accept, Alyosha, only I most respectfully return Him the ticket."

"That's rebellion," murmured Alyosha, looking down.

"Rebellion? I am sorry you call it that," said Ivan earnestly. "One can hardly live in rebellion, and I want to live. Tell me yourself, I challenge you —answer. Imagine that you are creating a fabric of human destiny with the object of making men happy in the end, giving them peace and rest at last, but that it was essential and inevitable to torture to death only one tiny creature —that baby beating its breast with its fist, for instance—and to found that edifice on its unavenged tears, would you consent to be the architect on those conditions? Tell me, and tell the truth."

"No, I wouldn't consent," said Alyosha softly. . . .

27

FREDERICK R. TENNANT (1866–1957)

A Theist's Account of Evil

Frederick Tennant was educated at Cambridge University and spent his career there as a lecturer in philosophy of religion. He is principally known as an eloquent apologist for ethical theism. His two-volume *Philosophical Theology* (1928–1930) attempts to apply "the inductive method of science" to the problem of religious knowledge. It includes an important and original formulation of the teleological argument for the existence of God as well as a non-Augustinian treatment of the problem of evil.

Tennant's thesis, like that of Leibniz, is that this is the best of all possible worlds. However, according to Tennant, the world is "best" in the sense that it is ideally designed for the development of *moral worth*. Tennant asserts that it is inconsistent with theism's concept of God to suppose that, in creating the world, God sought to create the "happiest, or sensuously pleasantest." Such a world, he argues, would not be the *best* world. Consequently, the fact that there are pain, suffering, and other evils in the world does not contradict the claim that this is the best of all possible worlds.

. . . .

Since theism teaches that the world-ground is an ethical Spirit, or that God is love, it must also teach that, in some sense, the world is the 'best possible' of its kind. And it may now be submitted that this implication is defensible, so long as we are consistent and in earnest in the use of both the words 'best' and 'possible.'

There is no sense in calling a world a best world unless we specify the *kind* of goodness or worth which that world is said to manifest in the fullest measure. Different values may not be actually compossible, especially if each of them is to be present in its superlative degree; so the notion of a world as an *omnitudo* of values may be as 'impossible' as is the notion of God as the *omnitudo* of all positive attributes. What the theist means by 'best', in this

From Frederick Tennant, *Philosophical Theology,* Volume II, Chapter VII (New York: Cambridge University Press, 1903), pp. 186–191. Reprinted by permission of the publisher.

connexion, is best in respect of moral worth, or of instrumentality thereto. But those who have allowed themselves to "charge God foolishly" have substituted for this meaning that of happiest, or sensuously pleasantest. Certainly our world is not, in this sense, the best that we can imagine. Equally certainly, the theist maintains, it was not meant to be. If it were, it would not be truly the best; for we cannot go behind our judgement, rational or non-rational, that the highest value in the hierarchy of values is moral worth, or—what is the ultimate essence of all morality—personal love. The hedonistic theory that pleasure is what gives worth to life, the ultimate good to be striven for, is generally acknowledged to be untenable: at any rate it is out of court for the theist. Happiness may be a constituent element in the highest complex good that we can conceive, and may accompany the attainment of a higher good; but the ultimate standard for the valuation of human life it cannot be. The 'best possible' world, then, or the world that is worthiest of God and man, must be a moral order, a theatre of moral life and love. Moral character and moral progress must be its purpose, as the best things which any world can realise. To dispense with them would be, for the Creator, to prefer a worse world. Unalloyed pleasure is condemned by man himself as unworthy to be his "life's crown". No pain or want, no effort; no effort, no progress; no progress, no attainment. *Necessity* is the mother of invention; experience is the "becoming expert *by experiment*": mere happiness would entail stagnation.

Thus we cannot have it both ways: the best world cannot be the most pleasurable; and it cannot lack its crown in moral agents.

The word 'cannot' leads on to a discussion of our second leading term, 'possible': on this occasion in connexion with the notion of divine omnipotence. It has already been found vain to speak of a *prius* of possibilities independent of actualities. It may now be added that, possibilities and impossibilities being once constituted by an actual order, omnipotence cannot be conceived as power or control over the possible and the impossible alike, as if both were the same to God. That leads to absurdity. Yet when theism has been rejected on the ground that the evil in the world furnishes an argument against the goodness, or even the existence, of God, it would seem to have been generally assumed that such a being must, by arbitrary exercise of will, be the author of possibility as well as of actuality.

That whatever power may be called omnipotence must be limited by the impossible has been maintained in at least two ways. One of these is to assert that the laws of thought, *i.e.* the laws of identity, contradiction, etc., are valid independently of God as well as of the world, and impose themselves upon Him as well as upon ourselves with necessity. If this be so, we at once reach a distinction between the possible and the impossible which must be eternally binding upon the Supreme Being. Such a doctrine will not be unacceptable to common sense, but it does not commend itself to all philosophers. It has several times been insisted in this work that the valid, abstracted from that of which it is valid, is a mental figment, not an 'existent' *prius*. And it may be argued that this is so even in the case of the fundamental laws of thought, as well as in that of the empirical laws of Nature. The sum of eternal truths cannot exist, so to say, *in vacuo,* prior both to the things in which they are embodied and to the thinker in whose mind they are ideas, etc. When we speak of God as recognising truths independent of Him, or as establishing truth or validity by fiat, and when we try to conceive of God as able to obliterate the difference between the logically possible and impossible, or to set up that difference as if it once did not exist, we are endeavouring to think of Him as a being for whom truth is not as yet truth, and therefore as an indeterminate being eventually indistinguishable from nothing.

On the other hand, if the thinker of the eternal truths is determinate, self-consistent, and so forth, with a definite nature and mode of activity, other modes of being and conceivable or possible activities are *ipso facto* precluded. Hence the sum of eternal truths becomes the mode of God's being and activity, and is neither their *prius* nor their product. And this is the better answer to the supposition that the possible is an arbitrary creation of God, and that the possible and the impossible are alike to omnipotence. In that God is love, He is not hate: in that He wills a developing moral order He is not the creator of a paradise of angels. Possibilities are thus determined by what God is; and God is limited by His very determinateness, not an indeterminate Absolute in whom all differences are lost. Theism has no concern with such an Absolute, and the puzzles set up by the adoption of such a notion constitute no difficulties for theism. Nor is determinateness, or the kind of finiteness which it implies, any derogation from such 'almightiness' as theology can predicate of the Deity without self-stultification.

But, granted that God is a determinate being, restricted to consistency and compatibility in His action, and granted that His world is to be a developing moral order—the highest ideal of a world that we can conceive—then it must follow that there be a possibility and a risk of moral evil in that world. There cannot be moral goodness in a creature such as man without the possibility of his sinning. Without freedom to choose the evil, or the lower good, a man might be a well-behaved puppet or a sentient automaton, but not a moral agent. But the best possible world implies the existence of moral agents; its crown cannot be the puppet or the automaton. Were our conduct determined like the movements of the machinery of a clock, our world might manifest a preëstablished harmony and fulfil the purpose of a clock-maker. But it could not fulfil any ideal of its own, and could not have one. Nor could it realise the purpose of a God willing a best possible world. In both these respects a world from which the possibility of moral evil was excluded would be other than a moral order. It is idle, then, wistfully to contemplate the happiness which the world might have known had its creator made us capable only of what is right; to profess, like Huxley, our readiness to close with an offer to remove our capacity to do wrong and cause misery; or to indulge the wish that we had been made good at the expense of freedom. There is no moral goodness in a clock, however perfectly it may keep time. Freedom to do good alone, except after suppression of lower motives by moral conflict, is not freedom. Such regrets as these, to which the ablest of men have occasionally allowed themselves to give expression, do but shew how hard it is to avoid playing fast and loose with plain words when we would apply logic to a question which excites emotion.

The best world, then, must include free agents, creatures that are in turn 'creators' in the sense that their 'utterances' are not God's positings but their own. And freewill introduces contingencies, new causal series, and new possibilities. God stands "a hand-breadth off " to give His creatures room to act and grow: and here another limitation is involved—the self-limitation of love. The Actual world, including human society and human achievements, is due to man as well as to God. We are fellow-workers together with God in the actualisation of a moral order: otherwise the world were not a moral order at all. For the possibility of moral evil entering into this moral order, God, who foreknew it, is responsible: He permits, so to say, the evil in order that there may be the good. But for the actual emergence of man's moral evil we cannot say that He is responsible: our sin, when 'sin' is strictly and correctly defined, is not God's act but the product of our volition, or devolved freedom. Conceivably moral evil *might* not have emerged, though the basic motivations to it, themselves morally neutral or non-moral, are inevitable consequences of the evolutionary process through which phenomenal man came to be.

. . . .

Thus the difficulties raised by the existence of sin are of an insuperable kind only on one or both of the suppositions, (1) that to God there must be no difference between the possible and the impossible, and (2) that the best possible world must be the happiest world and not a moral order. But theism repudiates omnipotence, in this sense, in its characterisation of the Deity; and it asserts that the instrumentality of the world to the production of a moral order is an expression or revelation of the nature of God, the empirically suggested world-ground. And if the moral ideal be the best or the highest that a world conceivably can fulfil, the process by which alone it is attainable is also good, despite the evil incidental to it. Theism *requires* that the world be an imperfect or mixed world, in that it takes the purpose of the world to consist in the realisation of the highest values by finite and developing creatures, with which an omnipotent establishment of non-moral or static perfection would have nothing in common.

If we suppose the ethical status of man to be less than the whole of the divine purpose, and but a stage to something higher but transcending our power to conceive, the further elements in the world-purpose may condition the evils with which we men are confronted, in respects that are beyond our ken. But, however this may be—and it is practically useless, if theoretically wholesome, to invoke the limitations of our knowledge and the inscrutability of the divine purpose in its fulness—theism is not unable to find a place and a meaning for moral evil in the world of an all-good God, in so far as the world is knowable and its purpose can reasonably be assigned.

.   .   .

For Further Reading

Adams, Robert Merrihew. "Must God Create the Best?" *The Philosophical Review,* 81 (1972), 317–332.

Ahorn, M. B. *The Problem of Evil.* New York: Schocken Books, 1971. Argues that the problem of evil leaves the existence of God an undecided issue.

Augustine, St. *On Free Will.* Several editions.

——————. *The Nature of the Good.* Several editions.

Bayle, Pierre. *Bayle's Historical and Critical Dictionary—Selections,* ed. by Richard Popkin. Indianapolis, Ind.: Bobbs-Merrill, 1965 (paperbound). Contains Bayle's objection to theism based on the problem of evil. Leibniz seeks to answer Bayle in his theodicy.

Farrer, Austin. *Love Almighty and Ills Unlimited.* Garden City, N.Y.: Doubleday, 1961.

Ferre, Nels. *Evil and the Christian Faith.* New York: Harper & Row, 1947. A defense of theism.

Hick, John. *Evil and the God of Love.* New York: Harper & Row, 1966. From a theistic standpoint.

Lewis, C. S. *The Problem of Pain.* New York: Macmillan, 1962. A readable defense of theism.

Madden, E. H., and P. H. Hare. *Evil and the Concept of God.* Springfield, Ill.: Charles C Thomas, 1968. Critical of theism.

Martin, M. "Is Evil Evidence against the Existence of God?" *Mind,* 87 (1978), 429–432. Argues *contra* Pargetter (see below), that it is.

McCloskey, H. J. *God and Evil.* The Hague: Martinus Hijhoff, 1974. Argues that the attempts of theists to reconcile the fact of evil with belief in God are not successful.

——————. "God and Evil," *The Philosophical Quarterly,* 10 (1960), 97–114. Argues against the theist's appeal to natural law as a solution to the problem of evil.

Mill, John Stuart. *Three Essays on Religion.* New York: Henry Holt, 1874.

Pargetter, R. "Evil as Evidence against the Existence of God," *Mind,* 85 (1976), 242–245. Argues that the claim that the existence of evil is strong evidence against the existence of God has not been established.

Pike, Nelson (ed.). *God and Evil.* Englewood Cliffs, N.J.: Prentice-Hall, 1964 (paperbound). Contains Pike's reply to Hume.

Plantinga, A. *God, Freedom and Evil.* Grand Rapids, Mich.: Eerdmans, 1978. Argues that the fact of evil does not contradict belief in the existence of God.

——————, R. M. Adams, and W. L. Rowe. "God and Possible Worlds," a symposium recorded in *The Journal of Philosophy,* 70 (1973), pp. 539–555. A discussion of Leibniz' thesis that this is the best of all possible worlds.

Reichenbach, B. "Natural Evils and Natural Laws: A Theodicy for Natural Evils," *International Philosophical Quarterly,* 16 (1976), 179–196. A critique of McCloskey (see above).

Sutherland, S. R. *Atheism and the Rejection of God: Contemporary Philosophy and 'The Brothers Karamazov.'* Oxford: Blackwell, 1977.

PART VII

Mind and Body

The common-sense view regarding mind and body may be summarized in two propositions: (1) minds and bodies are fundamentally different kinds of entities, minds being spiritual and bodies being physical, and (2) minds and bodies mutually influence one another. The first proposition states the central thesis of what is called *anthropological dualism,* the second that of *interactionism.* The two propositions together constitute what philosophers call *dualistic interactionism.*

To say that bodies are physical is only to say they share the characteristics of all physical objects: they have shape, size, weight, temperature, and a position in space. But what does it mean to say that minds are "spiritual"? It means that they do *not* share the characteristics of physical objects, yet they are real entities or real agents of certain sorts of activities. If it is with our bodies that we run, jump, and lift, it is with our minds, according to dualism, that we perceive, remember, ponder, and decide. Bodies are the subjects of physical activities, minds of mental activities. Bodies are located in space; minds are not. The activities of bodies are publicly observable; those of minds are not.

Bodies have causal effects on minds, according to the common-sense view. The physical acts of looking and seeing cause a mental awareness of what is seen; the physical act of touching causes a mental awareness of the texture of what is touched, and so on for each of the senses. And, according to dualism, minds have causal effects on bodies. For example, I consider watching a late-night movie, but I wisely decide not to. Then, I act on that decision. My decision (a mental activity) seems clearly to be causally related to the fact that I turn off the television, brush my teeth, and go to bed (physical activities).

169

The mind-body problem raises two questions concerning this account of mind and body. First, *are* mind and body two irreducibly different kinds of entity, or are they not? Second, what is occurring when mind and body seem to mutually influence one another, as in perception (body influencing mind) and volition (mind influencing body)?

The common-sense view—dualistic interactionism—is unacceptable to philosophical naturalism because dualism regards minds as "spiritual," and, according to naturalism, spiritual entities do not exist. The task of the naturalist, therefore, is to account for mental phenomena by reducing mind to some physical entity (for example, to identify it with the brain). The collective name for theories that attempt to explain the relationship between body and mind in this way is *identity materialism.*

The other principal alternative to dualism, the obverse of identity materialism, is *panpsychism,* which holds that body is ultimately reducible to mind.

28

RENÉ DESCARTES (1596–1650)

Thinking Things and Extended Things

René Descartes is regarded as the father of modern Western philosophy. Educated in French Jesuit schools, Descartes became disenchanted with Scholastic (medieval) philosophy at an early age and sought a new path toward philosophical truth. He used mathematics as his model. His first important work was a treatise called *A Discourse on Method,* in which he attempted to show that the method that mathematicians use to reach conclusions can be applied to all areas of human knowledge. The *Discourse* was followed by many other writings, among which *Meditations on the First Philoso-*

From René Descartes, *Meditations on the First Philosophy,* Meditations II and VI, and *A Discourse on Method,* Part V, in *The Method, Meditations, and Selections from the Principles of Descartes,* trans. J. Veitch (London: William Blackwood & Sons, 1913), pp. 41–58, 104–114, and 151–169.

phy is perhaps the best known. His influence on continental philosophy was enormous, and it can still be seen in the writings of such twentieth-century philosophers as Martin Heidegger and Jean Paul Sartre.

Descartes is so closely identified with the dualist-interactionist view of mind and body that "Cartesianism" has become another name for that view. In his quest for some truth that could not be doubted, Descartes concluded that his own existence was the first truth that he could safely assent to. "But what, then, am I?" he asks. His answer is "a thinking thing"—that is, a mind. But, he then asks, only a mind? He concludes that mind is conjoined with body so intimately that mind and body "compose a certain unity." Mind is a thinking unextended substance; body is an unthinking extended substance. In human beings the two are united.

The Meditation of yesterday has filled my mind with so many doubts, that it is no longer in my power to forget them. Nor do I see, meanwhile, any principle on which they can be resolved; and, just as if I had fallen all of a sudden into very deep water, I am so greatly disconcerted as to be unable either to plant my feet firmly on the bottom or sustain myself by swimming on the surface. I will, nevertheless, make an effort, and try anew the same path on which I had entered yesterday, that is, proceed by casting aside all that admits of the slightest doubt, not less than if I had discovered it to be absolutely false; and I will continue always in this track until I shall find something that is certain, or at least, if I can do nothing more, until I shall know with certainty that there is nothing certain. Archimedes, that he might transport the entire globe from the place it occupied to another, demanded only a point that was firm and immoveable; so also, I shall be entitled to entertain the highest expectations, if I am fortunate enough to discover only one thing that is certain and indubitable.

I suppose, accordingly, that all the things which I see are false (fictitious); I believe that none of those objects which my fallacious memory represents ever existed; I suppose that I possess no senses; I believe that body, figure, extension, motion, and place are merely fictions of my mind. What is there, then, that can be esteemed true? Perhaps this only, that there is absolutely nothing certain.

But how do I know that there is not something different altogether from the objects I have now enumerated, of which it is impossible to entertain the slightest doubt? Is there not a God, or some being, by whatever name I may designate him, who causes these thoughts to arise in my mind? But why suppose such a being, for it may be I myself am capable of producing them? Am I, then, at least not something? But I before denied that I possessed senses or a body; I hesitate, however, for what follows from that? Am I so dependent on the body and the senses that without these I cannot exist? But I had the persuasion that there was absolutely nothing in the world, that there was no sky and no earth, neither minds nor bodies; was I not, therefore, at the same time, persuaded that I did not exist? Far from it; I assuredly existed, since I was persuaded. But there is I know not what being, who is possessed at once of the highest power and the deepest cunning, who is constantly employing all his ingenuity in deceiving me. Doubtless, then, I exist, since I am deceived; and, let him deceive me as he may, he can never bring it about that I am nothing, so long as I shall be conscious that I am something. So that it must, in fine, be maintained, all things being maturely and carefully considered, that this proposition *(pronunciatum)* I am, I exist, is necessarily true each time it is expressed by me, or conceived in my mind.

. . .

But what, then, am I? A thinking thing, it has been said. But what is a thinking thing? It is a thing that doubts, understands, [conceives], affirms, denies, wills, refuses, that imagines also, and perceives. Assuredly it is not little, if all these properties belong to my nature. But why should they not belong to it? Am I not that very being who now doubts of almost everything; who, for all that, understands and conceives certain things; who affirms one alone as true, and denies the others; who desires to know more of them, and does not wish to be deceived; who imagines many things, sometimes even despite his will; and is likewise percipient of many, as if through the medium of the senses. Is there nothing of all this as true as that I am, even although I should be always dreaming, and although he who gave me being employed all his ingenuity to deceive me? Is there also any one of these attributes that can be properly distinguished from my thought, or that can be said to be separate from myself? For it is of itself so evident that it is I who doubt, I who understand, and I who desire, that it is here unnecessary to add anything by way of rendering it more clear. And I am as certainly the same being who imagines; for, although it may be (as I before supposed) that nothing I imagine is true, still the power of imagination does not cease really to exist in me and to form part of my thought. In fine, I am the same being who perceives, that is, who apprehends certain objects as by the organs of sense, since, in truth, I see light, hear a noise, and feel heat. But it will be said that these presentations are false, and that I am dreaming. Let it be so. At all events it is certain that I seem to see light, hear a noise, and feel heat; this cannot be false, and this is what in me is properly called perceiving *(sentire)*, which is nothing else than thinking. From this I begin to know what I am with somewhat greater clearness and distinctness than heretofore. . . .

. . .

. . . and, therefore, merely because I know with certitude that I exist, and because, in the meantime, I do not observe that aught necessarily belongs to my nature or essence beyond my being a thinking thing, I rightly conclude that my essence consists only in my being a thinking thing, [or a substance whose whole essence or nature is merely thinking]. And although I may, or rather, as I will shortly say, although I certainly do possess a body with which I am very closely conjoined; nevertheless, because, on the one hand, I have a clear and distinct idea of myself, in as far as I am only a thinking and unextended thing, and as, on the other hand, I possess a distinct idea of body, in as far as it is only an extended and unthinking thing, it is certain that I, [that is, my mind, by which I am what I am], is entirely and truly distinct from my body, and may exist without it.

.   .   .

Nature likewise teaches me by these sensations of pain, hunger, thirst, etc., that I am not only lodged in my body as a pilot in a vessel, but that I am besides so intimately conjoined, and as it were intermixed with it, that my mind and body compose a certain unity. For if this were not the case, I should not feel pain when my body is hurt, seeing I am merely a thinking thing, but should perceive the wound by the understanding alone, just as a pilot perceives by sight when any part of his vessel is damaged; and when my body has need of food or drink, I should have a clear knowledge of this, and not be made aware of it by the confused sensations of hunger and thirst: for, in truth, all these sensations of hunger, thirst, pain, etc., are nothing more than certain confused modes of thinking, arising from the union and apparent fusion of mind and body.

.   .   .

To commence this examination accordingly, I here remark . . . that there is a vast difference between mind and body, in respect that body, from its nature, is always divisible, and that mind is entirely indivisible. For in truth, when I consider the mind, that is, when I consider myself in so far only as I am a thinking thing, I can distinguish in myself no parts, but I very clearly discern that I am somewhat absolutely one and entire; and although the whole mind seems to be united to the whole body, yet, when a foot, an arm, or any other part is cut off, I am conscious that nothing has been taken from my mind; nor can the faculties of willing, perceiving, conceiving, etc., properly be called its parts, for it is the same mind that is exercised [all entire] in willing, in perceiving, and in conceiving, etc. But quite the opposite holds in corporeal or extended things; for I cannot imagine any one of them [how small soever it may be], which I cannot easily sunder in thought, and which, therefore, I do not know to be divisible. This would be sufficient to teach me that the mind or soul of man is entirely different from the body, if I had not already been apprised of it on other grounds.

.   .   .

I had expounded all these matters with sufficient minuteness in the Treatise which I formerly thought of publishing. And after these, I had shewn what must be the fabric of the nerves and muscles of the human body to give the animal spirits contained in it the power to move the members, as when we see heads shortly after they have been struck off still move and bite the earth, although no longer animated; what changes must take place in the brain to produce waking, sleep, and dreams; how light, sounds, odours, tastes, heat, and all the other qualities of external objects impress it with different ideas by means of the senses; how hunger, thirst, and the other internal affections can likewise impress upon it divers ideas; what must be understood by the common sense *(sensus communis)* in which these ideas are received, by the memory which retains them, by the fantasy which can change them in various ways, and out of them compose new ideas, and which, by the same means, distributing the animal spirits through the muscles, can cause the members of such a body to move in as many different ways, and in a manner as suited, whether to the objects that are presented to its senses or to its internal affections, as can take place in our own case apart from the guidance of the will. Nor will this appear at all strange to those who are acquainted with the variety of movements performed by the different automata, or moving machines fabricated by human industry, and that with help of but few pieces compared with the great multitude of bones, muscles, nerves, arteries, veins, and other parts that are found in the body of each animal. Such persons will look upon this body as a machine made by the hands of God, which is incomparably better arranged, and adequate to movements more admirable than is any machine of human invention. And here I specially stayed to show that, were there such machines exactly resembling in organs and outward form an ape or any other irrational animal, we could have no means of knowing that they were in any respect of a different nature from these animals; but if there were machines bearing the image of our bodies, and capable of imitating our actions as far as it is morally possible, there would still remain two most certain tests whereby to know that they were not therefore really men. Of these the first is that they could never use words or other signs arranged in such a manner as is competent to us in order to declare our thoughts to others: for we may easily conceive a machine to be so constructed that it emits vocables, and even that it emits some correspondent to the action upon it of external objects which cause a change in the organs; for example, if touched in a particular place it may demand what we wish to say to it; if in another it may cry out that it is hurt, and such like; but not that it should arrange them variously so as appositely to reply to what is said in its presence, as men of the lowest grade of intellect can do. The second test is that although such machines might execute many things with equal or perhaps greater perfection than any of us, they would, without doubt, fail in certain others from which it could be

discovered that they did not act from knowledge, but solely from the disposition of their organs: for while Reason is an universal instrument that is alike
available on every occasion, these organs, on the contrary, need a particular
arrangement for each particular action; whence it must be morally impossible
that there should exist in any machine a diversity of organs sufficient to enable
it to act in all the occurrences of life, in the way in which our reason enables
us to act. . . .

29

MARVIN L. MINSKY (1927– ———)

I Think, Therefore I Am

Marvin Minsky is professor of electrical engineering and director of the artificial
intelligence laboratory at the Massachusetts Institute of Technology. He is the author
of *Computation* (1967), *Semantic Information Processing* (1968), and *Perceptrons*
(with S. Papert, 1968).

Descartes had suggested that the human body might be looked upon as "a machine
made by the hands of God." Descartes was confident, however, that this body could
never be mistaken for a mere machine because (1) a machine could not produce
intelligent speech, and (2) a machine could not produce intelligent behavior.

Minsky challenges this argument in two ways. First, he suggests that the day is not
far off when our most advanced computers *will* behave intelligently, and when it will
be appropriate to call them intelligent for the same reasons that we call human beings
intelligent. Second, he holds that there is something inherent in the structure of
knowledge that makes it almost inevitable that the *self-concept* (or model of itself)
of anything that thinks (be it a human being or a computer) will be dualistic.

From Marvin Minsky, "I Think, Therefore I Am," *Psychology Today,* (April 1969), pp. 30–32.
Reprinted from *Psychology Today.* Copyright © 1969 Ziff-Davis Publishing Company.

I believe that we are on the threshold of an era that will be based on, and quite possibly dominated by, the activity of intelligent problem-solving machines.

Many people are skeptical about whether machines will ever be intelligent. Since people are intelligent, then the skeptics must be quite sure that they are not machines themselves. For example, Thomas J. Watson Jr. of IBM states that:

"Machines can perform arithmetic calculations with great rapidity. They can exercise prodigious feats of memory ... but ... no machine can understand the idea of liberty or recognize injustice or fight for human dignity." And Mortimer Taube, a specialist in documentation systems, argues that: "A program is a set of numbers in a certain order, and without human interpretation it remains only that. ..."

Certainly, the average person would say: "I don't feel like a machine." In this essay I am going to argue that this feeling is not a good guide. I could simply ask: "If you have never been a machine how could you know what it feels like?" But instead, I will show why certain kinds of machines will also say, "I don't feel like a machine," and suggest how our antipathy to the idea might be a by-product of a certain internal mechanism designed for another purpose.

Slowly, but (I am confident) surely we are devising programs that will make computers behave more and more intelligently. In many ways programs already pursue complex goals, use analogies, recognize patterns, and reason by making simplified models and then adapting them to the immediate problem. No single program yet does many of these things. But as these features are combined we will see increasingly resourceful and creative performances from our machines. I do not expect that we will find, in these programs of the future, any single principle, or "seat" of intelligence, for this will lie in the general quality of the organization—as in any successful administration. But I do think that much of such a machine's ability to deal with the real problems will be based on the use of "internal models"—structures built by the machine to embody its knowledge about itself, the world, and about methods that are helpful in achieving goals and subgoals.

At first we will have to build these models; later we should be able to give the machine methods it can use to set up models for itself. Self-improvement, after a point, should be regenerative and there is no reason to suppose (as many do) that machines will become almost as intelligent as man and then stop. But let us return to the idea of a model.

If the machine can answer a question about a hypothetical experiment without actually performing that experiment, then the answer must have been obtained from a sub-machine or model inside the machine. This internal model acts like the environment, and to the extent that the machine's own actions affect the environment, a good model will have to include some representation of the machine itself.

If we ask the machine an ordinary question about itself, such as how big it is, this can be answered directly by its internal model. But if we ask the machine a question about its own general nature, such as what sort of being it is, the answer will have to be made by the machine's model of its model. (A low-level machine will not have this model and will simply be unable to comprehend such a question.)

When a man inspects his own model, he usually concludes that it seems to be a dual thing: he has a "body" and a "mind." I will suggest a reason why this seems so, why it might reflect a useful mechanism, and why it might be difficult to avoid in machines. Briefly, it is hard to avoid dividing knowledge-structures into two main areas.

One area concerns *"mechanical,"* *geometrical,* and *physical* matters; the other deals with things like *goals, meanings* and *social interactions.* When we see an object we account for its mechanical support in the first domain—we ask who put it there and why in the second. Our language and thought have well-developed methods for each.

The two domains overlap, of course. The child finds mechanical limitations —in reach, mobility, strength—to psychological goals; he learns to connect postures with intentions, and emotions with the changing geometry of faces. (It is beside the point if some of these are "built-in.") But the domains are mainly separate. It could be otherwise only for a superpsychologist who has a reasonable model of how the brain works—and even then it would usually be most efficient not to use it in everyday life.

So my proposal is that a man's statement—indeed, his belief—that he has a mind and a body is just the conventional way to describe his dumbbell-shaped model of himself. And since this two-part form seems so terribly useful, we should not be surprised to find intelligent machines developing the same sort of dualistic belief-structure.

The idea that knowledge must be embedded in models also suggests why people are so insistent about their "freedom of will" yet are so extraordinarily unable to say anything sensible about it. My theory of this begins with the observation that in childhood we learn to recognize and dislike various forms of aggression and compulsion. We resent compulsion no matter from *whom,* whether we submit or resist. Later, when we learn that our behavior is con-trolled by such-and-such a set of laws, we insert this fact in our social model (inappropriately) along with other threats of compulsion.

In areas where we don't know the rules, we could fill in by postulating random or chance activity. But this leads only to a more subtle indignity of external control. We resolve this unpleasantness by postulating a third part of the model—which we call *will* or *spirit* or *conscious agent.* Naturally, we can't say anything meaningful about it: any regularity that we understand is promptly transferred to another part of the model. The "will" box is con-structed with an automatic emptying device, precisely so that it will contain no rules. Now, if we do not know that this is happening—that is, if it is not represented in our model of our model—it is no wonder that we are so perplexed when we ask ourselves questions about it and have every proposed answer neatly snatched away.

Unless we take steps to prevent it, there is no reason that intelligent machines will not follow the same path, and come to believe that they, too, have "free will."

When this happens, man will find his machines are as confused and as stubborn as he is in their convictions about mind-matter, consciousness, and free will, unless they are equipped with a satisfactory theory of intelligence.

As you can see, I believe that the "mind-body problem" is not so much an elusive and difficult philosophical problem as it is an elusive and difficult engineering problem. In the years ahead I hope that we will develop powerful technical and analytical tools for the theory of intelligent machines and their knowledge-structures.

But even now, I think we may be beginning to see why people have had so much trouble with these questions in the past.

30

HOWARD W. HINTZ (1903–1964)

Whitehead's Concept of Organism and the Mind-Body Problem

Howard Hintz spent virtually his entire life in New York City. He was born in Brooklyn, received his education at City College of New York, Columbia University, and New York University, and was on the Brooklyn College faculty almost continuously from 1930 to 1963. His lifelong interest in theology, literature, and philosophy resulted in the publication of books and articles in all three fields. His best-known book in philosophy is *Philosophy and the Social Order* (1960).

Hintz argues that the alleged similarity between advanced computers and the human brain has no relevance to the mind-body problem, because the problem concerns the relationship between *mind* and body, not *brain* and body. Minds can create brain-like machines, but they cannot create mind-like machines. Therefore, all talk about artificial intelligence is irrelevant.

What, then is the relationship between *mind* and body? The answer, Hintz argues, is to be found in A. N. Whitehead's view of nature; that is, it is a process in which mind and matter are inextricably interwoven *at every level* (and not limited to humans). All natural processes are mental as well as physical. Wherever anything exists, mind, as well as matter, is present. The mind-body problem is the problem that results when one makes the mistake, like Descartes, of separating mind from matter and then trying to figure out how to get them together again. When this mistake is eliminated, Hintz claims, the problem disappears.

It is my contention that the solution of the mind-body problem (to the extent that it *is* a "problem" and to the extent that it can be "solved") will never be reached if it is sought solely within the naturalistic-scientific framework and by the investigation of empirical data alone. It is my further contention that a much more fruitful approach to the problem, and one offering much greater promise of clarifying rather than confusing the issues is the approach suggested by Whitehead and his concept of "organism."

Before indicating more specifically the applications of Whitehead's theories to this problem I should like to suggest certain unique properties of "mind" as distinguished from "brain" which are of the utmost importance in any consideration of either mind-body or mind-machine relationship.

Briefly stated, the crucial question, then, is this: Could any brain-machine or group of machines carry on the type of discussion which has produced the present book? This leads to a host of corollary questions involving feeling, volition, curiosity, aspiration, evaluation, etc. What would be the machines' purposes and desires? What would be their incentives and objective? What manner of *self-consciousness* would the machines possess which would enable them to attach value to or to derive satisfaction from their enterprises? In what sense would they *feel* a sense of frustration, success, failure, achievement, or self-satisfaction? And let it be remembered and emphasized that "thought" in relation to these "states of mind" is inseparable from feeling and that to this extent mind is inseparable from the body which *includes* the brain.

The underlying fallacy of the conventional and traditional "naturalistic" approach to the mind-body problem is indeed graphically exposed by the very introduction of the "brain-machine" issue into the discussion. I contend that the brain-machine has no relevance to the philosophical question confronting us and that the investigation and discovery of mechanical or physical parallels between brain activity and brain-machine activity can throw no significant light on the issue. For the problem, let it be remembered, is not and never has been the brain-body relationship, but the *mind-body* relationship. The machine does indeed bear striking and startling resemblances to the human brain in terms of certain types of processes, functions, and activities. But it bears little or no resemblance to the *mind.* At best and at most, the brain-machine is an extension, however ingeniously contrived, of the human brain. But it is not primarily a creation of the brain. It is essentially a creation of the human mind, which, having willed to create it, created it, and which, should it will to destroy it, can also destroy it. Study of machine-brain and human-brain resemblances might disclose information of importance to the physician or to the brain physiologist. It is extremely doubtful whether such study can reveal anything important to the psychologist, for his concerns are much more with the mind than with that physical organ known as the brain.

The point to be stressed, of course, is the uniqueness of those qualities of the human entity that are identified with mind and that, although they involve the brain, also involve many other parts and elements of the human organism and that have traditionally been associated with such etymologically-related and synonymous terms as "spirit" and "soul." Thus the non-rational forms of thought and behavior are as fully embraced by the concept of mind as are the rational forms. Therefore, as has been noted, feeling (even more than thought), and the unconscious and irrational activities of the *brain,* as well as the rational and conscious activities, are represented by the term "mind." Now it is precisely that kind of "thinking" which is most closely associated with feeling—with pain and sorrow, love, hate, aspiration, purpose, and above all valuing and evaluation—it is that kind of thinking which the machine-brain does not do. Hence we need not be at all concerned about that absurd fear expressed by Dr. Wiener that the brain-machine may some day control men. Here is the Frankenstein fantasy all over again, but this time on the part of a man who is strangely confusing the mechanical brains he has helped to create with the "minds" which conceived them, built them, and must continue to operate or "prepare" them. Surely Dr. Wiener does not want to fall into the Cartesian error of believing that he can locate and install some "soul" object into the brain-machine, albeit an electronic or mechanical one! No one, I submit, who understands the true nature of the mind-body problem could possibly be misled by the false analogy between either the human mind and the brain-machine, or for that matter between the human brain and the machine-brain.

Observe what has now happened as a result of this confusion. The scientific-naturalist who is foremost among those who will admit of no separation of mind and body, now unwittingly makes that separation complete by endowing the non-human and hence disembodied machine with those attributes of mind that would presumably enable it to operate independently, not only of human minds, but of a biophysical body. Thus has the naturalist-physicist disembodied a mind and given it non-bodily existence. This, I suggest is indeed *meta*-physics in a new dimension, and in itself a complete refutation of the premise of mind-body inseparability. I submit further that if the inseparability premise negates the possibility of the separate and independent existence of "mind" in the traditional metaphysical or religious senses, it also negates it in every other sense. For either mind is separable from body or it is not. Whichever way it turns out, the *fact* will apply right down the line. If there cannot be disembodied minds invisibly floating about in the ether, there cannot be disembodied "minds" (or even "brains" except in a highly metaphorical sense) in the form of electronic monsters.

We return then to the essential *philosophical* problems on which the mechanical investigations, whether they take the form of noting resemblances between calculating machines and human brains or of measuring electrical brain impulses, have shed little or no light. In its traditional form, the problem can be simply stated. Are mind and body two separate and distinct entities? Can "soul," "spirit," "mind," exist independently of the physical body as we know it? Is reality monistic or is it dualistic, containing two separate life elements to be roughly designated as the physical and the spiritual, the "natural" and the "supernatural"?

The confusions about the issue revealed by scientists as noted above are indeed paralleled by similar confusions long prevalent among theologians and among philosophers of all stamps—metaphysicians and philosophers of science, empiricists *and* rationalists, naturalists and idealists. The confusion is, perhaps, inevitable, as Whitehead suggests, and due to a failure to understand the nature of the problem, or, to put it more precisely, the failure to recognize that it is not a real problem at all, but a pseudoproblem. Once reality is seen as "process" and nature as "organism," the problem disappears.

Keeping within the naturalistic-empirical restrictions of "evidence" (as Whitehead does), a few basic conclusions about the mind-body relationship can be drawn:

1. Mind, as far as we have any *direct* knowledge of this entity, is in its natural-human manifestations, inseparably associated with and dependent upon the physical organism known as body. If mind has any other form or kind of existence in a non-physical or non-corporeal realm we have no acceptable evidence to establish such existence.

2. We have no real knowledge of the source, cause, origin, or essential nature of those activities or phenomena (seemingly centered in the brain) which are most exclusively associated with mind, and especially with the human mind—namely, qualities of *feeling,* such as emotional states, moral and aesthetic evaluation, the search for meaning, etc. The activities of glands and other physical organs under the stimulation of emotional or mental states may be as much *effects* of these states as causes. (Does the adrenal secretion induce my fear or does my fear induce the secretion?) It is a mistake to say that fear

or any other emotional state is ever either purely mental or purely physical. It is always, invariably and necessarily, both.

3. Mind and body are equally part of the natural order. In other words, mental phenomena of all types are as much a part of natural-physical phenomena as are earthquakes, floods, electromagnetism, gravitation, the color of grass, the web of the spider, and the birth and death of organisms.

4. All theoretical explanations of mental and spiritual phenomena which extend beyond the realm of the natural and empirically demonstrable are to the present moment untested and unproved. At best, they might be described as symbolic or poetic representations of natural reality. Whitehead, following Hume on this point, insists that scientific "explanations," like metaphysical ones, have never approached the determination of ultimate causality. "Causal nature," says Whitehead, "is a metaphysical chimera."

5. To sum up, nature cannot be "bifurcated" by making a separation between the green which the mind perceives and the molecules which produce the green. We do not, maintains Whitehead, "explain" the natural phenomena by saying that they exist in the mind. They exist in the objects as well as in the mind.

The most satisfactory solution to the mind-body problem would seem to me to be found along the lines thus indicated by Whitehead. It is to be found in the concept of organism which removes the "problem" simply because it permits of no essential dichotomy in reality. Mind is as much a part of nature as is body. We cannot even legitimately refer to them as separate entities. They are types of phenomena resulting equally from the operation of molecules which meet in time and space. Indeed, the question of ultimate causation is beyond our reach, but the point too often missed is that the so-called physical phenomena are as much beyond our reach in terms of ultimate causation or complete comprehension as are the so-called mental or spiritual phenomena.

In a germinal passage in *The Concept of Nature* Whitehead has this to say about the "bifurcation" fallacy:

> [The] theory which I am arguing against is to bifurcate nature into two divisions, namely into the nature apprehended in awareness and the nature which is the cause of awareness. The nature which is the fact apprehended in awareness holds within it the greenness of the trees, the song of the birds, the warmth of the sun, the hardness of the chairs, and the feel of the velvet. The nature which is the cause of awareness is the conjectured system of molecules and electrons which so affects the mind as to produce the awareness of apparent nature. The meeting point of these two natures is the mind. . . .

In another section Whitehead makes some observations particularly relevant to the type of approach to the mind-body relationship engaged in by empirical scientists in various disciplines.

The modern account of nature is not, as it should be, merely an account of what the mind knows of nature; but it is also confused with an account of what nature does to the mind. *The result has been disastrous to both science and to philosophy, but chiefly to philosophy.* It has transformed the grand question of the relation between nature and mind into the petty form of the interaction between the human body and mind (my italics).

Why is this mistaken approach a disaster to science? Because it has led scientists to probe into realms beyond their legitimate scope and to speculate upon questions to which they do not and cannot have the tools for deriving precise and empirically-demonstrated answers. The error is in part due to the acceptance of unproved premises regarding the *limitations* of natural phenomena, and in part to the resultant confusion, already discussed at some length, about some presumed and hypothetical "bifurcation" between natural and mental phenomena—both of which may more likely be different aspects of the same fundamental natural reality and therefore not organically separable.

Another way of stating the issue is by suggesting that a basic fallacy may be involved in talking about mind and body, or about mind and external nature, as though they were separate entities or entailed separate kinds of realities. In the philosophy of organism, *all* of nature (not just the fraction of it which is animate) is infected with mind, just as all of mind is infected with body. Once we get rid of the stubborn and conventional notion that there is external reality on the one hand, and internal, perceptual reality on the other hand, as two different kinds of reality, the mind-body "problem" literally vanishes. In the concept of organism, all phenomena are of one piece. All *natural* processes are as well mental processes of a sort. To put it still another way, all "natural" or physical processes partake of mental events, and all mental processes involve physical events. If mind permeates the whole of reality the existence of it in animate objects does not differentiate these objects in kind from any other natural phenomena, but only in degree.

Why is this erroneous bifurcation a "disaster to philosophy"?—Because in Whitehead's words, it has transformed the "grand question" (by which he means the *philosophical* question) into the petty form of the "interaction between the *human body* and mind." This is the scientist's problem, properly narrow and essentially manageable in scope. But the philosophers have been deluded into believing that this also constitutes the nature and limits of the philosophical problem. But note: the "grand question" is the relation between nature and mind—the mind in nature, and the nature in mind—which is a very different question from that which merely involves the interaction between individual human bodies and individual human minds.

One further significant aspect of the "disaster" to which Whitehead refers involves metaphysics. We are confronted with the paradoxical situation in which the scientists draw broad metaphysical inferences from their limited study of mind-body interactions, while the philosophers either accept these inferences without careful scrutiny of their foundations, or reject the inferences and refuse to engage in further metaphysical inquiries of their own. Whitehead states at one point: "... any metaphysical interpretation is an illegitimate importation into the philosophy of natural science.... [The Philosophy of Science] is the philosophy of the thing perceived and is not to be confused with the metaphysics of reality of which the scope embraces both perceiver and perceived."

Thus the so-called "mind-body" problem as it continues to be posed and discussed implies and assumes not only that nature is somehow bifurcated but that reality as a whole is in some sense divided or separated as well. Those who refuse to accept this bifurcation on naturalistic or scientific grounds tend to eliminate the dualism by reducing reality to the physical and material, and by somehow rendering the mental or spiritual aspects of reality subservient to, or dependent upon, or derivative from, the physical-material. The reverse may just as likely be true. The philosophy of organism, however, would permit of no such discrimination, simply on the grounds that there is no empirical or rational evidence to support it. All reality as *process* partakes equally and interdependently of both phenomena.

Certain theologians, metaphysicians, and non-naturalistic philosophers, on the other hand, tend to resolve the supposed dilemma by rejecting altogether the depreciation and subjugation of the mental to the physical-material realm. They accept a metaphysical rather than a naturalistic bifurcation concept by returning to the ancient and traditional dichotomy between "Body" and "Soul" regarded as two separate entities or realities. And in returning to this solution they are of course laying themselves open to all of the traditional and familiar strictures of naturalism, empiricism, and logical analysis.

The philosophy of organism in denying the very validity of the dichotomy on strictly naturalistic and empirical, as well as on rationalistic grounds, removes the necessity for reducing all reality to physical and material entities. It also renders unnecessary, as an alternative, the acceptance of logically and empirically untenable dualisms. It simply removes the dilemma by revealing it not to have been a real dilemma in the first place. Moreover, it opens the way for potentially fruitful inquiries on the part of both scientists and philosophers into the nature of a reality which, while remaining wholly within the frame of naturalism, is as much Mind as it is Matter and in which neither can conceivably exist or operate without the other.

31

HERBERT FEIGL (1902– ————)

The Identity Theory

Herbert Feigl was a member of the Vienna Circle, a group of philosophers who initiated an influential movement in modern philosophy known as logical empiricism. Feigl later came to the United States, where, for many years, he was professor of philosophy at the University of Minnesota and director of the Minnesota Center for the Philosophy of Science. He has written on a wide variety of philosophical topics, especially on those relating to the philosophy of science.

The essay that follows is a compact statement of identity materialism. Mind *is* brain, according to Feigl. The mind-body problem arises because we have two different languages—the language of subjective experience ("phenomenal") and the language of objective description ("neurophysiological")—to describe the same single reality. The *sense* meaning of "He is weighing alternatives" is quite different from the *sense* meaning of "Certain microelectrical processes are occurring in his brain," but the *state of affairs* that is being described—what Feigl calls the "referent"—is one and the same.

Feigl's view should not be confused with *epiphenomenalism*. This view, which Feigl attempts to refute, affirms that bodily processes cause effects in minds, but minds do not cause effects in bodies. Physical events (including the behavior of human beings) are caused entirely by antecedent physical events, but these events may also create superfluous side effects, in the form of feelings or awarenesses, that have no effect on subsequent events. One way to read the following essay, then, would be to understand the epiphenomenalist view, then consider what Feigl finds deficient in the theory and, finally, note the ways in which Feigl's own view differs from epiphenomenalism.

. . . .

The crucial and central puzzle of the mind-body problem, at least since Descartes, has consisted in the challenge to render an adequate account of the relation of the "raw feels," as well as of other mental facts (intentions, thoughts, volitions, desires, etc.) to the corresponding neurophysiological pro-cesses. The problems may fairly clearly be divided into scientific and philo-sophical components. The scientific task is pursued by psychophysiology, *i.e.*, an exploration of the empirically ascertainable correlations of "raw feels," phenomenal patterns, etc., with the events and processes in the organism, especially in its central nervous system (if not in the cerebral cortex alone). The philosophical task consists in a logical and epistemological clarification of the concepts by means of which we may formulate and/or interpret those correla-tions.

Scientifically, the most plausible view to date is that of a one-one (or at least a one-many) correspondence of mental states to neurophysiological process-patterns. The investigations of Wolfgang Köhler, E. D. Adrian, W. Penfield, D. O. Hebb, W. S. McCulloch, *et al.,* strongly confirm such a correspondence in the form of an isomorphism of the patterns in the phenomenal fields with the simultaneous patterns of neural processes in various areas of the brain. The philosopher must of course regard this isomorphism as empirically establisha-ble or refutable, and hence as *logically* contingent. It is conceivable that further empirical evidence may lead the psychophysiologists to abandon or to modify this view which on the whole has served so well at least as a fruitful working hypothesis. It is conceivable that some of the as yet more obscure psy-chosomatic phenomena or possibly the still extremely problematic and contro-versial "facts" of parapsychology will require emergentist or even interactionistic explanations. (As an empiricist I must at least go through the motions of an "open mind" in these regards!) But tentatively assuming isomor-phism of some sort, a hypothesis which is favored by many "naturalistic" philosophers, are we then to interpret it philosophically along the lines of traditional epiphenomenalism? Although Professor Köhler does not commit himself expicitly to this view, I am practically certain that this is the general outlook within which he operates. If the basic physical laws of the universe should be sufficient for the derivation of biological and neurophysiological regularities, if the occurrence of neural patterns (physical *Gestalten*) is not a case of genuine emergent novelty but a matter of the combination of more elementary physical configurations, and if, finally, the experiential patterns correspond in some way isomorphically to neural process patterns, then this *is* epiphenomenalism in modern dress.

It will be best here not to use the somewhat ambiguous label "parallelism." Psychophysiological parallelism, as held by some thinkers in an earlier period, allowed for a "mental causality" to correspond to "physical (*i.e.,* neurophysio-logical) causality." Sometimes it even connoted an all-pervasive correspon-dence of mental and physical attributes (in the manner of Spinoza), and thus amounted to a form of panpsychism. But the favored outlook of modern psychophysiology amounts to postulating causal relations, *i.e.,* dynamic func-tional dependencies only on the physical side, and then to connect the neural process patterns merely by laws of (simultaneous) coexistence or co-occurrence with the corresponding mental states. Only a small subset of neural processes is thus accompanied by mental processes.

Traditionally the most prominent objection to epiphenomenalism has been the argument from the "efficacy of consciousness." We seem to know from our direct experience that moods, pleasure, displeasure, pain, attention, vigilance, intention, deliberation, choice, etc., make a difference in the ensuing behavior. But, of course, this subjective impression of the causal relevance and efficacy of mental states can easily be explained by the epiphenomenalist: Since, *ex hypothesi,* some dynamically relevant physical conditions are invariably accompanied by mental states, there is, then, also a regular occurrence of certain types of behavior (or of intra-organismic events) consequent upon mental states. For empiricists holding an essentially Humean conception of causality, it is then quite permissible in this sense to speak of the causal efficacy of mental states. There are, it should be noted, countless highly "teleological" processes that occur in our organism evidently without the benefit of any mental influence, guidance, or instigation. For example, the kinds of regenerations and restitutions that are involved in recoveries from many types of physical injury or disease appear as if they were most cleverly "designed," yet for many of these phenomena purely physiological (and perhaps ultimately physiochemical) explanations are available. Yet according to the epiphenomenalistic doctrine such explanations are sufficient also for behavior which we ordinarily consider instigated, regulated, or modulated by mental factors. If an effort of concentration facilitates learning algebra, piano playing, or the like, then consciousness cannot be regarded as a causally irrelevant or superfluous "luxury." I don't think we need to apologize for arguments of this sort. It is true, radical Materialists and Behaviorists reject such arguments as "tender-minded," but then radical Materialism or Behaviorism typically *represses* or *evades* the mind-body problem. They do not offer a genuine solution. Epiphenomenalism, while not evading the problem, offers a very queer solution. It accepts two fundamentally different sorts of laws—the usual causal laws and laws of psychophysiological correspondence. The physical (causal) laws connect the events in the physical world in the manner of a complex network, while the correspondence laws involve relations of physical events with purely mental "danglers." These correspondence laws are peculiar in that they may be said to postulate "effects" (mental states as dependent variables) which by themselves do not function, or at least do not seem to be needed, as "causes" (independent variables) for any observable behavior.

Laws of concomitance in the physical world could usually be accounted for in terms of underlying *identical* structures. Thus, for example, the correspondence of certain optical, electrical, and magnetic properties of various substances, as expressed in simple functional relations between the refraction index, the dielectric constant, and the magnetic permeability, is explainable on the basis of the atomic structure of those substances. Or, to take a slightly different example, it is in terms of a theory of *one* (unitary) electric current that we explain the thermal, chemical, magnetic, and optical effects which may severally or jointly be used in an "operational definition" of the intensity of the current. Similarly, it is at least a partially successful working program of psychophysiology to reduce certain correlated macrobehavioral features to underlying identical neurophysiological structures and processes. It should be emphasized, however, that a further step is needed if we are to overcome the dualism in the epiphenomenalist interpretation of the correlation of subjective mental states with brain states.

The classical attempts in the direction of such unification or of a monistic solution are well known: double-aspect, double-knowledge, twofold-access, or double-language doctrines have been proposed in various forms. The trouble with most of these is that they rely on vague metaphors or analogies and that it is extremely difficult to translate them into straightforward language. I can here only briefly indicate the lines along which I think the "world knot"—to use Schopenhauer's striking designation for the mind-body puzzles—may be disentangled. The indispensable step consists in a critical reflection upon the meanings of the terms "mental" and "physical," and along with this a thorough clarification of such traditional philosophical terms as "private" and "public," "subjective" and "objective," "psychological space(s)" and "physical space," "intentionality," "purposiveness," etc. The solution that appears most plausible to me, and that is entirely consistent with a thoroughgoing naturalism, is an *identity theory* of the mental and the physical, as follows: Certain neurophysiological terms denote (refer to) the very same events that are also denoted (referred to) by certain phenomenal terms. The identification of the objects of this twofold reference is of course logically contingent, although it constitutes a very fundamental feature of our world as we have come to conceive it in the modern scientific outlook. Utilizing Frege's distinction between *Sinn* ("meaning," "sense," "intension") and *Bedeutung* ("referent," *"denotatum,"* "extension"), we may say that neurophysiological terms and the corresponding phenomenal terms, though widely differing in *sense,* and hence in the modes of confirmation of statements containing them, do have identical *referents.* I take these referents to be the immediately experienced qualities, or their configurations in the various phenomenal fields.

Well-intentioned critics have tried to tell me that this is essentially the metaphysics of panpsychism. To this I can only reply: (1) If this be metaphysics, make the least of it!; (2) It is not panpsychism at all—either the "pan" or the "psyche" has to be deleted in the formulation. By way of very brief and unavoidably crude and sketchy comments let me explain my view a little further. The transition from the Logical Positivism of the Vienna Circle to the currently prevalent form of Logical Empiricism, as I interpret it, involved a complete emancipation from radical phenomenalism, behaviorism, operationism and their all-too-restrictive criteria of factual meaningfulness. Parallel with the critique of philosophical doubt by the Neo-Wittgensteinians, Logical

Empiricists nowadays have no patience with skeptical questions regarding the existence of physical objects or of other minds. "Skeptical doubts" of these sorts are illegitimate not because the beliefs in question are incapable of confirmation or disconfirmation, but because doubts of this pervasive character would call into question the very principles of confirmation and disconfirmation that underlie all empirical inquiry—both on the level of commonsense and on that of science. There can be no question that assertions of the existence of stars and atoms, or of the occurrence of conscious and unconscious mental processes, are subject to the normal procedures of inductive, analogical, or hypothetico-deductive confirmation or disconfirmation. It is preposterous (not to say philosophically perverse or naughty) to deny that we have well-confirmed knowledge concerning imperceptible physical objects or concerning the mental states of other human beings. A mature epistemology can make explicit the principles of such, often highly indirect, confirmations or disconfirmations. And along with this a liberalized meaning-criterion can be formulated, broad enough to include whatever is needed by way of commonsense or scientific hypotheses, and yet sufficiently restrictive to exclude transcendent metaphysical (pseudo-)beliefs. Freed from the torments of philosophical doubt and from the associated reductive tendencies and fallacies of phenomenalism as well as of radical behaviorism, we can now with a good intellectual conscience embrace a genuinely critical and empirical realism.

Once this position is attained, a mind-body-identity theory of the kind sketched above appears as the most adequate interpretation of all the relevant facts and considerations. This is not panpsychism for the simple reason that nothing in the least like a psyche is ascribed to lifeless matter, and certainly at most something very much less than a psyche is ascribed to plants or lower animals. The panpsychists claimed to reason by analogy, but this is precisely what they did not do in fact. The difference between the nervous system of, say, an earthworm and of a human being is so tremendous that we should in all consistency assume a correspondingly large difference in their respective mental states. And even on the human level there is no need whatever for the assumption of a psyche in the traditional sense of a soul that could act upon the brain, let alone be separable from it. One may, of course, doubt whether a purely Humean conception of the *self* (as a bundle and succession of direct data) will be sufficient for an adequate psychology. Nevertheless no substantial entity is required. Events, processes, and their properly defined organization and integration, should be perfectly sufficient. Professor Stephen C. Pepper suggested to me in conversation that my view might be labeled "pan-quality-ism." While this locution is not pleasant to the ear, it does come much closer to a correct characterization than "panpsychism." But since Paul E. Meehl, who understands my view at least as thoroughly as does Professor Pepper, has designated me a "materialist," perhaps one last word of elucidation may be in order.

I am indeed in agreement with one main line of traditional materialism in that I assume, as does Professor Köhler, that the basic *laws* of the universe are the *physical* ones. But (and this is so brief and crude a formulation that I fear I shall be misunderstood again) this does not commit me in the least as to the nature of the *reality* whose regularities are formulated in the physical laws. This reality is known to us by acquaintance only in the case of our direct experience which, according to my view, is the referent also of certain neurophysiological concepts. And if we are realists in regard to the physical world, we must assume that the concepts of theoretical physics, to the extent that they are instantialized in particulars, are not merely calculational devices for the prediction of observational data, but that they denote realities which are unknown by acquaintance, but which may in some way nevertheless be not entirely discontinuous with the qualities of direct experience. But—"whereof we cannot speak, thereof we must be silent." If this is metaphysics, it seems to me entirely innocuous. I have little sympathy with the mysticism of Eddington or the psychovitalism of Bergson. I reject the former because there is literally nothing that can be responsibly said in a phenomenal language about qualities that do not fall within the scope of acquaintance. Extrapolation will carry us at most to the concepts of unconscious wishes, urges or conflicts as postulated by such "depth-psychologies" as psychoanalysis. And even here, future scientific developments may be expected to couch these concepts much more fruitfully in the language of neurophysiology and endocrinology. And I reject psychovitalism because it involves dualistic interaction. At the very best "intuition" (empathetic imagination) may be heuristically helpful in that it can suggest scientific hypotheses in psychology (possibly even in biology), but these suggestions are extremely precarious, and hence must always be relentlessly scrutinized in the light of objective evidence.

Does the identity theory simplify our conception of the world? I think it does. Instead of conceiving of two realms or two concomitant types of events, we have only one reality which is represented in two different conceptual systems—on the one hand, that of physics and, on the other hand, where applicable (in my opinion only to an extremely small part of the world) that of phenomenological psychology. I realize fully that the simplification thus achieved is a matter of *philosophical* interpretation. For a synoptic, coherent account of the relevant facts of perception, introspection, and psychosomatics, and of the logic of theory-construction in the physical sciences, I think that the identity view is preferable to any other proposed solution of the mind-body problem. Call my view metaphysical if you must; I would rather call it *metascientific,* in the sense that it is the result of a comprehensive reflection on the *results* of science as well as on the logic and epistemology of scientific *method.* But I admit that for the ordinary purposes of psychology, psychophysiology, and psychiatry an epiphenomenalist position is entirely adequate, if only the traditional, picturesque but highly misleading locutions (*e.g.*, "substantial material reality and its shadowy mental accompaniments") are carefully avoided.

I conclude that the mind-body problem is not a pseudoproblem. There are, first, a great many genuine but unanswered questions in psychophysiology. And, secondly, there is plenty of work left for philosophers in the logical analysis of the intricate relations between phenomenal and physical terms. Problems of this complexity cannot be relegated to the limbo of nonsensical questions. I doubt quite generally whether many issues in modern epistemology can be simply "dissolved" in the manner in which some artificially concocted pseudoproblems can be disposed of by a minimum of reflection on the proper use of terms. Questions like "How fast does Time flow?", "Do we really see physical objects?", "Why is there anything at all rather than nothing?", "Why is the world the way it is?", etc., can indeed be very quickly shown to rest on elementary conceptual confusions. But the issues of perception, of reality, and of the mental and the physical require circumspect, perspicacious and painstaking analyses.

For Further Reading

Armstrong, D. M. *A Materialist Theory of the Mind.* London: Routledge and Kegan Paul, 1967.

Aune, Bruce. "Feelings, Moods, and Introspection," *Mind,* 72 (1963), 187–207.

————. "The Problem of Other Minds," *The Philosophical Review,* 70 (1961), 320–339.

Borowski, E. J. "Identity and Personal Identity," *Mind,* 85 (1976), 481–502.

Borst, C. V. *The Mind-Brain Identity Theory.* London: Macmillan, 1970 (paperbound). A collection of papers pro and con.

Broad, C. D. *The Mind and Its Place in Nature.* Paterson, N.J.: Littlefield, Adams, 1960, Chaps. 3 and 14 (paperbound).

Campbell, Keith. *Body and Mind.* Garden City, N.Y.: Doubleday, 1970 (paperbound). Contains a good bibliography.

Cornman, James W. *Materialism and Sensations.* New Haven, Conn.: Yale University Press, 1971. Defends an adverbial theory.

Dewey, John. *Experience and Nature.* LaSalle, Ill.: Open Court Publishing Co., 1958 (paperbound).

Dilman, I. *Matter and Mind.* London: Macmillan, 1975.

Ducasse, C. J. *Nature, Mind and Death.* LaSalle, Ill.: Open Court Publishing Co., 1951.

Evans, C. O. *The Subject of Consciousness.* London: G. Allen & Unwin, 1970.

Ewing, A. C. *The Fundamental Questions of Philosophy.* New York: Macmillan, 1951, Chap. 6.

Feigl, Herbert. *The "Mental" and the "Physical."* London: Oxford University Press, 1968 (paperbound).

————. "The Mind-Body Problem in the Development of Logical Empiricism," in M. Brodbeck and H. Feigl (eds.). *Readings in the Philosophy of Science.* New York: Appleton-Century-Crofts, 1953, pp. 612–626.

Grossman, Reinhardt. *The Structure of Mind.* Madison: University of Wisconsin Press, 1965. Detailed critique of arguments for phenomenalism from a realist perspective.

Hume, David. *A Treatise of Human Nature.* Many editions. See Book I. Section VI.

Joske, W. D. "Behaviorism as a Scientific Theory," *Philosophy and Phenomenological Research,* 22 (1961), 61–68.

Krikorian, Y. "A Naturalistic View of Mind," in Y. Krikorian (ed.). *Naturalism and the Human Spirit.* New York: Columbia University Press, 1944, pp. 242–269.

————. "The Publicity of Mind," *Philosophy and Phenomenological Research,* 22 (1962), 317–325.

Lachs, John. "Epiphenomenalism and the Notion of Cause," *The Journal of Philosophy,* 60 (1963), 141–146.

Laird, John. *Our Minds and Their Bodies.* London: Oxford University Press, 1925.

Laslett, Peter (ed.). *The Physical Basis of Mind.* Oxford: Basil Blackwell, 1951.

Lewis, H. D. *The Elusive Mind.* London: G. Allen & Unwin, 1970. Defends mind-body dualism against its major contemporary critics.

Locke, Don. *Myself and Others: A Study in Our Knowledge of Minds.* London: Oxford University Press, 1968. Current and lucid.

Malcom, Norman. "Knowledge of Other Minds," *The Journal of Philosophy,* 55 (1958), 969–978.

Mucciolo, L. F. "The Identity Theory and Critieria for the Mental," *Philosophy and Phenomenological Research,* 35 (1974–1975), 167–180. Examines the logic of the identity theory.

Nelson, R. J. "Mechanism, Functionalism, and the Identity Theory," *The Journal of Philosophy,* 73 (1976), 365–385.

O'Connor, John (ed.). *Modern Materialism: Readings on Mind-Body Identity.* New York: Harcourt, Brace & World, 1969. Useful bibliography.

Polten, E. P. *Critique of the Psycho-physical Identity Theory.* The Hague: Mouton, 1973. Attacks identity materialism as represented by Herbert Feigl.

Popper, K. R. "Some Remarks on Panpsychism and Epiphenomenalism," *Dialectica,* 31 (1977), 177–186. A critique of the two theories in the title.

Rosenthal, D. M. (ed.). *Materialism and the Mind-Body Problem,* Englewood Cliffs, N.J.: Prentice-Hall, 1971.

Russell, Bertrand, *The Analysis of Mind.* New York: Humanities Press, 1958.

Ryle, Gilbert. *The Concept of Mind.* New York: Barnes & Noble, 1965 (paperbound).

Shaffer, Jerome. "Could Mental States Be Brain Processes?" *The Journal of Philosophy,* 58 (1961), 813–822.

Skinner, B. F. *Science and Human Behavior.* New York: Macmillan, 1953. See "The Self," pp. 283–294.

Smart, J. J. C. *Philosophy and Scientific Realism.* New York: Humanities Press, 1963, Chap. 5. Defends identity materialism.

Smythies, J. R. (ed.). *Brain and Mind.* London: Routledge and Kegan Paul, 1965. A valuable collection of essays by various writers.

Spicker, Stuart F. (ed.). *The Philosophy of the Body.* New York: Quadrangle Books, 1970 (paperbound). Classical and contemporary selections.

Stevenson, L. "Mind, Brain and Mental Illness," *Philosophy,* 52 (1977), 27–43. Explores the psychiatric implications of materialist theories of mind.

Strawson, P. F. *Individuals.* Garden City, N.Y.: Doubleday, 1959, pp. 87–116.

Teichman, J. *The Mind and the Soul.* New York: Humanities Press, 1974. A short, well-written introduction to the mind-body problem.

Vesey, G. N. A. *The Embodied Mind.* London: G. Allen & Unwin, 1965. A Cartesian view in modern dress.

Wiggins, D. *Identity and Spatio-Temporal Continuity.* Oxford: Basil Blackwell, 1967.

Wilkerson, T. E. *Minds, Brains and People.* London: Oxford University Press, 1974. Critique of identity materialism, see especially Chap. 7.

Wisdom, John. *Other Minds.* New York: Philosophical Library, 1952.

——————. *Philosophy and Psychoanalysis.* New York: Philosophical Library, 1953.

——————. *Problems of Mind and Matter.* New York: Cambridge University Press, 1963 (paperbound).

Woodhouse, M. "A New Epiphenomenalism?" *Australasian Journal of Philosophy,* 52 (1974), 163–169. A critique of Keith Campbell's theory (see above).

PART VIII

Freedom and Determinism

The problem of freedom and determinism starts from the fact that we generally hold people responsible for their actions. The evidence supporting this is that we praise people for some actions and blame them for others. We use words such as "courageous," "self-sacrificing," and "noble" to describe actions we consider praiseworthy, "shameful," "cowardly," and "selfish" to describe actions that we consider blameworthy.

Only human beings are subject to moral praise or blame. We do not regard plants, insects, birds, or animals as appropriate candidates for moral appraisal. Why? The common-sense answer appears to be that we believe human beings to have freedom—a power of choice—that other creatures do not possess. Human beings appear to behave as they do because they *choose* to. When they choose to behave in a way that we approve of, we praise them. When they choose to behave in a way that we disapprove of, we blame them. It surely *seems* to be the case, then, that belief in human moral responsibility presupposes belief in freedom of choice.

Other considerations, however, tend to support a theory that appears to be in conflict with these beliefs. This theory is called *universal determinism*. Universal determinism maintains that every event in the universe—including, therefore, every action of every human being—is the theoretically predictable consequence of antecedent causes. Human beings may have the illusion of free choice—they may believe that they choose among alternatives—but, according to this theory, their actions are as determined as are all other events in the universe. An omniscient observer (if one existed) could predict exactly where you will be and what you will be doing at any future moment, just as astronomers can predict the exact time of the next solar eclipse. Such a prediction is theoretically possible because your behavior, and that of all of the elements in your environment that may influence your behavior, is strictly determined by the various forces that will produce that behavior. Everything that happens, including the minutest details of a person's behavior, happens according to the laws of nature.

The problem of freedom and determinism is the problem of the apparent conflict between the belief in the moral responsibility and freedom of human beings and the belief that the universe is strictly ordered. The problem might be stated thus: Is the freedom that is a condition of moral responsibility indeed incompatible with universal determinism, and if so, which is the case?

This question can be answered in three ways. One way is to say, "Yes, the two are incompatible, and determinism is the case; therefore, human beings are not free and not morally responsible." This view is called *hard determinism*.

The second possible answer is, "Yes, the two are incompatible, but human beings are morally responsible and free in the way required to render them morally responsible; therefore, universal determinism is not the case." This view is called *libertarianism*.

Finally, it is possible to argue that the freedom that is a condition of moral responsibility is compatible with universal determinism. In this view, it is possible to affirm the moral freedom and responsibility of human beings even though universal determinism is true. This view is called *soft determinism* or *compatibilism*.

Note well: both soft determinists and hard determinists are determinists. Both affirm that determinism is true without exception, that *every* event in the universe (including every action of every human being) is the theoretically predictable consequence of antecedent causes. The difference between them is that the hard determinist draws the "hard" conclusion that human beings are not morally responsible, while the soft determinist draws the "soft" conclusion that they are, nonetheless, morally responsible.

To reject determinism—to affirm that there are some events in the universe that are not the theoretically predictable consequences of antecedent causes—is to adopt the theory of *indeterminism*. Again, note well: indeterminism is simply the view that *some* events in the universe are exempt from universal causation. Libertarians are, therefore, obliged to affirm indeterminism (that is, to reject universal determinism). They are not, however, obliged to affirm the patently absurd view that the universe is an utter chaos.

32

JOHN STUART MILL (1806–1873)

Necessity and Moral Freedom

John Stuart Mill was an articulate spokesman for *soft determinism.* What Mill calls "the doctrine of Necessity"—the view that "human volitions and actions are necessary and inevitable"—is simply determinism applied to human behavior. According to this theory, which Mill endorses, a person's behavior is always the theoretically predictable product of that person's character. "If we knew the person thoroughly," Mill writes, "and knew all the inducements which are acting upon him, we could foretell his conduct with as much certainty as we can predict any physical event."

Does it follow, then, that human beings are not responsible for their behavior? No, replies Mill, for here there is no *coercion* or *compulsion.* We are responsible for our actions insofar as we do what we want to do. The question of why we want to do this or that—why we are the kind of person we are—does not enter the picture at all. Thus, says Mill, the "feeling of being free," which everyone has most of the time, is not a feeling of having a *free will* that is wholly exempt from the causal nexus, but the awareness of being under no compulsion to act as one does. (See p. 95 for a biographical note on John Stuart Mill.)

---

1. THE question, whether the law of causality applies in the same strict sense to human actions as to other phenomena, is the celebrated controversy concerning the freedom of the will: which, from at least as far back as the time of Pelagius, has divided both the philosophical and the religious world. The affirmative opinion is commonly called the doctrine of Necessity, as asserting human volitions and actions to be necessary and inevitable. The negative maintains that the will is not determined, like other phenomena, by antecedents, but determines itself; that our volitions are not, properly speaking, the effects of causes, or at least have no causes which they uniformly and implicitly obey.

I have already made it sufficiently apparent that the former of these opinions is that which I consider the true one; but the misleading terms in which it is

From John Stuart Mill, *A System of Logic,* 5th ed., Volume II, Book VI, Chapter II (London: Parker, Son & Brown, 1862), pp. 413–421.

often expressed, and the indistinct manner in which it is usually apprehended, have both obstructed its reception, and perverted its influence when received. The metaphysical theory of free will, as held by philosophers, (for the practical feeling of it, common in a greater or less degree to all mankind, is in no way inconsistent with the contrary theory,) was invented because the supposed alternative of admitting human actions to be *necessary*, was deemed inconsistent with every one's instinctive consciousness, as well as humiliating to the pride and even degrading to the moral nature of man. Nor do I deny that the doctrine, as sometimes held, is open to these imputations; for the misapprehension in which I shall be able to show that they originate, unfortunately is not confined to the opponents of the doctrine, but participated in by many, perhaps we might say by most, of its supporters.

2. Correctly conceived, the doctrine called Philosophical Necessity is simply this: that, given the motives which are present to an individual's mind, and given likewise the character and disposition of the individual, the manner in which he will act may be unerringly inferred: that if we knew the person thoroughly, and knew all the inducements which are acting upon him, we could foretell his conduct with as much certainty as we can predict any physical event. This proposition I take to be a mere interpretation of universal experience, a statement in words of what every one is internally convinced of. No one who believed that he knew thoroughly the circumstances of any case, and the characters of the different persons concerned, would hesitate to foretell how all of them would act. Whatever degree of doubt he may in fact feel, arises from the uncertainty whether he really knows the circumstances, or the character of some one or other of the persons, with the degree of accuracy required: but by no means from thinking that if he did know these things, there could be any uncertainty what the conduct would be. Nor does this full assurance conflict in the smallest degree with what is called our feeling of freedom. We do not feel ourselves the less free, because those to whom we are intimately known are well assured how we shall will to act in a particular case. We often, on the contrary, regard the doubt what our conduct will be, as a mark of ignorance of our character, and sometimes even resent it as an imputation. The religious metaphysicians who have asserted the freedom of the will, have always maintained it to be consistent with divine foreknowledge of our actions; and if with divine, then with any other foreknowledge. We may be free, and yet another may have reason to be perfectly certain what use we shall make of our freedom. It is not, therefore, the doctrine that our volitions and actions are invariable consequents of our antecedent states of mind, that is either contradicted by our consciousness, or felt to be degrading.

But the doctrine of causation, when considered as obtaining between our volitions and their antecedents, is almost universally conceived as involving more than this. Many do not believe, and very few practically feel, that there is nothing in causation but invariable, certain, and unconditional sequence. There are few to whom mere constancy of succession appears a sufficiently stringent bond of union for so peculiar a relation as that of cause and effect. Even if the reason repudiates, the imagination retains, the feeling of some more intimate connexion, of some peculiar tie, or mysterious constraint exercised by the antecedent over the consequent. Now this it is which, considered as applying to the human will, conflicts with our consciousness, and revolts our feelings. We are certain that, in the case of our volitions, there is not this mysterious constraint. We know that we are not compelled, as by a magical spell, to obey any particular motive. We feel, that if we wished to prove that we have the power of resisting the motive, we could do so, (that wish being, it needs scarcely be observed, a *new antecedent;*) and it would be humiliating to our pride and paralyzing to our desire of excellence if we thought otherwise. But neither is any such mysterious compulsion now supposed, by the best philosophical authorities, to be exercised by *any* cause over its effect. Those who think that causes draw their effects after them by a mystical tie, are right in believing that the relation between volitions and their antecedents is of another nature. But they should go farther, and admit that this is also true of all other effects and their antecedents. If such a tie is considered to be involved in the word necessity, the doctrine is not true of human actions; but neither is it then true of inanimate objects. It would be more correct to say that matter is *not* bound by necessity than that mind *is* so.

That the free-will metaphysicians, being mostly of the school which rejects Hume's and Brown's analysis of Cause and Effect, should miss their way for want of the light which that analysis affords, cannot surprise us. The wonder is, that the necessarians, who usually admit that philosophical theory, should in practice equally lose sight of it. The very same misconception of the doctrine called Philosophical Necessity, which prevents the opposite party from recognising its truth, I believe to exist more or less obscurely in the minds of most necessarians, however they may in words disavow it. I am much mistaken if they habitually feel that the necessity which they recognise in actions is but uniformity of order, and capability of being predicted. They have a feeling as if there were at bottom a stronger tie between the volitions and their causes: as if, when they asserted that the will is governed by the balance of motives, they meant something more cogent than if they had only said, that whoever knew the motives, and our habitual susceptibilities to them, could predict how we should will to act. They commit, in opposition to their own scientific system, the very same mistake which their adversaries commit in obedience to theirs; and in consequence do really in some instances suffer those depressing consequences, which their opponents erroneously impute to the doctrine itself.

3. I am inclined to think that this error is almost wholly an effect of the associations with a word; and that it would be prevented, by forbearing to employ, for the expression of the simple fact of causation, so extremely inappropriate a term as Necessity. That word, in its other acceptations, involves much more than mere uniformity of sequence: it implies irresistibleness. Ap-

plied to the will, it only means that the given cause will be followed by the effect, subject to all possibilities of counteraction by other causes: but in common use it stands for the operation of those causes exclusively, which are supposed too powerful to be counteracted at all. When we say that all human actions take place of necessity, we only mean that they will certainly happen if nothing prevents:—when we say that dying of want, to those who cannot get food, is a necessity, we mean that it will certainly happen whatever may be done to prevent it. The application of the same term to the agencies on which human actions depend, as is used to express those agencies of nature which are really uncontrollable, cannot fail, when habitual, to create a feeling of uncontrollableness in the former also. This however is a mere illusion. There are physical sequences which we call necessary, as death for want of food or air; there are others which are not said to be necessary, as death from poison, which an antidote, or the use of the stomach-pump, will sometimes avert. It is apt to be forgotten by people's feelings, even if remembered by their understandings, that human actions are in this last predicament: they are never (except in some cases of mania) ruled by any one motive with such absolute sway, that there is no room for the influence of any other. The causes, therefore, on which action depends, are never uncontrollable; and any given effect is only necessary provided that the causes tending to produce it are not controlled. That whatever happens, could not have happened otherwise unless something had taken place which was capable of preventing it, no one surely needs hesitate to admit. But to call this by the name necessity is to use the term in a sense so different from its primitive and familiar meaning, from that which it bears in the common occasions of life, as to amount almost to a play upon words. The associations derived from the ordinary sense of the term will adhere to it in spite of all we can do: and though the doctrine of Necessity, as stated by most who hold it, is very remote from fatalism, it is probable that most necessarians are fatalists, more or less, in their feelings.

A fatalist believes, or half believes (for nobody is a consistent fatalist), not only that whatever is about to happen, will be the infallible result of the causes which produce it, (which is the true necessarian doctrine,) but moreover that there is no use in struggling against it; that it will happen however we may strive to prevent it. Now, a necessarian, believing that our actions follow from our characters, and that our characters follow from our organization, our education, and our circumstances, is apt to be, with more or less of consciousness on his part, a fatalist as to his own actions, and to believe that his nature is such, or that his education and circumstances have so moulded his character, that nothing can now prevent him from feeling and acting in a particular way, or at least that no effort of his own can hinder it. In the words of the sect which in our own day has most perseveringly inculcated and most perversely misunderstood this great doctrine, his character is formed *for* him, and not *by* him; therefore his wishing that it had been formed differently is of no use; he has no power to alter it. But this is a grand error. He has, to a certain extent, a power to alter his character. Its being, in the ultimate resort, formed for him, is not inconsistent with its being, in part, formed *by* him as one of the intermediate agents. His character is formed by his circumstances (including among these his particular organization); but his own desire to mould it in a particular way, is one of those circumstances, and by no means one of the least influential. We cannot, indeed, directly will to be different from what we are. But neither did those who are supposed to have formed our characters, directly will that we should be what we are. Their will had no direct power except over their own actions. They made us what they did make us, by willing, not the end, but the requisite means; and we, when our habits are not too inveterate, can, by similarly willing the requisite means, make ourselves different. If they could place us under the influence of certain circumstances, we, in like manner, can place ourselves under the influence of other circumstances. We are exactly as capable of making our own character, *if we will,* as others are of making it for us.

Yes (answers the Owenite), but these words, "if we will," surrender the whole point: since the will to alter our own character is given us, not by any efforts of ours, but by circumstances which we cannot help; it comes to us either from external causes, or not at all. Most true: if the Owenite stops here, he is in a position from which nothing can expel him. Our character is formed by us as well as for us; but the wish which induces us to attempt to form it is formed for us: and how? Not, in general, by our organization, nor wholly by our education, but by our experience; experience of the painful consequences of the character we previously had: or by some strong feeling of admiration or aspiration, accidentally aroused. But to think that we have no power of altering our character, and to think that we shall not use our power unless we desire to use it, are very different things, and have a very different effect on the mind. A person who does not wish to alter his character, cannot be the person who is supposed to feel discouraged or paralyzed by thinking himself unable to do it. The depressing effect of the fatalist doctrine can only be felt where there *is* a wish to do what that doctrine represents as impossible. It is of no consequence what we think forms our character, when we have no desire of our own about forming it; but it is of great consequence that we should not be prevented from forming such a desire by thinking the attainment impracticable, and that if we have the desire, we should know that the work is not so irrevocably done as to be incapable of being altered.

And indeed, if we examine closely, we shall find that this feeling, of our being able to modify our own character *if we wish,* is itself the feeling of moral freedom which we are conscious of. A person feels morally free who feels that his habits or his temptations are not his masters, but he theirs: who even in yielding to them knows that he could resist; that were he desirous of altogether throwing them off, there would not be required for that purpose a stronger desire than he knows himself to be capable of feeling. It is of course necessary, to render our consciousness of freedom complete, that we should have succeeded in making our character all we have hitherto attempted to make it; for if we have wished and not attained, we have not power over our own character, we are not free. Or at least, we must feel that our wish, if not strong enough to alter our character, is strong enough to conquer our character when the two are brought into conflict in any particular case of conduct.

.   .   .

A habit of willing is commonly called a purpose; and among the causes of our volitions, and of the actions which flow from them, must be reckoned not only likings and aversions, but also purposes. It is only when our purposes have become independent of the feelings of pain or pleasure from which they originally took their rise, that we are said to have a confirmed character. "A character," says Novalis, "is a completely fashioned will": and the will, once so fashioned, may be steady and constant, when the passive susceptibilities of pleasure and pain are greatly weakened, or materially changed.

With the corrections and explanations now given, the doctrine of the causation of our volitions by motives, and of motives by the desirable objects offered to us, combined with our particular susceptibilities of desire, may be considered, I hope, as sufficiently established for the purposes of this treatise.

33

WILLIAM JAMES (1842–1910)

The Dilemma of Determinism

William James, along with C. S. Peirce (1839–1914) and John Dewey (1859–1952), was one of the major proponents of a philosophical movement known as pragmatism. Trained as a physician, James began his professional career as an instructor in physiology at Harvard University, but his interests moved swiftly from physiology to psy-

From William James, *The Will to Believe and Other Essays in Popular Philosophy* (copyrighted by William James, 1896), pp. 145–179.

chology and, ultimately, to philosophy. His writings include *The Principles of Psychology* (1890), *The Will to Believe and Other Essays in Popular Philosophy* (1897), *Human Immortality* (1898), *Varieties of Religious Experience* (1902), *Pragmatism* (1907), *The Meaning of Truth* (1909), *A Pluralistic Universe* (1909), and *Essays in Radical Empiricism* (1912).

Although James was greatly influenced by Darwinism, he did not draw the behavioristic-deterministic consequences that others claimed were implicit in the evolutionary theory. Indeed, much of James' work as a philosopher was devoted to preserving cherished beliefs, such as the existence of God, the objectivity of good and evil, free will, and human immortality, in the face of the growing naturalistic outlook of his day. The essay that follows shows that James pursued this task with great imagination and argumentative skill.

James has little respect for the position taken by writers such as John Stuart Mill. He describes that position with unconcealed contempt as "a *soft* determinism which abhors harsh words, and, repudiating fatality, necessity, and even predetermination, says that its real name is freedom." You must choose, James says, between *hard* determinism, which accepts the unpalatable consequences of the determinist hypothesis, and libertarianism, which frankly rejects determinism. And, he claims that if you want to make moral sense out of the universe, you will choose the latter.

A common opinion prevails that the juice has ages ago been pressed out of the free-will controversy, and that no new champion can do more than warm up stale arguments which every one has heard. This is a radical mistake. I know of no subject less worn out, or in which inventive genius has a better chance of breaking open new ground,—not, perhaps, of forcing a conclusion or of coercing assent, but of deepening our sense of what the issue between the two parties really is, of what the ideas of fate and of free-will imply. At our very side almost, in the past few years, we have seen falling in rapid succession from the press works that present the alternative in entirely novel lights. Not to speak of the English disciples of Hegel, such as Green and Bradley; not to speak of Hinton and Hodgson, nor of Hazard here,—we see in the writings of Renouvier, Fouillée, and Delbœuf how completely changed and refreshed is the form of all the old disputes. I cannot pretend to vie in originality with any of the masters I have named, and my ambition limits itself to just one little point. If I can make two of the necessarily implied corollaries of determinism clearer to you than they have been made before, I shall have made it possible for you to decide for or against that doctrine with a better understanding of what you are about. And if you prefer not to decide at all, but to remain doubters, you will at least see more plainly what the subject of your hesitation is. I thus disclaim openly on the threshold all pretension to prove to you that the freedom of the will is true. The most I hope is to induce some of you to follow my own example in assuming it true, and acting as if it were true. If it be true, it seems to me that this is involved in the strict logic of the case. Its truth ought not to be forced willy-nilly down our indifferent throats. It ought to be freely espoused by men who can equally well turn their backs upon it. In other words, our first act of freedom, if we are free, ought in all inward propriety to be to affirm that we are free. This should exclude, it seems to me, from the free-will side of the question all hope of a coercive demonstration, —a demonstration which I, for one, am perfectly contented to go without.

With thus much understood at the outset, we can advance. But not without one more point understood as well. The arguments I am about to urge all proceed on two suppositions: first, when we make theories about the world and discuss them with one another, we do so in order to attain a conception of things which shall give us subjective satisfaction; and, second, if there be two conceptions, and the one seems to us, on the whole, more rational than the other, we are entitled to suppose that the more rational one is the truer of the two. I hope that you are all willing to make these suppositions with me; for I am afraid that if there be any of you here who are not, they will find little edification in the rest of what I have to say. I cannot stop to argue the point; but I myself believe that all the magnificent achievements of mathematical and physical science—our doctrines of evolution, of uniformity of law, and the rest —proceed from our indomitable desire to cast the world into a more rational shape in our minds than the shape into which it is thrown there by the crude order of our experience. The world has shown itself, to a great extent, plastic to this demand of ours for rationality. How much farther it will show itself plastic no one can say. Our only means of finding out is to try; and I, for one, feel as free to try conceptions of moral as of mechanical or of logical rationality. If a certain formula for expressing the nature of the world violates my moral demand, I shall feel as free to throw it overboard, or at least to doubt it, as if it disappointed my demand for uniformity of sequence, for example; the one demand being, so far as I can see, quite as subjective and emotional as the other is. The principle of causality, for example,—what is it but a postulate, an empty name covering simply a demand that the sequence of events shall some day manifest a deeper kind of belonging of one thing with another than the mere arbitrary juxtaposition which now phenomenally appears? It is as much an altar to an unknown god as the one that Saint Paul found at Athens. All our scientific and philosophic ideals are altars to unknown gods. Uniformity is as much so as is free-will. If this be admitted, we can debate on even terms. But if any one pretends that while freedom and variety are, in the first instance, subjective demands, necessity and uniformity are something altogether different, I do not see how we can debate at all.

To begin, then, I must suppose you acquainted with all the usual arguments on the subject. I cannot stop to take up the old proofs from causation, from statistics, from the certainty with which we can foretell one another's conduct, from the fixity of character, and all the rest. But there are two *words* which usually encumber these classical arguments, and which we must immediately dispose of if we are to make any progress. One is the eulogistic word *freedom,* and the other is the opprobrious word *chance.* The word 'chance' I wish to keep, but I wish to get rid of the word 'freedom.' Its eulogistic associations have so far overshadowed all the rest of its meaning that both parties claim the sole right to use it, and determinists to-day insist that they alone are freedom's champions. Old-fashioned determinism was what we may call *hard* determinism. It did not shrink from such words as fatality, bondage of the will, necessitation, and the like. Nowadays, we have a *soft* determinism which abhors harsh words, and, repudiating fatality, necessity, and even predetermination, says that its real name is freedom; for freedom is only necessity understood, and bondage to the highest is identical with true freedom. Even a writer as little used to making capital out of soft words as Mr. Hodgson hesitates not to call himself a 'free-will determinist.'

Now, all this is a quagmire of evasion under which the real issue of fact has been entirely smothered. Freedom in all these senses presents simply no problem at all. No matter what the soft determinist mean by it,—whether he mean the acting without external constraint; whether he mean the acting rightly, or whether he mean the acquiescing in the law of the whole,—who cannot answer him that sometimes we are free and sometimes we are not? But there *is* a problem, an issue of fact and not of words, an issue of the most momentous importance, which is often decided without discussion in one sentence,—nay, in one clause of a sentence,—by those very writers who spin out whole chapters in their efforts to show what 'true' freedom is; and that is the question of determinism, about which we are to talk to-night.

Fortunately, no ambiguities hang about this word or about its opposite, indeterminism. Both designate an outward way in which things may happen, and their cold and mathematical sound has no sentimental associations that can bribe our partiality either way in advance. Now, evidence of an external kind to decide between determinism and indeterminism is, as I intimated a while back, strictly impossible to find. Let us look at the difference between them and see for ourselves. What does determinism profess?

It professes that those parts of the universe already laid down absolutely appoint and decree what the other parts shall be. The future has no ambiguous possibilities hidden in its womb: the part we call the present is compatible with only one totality. Any other future complement than the one fixed from eternity is impossible. The whole is in each and every part, and welds it with the rest into an absolute unity, an iron block, in which there can be no equivocation or shadow of turning.

> With earth's first clay they did the last man knead,
> And there of the last harvest sowed the seed.
> And the first morning of creation wrote
> What the last dawn of reckoning shall read.

Indeterminism, on the contrary, says that the parts have a certain amount of loose play on one another, so that the laying down of one of them does not necessarily determine what the others shall be. It admits that possibilities may be in excess of actualities, and that things not yet revealed to our knowledge may really in themselves be ambiguous. Of two alternative futures which we conceive, both may now be really possible; and the one become impossible only at the very moment when the other excludes it by becoming real itself. Indeterminism thus denies the world to be one unbending unit of fact. It says there is a certain ultimate pluralism in it; and, so saying, it corroborates our ordinary unsophisticated view of things. To that view, actualities seem to float in a wider sea of possibilities from out of which they are chosen; and, *somewhere,* indeterminism says, such possibilities exist, and form a part of truth.

Determinism, on the contrary, says they exist *nowhere,* and that necessity on the one hand and impossibility on the other are the sole categories of the real. Possibilities that fail to get realized are, for determinism, pure illusions: they never were possibilities at all. There is nothing inchoate, it says, about this universe of ours, all that was or is or shall be actual in it having been from eternity virtually there. The cloud of alternatives our minds escort this mass of actuality withal is a cloud of sheer deceptions, to which 'impossibilities' is the only name that rightfully belongs.

The issue, it will be seen, is a perfectly sharp one, which no eulogistic terminology can smear over or wipe out. The truth *must* lie with one side or the other, and its lying with one side makes the other false.

The question relates solely to the existence of possibilities, in the strict sense of the term, as things that may, but need not, be. Both sides admit that a volition, for instance, has occurred. The indeterminists say another volition might have occurred in its place: the determinists swear that nothing could possibly have occurred in its place. Now, can science be called in to tell us which of these two point-blank contradicters of each other is right? Science professes to draw no conclusions but such as are based on matters of fact, things that have actually happened; but how can any amount of assurance that something actually happened give us the least grain of information as to whether another thing might or might not have happened in its place? Only facts can be proved by other facts. With things that are possibilities and not facts, facts have no concern. If we have no other evidence than the evidence of existing facts, the possibility-question must remain a mystery never to be cleared up.

And the truth is that facts practically have hardly anything to do with making us either determinists or indeterminists. Sure enough, we make a flourish of quoting facts this way or that; and if we are determinists, we talk about the infallibility with which we can predict one another's conduct; while if we are indeterminists, we lay great stress on the fact that it is just because we cannot foretell one another's conduct, either in war or statecraft or in any of the great and small intrigues and businesses of men, that life is so intensely anxious and hazardous a game. But who does not see the wretched insufficiency of this so-called objective testimony on both sides? What fills up the gaps in our minds is something not objective, not external. What divides us into possibility men and anti-possibility men is different faiths or postulates, —postulates of rationality. To this man the world seems more rational with possibilities in it,—to that man more rational with possibilities excluded; and talk as we will about having to yield to evidence, what makes us monists or pluralists, determinists or indeterminists, is at bottom always some sentiment like this.

The stronghold of the deterministic sentiment is the antipathy to the idea of chance. As soon as we begin to talk indeterminism to our friends, we find a number of them shaking their heads. This notion of alternative possibility, they say, this admission that any one of several things may come to pass, is, after all, only a roundabout name for chance; and chance is something the notion of which no sane mind can for an instant tolerate in the world. What is it, they ask, but barefaced crazy unreason, the negation of intelligibility and law? And if the slightest particle of it exist anywhere, what is to prevent the whole fabric from falling together, the stars from going out, and chaos from recommencing her topsy-turvy reign?

Remarks of this sort about chance will put an end to discussion as quickly as anything one can find. I have already told you that 'chance' was a word I wished to keep and use. Let us then examine exactly what it means, and see whether it ought to be such a terrible bugbear to us. I fancy that squeezing the thistle boldly will rob it of its sting.

The sting of the word 'chance' seems to lie in the assumption that it means something positive, and that if anything happens by chance, it must needs be something of an intrinsically irrational and preposterous sort. Now, chance means nothing of the kind. It is a purely negative and relative term,[1] giving us no information about that of which it is predicated, except that it happens to be disconnected with something else,—not controlled, secured, or necessitated by other things in advance of its own actual presence. As this point is the most subtle one of the whole lecture, and at the same time the point on which all the rest hinges, I beg you to pay particular attention to it. What I say is that it tells us nothing about what a thing may be in itself to call it 'chance.' It may be a bad thing, it may be a good thing. It may be lucidity, transparency, fitness incarnate, matching the whole system of other things, when it has once befallen, in an unimaginably perfect way. All you mean by calling it 'chance' is that this is not guaranteed, that it may also fall out otherwise. For the system of other things has no positive hold on the chance-

[1]Speaking technically, it is a word with a positive denotation, but a connotation that is negative. Other things must be silent about *what* it is: it alone can decide that point at the moment in which it reveals itself.

thing. Its origin is in a certain fashion negative: it escapes, and says, Hands off! coming, when it comes, as a free gift, or not at all.

This negativeness, however, and this opacity of the chance-thing when thus considered *ab extra,* or from the point of view of previous things or distant things, do not preclude its having any amount of positiveness and luminosity from within, and at its own place and moment. All that its chance-character asserts about it is that there is something in it really of its own, something that is not the unconditional property of the whole. If the whole wants this property, the whole must wait till it can get it, if it be a matter of chance. That the universe may actually be a sort of joint-stock society of this sort, in which the sharers have both limited liabilities and limited powers, is of course a simple and conceivable notion.

Nevertheless, many persons talk as if the minutest dose of disconnectedness of one part with another, the smallest modicum of independence, the faintest tremor of ambiguity about the future, for example, would ruin everything, and turn this goodly universe into a sort of insane sand-heap or nulliverse, no universe at all. Since future human volitions are as a matter of fact the only ambiguous things we are tempted to believe in, let us stop for a moment to make ourselves sure whether their independent and accidental character need be fraught with such direful consequences to the universe as these.

What is meant by saying that my choice of which way to walk home after the lecture is ambiguous and matter of chance as far as the present moment is concerned? It means that both Divinity Avenue and Oxford Street are called; but that only one, and that one *either* one, shall be chosen. Now, I ask you seriously to suppose that this ambiguity of my choice is real; and then to make the impossible hypothesis that the choice is made twice over, and each time falls on a different street. In other words, imagine that I first walk through Divinity Avenue, and then imagine that the powers governing the universe annihilate ten minutes of time with all that it contained, and set me back at the door of this hall just as I was before the choice was made. Imagine then that, everything else being the same, I now make a different choice and traverse Oxford Street. You, as passive spectators, look on and see the two alternative universes,—one of them with me walking through Divinity Avenue in it, the other with the same me walking through Oxford Street. Now, if you are determinists you believe one of these universes to have been from eternity impossible: you believe it to have been impossible because of the intrinsic irrationality or accidentality somewhere involved in it. But looking outwardly at these universes, can you say which is the impossible and accidental one, and which the rational and necessary one? I doubt if the most ironclad determinist among you could have the slightest glimmer of light on this point. In other words, either universe *after the fact* and once there would, to our means of observation and understanding, appear just as rational as the other. There would be absolutely no criterion by which we might judge one necessary and the other matter of chance. Suppose now we relieve the gods of their hypothetical task and assume my choice, once made, to be made forever. I go through Divinity Avenue for good and all. If, as good determinists, you now begin to affirm, what all good determinists punctually do affirm, that in the nature of things I *couldn't* have gone through Oxford Street,—had I done so it would have been chance, irrationality, insanity, a horrid gap in nature,—I simply call your attention to this, that your affirmation is what the Germans call a *Machtspruch,* a mere conception fulminated as a dogma and based on no insight into details. Before my choice, either street seemed as natural to you as to me. Had I happened to take Oxford Street, Divinity Avenue would have figured in your philosophy as the gap in nature; and you would have so proclaimed it with the best deterministic conscience in the world.

But what a hollow outcry, then, is this against a chance which, if it were present to us, we could by no character whatever distinguish from a rational necessity! I have taken the most trivial of examples, but no possible example could lead to any different result. For what are the alternatives which, in point of fact, offer themselves to human volition? What are those futures that now seem matters of chance? Are they not one and all like the Divinity Avenue and Oxford Street of our example? Are they not all of them *kinds* of things already here and based in the existing frame of nature? Is any one ever tempted to produce an *absolute* accident, something utterly irrelevant to the rest of the world? Do not all the motives that assail us, all the futures that offer themselves to our choice, spring equally from the soil of the past; and would not either one of them, whether realized through chance or through necessity, the moment it was realized, seem to us to fit that past, and in the completest and most continuous manner to interdigitate with the phenomena already there?[2]

The more one thinks of the matter, the more one wonders that so empty and gratuitous a hubbub as this outcry against chance should have found so great an echo in the hearts of men. It is a word which tells us absolutely nothing about what chances, or about the *modus operandi* of the chancing; and the use of it as a war-cry shows only a temper of intellectual absolutism, a demand that the world shall be a solid block, subject to one control,—which temper, which demand, the world may not be bound to gratify at all. In every outwardly verifiable and practical respect, a world in which the alternatives that now actually distract *your* choice were decided by pure chance would be by

[2]A favorite argument against free-will is that if it be true, a man's murderer may as probably be his best friend as his worst enemy, a mother be as likely to strangle as to suckle her first-born, and all of us be as ready to jump from the fourth-story windows as to go out of front doors, etc. Users of this argument should properly be excluded from debate till they learn what the real question is. "Free-will" does not say that everything that is physically conceivable is also morally possible. It merely says that of alternatives that really *tempt* our will more than one is really possible. Of course, the alternatives that do thus tempt our will are vastly fewer than the physical possibilities we can coldly fancy. Persons really tempted often do murder their best friends, mothers do strangle their first-borns, people do jump out of fourth-story windows, etc.

me absolutely undistinguished from the world in which I now live. I am, therefore, entirely willing to call it, so far as your choices go, a world of chance for me. To *yourselves,* it is true, those very acts of choice, which to me are so blind, opaque, and external, are the opposites of this, for you are within them and effect them. To you they appear as decisions; and decisions, for him who makes them, are altogether peculiar psychic facts. Self-luminous and self-justifying at the living moment at which they occur, they appeal to no outside moment to put its stamp upon them or make them continuous with the rest of nature. Themselves it is rather who seem to make nature continuous; and in their strange and intense function of granting consent to one possibility and withholding it from another, to transform an equivocal and double future into an inalterable and simple past.

But with the psychology of the matter we have no concern this evening. The quarrel which determinism has with chance fortunately has nothing to do with this or that psychological detail. It is a quarrel altogether metaphysical. Determinism denies the ambiguity of future volitions, because it affirms that nothing future can be ambiguous. But we have said enough to meet the issue. Indeterminate future volitions *do* mean chance. Let us not fear to shout it from the house-tops if need be; for we now know that the idea of chance is, at bottom, exactly the same thing as the idea of gift,—the one simply being a disparaging, and the other a eulogistic, name for anything on which we have no effective *claim.* And whether the world be the better or the worse for having either chances or gifts in it will depend altogether on *what* these uncertain and unclaimable things turn out to be.

And this at last brings us within sight of our subject. We have seen what determinism means: we have seen that indeterminism is rightly described as meaning chance; and we have seen that chance, the very name of which we are urged to shrink from as from a metaphysical pestilence, means only the negative fact that no part of the world, however big, can claim to control absolutely the destinies of the whole. But although, in discussing the word 'chance,' I may at moments have seemed to be arguing for its real existence, I have not meant to do so yet. We have not yet ascertained whether this be a world of chance or no; at most, we have agreed that it seems so. And I now repeat what I said at the outset, that, from any strict theoretical point of view, the question is insoluble. To deepen our theoretic sense of the *difference* between a world with chances in it and a deterministic world is the most I can hope to do; and this I may now at last begin upon, after all our tedious clearing of the way.

I wish first of all to show you just what the notion that this is a deterministic world implies. The implications I call your attention to are all bound up with the fact that it is a world in which we constantly have to make what I shall, with your permission, call judgments of regret. Hardly an hour passes in which we do not wish that something might be otherwise; and happy indeed are those of us whose hearts have never echoed the wish of Omar Khayam—

> That we might clasp, ere closed, the book of fate,
>   And make the writer on a fairer leaf
> Inscribe our names, or quite obliterate.
>
> Ah! Love, could you and I with fate conspire
> To mend this sorry scheme of things entire,
>   Would we not shatter it to bits, and then
> Remould it nearer to the heart's desire?

Now, it is undeniable that most of these regrets are foolish, and quite on a par in point of philosophic value with the criticisms on the universe of that friend of our infancy, the hero of the fable The Atheist and the Acorn,—

> Fool! had that bough a pumpkin bore,
> Thy whimsies would have worked no more, etc.

Even from the point of view of our own ends, we should probably make a botch of remodelling the universe. How much more then from the point of view of ends we cannot see! Wise men therefore regret as little as they can. But still some regrets are pretty obstinate and hard to stifle,—regrets for acts of wanton cruelty or treachery, for example, whether performed by others or by ourselves. Hardly any one can remain *entirely* optimistic after reading the confession of the murderer at Brockton the other day: how, to get rid of the wife whose continued existence bored him, he inveigled her into a desert spot, shot her four times, and then, as she lay on the ground and said to him, "You didn't do it on purpose, did you, dear?" replied, "No, I didn't do it on purpose," as he raised a rock and smashed her skull. Such an occurrence, with the mild sentence and self-satisfaction of the prisoner, is a field for a crop of regrets, which one need not take up in detail. We feel that, although a perfect mechanical fit to the rest of the universe, it is a bad moral fit, and that something else would really have been better in its place.

But for the deterministic philosophy the murder, the sentence, and the prisoner's optimism were all necessary from eternity; and nothing else for a moment had a ghost of a chance of being put into their place. To admit such a chance, determinists tell us, would be to make a suicide of reason; so we must steel our hearts against the thought. And here our plot thickens, for we see the first of those difficult implications of determinism and monism which it is my purpose to make you feel. If this Brockton murder was called for by the rest of the universe, if it had to come at its preappointed hour, and if nothing else would have been consistent with the sense of the whole, what are we to think of the universe? Are we stubbornly to stick to our judgment of regret, and say, though it *couldn't* be, yet it *would* have been a better universe with something different from this Brockton murder in it? That, of course, seems the natural and spontaneous thing for us to do; and yet it is nothing short of deliberately espousing a kind of pessimism. The judgment of regret calls the murder bad. Calling a thing bad means, if it mean anything at all, that the thing ought not to be, that something else ought to be in its stead. Determinism, in denying that anything else can be in its stead, virtually defines the universe as a place in which what ought to be is impossible,—in other words, as an organism whose constitution is afflicted with an incurable taint, an irremediable flaw. The pessimism of a Schopenhauer says no more than this,—that the murder is a symptom; and that it is a vicious symptom because it belongs to a vicious whole, which can express its nature no otherwise than by bringing forth just such a symptom as that at this particular spot. Regret for the murder must transform itself, if we are determinists and wise, into a larger regret. It is absurd to regret the murder alone. Other things being what they are, *it* could not be different. What we should regret is that whole frame of things of which the murder is one member. I see no escape whatever from this pessimistic conclusion, if, being determinists, our judgment of regret is to be allowed to stand at all.

The only deterministic escape from pessimism is everywhere to abandon the judgment of regret. That this can be done, history shows to be not impossible. The devil, *quoad existentiam*, may be good. That is, although he be a *principle* of evil, yet the universe, with such a principle in it, may practically be a better universe than it could have been without. On every hand, in a small way, we find that a certain amount of evil is a condition by which a higher form of good is bought. There is nothing to prevent anybody from generalizing this view, and trusting that if we could but see things in the largest of all ways, even such matters as this Brockton murder would appear to be paid for by the uses that follow in their train. An optimism *quand même*, a systematic and infatuated optimism like that ridiculed by Voltaire in his Candide, is one of the possible ideal ways in which a man may train himself to look on life. Bereft of dogmatic hardness and lit up with the expression of a tender and pathetic hope, such an optimism has been the grace of some of the most religious characters that ever lived.

> Throb thine with Nature's throbbing breast,
> And all is clear from east to west.

Even cruelty and treachery may be among the absolutely blessed fruits of time, and to quarrel with any of their details may be blasphemy. The only real blasphemy, in short, may be that pessimistic temper of the soul which lets it give way to such things as regrets, remorse, and grief.

Thus, our deterministic pessimism may become a deterministic optimism at the price of extinguishing our judgments of regret.

But does not this immediately bring us into a curious logical predicament? Our determinism leads us to call our judgments of regret wrong, because they are pessimistic in implying that what is impossible yet ought to be. But how then about the judgments of regret themselves? If they are wrong, other judgments, judgments of approval presumably, ought to be in their place. But as they are necessitated, nothing else *can* be in their place; and the universe is just what it was before,—namely, a place in which what ought to be appears impossible. We have got one foot out of the pessimistic bog, but the other one sinks all the deeper. We have rescued our actions from the bonds of evil, but our judgments are now held fast. When murders and treacheries cease to be sins, regrets are theoretic absurdities and errors. The theoretic and the active life thus play a kind of seesaw with each other on the ground of evil. The rise of either sends the other down. Murder and treachery cannot be good without regret being bad: regret cannot be good without treachery and murder being bad. Both, however, are supposed to have been foredoomed; so something must be fatally unreasonable, absurd, and wrong in the world. It must be a place of which either sin or error forms a necessary part . . .

.   .   .

We have thus clearly revealed to our view what may be called the dilemma of determinism, so far as determinism pretends to think things out at all. A merely mechanical determinism, it is true, rather rejoices in not thinking them out. It is very sure that the universe must satisfy its postulate of a physical continuity and coherence, but it smiles at any one who comes forward with a postulate of moral coherence as well. I may suppose, however, that the number of purely mechanical or hard determinists among you this evening is small. The determinism to whose seductions you are most exposed is what I have called soft determinism,—the determinism which allows considerations of good and bad to mingle with those of cause and effect in deciding what sort of a universe this may rationally be held to be. The dilemma of this determinism is one whose left horn is pessimism and whose right horn is subjectivism. In other words, if determinism is to escape pessimism, it must leave off looking at the goods and ills of life in a simple objective way, and regard them as materials, indifferent in themselves, for the production of consciousness, scientific and ethical, in us.

.   .   .

But this brings us right back, after such a long détour, to the question of indeterminism and to the conclusion of all I came here to say to-night. For the only consistent way of representing a pluralism and a world whose parts may affect one another through their conduct being either good or bad is the indeterministic way. What interest, zest, or excitement can there be in achieving the right way, unless we are enabled to feel that the wrong way is also a possible and a natural way,—nay, more, a menacing and an imminent way? And what sense can there be in condemning ourselves for taking the wrong way, unless we need have done nothing of the sort, unless the right way was open to us as well? I cannot understand the willingness to act, no matter how we feel, without the belief that acts are really good and bad. I cannot understand the belief that an act is bad, without regret at its happening. I cannot understand regret without the admission of real, genuine possibilities in the world. Only *then* is it other than a mockery to feel, after we have failed to do our best, that an irreparable opportunity is gone from the universe, the loss of which it must forever after mourn.

If you insist that this is all superstition, that possibility is in the eye of science and reason impossibility, and that if I act badly 'tis that the universe was foredoomed to suffer this defect, you fall right back into the dilemma, the labyrinth, of pessimism and subjectivism, from out of whose toils we have just wound our way.

Now, we are of course free to fall back, if we please. For my own part, though, whatever difficulties may beset the philosophy of objective right and wrong, and the indeterminism it seems to imply, determinism, with its alternative of pessimism or romanticism, contains difficulties that are greater still. But you will remember that I expressly repudiated awhile ago the pretension to offer any arguments which could be coercive in a so-called scientific fashion in this matter. And I consequently find myself, at the end of this long talk, obliged to state my conclusions in an altogether personal way. This personal method of appeal seems to be among the very conditions of the problem; and the most any one can do is to confess as candidly as he can the grounds for the faith that is in him, and leave his example to work on others as it may.

Let me, then, without circumlocution say just this. The world is enigmatical enough in all conscience, whatever theory we may take up toward it. The indeterminism I defend, the free-will theory of popular sense based on the judgment of regret, represents that world as vulnerable, and liable to be injured by certain of its parts if they act wrong. And it represents their acting wrong as a matter of possibility or accident, neither inevitable nor yet to be infallibly warded off. In all this, it is a theory devoid either of transparency or of stability. It gives us a pluralistic, restless universe, in which no single point of view can ever take in the whole scene; and to a mind possessed of the love of unity at any cost, it will, no doubt, remain forever inacceptable. A friend with such a mind once told me that the thought of my universe made him sick, like the sight of the horrible motion of a mass of maggots in their carrion bed.

But while I freely admit that the pluralism and the restlessness are repugnant and irrational in a certain way, I find that every alternative to them is irrational in a deeper way. The indeterminism with its maggots, if you please to speak so about it, offends only the native absolutism of my intellect,—an absolutism which, after all, perhaps, deserves to be snubbed and kept in check. But the determinism with its necessary carrion, to continue the figure of speech, and with no possible maggots to eat the latter up, violates my sense of moral reality through and through. When, for example, I imagine such carrion as the Brockton murder, I cannot conceive it as an act by which the universe, as a whole, logically and necessarily expresses its nature without shrinking from complicity with such a whole. And I deliberately refuse to keep on terms of loyalty with the universe by saying blankly that the murder, since it does flow from the nature of the whole, is not carrion. There are *some* instinctive reactions which I, for one, will not tamper with. The only remaining alternative, the attitude of gnostical romanticism, wrenches my personal instincts in quite as violent a way. It falsifies the simple objectivity of their deliverance. It makes the goose-flesh the murder excites in me a sufficient reason for the perpetration of the crime. It transforms life from a tragic reality into an insincere melodramatic exhibition, as foul or as tawdry as any one's diseased curiosity pleases to carry it out. And with its consecration of the 'roman naturaliste' state of mind, and its enthronement of the baser crew of Parisian *littérateurs* among the eternally indispensable organs by which the infinite spirit of things attains to that subjective illumination which is the task of its life, it leaves me in presence of a sort of subjective carrion considerably more noisome than the objective carrion I called it in to take away.

No! better a thousand times, than such systematic corruption of our moral sanity, the plainest pessimism, so that it be straightforward; but better far than that the world of chance. Make as great an uproar about chance as you please, I know that chance means pluralism and nothing more. If some of the members of the pluralism are bad, the philosophy of pluralism, whatever broad views it may deny me, permits me, at least, to turn to the other members with a clean breast of affection and an unsophisticated moral sense. And if I still wish to think of the world as a totality, it lets me feel that a world with a *chance* in it of being altogether good, even if the chance never comes to pass, is better than a world with no such chance at all. That 'chance' whose very notion I am exhorted and conjured to banish from my view of the future as the suicide of reason concerning it, that 'chance' is—what? Just this,—the chance that in moral respects the future may be other and better than the past has been. This is the only chance we have any motive for supposing to exist. Shame, rather, on its repudiation and its denial! For its presence is the vital air which lets the world live, the salt which keeps it sweet.

.   .   .

34

JOHN HOSPERS (1918– ————)

What Means This Freedom?

When should human beings be held responsible for their behavior? According to Mill and other soft determinists, the answer is "Whenever they are doing what they want to do, that is, whenever they act without compulsion." Hospers questions whether this will do as a criterion for moral responsibility, and he considers some alternatives. He then goes on to discuss the far more disturbing question of "whether we are, in the final analysis, *responsible for any of our actions at all.*" His answer is that we probably are not, for reasons that are set forth in some detail in the following essay. Hospers' final position is, therefore, a version of *hard determinism.* (See p. 65 for a biographical note on John Hospers.)

. . . As a preparation for developing my own views on the subject, I want to mention a factor that I think is of enormous importance and relevance: namely, unconscious motivation. There are many actions—not those of an insane person (however the term "insane" be defined), nor of a person ignorant of the effects of his action, nor ignorant of some relevant fact about the situation, nor in any obvious way mentally deranged—for which human beings in general and the courts in particular are inclined to hold the doer responsible, and for which, I would say, he should not be held responsible. The deed may be planned, it may be carried out in cold calculation, it may spring from the agent's character and be continuous with the rest of his behavior, and it may be perfectly true that he could have done differently *if* he had wanted to; nonetheless his behavior was brought about by unconscious conflicts developed in infancy, over which he had no control and of which (without training in psychiatry) he does not even have knowledge. He may even *think* he knows why he acted as he did, he may *think* he has conscious control over his actions, he may even *think* he is fully responsible for them; but he is not. Psychiatric casebooks provide hundreds of examples. The law and common sense, though puzzled sometimes by such cases, are gradually becoming aware that they exist; but at this early stage countless tragic blunders still occur because neither the law nor the public in general is aware of the genesis of criminal actions. The mother blames her daughter for choosing the wrong men as candidates for husbands; but though the daughter thinks she is choosing freely and spends a considerable amount of time "deciding" among them, the identification with her sick father, resulting from Oedipal fantasies in early childhood, prevents her from caring for any but sick men, twenty or thirty years older than herself. Blaming her is beside the point; she cannot help it, and she cannot change it. Countless criminal acts are thought out in great detail; yet the participants are (without their own knowledge) acting out fantasies, fears, and defenses from early childhood, over whose coming and going they have no conscious control.

Now, I am not saying that none of these persons should be in jails or asylums. Often society must be protected against them. Nor am I saying that people should cease the practices of blaming and praising, punishing and rewarding; in general these devices are justified by the results—although very often they have practically no effect; the deeds are done from inner compulsion, which is not lessened when the threat of punishment is great. I am only saying that frequently persons we think responsible are not properly to be called so; we mistakenly think them responsible because we assume they are like those in whom no unconscious drive (toward this type of behavior) is present, and that their behavior can be changed by reasoning, exhorting, or threatening.

I

I have said that these persons are not responsible. But what is the criterion for responsibility? Under precisely what conditions is a person to be held morally responsible for an action? Disregarding here those conditions that have to do with a person's *ignorance* of the situation or the effects of his action, let us concentrate on those having to do with his "inner state." There are several criteria that might be suggested:

1. The first idea that comes to mind is that responsibility is determined by the presence or absence of *premeditation*—the opposite of "premeditated" being, presumably, "unthinking" or "impulsive." But this will not do—both because some acts are not premeditated but responsible, and because some are premeditated and not responsible.

Many acts we call responsible can be as unthinking or impulsive as you please. If you rush across the street to help the victim of an automobile collision, you are (at least so we would ordinarily say) acting responsibly, but you did not do so out of premeditation; you saw the accident, you didn't think, you rushed to the scene without hesitation. It was like a reflex action. But you acted responsibly: unlike the knee jerk, the act was the result of past training and past thought about situations of this kind; that is why you ran to help instead of ignoring the incident or running away. When something done originally from conviction or training becomes habitual, it becomes *like* a reflex action. As Aristotle said, virtue should become second nature through habit: a virtuous act should be performed *as if* by instinct; this, far from detracting from its moral worth, testifies to one's mastery of the desired type of behavior; one does not have to make a moral effort each time it is repeated.

There are also premeditated acts for which, I would say, the person is not responsible. Premeditation, especially when it is so exaggerated as to issue in no action at all, can be the result of neurotic disturbance or what we sometimes call an emotional "block," which the person inherits from long-past situations. In Hamlet's revenge on his uncle (I use this example because it is familiar to all of us), there was no lack, but rather a surfeit, of premeditation; his actions were so exquisitely premeditated as to make Freud and Dr. Ernest Jones look more closely to find out what lay behind them. The very premeditation camouflaged unconscious motives of which Hamlet himself was not aware. I think this is an important point, since it seems that the courts often assume that premeditation is a criterion of responsibility. If failure to kill his uncle had been considered a crime, every court in the land would have convicted Hamlet. Again: a woman's decision to stay with her husband in spite of endless "mental cruelty" is, if she is the victim of an unconscious masochistic "will to punishment," one for which she is not responsible; she is the victim and not the agent, no matter how profound her conviction that she is the agent; she is caught in a masochistic web (of complicated genesis) dating back to babyhood, perhaps a repetition of a comparable situation involving her own parents, a repetition-compulsion that, as Freud said, goes "beyond the pleasure principle." Again: a criminal whose crime was carefully planned step by step is usually considered responsible, but as we shall see in later examples, the overwhelming impulse toward it, stemming from an unusually humiliating ego defeat in early childhood, was as compulsive as any can be.

2. Shall we say, then, that a person is not responsible for his act unless he can *defend it with reasons?* I am afraid that this criterion is no better than the previous one. First, intellectuals are usually better at giving reasons than nonintellectuals, and according to this criterion would be more responsible than persons acting from moral conviction not implemented by reasoning; yet it is very doubtful whether we should want to say that the latter are more responsible. Second, the giving of reasons itself may be suspect. The reasons may be rationalizations camouflaging unconscious motives of which the agent knows nothing. Hamlet gave many reasons for not doing what he felt it was his duty to do: the time was not right, his uncle's soul might go to heaven, etc. His various "reasons" contradicted one another, and if an overpowering compulsion had not been present, the highly intellectual Hamlet would not have been taken in for a moment by these rationalizations. The real reason, the

Oedipal conflict that made his uncle's crime the accomplishment of his own deepest desire, binding their fates into one and paralyzing him into inaction, was unconscious and of course unknown to him. One's intelligence and reasoning power do not enable one to escape from unconsciously motivated behavior; it only gives one greater facility in rationalizing that behavior; one's intelligence is simply used in the interests of the neurosis—it is pressed into service to justify with reasons what one does quite independently of the reasons.

If these two criteria are inadequate, let us seek others.

3. Shall we say that a person is responsible for his action unless it is the *result of unconscious forces* of which he knows nothing? Many psychoanalysts would probably accept this criterion. If it is not largely reflected in the language of responsibility as ordinarily used, this may be due to ignorance of fact; most people do not know that there are such things as unconscious motives and unconscious conflicts causing human beings to act. But it may be that if they did, perhaps they would refrain from holding persons responsible for certain actions.

I do not wish here to quarrel with this criterion of responsibility. I only want to point out the fact that if this criterion is employed a far greater number of actions will be excluded from the domain of responsibility than we might at first suppose. Whether we are neat or untidy, whether we are selfish or unselfish, whether we provoke scenes or avoid them, even whether we can exert our powers of will to change our behavior—all these may, and often do, have their source in our unconscious life.

4. Shall we say that a person is responsible for his act unless it is *compelled?* Here we are reminded of Aristotle's assertion (*Nicomachean Ethics,* Book III) that a person is responsible for his act except for reasons of either ignorance or compulsion. Ignorance is not part of our problem here (unless it is unconsciously induced ignorance of facts previously remembered and selectively forgotten—in which case the forgetting is again compulsive), but compulsion is. How will compulsion do as a criterion? The difficulty is to state just what . it means. When we say an act is compelled in a psychological sense, our language is metaphorical—which is not to say that there is no point in it or that, properly interpreted, it is not true. Our actions are compelled in a literal sense if someone has us in chains or is controlling our bodily movements. When we say that the storm compelled us to jettison the cargo of the ship (Aristotle's example), we have a less literal sense of compulsion, for at least it is open to us to go down with the ship. When psychoanalysts say that a man was compelled by unconscious conflicts to wash his hands constantly, this is also not a literal use of "compel"; for nobody forced his hands under the tap. Still, it is a typical example of what psychologists call *compulsive* behavior: it has unconscious causes inaccessible to introspection, and moreover nothing can change it—it is as inevitable for him to do it as it would be if someone were forcing his hands under the tap. In this it is exactly like the action of a powerful external force; it is just as little within one's conscious control.

In its area of application this interpretation of responsibility comes to much the same as the previous one. And this area is very great indeed. For if we cannot be held responsible for the infantile situations (in which we were after all passive victims), then neither, it would seem, can we be held responsible for compulsive actions occurring in adulthood that are inevitable consequences of those infantile situations. And, psychiatrists and psychoanalysts tell us, actions fulfilling this description are characteristic of all people some of the time and some people most of the time. Their occurrence, once the infantile events have taken place, is inevitable, just as the explosion is inevitable once the fuse has been lighted; there is simply more "delayed action" in the psychological explosions than there is in the physical ones.

5. There is still another criterion, which I prefer to the previous ones, by which a man's responsibility for an act can be measured: the degree to which that act can (or could have been) *changed by the use of reasons.* Suppose that the man who washes his hands constantly does so, he says, for hygienic reasons, believing that if he doesn't do so he will be poisoned by germs. We now convince him, on the best medical authority, that his belief is groundless. Now, the test of his responsibility is whether the changed belief will result in changed behavior. If it does not, as with the compulsive hand washer, he is not acting responsibly, but if it does, he is. It is not the *use* of reasons, but their *efficacy in changing behavior,* that is being made the criterion of responsibility. And clearly in neurotic cases no such change occurs; in fact, this is often made the defining characteristic of neurotic behavior: it is unchangeable by any rational considerations.

II

I have suggested these criteria to distinguish actions for which we can call the agent responsible from those for which we cannot. Even persons with extensive knowledge of psychiatry do not, I think, use any one of these criteria to the exclusion of the others; a conjunction of two or more may be used at once. But however they may be combined or selected in actual application, I believe we can make the distinction along some such lines as we have suggested.

But is there not still another possible meaning of "responsibility" that we have not yet mentioned? Even after we have made all the above distinctions, there remains a question in our minds whether we are, in the final analysis, *responsible for any of our actions at all.* The issue may be put this way: How can anyone be responsible for his actions, since they grow out of his character, which is shaped and molded and made what it is by influences—some hereditary, but most of them stemming from early parental environment—that were not of his own making or choosing? This question, I believe, still troubles many people who would agree to all the distinctions we have just made but still have the feeling that "this isn't all." They have the uneasy suspicion that there is a more ultimate sense, a "deeper" sense, in which we are *not* responsible for our actions, since we are not responsible for the character out of which those actions spring. . . .

Let us take as an example a criminal who, let us say, strangled several persons and is himself now condemned to die in the electric chair. Jury and public alike hold him fully responsible (at least they utter the words "he is responsible"), for the murders were planned down to the minutest detail, and the defendant tells the jury exactly how he planned them. But now we find how it all came about; we learn of parents who rejected him from babyhood, of the childhood spent in one foster home after another, where it was always plain to him that he was not wanted; of the constantly frustrated early desire for affection, the hard shell of nonchalance and bitterness that he assumed to cover the painful and humiliating fact of being unwanted, and his subsequent attempts to heal these wounds to his shattered ego through defensive aggression.

> The criminal is the most passive person in this world, helpless as a baby in his motorically inexpressible fury. Not only does he try to wreak revenge on the mother of the earliest period of his babyhood; his criminality is based on the inner feeling of being incapable of making the mother even feel that the child seeks revenge on her. The situation is that of a dwarf trying to annoy a giant who superciliously refuses to see these attempts. . . . Because of his inner feeling of being a dwarf, the criminotic uses, so to speak, dynamite. Of that the giant must take cognizance. True, the "revenge" harms the avenger. He may be legally executed. However, the primary inner aim of forcing the giant to acknowledge the dwarf's fury is fulfilled.[1]

The poor victim is not conscious of the inner forces that exact from him this ghastly toll; he battles, he schemes, he revels in pseudo-aggression, he is miserable, but he does not know what works within him to produce these catastrophic acts of crime. His aggressive actions are the wriggling of a worm on a fisherman's hook. And if this is so, it seems difficult to say any longer, "He is responsible." Rather, we shall put him behind bars for the protection of society, but we shall no longer flatter our feeling of moral superiority by calling him personally responsible for what he did.

Let us suppose it were established that a man commits murder only if, sometime during the previous week, he has eaten a certain combination of foods—say, tuna fish salad at a meal also including peas, mushroom soup, and blueberry pie. What if we were to track down the factors common to all murders committed in this country during the last twenty years and found this

[1]Edmund Bergler, *The Basic Neurosis* (New York: Grune and Stratton, 1949), p. 305.

factor present in all of them, and only in them? The example is of course empirically absurd; but may it not be that there is *some* combination of factors that regularly leads to homicide, factors such as are described in general terms in the above quotation? (Indeed the situation in the quotation is less fortunate than in our hypothetical example, for it is easy to avoid certain foods once we have been warned about them, but the situation of the infant is thrust on him; something has already happened to him once and for all, before he knows it has happened.) When such specific factors are discovered, won't they make it clear that it is foolish and pointless, as well as immoral, to hold human beings responsible for crimes? Or, if one prefers biological to psychological factors, suppose a neurologist is called in to testify at a murder trial and produces X-ray pictures of the brain of the criminal; anyone can see, he argues, that the *cella turcica* was already calcified at the age of nineteen; it should be a flexible bone, growing, enabling the gland to grow.[2] All the defendant's disorders might have resulted from this early calcification. Now, this particular explanation may be empirically false; but who can say that no such factors, far more complex, to be sure, exist?

When we know such things as these, we no longer feel so much tempted to say that the criminal is responsible for his crime; and we tend also (do we not?) to excuse him—not legally (we still confine him to prison) but morally; we no longer call him a monster or hold him personally responsible for what he did. Moreover, we do this in general, not merely in the case of crime: "You must excuse Grandmother for being irritable; she's really quite ill and is suffering some pain all the time." Or: "The dog always bites children after she's had a litter of pups; you can't blame her for it: she's not feeling well, and besides she naturally wants to defend them." Or: "She's nervous and jumpy, but do excuse her: she has a severe glandular disturbance."

Let us note that the more *thoroughly* and *in detail* we know the causal factors leading a person to behave as he does, the more we tend to exempt him from responsibility. When we know nothing of the man except what we see him do, we say he is an ungrateful cad who expects much of other people and does nothing in return, and we are usually indignant. When we learn that his parents were the same way and, having no guilt feelings about this mode of behavior themselves, brought him up to be greedy and avaricious, we see that we could hardly expect him to have developed moral feelings in this direction. When we learn, in addition, that he is not aware of being ungrateful or selfish, but unconsciously represses the memory of events unfavorable to himself, we feel that the situation is unfortunate but "not really his fault." When we know that this behavior of his, which makes others angry, occurs more constantly when he feels tense or insecure, and that he now feels tense and insecure, and that relief from pressure will diminish it, then we tend to "feel sorry for the poor guy" and say he's more to be pitied than censured. We no longer want

[2]Meyer Levin, *Compulsion* (New York: Simon and Schuster, 1956), p. 403.

to say that he is personally responsible; we might rather blame nature or his parents for having given him an unfortunate constitution or temperament.

> In recent years a new form of punishment has been imposed on middle-aged and elderly parents. Their children, now in their twenties, thirties or even forties, present them with a modern grievance: "My analysis proves that *you* are responsible for my neurosis." Overawed by these authoritative statements, the poor tired parents fall easy victims to the newest variations on the scapegoat theory.
>
> In my opinion, this senseless cruelty—which disinters educational sins which had been burned for decades, and uses them as the basis for accusations which the victims cannot answer—is unjustified. Yes "the truth loves to be centrally located" (Melville), and few parents—since they are human—have been perfect. But granting their mistakes, they acted as *their* neurotic difficulties forced them to act. To turn the tables and declare the children not guilty because of the *impersonal* nature of their own neuroses, while at the same time the parents are *personally* blamed, is worse than illogical; it is profoundly unjust.[3]

And so, it would now appear, neither of the parties is responsible: "they acted as their neurotic difficulties forced them to act." The patients are not responsible for their neurotic manifestations, but then neither are the parents responsible for theirs; and so, of course, for their parents in turn, and theirs before them. It is the twentieth-century version of the family curse, the curse on the House of Atreus.

"But," a critic complains, "it's immoral to exonerate people indiscriminately in this way. I might have thought it fit to excuse somebody because he was born on the other side of the tracks, if I didn't know so many bank presidents who were also born on the other side of the tracks." Now, I submit that the most immoral thing in this situation is the critic's caricature of the conditions of the excuse. Nobody is excused merely because he was born on the other side of the tracks. But if he was born on the other side of the tracks *and* was a highly narcissistic infant to begin with *and* was repudiated or neglected by his parents *and* . . . (here we list a finite number of conditions), and if this complex of factors is *regularly* followed by certain behavior traits in adulthood, and moreover *unavoidably* so—that is, they occur no matter what he or anyone else tries to do—then we excuse him morally and say he is not responsible for his deed. If he is not responsible for *A*, a series of events occurring in his babyhood, then neither is he responsible for *B*, a series of things he does in adulthood, provided that *B* inevitably—that is, unavoidably— follows upon the occurrence of *A*. And according to psychiatrists and psychoanalysts, this often happens.

But one may still object that so far we have talked only about neurotic behavior. Isn't nonneurotic or normal or not unconsciously motivated (or whatever you want to call it) behavior still within the area of responsibility?

[3]Edmund Bergler, *The Superego* (New York: Grune and Stratton, 1952), p. 320.

There are reasons for answering "No" even here, for the normal person no more than the neurotic one has caused his own character, which makes him what he is. Granted that neurotics are not responsible for their behavior (that part of it which we call neurotic) because it stems from undigested infantile conflicts that they had no part in bringing about, and that are external to them just as surely as if their behavior had been forced on them by a malevolent deity (which is indeed one theory on the subject); but the so-called normal person is equally the product of causes in which his volition took no part. And if, unlike the neurotic's, his behavior is changeable by rational considerations, and if he has the will power to overcome the effects of an unfortunate early environment, this again is no credit to him; he is just lucky. If energy is available to him in a form in which it can be mobilized for constructive purposes, this is no credit to him, for this too is part of his psychic legacy. Those of us who can discipline ourselves and develop habits of concentration of purpose tend to blame those who cannot, and call them lazy and weak-willed; but what we fail to see is that they literally *cannot* do what we expect; if their psyches were structured like ours, they could, but as they are burdened with a tyrannical super-ego (to use psychoanalytic jargon for the moment), and a weak defenseless ego whose energies are constantly consumed in fighting endless charges of the supergo, they simply cannot do it, and it is irrational to expect it of them. We cannot with justification blame them for their inability, any more than we can congratulate ourselves for our ability. This lesson is hard to learn, for we constantly and naively assume that other people are constructed as we ourselves are.

For example: A child raised under slum conditions, whose parents are socially ambitious and envy families with money, but who nevertheless squander the little they have on drink, may simply be unable in later life to mobilize a drive sufficient to overcome these early conditions. Common sense would expect that he would develop the virtue of thrift; he would make quite sure that he would never again endure the grinding poverty he had expeienced as a child. But in fact it is not so: the exact conditions are too complex to be specified in detail here, but when certain conditions are fulfilled (concerning the subject's early life), he will always thereafter be a spendthrift, and no rational considerations will be able to change this. He will listen to the rational considerations and see the force of these, but they will not be able to change him, even if he tries; he cannot change his wasteful habits any more than he can lift the Empire State Building with his bare hands. We moralize and plead with him to be thrifty, but we do not see how strong, how utterly overpowering, and how constantly with him, is the opposite drive, which is so easily manageable with us. But he is possessed by the all-consuming, all-encompassing urge to make the world see that he belongs, that he has arrived, that he is just as well off as anyone else, that the awful humiliations were not real, that they never actually occurred, for isn't he now able to spend and spend? The humiliation must be blotted out; and conspicuous, flashy, expensive, and wasteful buying will do this; it shows the world what the world must know! True, it is only for the moment; true, it is in the end self-defeating, for wasteful consumption is the best way to bring poverty back again; but the person with an overpowering drive to mend a lesion to his narcissism cannot resist the avalanche of that drive with his puny rational consideration. A man with his back against the wall and a gun at his throat doesn't think of what may happen ten years hence. (Consciously, of course, he knows nothing of this drive; all that appears to consciousness is its shattering effects; he knows only that he must keep on spending—not why—and that he is unable to resist.) He hasn't in him the psychic capacity, the energy to stem the tide of a drive that at the moment is all-powerful. We, seated comfortably away from this flood, sit in judgment on him and blame him and exhort him and criticize him; but he, carried along by the flood, cannot do otherwise than he does. He may fight with all the strength of which he is capable, but it is not enough. And we, who are rational enough at least to exonerate a man in a situation of "overpowering impulse" when we recognize it to be one, do not even recognize this as an example of it, and so, in addition to being swept away in the flood that childhood conditions rendered inevitable, he must also endure our lectures, our criticisms, and our moral excoriation.

But, one will say, he could have overcome his spendthrift tendencies; some people do. Quite true: some people do. They are lucky. They have it in them to overcome early deficiencies by exerting great effort, and they are capable of exerting the effort. Some of us, luckier still, can overcome them with but little effort; and a few, the luckiest, haven't the deficiencies to overcome. It's all a matter of luck. The least lucky are those who can't overcome them, even with great effort, and those who haven't the ability to exert the effort.

But, one persists, it isn't a matter simply of luck; it *is* a matter of effort. Very well then, it's a matter of effort; without exerting the effort you may not overcome the deficiency. But whether or not you are the kind of person who has it in him to exert the effort is a matter of luck.

All this is well known to psychoanalysts. They can predict, from minimal cues that most of us don't notice, whether a person is going to turn out to be lucky or not. "The analyst," they say, "must be able to use the residue of the patient's unconscious guilt so as to remove the symptom or character trait that creates the guilt. The guilt must not only be present, but *available* for use, *mobilizable*. If it is used up (absorbed) in criminal activity, or in an excessive amount of self-damaging tendencies, then it cannot be used for therapeutic purposes, and the prognosis is negative." Not all philosophers will relish the analyst's way of putting the matter, but at least as a physician he can soon detect whether the patient is lucky or unlucky—and he knows that whichever it is, it *isn't the patient's fault.* The patient's conscious volition cannot remedy the deficiency. Even whether he will co-operate with the analyst is really out of the patient's hands: if he continually projects the denying-mother fantasy on the analyst and unconsciously identifies him always with the cruel, harsh forbidder of the nursery, thus frustrating any attempt at impersonal observation, the sessions are useless; yet if it happens that way, he can't help that either. That fatal projection is not under his control; whether it occurs or not depends on how his unconscious identifications have developed since his infancy. He can try, yes—but the ability to try enough for the therapy to have effect is also beyond his control; the capacity to try more than just so much is either there or it isn't—and either way "it's in the lap of the gods."

The position, then, is this: if we *can* overcome the effects of early environment, the ability to do so is itself a product of the early environment. We did not give ourselves this ability; and if we lack it we cannot be blamed for not having it. Sometimes, to be sure, moral exhortation brings out an ability that is there but not being used, and in this lies its *occasional* utility; but very often its use is pointless, because the ability is not there. The only thing that can overcome a desire, as Spinoza said, is a stronger contrary desire; and many times there simply is no wherewithal for producing a stronger contrary desire. Those of us who do have the wherewithal are lucky.

There is one possible practical advantage in remembering this. It may prevent us (unless we are compulsive blamers) from indulging in righteous indignation and committing the sin of spiritual pride, thanking God that we are not as this publican here. And it will protect from our useless moralizings those who are least equipped by nature for enduring them. As with responsibility, so with deserts. Someone commits a crime and is punished by the state; "he deserved it," we say self-righteously—as if we were moral and he immoral, when in fact we are lucky and he is unlucky—forgetting that there, but for the grace of God and a fortunate early environment, go we. Or, as Clarence Darrow said in his speech for the defense in the Loeb-Leopold case:

> I do not believe that people are in jail because they deserve to be. . . . I know what causes the emotional life. . . . I know it is practically left out of some. Without it they cannot act with the rest. They cannot feel the moral shocks which safeguard others. Is [this man] to blame that his machine is imperfect? Who is to blame? I do not know. I have never in my life been interested so much in fixing blame as I have in relieving people from blame. I am not wise enough to fix it.[4]

.   .   .

[4]Levin, *op. cit.,* pp. 439–440, 469.

35

PHILIPPA FOOT (1920– ————)

Free Will as Involving Determinism

Philippa Foot was born and educated in England and has taught at several universities in the United States as well as at Oxford University in England. She is now professor of philosophy at the University of California in Los Angeles and senior research fellow, Somerville College, Oxford University. She is the editor of *Theories of Ethics* (1967), a collection of essays dealing with various problems in contemporary ethical theory.

Soft determinism, as we have seen, is the view that universal determinism is consistent with—compatible with—the view that human beings may be free in the way required to render them morally responsible even though determinism is the case. Some philosophers have argued, however, that not only is determinism *compatible* with moral freedom, but it is an *essential condition* of such freedom. It is this latter thesis that Professor Foot attempts to refute in the essay that follows. She attacks three arguments that have been put forward in support of the freedom-requires-determinism thesis: (1) that an undetermined act could not properly be called an *action* at all, and thus could not be fittingly praised or blamed, (2) that an undetermined act would not be the action of a rational agent, who alone is capable of being morally responsible, and (3) that an undetermined act would not be connected with anything permanent in the character of the agent, and for this reason would not be a fitting occasion for praise, blame, reward, or punishment. Professor Foot finds all three arguments unconvincing, and her article is devoted to pointing out in careful detail just where each argument, in her opinion, fails.

The idea that free will can be reconciled with the strictest determinism is now very widely accepted. To say that a man acted freely is, it is often suggested, to say that he was not constrained, or that he could have done otherwise if he had chosen, or something else of that kind; and since these things could be true

From Philippa Foot, "Free Will as Involving Determinism," in *The Philosophical Review,* 66 (1957), pp. 439–450. Reprinted by permission of the author and the publisher.

even if his action was determined it seems that there could be room for free will even within a universe completely subject to causal laws. Hume put forward a view of this kind in contrasting the "liberty of spontaneity . . . which is oppos'd to violence" with the nonexistent "liberty of indifference . . . which means a negation of necessity and causes."[1] A. J. Ayer, in his essay "Freedom and Necessity"[2] was summing up such a position when he said, "from the fact that my action is causally determined . . . it does not necessarily follow that I am not free"[3] and "it is not when my action has any cause at all, but only when it has a special sort of cause, that it is reckoned not to be free."[4]

I am not here concerned with the merits of this view but only with a theory which appears more or less incidentally in the writings of those who defend it. This is the argument that so far from being incompatible with determinism, free will actually requires it. It appears briefly in Hume's *Treatise* and was set out in full in an article by R. E. Hobart.[5] P. H. Nowell-Smith was expressing a similar view when he said of the idea that determinism is opposed to free will that "the clearest proof that it is mistaken or at least muddled lies in showing that I could not be free to choose what I do *unless* determinism is correct. . . . Freedom, so far from being incompatible with causality implies it."[6] Ayer has taken up a similar position, arguing that the absence of causal laws governing action "does not give the moralist what he wants. For he is anxious to show that men are capable of acting freely in order to infer that they can be morally responsible for what they do. But if it is a matter of pure chance that a man should act in one way rather than another, he may be free but he can hardly be responsible."[7]

This argument is not essential to the main thesis of those who use it; their own account of free will in such terms as the absence of *constraining* causes might be correct even though there were no inconsistencies in the suggestion put forward by their libertarian opponents. But if valid the argument would be a strong argument, disposing of the position of anyone who argued both that free will required the absence of determining causes and that free will was a possibility. That the argument is not valid, and indeed that it is singularly implausible, I shall now try to show. It is, I think, surprising that it should have survived so long; this is perhaps because it has not had to bear much weight. In any case the weapons which can be used against it are ones which are in general use elsewhere.

In discussing determinism and free will it is important to be clear about the sense which is given in this context to words such as "determined" and "caused." Russell gave this account:

[1] *Treatise,* bk. II, pt. III, sec. 2.
[2] *Polemic,* no. 5 (1946); reprinted in his *Philosophical Essays* (London, 1954).
[3] *Philosophical Essays,* p. 278.
[4] *Ibid.,* p. 281.
[5] "Freewill as Involving Determinism," *Mind,* XLIII (1934), 1–27.
[6] "Freewill and Moral Responsibility," *Mind,* LVII (1948), 46.
[7] *Philosophical Essays,* p. 275.

The law of universal causation . . . may be enunciated as follows: There are such invariable relations between different events at the same or different times that, given the state of the whole universe throughout any finite time, however short, every previous and subsequent event can theoretically be determined as a function of the given events during that time.[8]

This seems to be the kind of determinism which worries the defender of free will, for if human action is subject to a universal law of causation of this type, there will be for any action a set of sufficient conditions which can be traced back to factors outside the control of the agent.

We cannot of course take it for granted that whenever the word "determined" or the word "cause" is used this is what is implied, and what is intended may be in no way relevant to the question of free will. For instance, an action said to be determined by the desires of the man who does it is not necessarily an action for which there is supposed to be a sufficient condition. In saying that it is determined by his desires we may mean merely that he is doing something that he wants to do, or that he is doing it for the sake of something else that he wants. There is nothing in this to suggest determinism in Russell's sense. On the whole it is wise to be suspicious of expressions such as "determined by desire" unless these have been given a clear sense, and this is particularly true of the phrase "determined by the agent's character." Philosophers often talk about actions being determined by a man's character, but it is not certain that anyone else does, or that the words are given any definite sense. One might suppose that an action was so determined if it was *in* character, for instance the generous action of a generous man; but if this is so we will not have the kind of determinism traditionally supposed to raise difficulties for a doctrine of free will. For nothing has been said to suggest that where the character trait can be predicated the action will invariably follow; it has not been supposed that a man who can truly be said to be generous never acts ungenerously even under given conditions.

Keeping the relevant sense of "determinism" in mind, we may now start to discuss the view that free will requires determinism. The first version which I shall consider is that put forward by Hobart, who suggests that an action which is not determined cannot properly be called an *action* at all, being something that happened to the agent rather than something he *did*. Hobart says, "*In proportion* as it [the action] is undetermined, it is just as if his legs should suddenly spring up and carry him off where he did not prefer to go." To see how odd this suggestion is we have only to ask when we would say that a man's legs were carrying him where he did not prefer to go. One can imagine the scene: he is sitting quietly in his chair and has said that he is going to go on reading his book; suddenly he cries, "Good heavens, I can't control my legs!" and as he moves across the room, he hangs on to the furniture or asks

<hr>

[8]"On the Notion of Cause," in *Our Knowledge of the External World* (London, 1914), p. 221.

someone else to hold him. Here indeed his legs are carrying him where he does not want to go, but what has this to do with indeterminism, and what has the ordinary case, where he walks across the room, to do with determinism? Perhaps Hobart thinks that when a man does something meaning to do it, he does what he wants to do, and so his action is determined by his desire. But to do something meaning to do it is to do it in a certain way, not to do it as the result of the operation of a causal law. When one means to do something, one does not call out for help in preventing the movement of one's limbs; on the contrary, one is likely to stop other people from interfering, saying, "I want to do this." It is by such factors that walking across the room is distinguished from being carried off by one's legs. It is to be explained in terms of the things said and done by the agent, not in terms of some force, "the desire," present before the action was done and still less in terms of some law telling us that whenever this "desire" is found it will be followed by the action. The indeterminist has no difficulty in distinguishing an action from something that happens to the agent; he can say exactly the same as anyone else.

Nowell-Smith seems to be thinking along somewhat the same lines as Hobart when he attacks C. A. Campbell for saying that free will requires indeterminism:

> The essence of Campbell's account is that the action should not be predictable from a knowledge of the agent's character. But, if this is so, can what he does be called *his* action at all? Is it not rather a *lusus naturae,* an Act of God or a miracle? If a hardened criminal, bent on robbing the poor-box, suddenly and *inexplicably* fails to do so, we should not say that he *chose* to resist or deserves *credit* for resisting the temptation; we should say, if we were religious, that he was the recipient of a sudden outpouring of Divine Grace or, if we were irreligious, that his "action" was due to chance, which is another way of saying that it was inexplicable. In either case we should refuse to use the active voice.[9]

It is hard to see why a man who does something inexplicably does not really *do* it. Let us suppose that the hardened criminal's action really is inexplicable; we can only say, "He just turned away," and not why he did so; this does not mean that he did it by accident, or unintentionally, or not of his own free will, and I see no reason for refusing to use the active voice. In any case, to explain an action is not necessarily to show that it could have been predicted from some fact about the agent's character—that he is weak, greedy, sentimental, and so forth. We may if we like say that an action is never *fully* explained unless it has been shown to be covered by a law which connects it to such a character trait; but then it becomes even more implausible to say that an action must be explicable if we are to admit it as something genuinely *done*. In the ordinary sense we explain the criminal's action if we say, for instance, that a

[9] *Ethics* (London, 1954), pp. 281–282.

particular thought came into his mind; we do not also have to find a law about the way such thoughts do come into the minds of such men.

A rather different version of this argument runs as follows. We hold responsible only a man who is a rational agent; if someone were always to do things out of the blue, without having any reason to do them, we should be inclined to count him as a lunatic, one who could not be held responsible for his actions, so that even if he *did* things he would do things for which he could not be held responsible. And is it not through being determined by motives that actions are those of a rational agent whom we can praise or blame?

It certainly would be odd to suppose that free will required the absence of motives for action. We do not of course expect that everything that the rational man does should be done with a motive; if he gets up and walks about the room he need not be doing so in order to take exercise; it is quite usual for people to do this kind of thing without any particular purpose in view, and no one is counted irrational for doing so. And yet we do expect a man to have a motive for a great number of the things that he does, and we would count anyone who constantly performed troublesome actions without a motive as irrational. So it looks as if a moral agent is a man whose actions are in general determined, if determinism is involved in "having a motive" for what he does.

What does it mean to say that someone had a motive for doing what he did? Often this particular expression means that he did it with a particular intention, so we should first say something about intentions and the sense in which they can be said to determine action. We say that a man had a certain intention in acting when he aimed at a certain thing, and "his motive for such and such" often means "his aim in doing such and such," for instance, "His motive for going to the station was to take a train to London." But where motives are intentions it is clear that they cannot be determining causes; for intending to do x and being ready to take the steps thought necessary to do x are connected not empirically but analytically. A man cannot be said to have an intention unless he is reconciled to what he believes to be the intermediate steps. We cannot speak as if the intention were something which could be determined first, and "being ready to take the necessary steps" were a second stage following on the first.

It might be objected that this does not cover the case of "doing y because one wants x" where "wanting x" does not imply trying to get x. In one sense of "want" it is possible to say, "He wants x" without knowing whether he is prepared to take steps to get it. (One might, for instance, want to go to London but not be prepared to spend the money to get there.) So that *wanting* seems here to be a separate condition, which might in certain cases be connected by an empirical law to the adoption of particular courses of action. Certainly wanting is not an event, but one gets rid of wanting as a determining factor too easily if one merely says that desires are not causes because they are not occurrences.

We say "He wants" in this sense where he would adopt certain policies *if* there were no reasons for not doing so. We can say, "He wants to get to London," even when he is not prepared to take the necessary steps to get to London, provided he can say, "Trains are too expensive," or "Hitchhiking is too uncomfortable." If we offered him a spare railway ticket or otherwise disposed of his reasons against going, and he still did not go, we would have to say, "He didn't really want to go after all." So wanting in this sense is being prepared to act under certain conditions, though not being prepared to act under the given conditions. It is a description which could be applied to a man before we knew whether he was ready to act in a given situation, and it seems that there might then be a causal relation between the wanting and the acting where the latter took place. This is quite true; there could be a law to the effect that when the description "He wants x" applied at t_1, the description "He is taking the necessary steps to get x" applied at t_2. It would be possible to say this without making a mistake about what it is to *want* and inventing a hidden condition of body or mind. One could say, "Wanting in this sense just is being prepared to act under some conditions," and still maintain that there could be an empirical law connecting wanting with acting under a particular set of conditions. The mistake lies not in the idea that such laws are *possible* but in the thought that there is a reference to them in the statement that a man did one thing because he wanted something else.

So far we have been dealing only with cases in which a question about a motive was answered by specifying something aimed at or wanted. Now we should turn to the cases in which the motive is said to be kindness, vanity, ambition, meanness, jealousy, and so on, to see whether determinism is involved.

It is easy to show that a motive is not a cause in Russell's sense, for it is clearly not an antecedent cause. Professor Gilbert Ryle has pointed out that a man who acts out of vanity is not a man who had a feeling of vanity immediately before he acted, and if it is objected that the vanity which preceded the action need not have manifested itself in a feeling, one may ask what else *would* count as the vanity which was causing him to act. A man's motives are not given by what was happening to him immediately before he started to act. Nor do we discover some independent condition contemporaneous with the action and a law linking the two, for again there is nothing which would count as vanity except the tendency to do this kind of thing.

So much is implied in what Ryle says about acting out of vanity, but his own account of what it is to do so still uses something which is objectionably like a causal model. The analogy which he thinks apt is that between saying a man acted out of vanity and saying a piece of glass broke because it was brittle: "To explain an act as done from a certain motive is not analogous to saying that the glass broke because a stone hit it, but to the quite different type of statement that the glass broke, when the stone hit it, because the glass was brittle."[10]

---

[10] *Concept of Mind* (London, 1949), pp. 86–87.

The positive part of this statement seems to me mistaken. Acting out of vanity is not so closely connected with being vain as Ryle must suppose it to be. Let us suppose that his account of what it is to be vain is entirely correct; to say that a man is vain is to say that he tends to behave in certain ways, to feel aggrieved in particular situations, and so on.[11] It does not follow that ascribing vanity as a motive for an action is bringing this action under the "lawlike" proposition that the agent is a man who tends to do these things. For it makes sense to say that a man acts out of vanity on a particular occasion although he is not in general vain, or even vain about this kind of thing. It cannot therefore be true that when we speak of an agent's motive for a particular action we are explaining it in terms of his character, as Ryle suggests; we are not saying "he *would* do that." It is of course possible to give a motive *and* to say that the agent has the character trait concerned, but the latter cannot be included in an account of what it is to assign a motive to a particular action.

The explanation of why Ryle says what he does seems to lie in the fact that he has taken a false example of explaining an action by giving a motive. He considers as his example the explanation, "He boasted because he is vain," which is not in fact an explanation of the right type; considered as a statement assigning a motive to a particular action it would be uninformative, for except in very special cases *boasting is* acting out of vanity. It is not surprising that this particular sentence has a different function—that of relating this act of vanity to the character trait. What Ryle says about the example is correct, but it is not an example of the kind of thing he is trying to describe.

It might seem as if we could reformulate the theory to meet the objection about the man who acts out of vanity on one occasion by saying that a man's acting out of vanity is like glass breaking because of a brittleness which could be temporary. "He acted out of vanity" would then be explained as meaning that at that particular time he tended to react in the ways described by Ryle. (If he finds a chance of securing the admiration and envy of others, he does whatever he thinks will produce this admiration and envy.) This is wrong because, whereas glass which is even temporarily brittle has all the reactions which go by this name, a man who is temporarily acting out of vanity is not liable to do other things of this kind. To find concepts which this model would fit one must turn to such descriptions as "a boastful mood," "a savage frame of mind," or "a fit of bad temper."

Assigning a motive to an action is not bringing it under any law; it is rather saying something about the kind of action it was, the direction in which it was tending, or what it was done *as*. A possible comparison would be with the explanation of a movement in a dance which consisted in saying what was being danced. Often in diagnosing motives we should look to purposes—to what the action was done for. This we should discover if we found out what the agent was prepared to go without and what he insisted on having; the fact

[11] *Ibid.,* p. 86.

that visitors are made to admire a garden even in the rain is strong evidence that they were invited out of vanity rather than kindness. In other cases finding the motive will be better described as finding what was being done—finding, for instance, that someone was *taking revenge.* We should take it that a man's motive was revenge if we discovered that he was intentionally harming someone and that his doing so was conditional on his believing that that person had injured him. In the same way we should take it that someone was acting out of gratitude if he (1) intended to confer a benefit and (2) saw this as called for by a past kindness. The fact that it is only the character of the particular action which is involved shows how far we are from anything which could involve motives as determining causes.

We have now considered two suggestions: (1) that an undetermined action would not be one which could properly be attributed to an agent as something that he *did* and (2) that an undetermined action would not be the action of a *rational* agent. A third version, the one put forward by Hume, suggests that an undetermined action would be one for which it would be impossible to praise or blame, punish or reward a man, because it would be connected with nothing permanent in his nature.

> 'Tis only [Hume says] upon the principles of necessity, that a person acquires any merit or demerit from his actions. . . . Actions are by their very nature temporary and perishing; and where they proceed not from some cause in the characters and disposition of the person, who perform'd them, they infix not themselves upon him, and can neither redound to his honour, if good, nor infamy, if evil. The action in itself may be blameable. . . . But the person is not responsible for it; and as it proceeded from nothing in him, that is durable and constant, and leaves nothing of that nature behind it, 'tis impossible he can, upon its account, become the object of punishment or vengeance.[12]

Hume is surely wrong in saying that we could not praise or blame, punish or reward, a person in whose character there was nothing "permanent or durable." As he was the first to point out, we do not need any *unchanging* element in order to say that a person is the same person throughout a period of time, and our concept of merit is framed to fit our concept of personal identity. We honor people as well as nations for what they have done in the past and do not consider what has been done merely as an indication of what may be expected in the future. Moreover, it is perfectly rational to punish people for what they have done, even if there is no reason to think that they would be likely to do it again. The argument that it will be a different *me* who will be beaten tomorrow carries no weight, for "different" or not the back which will be beaten is the one about which I am concerned today. So we have no reason to invent something durable and constant underlying the actions which we punish or reward. And it is not in fact our practice to pick out for

[12] *Treatise,* bk. II, pt. III, sec. 2.

praise or blame only those actions for which something of the kind can be found. It would be possible, of course, that we should do this, punishing the cruel action of the cruel man but not that of one usually kind. But even in such a situation there would be no argument against the man who said that moral responsibility depended upon indeterminism; for a motive is not a determining cause, nor is an habitual motive. If we say that a man constantly acts out of cruelty, we no more say that his actions are determined than if we say that he acts out of cruelty on a particular occasion. There could of course be a law to the effect that no one who has been cruel for thirty years can turn to kindness after that, and this would throw responsibility back from the later to the earlier acts. But it is clear that this is a special assumption in no way involved in the statement that cruelty is a "durable and constant" element in someone's character.

I have already mentioned Ayer's argument that moral responsibility cannot be defended on the basis of indeterminism and will now consider his version in detail. Ayer says that the absence of a cause will not give the moralist what he wants, because "if it is a matter of pure chance that a man should act in one way rather than another, he may be free but he can hardly be responsible."[13] To the suggestion that "my actions are the result of my own free choice," Ayer will reply with a question about how I came to make my choice:

> Either it is an accident that I choose to act as I do or it is not. If it is an accident, then it is merely a matter of chance that I did not choose otherwise; and if it is merely a matter of chance that I did not choose otherwise, it is surely irrational to hold me morally responsible for choosing as I did. But if it is not an accident that I chose to do one thing rather than another, then presumably there is some causal explanation of my choice: and in that case we are led back to determinism.[14]

The "presumably" seems to be the weak link in the argument, which assumes a straightforward opposition between causality and chance that does not in general exist. It is not at all clear that when actions or choices are called "chance" or "accidental" this has anything to do with the absence of causes, and if it has not we will not be saying that they are in the ordinary sense a matter of chance if we say that they are undetermined.

When should we say that it was a matter of chance that a man did what he did? A typical example would be the case in which a man killed someone with a bullet which glanced off some object in a totally unforseeable way; here he could disclaim responsibility for the act. But in this instance, and that of something done "by accident," we are dealing with what is done unintentionally, and this is not the case which Ayer has in mind. We may turn, as he does, to the actions which could be said to have been "chosen" and ask how the

[13] *Philosophical Essays,* p. 275.
[14] *Ibid.*

words "chance" and "accident" apply to choices. Ayer says, "Either it is an accident that I choose to act as I do, or it is not." The notion of choosing by accident to do something is on the face of it puzzling; for usually choosing to do something is opposed to doing it by accident. What does it mean to say that the choice itself was accidental? The only application I can think of for the words "I chose by accident" is in a case such as the following. I choose a firm with which to have dealings without meaning to pick on one run by an international crook. I can now rebut the charge of *choosing a firm run by an international crook* by saying that I chose it by accident. I cannot be held responsible for this but only for any carelessness which may have been involved. But this is because the relevant action—the one with which I am being charged—was unintentional; it is for this reason and not because my action was uncaused that I can rebut the charge. Nothing is said about my action being uncaused, and if it were, this could not be argued on my behalf; the absence of causes would not give me the same right to make the excuse.

Nor does it make any difference if we substitute "chance" for "accident." If I say that it was a matter of chance that I chose to do something, I rebut the suggestion that I chose it for this reason or for that, and this can be a plea against an accusation which has to do with my reasons. But I do not imply that there was no reason for my doing what I did, and I say nothing whatsoever about my choice being undetermined. If we use "chance" and "accident" as Ayer wants to use them, to signify the absence of causes, we shall have moved over to a totally different sense of the words, and "I chose it by chance" can no longer be used to disclaim responsibility.

For Further Reading

Adler, Mortimer, et al. *The Idea of Freedom.* Garden City, N.Y.: Doubleday, 1958.

Ayers, M. R. *The Refutation of Determinism.* London: Methuen, 1968.

Beardsley, Elizabeth L. "Determinism and Moral Perspectives," *Philosophy and Phenomenological Research,* 21 (1960), 1–20.

Bergson, Henri. *Time and Free Will.* New York: Harper & Row, 1962 (paperbound).

Berofsky, Bernard. *Determinism.* Princeton, N.J.: Princeton University Press, 1971.

————— (ed.). *Free Will and Determinism.* New York: Harper & Row, 1966. A valuable collection of writings from many sources.

Brand, Myles (ed.). *The Nature of Human Action.* Glenview, Ill.: Scott, Foresman, 1970 (paperbound). An anthology that deals with a basic issue: can sufficient explanations of human actions be given by references to causes?

Campbell, C. A. *In Defense of Free Will.* London: G. Allen & Unwin, 1967. A collection of essays by a prominent proponent of libertarianism.

—————. "Is 'Free Will' a Pseudo-Problem?" *Mind,* 60 (1951), 441–465.

—————. *On Selfhood and Godhood.* New York: Humanities Press, 1957.

Cranston, M. *Freedom—A New Analysis.* London: Longmans, Green, 1953.

Dworkin, Gerald (ed.). *Determinism, Free Will and Moral Responsibility.* Englewood Cliffs, N.J.: Prentice-Hall, 1970 (paperbound).

Eddington, A. S. *The Nature of the Physical World.* Ann Arbor: University of Michigan Press, 1958, Chap. 14 (paperbound).

Edwards, Jonathan. *Inquiry Concerning the Freedom of the Will,* ed. by Paul Ramsey. New Haven, Conn.: Yale University Press, 1957.

Ezorsky, G. (ed.). *Philosophical Perspectives on Punishment.* Albany, N.Y.: State University of New York Press, 1972. Classical and contemporary selections.

Farrer, Austin. *The Freedom of the Will.* New York: Scribner, 1960.

Fingarette, Herbert. *The Meaning of Criminal Insanity.* Berkeley: University of California Press, 1974 (paperbound).

Flew, Antony. *Crime or Disease?* New York: Harper & Row, 1973. An examination of the concept of mental illness as it relates to the legal and moral issues raised.

Foley, R. "Compatibilism," *Mind,* 88 (1948), 421–428. Defends soft determinism (compatibilism) by means of a careful analysis of the meaning of "able to do otherwise."

Frankfurt, H. "Alternate Possibilities and Moral Responsibility," *Journal of Philosophy,* 65 (1969), 829–839. Argues that ability to do otherwise is not a condition of being morally responsible.

Franklin, R. L. *Freewill and Determinism.* London: Routledge and Kegan Paul, 1968.

Glover, J. *Responsibility.* London: Routledge and Kegan Paul, 1970. Defends soft determinism.

Halverson, W. H. "The Bogy of Chance," *Mind,* 73 (1964), 567–570.

Hampshire, Stuart. *Freedom of Mind and Other Essays.* Princeton, N.J.: Princeton University Press, 1971. Favors "free will."

Honderich, T. (ed.). *Essays in the Freedom of Action.* London: Routledge and Kegan Paul, 1973. Contemporary sources.

Hook, Sidney (ed.). *Determinism and Freedom in the Age of Modern Science.* New York: New York University Press, 1958.

Hospers, John. "Free-Will and Psychoanalysis," in W. Sellars and J. Hospers (eds.). *Readings in Ethical Theory.* New York: Appleton-Century-Crofts, 1952.

Hume, David. *A Treatise of Human Nature.* Many editions. See Book II, Part III.

Laird, John. *On Human Freedom.* New York: Hillary House, 1947.

Lehrer, Keith. "Can We Know that We Have Free Will by Introspection?" *The Journal of Philosophy,* 57 (1960), 145–157.

MacMurray, John. *The Self as Agent.* New York: Humanities Press, 1957.

Matson, W. I. "On the Irrelevance of Free-Will to Moral Responsibility," *Mind,* 65 (1956), 489–497.

Nathan, N. M. L. "Compatibilism and Natural Necessity," *Mind,* 84 (1975), 277–280. A critique of Glover's defense of soft determinism (see above).

O'Connor, D. J. *Free Will.* London: Macmillan, 1972. An introductory discussion of the problem.

Pears, D. F. (ed.). *Freedom and the Will.* New York: St. Martin's Press, 1963.

Pike, N. "Divine Foreknowledge, Human Freedom and Possible Worlds," *Philosophical Review,* 86 (1977), 209–216. A defense of his 1965 thesis (see below) against a critique by Alvin Plantinga (see below).

——————. "Divine Omniscience and Voluntary Action," *Philosophical Review,* 74 (1965), 27–46. Argues that if God (as traditionally conceived) exists, no human actions are free.

Rankin, K. W. *Choice and Chance: A Libertarian Analysis.* Oxford: Basil Blackwell, 1961.

Rashdall, Hastings. *The Theory of Good and Evil.* Oxford: Oxford University Press, 1924, Book III, Chap. 3.

Rolston, H., III. "Schlick's Responsible Man," *Philosophy and Phenomenological Research,* 36 (1975), 261–267. A critique of Moritz Schlick's soft determinism.

Schlick, Moritz. *Problems of Ethics,* trans. by David Rynin. Englewood Cliffs, N.J.: Prentice-Hall, 1939, Chap. 7 (originally published in German in 1931).

Sidgwick, Henry. *The Methods of Ethics,* 7th ed., rev. by Constance Jones. Chicago: University of Chicago Press, 1962.

Skinner, B. F. *Beyond Freedom and Dignity.* New York: Knopf, 1971. A famous psychologist argues that the concept of free will has adverse social consequences and offers an alternative approach to various social problems.

——————. *Science and Human Behavior.* New York: Macmillan, 1953, Chap. 1.

Smart, J. J. C. "Free Will, Praise and Blame," *Mind,* 70 (1961), 291–306.

Stebbing, L. S. *Philosophy and the Physicists.* New York: Dover, 1958 (paperbound).

Stevenson, C. L. *Ethics and Language.* New Haven, Conn.: Yale University Press, 1960, Chap. 14 (paperbound).

van Inwagen, P. "Ability and Responsibility," *Philosophical Review,* 87 (1978), 201–224. A critique of Frankfurt's thesis (see above).

Walter, E. "Is Libertarianism Logically Coherent?" *Philosophy and Phenomenological Research,* 38 (1977–1978), 505–513. Argues that libertarianism is "not a logically possible state of affairs."

Watson, G. "Free Agency," *The Journal of Philosophy,* 72 (1975), 205–220. An attempt to elucidate some key concepts.

Wilson, John. "Freedom and Compulsion," *Mind,* 67 (1958), 60–69.

Young, R. *Freedom, Responsibility and God.* London: Macmillan, 1975. Defends a soft determinist view.

PART IX

Freedom and Authority

There is a law in the United States prescribing that the maximum speed on any highway shall be 55 miles per hour. There are also laws requiring income earners to pay taxes, property owners to maintain their sidewalks in good repair, drivers of automobiles to be properly licensed, motorcyclists to wear helmets, and so on. To live in society is to be governed by laws that restrict our freedom. They require us to do things we we might find disagreeable (pay taxes, for example) or prohibit us from doing other things that we might like to do (perhaps, drive our Porsche 90 miles per hour on an interstate highway).

Every law restricts, in some way, the freedom of those subject to that law. If the law of a city prescribes that no beer or wine may be sold on Sunday, then the freedom of the purveyors of beer and wine to sell their products in that city on Sunday is restricted. If the law of a state requires that anyone operating a motor vehicle must possess a valid driver's license, then the freedom of every driver to operate a motor vehicle in that state without possessing such a license is denied. Indeed, the very existence of a law presupposes the necessity or the desirability of restricting individual freedom in some way. It is not necessary to require people to do by law what they would do willingly and freely in the absence of law.

This state of affairs raises an interesting philosophical question: Does society have a *right* to limit the freedom of the individual in this way, and, if so, what is the basis of that right? This, in turn, leads to a related question: If it can be shown that society has some right to limit the freedom of the indivudual, what, if any, are the *limits* of that right?

When, if ever, is the exercise of authority legitimate, and when is it merely arbitrary?

These questions are of practical as well as theoretical interest. History is replete with examples of laws that, in retrospect, have been generally regarded as oppressive and unjustifiable: the pre–Civil War Fugitive Slave Law in this country and the anti-Jewish laws of Hitler's Germany are examples. By what standard, or standards, do we judge these laws to be unjust? On what basis can citizens distinguish between a legitimate and an illegitimate curtailment of freedom? When, if ever, do we have a right (perhaps a duty) to oppose the government and the law? Answers to such questions are determined by one's view of the authority of society to restrict the freedom of the individual.

The principal alternatives available with respect to the fundamental question are the natural law theory, the social contract theory, social utilitarianism, and theoretical anarchism. According to the *natural law* theory, all legitimate law is derived from eternal law—that is, God's will and plan for the governance of the world—which, insofar as it can be known by human beings, is called natural law. The *social contract* theory bases the legitimacy of law (and, by implication, the right of government to enforce that law) on the consent of the governed—that is, the members of society make a "deal" with one another in order to avoid inevitable warfare against each other. *Social utilitarianism* finds the justification for government and its laws in the ethical principle that it is always right to do that which will promote the greatest happiness for the greatest number of people. And, finally, *theoretical anarchism* holds that there is no theoretical justification for the authority of government, that the practice of imposing the will of some upon all derives simply from superior power, not from right.

36

THOMAS AQUINAS (1225–1274)

Four Kinds of Law

The natural law theory has never been more succinctly stated than by Thomas Aquinas in what is sometimes called his Treatise on Law (*Summa Theologica*, Part II-II, Questions 90–108). Aquinas defines law as "an ordinance of reason for the common good, promulgated by him who has the care of the community." But clearly, says Aquinas, God is responsible for the care of "the whole community of the universe." Therefore, all valid law is derived from God's will and plan for the government of the universe (what Aquinas calls "eternal" law). He then goes on to distinguish three kinds of law that are derived from eternal law: natural law, human law, and divine (that is, revealed) law. His account of human law should be read with special care, since it is the validation of such law that is most relevant to the problem with which we are concerned. (See p. 125 for a biographical note on Thomas Aquinas and a brief description of the five-part structure of Aquinas' exposition in the *Summa Theologica*.)

FIRST ARTICLE.

Whether There Is an Eternal Law?

We proceed thus to the First Article :—

Objection 1. It seems that there is no eternal law. Because every law is imposed on someone. But there was not someone from eternity on whom a law could be imposed: since God alone was from eternity. Therefore no law is eternal.

From Thomas Aquinas, *Summa Theologica*, First part of the Second part, Question 91, Articles 1–4, trans. the Fathers of the English Dominican Province (New York: Benziger Brothers, 1915), pp. 9–21.

Obj. 2. Further, promulgation is essential to law. But promulgation could not be from eternity: because there was no one to whom it could be promulgated from eternity. Therefore no law can be eternal.

Obj. 3. Further, a law implies order to an end. But nothing ordained to an end is eternal: for the last end alone is eternal. Therefore no law is eternal.

On the contrary, Augustine says (*De Lib. Arb.* i.): *That Law which is the Supreme Reason cannot be understood to be otherwise than unchangeable and eternal.*

I answer that, As stated above (Q. XC., A. 1 *ad* 2; AA. 3, 4), a law is nothing else but a dictate of practical reason emanating from the ruler who governs a perfect community. Now it is evident, granted that the world is ruled by Divine Providence, as was stated in the First Part (Q. XXII., AA. 1, 2), that the whole community of the universe is governed by Divine Reason. Wherefore the very Idea of the government of things in God the Ruler of the universe, has the nature of a law. And since the Divine Reason's conception of things is not subject to time but is eternal, according to Prov. viii. 23, therefore it is that this kind of law must be called eternal.

Reply Obj. 1. Those things that are not in themselves, exist with God, inasmuch as they are foreknown and preordained by Him, according to Rom. iv. 17: *Who calls those things that are not, as those that are.* Accordingly the eternal concept of the Divine law bears the character of an eternal law, in so far as it is ordained by God to the government of things foreknown by Him.

Reply Obj. 2. Promulgation is made by word of mouth or in writing; and in both ways the eternal law is promulgated: because both the Divine Word and the writing of the Book of Life are eternal. But the promulgation cannot be from eternity on the part of the creature that hears or reads.

Reply Obj. 3. The law implies order to the end actively, in so far as it directs certain things to the end; but not passively,—that is to say, the law itself is not ordained to the end,—except accidentally, in a governor whose end is extrinsic to him, and to which end his law must needs be ordained. But the end of the Divine government is God Himself, and His law is not distinct from Himself. Wherefore the eternal law is not ordained to another end.

SECOND ARTICLE.

Whether There Is in Us a Natural Law?

We proceed thus to the Second Article :—

Objection 1. It seems that there is no natural law in us. Because man is governed sufficiently by the eternal law: for Augustine says (*De Lib. Arb.* i.) that *the eternal law is that by which it is right that all things should be most orderly.* But nature does not abound in superfluities as neither does she fail in necessaries. Therefore no law is natural to man.

Obj. 2. Further, by the law man is directed, in his acts, to the end, as stated above (Q. XC., A. 2). But the directing of human acts to their end is not a function of nature, as is the case in irrational creatures, which act for an end solely by their natural appetite; whereas man acts for an end by his reason and will. Therefore no law is natural to man.

Obj. 3. Further, the more a man is free, the less is he under the law. But man is freer than all the animals, on account of his free-will, with which he is endowed above all other animals. Since therefore other animals are not subject to a natural law, neither is man subject to a natural law.

On the contrary, The gloss on Rom. ii. 14: *When the Gentiles, who have not the law, do by nature those things that are of the law,* comments as follows: *Although they have no written law, yet they have the natural law, whereby each one knows, and is conscious of, what is good and what is evil.*

I answer that, As stated above (Q. XC., A. 1 *ad* 1), law, being a rule and measure, can be in a person in two ways: in one way, as in him that rules and measures; in another way, as in that which is ruled and measured, since a thing is ruled and measured, in so far as it partakes of the rule or measure. Wherefore, since all things subject to Divine Providence are ruled and measured by the eternal law, as was stated above (A. 1); it is evident that all things partake somewhat of the eternal law, in so far as, namely, from its being imprinted on them, they derive their respective inclinations to their proper acts and ends. Now among all others, the rational creature is subject to Divine Providence in the most excellent way, in so far as it partakes of a share of providence, by being provident both for itself and for others. Wherefore it has a share of the Eternal Reason, whereby it has a natural inclination to its proper act and end: and this participation of the eternal law in the rational creature is called the natural law. Hence the Psalmist after saying (Ps. iv. 6): *Offer up the sacrifice of justice,* as though someone asked what the works of justice are, adds: *Many say, Who showeth us good things?* in answer to which question he says: *The light of Thy countenance, O Lord, is signed upon us:* thus implying that the light of natural reason, whereby we discern what is good and what is evil, which is the function of the natural law, is nothing else than an imprint on us of the Divine light. It is therefore evident that the natural law is nothing else than the rational creature's participation of the eternal law.

Reply Obj. 1. This argument would hold, if the natural law were something different from the eternal law: whereas it is nothing but a participation thereof, as stated above.

Reply Obj. 2. Every act of reason and will in us is based on that which is according to nature, as stated above (Q.X., A. 1): for every act of reasoning is based on principles that are known naturally, and every act of appetite in respect of the means is derived from the natural appetite in respect of the last end. Accordingly the first direction of our acts to their end must needs be in virtue of the natural law.

Reply Obj. 3. Even irrational animals partake in their own way of the

Eternal Reason, just as the rational creature does. But because the rational creature partakes thereof in an intellectual and rational manner, therefore the participation of the eternal law in the rational creature is properly called a law, since a law is something pertaining to reason, as stated above (Q. XC., A. 1). Irrational creatures, however, do not partake thereof in a rational manner, wherefore there is no participation of the eternal law in them, except by way of similitude.

THIRD ARTICLE.

Whether There Is a Human Law?

We proceed thus to the Third Article :—

Objection 1. It seems that there is not a human law. For the natural law is a participation of the eternal law, as stated above (A. 2). Now through the eternal law *all things are most orderly,* as Augustine states (*De Lib. Arb.* i.). Therefore the natural law suffices for the ordering of all human affairs. Consequently there is no need for a human law.

Obj. 2. Further, a law bears the character of a measure, as stated above (Q. XC., A. 1). But human reason is not a measure of things, but vice versa (*cf. Metaph.* x.). Therefore no law can emanate from human reason.

Obj. 3. Further, a measure should be most certain, as stated in *Metaph.* x. But the dictates of human reason in matters of conduct are uncertain, according to Wis. ix. 14: *The thoughts of mortal men are fearful, and our counsels uncertain.* Therefore no law can emanate from human reason.

On the contrary, Augustine (*De Lib. Arb.* i.) distinguishes two kinds of law, the one eternal, the other temporal, which he calls human.

I answer that, As stated above (Q. XC., A. 1, *ad* 2), a law is a dictate of the practical reason. Now it is to be observed that the same procedure takes place in the practical and in the speculative reason: for each proceeds from principles to conclusions, as stated above (*ibid.*). Accordingly we conclude that just as, in the speculative reason, from naturally known indemonstrable principles, we draw the conclusions of the various sciences, the knowledge of which is not imparted to us by nature, but acquired by the efforts of reason, so too it is from the precepts of the natural law, as from general and indemonstrable principles, that the human reason needs to proceed to the more particular determination of certain matters. These particular determinations, devised by human reason, are called human laws, provided the other essential conditions of law be observed, as stated above (Q. XC., AA. 2, 3, 4). Wherefore Tully says in his *Rhetoric* (*De Invent. Rhet.* ii.) that *justice has its source in nature; thence certain things came into custom by reason of their utility; afterwards these things which emanated from nature and were approved by custom, were sanctioned by fear and reverence for the law.*

Reply Obj. 1. The human reason cannot have a full participation of the dictate of the Divine Reason, but according to its own mode, and imperfectly. Consequently, as on the part of the speculative reason, by a natural participation of Divine Wisdom, there is in us the knowledge of certain general principles, but not proper knowledge of each single truth, such as that contained in the Divine Wisdom; so too, on the part of the practical reason, man has a natural participation of the eternal law, according to certain general principles, but not as regards the particular determinations of individual cases, which are, however, contained in the eternal law. Hence the need for human reason to proceed further to sanction them by law.

Reply Obj. 2. Human reason is not, of itself, the rule of things: but the principles impressed on it by nature, are general rules and measures of all things relating to human conduct, whereof the natural reason is the rule and measure, although it is not the measure of things that are from nature.

Reply Obj. 3. The practical reason is concerned with practical matters, which are singular and contingent: but not with necessary things, with which the speculative reason is concerned. Wherefore human laws cannot have that inerrancy that belongs to the demonstrated conclusions of sciences. Nor is it necessary for every measure to be altogether unerring and certain, but according as it is possible in its own particular genus.

FOURTH ARTICLE.

Whether There Was Any Need for a Divine Law?

We proceed thus to the Fourth Article :—

Objection 1. It seems that there was no need for a Divine law. Because, as stated above (A. 2), the natural law is a participation in us of the eternal law. But the eternal law is a Divine law, as stated above (A. 1). Therefore there is no need for a Divine law in addition to the natural law, and human laws derived therefrom.

Obj. 2. Further, it is written (Ecclus. xv. 14) that *God left man in the hand of his own counsel.* Now counsel is an act of reason, as stated above (Q. XIV., A. 1). Therefore man was left to the direction of his reason. But a dictate of human reason is a human law, as stated above (A. 3). Therefore there is no need for man to be governed also by a Divine law.

Obj. 3. Further, human nature is more self-sufficing than irrational creatures. But irrational creatures have no Divine law besides the natural inclination impressed on them. Much less, therefore, should the rational creature have a Divine law in addition to the natural law.

On the contrary, David prayed God to set His law before him, saying: *Set before me for a law the way of Thy justifications, O Lord.*

I answer that, Besides the natural and the human law it was necessary for the directing of human conduct to have a Divine law. And this for four reasons. First, because it is by law that man is directed how to perform his proper acts in view of his last end. And indeed if man were ordained to no other end than that which is proportionate to his natural faculty, there would be no need for man to have any further direction on the part of his reason, besides the natural law and human law which is derived from it. But since man is ordained to an end of eternal happiness which is inproportionate to man's natural faculty, as stated above (Q. V., A. 5), therefore it was necessary that, besides the natural and the human law, man should be directed to his end by a law given by God.

Secondly, because, on account of the uncertainty of human judgment, especially on contingent and particular matters, different people form different judgments on human acts; whence also different and contrary laws result. In order, therefore, that man may know without any doubt what he ought to do and what he ought to avoid, it was necessary for man to be directed in his proper acts by a law given by God, for it is certain that such a law cannot err.

Thirdly, because man can make laws in those matters of which he is competent to judge. But man is not competent to judge of interior movements, that are hidden, but only of exterior acts which appear: and yet for the perfection of virtue it is necessary for man to conduct himself aright in both kinds of acts. Consequently human law could not sufficiently curb and direct interior acts; and it was necessary for this purpose that a Divine law should supervene.

Fourthly, because, as Augustine says (*De Lib. Arb.* i.), human law cannot punish or forbid all evil deeds: since while aiming at doing away with all evils, it would do away with many good things, and would hinder the advance of the common good, which is necessary for human intercourse. In order, therefore, that no evil might remain unforbidden and unpunished, it was necessary for the Divine law to supervene, whereby all sins are forbidden.

And these four causes are touched upon in Ps. cxviii. 8, where it is said: *The law of the Lord is unspotted, i.e.,* allowing no foulness of sin; *converting souls,* because it directs not only exterior, but also interior acts; *the testimony of the Lord is faithful,* because of the certainty of what is true and right; *giving wisdom to little ones,* by directing man to an end supernatural and Divine.

Reply Obj. 1. By the natural law the eternal law is participated proportionately to the capacity of human nature. But to his supernatural end man needs to be directed in a yet higher way. Hence the additional law given by God, whereby man shares more perfectly in the eternal law.

Reply Obj. 2. Counsel is a kind of inquiry: hence it must proceed from some principles. Nor is it enough for it to proceed from principles imparted by nature, which are the precepts of the natural law, for the reasons given above: but there is need for certain additional principles, namely, the precepts of the Divine law.

Reply Obj. 3. Irrational creatures are not ordained to an end higher than that which is proportionate to their natural powers: consequently the comparison fails.

37

JEAN JACQUES ROUSSEAU (1712–1778)

The Social Contract

Jean Jacques Rousseau was born in Switzerland, but, after leaving home at the age of sixteen, he lived a more or less tempestuous life in Savoy, France, Switzerland, England, and finally again in France. He was acquainted with most of the intellectual leaders of his day, including David Hume. During his lifetime, his writings exerted such influence that he was frequently involved in public controversy.

Rousseau would have nothing to do with the natural law theory, because he believed it gave credence to the claims to power of aristocrats and despots. According to Rousseau, the authority of the state resides in the sovereign authority of the people who constitute the state, not in the decrees of God. Regardless of their social rank or status, those people are born free and equal and have certain natural and inalienable rights that must not be transgressed. Those rights are, however, endangered in the state of nature, and it is in order to defend more securely those rights that people create those voluntary associations called states. The act of establishing such a voluntary association is what Rousseau calls "the social contract."

Had I granted all which I have refuted, the favourers of despotism would not have found their cause advanced by it. There is a wide difference between subduing a multitude, and governing a society.

When uncivilized men are successively subjugated by an individual, whatever number there may be of them, they appear to me only as a master and his slaves; I cannot regard them as a people and their chief. They are, if you

From Jean Jacques Rousseau, *An Inquiry into the Nature of the Social Contract,* Chapters V–VIII (London: G. G. J. & J. Robinson, 1791), pp. 29–51.

please, an *aggregation,* but they are not an *association;* for there is neither public property, or a political body, amongst them.

A man may have enslaved half the world, and yet continue a private individual, if his interest is separate from the general interest, and confined to himself alone. When such a man falls, his empire remains unconnected, and without any bond of union; as an oak dissolves, and becomes a mass of ashes, when consumed by fire.

"A people (says GROTIUS) can give themselves to a king." According to Grotius, then, they are a people before they give themselves to the king. The donation itself is a civil act, and supposes a public consultation by an assembly of the people: it will therefore be necessary, before we examine the act by which they elected a king, to enquire into that by which they became a people: for that act, being anterior to the other, is the true foundation of the society.

In fact, if there was no prior convention, where would be (unless the election of a chief was unanimous) the obligation which should bind the lesser number to submit to the choice of the greater? And from whence would a hundred men, who wished to submit to a master, derive the right of binding by their votes ten other men who were not disposed to acknowledge any chief? The law which gives a majority of suffrages the power of deciding for the whole body, can only be established by a convention, and proves that there must have been at some former period a unanimous will.

We will suppose that men in a state of nature are arrived at that crisis, when the strength of each individual is insufficient to defend him from the attacks he is subject to. This primitive state can therefore subsist no longer; and the human race must perish, unless they change their manner of life.

As men cannot create for themselves new forces, but merely unite and direct those which already exist, the only means they can employ for their preservation is to form by aggregation an assemblage of forces that may be able to resist all assaults, be put in motion as one body, and act in concert upon all occasions.

This assemblage of forces must be produced by the concurrence of many: and as the force and the liberty of a man are the chief instruments of his preservation, how can he engage them without danger, and without neglecting the care which is due to himself? This doubt, which leads directly to my subject, may be expressed in these words: "Where shall we find a form of association which will defend and protect with the whole aggregate force the person and the property of each individual; and by which every person, while united with ALL, shall obey only HIMSELF, and remain as free as before the union?" Such is the fundamental problem, of which the Social Contract gives the solution.

The articles of this contract are so unalterably fixed by the nature of the act, that the least modification renders them vain and of no effect. They are the same every where, and are every where understood and admitted, even though they may never have been formally announced: so that, when once the social pact is violated in any instance, all the obligations it created cease; and each individual is restored to his original rights, and resumes his native liberty, as the consequence of losing that conventional liberty for which he exchanged them.

All the articles of the social contract will, when clearly understood, be found reducible to this single point—THE TOTAL ALIENATION OF EACH ASSOCIATE, AND ALL HIS RIGHTS, TO THE WHOLE COMMUNITY. For every individual gives himself up entirely—the condition of every person is alike; and being so, it would not be the interest of any one to render himself offensive to others.

Nay, more than this—the alienation is made without any reserve; the union is as complete as it can be, and no associate has a claim to any thing: for if any individual was to retain rights not enjoyed in general by all, as there would be no common superior to decide between him and the public, each person being in some points his own proper judge, would soon pretend to be so in every thing; and thus would the state of nature be revived, and the association become tyrannical or be annihilated.

In fine, each person gives himself to ALL but not to any INDIVIDUAL: and as there is no one associate over whom the same right is not acquired which is ceded to him by others, each gains an equivalent for what he loses, and finds his force increased for preserving that which he possesses.

If, therefore, we exclude from the social compact all that is not essentially necessary, we shall find it reduced to the following terms:

"We each of us place, in common, his person, and all his power, under the supreme direction of the general will; and we receive into the body each member as an indivisible part of the whole."

From that moment, instead of so many separate persons as there are contractors, this act of association produces a moral collective body, composed of as many members as there are voices in the assembly; which from this act receives its unity, its common self, its life, and its will. This public person, which is thus formed by the union of all the private persons, took formerly the name of *city,* and now takes that of *republic* or *body politic.* It is called by its members *state* when it is passive, and *sovereign* when in activity: and whenever it is spoken of with other bodies of a similar kind, it is denominated *power.* The associates take collectively the name of *people,* and separately that of *citizens,* as participating the sovereign authority: they are also styled *subjects,* because they are subjected to the laws. But these terms are frequently confounded, and used one for the other; and a man must understand them well to distinguish when they are properly employed.

It appears from this form that the act of association contains a reciprocal engagement between the public and individuals; and that each individual contracting as it were with himself, is engaged under a double character; that is, as a part of the *sovereign power* engaging with individuals, and as a member of the *state* entering into a compact with the *sovereign power.* But we cannot apply here the maxim of civil right, that no person is bound by any engagement which he makes with himself; for there is a material difference between an obligation contracted towards *one's self* individually, and towards a collective body of which *one's self* constitutes a part.

It is necessary to observe here, that the will of the public, expressed by a majority of votes, which can enforce obedience from the subjects to the sovereign power, in consequence of the double character under which the members of that body appear, cannot bind the sovereign power to itself; and that it is against the nature of the body politic for the sovereign power to impose any one law which it cannot alter. Were they to consider themselves as acting under one character only, they would be in the situation of individuals forming each a contract with himself: but this is not the case; and therefore there can be no fundamental obligatory law established for the body of the people, not even the social contract. But this is of little moment, as that body could not very well engage itself to others in any manner which would not derogate from the contract. With respect to foreigners, it becomes a single being, an individual only.

But the body politic, or sovereign power, which derives its existence from the sacredness of the contract, can never bind itself, even towards others, in any thing that would derogate from the original act; such as alienating any portion of itself, or submitting to another sovereign: for by violating the contract its own existence would be at once annihilated; and by nothing nothing can be performed.

As soon as the multitude is thus united in one body, you cannot offend one of its members without attacking the whole; much less can you offend the whole without incurring the resentment of all the members. Thus duty and interest equally oblige the two contracting parties to lend their mutual aid to each other; and the same men must endeavour to unite under this double character all the advantages which attend it.

The sovereign power being formed only of the individuals which compose it, neither has, or can have, any interest contrary to theirs; consequently the sovereign power requires no guarantee towards its subjects, because it is impossible that the body should seek to injure all its members: and we shall see presently that it can do no injury to any individual. The sovereign power, by its nature, must, while it exists, be every thing it ought to be: but it is not so with subjects towards the sovereign power; to which, notwithstanding the common interest subsisting between them, there is nothing to answer for the performance of their engagements, if some means is not found of ensuring their fidelity.

In fact, each individual may, as a man, have a private will, dissimilar or contrary to the general will which he has as a citizen. His own particular interest may dictate to him very differently from the common interest; his mind, naturally and absolutely independent, may regard what he owes to the common cause as a gratuitous contribution, the omission of which would be less injurious to others than the payment would be burdensome to himself; and considering the moral person which constitutes the state as a creature of the imagination, because it is not a man, he may wish to enjoy the rights of a citizen, without being disposed to fulfil the duties of a subject: an injustice which would in its progress cause the ruin of the body politic.

In order therefore to prevent the social compact from becoming a vain form, it tacitly comprehends this engagement, which alone can give effect to the others—That whoever refuses to obey the general will, shall be compelled to it by the whole body, which is in fact only forcing him to be free; for this is the condition which guarantees his absolute personal independence to every citizen of the country: a condition which gives motion and effect to the political machine; which alone renders all civil engagements legal; and without which they would be absurd, tyrannical, and subject to the most enormous abuses.

The passing from a state of nature to a civil state, produces in man a very remarkable change, by substituting justice for instinct, and giving to his actions a moral character which they wanted before.

It is at the moment of that transition that the voice of duty succeeds to physical impulse; and a sense of what is right, to the incitements of appetite. The man who had till then regarded none but himself, perceives that he must act on other principles, and learns to consult his reason before he listens to his propensities.

Although he is deprived in this new state of many advantages which he enjoyed from nature, he gains others of equal consequence. His faculties unfold themselves by being exercised; his ideas are extended; his sentiments exalted; and his whole mind becomes so enlarged and refined, that if, by abusing his new condition, he sometimes degrades it even below that from which he emerged, he ought still to bless, without ceasing, the happy moment that snatched him forever from it, and transformed him from a circumscribed and stupid animal to a free intelligent being: in a word, to a man.

In order to draw a balance between the advantages and disadvantages attending his new situation, let us state them in such a manner, that they may be easily compared.

A man loses by the social contract his natural liberty, and an unlimited right to all which tempts him, and which he can obtain. In return he acquires civil liberty, and a just right to all he possesses.

That we may not be deceived in the value of these compensations, we must distinguish natural liberty, which knows no bounds but the power of the individual, from civil liberty, which is limited by the general will: and between that possession which is only the effect of force, or of first occupancy, from that property which must be founded on a positive title.

We may add to the other acquisitions of the civil state, that of moral liberty, which alone renders a man master of himself: for it is slavery to be under the impulse of appetite; and freedom to obey the laws. But I have already said too much on this head: and the philosophical sense of the word liberty is not at present my subject.

·   ·   ·

38

JOHN STUART MILL (1806–1873)

The Utilitarian Basis of Civil Authority

John Stuart Mill was more concerned with developing a philosophical defense of the freedom of the individual than in finding a philosophical basis for the authority of society. He believed that, as a practical matter, individual freedom was perpetually in greater jeopardy than was the authority of society. However, in order to define the sphere of the freedom of the individual vis-à-vis society, one must set limits to the authority of society, and if this is to be done in a nonarbitrary way, those limits must be derived from some higher principle.

For Mill, the principle is utility: the ultimate standard of right and wrong is the tendency of any act to produce the greatest happiness for the greatest number of people. The only morally defensible purpose of government, according to this view, is to promote the greatest happiness for the greatest number. It follows, then, that the only purpose for which the power of government can legitimately be imposed on an individual citizen is to protect the rest of society from some harm that would otherwise result.

It is interesting to note that while Rousseau's theory of the social contract carries with it the implication that pure democracy is the only "right" form of government, Mill's theory does not. Mill explicitly accepts the implication that, under certain circumstances, the "best" government may be quite different from either pure or representative democracy—that is, monarchy, dictatorship, or whatever. (See p. 95 for a biographical note on John Stuart Mill.)

The subject of this Essay is not the so-called Liberty of the Will, so unfortunately opposed to the misnamed doctrine of Philosophical Necessity; but Civil, or Social Liberty: the nature and limits of the power which can be legitimately exercised by society over the individual. A question seldom stated, and hardly ever discussed, in general terms, but which profoundly influences the practical

From John Stuart Mill, *On Liberty,* Chapter 1 (1859).

controversies of the age by its latent presence, and is likely soon to make itself recognized as the vital question of the future. It is so far from being new, that, in a certain sense, it has divided mankind, almost from the remotest ages, but in the stage of progress into which the more civilized portions of the species have now entered, it presents itself under new conditions, and requires a different and more fundamental treatment.

.   .   .

Like other tyrannies, the tyranny of the majority was at first, and is still vulgarly, held in dread, chiefly as operating through the acts of the public authorities. But reflecting persons perceived that when society is itself the tyrant—society collectively, over the separate individuals who compose it— its means of tyrannizing are not restricted to the acts which it may do by the hands of its political functionaries. Society can and does execute its own mandates: and if it issues wrong mandates instead of right, or any mandates at all in things with which it ought not to meddle, it practises a social tyranny more formidable than many kinds of political oppression, since, though not usually upheld by such extreme penalties, it leaves fewer means of escape, penetrating much more deeply into the details of life, and enslaving the soul itself. Protection, therefore, against the tyranny of the magistrate is not enough; there needs protection also against the tyranny of the prevailing opinion and feeling; against the tendency of society to impose, by other means than civil penalties, its own ideas and practices as rules of conduct on those who dissent from them; to fetter the development, and, if possible, prevent the formation, of any individuality not in harmony with its ways, and compel all characters to fashion themselves upon the model of its own. There is a limit to the legitimate interference of collective opinion with individual independence; and to find that limit, and maintain it against encroachment, is as indispensable to a good condition of human affairs, as protection against political despotism.

But though this proposition is not likely to be contested in general terms, the practical question, where to place the limit—how to make the fitting adjustment between individual independence and social control—is a subject on which nearly everything remains to be done. All that makes existence valuable to any one, depends on the enforcement of restraints upon the actions of other people. Some rules of conduct, therefore, must be imposed, by law in the first place, and by opinion on many things which are not fit subjects for the operation of law. What these rules should be, is the principal question in human affairs; but if we except a few of the most obvious cases, it is one of those which least progress has been made in resolving.

.   .   .

There is, in fact, no recognized principle by which the propriety or impropriety of government interference is customarily tested. People decide according to their personal preferences. Some, whenever they see any good to be done, or evil to be remedied, would willingly instigate the government to undertake the business; while others prefer to bear almost any amount of social evil, rather than add one to the departments of human interests amenable to governmental control. And men range themselves on one or the other side in any particular case, according to this general direction of their sentiments; or according to the degree of interest which they feel in the particular thing which it is proposed that the government should do; or according to the belief they entertain that the government would, or would not, do it in the manner they prefer; but very rarely on account of any opinion to which they consistently adhere, as to what things are fit to be done by a government. And it seems to me that, in consequence of this absence of rule or principle, one side is at present as often wrong as the other; the interference of government is, with about equal frequency, improperly invoked and improperly condemned.

The object of this Essay is to assert one very simple principle, as entitled to govern absolutely the dealings of society with the individual in the way of compulsion and control, whether the means used be physical force in the form of legal penalties, or the moral coercion of public opinion. That principle is, that the sole end for which mankind are warranted, individually or collectively in interfering with the liberty of action of any of their number, is self-protection. That the only purpose for which power can be rightfully exercised over any member of a civilized community, against his will, is to prevent harm to others. His own good, either physical or moral, is not a sufficient warrant. He cannot rightfully be compelled to do or forbear because it will be better for him to do so, because it will make him happier, because, in the opinions of others, to do so would be wise, or even right. These are good reasons for remonstrating with him, or reasoning with him, or persuading him, or entreating him, but not for compelling him, or visiting him with any evil, in case he do otherwise. To justify that, the conduct from which it is desired to deter him must be calculated to produce evil to some one else. The only part of the conduct of any one, for which he is amenable to society, is that which concerns others. In the part which merely concerns himself, his independence is, of right, absolute. Over himself, over his own body and mind, the individual is sovereign.

It is, perhaps, hardly necessary to say that this doctrine is meant to apply only to human beings in the maturity of their faculties. We are not speaking of children, or of young persons below the age which the law may fix as that of manhood or womanhood. Those who are still in a state to require being taken care of by others, must be protected against their own actions as well as against external injury. For the same reason, we may leave out of consideration those backward states of society in which the race itself may be considered as in its nonage. The early difficulties in the way of spontaneous progress are so great, that there is seldom any choice of means for overcoming them; and a ruler full of the spirit of improvement is warranted in the use of any expedients that will attain an end, perhaps otherwise unattainable. Despotism is a legitimate mode of government in dealing with barbarians, provided the end be their improvement, and the means justified by actually effecting that end. Liberty, as a principle, has no application to any state of things anterior to the time when mankind have become capable of being improved by free and equal discussion. Until then, there is nothing for them but implicit obedience to an Akbar or a Charlemagne, if they are so fortunate as to find one. But as soon as mankind have attained the capacity of being guided to their own improvement by conviction or persuasion (a period long since reached in all nations with whom we need here concern ourselves), compulsion, either in the direct form or in that of pains and penalties for non-compliance, is no longer admissible as a means to their own good, and justifiable only for the security of others.

It is proper to state that I forego any advantage which could be derived to my argument from the idea of abstract right as a thing independent of utility. I regard utility as the ultimate appeal on all ethical questions; but it must be utility in the largest sense, grounded on the permanent interests of man as a progressive being. Those interests, I contend, authorize the subjection of individual spontaneity to external control, only in respect to those actions of each, which concern the interest of other people. If any one does an act hurtful to others, there is a *prima facie* case for punishing him, by law, or, where legal penalties are not safely applicable, by general disapprobation. There are also many positive acts for the benefit of others, which he may rightfully be compelled to perform; such as, to give evidence in a court of justice; to bear his fair share in the common defence, or in any other joint work necessary to the interest of the society of which he enjoys the protection; and to perform certain acts of individual beneficence, such as saving a fellow-creature's life, or interposing to protect the defenceless against ill-usage, things which whenever it is obviously a man's duty to do, he may rightfully be made responsible to society for not doing. A person may cause evil to others not only by his actions but by his inaction, and in either case he is justly accountable to them for the injury. The latter case, it is true, requires a much more cautious exercise of compulsion than the former. To make any one answerable for doing evil to others, is the rule; to make him answerable for not preventing evil, is, comparatively speaking, the exception. Yet there are many cases clear enough and grave enough to justify that exception. In all things which regard the external relations of the individual, he is *de jure* amenable to those whose interests are concerned, and if need be, to society as their protector. There are often good reasons for not holding him to the responsibility; but these reasons must arise from the special expediencies of the case: either because it is a kind of case in which he is on the whole likely to act better, when left to his own discretion, than when controlled in any way in which society have it in their power to control him; or because the attempt to exercise control would produce other evils, greater than those which it would prevent. When such reasons as these preclude the enforcement of responsibility, the conscience of the agent himself should step into the vacant judgment-seat, and protect those interests of others which have no external protection; judging himself all the more rigidly, because the case does not admit of his being made accountable to the judgment of his fellow-creatures.

But there is a sphere of action in which society, as distinguished from the individual, has, if any, only an indirect interest; comprehending all that portion of a person's life and conduct which affects only himself, or, if it also affects others, only with their free, voluntary, and undeceived consent and participation. When I say only himself, I mean directly, and in the first instance: for whatever affects himself, may affect others *through* himself; and the objection which may be grounded on this contingency, will receive consideration in the sequel. This, then, is the appropriate region of human liberty. It comprises, first, the inward domain of consciousness; demanding liberty of conscience, in the most comprehensive sense; liberty of thought and feeling; absolute freedom of opinion and sentiment on all subjects, practical or speculative, scientific, moral, or theological. The liberty of expressing and publishing opinions may seem to fall under a different principle, since it belongs to that part of the conduct of an individual which concerns other people; but, being almost of as much importance as the liberty of thought itself, and resting in great part on the same reasons, is practically inseparable from it. Secondly, the principle requires liberty of tastes and pursuits; of framing the plan of our life to suit our own character; of doing as we like, subject to such consequences as may follow; without impediment from our fellow-creatures, so long as what we do does not harm them even though they should think our conduct foolish, perverse, or wrong. Thirdly, from this liberty of each individual, follows the liberty, within the same limits, of combination among individuals; freedom to unite, for any purpose not involving harm to others: the persons combining being supposed to be of full age, and not forced or deceived.

No society in which these liberties are not, on the whole, respected, is free, whatever may be its form of government; and none is completely free in which they do not exist absolute and unqualified. The only freedom which deserves the name, is that of pursuing our own good in our own way, so long as we do not attempt to deprive others of theirs, or impede their efforts to obtain it. Each is the proper guardian of his own health, whether bodily, or mental or spiritual. Mankind are greater gainers by suffering each other to live as seems good to themselves, than by compelling each to live as seems good to the rest.

39

HANNA PITKIN (1931– ————)

Obligation and Consent

Hanna Pitkin is a political scientist with a special interest in the relevance of contemporary linguistic philosophy for the analysis of problems of political theory. Her writings include *The Concept of Representation* (1967), *Representation* (an anthology, 1969), and *Wittgenstein and Justice* (1972). She has taught at San Francisco State College and at the University of Wisconsin and is now on the faculty at the University of California at Berkeley.

Pitkin's view regarding the authority of the state is a form of social contract theory, though she is explicitly critical of many of the traditional forms of that theory. According to her theory, which she calls the doctrine of "hypothetical consent," the authority of government depends on its being the kind of government that deserves to be obeyed. A legitimate government is one whose actions "are in accord with the authority a hypothetical group of rational men in a hypothetical state of nature would have (had) to give to any government they were founding." A government is deserving of obedience if it is "a good, just government doing what a government should." It merits no such obedience if it is "a tyrannical, unjust government trying to do what no government may."

Much of Pitkin's essay is devoted to an examination, in the light of this theory of governmental authority, of the question, How, in a concrete case, can I know whether I ought to obey or disobey the commands of government? With the aid of several examples, notably that of Socrates in his prison cell, the relevance of the theory to this difficult question is explored. The author then attempts to relate her theory to the even more difficult question to which each of the preceding writers has attempted to give an answer: Why is anyone *ever* obligated to obey a government, even a so-called legitimate government? What is the "ultimate" justification of the authority of the state?

From Hanna Pitkin, "Obligation and Consent," *The American Political Science Review,* 60 (1966), pp. 39–49. Reprinted by permission of the publisher.

A reexamination of even the most venerable traditional problems of political theory can sometimes yield surprisingly new and relevant results.[1] The problem of political obligation, for example, and its most popular "solution," based on consent, turn out on reexamination to be rather different from what we have come to assume about them. The problem of political obligation resolves itself into at least four mutually related but partially independent questions:

1. The limits of obligation ("*When* are you obligated to obey, and when not?")
2. The locus of sovereignty ("*Whom* are you obligated to obey?")
3. The difference between legitimate authority and mere coercion ("Is there *really* any difference; are you ever *really* obligated?")
4. The justification of obligation ("*Why* are you ever obligated to obey even a legitimate authority?")

And the consent theory of obligation, as exemplified in Locke's *Second Treatise* and Joseph Tussman's *Obligation and the Body Politic,* turns out to yield a new formulation—perhaps a new interpretation of consent theory, perhaps an alternative to it—that might be labelled either the doctrine of the "nature of the government" or the doctrine of "hypothetical consent."[2]

It teaches that your obligation depends not on any actual act of consenting, past or present, by yourself or your fellow-citizens, but on the character of the government. If it is a good, just government doing what a government should, then you must obey it; if it is a tyrannical, unjust government trying to do what no government may, then you have no such obligation. Or to put it another way, your obligation depends not on whether you have consented but on whether the government is such that you *ought* to consent to it, whether its actions are in accord with the authority a hypothetical group of rational men in a hypothetical state of nature would have (had) to give to any government they were founding. Having shown how this formulation emerges from Locke's and Tussman's ideas, I want now to defend it as a valid response to what troubles us about political obligation, and as a response more consonant than most with the moral realities of human decisions about obedience and resistance. At the same time the discussion should also demonstrate how many different or even conflicting things that one might want to call "consent" continue to be relevant—a fact which may help to explain the tenacity of traditional consent theory in the face of its manifest difficulties. Such a defense and demonstration, with detailed attention to such decisions, are difficult; the discussion from here on will be more speculative, and will raise more questions than it answers.

[1]This and part of the following paragraph are intended to summarize the argument of "Obligation and Consent—I," This REVIEW, 59 (December, 1965), pp. 990–999.

[2]John Locke, *Second Treatise of Civil Government;* Joseph Tussman, *Obligation and the Body Politic* (New York: Oxford, 1960).

I. THE THEORY APPLIED

Our new doctrine seems most obviously satisfactory as a response to question three, concerning the difference between legitimate authority and mere coercion. For it teaches that legitimate authority is precisely that which *ought* to be obeyed, to which one ought to consent, which deserves obedience and consent, to which rational men considering all relevant facts and issues would consent, to which consent can be justified. Anything or anyone else who tries to command us is then merely coercing, and is not entitled to our obedience. This answer to the question is essentially what Wittgenstein calls a "point of grammar"; it reminds us of the way concepts like "authority," "legitimacy," "law" are related in our language (and therefore in our world) to concepts like "consent" and "obedience."[3] To call something a legitimate authority is normally to imply that it ought to be obeyed. You cannot, without further rather elaborate explanation, maintain simultaneously *both* that this government has legitimate authority over you *and* that you have no obligation to obey it. Thus if you say that you consent to it (recognize it as an authority), that statement itself is normally a recognition of the obligation to obey, at least at the moment it is uttered. Part of what "authority" means is that those subject to it are obligated to obey. As an answer to question three, then, this doctrine tells us (something about) what legitimate authority *is* by reminding us of something about what "legitimate authority" *means*. But of course that is not yet to provide criteria for telling apart the two species—legitimate authority and mere coercion—when you encounter them in reality.

Thus, insofar as our *real* need is for a practical way of deciding whether to obey or resist this government right now, or which of two rival authorities to follow, our new theory seems less adequate. Its response to our question three does not seem immediately helpful with questions one and two; and surely those are of the most concern to real people confronted with decisions about action. It just does not seem very helpful to tell a man considering resistance to authority: you must obey if the government is such that you ought to obey. But neither is traditional consent theory very helpful to this man; indeed, one of its weaknesses has always been this matter of detailed application. Perhaps it is even a mistake to assume that a theory of political obligation is supposed to tell a man directly what to do in particular cases.[4]

One might argue, however, that such a theory should at least tell him what sorts of considerations are relevant to his decision, direct his attention and tell

[3]Ludwig Wittgenstein, *Philosophical Investigations* (New York: Macmillan, 1953). See also Stanley Louis Cavell, "The Claim to Rationality" (Unpublished Ph.D. dissertation, Harvard University, 1961), esp. Chapter 1.

[4]See, for example, Margaret Macdonald, "The Language of Political Theory," in A. Flew, ed., *Logic and Language: First Series* (Oxford: Basil Blackwell, 1960), pp. 167–186.

him where to look.[5] And in that regard, I suggest that traditional consent theory is defective, for it directs such a man's attention to the wrong place. It teaches him to look at himself (for his own consent) or at the people around him (for theirs), rather than at the merits of the government. Where it demands obedience, consent theory does so on the grounds that he or the majority have consented; where it justifies resistance, it does so on the grounds that consent was never given or has been exceeded. Thus the man who must choose is directed to the question: have I (we) consented to this? The new doctrine formulated in this essay seems at least to have the virtue of pointing such a man in the right direction. For it tells him: look to the nature of the government—its characteristics, structure, activities, functioning. This is not much of a guide, but it is a beginning much more usefully related to what men need to think about when they make such choices.

Let us consider seriously what sorts of things people really think about when they confront a genuine decision about obedience and resistance, and what sorts of things they ought to think about. But anyone who undertakes to do that is immediately overwhelmed by the complexity and multiplicity of what seems relevant, and by the many different imaginable cases. We need to consider a list of specific cases at least as diverse as these:

Socrates, as presented in the *Crito* and the *Apology.*
An ordinary criminal.
An American student engaging in civil disobedience.
A Mississippi Negro who decides to join a revolutionary group.
A South African Negro who decides to join a revolutionary group.
A minor official in Nazi Germany, who continues to carry out his functions.

Even a brief review of such cases teaches at least this much: the occasions for contemplating and possibly engaging in disobedience are extremely varied; and a great many kinds of non-obedience are available, from flight through crime to attempted revolution.[6] Some forms of non-obedience are violent, others not; some are personal and others organized; some are isolated actions and others a systematic program of action; some are directed against a particular law or decree and others against an entire system of government. To a person confronted with a real decision about resistance or obedience, it makes an enormous difference what kind of action is contemplated. Circumstances that may justify escape or isolated refusal to obey a particular law may not suffice to justify revolution; indeed, some forms of resistance (like civil disobedience) may even be provided for within a political system.

[5]This suggestion is advanced, against Miss Macdonald's argument, in S. I. Benn and R. S. Peters, *Social Principles and the Democratic State* (London: George Allen & Unwin, 1959), pp. 299–301.
[6]Something like this point is suggested by Tussman, *op. cit.,* p. 43.

Next, we may notice that all of our examples are, or could reasonably be, people in conflict. Socrates may never have been in doubt as to what he would do, but his friends certainly disagreed with him at first; and he cast his own argument in the form of a confrontation between the desire "to play truant" and the admonitions of the laws. All of our examples (with the exception of the criminal?) might have good, serious reasons for resistance. None of them ought to feel entirely free to pursue those reasons without first weighing them against something else—his *prima facie* obligation to obey. One might say: all these men ought to feel a certain tie to their governments, their societies, in the sense in which Socrates feels such a tie, but some of them might nevertheless be justified in disobeying or resisting. That he does not sufficiently feel such a tie, that he has no (good) reason, no justification for disobedience, is precisely what makes the case of an "ordinary" criminal different from the rest. This is at least in accord with the formula offered by our new theory: normally law, authority, government are to be obeyed and resistance requires justification. You are not morally free to resist as a matter of whim.

The real person confronted by a problematic situation about obedience needs to know that, but he obviously needs to know much more. He needs to know much more specifically when resistance is justified and what might count as a justification. Does he learn this by thinking about his own past consent or that of his fellow-citizens, as traditional consent theory would suggest? Or does he learn it by assessing the nature and quality of the government?

Our cases of potential disobedience show an interesting division in this respect. Three of them—the student and the two Negroes—seem quite unlikely to think much about their own past consent—when and whether they consented, how often and how seriously, expressly or tacitly, and so on. What they are likely to think about is the "outrageous" conduct and "oppressive, unjust" structure of the government, and of the possible consequences of resistance. The criminal (since we have defined him as "ordinary") is not likely to think about either obligations to obey or justifications for his action. The Nazi might well cite his consent to the Fuehrer, his oath of office, pledges of absolute obedience, and so on, as a justification for continued obedience despite "certain unpleasant government measures that perhaps ought not to have been taken." And Socrates is passionately aware of his ties to the Athenian laws, the gratitude he owes them for past favors, the power of his past consent to them.

Thus both Socrates and the Nazi do seem to look to past consent rather than to the nature of the government. But the significance of this fact has yet to be assessed; for on closer examination, each of their cases reveals an important weakness in traditional consent theory. From the case of the Nazi we can learn that even express consent may not be enough; and from that of Socrates, the difficulties of applying past consent as a guide to action.

It might be tempting to say that of our six cases, only Socrates is truly moral, for only he thinks about his obligations and commitments to the laws. But the example of the Nazi saves us from this simplistic response, by showing that sometimes past promises and oaths are not enough to determine present obligations. Sometimes a man who cites even an express oath to obedience, is being not admirable but hypocritical, refusing to recognize where his real duty lies. We would not want to say that past oaths and promises count for nothing, that they can be ignored at will. We all feel the power of the argument that you ought to be consistent, that it isn't fair to pick up your marbles and go home just because it's your turn to lose under the rules you have accepted so far. But that is partly because such a partisan assessment of the rules is likely to be biased. If you can in fact show that the rules are really unfair, then any time is a good time to change them. Again, normally rules and authorities are to be obeyed; when occasions for questioning this obligation arise, what is ultimately needed is an assessment of the rules or authorities. Mere reference to your "going along with them" in the past is not enough.

No doubt if a man had no political obligation he could acquire one by a promise or contract. But that by no means proves that political obligation can be acquired *only* by promise or contract; it may be that a quite independent political obligation is sometimes reinforced by an oath to obey, at other times (partly) countered by a promise to resist. A personal past commitment to obey need not settle the matter.

Indeed, the case of the Nazi calls attention to something traditional consent theory seems to have overlooked: the duty to resist. There are times in human history when men are not merely free(d) from an obligation to obey, but positively obligated to oppose the powers that be. The authors of the Declaration of Independence recognized this, despite their heavy reliance on Locke; for they saw resistance to tyranny not merely as man's right but as his duty. Locke, and traditional consent theory in general, make no provision for such a duty, nor can it be easily accommodated within their framework. There is provision in Locke's system for majority resistance to a tyrannical government, and a duty to follow such a majority. But *individual* resistance has a highly ambiguous status at best, and is certainly *not* a duty.[7] For if political obligation arises from contract, the violation or overstepping of this contract leaves each individual free to do as he likes with regard to the tyranny. True, the individual is still then bound by natural law; but natural law does not command the punishment of offenders, it only permits it. And amending the Lockeian system on this score would obviously require fundamental changes in its individualistic presuppositions.

Similarly, traditional consent theory teaches that at times of civil war or successful revolution, when an old authority structure collapses, each individual is free to place his consent anew wherever he wishes and thinks best for himself. If he thinks fit to follow a highway robber then, he is free to do so. But when we contemplate real cases, would we not rather want to maintain that even in chaos there is responsibility, that even then the individual has

[7]Locke, *op. cit.,* pars. 121, 149, 168, 203–4, 208–9, 211–12, 220, 232, 240–3.

some obligation to think of others as well as himself, the welfare of society or mankind as well as his own?

It seems that insufficient attention has been given to the failure of traditional consent theory to provide for any obligation to resist, or any obligation to choose responsibly when new authorities must be chosen. Indeed, divine right, prescription and utilitarianism can accommodate such obligations far more easily than a contract theory can. As for the "nature of the government" or "hypothetical consent" doctrine developed in this essay, it too would presumably require amendment on this score. An enlarged version might hold: your obligation is to obey what deserves obedience and consent, and to resist what deserves resistance and rejection (leaving the important possibility that many persons or agencies deserve neither obedience nor resistance). But it is not obvious to me whether the obligation to resist tyranny should be construed as a part of political obligation at all, or as an occasional alternative to it. The question seems related to that of whether revolution is a special part of political life or a breakdown of the political.

II. THE CASE OF SOCRATES

Though the Nazi may continue to obey on the grounds that he has sworn to do so, we may find that he thereby fails to perform his true obligations. Why, then, does Socrates' position—equally founded on past personal consent— strike us as so exemplary and moral? I would suggest that the distinguishing thing about Socrates' situation is this: he can find no fault with the Athenian laws, nor even with the Athenian way of administering them. Only his own particular conviction and sentence are (almost fortuitously) unjust. And his dialogue with the laws is essentially a way of expressing or establishing this fact. Socrates' past consent is not so much compelling in its own right, as it is a way of expressing and reinforcing his present judgment that there is nothing basically wrong with the system, no justification for resistance. What amazes us about him is not this judgment, nor the refusal to accept a single case of injustice as a justification for disobedience. These are relatively ordinary positions to take. What amazes us about him is that he construes disobedience so widely, to include even flight; and that he is willing to perform his obligation down to the minutest detail, even at the cost of his life.[8]

The suggestion is, then, that Socrates' focus on his past acceptance of the laws and his gratitude to them is in fact an evaluation of the Athenian government (or the expression of such an evaluation). We need to recall that this same moral Socrates refused to carry out an "authoritative" order given him in the

[8]Plato, *Crito* [50]: "are you not going by an act of yours to overturn us—the laws, and the whole state, as far as in you lies?" B. Jowett translation (New York: Random House, 1937).

time of the Thirty Tyrants, because it was unjust, and would apparently have refused to carry out injustice voted by a democratic majority as well.[9] In those earlier situations, one may suppose, what Socrates thought about was the injustice of what he had been ordered to do, and of those who issued the order, not his own (tacit?) consent to them.

To this line of argument a traditional consent theorist might respond: Socrates looks to his own past consent in order to find and determine its limits, in order to see whether this new governmental action does not exceed what he had consented to. But if we take that seriously as a model of what the moral man must do when he contemplates resistance, we set him an extremely difficult task. How is Socrates to know *to what* he has consented, particularly if his consent has been tacit? Surely it is not enough to say that he has consented only to those precise things the government did in the past, so that any new or unprecedented action is automatically *ultra vires.* But if not that, then to what does one give tacit consent? Is it to the particular people then in authority, or to the authority of the office they hold, or to the laws that define and limit that office, or to the body that makes those laws, or to the Constitution that lays down rules and procedures for the making of laws, or to the principles behind that Constitution, or to the fellow-members of the society, or even to all of mankind? In particular cases, these various foci of loyalty may come into conflict; then knowing that one has consented to them all at a time when they were in agreement is no help for deciding what to do.

In short, though two of our examples do look to their own past consent in deciding what to do, one of them thereby fails to perform his true obligation, and the other seems to be using the language of consent to express a favorable assessment of the government. Furthermore, we have noted at least two disadvantages of personal consent as a criterion: the difficulty of knowing *to what* you have consented (especially if consent was tacit), and the fact that even an express oath to obey may sometimes be outweighed by an obligation to resist.

Besides an individual's personal consent, traditional consent theory offers as an alternative criterion the "consent of the governed," the consent of all, or a majority of one's fellow-citizens. Of such consent, too, we would have to say that it cannot simply be dismissed as irrelevant. Even our Negro in Mississippi or South Africa might think about how widely shared his grievances are. But again, the consent or dissent of the majority cannot by itself be decisive for defining your obligation. Majorities are sometimes wrong, and have been known to do evil. Resistance might be justified in Athens under the Thirty Tyrants or in Nazi Germany despite the majority.

But majority consent does enter the argument at another level, in a way quite different from the relevance of personal consent. Majority consent may be relevant as a *way* of assessing, as *evidence about* the nature of the government, given that the nature of the government bears on political obligation.

[9]Plato, *Apology,* 32.

In fact, a variety of considerations each of which we might want to call "consent of the governed" can be used in the process of evaluating a government. They may come into conflict with each other, and their relative weight and importance will be a matter of one's political values, of what kind of government he thinks desirable or even tolerable.

It is useful to distinguish here between the "procedural" criteria yielded by the consent of the governed for assessing a government, and the "substantive" ones. Procedural criteria are those which concern the institutional structure and political functioning of the government, the way in which it makes decisions and takes actions. To assess its nature, we want to know about the way a government functions in relation to the governed—whether it is responsive to them or forces its policies on them. Thus we look for machinery for the expression of popular desires; we look for the degree of popular participation in or control over decisions, for channels for the redress of grievances, for access to power. At the same time we look also for signs of repression, of propaganda, of coercion. We look, of course, not merely at the institutions defined on paper, but at their actual functioning in the largest social sense. Denial of suffrage to Negroes in South Africa is very different from denial of suffrage to women in Switzerland (and theorists would do well to think about why this is so). But roughly speaking, a government is likely to seem to us deserving if it is open to the governed, reprehensible if it rules them against their will. This general criterion may well be expressed by some formula like "the consent of the governed"; but that formula must not be taken too simply, and that criterion must not be regarded as our only one.

Besides this vague cluster of procedural criteria, we have in addition substantive ones. We may look also at the substance of what the government does —whether it pursues good, benevolent, justifiable policies. A government that systematically harms its subjects, whether out of misguided good intentions or simply for the selfish gain of the rulers, is to that extent illegitimate—even if the subjects do not know it, even if they "consent" to being abused. But even here "the consent of the governed" is *relevant* as important evidence, for one of the main ways we estimate whether people are being well treated is by whether they seem to like what they get. Only we may sometimes need to consider other evidence as well; the consent or dissent of the governed need not be decisive as to the goodness or justness of a government's policies.

It is the relationship between at least these two kinds of criteria that is likely to determine our assessment of a government, whether it deserves support or opposition. Thus we may all agree that a government pursuing very bad policies and forcing them on its subjects, so that it is obviously doing great harm to them and other countries, and doing so despite their attempts at protest and without their consent—such a government clearly is the occasion for resistance. Conversely, if we find a government that truly has the consent of its subjects although they have wide sources of information and true opportunities to dissent and criticize, and if that government pursues only the most praiseworthy policies, then few of us would urge revolution or resistance to it. The problematic cases are, of course, the ones in between, where procedure and substance are partly good, partly bad, and you need to make evaluations and decisions. Here it begins to be a matter of your metapolitics—how you think of men and societies, what positions you are willing to take and defend, and take responsibility for.

Suppose, for example, that a government is procedurally open, with genuine channels for controlling policy from below, but it engages in vicious policies. Then, one might want to say, the citizen is not free to engage in revolution; he has channels available and it is his duty to use them, to change the policy. But what if he tries to do so, and fails because the majority continues to approve of the wickedness? What if he is a member of a permanent minority group, being systematically abused and exploited by an eager, consenting majority? Then the seemingly open channels of consent are not truly open to him. Might there not come a point when violent minority resistance of some sort is justified?

Or suppose that a government is benevolent, so no one can criticize its actions, but in procedure it is simply autocratic and dictatorial. Is revolution justified against a benevolent dictatorship? This might be the case, for example, if men need political participation in order to be really well, in order to reach their full human potential. Then bad procedure would itself become a substantive grievance.

The theoretical complications possible here are legion, but at least this much seems clear: evaluating a government in order to decide whether it deserves obedience or resistance, requires attention both to the way it works and to what it does. In both cases something like consent is relevant; it may be a formula for expressing some rather complex requirements concerning opportunities for dissent and participation, or it may be evidence of good policies. Thus even if we adhere to the doctrine of hypothetical consent or the nature of government, majority consent may still be relevant in a subordinate capacity for assessing a government, for working out more detailed answers to our questions one and two about consent, the specific practical "when" and "whom" of obedience. But here "the consent of the governed" is not one simple thing, decisive for obligation; rather, it is relevant in a number of different, potentially conflicting ways.

And all of these ways put together differ, in turn, not merely from personal consent, but also from the doctrine of hypothetical consent developed in this essay.[10] That legitimate authority is such that one ought to consent to it, is a precept built into English grammar, into the meanings of these terms. That a legitimate government is one which has the consent of (a majority of) the governed—is procedurally responsive to them or looks after their interests, or both—is one particular position about what kind of government is desirable

[10]For the latter distinction, compare Benn and Peters, *op. cit.*, pp. 329–31.

for men. More accurately, it is a cluster of positions, depending on the relative weight given to procedural and substantive criteria. Though these positions are very widely shared today, and though they were shared by almost all traditional consent theorists, they are not the only conceivable positions on this subject. Someone might undertake to argue, for example, that a government is legitimate only to the extent that it fosters high culture, or to the extent that it promotes the evolution of a master race. That would be to reject majority consent as any sort of criterion for assessing a government. But the doctrine of hypothetical consent holds even for someone taking such an unorthodox position; even for him, a legitimate government would be the one that deserves consent, to which everyone ought to consent. Both the philosophical weakness and the historical persistence and strength of traditional consent theory rest in its failure to distinguish these very different arguments.

Finally, even if we succeed in evaluating a government, that does not seem fully to settle how we must behave toward it. One final, important consideration seems relevant: the action taken must be appropriate. To the diversity of ways in which one can obey or support, resist or overthrow a government, there correspond a diversity of conditions when the various actions may be appropriate or justified. The fact that some action is justified, that some abuse has taken place, does not mean that just any action will do. A man mistreated by his superior may kick his dog. We can understand, and perhaps even sympathize, but surely the action is not justified. Not just any violation of law will qualify as civil disobedience or attempted revolution. This observation is presumably related to the traditional assertion of consent theorists, that it is necessary to "exhaust the remedies" available, to suffer "a long train of abuses" before violent resistance is justified. Where other actions are appropriate, revolution may not be called for.

Thus it begins to seem that a decision about obedience and resistance ought to be measured not merely against the character of the government, but against all the relevant social circumstances—what alternatives one can envision, and what consequences resistance is likely to have. Revolution would not seem justified, for example, if one had no hope of its being followed by an improvement in conditions. If it would simply substitute one tyranny for another, or if it would annihilate the human race through the resulting violence, then it does not seem justified.

But a doctrine that casts its net so wide, making all social circumstances at least potentially relevant, that sees both an obligation to obey and an obligation to resist, and that stresses so much the individual burden of decision, seems very close to the social utilitarianism examined in the first half of this essay. It seems to say, with the social utilitarian, you are obligated to obey when that is best on the whole for society (all of mankind?), and obligated to resist when *that* is best on the whole. But that formula, and social utilitarianism, seem to neglect again the obligatory nature of law and authority in normal circumstances, the *prima facie* obligation to obey. Being subject to law, government, authority means precisely an obligation (normally) to do what *they* say is best, rather than judge the welfare of society for yourself and act on your private judgment. Yet there are times when you must resist in the name of something very like the welfare of society. Whether these two positions are compatible remains somehow problematic; but before we can make a final stab at the matter, we must finish applying our new doctrine to our four questions about political obligation.

III. JUSTIFYING POLITICAL OBLIGATION

We come now to question four, the matter of justification: "why are you ever obligated to obey even legitimate authority?" Here again our "nature of the government" doctrine does not at first seem a very useful answer. For it can only say: because of the nature of the government, because the government is such that you ought to obey it and consent to it, because a rational man would do so. But that answer is not likely to still the question. For someone genuinely puzzled about obligation in this (philosophical) way is likely to persist: "how does that 'ought' bind me, *why* must I do what a rational man would do, what if I don't *want* to be rational?"

But the reader may have noticed by now that all of the theories and versions of theories we have considered are subject to this same difficulty to some extent. Some seem better designed to cope with it than others; yet we can always push the question further back: why must I do what God commands, why must I do what history teaches, why must I do what is best for me personally, why must I do what I have promised? Even traditional consent theory is liable to this difficulty; and it is remarkable that despite Hume's early criticism, we continue to believe in consent theory while ignoring this problem. For Hume had already told the consent theorist:

> You find yourself embarrassed when it is asked, *Why we are bound to keep our word?* Nor can you give any answer but what would, immediately, without any circuit, have accounted for our obligation to allegiance.[11]

The obligation to keep one's word is no more "natural" and self-evident and indubitable than political obligation itself; though either may sometimes reinforce the other, neither can give the other absolute justification. The two obligations are essentially separate and equal in status. Why, then, does the traditional consent theorist, so doubtful about the validity of political obligation, take the obligation of keeping contracts as obvious? Why, if he imagines a state of nature, is it always stripped of political authority but inevitably equipped with a natural law that dictates the keeping of one's word? Hume

[11]David Hume, "Of the Original Contract," in Sir Ernest Barker, ed., *The Social Contract* (New York: Oxford, 1960), p. 161.

uses these questions as a rhetorical device to attack consent theory, but they can also be taken seriously as a way of learning something more about the consent theorist.

For a theorist does not choose his beliefs and his doubts. The traditional consent theorist simply finds himself in doubt about (the justification of, or limits of, or validity of) political obligation; it just seems obvious to him that there is a problem about it. And he simply is not in doubt about promises or contracts; it just seems obvious to him that they oblige.

At one level one can argue that both the consent theorist's doubt and his assumption spring from the peculiar picture of man and society he seems to hold. If your picture of man in the abstract is of a man fully grown, complete with his own private needs, interests, feelings, desires, beliefs and values, and if you therefore never think about how he grew up and became the particular person he became, then he may well seem to you an ineluctably *separate* unit, his ties to other individuals may seem mysterious or illusory and will require explanation. Given man as such a separate, self-contained unit, it does indeed seem strange that he might have obligations not of his own choosing, perhaps even without being aware of them, or even against his will. Furthermore, self-assumed obligations may then strike you as a way of overcoming this separateness. For it is easy to confuse the fact that promises and contracts are self-assumed, with the idea that the *obligation to keep* them is self-assumed as well. That is, the person who makes a promise seems to recognize and commit himself to the institution of promises; the person who makes a contract seems to acknowledge thereby the binding character of contracts, so that a later refusal to accept them as binding strikes one as a kind of self-contradiction. But of course this is a confusion. The making of particular promises or contracts presupposes the social institution of promising or contracts, and the obligation to keep promises cannot itself be founded on a promise.

In truth, there is something profoundly wrong with the consent theorist's picture of man. Every free, separate, adult, consenting individual was first shaped and molded by his parents and (as we say) society. It is only as a result of their influence that he becomes the particular person he does become, with his particular interests, values, desires, language and obligations. The only thing truly separate about us is our bodies; our selves are manifestly social. But surely even the consent theorist knows this, so the problem becomes why he nevertheless holds, or is held captive by, a different and peculiar picture. Could that picture be not so much the cause as the by-product of his philosophical doubt?

After all, consent theorists are not the only ones troubled about political obligation. Political theorists of other persuasions have also been led, or have led themselves sometimes to ask "why are you ever obligated to obey even legitimate authority?" But if none of the theories of political obligation is able to deal adequately with that question, it must be quite peculiar, not nearly as straightforward as it looks. Perhaps it is a question that cannot be fully

answered in the ordinary way. But what sort of question is that; and if it cannot
be answered, how should it be treated? Tussman rejects it as a symptom of
"moral disorder"; I would suggest instead that it is a symptom of philosophical
disorder, the product of a philosophical paradox. If so, it will not disappear
—the theorist will not stop being bothered by it—unless we can show how and
why it arises, why anyone should so much as suppose that political obligation
in general needs (or can have) a general justification. But that would require
a discussion of the nature of philosophical puzzlement far beyond the scope
of this essay.

What can be done here is something much more limited and less effective.
Having suggested that the status of political obligation and of the obligation
to keep promises is essentially the same—that neither is more "natural" than
or can serve as an absolute justification for the other—we can approach our
question four about political obligation by first pursuing a parallel question
about promises. For in the area of promises some extremely useful work has
been done in philosophy in recent years—work which can be applied to the
problem of political obligation.[12]

Philosophers have sometimes asked a question like our question four about
promises: "why are you (ever) obligated to keep (any of) your promises
(whatsoever); why do promises oblige?" This question, too, can be answered
in terms of divine commandment or utilitarian consequences, social or individual; and here, too, the answers are less than satisfactory. "God commands you
to keep your word" is no answer to the nonbeliever, nor to someone heretical
enough to demand proof of God's will. The utilitarian response tends to
dissolve the obligation altogether, so that your duty is always to do what
produces the best results, quite apart from whether you have made any promises on the subject. And, of course, a consent argument is out of the question
here ("you have promised to keep your promises"?).

What has been suggested by philosophers is this: "promise" is not just a
word. Promising is a social practice, something we *do,* something children
have to learn *how* to do. It has rules, penalties, roles, and moves, almost in
the way that games have them. Children do not learn what a promise is by
having one pointed out to them; they learn gradually about what it means to
"make a promise," "keep (or break) a promise," "be unable to promise but
certainly intend to try," "have said something which, in the circumstances,
amounted to a promise," and so on. Promising is not just producing certain
sounds ("I promise"), for a phonograph might make those sounds, or a man
rehearsing a play, or a philosopher explaining the practice, yet none of these
would actually be promising. Promising, rather, is taking on an obligation.

---

[12]See particularly J. L. Austin, *Philosophical Papers* (Oxford: Clarendon, 1961), chs.
3, 6 and 10; John Rawls, "Two Concepts of Rules," *Philosophical Review,* LXIV
(January, 1955), 3–32; and S. L. Cavell, "Must We Mean What We Say?" in V. C.
Chappell, *Ordinary Language* (Englewood Cliffs, N. J.: Prentice-Hall, 1964), esp. pp.
94–101.

That is, "to promise" does not mean "to make certain sounds," but rather "to take on an obligation."

Now, of course, we do not always do what we have promised. Sometimes we act contrary to our obligations, and sometimes we are wholly or partly excused from performing what we had promised. If, for example, keeping a promise would frustrate the purpose for which it was made, or would lead to great evil, or has become impossible, we may be excused from performing. So about any particular promise we have made it may sometimes be relevant to ask: am I still obligated to perform or not? That is, normally, in principle promises oblige; a promise is a certain kind of obligation. But sometimes, under certain circumstances, there is reason to question or withdraw or cancel that obligation in a particular case. In such circumstances we weigh the alternatives, the possible consequences of performance and failure to perform. But our obligations, including that of the promise, continue to be among the factors that must be weighed in the decision. The obligation of a promise does not simply disappear when there is occasion to question it; it only is sometimes outweighed.

But philosophers are sometimes led to wonder *categorically,* about *all* promises: do they oblige; what are the reasons pro and con; why am I ever obligated to keep any promise? And here, of course, there are no *particular* circumstances to weigh in the balance; the question is abstract and hypothetical. What sort of answer is possible to this question? First, that this is what a promise *is,* what "promise" means. A promise is a self-assumed obligation. If you *assume* an obligation and have not yet performed it, nor been excused from it, then you *have* an obligation; in much the same way as someone who puts on a coat, has a coat on.[13] To ask why promises oblige is to ask why (self-assumed) obligations oblige. And to the question why obligations oblige the only possible answer would seem to be that this is what the words mean.

Beyond this one can only paraphrase Wittgenstein: there are a hundred reasons; there is no reason. There is no absolute, deductive answer to the question "why does any promise ever oblige?" beyond calling attention to the meaning of the words. There is no absolute, indubitable principle from which the obligation can be deduced. It is, to be sure, related to any number of other principles, obligations and values; but the relationship is more like a network (or patchwork) than like a hierarchical pyramid. It is simply a mistake to suppose that there might be such an absolute principle, such a deductive proof. We have no right to expect one. (Why, then, does the philosopher expect one; why can we ourselves be led to share his expectation when we are in a "philosophical mood"?)

John Rawls has pointed out that utilitarianism will not do as a criterion for the keeping of particular promises—as a standard for *when* promises oblige.[14]

---

[13]Compare Cavell, "Must We Mean What We Say?" *op. cit.,* pp. 96, 99.
[14]*Op. cit.,* Part II.

To say "keep your promises only when that maximizes pleasure and minimizes pain" is to miss precisely the *obligatory* nature of a promise; having once promised you are not free to decide what to do merely on utilitarian grounds. But, Rawls says, utilitarian considerations *are* relevant at a different level of argument, for assessing the social practice of promising. For we can ask "must we (should we) have an institution like promising and promise-keeping at all?" And here utilitarian reasons seem relevant; we may try to justify the social practice by its useful consequences.

Stanley Cavell has argued that this implies a degree of freedom of choice on our parts which we do not in fact have.[15] To evaluate the practice of promising pro and con, we would have to envision alternatives. And how shall we envision a society which knows no obligation to keep one's word? (For it is not, of course, the particular English locution "I promise" that is being assessed, but the practice of assuming obligations and holding people to their word.) We seem to have no choice about the pros and cons of such an institution. It is not socially useful; it is indispensable to the very concept of society and human life.

But even if we could and did evaluate as Rawls suggests, and "decide" that the institution of promising is on balance socially useful, even this would not provide an absolute justification for the keeping of particular promises. For what are we to answer the man who says: "granted that we must have the practice of promising, and granted promising means taking on an obligation; still, why am *I* obliged to keep my promise? Why can't *I* be an exception?" To him we can only say, that is how obligation and promises work. Of course you *can* refuse to keep your promise, but then you are failing to perform an obligation.

Now the same line of reasoning can be applied to the question "why does even a legitimate government, a valid law, a genuine authority ever obligate me to obey?" As with promises, and as our new doctrine about political obligation suggests, we may say that this is what "legitimate government," "valid law," "genuine authority" *mean*. It is part of the concept, the meaning of "authority" that those subject to it are required to obey, that it has a right to command. It is part of the concept, the meaning of "law," that those to whom it is applicable are obligated to obey it. As with promises, so with authority, government and law: there is a *prima facie* obligation involved in each, and normally you must perform it. Normally a man is not free to decide on utilitarian grounds whether or not he will do a certain thing, if that thing happens to be against the law or required by law; he is not free to make a decision on his own the way he would be free where the law is silent. The existence of the law on this subject normally constitutes an obligation, just as having promised normally constitutes an obligation, so that one is not free to decide what to do just as if no promise had been made. (This is not, of course,

[15]"The Claim to Rationality," Chapter VIII.

to say that everything claiming to be law is law, that everyone claiming to have authority has it, that every statement alleged to be a promise is in fact one. It says only: *if* something is a promise, law, obligation, *then* normally it obliges.) This kind of response to question four is obviously almost the same as the one our doctrine of hypothetical consent yielded to question three: government and authority are concepts grammatically related to obligation and obedience. A legitimate government is one that you ought to obey and ought to consent to because that is what the words mean. But as before, this answer is likely to seem purely formal, and empty. It will not satisfy someone genuinely puzzled about the justification of political obligation.

But as with promises, all that one can say beyond calling attention to the meanings of the words, is that no absolute, deductive justification exists or is necessary. There are no absolute first principles from which this obligation could be derived. It is related to all kinds of other obligations in all kinds of ways, to be sure, but the relationship is not hierarchical and deductive. In particular, as we have seen, the obligatory nature of promises is no more or no less absolute and indubitable than the obligation to obey laws. Again, following Rawls' suggestion, one might attempt a utilitarian assessment of such institutions or practices as law, government and authority. And here, I suppose, there may be somewhat more room for discussion than with promises. For it is not at all obvious that government and law are indispensable to human social life. But can we conceive society without any such thing as authority? One function of the idea of the state of nature in classical consent theories does seem to be a kind of indirect demonstration of the utilitarian advantages of having governments and laws. If such things did not exist, Locke seems to argue, we would have to invent them.

But as with promises, even a recognition of the necessity or utilitarian advantages of such things as authority, law and government is no absolute answer to the man who is questioning his particular obligation to obey, who wants to be an exception. There is no such absolute answer, and can be none. Nothing we say is absolutely beyond question. Again, you *can* disobey but in the absence of excuses or justifications you violate an obligation when you do so.

The parallel between promises and authority as obligations is not perfect. For one thing, promises are explicitly taken on oneself; political obligation (I have argued) need not be. Furthermore, promises are normally made to particular persons, whereas political obligation is sometimes confounded by our question two, by the problem of rival authorities. We have noted the difficulty of determining to whom or what consent is given: particular officials, their positions, the laws, the Constitution, the people of the society. This means, among other things, that political obligation is open to a kind of challenge not normally relevant to promises. We saw that, following Rawls, both promises and political obligation can be challenged at two very different levels: sometimes we may claim to be excused from performing in a particular case (for instance because of conflicting obligations or overwhelming difficulties). And sometimes we may want to challenge and assess the whole institution with the obligations it defines. But in addition, political obligation can be challenged also on a third level. Sometimes we may refuse to obey neither because our particular case is exceptional, nor because we question such obligation categorically, but because the one who is claiming authority over us does not in fact have it. We may resist a government that has become tyrannical not as a special, personal exception, and not because we are against government, but because *this* government no longer deserves obedience. Such a challenge is made on principle, *in accord* (as it were) with the "rules" of political obligation.

But the differences between promises and political obligation do not affect the point to be made here. That point concerns our question four, the search for a justification for having to obey (or having to keep a promise); and it is essentially twofold. First, we have said, "authority," "law," and "government" are grammatically, conceptually related to obligation, as is "promise." And beyond this, the quest for some "higher," absolute, deductive justification is misguided. Insofar, then, as the grammatical point does not seem to still the question, does not get at what someone philosophically puzzled wants to ask, what is needed is not a better justification, but an account of why the philosopher is driven to ask the question in the first place. . . .

40

ROBERT PAUL WOLFF (1933– ———)

Beyond the Legitimate State

Robert Paul Wolff, a contemporary American philosopher, was born in New York City, educated at Harvard University, and is now professor of philosophy at the University of Massachusetts. He previously taught at Harvard, the University of Chicago, and Columbia University. His writings have focused on the philosophy of

From Robert Paul Wolff, *In Defense of Anarchism*, Chapter III (New York: Harper & Row, 1970), pp. 69–82. Copyright © 1970 by Robert Paul Wolff. Reprinted by permission of the publisher.

Kant and on political philosophy. He has authored four books in political philosophy: *A Critique of Pure Tolerance* (1965), *Political Man and Social Man* (1966), *The Poverty of Liberalism* (1968), and *In Defense of Anarchism* (1970).

In the preface to the book from which the following selection is taken, Wolff tells of his unsuccessful search for a political theory that would legitimize the state's authority over an individual citizen. He was finally forced to conclude that no such theory is possible. "My failure to find any theoretical justification for the authority of the state," he writes, "had convinced me that there was no justification. In short, I had become a philosophical anarchist."[1]

Is it possible, then, to have a stable political order that preserves the absolute freedom (autonomy) of the individual—a state *without authority?* Wolff wants to answer "Yes," and in the reading that follows he tries to suggest the outlines of such a political order.

1. THE QUEST FOR THE LEGITIMATE STATE

We have come to a dead end in our search for a viable form of political association which will harmonize the moral autonomy of the individual with the legitimate authority of the state. The one proposal which appears genuinely to resolve the conflict, namely unanimous direct democracy, is so restricted in its application that it offers no serious hope of ever being embodied in an actual state. Indeed, since it achieves its success only by ruling out precisely the conflicts of opinion which politics is designed to resolve, it may be viewed as the limiting case of a solution rather than as itself a true example of a legitimate state.

A contractual democracy is legitimate, to be sure, for it is founded upon the citizens' promise to obey its commands. Indeed, any state is legitimate which is founded upon such a promise. However, all such states achieve their legitimacy only by means of the citizens' forfeit of their autonomy, and hence are not solutions to the fundamental problem of political philosophy. Majoritarian democracy claims a deeper justification than merely an original promise. It presents itself as the only viable form of political community in which the citizenry rule themselves, and thus preserve their autonomy while collecting their individual authority into the authority of the state. Unfortunately, our examination of the various arguments in support of majority rule has revealed that this additional claim is unfounded. Whatever else may be said for a majoritarian democracy, it does not appear to be true that the minority remain free and self-ruled while submitting to the majority.

Our failure to discover a form of political association which could combine moral autonomy with legitimate authority is not a result of the imperfect

[1] *In Defense of Anarchism* (New York, Evanston, and London: Harper & Row, 1970), p. viii.

rationality of men, nor of the passions and private interests which deflect men from the pursuit of justice and the general good. Many political philosophers have portrayed the state as a necessary evil forced upon men by their own inability to abide by the principles of morality, or as a tool of one class of men against the others in the never-ending struggle for personal advantage. Marx and Hobbes agree that in a community of men of good will, where the general good guided every citizen, the state would be unnecessary. They differ only in the degree of their hope that so happy a condition can ever be realized.

Nor does our dilemma grow out of the familiar limitations of intellect and knowledge which afflict all but the most extraordinary men. It may be that in a technologically complex world only a few men can hope to master the major political issues well enough to have genuinely personal convictions about them. By positing a society of rational men of good will, however, we have eliminated such well-known obstacles to the fully just state. The magnitude of our problem is indicated by our inability to solve the dilemma of autonomy and authority even for a utopian society! By and large, political philosophers have supposed that utopia was logically possible, however much they may have doubted that it was even marginally probable. But the arguments of this essay suggest that the just state must be consigned the category of the round square, the married bachelor, and the unsensed sense-datum.

If autonomy and authority are genuinely incompatible, only two courses are open to us. Either we must embrace philosophical anarchism and treat *all* governments as nonlegitimate bodies whose commands must be judged and evaluated in each instance before they are obeyed; or else, we must give up as quixotic the pursuit of autonomy in the political realm and submit ourselves (by an implicit promise) to whatever form of government appears most just and beneficent at the moment. (I cannot resist repeating yet again that if we take this course, *there is no universal or* a priori *reason for binding ourselves to a democratic government rather than to any other sort.* In some situations, it may be wiser to swear allegiance to a benevolent and efficient dictatorship than to a democracy which imposes a tyrannical majority on a defenseless minority. *And in those cases where we have sworn to obey the rule of the majority, no additional binding force will exist beyond what would be present had we promised our allegiance to a king!*)

It is out of the question to give up the commitment to moral autonomy. Men are no better than children if they not only accept the rule of others from force of necessity, but embrace it willingly and forfeit their duty unceasingly to weigh the merits of the actions which they perform. When I place myself in the hands of another, and permit him to determine the principles by which I shall guide my behavior, I repudiate the freedom and reason which give me dignity. I am then guilty of what Kant might have called the sin of willful heteronomy.

There would appear to be no alternative but to embrace the doctrine of anarchism and categorically deny *any* claim to legitimate authority by one man over another. Yet I confess myself unhappy with the conclusion that I must simply leave off the search for legitimate collective authority. Perhaps it might be worth saying something about the deeper philosophical reasons for this reluctance.

Man confronts a natural world which is irreducibly *other,* which stands over against him, independent of his will and indifferent to his desires. Only religious superstition or the folly of idealist metaphysics could encourage us to assume that nature will prove ultimately rational, or that the opposition between man and objects must in principle be surmountable. Man also confronts a social world which *appears* other, which *appears* to stand over against him, at least partially independent of his will and frequently capricious in its frustration of his desires. Is it also folly to suppose that this opposition can be overcome, and that man can so perfectly conquer society as to make it his tool rather than his master? To answer this question, we must determine whether the appearance of the objectivity of society is also reality, or whether perhaps here, in the realm of institutions and interpersonal relationships, man's estrangement from the society which dominates him is accidental, adventitious, and ultimately eradicable.

Each individual is born into a social world which is already organized into regular patterns of behavior and expectation. At first, he is aware only of the few persons in his immediate physical environment and of their qualities and appearance. Very soon, the infant learns to expect repeated sequences of behavior from those around him. Later still, the child comes to see these significant persons as playing certain defined roles (mother, father, teacher, policeman) which are also played by other persons in different situations (other children also have mothers and fathers, etc.). The learning of language reinforces this awareness, for built into the word "father" is the notion that there may be many fathers to many children. The child matures and develops a personality by identifying with various role-bearers in his world and internalizing as his own the patterns of behavior and belief which constitute the roles. He *becomes* someone in this way, and also *discovers* who he is by reflecting on the alternatives which life offers him. Characteristically, the adolescent goes through a period of role definition during which he tentatively tries on a variety of roles, in order to test their appropriateness for him. (This is perhaps a description biased by contemporary Western experience. In some cultures, of course, the uncertainty over roles which produces an "identity crisis" never occurs since it is laid down by the society what set of roles the individual shall internalize and act out. For the purposes of this discussion, however, that point is not significant.)

Thus, the social world presents to each individual an objective reality with independently existing structures, just as the physical world does. The infant learns where his body ends and the objects around him begin. He distinguishes between what is within his control (various movements of his body) and what does not respond to his will. In exactly the same way, he learns to recognize the intractable realities of his social environment. When a boy is asked what he wants to be, he is really being asked which already existing social role he wishes to adopt as an adult. His answer—that he wants to be a fireman, or an engineer, or an explorer—indicates that he understands perfectly well the nature of the question. He may see himself, at least in a society like ours, as exercising some control over the roles which he shall adopt; but neither the questioner nor the boy would suppose that either of them has any control over the existence and nature of the roles themselves! Even the social rebel characteristically opts for an existing role, that of bohemian, or beatnik, or revolutionary. Like all role-players, such rebels wear the clothes, live in the quarters, and use the language appropriate to the role which they have chosen.

In any reasonably complex society, social roles are in turn organized into even more extensive patterns of behavior and belief, to which we apply the term "institutions." The church, the state, the army, the market are all such systems of roles. The characteristic interactions of the constituent roles of an institution are determined independently of particular individuals, just as the roles themselves are. At this level of complexity of organization, however, a new phenomenon appears which vastly increases the apparent objectivity of social reality, namely what has come to be known as the "paradox of unintended consequences." Each person in an institutional structure pursues goals and follows patterns at least partially laid down for him by the society—that is, already existing when he takes on the role and hence *given* to him. In his roles, however, he should be able to see the relationship between what he does and what results, even though he may not feel free to alter his goals or try new means. In the process of interaction with other individual role-players, more far-reaching results will be produced which may be neither anticipated nor particularly desired by any person in the system. These unintended consequences will therefore appear to the role-players as somehow not their doing, and hence objective in just the way that natural occurrences are objective. To cite a classic example, as each entrepreneur strives to increase his profit by cutting his price slightly, hoping thereby to seize a larger portion of the total market, the market price of his commodity falls steadily and everyone experiences a decline in profits. If he thinks about it at all, the entrepreneur will characteristically suppose himself to be caught in the grip of a "falling market," which is to say a natural or objective force over which he has no control. Even after he recognizes the causal relationship between his individual act of pricecutting and the drop in the market price, he is liable to think himself powerless to reverse the workings of the "laws of the marketplace." (Perhaps it is worth noting that, contrary to the assumptions of classical liberal economic theory, the entrepreneur is as much in the grip of social forces when he plays the role of capitalist as when he feels the pinch of the market. Even the most casual cross-cultural comparison reveals that "economic man" is a social role peculiar to certain cultures, and not at all the natural man who emerges when the distorting forces of tradition and superstition are lifted.)

The experience of the entrepreneur is reduplicated endlessly, so that men come to imagine themselves more completely enslaved by society than they ever were by nature. Yet their conviction is fundamentally wrong, for while the natural world really does exist independently of man's beliefs or desires, and therefore exercises a constraint on his will which can at best be mitigated or combatted, the social world is nothing in itself, and consists merely of the totality of the habits, expectations, beliefs, and behavior patterns of all the individuals who live in it. To be sure, insofar as men are ignorant of the total structures of the institutions within which they play their several roles, they will be the victims of consequences unintended by anyone; and, of course, to the extent that men are set against one another by conflicting interests, those whose institutional roles give them advantages of power or knowledge in the social struggle will prevail over those who are relatively disadvantaged. But since each man's unfreedom is entirely a result either of ignorance or of a conflict of interests, it ought to be in principle possible for a society of rational men of good will to eliminate the domination of society and subdue it to their wills in a manner that is impossible in the case of nature.

Consider as an example the economic institutions of society. At first, men play their several economic roles (farmer, craftsman, trader, fisherman) in complete ignorance of the network of interactions which influence the success of their endeavors and guide them into sequences of decisions, for good or ill, whose structure and ultimate outcome they cannot see. These same men imagine themselves encapsulated in a set of unchanging economic roles whose patterns, rewards, and systematic relationships are quite independent of their wills. Slowly, as the systematic interconnections themselves become more complex and mutually dependent, man's understanding of the economy as a whole grows, so that, for example, entrepreneurs begin to realize that their profits depend upon the total quantity of goods produced by themselves and their fellow capitalists, and the accumulation of individual desires for those goods which, collectively, constitute the level of demand. The first stage in the mastery of the economy may consist simply in the discovery of such aggregate quantities as demand, supply, interest rate, profit level, and even market price. That is to say, men must *discover* that the interaction of many individual acts of buying and selling establishes a single market price, which reflects the relation of supply to demand of the commodity being marketed. After realizing that such a marketwide price exists, men can begin to understand how it is determined. Only then can they consider the possibility of making that price a direct object of decision, and thus finally free themselves from the tyranny of the market.

In addition to the ignorance which enslaves even those in positions of power in the economy (the capitalists in a laissez-faire system), the pursuit of private interest results in the exploitation and enslavement of those whose roles in the economy carry relatively little power. Hence even the farthest advance imaginable of social knowledge would not suffice to liberate all men from their social bonds unless it were accompanied by a transformation of private interest into a concern for the general good. But if so utopian a condition were achieved, then surely men could once and for all reconquer their common product, society, and at least within the human world, move from the realm of necessity into the realm of freedom. Death and taxes, it is said, are the only certainties in this life; a folk maxim which reflects the deep conviction that men cannot escape the tyranny of either nature or society. Death will always be with us, reminding us that we are creatures of nature. But taxes, along with all the other instruments of social action, are human products, and hence must in the end submit to the collective will of a society of rational men of good will.

It should now be clear why I am unwilling to accept as final the negative results of our search for a political order which harmonizes authority and autonomy. The state is a social institution, and therefore no more than the totality of the beliefs, expectations, habits, and interacting roles of its members and subjects. When rational men, in full knowledge of the proximate and distant consequences of their actions, determine to set private interest aside and pursue the general good, it *must* be possible for them to create a form of association which accomplishes that end without depriving some of them of their moral autonomy. The state, in contrast to nature, cannot be ineradicably *other*.

2. UTOPIAN GLIMPSES OF A WORLD WITHOUT STATES

Through the exercise of *de facto* legitimate authority, states achieve what Max Weber calls the imperative coordination of masses of men and women. To some extent, of course, this coordination consists in the more-or-less voluntary submission by large numbers of people to institutional arrangements which are directly contrary to their interests. Threats of violence or economic sanction play a central role in holding the people in line, although as Weber very persuasively argues, the myth of legitimacy is also an important instrument of domination.

But even if there were no exploitation or domination in society, it would still be in men's interest to achieve a very high level of social coordination, for reasons both of economic efficiency and of public order. At our present extremely advanced stage of division of labor, relatively minor disruptions of social coordination can produce a breakdown of the flow of goods and services necessary to sustain life.

Consequently, it is worth asking whether a society of men who have been persuaded of the truth of anarchism—a society in which no one claims legitimate authority or would believe such a claim if it were made—could through alternative methods achieve an adequate level of social coordination.

There are, so far as I can see, three general sorts of purposes, other than the domination and exploitation of one segment of society by another, for which

men might wish to achieve a high order of social coordination. First, there is
the collective pursuit of some *external* national goal such as national defense,
territorial expansion, or economic imperialism. Second, there is the collective
pursuit of some *internal* goal which requires the organization and coordination of the activities of large numbers of people, such as traffic safety, to cite
a trivial example, or the reconstruction of our cities, to cite an example not
so trivial. Finally, there is the maintenance of our industrial economy whose
functional differentiation and integration—to use the sociologist's jargon—are
advanced enough to sustain an adequately high level of production. Is there
any way in which these ends could be served other than by commands enforced
by coercion and by the myth of legitimacy?

I do not now have a complete and coherent answer to this question, which
is in a way the truest test of the political philosophy of anarchism, but I shall
make a few suggestions which may open up fruitful avenues of investigation.

With regard to matters of national defense and foreign adventure, it seems
to me that there is much to be said for the adoption of a system of voluntary
compliance with governmental directives. If we assume a society of anarchists
—a society, that is to say, which has achieved a level of moral and intellectual
development at which superstitious beliefs in legitimacy of authority have
evaporated—then the citizenry would be perfectly capable of choosing freely
whether to defend the nation and carry its purpose beyond the national bor-
ders. The army itself could be run on the basis of voluntary commitments and
submission to orders. To be sure, the day might arrive when there were not
enough volunteers to protect the freedom and security of the society. But if
that were the case, then it would clearly be illegitimate to command the
citizens to fight. Why should a nation continue to exist if its populace does not
wish to defend it? One thinks here of the contrast between the Yugoslav
partisans or Israeli soldiers, on the one hand, and the American forces in
Vietnam on the other.

The idea of voluntary compliance with governmental directives is hardly
new, but it inevitably provokes the shocked reaction that social chaos would
result from any such procedure. My own opinion is that superstition rather
than reason lies behind this reaction. I personally would feel quite safe in an
America whose soldiers were free to choose when and for what they would
fight.

Voluntary compliance would go far toward generating sufficient social coordination to permit collective pursuit of domestic goals as well. In addition, I
believe that much could be done through the local, community-based development of a consensual or general will with regard to matters of collective rather
than particular interest. In the concluding chapter of my book, *The Poverty
of Liberalism,* I have offered a conceptual analysis of the several modes of
community. I will simply add that achievement of the sorts of community I
analyzed there would require a far-reaching decentralization of the American
economy.

This last point brings me to the most difficult problem of all—namely, the maintenance of a level of social coordination sufficient for an advanced industrial economy. As Friedrich Hayek and a number of other classical liberal political economists have pointed out, the natural operation of the market is an extremely efficient way of coordinating human behavior on a large scale without coercion or appeal to authority. Nevertheless, reliance on the market is fundamentally irrational once men know how to control it in order to avoid its undesired consequences. The original laissez-faire liberals viewed the laws of the market as objective laws of a benevolent nature; modern laissez-faire liberals propose that we go on confusing nature and society, even though we have the knowledge to subordinate the market to our collective will and decision.

Only extreme economic decentralization could permit the sort of voluntary economic coordination consistent with the ideals of anarchism and affluence. At the present time, of course, such decentralization would produce economic chaos, but if we possessed a cheap, local source of power and an advanced technology of small-scale production, and if we were in addition willing to accept a high level of economic waste, we might be able to break the American economy down into regional and subregional units of manageable size. The exchanges between the units would be inefficient and costly—very large inventory levels, inelasticities of supply and demand, considerable waste, and so forth. But in return for this price, men would have increasing freedom to act autonomously. In effect, such a society would enable all men to be autonomous agents, whereas in our present society, the relatively few autonomous men are —as it were—parasitic upon the obedient, authority-respecting masses.

These remarks fall far short of a coherent projection of an anarchist society, but they may serve to make the ideal seem a bit less like a mere fantasy of utopian political philosophy.

For Further Reading

Aristotle. *Politics.* Many editions. See especially Book VII.

Beran, H. "In Defense of the Consent Theory of Political Obligation and Authority," *Ethics,* 87 (1977), 260–271.

Barry, Brian. *Political Argument.* New York: Humanities Press, 1965.

—————. *The Liberal Theory of Justice: A Critical Examination of the Principal Doctrines in "A Theory of Justice" by John Rawls.* New York: Oxford University Press, 1973.

Berlin, Isaiah. *Four Essays on Liberty.* New York: Oxford University Press, 1969 (paperbound).

Bosanquet, Bernard. *Philosophical Theory of the State.* London: Macmillan, 1920.

Brown, D. G. "Mill on Liberty and Morality," *The Philosophical Review,* 81 (1972), 133–158.

Cohen, Carl. *Democracy.* Athens: University of Georgia Press, 1971. A comprehensive analysis.

Crocker, L. G. *Rousseau's Social Contract.* Cleveland, Ohio: Cleveland Press of Case Western Reserve University, 1968.

d'Entreves, A. P. *Natural Law.* London: Hutchinson, 1951.

Feinberg, Joel. *Social Philosophy.* Englewood Cliffs, N.J.: Prentice-Hall, 1973 (paperbound).

Fuller, Lon L. *The Morality of Law.* New Haven, Conn.: Yale University Press, 1964. Deals with the status of law and its relation to moral rules.

Gierke, Otto. *Natural Law and the Theory of Society.* New York: Cambridge University Press, 1934.

Gilson, Etienne. *Medieval Universalism and Its Present Value.* New York: Sheed and Ward, 1937.

Gough, J. W. *The Social Contract,* 2nd ed. Oxford: Clarendon Press, 1957.

Grimsley, Ronald. *The Philosophy of Rousseau.* London: Oxford University Press, 1973 (paperbound). Includes an examination of social contract theory.

Hart, H. L. A. *The Concept of Law.* New York: Oxford University Press, 1961.

————. *Law, Liberty and Morality.* New York: Random House, 1963. Three lectures regarding "the proper scope of criminal law."

Hobbes, Thomas. *Leviathan.* Many editions. Originally published in 1651. See especially Part 1, Chaps. 13–15.

Hobhouse, L. T. *The Metaphysical Theory of the State.* New York: Macmillan, 1918.

Hutchins, Robert M., et al. *Natural Law and Modern Society.* Cleveland, Ohio: World, 1963.

Kaplan, Abraham (ed.). *Individuality and the New Society.* Seattle: University of Washington Press, 1970.

Levine, A. "A Conceptual Problem for Liberal Democracy," *The Journal of Philosophy,* 75 (1978), 302–308.

Lewis, H. D. "Freedom and Authority in Rousseau," *Philosophy,* 53 (1978), 353–362.

Locke, John. *Two Treatises of Government.* Many editions.

McPherson, Thomas. *Political Obligation.* London: Routledge and Kegan Paul, 1967. Reviews and criticizes several theories as to the basis for civil authority.

Maritain, Jacques. *The Rights of Man and Natural Law.* New York: Scribner, 1945.

Melden, A. I. (ed.). *Human Rights.* Belmont, Calif.: Wadsworth, 1970 (paperbound). Contains classical and contemporary selections as well as such documents as the Universal Declaration of Human Rights.

Montesquieu, Charles de. *Spirit of the Laws,* trans. by Thomas Nugent. New York: Hafner, 1949.

Nagel, Thomas. "Rawls on Justice," *The Philosophical Review,* 82 (1973), 220–234.

Negley, Glenn. *Political Authority and Moral Judgment.* Durham, N.C.: Duke University Press, 1965. Critique of several theories regarding the basis of civil authority.

Nozick, R. *Anarchy, State, and Utopia.* New York: Basic Books, 1974. A thoughtful and witty presentation of a social contract theory on the basis of which the author defends the authority of what he calls a "minimal" state.

Popper, Karl R. *The Open Society and Its Enemies.* Princeton, N.J.: Princeton University Press, 1950.

Rawls, John. *A Theory of Justice.* Cambridge, Mass.: Harvard University Press, 1971 (paperbound). A contemporary classic. Draws from social contract tradition.

Russell, Bertrand. *Authority and the Individual.* New York: Simon and Schuster, 1949.

Sen, A. K. *Collective Choice and Social Welfare.* San Francisco, Calif.: Holden Day, 1970, Chap. 6.

——————. "The Impossibility of a Paretian Liberal," *Journal of Political Economy,* 78 (1970), 152–157.

Tassi, A. "Anarchism, Autonomy, and the Concept of the Common Good," *International Philosophical Quarterly,* 17 (1977), 273–283. A critique of anarchism.

Taylor, Richard. *Freedom, Anarchy, and the Law: An Introduction to Political Philosophy.* Englewood Cliffs, N.J.: Prentice-Hall, 1973 (paperbound).

Weil, Simone. *Oppression and Liberty,* trans. by Arthur Wills and John Petrie. Amherst: University of Massachusetts Press, 1973.

Wild, John. *Plato's Modern Enemies and the Theory of Natural Law.* Chicago: University of Chicago Press, 1953.

PART X

The Highest Good

Human beings sometimes appraise human behavior—both their own and that of others—in moral terms. Acts are described as right or wrong, kind or cruel, generous or selfish. Indeed, there exists a large vocabulary of moral-appraisal terms that are used to express moral values and judgments.

What makes an act right or wrong, praiseworthy or blameworthy? One plausible answer is that it is the tendency of the act in question (or of acts of that type) to enhance or diminish the well-being of other human beings. Feeding the hungry is praiseworthy because it eliminates hunger and, thus, enhances human well-being. Caring for the sick, comforting the bereaved, cheering the sorrowful, visiting the lonely—such acts appear to derive their moral value at least in part from the fact that they diminish human suffering and increase human well-being. They contribute, one could say, to the realization (that is, the making real) of that which is *good for human beings.*

However, if the moral value of an act consists in its tendency to enhance or diminish human well-being, then, in order to make appropriate judgments about any act, we must have some opinion about what it is that constitutes human well-being. If we think, for example, that human well-being consists in experiencing as much pleasure as is possible, then we will consider praiseworthy everything that enhances human pleasure, and we will consider blameworthy everything that diminishes it. If, however, we consider human well-being to consist primarily in something other than pleasure—such as knowledge or saintliness—then our judgments about the moral value of various acts will be different.

We must distinguish between that which is *instrumentally* good and that which is *intrinsically* good, between that which is *good as a means* and that which is *good as an end*. The instrumentally good is that which is worthy of being desired because it tends to bring into being that which is intrinsically good. The intrinsically good is that which is worthy of being desired for its own sake.

What, then, is worthy of being desired for its own sake? What is intrinsically good for human beings? Health? Pleasure? Knowledge? Virtue? all, or none, of the above? And if more than one thing is worthy of being desired for its own sake, which is *most* worthy of being so desired? What is the *highest* good—the *summum bonum*—for a human being? This is the issue under consideration here.

To say that something is the *highest* human good is to say that nothing else—not even other intrinsic goods—should be allowed to stand in the way of its realization. If pleasure is the highest good, then any pursuit of knowledge, for example, that results in less total pleasure than some other kind of activity is morally indefensible. If knowledge is the highest good, then any pursuit of pleasure, or anything else, that detracts from the achievement of knowledge is similarly wrong. That which is good ceases to be good if it detracts from the realization of that which is best.

The question, What is the highest human good? could be answered in a wide variety of ways. However, only a few of these possible answers have seemed plausible to those who have given some thought to the question. It is those few that are considered in the readings that follow. The theories that we will examine are *rational eudemonism* (Aristotle), *hedonism* (Epicurus and Mill), the *inner tranquility theory* (Epictetus), *theological eudemonism* (St Augustine), and *ethical pluralism* (Ross). Each theory is defined in the introduction to the relevant reading.

41

ARISTOTLE (384–322 B.C.)

Activity According to Reason as the Highest Good for Man

How does one begin to answer the question, What is the highest good for a human being? Aristotle believed that the first step is to isolate a human being's unique endowment. Then, it will follow that the highest good will be the maximum fulfillment or realization of that unique endowment. In short, it is necessary to determine what a human being is *for*, what his or her natural *function* is. "For as the goodness and the excellence of a piper or a sculptor, or the practicer of any art, and generally of those who have any function or business to do, lies in that function," Aristotle writes, "so man's good would seem to lie in his function, if he has one."

What, then, is the unique function of human beings? Aristotle concludes that it is the exercise of their vital faculties in accordance with their rational nature. Since part of the task of reason is to teach human beings how to act virtuously, it follows that the good of human beings is activity—the exercise of their faculties—in accordance with virtue. This, according to Aristotle, is the essence of human good. This is the essence of human happiness, although that happiness may be enhanced by other, albeit lesser, goods. This view is sometimes called *rational eudemonism:* "eudemonism" from the Greek word *eudemonia,* which mean "happiness," and "rational" because the happiness of human beings is based in their rational nature. (See p. 51 for a biographical note on Aristotle.)

· · ·

7. Leaving these matters, then, let us return once more to the question, what this good can be of which we are in search.

It seems to be different in different kinds of action and in different arts,— one thing in medicine and another in war, and so on. What then is the good in each of these cases? Surely that for the sake of which all else is done. And

From Aristotle, *Nicomachean Ethics,* 1097a 15–1100 a 10, in *The Nicomachean Ethics of Aristotle,* trans. F. Peters (London: Kegan Paul, Trench, Trubner & Co., Ltd., 1904), pp. 12–23.

that in medicine is health, in war is victory, in building is a house,—a different thing in each different case, but always, in whatever we do and in whatever we choose, the end. For it is always for the sake of the end that all else is done.

If then there be one end of all that man does, this end will be the realizable good,—or these ends, if there be more than one.

... This point we must try to explain more clearly.

We see that there are many ends. But some of these are chosen only as means, as wealth, flutes, and the whole class of instruments. And so it is plain that not all ends are final.

But the best of all things must, we conceive, be something final.

If then there be only one final end, this will be what we are seeking,—or if there be more than one, then the most final of them.

Now that which is pursued as an end in itself is more final than that which is pursued as means to something else, and that which is never chosen as means than that which is chosen both as an end in itself and as means, and that is strictly final which is always chosen as an end in itself and never as means.

Happiness seems more than anything else to answer to this description: for we always choose it for itself, and never for the sake of something else; while honour and pleasure and reason, and all virtue or excellence, we choose partly indeed for themselves (for, apart from any result, we should choose each of them), but partly also for the sake of happiness, supposing that they will help to make us happy. But no one chooses happiness for the sake of these things, or as a means to anything else at all.

We seem to be led to the same conclusion when we start from the notion of self-sufficiency.

The final good is thought to be self-sufficing [or all-sufficing]. In applying this term we do not regard a man as an individual leading a solitary life, but we also take account of parents, children, wife, and in short, friends and fellow-citizens generally, since man is naturally a social being. Some limit must indeed be set to this; for if you go on to parents and descendants and friends of friends, you will never come to a stop. But this we will consider further on: for the present we will take self-sufficing to mean what by itself makes life desirable and in want of nothing. And happiness is believed to answer to this description.

And further, happiness is believed to be the most desirable thing in the world, and that not merely as one among other good things: if it were merely one among other good things [so that other things could be added to it], it is plain that the addition of the least of other goods must make it more desirable; for the addition becomes a surplus of good, and of two goods the greater is always more desirable.

Thus it seems that happiness is something final and self-sufficing, and is the end of all that man does.

But perhaps the reader thinks that though no one will dispute the statement that happiness is the best thing in the world, yet a still more precise definition of it is needed.

This will best be gained, I think, by asking, What is the function of man? For as the goodness and the excellence of a piper or a sculptor, or the practiser of any art, and generally of those who have any function or business to do, lies in that function, so man's good would seem to lie in his function, if he has one.

But can we suppose that, while a carpenter or a cobbler has a function and a business of his own, man has no business and no function assigned him by nature? Nay, surely as his several members, eye and hand and foot, plainly have each his own function, so we must suppose that man also has some function over and above all these.

What then is it?

Life evidently he has in common even with the plants, but we want that which is peculiar to him. We must exclude, therefore, the life of mere nutrition and growth.

Next to this comes the life of sense; but this too he plainly shares with horses and cattle and all kinds of animals.

There remains then the life whereby he acts—the life of his rational nature, with its two sides or divisions, one rational as obeying reason, the other rational as having and exercising reason.

But as this expression is ambiguous, we must be understood to mean thereby the life that consists in the exercise of the faculties; for this seems to be more properly entitled to the name.

The function of man, then, is exercise of his vital faculties [or soul] on one side in obedience to reason, and on the other side with reason.

But what is called the function of a man of any profession and the function of a man who is good in that profession are generically the same, *e.g.* of a harper and of a good harper; and this holds in all cases without exception, only that in the case of the latter his superior excellence at his work is added; for we say a harper's function is to harp, and a good harper's to harp well.

(Man's function then being, as we say, a kind of life—that is to say, exercise of his faculties and action of various kinds with reason—the good man's function is to do this well and beautifully [or nobly]. But the function of anything is done well when it is done in accordance with the proper excellence of that thing.)

If this be so the result is that the good of man is exercise of his faculties in accordance with excellence or virtue, or, if there be more than one, in accordance with the best and most complete virtue.

But there must also be a full term of years for this exercise; for one swallow or one fine day does not make a spring, nor does one day or any small space of time make a blessed or happy man.

This, then, may be taken as a rough outline of the good; for this, I think, is the proper method,—first to sketch the outline, and then to fill in the details. But it would seem that, the outline once fairly drawn, any one can carry on the work and fit in the several items which time reveals to us or helps us to find. And this indeed is the way in which the arts and sciences have grown; for it requires no extraordinary genius to fill up the gaps.

We must bear in mind, however, what was said above, and not demand the same degree of accuracy in all branches of study, but in each case so much as the subject-matter admits of and as is proper to that kind of inquiry. The carpenter and the geometer both look for the right angle, but in different ways: the former only wants such an approximation to it as his work requires, but the latter wants to know what constitutes a right angle, or what is its special quality; his aim is to find out the truth. And so in other cases we must follow the same course, lest we spend more time on what is immaterial than on the real business in hand.

Nor must we in all cases alike demand the reason why; sometimes it is enough if the undemonstrated fact be fairly pointed out, as in the case of the starting-points or principles of a science. Undemonstrated facts always form the first step or starting-point of a science; and these starting-points or principles are arrived at some in one way, some in another—some by induction, others by perception, others again by some kind of training. But in each case we must try to apprehend them in the proper way, and do our best to define them clearly; for they have great influence upon the subsequent course of an inquiry. A good start is more than half the race, I think, and our starting-point or principle, once found, clears up a number of our difficulties.

8. We must not be satisfied, then, with examining this starting-point or principle of ours as a conclusion from our data, but must also view it in its relation to current opinions on the subject; for all experience harmonizes with a true principle, but a false one is soon found to be incompatible with the facts.

Now, good things have been divided into three classes, external goods on the one hand, and on the other goods of the soul and goods of the body; and the goods of the soul are commonly said to be goods in the fullest sense, and more good than any other.

But "actions and exercises of the vital faculties or soul" may be said to be "of the soul." So our account is confirmed by this opinion, which is both of long standing and approved by all who busy themselves with philosophy.

But, indeed, we secure the support of this opinion by the mere statement that certain actions and exercises are the end; for this implies that it is to be ranked among the goods of the soul, and not among external goods.

Our account, again, is in harmony with the common saying that the happy man lives well and does well; for we may say that happiness, according to us, is a living well and doing well.

And, indeed, all the characteristics that men expect to find in happiness seem to belong to happiness as we define it.

Some hold it to be virtue or excellence, some prudence, others a kind of wisdom; others, again, hold it to be all or some of these, with the addition of pleasure, either as an ingredient or as a necessary accompaniment; and some even include external prosperity in their account of it.

Now, some of these views have the support of many voices and of old authority; others have few voices, but those of weight; but it is probable that neither the one side nor the other is entirely wrong, but that in some one point at least, if not in most, they are both right.

First, then, the view that happiness is excellence or a kind of excellence harmonizes with our account; for "exercise of faculties in accordance with excellence" belongs to excellence.

But I think we may say that it makes no small difference whether the good be conceived as the mere possession of something, or as its use—as a mere habit or trained faculty, or as the exercise of that faculty. For the habit or faculty may be present, and yet issue in no good result, as when a man is alseep, or in any other way hindered from his function; but with its exercise this is not possible, for it must show itself in acts and in good acts. And as at the Olympic games it is not the fairest and strongest who receive the crown, but those who contend (for among these are the victors), so in life, too, the winners are those who not only have all the excellences, but manifest these in deed.

And, further, the life of these men is in itself pleasant. For pleasure is an affection of the soul, and each man takes pleasure in that which he is said to love,—he who loves horses in horses, he who loves sight-seeing in sight-seeing, and in the same way he who loves justice in acts of justice, and generally the lover of excellence or virtue in virtuous acts or the manifestation of excellence.

And while with most men there is a perpetual conflict between the several things in which they find pleasure, since these are not naturally pleasant, those who love what is noble take pleasure in that which is naturally pleasant. For the manifestations of excellence are naturally pleasant, so that they are both pleasant to them and pleasant in themselves.

Their life, then, does not need pleasure to be added to it as an appendage, but contains pleasure in itself.

Indeed, in addition to what we have said, a man is not good at all unless he takes pleasure in noble deeds. No one would call a man just who did not take pleasure in doing justice, nor generous who took no pleasure in acts of generosity, and so on.

If this be so, the manifestations of excellence will be pleasant in themselves. But they are also both good and noble, and that in the highest degree—at least, if the good man's judgment about them is right, for this is his judgment.

Happiness, then, is at once the best and noblest and pleasantest thing in the world, and these are not separated, as the Delian inscription would have them to be:—

> What is most just is noblest, health is best,
> Pleasantest is to get your heart's desire.

For all these characteristics are united in the best exercises of our faculties; and these, or some one of them that is better than all the others, we identify with happiness.

But nevertheless happiness plainly requires external goods too, as we said; for it is impossible, or at least not easy, to act nobly without some furniture of fortune. There are many things that can only be done through instruments, so to speak, such as friends and wealth and political influence: and there are some things whose absence takes the bloom off our happiness, as good birth, the blessing of children, personal beauty; for a man is not very likely to be happy if he is very ugly in person, or of low birth, or alone in the world, or childless, and perhaps still less if he has worthless children or friends, or has lost good ones that he had.

As we said, then, happiness seems to stand in need of this kind of prosperity; and so some identify it with good fortune, just as others identify it with excellence.

9. This has led people to ask whether happiness is attained by learning, or the formation of habits, or any other kind of training, or comes by some divine dispensation or even by chance.

Well, if the gods do give gifts to men, happiness is likely to be among the number, more likely, indeed, than anything else, in proportion as it is better than all other human things.

This belongs more properly to another branch of inquiry; but we may say that even if it is not heavensent, but comes as a consequence of virtue or some kind of learning or training, still it seems to be one of the most divine things in the world; for the prize and aim of virtue would appear to be better than anything else and something divine and blessed.

Again, if it is thus acquired it will be widely accessible; for it will then be in the power of all except those who have lost the capacity for excellence to acquire it by study and diligence.

And if it be better that men should attain happiness in this way rather than by chance, it is reasonable to suppose that it is so, since in the sphere of nature all things are arranged in the best possible way, and likewise in the sphere of art, and of each mode of causation, and most of all in the sphere of the noblest mode of causation. And indeed it would be too absurd to leave what is noblest and fairest to the dispensation of chance.

But our definition itself clears up the difficulty; for happiness was defined as a certain kind of exercise of the vital faculties in accordance with excellence or virtue. And of the remaining goods [other than happiness itself], some must be present as necessary conditions, while others are aids and useful instruments to happiness. And this agrees with what we said at starting. We then laid down that the end of the art political is the best of all ends; but the chief business of that art is to make the citizens of a certain character—that is, good and apt to do what is noble. It is not without reason, then, that we do not call an ox, or a horse, or any brute happy; for none of them is able to share in this kind of activity.

For the same reason also a child is not happy; he is as yet, because of his age, unable to do such things. If we ever call a child happy, it is because we hope he will do them. For, as we said, happiness requires not only perfect excellence or virtue, but also a full term of years for its exercise. For our circumstances are liable to many changes and to all sorts of chances, and it is possible that he who is now most prosperous will in his old age meet with great disasters, as is told of Priam in the tales of Troy; and a man who is thus used by fortune and comes to a miserable end cannot be called happy.

42

EPICURUS (341–270 B.C.)

Pleasure Is the Highest Good

Epicurus was not the first philosopher to assert that pleasure is the highest human good, but he was the first to establish a philosophical movement based on this principle. Indeed, during the years immediately following Aristotle's death, it was not to the three great philosophers of the Golden Age of Greek philosophy—Socrates, Plato, and Aristotle—that the Hellenistic world looked for its wisdom. It turned, instead, to Epicurus of Athens and Zeno the Stoic.

Knowing that Epicurus held that pleasure is the highest good, one might suppose that he and his followers were base and ignoble men who spent their lives in the mad pursuit of sensual thrills. Such, however, was not the case. Epicurus was something of an ascetic, and it seems, from the few of his writings that have survived, that he was more interested in the avoidance of pain than in the pursuit of pleasure. Moreover, the pains that distressed him most were the pains of fear and superstition. An important aspect of his philosophy was to teach his followers to conquer those pains. He taught, therefore, that the soul, as well as the body, is composed of matter, and that when the body dies, the soul also dies. This belief allowed him to write to his friend Menoeceus, "So death, the most terrifying of ills, is nothing to us, since so long as we exist death is not with us; but when death comes, we are no more."

The view that pleasure is the highest human good is called *hedonism*, from the Greek word *hedone*, which means "pleasure."

From Epicurus, "Letter to Menoeceus," in *The Extant Remains,* trans. Cyril Bailey (Oxford: Oxford University Press, 1926), pp. 87–93. Reprinted by permission of Oxford University Press.

. . .

We must consider that of desires some are natural, others vain, and of the natural some are necessary and others merely natural; and of the necessary some are necessary for happiness, others for the repose of the body, and others for very life. The right understanding of these facts enables us to refer all choice and avoidance, to the health of the body and (the soul's) freedom from disturbance, since this is the aim of the life of blessedness. For it is to obtain this end that we always act, namely, to avoid pain and fear. And when this is once secured for us, all the tempest of the soul is dispersed, since the living creature has not to wander as though in search of something that is missing, and to look for some other thing by which he can fulfil the good of the soul and the good of the body. For it is then that we have need of pleasure, when we feel pain owing to the absence of pleasure; (but when we do not feel pain), we no longer need pleasure. And for this cause we call pleasure the beginning and end of the blessed life. For we recognize pleasure as the first good innate in us, and from pleasure we begin every act of choice and avoidance, and to pleasure we return again, using the feeling as the standard by which we judge every good.

And since pleasure is the first good and natural to us, for this very reason we do not choose every pleasure, but sometimes we pass over many pleasures, when greater discomfort accrues to us as the result of them: and similarly we think many pains better than pleasures, since a greater pleasure comes to us when we have endured pains for a long time. Every pleasure then because of its natural kinship to us is good, yet not every pleasure is to be chosen: even as every pain also is an evil, yet not all are always of a nature to be avoided. Yet by a scale of comparison and by the consideration of advantages and disadvantages we must form our judgement on all these matters. For the good on certain occasions we treat as bad, and conversely the bad as good.

And again independence of desire we think a great good—not that we may at all times enjoy but a few things, but that, if we do not possess many we may enjoy the few in the genuine persuasion that those have the sweetest pleasure in luxury who least need it, and that all that is natural is easy to be obtained, but that which is superfluous is hard. And so plain savours bring us a pleasure equal to a luxurious diet, when all the pain due to want is removed; and bread and water produce the highest pleasure, when one who needs them puts them to his lips. To grow accustomed therefore to simple and not luxurious diet gives us health to the full, and makes a man alert for the needful employments of life, and when after long intervals we approach luxuries disposes us better towards them, and fits us to be fearless of fortune.

When, therefore, we maintain that pleasure is the end, we do not mean the pleasures of profligates and those that consist in sensuality, as is supposed by some who are either ignorant or disagree with us or do not understand, but freedom from pain in the body and from trouble in the mind. For it is not continuous drinkings and revellings, nor the satisfaction of lusts, nor the enjoyment of fish and other luxuries of the wealthy table, which produce a pleasant life, but sober reasoning, searching out the motives for all choice and avoidance, and banishing mere opinions, to which are due the greatest disturbance of the spirit.

Of all this the beginning and the greatest good is prudence. Wherefore prudence is a more precious thing even than philosophy: for from prudence are sprung all the other virtues, and it teaches us that it is not possible to live pleasantly without living prudently and honourably and justly, (nor, again, to live a life of prudence, honour, and justice) without living pleasantly. For the virtues are by nature bound up with the pleasant life, and the pleasant life is inseparable from them. For indeed who, think you, is a better man than he who holds reverent opinions concerning the gods, and is at all times free from fear of death, and has reasoned out the end ordained by nature? He understands that the limit of good things is easy to fulfil and easy to attain, whereas the course of ills is either short in time or slight in pain: he laughs at destiny, whom some have introduced as the mistress of all things. He thinks that with us lies the chief power in determining events, some of which happen by necessity and some by chance, and some are within our control; for while necessity cannot be called to account, he sees that chance is inconstant, but that which is in our control is subject to no master, and to it are naturally attached praise and blame. For, indeed, it were better to follow the myths about the gods than to become a slave to the destiny of the natural philosophers: for the former suggests a hope of placating the gods by worship, whereas the latter involves a necessity which knows no placation. As to chance, he does not regard it as a god as most men do (for in a god's acts there is no disorder), nor as an uncertain cause of all things: for he does not believe that good and evil are given by chance to man for the framing of a blessed life, but that opportunities for great good and great evil are afforded by it. He therefore thinks it better to be unfortunate in reasonable action than to prosper in unreason. For it is better in a man's actions that what is well chosen should fail, rather than that what is ill chosen should be successful owing to chance.

Meditate therefore on these things and things akin to them night and day by yourself, and with a companion like to yourself, and never shall you be disturbed waking or asleep, but you shall live like a god among men. For a man who lives among immortal blessings is not like to a mortal being.

43

EPICTETUS (ca. 60–100 A.D.)

Tranquility Is the Highest Good

Epictetus was a Greek who lived most of his life in Rome. Born a slave, he was said to have been lame as a result of cruel mistreatment by his master. He became, however, an ardent and eloquent spokesman for Stoicism, which included among its adherents some of the finest representatives of the Roman world of the first and second centuries.

According to the Stoics, the beginning of wisdom is the realization that "whatever will be will be." This is a deterministic universe, and we can do nothing to alter the course of events. But we can control *how we will regard* what occurs, and this, according to the Stoics, is the secret to happiness. To be happy, they argue, we must learn not to be affected internally by what happens externally. We must cultivate *tranquility* as the highest good. Then whatever follows—suffering, poverty, bereavement, death—will not affect us, for our tranquility does not depend on circumstances but on our inner determination to accept, willingly and with dignity, whatever may befall us.

Of all existing things some are in our power, and others are not in our power. In our power are thought, impulse, will to get and will to avoid, and, in a word, everything which is our own doing. Things not in our power include the body, property, reputation, office, and, in a word, everything which is not our own doing. Things in our power are by nature free, unhindered, untrammelled; things not in our power are weak, servile, subject to hindrance, dependent on others. Remember then that if you imagine that what is naturally slavish is free, and what is naturally another's is your own, you will be hampered, you will mourn, you will be put to confusion, you will blame gods and men; but if you think that only your own belongs to you, and that what is another's is indeed another's, no one will ever put compulsion or hindrance on you, you

From Epictetus, *The Manual of Epictetus,* Volume II, Selections 1, 5, 8, 9, 11, 12, and 14, in *Epictetus: The Discourses and Manual,* trans. P. E. Matheson (Oxford: Oxford University Press, 1916), pp. 213–218. Reprinted by permission of Oxford University Press.

will blame none, you will accuse none, you will do nothing against your will, no one will harm you, you will have no enemy, for no harm can touch you.

Aiming then at these high matters, you must remember that to attain them requires more than ordinary effort; you will have to give up some things entirely, and put off others for the moment. And if you would have these also —office and wealth—it may be that you will fail to get them, just because your desire is set on the former, and you will certainly fail to attain those things which alone bring freedom and happiness.

Make it your study then to confront every harsh impression with the words, 'You are but an impression, and not at all what you seem to be'. Then test it by those rules that you possess; and first by this—the chief test of all—'Is it concerned with what is in our power or with what is not in our power?' And if it is concerned with what is not in our power, be ready with the answer that it is nothing to you.

· · ·

What disturbs men's minds is not events but their judgements on events. For instance, death is nothing dreadful, or else Socrates would have thought it so. No, the only dreadful thing about it is men's judgement that it is dreadful. And so when we are hindered, or disturbed, or distressed, let us never lay the blame on others, but on ourselves, that is on our own judgements. To accuse others for one's own misfortunes is a sign of want of education: to accuse oneself shows that one's education has begun; to accuse neither oneself nor others shows that one's education is complete.

· · ·

Ask not that events should happen as you will, but let your will be that events should happen as they do, and you shall have peace.

Sickness is a hindrance to the body, but not to the will, unless the will consent. Lameness is a hindrance to the leg, but not to the will. Say this to yourself at each event that happens, for you shall find that though it hinders something else it will not hinder you.

· · ·

Never say of anything, 'I lost it', but say, 'I gave it back'. Has your child died? It was given back. Has your wife died? She was given back. Has your estate been taken from you? Was not this also given back? But you say, 'He who took it from me is wicked'. What does it matter to you through whom the Giver asked it back? As long as He gives it you, take care of it, but not as your own; treat it as passers-by treat an inn.

If you wish to make progress, abandon reasonings of this sort: 'If I neglect my affairs I shall have nothing to live on'; 'If I do not punish my son, he will be wicked.' For it is better to die of hunger, so that you be free from pain and free from fear, than to live in plenty and be troubled in mind. It is better for your son to be wicked than for you to be miserable. Wherefore begin with little things. Is your drop of oil spilt? Is your cup of wine stolen? Say to yourself, 'This is the price paid for freedom from passion, this is the price of a quiet mind.' Nothing can be had without a price. When you call your slave-boy, reflect that he may not be able to hear you, and if he hears you, he may not be able to do anything you want. But he is not so well off that it rests with him to give you peace of mind.

.   .   .

It is silly to want your children and your wife and your friends to live for ever, for that means that you want what is not in your control to be in your control, and what is not your own to be yours. In the same way if you want your servant to make no mistakes, you are a fool, for you want vice not to be vice but something different. But if you want not to be disappointed in your will to get, you can attain to that.

Exercise yourself then in what lies in your power. Each man's master is the man who has authority over what he wishes or does not wish, to secure the one or to take away the other. Let him then who wishes to be free not wish for anything or avoid anything that depends on others; or else he is bound to be a slave.

44

AUGUSTINE OF HIPPO (354–430)

Man's Ultimate Happiness

Augustine argues that human happiness cannot be found in this life, for (1) every good thing that this life has to offer is inherently precarious and may be taken from us, and (2) even virtue, which is the highest earthly good, is not fully attainable by any human being. He speaks scornfully of the Stoic view, which claims that tranquility is the highest good. He argues that there is a contradiction between the claim that pursuit of this good will assure happiness and the accompanying recommendation to commit suicide if life becomes unendurable. The highest human good, Augustine insists, lies not in this world but in the world to come. "Salvation," he writes, "should itself be our final happiness" (See p. 144 for a biographical note on St. Augustine.)

If, then, we be asked what the city of God has to say upon these points, and, in the first place, what its opinion regarding the supreme good and evil is, it will reply that life eternal is the supreme good, death eternal the supreme evil, and that to obtain the one and escape the other we must live rightly. And thus it is written, "The just lives by faith,"[1] for we do not as yet see our good, and must therefore live by faith; neither have we in ourselves power to live rightly, but can do so only if He who has given us faith to believe in His help does help us when we believe and pray. As for those who have supposed that the sovereign good and evil are to be found in this life, and have placed it either in the soul or the body, or in both, or, to speak more explicitly, either in pleasure or in virtue, or in both; in repose or in virtue, or in both; in pleasure and repose, or in virtue, or in all combined; in the primary objects of nature, or in virtue, or in both,—all these have, with a marvelous shallowness, sought to find their blessedness in this life and in themselves. Contempt has been poured upon such ideas by the Truth, saying by the prophet, "The Lord

From Augustine of Hippo, *The City of God,* Book XIX, Chapter 4, in *Nicene and Post-Nicene Fathers of the Christian Church,* Volume II, ed. P. Schaff (New York: Charles Scribner's Sons, 1907), pp. 401–403.
[1]Hab. ii. 4.

knoweth the thoughts of men" (or, as the Apostle Paul cites the passage, "The Lord knoweth the thoughts of the *wise*") "that they are vain."[2]

For what flood of eloquence can suffice to detail the miseries of this life? Cicero, in the *Consolation* on the death of his daughter, has spent all his ability in lamentation; but how inadequate was even his ability here? For when, where, how, in this life can these primary objects of nature be possessed so that they may not be assailed by unforeseen accidents? Is the body of the wise man exempt from any pain which may dispel pleasure, from any disquietude which may banish repose? The amputation or decay of the members of the body puts an end to its integrity, deformity blights its beauty, weakness its health, lassitude its vigor, sleepiness or sluggishness its activity,—and which of these is it that may not assail the flesh of the wise man? Comely and fitting attitudes and movements of the body are numbered among the prime natural blessings; but what if some sickness makes the members tremble? what if a man suffers from curvature of the spine to such an extent that his hands reach the ground, and he goes upon all-fours like a quadruped? Does not this destroy all beauty and grace in the body, whether at rest or in motion? What shall I say of the fundamental blessings of the soul, sense and intellect, of which the one is given for the perception, and the other for the comprehension of truth? But what kind of sense is it that remains when a man becomes deaf and blind? where are reason and intellect when disease makes a man delirious? We can scarcely, or not at all, refrain from tears, when we think of or see the actions and words of such frantic persons, and consider how different from and even opposed to their own sober judgment and ordinary conduct their present demeanor is. And what shall I say of those who suffer from demoniacal possession? Where is their own intelligence hidden and buried while the malignant spirit is using their body and soul according to his own will? And who is quite sure that no such thing can happen to the wise man in this life? Then, as to the perception of truth, what can we hope for even in this way while in the body, as we read in the true book of Wisdom, "The corruptible body weigheth down the soul, and the earthly tabernacle presseth down the mind that museth upon many things?"[3] And eagerness, or desire of action, if this is the right meaning to put upon the Greek ὁρμή, is also reckoned among the primary advantages of nature; and yet is it not this which produces those pitiable movements of the insane, and those actions which we shudder to see, when sense is deceived and reason deranged?

In fine, virtue itself, which is not among the primary objects of nature, but succeeds to them as the result of learning, though it holds the highest place among human good things, what is its occupation save to wage perpetual war with vices,—not those that are outside of us, but within; not other men's, but our own,—a war which is waged especially by that virtue which the Greeks

[2] Ps. xciv. 11, and I Cor. iii. 20.
[3] Wisdom ix. 15.

call σωφροσμνη, and we temperance,[4] and which bridles carnal lusts, and prevents them from winning the consent of the spirit to wicked deeds? For we must not fancy that there is no vice in us, when, as the apostle says, "The flesh lusteth against the spirit:"[5] for to this vice there is a contrary virtue, when, as the same writer says, "The spirit lusteth against the flesh." "For these two," he says, "are contrary one to the other, so that you cannot do the things which you would." But what is it we wish to do when we seek to attain the supreme good, unless that the flesh should cease to lust against the spirit, and that there be no vice in us against which the spirit may lust? And as we cannot attain to this in the present life, however ardently we desire it, let us by God's help accomplish at least this, to preserve the soul from succumbing and yielding to the flesh that lusts against it, and to refuse our consent to the perpetration of sin. Far be it from us, then, to fancy that while we are still engaged in this intestine war, we have already found the happiness which we seek to reach by victory. And who is there so wise that he has no conflict at all to maintain against his vices?

What shall I say of that virtue which is called prudence? Is not all its vigilance spent in the discernment of good from evil things, so that no mistake may be admitted about what we should desire and what avoid? And thus it is itself a proof that we are in the midst of evils, or that evils are in us; for it teaches us that it is an evil to consent to sin, and a good to refuse this consent. And yet this evil, to which prudence teaches and temperance enables us not to consent, is removed from this life neither by prudence nor by temperance. And justice, whose office it is to render to every man his due, whereby there is in man himself a certain just order of nature, so that the soul is subjected to God and the flesh to the soul, and consequently both soul and flesh to God, —does not the virtue demonstrate that it is as yet rather laboring towards its end than resting in its finished work? For the soul is so much the less subjected to God as it is less occupied with the thought of God; and the flesh is so much the less subjected to the spirit as it lusts more vehemently against the spirit. So long, therefore, as we are beset by this weakness, this plague, this disease, how shall we dare to say that we are safe? and if not safe, then how can we be already enjoying our final beatitude? Then that virtue which goes by the name of fortitude is the plainest proof of the ills of life, for it is these ills which it is compelled to bear patiently. And this holds good, no matter though the ripest wisdom co-exists with it. And I am at a loss to understand how the Stoic philosophers can presume to say that these are no ills, though at the same time they allow the wise man to commit suicide and pass out of this life if they become so grievous that he cannot or ought not to endure them. But such is the stupid pride of these men who fancy that the supreme good can be found in this life, and that they can become happy by their own resources, that their

---

[4]Cicero, *Iuse. Quast.* iii. 8.
[5]Gal. v. 17.

wise man, or at least the man whom they fancifully depict as such, is always happy, even though he become blind, deaf, dumb, mutilated, racked with pains, or suffer any conceivable calamity such as may compel him to make away with himself; and they are not ashamed to call the life that is beset with these evils happy. O happy life, which seeks the aid of death to end it? If it is happy, let the wise man remain in it; but if these ills drive him out of it, in what sense is it happy? Or how can they say that these are not evils which conquer the virtue of fortitude, and force it not only to yield, but so to rave that it in one breath calls life happy and recommends it to be given up? For who is so blind as not to see that if it were happy it would not be fled from? And if they say we should flee from it on account of the infirmities that beset it, why then do they not lower their pride and acknowledge that it is miserable? Was it, I would ask, fortitude or weakness which prompted Cato to kill himself? for he would not have done so had he not been too weak to endure Cæsar's victory. Where, then, is his fortitude? It has yielded, it has succumbed, it has been so thoroughly overcome as to abandon, forsake, flee this happy life. Or was it no longer happy? Then it was miserable. How, then, were these not evils which made life miserable, and a thing to be escaped from?

And therefore those who admit that these are evils, as the Peripatetics do, and the Old Academy, the sect which Varro advocates, express a more intelligible doctrine; but theirs also is a surprising mistake, for they contend that this is a happy life which is beset by these evils, even though they be so great that he who endures them should commit suicide to escape them. "Pains and anguish of body," says Varro, "are evils, and so much the worse in proportion to their severity; and to escape them you must quit this life." What life, I pray? This life, he says, which is oppressed by such evils. Then it is happy in the midst of these very evils on account of which you say we must quit it? Or do you call it happy because you are at liberty to escape these evils by death? What, then, if by some secret judgment of God you were held fast and not permitted to die, nor suffered to live without these evils? In that case, at least, you would say that such a life was miserable. It is soon relinquished, no doubt, but this does not make it not miserable; for were it eternal, you yourself would pronounce it miserable. Its brevity, therefore, does not clear it of misery; neither ought it to be called happiness because it is a brief misery. Certainly there is a mighty force in these evils which compel a man—according to them, even a wise man—to cease to be a man that he may escape them, though they say, and say truly, that it is as it were the first and strongest demand of nature that a man cherish himself, and naturally therefore avoid death, and should so stand his own friend as to wish and vehemently aim at continuing to exist as a living creature, and subsisting in this union of soul and body. There is a mighty force in these evils to overcome this natural instinct by which death is by every means and with all a man's efforts avoided, and to overcome it so completely that what was avoided is desired, sought after, and if it cannot in any other way be obtained, is inflicted by the man on himself. There is a mighty force in these evils which make fortitude a homicide,—if, indeed, that is to be called fortitude which is so thoroughly overcome by these evils, that it not only cannot preserve by patience the man whom it undertook to govern and defend, but is itself obliged to kill him. The wise man, I admit, ought to bear death with patience, but when it is inflicted by another. If, then, as these men maintain, he is obliged to inflict it on himself, certainly it must be owned that the ills which compel him to this are not only evils, but intolerable evils. The life, then, which is either subject to accidents, or environed with evils so considerable and grievous, would never have been called happy, if the men who give it this name had condescended to yield to the truth, and to be conquered by valid arguments, when they inquired after the happy life, as they yield to unhappiness, and are overcome by overwhelming evils, when they put themselves to death, and if they had not fancied that the supreme good was to be found in this mortal life; for the very virtues of this life, which are certainly its best and most useful possessions, are all the more telling proofs of its miseries in proportion as they are helpful against the violence of its dangers, toils, and woes. For if these are true virtues,—and such cannot exist save in those who have true piety,—they do not profess to be able to deliver the men who possess them from all miseries; for true virtues tell no such lies, but they profess that by the hope of the future world this life, which is miserably involved in the many and great evils of this world, is happy as it is also safe. For if not yet safe, how could it be happy? And therefore the Apostle Paul, speaking not of men without prudence, temperance, fortitude, and justice, but of those whose lives were regulated by true piety, and whose virtues were therefore truer, says, "For we are saved by hope: now hope which is seen is not hope; for what a man seeth, why doth he yet hope for? But if we hope for that we see not, then do we with patience wait for it." As, therefore, we are saved, so we are made happy by hope. And as we do not as yet possess a present, but look for a future salvation, so is it with our happiness, and this "with patience;" for we are encompassed with evils, which we ought patiently to endure, until we come to the ineffable enjoyment of unmixed good; for there shall be no longer anything to endure. Salvation, such as it shall be in the world to come, shall itself be our final happiness. And this happiness these philosophers refuse to believe in, because they do not see it, and attempt to fabricate for themselves a happiness in this life, based upon a virtue which is as deceitful as it is proud.

45

JOHN STUART MILL (1806–1873)

In Defense of the Pleasure Principle

John Stuart Mill's view "that pleasure, and freedom from pain, are the only things desirable as ends" is identical to that of Epicurus, whom Mill greatly admired. Sensitive to the criticism that this view is "a doctrine worthy only of swine," Mill attempts to show that it is, nonetheless, "better to be a human being dissatisfied than a pig satisfied; better to be Socrates dissatisfied than a fool satisfied." Now there is no doubt that Mill held the latter view, but it is unclear how it can be derived from his principles. If pleasure is the only thing desirable as an end, how can one pleasure be more desirable than another except by virtue of being more pleasurable? And if it is true that it is better to be Socrates dissatisfied (perhaps even in pain) than a fool satisfied (that is, experiencing pleasure), does it not follow that the highest good is something other than pleasure? This is the problem Mill wrestles with in this selection. (See p. 95 for a biographical note on John Stuart Mill.)

. . .

The creed which accepts as the foundation of morals, Utility, or the Greatest Happiness Principle, holds that actions are right in proportion as they tend to promote happiness, wrong as they tend to produce the reverse of happiness. By happiness is intended pleasure, and the absence of pain; by unhappiness, pain, and the privation of pleasure. To give a clear view of the moral standard set up by the theory, much more requires to be said; in particular, what things it includes in the ideas of pain and pleasure; and to what extent this is left an open question. But these supplementary explanations do not affect the theory of life on which this theory of morality is grounded—namely, that pleasure, and freedom from pain, are the only things desirable as ends; and that all desirable things (which are as numerous in the utilitarian as in any other scheme) are desirable either for the pleasure inherent in themselves, or as means to the promotion of pleasure and the prevention of pain.

From John Stuart Mill, *Utilitarianism,* Chapter II (1861).

Now, such a theory of life excites in many minds, and among them in some of the most estimable in feeling and purpose, inveterate dislike. To suppose that life has (as they express it) no higher end than pleasure—no better and nobler object of desire and pursuit—they designate as utterly mean and grovelling; as a doctrine worthy only of swine, to whom the followers of Epicurus were, at a very early period, contemptuously likened; and modern holders of the doctrine are occasionally made the subject of equally polite comparisons by its German, French, and English assailants.

When thus attacked, the Epicureans have always answered, that it is not they, but their accusers, who represent human nature in a degrading light; since the accusation supposes human beings to be capable of no pleasures except those of which swine are capable. If this supposition were true, the charge could not be gainsaid, but would then be no longer an imputation; for if the sources of pleasure were precisely the same to human beings and to swine, the rule of life which is good enough for the one would be good enough for the other. The comparison of the Epicurean life to that of beasts is felt as degrading, precisely because a beast's pleasures do not satisfy a human being's conceptions of happiness. Human beings have faculties more elevated than the animal appetites, and when once made conscious of them, do not regard anything as happiness which does not include their gratification. I do not, indeed, consider the Epicureans to have been by any means faultless in drawing out their scheme of consequences from the utilitarian principle. To do this in any sufficient manner, many Stoic, as well as Christian elements require to be included. But there is no known Epicurean theory of life which does not assign to the pleasures of the intellect, of the feelings and imagination, and of the moral sentiments, a much higher value as pleasures than to those of mere sensation. It must be admitted, however, that utilitarian writers in general have placed the superiority of mental over bodily pleasures chiefly in the greater permanency, safety, uncostliness, etc., of the former—that is, in their circumstantial advantages rather than in their intrinsic nature. And on all these points utilitarians have fully proved their case; but they might have taken the other, and, as it may be called, higher ground, with entire consistency. It is quite compatible with the principle of utility to recognise the fact, that some *kinds* of pleasure are more desirable and more valuable than others. It would be absurd that while, in estimating all other things, quality is considered as well as quantity, the estimation of pleasures should be supposed to depend on quantity alone.

If I am asked, what I mean by difference of quality in pleasures, or what makes one pleasure more valuable than another, merely as a pleasure, except its being greater in amount, there is but one possible answer. Of two pleasures, if there be one to which all or almost all who have experience of both give a decided preference, irrespective of any feeling of moral obligation to prefer it, that is the more desirable pleasure. If one of the two is, by those who are competently acquainted with both, placed so far above the other that they prefer it, even though knowing it to be attended with a greater amount of discontent, and would not resign it for any quantity of the other pleasure which their nature is capable of, we are justified in ascribing to the preferred enjoyment a superiority in quality, so far outweighing quantity as to render it, in comparison, of small account.

Now it is an unquestionable fact that those who are equally acquainted with, and equally capable of appreciating and enjoying, both, do give a most marked preference to the manner of existence which employs their higher faculties. Few human creatures would consent to be changed into any of the lower animals, for a promise of the fullest allowance of a beast's pleasures; no intelligent human being would consent to be a fool, no instructed person would be an ignoramus, no person of feeling and conscience would be selfish and base, even though they should be persuaded that the fool, the dunce, or the rascal is better satisfied with his lot than they are with theirs. They would not resign what they possess more than he for the most complete satisfaction of all the desires which they have in common with him. If they ever fancy they would, it is only in cases of unhappiness so extreme, that to escape from it they would exchange their lot for almost any other, however undesirable in their own eyes. A being of higher faculties requires more to make him happy, is capable probably of more acute suffering, and certainly accessible to it at more points, than one of an inferior type; but in spite of these liabilities, he can never really wish to sink into what he feels to be a lower grade of existence. We may give what explanation we please of this unwillingness; we may attribute it to pride, a name which is given indiscriminately to some of the most and to some of the least estimable feelings of which mankind are capable; we may refer it to the love of liberty and personal independence, an appeal to which was with the Stoics one of the most effective means for the inculcation of it; to the love of power, or to the love of excitement, both of which do really enter into and contribute to it; but its most appropriate appellation is a sense of dignity, which all human beings possess in one form or other, and in some, though by no means in exact, proportion to their higher faculties, and which is so essential a part of the happiness of those in whom it is strong, that nothing which conflicts with it could be, otherwise than momentarily, an object of desire to them. Whoever supposes that this preference takes place at a sacrifice of happiness—that the superior being, in anything like equal circumstances, is not happier than the inferior—confounds the two very different ideas, of happiness, and content. It is indisputable that the being whose capacities of enjoyment are low, has the greatest chance of having them fully satisfied; and a highly endowed being will always feel that any happiness which he can look for, as the world is constituted, is imperfect. But he can learn to bear its imperfections, if they are at all bearable; and they will not make him envy the being who is indeed unconscious of the imperfections, but only because he feels not at all the good which those imperfections qualify. It is better to be a human being dissatisfied than a pig satisfied; better to be Socrates dissatisfied than a fool satisfied. And if the fool, or the pig, are of a different opinion, it is because they only know their own side of the question. The other party to the comparison knows both sides.

It may be objected, that many who are capable of the higher pleasures, occasionally, under the influence of temptation, postpone them to the lower. But this is quite compatible with a full appreciation of the intrinsic superiority of the higher. Men often, from infirmity of character, make their election for the nearer good, though they know it to be the less valuable; and this is no less when the choice is between two bodily pleasures, than when it is between bodily and mental. They pursue sensual indulgences to the injury of health, though perfectly aware that health is the greater good. It may be further objected, that many who begin with youthful enthusiasm for everything noble, as they advance in years sink into indolence and selfishness. But I do not believe that those who undergo this very common change, voluntarily choose the lower description of pleasures in preference to the higher. I believe that before they devote themselves exclusively to the one, they have already become incapable of the other. Capacity for the nobler feelings is in most natures a very tender plant, easily killed, not only by hostile influences, but by mere want of sustenance; and in the majority of young persons it speedily dies away if the occupations to which their position in life has devoted them, and the society into which it has thrown them, are not favourable to keeping that higher capacity in exercise. Men lose their high aspirations as they lose their intellectual tastes, because they have not time or opportunity for indulging them; and they addict themselves to inferior pleasures, not because they deliberately prefer them, but because they are either the only ones to which they have access, or the only ones which they are any longer capable of enjoying. It may be questioned whether any one who has remained equally susceptible to both classes of pleasures, ever knowingly and calmly preferred the lower; though many, in all ages, have broken down in an ineffectual attempt to combine both.

From this verdict of the only competent judges, I apprehend there can be no appeal. On a question which is the best worth having of two pleasures, or which of two modes of existence is the most grateful to the feelings, apart from its moral attributes and from its consequences, the judgment of those who are qualified by knowledge of both, or, if they differ, that of the majority among them, must be admitted as final. And there needs to be the less hesitation to accept this judgment respecting the quality of pleasures, since there is no other tribunal to be referred to even on the question of quantity. What means are there of determining which is the acutest of two pains, or the intensest of two pleasurable sensations, except the general suffrage of those who are familiar with both? Neither pains nor pleasures are homogeneous, and pain is always heterogeneous with pleasure. What is there to decide whether a particular pleasure is worth purchasing at the cost of a particular pain, except the feelings and judgment of the experienced? When, therefore, those feelings and judgment declare the pleasures derived from the higher faculties to be preferable *in kind,* apart from the question of intensity, to those of which the animal nature, disjoined from the higher faculties, is susceptible, they are entitled on this subject to the same regard.

I have dwelt on this point, as being a necessary part of a perfectly just conception of Utility or Happiness, considered as the directive rule of human conduct. But it is by no means an indispensable condition to the acceptance of the utilitarian standard; for that standard is not the agent's own greatest happiness, but the greatest amount of happiness altogether; and if it may possibly be doubted whether a noble character is always the happier for its nobleness, there can be no doubt that it makes other people happier, and that the world in general is immensely a gainer by it. Utilitarianism, therefore, could only attain its end by the general cultivation of nobleness of character, even if each individual were only benefited by the nobleness of others, and his own, so far as happiness is concerned, were a sheer deduction from the benefit. But the bare enunciation of such an absurdity as this last, renders refutation superfluous.

According to the Greatest Happiness Principle, as above explained, the ultimate end, with reference to and for the sake of which all other things are desirable (whether we are considering our own good or that of other people), is an existence exempt as far as possible from pain, and as rich as possible in enjoyments, both in point of quantity and quality; the test of quality, and the rule for measuring it against quantity, being the preference felt by those who in their opportunities of experience, to which must be added their habits of self-consciousness and self-observation, are best furnished with the means of comparison. This, being, according to the utilitarian opinion, the end of human action, is necessarily also the standard of morality; which may accordingly be defined, the rules and precepts for human conduct, by the observance of which an existence such as has been described might be, to the greatest extent possible, secured to all mankind; and not to them only, but, so far as the nature of things admits, to the whole sentient creation.

.   .   .

46

WILLIAM DAVID ROSS (1877– ————)

A Plurality of Intrinsic Goods

W. D. Ross is a world-renowned classical scholar, a respected authority on both Plato and Aristotle, and a prolific writer on philosophical ethics. His two books on ethics —*The Right and the Good* (1930) and *Foundations of Ethics* (1939)—are "must" reading for anyone interested in twentieth century ethical thought.

In attempting to determine "what kinds of things are intrinsically good," Ross uses the technique of *imaginative isolation.* This technique consists in imagining two states of the universe, one in which a given candidate for intrinsic goodness is present and another in which it is not. If one would prefer that state in which the candidate is present to that in which it is not, then we are judging that the candidate is intrinsically good.

Using this technique, Ross finds several things that are intrinsically good, that is, worthy of being desired for their own sake. The implication is that the highest human good consists in the attainment of all these intrinsic goods in such measure and proportion as one's circumstances may allow.

Our next step is to inquire what kinds of thing are intrinsically good. (1) The first thing for which I would claim that it is intrinsically good is virtuous disposition and action, *i.e.* action, or disposition to act, from any one of certain motives, of which at all events the most notable are the desire to do one's duty, the desire to bring into being something that is good, and the desire to give pleasure or save pain to others. It seems clear that we regard all such actions and dispositions as having value in themselves apart from any consequence. And if any one is inclined to doubt this and to think that, say, pleasure alone is intrinsically good, it seems to me enough to ask the question whether, of two states of the universe holding equal amounts of pleasure, we should really think no better of one in which the actions and dispositions of all the persons in it were thoroughly virtuous than of one in which they were highly vicious. To

From *The Right and the Good,* by W. D. Ross, published by Oxford University Press (1930). Reprinted by permission of Oxford University Press.

this there can be only one answer. Most hedonists would shrink from giving the plainly false answer which their theory requires, and would take refuge in saying that the question rests on a false abstraction. Since virtue, as they conceive it, is a disposition to do just the acts which will produce most pleasure, a universe full of virtuous persons would be bound, they might say, to contain more pleasure than a universe full of vicious persons. To this two answers may be made. *(a)* Much pleasure, and much pain, do not spring from virtuous or vicious actions at all but from the operation of natural laws. Thus even if a universe filled with virtuous persons were bound to contain more of the pleasure and less of the pain that springs from human action than a universe filled with vicious persons would, that inequality of pleasantness might easily be supposed to be precisely counteracted by, for instance, a much greater incidence of disease. The two states of affairs would then, on balance be equally pleasant; would they be equally good? And *(b)* even if we could not imagine any circumstances in which two states of the universe equal in pleas-antness but unequal in virtue could exist, the supposition is a legitimate one, since it is only intended to bring before us in a vivid way what is really self-evident, that virtue is good apart from its consequences.

(2) It seems at first sight equally clear that pleasure is good in itself. Some will perhaps be helped to realize this if they make the corresponding supposition to that we have just made; if they suppose two states of the universe including equal amounts of virtue but the one including also widespread and intense pleasure and the other widespread and intense pain. Here too it might be objected that the supposition is an impossible one, since virtue always tends to promote general pleasure, and vice to promote general misery. But this objection may be answered just as we have answered the corresponding objection above.

Apart from this, however, there are two ways in which even the most austere moralists and the most anti-hedonistic philosophers are apt to betray the conviction that pleasure is good in itself. *(a)* One is the attitude which they, like all other normal human beings, take towards kindness and towards cru-elty. If the desire to give pleasure to others is approved, and the desire to inflict pain on others condemned, this seems to imply the conviction that pleasure is good and pain bad. Some may think, no doubt, that the mere thought that a certain state of affairs would be *painful* for another person is enough to account for our conviction that the desire to produce it is bad. But I am inclined to think that there is involved the further thought that a state of affairs in virtue of being painful is *prima facie (i.e.* where other considerations do not enter into the case) one that a rational spectator would not approve, *i.e.* is *bad;* and that similarly our attitude towards kindness involves the thought that pleasure is good. *(b)* The other is the insistence, which we find in the most austere moralists as in other people, on the conception of merit. If virtue deserves to be rewarded by happiness (whether or not vice also deserves to be rewarded by unhappiness), this seems at first sight to imply that happiness and unhappiness are not in themselves things indifferent, but are good and bad respectively.

.   .   .

But reflection on the conception of merit does not support the view that pleasure is always good in itself and pain always bad in itself. For while this conception implies the conviction that pleasure when deserved is good, and pain when undeserved bad, it also suggests strongly that pleasure when un-deserved is bad and pain when deserved good.

There is also another set of facts which casts doubt on the view that pleasure is always good and pain always bad. We have a decided conviction that there are bad pleasures and (though this is less obvious) that there are good pains. We think that the pleasure taken either by the agent or by a spectator in, for instance, a lustful or cruel action is bad; and we think it a good thing that people should be pained rather than pleased by contemplating vice or misery.

Thus the view that pleasure is always good and pain always bad, while it seems to be strongly supported by some of our convictions, seems to be equally strongly opposed by others. The difficulty can, I think, be removed by ceasing to speak simply of pleasure and pain as good or bad, and by asking more carefully what it is that we mean. Consideration of the question is aided if we adopt the view (tentatively adopted already) that what is good or bad is always something properly expressed by a that-clause, *i.e.* an objective, or as I should prefer to call it, a *fact.* If we look at the matter thus, I think we can agree that the fact that a sentient being is in a state of pleasure is always in itself good, and the fact that a sentient being is in a state of pain always in itself bad, when this fact is not an element in a more complex fact having some other character-istic relevant to goodness or badness. And where considerations of desert or of moral good or evil do not enter, *i.e.* in the case of animals, the fact that a sentient being is feeling pleasure or pain is the whole fact (or the fact suffi-ciently described to enable us to judge of its goodness or badness), and we need not hesitate to say that the pleasure of animals is always good, and the pain of animals always bad, in itself and apart from its consequences. But when a moral being is feeling a pleasure or pain that is deserved or undeserved, or a pleasure or pain that implies a good or a bad disposition, the total fact is quite inadequately described if we say 'a sentient being is feeling pleasure, or pain'. The total fact may be that a sentient and moral being is feeling a pleasure that is undeserved, or that is the realization of a vicious disposition', and though the fact included in this, that 'a sentient being is feeling pleasure' would be good if it stood alone, that creates only a presumption that the total fact is good, and a presumption that is outweighed by the other element in the total fact.

Pleasure seems, indeed, to have a property analogous to that which we have previously recognized under the name of conditional or *prima facie* rightness.

An act of promise-keeping has the property, not necessarily of being right but of being something that is right if the act has no other morally significant characteristic (such as that of causing much pain to another person). And similarly a state of pleasure has the property, not necessarily of being good, but of being something that is good if the state has no other characteristic that prevents it from being good. The two characteristics that may interfere with its being good are *(a)* that of being contrary to desert, and *(b)* that of being a state which is the realization of a bad disposition. Thus the pleasures of which we can say without doubt that they are good are *(i)* the pleasures of non-moral beings (animals), *(ii)* the pleasures of moral beings that are deserved and are either realizations of good moral dispositions or realizations of neutral capacities (such as the pleasures of the senses).

In so far as the goodness or badness of a particular pleasure depends on its being the realization of a virtuous or vicious disposition, this has been allowed for by our recognition of virtue as a thing good in itself. But the mere recognition of virtue as a thing good in itself, and of pleasure as a thing *prima facie* good in itself, does not do justice to the conception of merit. If we compare two imaginary states of the universe, alike in the total amounts of virtue and vice and of pleasure and pain present in the two, but in one of which the virtuous were all happy and the vicious miserable, while in the other the virtuous were miserable and the vicious happy, very few people would hesitate to say that the first was a much better state of the universe than the second. It would seem then that, besides virtue and pleasure, we must recognize (3), as a third independent good, the apportionment of pleasure and pain to the virtuous and the vicious respectively. And it is on the recognition of this as a separate good that the recognition of the duty of justice, in distinction from fidelity to promises on the one hand and from beneficence on the other, rests.

(4) It seems clear that knowledge, and in a less degree what we may for the present call 'right opinion,' are states of mind good in themselves. Here too we may, if we please, help ourselves to realize the fact by supposing two states of the universe equal in respect of virtue and of pleasure and of the allocation of pleasure to the virtuous, but such that the persons in the one had a far greater understanding of the nature and laws of the universe than those in the other. Can any one doubt that the first would be a better state of the universe?

From one point of view it seems doubtful whether knowledge and right opinion, no matter what it is of or about, should be considered good. Knowledge of mere matters of fact (say of the number of stories in a building), without knowledge of their relation to other facts, might seem to be worthless; it certainly seems to be worth much less than the knowledge of general principles, or of facts as depending on general principles—what we might call insight or understanding as opposed to mere knowledge. But on reflection it seems clear that even about matters of fact right opinion is in itself a better state of mind to be in than wrong, and knowledge than right opinion.

There is another objection which may naturally be made to the view that knowledge is as such good. There are many pieces of knowledge which we in fact think it well for people *not* to have; e.g. we may think it a bad thing for a sick man to know how ill he is, or for a vicious man to know how he may most conveniently indulge his vicious tendencies. But it seems that in such cases it is not the knowledge but the consequences in the way of pain or of vicious action that we think bad.

It might perhaps be objected that knowledge is not a better state than right opinion, but merely a source of greater satisfaction to its possessor. It no doubt is a source of greater satisfaction. Curiosity is the desire to *know,* and is never really satisfied by mere opinion. Yet there are two facts which seem to show that this is not the whole truth. *(a)* While opinion recognized to be such is never thoroughly satisfactory to its possessor, there is another state of mind which is not knowledge—which may even be mistaken—yet which through lack of reflection is not distinguished from knowledge by its possessor, the state of mind which Professor Cook Wilson has called 'that of being under the impression that so-and-so is the case'.[1] Such a state of mind may be as great a source of satisfaction to its possessor as knowledge, yet we should all think it to be an inferior state of mind to knowledge. This surely points to a recognition by us that knowledge has a worth other than that of being a source of satisfaction to its possessor. *(b)* Wrong opinion, so long as its wrongness is not discovered, may be as great a source of satisfaction as right. Yet we should agree that it is an inferior state of mind, because it is to a less extent founded on knowledge and is itself a less close approximation to knowledge; which again seems to point to our recognizing knowledge as something good in itself.

Four things, then, seem to be intrinsically good—virtue, pleasure, the allocation of pleasure to the virtuous, and knowledge (and in a less degree right opinion). And I am unable to discover anything that is intrinsically good, which is not either one of these or a combination of two or more of them. And while this list of goods has been arrived at on its own merits, by reflection on what we really think to be good, it perhaps derives some support from the fact that it harmonizes with a widely accepted classification of the elements in the life of the soul. It is usual to enumerate these as cognition, feeling, and conation. Now knowledge is the ideal state of the mind, and right opinion an approximation to the ideal, on the cognitive or intellectual side; pleasure is its ideal state on the side of feeling; and virtue is its ideal state on the side of conation; while the allocation of happiness to virtue is a good which we recognize when we reflect on the ideal relation between the conative side and the side of feeling. It might of course be objected that there are or may be intrinsic goods that are not states of mind or relations between states of mind at all, but in this suggestion I can find no plausibility. Contemplate any imaginary universe from which you suppose mind entirely absent, and you will fail to find anything in it that you can call good in itself. That is not to say, of course, that the existence of a material universe may not be a necessary condition for the existence of many things that are good in themselves. Our

[1] *Statement and Inference,* i. 113.

knowledge and our true opinions are to a large extent about the material world, and to that extent could not exist unless it existed. Our pleasures are to a large extent derived from material objects. Virtue owes many of its opportunities to the existence of material conditions of good and material hindrances to good. But the value of material things appears to be purely instrumental, not intrinsic.

Of the three elements virtue, knowledge, and pleasure are compounded all the complex states of mind that we think good in themselves. Aesthetic enjoyment, for example, seems to be a blend of pleasure with insight into the nature of the object that inspires it. Mutual love seems to be a blend of virtuous disposition of two minds towards each other, with the knowledge which each has of the character and disposition of the other, and with the pleasure which arises from such disposition and knowledge. And a similar analysis may probably be applied to all other complex goods.

For Further Reading

Aquinas, St. Thomas. *Summa Contra Gentiles.* Many editions. See Book III, Chaps. 25–37, 48, and 60–63.

Augustine, St. *The Morals of the Catholic Church.* Many editions. See Chaps. 1–14.

Bennett, Jonathan. *Rationality: An Essay Towards an Analysis.* New York: Humanities Press, 1964.

Bentham, Jeremy. *An Introduction to the Principles of Morals and Legislation.* Several editions. See especially Chaps. 1, 2, 4, and 10. Of interest especially because of its description of the "hedonistic calculus."

Broad, C. D. *Five Types of Ethical Theory.* New York: Humanities Press, 1956.

DeWitt, N. W. *Epicurus and His Philosophy.* Minneapolis: University of Minnesota Press, 1954.

Ewing, Alfred C. *The Definition of Good.* New York: Macmillan, 1947.

Gosling, J. C. B. *Pleasure and Desire: The Case for Hedonism Reviewed.* Oxford: Clarendon Press, 1969.

Jones, H. "Mill's Argument for the Principle of Utility," *Philosophy and Phenomenological Research,* 38 (1977–1978), 338–354. A critique of Mill's arguments in support of his central thesis.

Lucretius. *On the Nature of Things.* Many editions. See Books III and IV. A well-known statement of the hedonistic view by an ancient admirer of Epicurus.

MacKinnon, D. M. *A Study of Ethical Theory.* London: A. and C. Black, 1957.

Moore, G. E. *Principia Ethica.* New York: Cambridge University Press, 1959. Chap. 3 is a detailed critique of hedonism; Chap. 6 is a statement of the pluralistic view.

Murdoch, Iris. *The Sovereignty of Good.* New York: Schocken Books, 1971.

Passmore, John. *The Perfectibility of Man.* New York: Scribner's, 1971.

Plato. *Philebus.* Many editions. Difficult reading, but of great interest for its critique of hedonism and its advocacy of a pluralistic view.

Ross, W. D. *Foundations of Ethics.* London: Oxford University Press, 1939.

Stocks, J. L. *Aristotle's Definition of the Human Good.* Oxford: Basil Blackwell, 1919.

Tsanoff, Radoslav A. *The Moral Ideals of Our Civilization.* New York: Dutton, 1942.

PART XI

The Language of Morals

The capacity for language is considered a distinctively human characteristic. Many birds and animals are able to make natural sounds, but it is only by the wildest stretch of the imagination that these sounds can be construed as a language, even a rudimentary language. Unlike human beings, they do not (so far as we know) make grammatical mistakes, have trouble with sentence structure, develop regional accents, use profanity, or get into arguments with one another. Depending on their species they may moo, neigh, caw, bleat, or whatever, but they cannot speak. Only human beings have the use of language.

Possessing this capacity, we use it in a variety of ways: to request information ("Where is my hat?"), to convey information ("Your hat is on the chair"), to direct behavior ("Please give me my hat"), and to express feeling ("That's a hat? Yuck!"). A single utterance may, of course, combine two or more of these functions. The sentence, "Please bring me the book that is on the table," for example, conveys the information (affirms) that a book is on the table and directs the hearer to bring that book to the speaker. The sentence, "Where is the package that came in yesterday's mail?" conveys the information (affirms) that a package arrived in yesterday's mail and requests information as to its present location. One could easily invent additional examples combining three or perhaps all four of the above-named functions in a single sentence.

Does language serve any purposes other than these four? It is difficult to say with certainty. As we reflect on the phenomenon of language as it is actually used, it certainly *seems* that this classification of functions is exhaustive, but further reflection might extend the list. In any event, it seems reasonable to proceed on the tentative assumption that our fourfold classification of the functions of language is exhaustive.

Let that be our assumption. How, then, are we using language when we say of something, in a moral sense, that it is good or bad, right or wrong? This is the central issue of what is called *metaethics.* Are we requesting information? Obviously, we are not. Perhaps, then, we are conveying information, affirming that something is the case. But what are we affirming? If the utterance "Honesty is good" is an assertion, precisely what is it that is being asserted? Several possibilities come to mind. (1) Perhaps, what is being asserted is that the practice of honesty results in the greatest happiness for the greatest number of people, that is, "morally good" means "productive of happiness." This is hedonism, which is a form of *ethical naturalism.* (2) Perhaps, what is being asserted is that the practice of honesty possesses the unique *non*natural quality of goodness, that is, "good" denotes no natural quality or qualities but rather a non-empirical quality or characteristic that is intuited (rationally discerned) rather than seen. This is *intuitionism,* or *nonnaturalism.* (3) Perhaps, what is being asserted is that the person uttering the sentence "Honesty is good" *approves* of honesty. To say that something is morally good, then, is not to say anything about the object that is said to be good; it is to say something about the speaker, namely that he or she likes, or approves of, the object in question. This is *subjectivism.* (4) Perhaps, the utterance "Honesty is good" means that honesty is generally approved of by some social group with whom the speaker is identified, such as the group Americans, Catholics, or the Society for the Prevention of Cruelty to Animals. This is *cultural relativism.*

These four theories are alike in that they regard ethical utterances as informative statements, statements that convey information of one kind or another. They are, therefore, *cognitivist* theories. According to all these theories, ethical utterances are assertions that are capable of being true or false. They differ in their view of what it is that is being asserted when something is said to be good or bad, right or wrong.

It is possible, however, that ethical utterances are not informative of anything—that is, they are instances of language being used directively or emotively rather than informatively. (5) It may be that ethical utterances are veiled commands, that an utterance like "Honesty is good" means, roughly, "Be honest!" This view is called *imperativism.* (6) Or, finally, it is possible that ethical utterances are instances of the expressive use of language, that "Honesty is good" means something like "Hurray for honesty!" This is the *emotivist* theory. Imperativism and emotivism are both *noncognitivist* theories regarding the meaning of ethical utterances.

Thus, we arrive at the following typology of metaethical theories:

I. Cognitivist Theories (language is being used informatively)
    A.   Objectivist Theories
        1.   Naturalism (1)
        2.   Intuitionism (2)
    B.   Subjectivist Theories
        1.   Private Subjectivism (3)
        2.   Cultural Relativism (4)
II. Noncognitivist theories (language is being used directively or emotively)
    A.   Imperativism (5)
    B.   Emotivism (6)

47

GEORGE EDWARD MOORE (1873–1958)

The Meaning of 'Good'

G. E. Moore was professor of philosophy at Cambridge University, and, for many years, editor of the influential philosophical journal *Mind*. He wrote on a wide variety of philosophical problems, but he is best known for his work in ethics (including metaethics) and his defense of common sense against what he called "philosophical paradoxes."

Moore's *Principia Ethica*, published in 1903, launched the modern discussion of the metaethical question, What does it *mean* to say of something that it is morally good? Moore's answer, reprinted below, is still the clearest formulation of the *intuitionist* theory: to affirm that something is good (in the ethical sense) is to affirm that it possesses the nonnatural (that is, nonempirical) quality of goodness. Once this is understood, Moore argues, we can go on to ask what things *are* good with a clearer understanding of what we are looking for.

From G. E. Moore, *Principia Ethica,* Chapter I (Cambridge, Eng: Cambridge University Press, 1903), pp. 6–9. Reprinted by permission of the publisher.

. . .

6. What, then, is good? How is good to be defined? Now, it may be thought that this is a verbal question. A definition does indeed often mean the expressing of one word's meaning in other words. But this is not the sort of definition I am asking for. Such a definition can never be of ultimate importance in any study except lexicography. If I wanted that kind of definition I should have to consider in the first place how people generally used the word 'good'; but my business is not with its proper usage, as established by custom. I should, indeed, be foolish, if I tried to use it for something which it did not usually denote: if, for instance, I were to announce that, whenever I used the word 'good,' I must be understood to be thinking of that object which is usually denoted by the word 'table.' I shall, therefore, use the word in the sense in which I think it is ordinarily used; but at the same time I am not anxious to discuss whether I am right in thinking that it is so used. My business is solely with that object or idea, which I hold, rightly or wrongly, that the word is generally used to stand for. What I want to discover is the nature of that object or idea, and about this I am extremely anxious to arrive at an agreement.

But, if we understand the question in this sense, my answer to it may seem a very disappointing one. If I am asked 'What is good?' my answer is that good is good, and that is the end of the matter. Or if I am asked 'How is good to be defined?' my answer is that it cannot be defined, and that is all I have to say about it. But disappointing as these answers may appear, they are of the very last importance. To readers who are familiar with philosophic terminology, I can express their importance by saying that they amount to this: That propositions about the good are all of them synthetic and never analytic; and that is plainly no trivial matter. And the same thing may be expressed more popularly, by saying that, if I am right, then nobody can foist upon us such an axiom as that 'Pleasure is the only good' or that 'The good is the desired' on the pretence that this is 'the very meaning of the word.'

7. Let us, then, consider this position. My point is that 'good' is a simple notion, just as 'yellow' is a simple notion; that, just as you cannot, by any manner of means, explain to any one who does not already know it, what yellow is, so you cannot explain what good is. Definitions of the kind that I was asking for, definitions which describe the real nature of the object or notion denoted by a word, and which do not merely tell us what the word is used to mean, are only possible when the object or notion in question is something complex. You can give a definition of a horse, because a horse has many different properties and qualities, all of which you can enumerate. But when you have enumerated them all, when you have reduced a horse to his simplest terms, then you can no longer define those terms. They are simply something which you think of or perceive, and to any one who cannot think of or perceive them, you can never, by any definition, make their nature known. It may perhaps be objected to this that we are able to describe to others, objects which they have never seen or thought of. We can, for instance, make a man understand what a chimaera is, although he has never heard of one or seen

one. You can tell him that it is an animal with a lioness's head and body, with a goat's head growing from the middle of its back, and with a snake in place of a tail. But here the object which you are describing is a complex object; it is entirely composed of parts, with which we are all perfectly familiar—a snake, a goat, a lioness; and we know, too, the manner in which those parts are to be put together, because we know what is meant by the middle of a lioness's back, and where her tail is wont to grow. And so it is with all objects, not previously known, which we are able to define: they are all complex; all composed of parts, which may themselves, in the first instance, be capable of similar definition, but which must in the end be reducible to simplest parts, which can no longer be defined. But yellow and good, we say, are not complex: they are notions of that simple kind, out of which definitions are composed and with which the power of further defining ceases.

8. When we say, as Webster says, 'The definition of horse is "A hoofed quadruped of the genus Equus," ' we may, in fact, mean three different things. (1) We may mean merely: 'When I say "horse," you are to understand that I am talking about a hoofed quadruped of the genus Equus.' This might be called the arbitrary verbal definition: and I do not mean that good is indefinable in that sense. (2) We may mean, as Webster ought to mean: 'When most English people say "horse," they mean a hoofed quadruped of the genus Equus.' This may be called the verbal definition proper, and I do not say that good is indefinable in this sense either; for it is certainly possible to discover how people use a word: otherwise, we could never have known that 'good' may be translated by 'gut' in German and by 'bon' in French. But (3) we may, when we define horse, mean something much more important. We may mean that a certain object, which we all of us know, is composed in a certain manner: that it has four legs, a head, a heart, a liver, etc., etc., all of them arranged in definite relations to one another. It is in this sense that I deny good to be definable. I say that it is not composed of any parts, which we can substitute for it in our minds when we are thinking of it. We might think just as clearly and correctly about a horse, if we thought of all its parts and their arrangement instead of thinking of the whole: we could, I say, think how a horse differed from a donkey just as well, just as truly, in this way, as now we do, only not so easily; but there is nothing whatsoever which we could so substitute for good; and that is what I mean, when I say that good is indefinable.

9. But I am afraid I have still not removed the chief difficulty which may prevent acceptance of the proposition that good is indefinable. I do not mean to say that *the* good, that which is good, is thus indefinable; if I did think so, I should not be writing on Ethics, for my main object is to help towards discovering that definition. It is just because I think there will be less risk of error in our search for a definition of 'the good,' that I am now insisting that *good* is indefinable. I must try to explain the difference between these two. I suppose it may be granted that 'good' is an adjective. Well 'the good,' 'that which is good,' must therefore be the substantive to which the adjective 'good' will apply: it must be the whole of that to which the adjective will apply, and

the adjective must *always* truly apply to it. But if it is that to which the adjective will apply, it must be something different from that adjective itself; and the whole of that something different, whatever it is, will be our definition of *the* good. Now it may be that this something will have other adjectives, beside 'good,' that will apply to it. It may be full of pleasure, for example; it may be intelligent: and if these two adjectives are really part of its definition, then it will certainly be true, that pleasure and intelligence are good. And many people appear to think that, if we say 'Pleasure and intelligence are good,' or if we say 'Only pleasure and intelligence are good,' we are defining 'good.' Well, I cannot deny that propositions of this nature may sometimes be called definitions; I do not know well enough how the word is generally used to decide upon this point. I only wish it to be understood that that is not what I mean when I say there is no possible definition of good, and that I shall not mean this if I use the word again. I do most fully believe that some true proposition of the form 'Intelligence is good and intelligence alone is good' can be found; if none could be found, our definition of *the* good would be impossible. As it is, I believe *the* good to be definable; and yet I still say that good itself is indefinable.

.   .   .   .

48

BRAND BLANSHARD (1892– ———)

In Defense of Naturalism

Brand Blanshard, a contemporary American philosopher, was, for many years, a professor at Yale University. He is something of a rarity among contemporary philosophers in that he is an advocate of both rationalism and objective idealism, neither of

From Brand Blanshard, "The Impasse in Ethics—and a Way Out," in *University of California Publications in Philosophy,* no. 28 (1954), pp. 107–110. Reprinted by permission of the publisher.

which can count many adherents among twentieth-century British or American philosophers. He has published several books, including *The Nature of Thought* (1939), *Reason and Goodness* (1961), and *Reason and Analysis* (1962).

Blanshard's metaethical theory is a form of *naturalism*. He writes: "To say of an experience that it is intrinsically good means . . . two things: first, that it satisfies; and second, that it fulfills." To say that it "satisfies" is to say that it is pleasurable; to say that it "fulfills" is to say that it is an expression or realization of some distinctively human aspect of our nature. According to Blanshard's theory, the reason that it is better to be Socrates dissatisfied than a fool satisfied is that in Socrates we find a richer fulfillment of human nature than we find in a fool.

.   .   .

. . . When Socrates set the fashion for Western thinkers in defining ethical terms, his method was a straightforward one; perceiving that even when we were uncertain what a term meant, we could often point with confidence to varying examples of it, he proposed that we discover our meaning by asking what it was in virtue of which we recognized these as examples, and that we do this by bringing to light what they had in common. This is regarded by some present-day analysts as too crude a method; for it is possible, they say, to find a set of characters that is always present when goodness is present, and yet is not strictly what goodness means. The proof of this is that we may use the word "goodness" significantly without any explicit thought of the characters named; and, further, that the question whether a thing could be good without these characters is not instantly seen to be meaningless.

I suggest that when analysis reaches this stage it has become so refined as to be self-defeating. Not only does the term "good" have no one meaning (Dr. Ewing has recently distinguished ten meanings), but even when used in the restricted sense of intrinsically good, I see no reason to think that its meaning is either clear or simple. Words are used very much as checks are used, to transfer accumulated stores, and the fact that no inventory is made of these at the time of transfer does not imply that the checks are irredeemable. Behind this term "good," which we bandy about so readily as a counter, there lies a massive wealth of meaning which for most purposes may be taken for granted, but which the analyst ignores at his peril. If he assumes that the word means only what is explicitly present whenever it is used, the result will be a triumph of precise and lucid superficiality, which must be repudiated at the first glimpse of what lies in its hinterland.

Very well, if goodness is not a quality but rather a complex of characters of which the word is merely the opening gate, what is included in this complex? Let me make such answer as I have to give with the help of a famous case in ethical history. John Stuart Mill, you will recall, concluded that goodness meant pleasure. Hence any state of mind that was intrinsically good, whether an experience of beauty or of wisdom or of champagne, was good in the precise degree of its pleasantness. This led to an attractively simple solution of nearly all the problems of ethics, and Mill regarded it with some complacency. But when his friend Carlyle began to berate it as a "pig" philosophy, he had second thoughts. He asked himself the classic question: if he had to choose between the life of a pig, supported in the style to which Mr. Wodehouse's Empress of Blanding was accustomed, or an equal period in the life of a harassed and henpecked Socrates, would he elect the porcine bliss or the philosophic struggle? Could he put his hand on his heart and say that the pleasure of the Socratic life was certainly greater? No. Did he have the slightest doubt, however, that it would be better to be Socrates in any case? No again, Mill confessed, with that honesty and candor that made him so persuasive. But then what became of his theory that the good lay in pleasure alone? His answer, of course, was that though the Socratic life might not contain *more* pleasure than the other life, the pleasure it did contain was so much better, so much higher in quality, as to outweigh any deficit in quantity. By pretty general agreement, this did more credit to his heart than to his head. You cannot consistently say that, with their pleasantness equal, one experience is better than another, and also that their goodness lies in their pleasantness alone. It was all too clear that Mill was making two major mistakes at once: first, in identifying goodness with pleasure; second, in trying to combine this view with the admission that goodness was other than pleasure.

Several generations of teachers and students have triumphantly pointed out Mill's blunders. But many, even in doing so, have felt that his sane and honest mind had carried him very near to the truth. I own to being one of these. I am inclined to think that goodness consists in two components, both of which Mill more or less clearly recognized, and that if he had seen the parts they really play, his theory on this point would have been beyond cavil.

In the first place, he recognized that pleasure, or, as I prefer to call it, satisfaction, is present in every state of mind that is intrinsically good, and is inseparable from the goodness. This, I submit, remains true even if goodness is not exhausted by pleasure. Take one example. We who are in academic life call knowledge or understanding good. Suppose that at one stroke we could achieve what we are seeking, and have at our command all the knowledge and understanding of what James calls the "quarto and folio editions of mankind," but with this one proviso added, that we should find no pleasure, take no satisfaction, in it. Would it have any value for us? I am not asking whether we might still choose it for its consequences to ourselves or others; that is a wholly different question. I am asking whether it would have intrinsic value for us, and suggesting that it would not. Indeed, this answer has over and over again been forced upon those who tried to evade it. It was forced upon the Stoics, who, in seeking to rid themselves of feeling, found that as they lived more exclusively in the gray light of reason, everything else turned gray. It was forced upon Mill himself by the nervous collapse of his earlier years, when, having lost the power to enjoy as the result of intellectual overforcing, he found that the goods for which he was living had suddenly turned to dust and ashes. Enjoyment is not all there is to goodness; at this date there is no need to stop over that. But it is so essential to any experience we call good that if it vanishes, the value vanishes with it.

Secondly, Mill recognized that of two states which are equally pleasant one may be better than the other, and through the example he took he set our feet on the right road, though he somehow missed it himself. What is it that makes the life of Socrates more worth living than that of the pig, whether pleasanter or not? Surely not the quality of his pleasure whatever that may mean, but something more obvious, something indeed that stares us in the face. *It is simply that in the mind of a great thinker we have a richer fulfillment of the faculties that make us men.* In respect to his intelligence, Socrates is more of a man than we are, more of what we want to be. The power, the need, the desire, to know is fundamental in all of us. Its presence at a certain level is a defining mark of human nature, the fulfillment in exceptional measure is what marks off the large mind from the little one.

The same fact marks off even a lowly human mind from the animal mind. Mill's essay appears to have been written before *The Origin of Species,* though it was published a year or two later. We see now, as he could not, that running through the whole development of mind, and determining its course, there is a continuous drive, or, rather, set of drives, of which human nature itself is only the most recent expression. One of these is the impulse to know, which is central in human nature because its roots run deep into animal nature. Even in the dim-witted four-footed cousin that Mill referred to, and in the midst of notorious appetites in other directions, it flickers up into a vagrant curiosity. In the higher apes it is far more active. In man, with his power to look before and after, it is more restless and inquiring still. And, despite Housman's gibe that the love of truth is the faintest of human passions, in a few men it burns up into a devouring, illuminating flame that seems to light up for miles ahead the road which intelligence must travel. Contact with such a mind is self-revelation; we seem to see for the first time that this is what we are really about, this is what we have been trying to do all along; we catch a glimpse, as Arnold would say, of "the hills where our life rose, and the sea where it goes." A great mind is a great mind because it does what we are all trying to do, only better. In sum, when we say that it is better to be Socrates than ourselves, and ourselves than a fool, and a fool than a pig, we are saying that in Socrates we have a completer fulfillment of a set of drives or impulses that are continuous from one extreme to the other.

To say of an experience that it is intrinsically good means, then, two things: first, that it satisfies; and second, that it fulfills. Pleasure without fulfillment, as Aristotle saw, is hardly possible. Fulfillment without pleasure, as Mill saw, is valueless. Of two experiences that equally fulfill, the one we enjoy more is

the better. Of two experiences that we equally enjoy, the one that fulfills more
is the better. Of course fulfillment does not mean meeting our demands for
enlightenment only; it means meeting all the other demands of our nature so
far as they can be met without mutual suppression. The quiver of human
nature is full of arrows of desire, big and little, desires that are fashioned from
what we are, desires for food and drink and play and friends and things of
beauty. If anything fulfills and satisfies such demands, it is *ipso facto* good; if
it is utterly out of relation to such demands, no one would think of calling it
good.

It may be said that there are impulses in human nature whose indulgence
is evil, such as those of aggression and fear. But Professor Pepper has shown
fine insight, I think, in pointing out that these are not drives with ends of their
own; they are summoned up when other drives are frustrated, and are nature's
means of intensifying these or safeguarding them. When they do get out of
hand and must be suppressed, it is not because they are evil in themselves but
because their fulfillment would block other fulfillments. The doctrine that men
are naturally evil, so current in some theological circles, is thus the precise
reverse of the truth. To fulfill and satisfy what nature prompts is not only good;
it is what goodness means.

·   ·   ·

49

ALFRED JULES AYER (1910– ————)

Emotivism

Ayer has been a leading spokesman for the philosophical school known as logical
positivism ever since the publication, in 1936, of his influential book, *Language, Truth
and Logic* (written when he was twenty-six years of age). He has written a number

From A. J. Ayer, *Language, Truth and Logic,* Chapter VI (New York: Dover, 1946), pp.
106–112. Reprinted by permission of the publisher.

of other books, including *The Foundations of Empirical Knowledge* (1940), *Philosophical Essays* (1954), *The Problem of Knowledge* (1956), *Philosophy and Language* (1960), and *The Concept of a Person and Other Essays* (1963).

The selection that follows is an exceptionally clear statement of *emotivism*. According to this theory, ethical utterances are not statements; they are simply expressions of the approval or disapproval of the person making the utterance. "Good" denotes neither a nonnatural quality (Moore) nor a natural quality (Blanshard): it denotes nothing at all. It merely expresses the approval of the person who says of something that it is "good," just as "bad" and "wrong" express disapproval.

.   .   .

Considering the use which we have made of the principle that a synthetic proposition is significant only if it is empirically verifiable, it is clear that the acceptance of an "absolutist" theory of ethics would undermine the whole of our main argument. And as we have already rejected the "naturalistic" theories which are commonly supposed to provide the only alternative to "absolutism" in ethics, we seem to have reached a difficult position. We shall meet the difficulty by showing that the correct treatment of ethical statements is afforded by a third theory, which is wholly compatible with our radical empiricism.

We begin by admitting that the fundamental ethical concepts are unanalysable, inasmuch as there is no criterion by which one can test the validity of the judgments in which they occur. So far we are in agreement with the absolutists. But, unlike the absolutists, we are able to give an explanation of this fact about ethical concepts. We say that the reason why they are unanalysable is that they are mere pseudo-concepts. The presence of an ethical symbol in a proposition adds nothing to its factual content. Thus if I say to someone, "You acted wrongly in stealing that money," I am not stating anything more than if I had simply said, "You stole that money." In adding that this action is wrong I am not making any further statement about it. I am simply evincing my moral disapproval of it. It is as if I had said, "You stole that money," in a peculiar tone of horror, or written it with the addition of some special exclamation marks. The tone, or the exclamation marks, adds nothing to the literal meaning of the sentence. It merely serves to show that the expression of it is attended by certain feelings in the speaker.

If now I generalise my previous statement and say, "Stealing money is wrong," I produce a sentence which has no factual meaning—that is, expresses no proposition which can be either true or false. It is as if I had written "Stealing money!!"—where the shape and thickness of the exclamation marks show, by a suitable convention, that a special sort of moral disapproval is the feeling which is being expressed. It is clear that there is nothing said here which can be true or false. Another man may disagree with me about the wrongness of stealing, in the sense that he may not have the same feelings about stealing as I have, and he may quarrel with me on account of my moral sentiments. But he cannot, strictly speaking, contradict me. For in saying that a certain type of action is right or wrong, I am not making any factual statement, not even a statement about my own state of mind. I am merely expressing certain moral sentiments. And the man who is ostensibly contradicting me is merely expressing his moral sentiments. So that there is plainly no sense in asking which of us is in the right. For neither of us is asserting a genuine proposition.

What we have just been saying about the symbol "wrong" applies to all normative ethical symbols. Sometimes they occur in sentences which record ordinary empirical facts besides expressing ethical feeling about those facts: sometimes they occur in sentences which simply express ethical feeling about a certain type of action, or situation, without making any statement of fact. But in every case in which one would commonly be said to be making an ethical judgement, the function of the relevant ethical word is purely "emotive." It is used to express feeling about certain objects, but not to make any assertion about them.

It is worth mentioning that ethical terms do not serve only to express feeling. They are calculated also to arouse feeling, and so to stimulate action. Indeed some of them are used in such a way as to give the sentences in which they occur the effect of commands. Thus the sentence "It is your duty to tell the truth" may be regarded both as the expression of a certain sort of ethical feeling about truthfulness and as the expression of the command "Tell the truth." The sentence "You ought to tell the truth" also involves the command "Tell the truth," but here the tone of the command is less emphatic. In the sentence "It is good to tell the truth" the command has become little more than a suggestion. And thus the "meaning" of the word "good," in its ethical usage, is differentiated from the word "duty" or the word "ought." In fact we may define the meaning of the various ethical words in terms both of the different feelings they are ordinarily taken to express, and also the different responses which they are calculated to provoke.

We can now see why it is impossible to find a criterion for determining the validity of ethical judgements. It is not because they have an "absolute" validity which is mysteriously independent of ordinary sense-experience, but because they have no objective validity whatsoever. If a sentence makes no statement at all, there is obviously no sense in asking whether what it says is true or false. And we have seen that sentences which simply express moral judgements do not say anything. They are pure expressions of feeling and as such do not come under the category of truth and falsehood. They are unverifiable for the same reason as a cry of pain or a word of command is unverifiable —because they do not express genuine propositions.

Thus, although our theory of ethics might fairly be said to be radically subjectivist, it differs in a very important respect from the orthodox subjectivist theory. For the orthodox subjectivist does not deny, as we do, that the sentences of a moralizer express genuine propositions. All he denies is that they express propositions of a unique non-empirical character. His own view is that they express propositions about the speaker's feelings. If this were so, ethical judgements clearly would be capable of being true or false. They would be true if the speaker had the relevant feelings, and false if he had not. And this is a matter which is, in principle, empirically verifiable. Furthermore they could be significantly contradicted. For if I say, "Tolerance is a virtue," and someone answers, "You don't approve of it," he would, on the ordinary subjectivist theory, be contradicting me. On our theory, he would not be contradicting me, because, in saying that tolerance was a virtue, I should not be making any statement about my own feelings or about anything else. I should simply be evincing my feelings, which is not at all the same thing as saying that I have them.

The distinction between the expression of feeling and the assertion of feeling is complicated by the fact that the assertion that one has a certain feeling often accompanies the expression of that feeling, and is then, indeed, a factor in the expression of that feeling. Thus I may simultaneously express boredom and say that I am bored, and in that case my utterance of the words, "I am bored," is one of the circumstances which make it true to say that I am expressing or evincing boredom. But I can express boredom without actually saying that I am bored. I can express it by my tone and gestures, while making a statement about something wholly unconnected with it, or by an ejaculation, or without uttering any words at all. So that even if the assertion that one has a certain feeling always involves the expression of that feeling, the expression of a feeling assuredly does not always involve the assertion that one has it. And this is the important point to grasp in considering the distinction between our theory and the ordinary subjectivist theory. For whereas the subjectivist holds that ethical statements actually assert the existence of certain feelings, we hold that ethical statements are expressions and excitants of feeling which do not necessarily involve any assertions.

We have already remarked that the main objection to the ordinary subjectivist theory is that the validity of ethical judgements is not determined by the nature of their author's feelings. And this is an objection which our theory escapes. For it does not imply that the existence of any feelings is a necessary and sufficient condition of the validity of an ethical judgement. It implies, on the contrary, that ethical judgements have no validity.

There is, however, a celebrated argument against subjectivist theories which our theory does not escape. It has been pointed out by Moore that if ethical statements were simply statements about the speaker's feelings, it would be impossible to argue about questions of value.[1] To take a typical example: if a man said that thrift was a virtue, and another replied that it was a vice, they

[1] cf. *Philosophical Studies,* "The Nature of Moral Philosophy."

would not, on this theory, be disputing with one another. One would be saying that he approved of thrift, and the other that *he* didn't; and there is no reason why both these statements should not be true. Now Moore held it to be obvious that we do dispute about questions of value, and accordingly concluded that the particular form of subjectivism which he was discussing was false.

It is plain that the conclusion that it is impossible to dispute about questions of value follows from our theory also. For as we hold that such sentences as "Thrift is a virtue" and "Thrift is a vice" do not express propositions at all, we clearly cannot hold that they express incompatible propositions. We must therefore admit that if Moore's argument really refutes the ordinary subjectivist theory, it also refutes ours. But, in fact, we deny that it does refute even the ordinary subjectivist theory. For we hold that one really never does dispute about questions of value.

This may seem, at first sight, to be a very paradoxical assertion. For we certainly do engage in disputes which are ordinarily regarded as disputes about questions of value. But, in all such cases, we find, if we consider the matter closely, that the dispute is not really about a question of value, but about a question of fact. When someone disagrees with us about the moral value of a certain action or type of action, we do admittedly resort to argument in order to win him over to our way of thinking. But we do not attempt to show by our arguments that he has the "wrong" ethical feeling towards a situation whose nature he has correctly apprehended. What we attempt to show is that he is mistaken about the facts of the case. We argue that he has misconceived the agent's motive: or that he has misjudged the effects of the action, or its probable effects in view of the agent's knowledge; or that he has failed to take into account the special circumstances in which the agent was placed. Or else we employ more general arguments about the effects which actions of a certain type tend to produce, or the qualities which are usually manifested in their performance. We do this in the hope that we have only to get our opponent to agree with us about the nature of the empirical facts for him to adopt the same moral attitude towards them as we do. And as the people with whom we argue have generally received the same moral education as ourselves, and live in the same social order, our expectation is usually justified. But if our opponent happens to have undergone a different process of moral "conditioning" from ourselves, so that, even when he acknowledges all the facts, he still disagrees with us about the moral value of the actions under discussion, then we abandon the attempt to convince him by argument. We say that it is impossible to argue with him because he has a distorted or undeveloped moral sense; which signifies merely that he employs a different set of values from our own. We feel that our own system of values is superior, and therefore speak in such derogatory terms of his. But we cannot bring forward any arguments to show that our system is superior. For our judgement that it is so is itself a judgement of value, and accordingly outside the scope of argument. It is because argument fails us when we come to deal with pure questions of value, as distinct from questions of fact, that we finally resort to mere abuse.

In short, we find that argument is possible on moral questions only if some system of values is presupposed. If our opponent concurs with us in expressing moral disapproval of all actions of a given type *t*, then we may get him to condemn a particular action *A*, by bringing forward arguments to show that *A* is of type *t*. For the question whether *A* does or does not belong to that type is a plain question of fact. Given that a man has certain moral principles, we argue that he must, in order to be consistent, react morally to certain things in a certain way. What we do not and cannot argue about is the validity of these moral principles. We merely praise or condemn them in the light of our own feelings.

If anyone doubts the accuracy of this account of moral disputes, let him try to construct even an imaginary argument on a question of value which does not reduce itself to an argument about a question of logic or about an empirical matter of fact. I am confident that he will not succeed in producing a single example. And if that is the case, he must allow that its involving the impossibility of purely ethical arguments is not, as Moore thought, a ground of objection to our theory, but rather a point in favour of it.

Having upheld our theory against the only criticism which appeared to threaten it, we may now use it to define the nature of all ethical enquiries. We find that ethical philosophy consists simply in saying that ethical concepts are pseudo-concepts and therefore unanalysable. The further task of describing the different feelings that the different ethical terms are used to express, and the different reactions that they customarily provoke, is a task for the psychologist. There cannot be such a thing as ethical science, if by ethical science one means the elaboration of a "true" system of morals. For we have seen that, as ethical judgements are mere expressions of feeling, there can be no way of determining the validity of any ethical system, and, indeed, no sense in asking whether any such system is true. All that one may legitimately enquire in this connection is, What are the moral habits of a given person or group of people, and what causes them to have precisely those habits and feelings? And this enquiry falls wholly within the scope of the existing social sciences.

50

STEPHEN TOULMIN (1922– ———)

Ethics and Society

Born and educated in England, Stephen Toulmin has lived in the United States since 1965, where he has held teaching positions at Brandeis University, Michigan State University, the University of California at Santa Cruz, and the University of Chicago. His writings, which cover a wide variety of philosophical topics, include *The Place of Reason in Ethics* (1950), *The Philosophy of Science: An Introduction* (1953), *The Uses of Argument* (1958), *Foresight and Understanding* (1961), a three-volume work entitled *The Ancestry of Science* (1961–1965), *Wittgenstein's Vienna* (1973), and *Knowing and Acting* (1976).

Although Toulmin does not give his metaethical theory a label, it can reasonably be interpreted as a form of *cultural relativism*. "Ethical language," he writes, "can be regarded as part of the process whereby, as members of a community, we moderate our impulses and adjust our demands so as to reconcile them as far as possible with those of our fellows." It follows, then, that the positive ethical terms ("good," "right," and the like) express the approval of a given community for whatever is so described, and the correlative negative terms ("bad," "wrong," and the like) express the community's disapproval.

. . .

10.2   THE NOTION OF 'DUTY'

Suppose . . . that two people are arguing about what to do. The one (A) begins by advocating course α; the other (B) rejects α and proposes β instead. They continue to argue, bringing forward all kinds of reasons for and against α and β. Finally, they come to a decision, agreeing that γ and δ are *really* the right

From Stephen Toulmin, *An Examination of the Place of Reason in Ethics,* Chapter 10 (New York: Cambridge University Press, 1950), pp. 132–133, 136–143. Reprinted by permission of the publisher.

things to do. What kinds of reasons would they have to bring for and against α, β, γ and δ in order for us to say that 'ethical' considerations had affected their decisions, and that they had refrained from α and β in favour of γ and δ because they recognised that it would be 'morally wrong' to do otherwise?

The answer to this question must, in the first place, be twofold. Two types of consideration, not at first sight comparable, cry out to be called 'moral':

(i) arguments showing that γ and δ fulfill a 'duty' in the 'moral code' of the community to which A and B belong, whereas α and β contraveⁿe this part of the 'code';

(ii) arguments showing that γ and δ will avoid causing to other members of the community some inconvenience, annoyance or suffering which would be caused by α and β.

The second type of consideration suggests that ethics and ethical language can be regarded as part of the process whereby, as members of a community, we moderate our impulses and adjust our demands so as to reconcile them as far as possible with those of our fellows. But what about the first type of consideration—arguments from 'duty'? How far does it falsify our notions to regard these as a part of the same process? And does it derogate from the 'absoluteness' of 'duty' to characterise it in terms of this process?

The answer is that the only context in which the concept of 'duty' is straightforwardly intelligible is one of communal life—it is, indeed, completely bound up with this very feature of communal life, that we learn to renounce our claims and alter our aims where they conflict with those of our fellows.

.   .   .

The concept of 'duty', in short, is inextricable from the 'mechanics' of social life, and from the practices adopted by different communities in order to make living together in proximity tolerable or even possible. We need not therefore worry about the apparent duality of ethical arguments—about the contrast between arguments from 'duty' and arguments from the welfare of our fellows. And we can fairly characterise ethics as a part of the process whereby the desires and actions of the members of a community are harmonised.

The central importance of 'disposition' in ethics is now understandable: there would be no use for ethical reasoning, either among people whose feelings were wholly unalterable (and who would therefore behave exactly the same whether exhorted to change or not) or, on the other hand, among angels, whose dispositions were always of the best (and who would therefore have no need to inquire or discuss what to do).

Further, the analysis of what I have called the 'function' of ethics can now be completed; we can provisionally define it as being 'to correlate our feelings and behaviour in such a way as to make the fulfilment of everyone's aims and desires as far as possible compatible'.

It is in the light of this function, and of its context of communal living, that
we must examine

(i) the development of morality and of ethical reasoning, and
(ii) the logical rules to be applied to ethical arguments.

10.3   THE DEVELOPMENT OF ETHICS (I)

Historically and psychologically alike, the development of ethics is most conveniently described in two contrasted stages. This division we shall find later
reflected in the logic of ethics.

The first and most obvious way of preventing conflicts of interest in a
community (whether a tribe or a family) is for all its members to have the same
aims, the same interests, the same desires, hopes and fears; in fact the same
dispositions. In its early stages, therefore, morality boils down to 'doing the
done thing': and this is true, both of the way in which a child learns from its
parents, and, in social pre-history, of moral codes. Primitive ethics is 'deontological', a matter of rigid duties, taboos, customs and commandments. It
prevents conflicts of interest by keeping the dispositions of all concerned
aligned, and condemns behaviour directed away from the prescribed aims.
Further, these aims are not advocated but imposed, the use of ethical language
being part of the behaviour adopted by 'those in authority' for enforcing
co-operation: so no wonder if ethical utterances are often 'rhetorical'.

Respect for fixed 'social practices' (or 'done things'), though most characteristic of primitive morality, continues throughout the later stages of development, and can be recognised in our own societies. Although 'doing the done
thing' may be merely conventionalism, it may equally be anything but that;
especially in those situations in which *some* common practice must be adopted
and, within limits, it does not matter what.

The Rule of the Road is a good example. By appealing to this practice, the
statements, 'It is right to drive on the left in England' and 'You ought to be
driving on the left', may be used to alter the hearer's disposition, so that in the
future he drives on the left. (The ethical judgements are here used 'persuasively'.) But the same utterances can also be used simply to draw attention to
the rule, or to evince the speaker's displeasure.

Now consider two more subtle examples: first, that of the schoolboy who
hears that he has been given his cricket colours. His immediate reaction will
probably be one of pleasure, and he will cry out, 'Why, that is good news!' But
his school-fellows may feel differently about it, especially if they suspect that
he has been given them only because the cricket captain is fond of him. Then
they will do their best to make him feel that his rejoicing is misplaced, pointing
out (for example) that another, better batsman has had to go without colours
as a result. If the schoolboy has a tender conscience, accepts the 'principle' that
cricket colours should go to the best cricketers, and not just to the captain's

favourites, and admits both that he is rather a friend of the captain's, and that the man who has had to go without has the better batting record and more 1st XI matches to his credit; then he may eventually say, 'Well, naturally I was pleased at the time, but I see now that I *ought not really* to have been given them'.

In this example, several of the most characteristic features of ethics are displayed. To start with, an ethical term is used simply to evince pleasure. Next, contrary feelings are aroused in, and evinced by others. These are concerned at the way in which the schoolboy's award has cut across another's interests—in this case, someone's 'natural right' to colours, based on a generally accepted practice. (The conflict between one schoolboy's winning his colours, and the other's failure to obtain them, is a typically ethical one, in that it is only possible for one of them to have them.) Reasons are advanced for the view that the award was not *really good.* The principle is appealed to as authority. Finally, the schoolboy admits the facts, accepts the principle, and agrees that, though the news originally *seemed* good to him, it was not *really* good.

Again, suppose that I am already rich, and then win £10,000 in a lottery. At first, I may excusably rejoice. But now someone may try to persuade me that I *ought not* to be so glad. He may remind me of all the shillings paid by labourers out of their wages, that went to make up my prize; he may point out that I already have as much money as I have any use for; and he may insist that the prize-money would do more good anywhere but in my bank. In the end, I may come to admit that, however pleased I was to win the prize, it was, all in all, not a good thing that I did. Though it *seemed* good to me at first, it was not *really* good. In this case, a number of 'principles' may be appealed to—for instance, the 'principles' that opportunities for satisfying people's needs should not be neglected; that no one should retain more than he needs of anything while others suffer through going without; and that one should not accept anything which has been got by unnecessary suffering.

Appeal to a 'principle' in ethics is like appeal to a 'law' in science: 'principles' and 'laws of nature' may both be thought of as shorthand summaries of experience—as condensed comparisons. If I explain the 'bending' of a stick in water by reference to the laws of optics, my purpose is to relate the present experience to past observations and experiments; the explanation in terms of 'Snell's Law' is then shorthand for, 'If you had put the stick above a bonfire, you'd have expected it to shimmer in the heated air, wouldn't you? And if. . . . And if. . . . So you see, the look of bentness in this case was to be expected.' Likewise, appeal to the 'principle' that you should not accept anything got by unnecessary suffering can be thought of as shorthand for, 'If you found out that your garden was being cultivated by a team of slaves, who were whipped until they produced all the flowers and vegetables you asked for, you wouldn't ask for them any more, would you? And if. . . . And if. . . . So you see, winning £10,000 in this lottery was nothing to be so pleased about.'

Like scientific theories again, all principles are not equally well established;

some refer to wider, some to narrower ranges of experience. There is an air of conventionality about the principle that the best cricketers shall be given their colours, which is absent from the principles involved in the second example. The principle that all promises ought to be kept may seem less compelling than the principle that unnecessary suffering ought to be prevented; but, equally, it is less conventional than the rules by which colours are distributed. We shall have to return to these differences in discussing the next stage of development.

10.4   THE DEVELOPMENT OF ETHICS (II)

In any particular community, certain principles are current—that is to say, attention is paid to certain types of argument, as appealing to accepted criteria of 'real goodness', 'real rightness', 'real obligation', etc. From these, the members of the community are expected to try and regulate their lives and judgements. And such a set of principles, of 'prima facie obligations',[1] of 'categorical imperatives',[2] is what we call the 'moral code' of the community.

At the primitive stage of development, this is something fixed and unalterable.[3] There is no room for criticism of the moral code as a whole, as there is of a particular action, expression of pleasure, or ethical judgement. However, the methods used in primitive communities to harmonise the desires and actions of their members are very crude and, although at first they may do their job, something always happens to throw doubt on them. New opportunities emerge. People discover that different principles of the code conflict. As a result of contact with other peoples having different codes, or of changes within the community, they begin to question not only the rightness of particular actions but also the standards laid down in the code. They realise that, as a result of these changes, the present code is causing frustration and suffering which, by making a specific alteration in the practices of the community, could be avoided—and avoided without incurring any comparable evil.

The same situation arises within the family, when the growing child, having learnt to accept appeal to a principle as an argument for and against actions, begins to question the need for some of the principles with which he has been brought up, and to argue that they cause needless annoyance. When this happens, he ceases to accept authority as the sole moral argument, and becomes himself a 'responsible being'.

[1] W. D. Ross, *The Right and the Good,* p. 19.
[2] Kant, op. cit. p. 37.
[3] As a matter of anthropology, this is not altogether exact: the features characteristic of my 'second phase of development' are probably present to a limited extent in all communities. The division I adopt is, however, an illuminating one; and this inaccuracy is not one which can affect the validity of the logical considerations of Chapter 11, to which we are leading up.

At this stage, there are two possible reactions: either for those in authority —those who enforce the existing 'code'—to assert its absolute rightness, and to attempt to legislate for every possibility; or for them to agree, first to criticism, and eventually to modification of the code, so as to remove its objectionable features. If the first course is adopted, the continual changes in the circumstances of the community tend only to aggravate the situation: the second course, on the other hand, represents a natural extension of the process by which moral codes themselves grow out of conflicts of interest—*i.e.* it takes account of the function of ethics.

When it is recognised that the members of a community have the right to criticise the existing practices, and to suggest new ones, a new phase in the development of ethics begins. In this phase, it is the *motives* of actions and the *results* of social practices, rather than 'the letter of the law', which are emphasised. The 'deontological'[4] code was at first supreme; the 'teleological'[5] criterion now amplifies it, and provides a standard by which to criticise it. This does not mean that morality becomes wholly teleological, as Utilitarianism[6] would suggest. All that happens is that the initially inflexible system of taboos is transformed into a *developing* moral code—a code which, in unambiguous cases, remains mandatory, but whose interpretation in equivocal cases and whose future development are controlled by appeal to the function of ethics; that is, to the general requirement that preventable suffering shall be avoided.

The contrast between the two main phases of development is strikingly reflected in the contrast between the Old and New Testaments. The moral code of the Israelites—a nomadic tribe in a hostile environment—was understandably strict; but, in the more settled atmosphere of Palestine under Roman rule, anomalies arose in this code. Jesus was therefore able to criticise contemporary ethical practices in a spirit to which the Pharisees could hardly take open exception. Whatever form their questions took, they could not get him to say that his teaching was meant to *supersede* the Law and the Prophets: in fact, whenever there was any discussion of the Jewish code, he made it clear that he took it as his starting-point. Instead, it was his aim throughout to get the existing code applied in a more intelligent manner: to point out that the prevention of human suffering is more important than formal respect for obsolete customs. Thus, when challenged in the Temple about the propriety of healing the sick on the Sabbath, he asked, 'Whether is it lawful on the

[4]"Deontological theories hold that there are ethical propositions of the form: "Such and such a kind of action would always be right (or wrong) in such and such circumstances, no matter what its consequences might be." ' (Broad, *Five Types of Ethical Theory,* p. 206.)

[5]"Teleological theories hold that the rightness or wrongness of an action is always determined by its tendency to produce certain consequences which are intrinsically good or bad.' (Broad, op. cit. p. 207.)

[6]"The doctrine that it is the duty of each to aim at the maximum happiness of all, and to subordinate everything else to this end.' (Broad, op. cit. p. 183.)

sabbath days to do good or to do evil? to save life or for to destroy it?',[7] and
went on to heal the man with a withered hand. Again, in a phrase echoed by
Kant[8] he declared, 'Whatsoever ye would that men should do to you, even so
do ye to them. This is the law and the Prophets.'[9] He was ready to criticise
the existing code, certainly; but only by reference to its function—the function
which he expressed, in his own way, as the 'New Commandment', to love one
another.

We can trace the beginnings of this new outlook further back: it is clearly
to be seen, breaking through the old, rigid morality, in the more 'advanced'
of the Greek tragedies. Contrast, for example, the approaches which different
dramatists adopted towards the same traditional stories, and the lessons which
they drew from them. Both Sophocles and Euripides wrote plays, which have
survived, using the story of Electra and Orestes as their foundation. Sophocles
produced an archaic 'drama of duty'. In his play, the central figures perform
their ritual act of vengeance—the murder of their own mother, Clytemnestra
—without emotion: 'there is no shrinking back, no question of conscience at
all.'[10] Euripides' play is in vivid contrast: it is a psychological 'drama of
motive'. After the murder, Orestes and Electra suffer 'a long agony of remorse';[11] and even the gods, through the mouth of Castor, are made to
condemn the act. For Euripides, the blood-feud has lost its absolute authority.
For Sophocles, however, old ways held good, and there could be no question
of blame.

We can now see how it is that different 'moral principles' have such different
degrees of 'conventionality'. To return to the three examples discussed before:
the 'duty' to give cricket-colours to the best cricketers, the 'duty' to keep a
promise, and the 'duty' to prevent unavoidable suffering. The reason why the
first of these appears comparatively conventional, the last comparatively compelling, is clear, when we bear in mind the overall requirement that, wherever
we can, we shall prevent suffering from being inflicted upon others. To abolish
the custom of giving cricket-colours would have a trivial effect by these standards; to abandon the social practice of promise-keeping might, by the same
standards, be expected to have intolerable results; and the third principle
cannot be rejected, without completely abandoning the very ideas of 'duty' and
of 'ethics'.

[7]Luke vi.
[8]Cf. *Fundamental Principles of the Metaphysic of Ethics* (tr. Abbott), p. 66: 'Act
always on such a maxim as thou canst at the same time will to be a universal law.'
[9]Matt. vii.
[10]Gilbert Murray, *Euripides and his Age,* p. 154.
[11]Op. cit. p. 156: the whole discussion of the contrast between Sophocles' and
Euripides' treatments of the story is well worth study (op. cit. pp. 152–7).

51

MARY MOTHERSILL (1923– ———)

Moral Knowledge

Mary Mothersill is professor of philosophy at Barnard College, Columbia University. Educated at the University of Toronto and Harvard University, she taught at Vassar College, Columbia University, the University of Connecticut, the University of Michigan, the University of Chicago, and City College of New York before joining the Barnard faculty in 1964. She is the editor of *Ethics* (1967), and has published articles on ethics and aesthetics in various philosophical journals.

In the essay that follows, Mothersill examines the arguments used by noncognitivists (emotivists and imperativists) to show that ethical utterances are not assertions and, therefore, are not capable of being true or false. Mothersill does not develop an independent argument in support of her view, which appears to be a form of naturalism. Rather, she attempts to show that the arguments against such a view are not sound. Her position appears to be that the common-sense view that moral knowledge is possible (like the view that there is a real, material world independent of our perception of it) is the starting point for everyone in this debate. In the absence of convincing arguments to the contrary, she believes it is the position we should continue to hold. This, obviously, leaves open the question of which cognitivist theory may be best supported by the relevant evidence.

To the philosophical skeptic common sense is always "naive." The skeptic is free from illusion; he sees through what others take to be simple truth. There is reasoned skepticism which commands respect and there is dogmatic skepticism which is mere affectation. It is important to distinguish the two. It was a vulgar mistake on the part of Dr. Johnson to think that by kicking a stone he had refuted Berkeley. Berkeley's analysis of the concept of material objects is developed in full cognizance of the fact that stones can be kicked and he takes great pains to show just how this fact bears on his skeptical thesis. In the present paper I am going to discuss a certain kind of moral skepticism.

From Mary Mothersill, "Moral Knowledge," *The Journal of Philosophy*, LVI (1959), pp. 755–763. Reprinted by permission of the author and the publisher.

Suppose I were to begin in a Johnsonian manner by describing a particular act which I personally know and can prove to have been wrong, and were to conclude from this that moral knowledge is really possible since in at least one case it is actual. Would it be right to say that I, too, had made a simple-minded blunder?

Let me describe the philosophers' position. Professor Frankena used the term "noncognitivist" to describe Stevenson and other so-called emotive theorists. I should like to extend it to include some other moral philosophers, for example, Hare and Nowell-Smith. Stevenson is squarely in the tradition of Hume, and thus a moral skeptic, but it would not be quite correct so to describe the others. What they share with Stevenson is the belief that the concepts of moral knowledge or moral truth are suspect and I think they would all agree that when we speak of knowing or proving moral truths we are in grave danger of being misled. To put our moral utterances in an epistemic idiom may be harmless in ordinary conversation but to take it seriously is to invite confusion. Thus the noncognitivist position is both vaguer and weaker than traditional skepticism. The common viewpoint might be expressed this way: Once we really understand the grammar of the sentence "I know that act A is wrong" we shall come to think either of the verb or of the substantive clause as enclosed in invisible quotation marks. That an act is wrong we may, so to speak, "know"; or, alternatively, we may know that an act is, as it were, "wrong." But at least one element in the phrase "knowing an act to be wrong" must be understood in a sense which is elliptical, ironic, or in some other respect atypical.

I want to argue that this rarefied skepticism is quite unwarranted and that its authors, while they have said much that is interesting about moral language, have not given us any reason for believing that when we say that we know that an act is right or wrong we are guilty of some subtle impropriety. The arguments which they do provide center around two related topics: the function of moral language and the meaning of ethical predicates. I shall consider each briefly.

The function of moral language may be treated in quasi-empirical terms or else as a question of definition. Thus simply as a matter of observation it may be remarked that debate over moral issues is likely to be more highly charged with emotion than dispute about factual questions, or that moral judgments are often pronounced for strategic reasons—e.g., with the intention of getting someone to do something. Moral language, as Hare observes, is associated with commending and is thus linked in rather complicated ways with problems of choice. Others have called attention to the fact that moral utterances, like legal verdicts, often have a ceremonial function as part of a ritual or performance. Taken informally these observations are illuminating but of course they cannot be taken strictly—that is, as assertions that moral language has some invariant characteristics. It is absurd to say that *every* moral judgment is part of a ritual or that it is said with the intention of getting someone to do something. There is the further complicating factor that the so-called "language of morals" has never been defined in such a way as would be required for systematic testing of such hypotheses. But even if this could be done and even if a great deal of evidence were collected in support of the claim, let us say, that every time someone pronounces a moral sentence (Act A is wrong) it is with a certain specified intention, the question remains: What bearing would this discovery have on the cognitive status of the sentence? Suppose I say that I know that act A is wrong. Of course I must be prepared to support this claim. Suppose that I do so by means of a simple enthymematic argument: Act A has characteristics C_1 and C_2 and is therefore wrong. There are all the ordinary possibilities of error; I may be mistaken in saying that Act A has characteristics C_1 and C_2 or there may be no reason for holding that the latter are what are called "wrong-making characteristics." In either case my claims to know would be disallowed. Suppose now that it is proved on empirical grounds that I uttered the sentence in question with a certain intention, for example, in order to get someone to do something. Would this fact in itself count as a *further* reason for saying that my claim had not been established? It seems clear that it would not. Showing that an act is wrong is like showing that a certain animal is a cat. In both cases it is necessary to know the appropriate criteria and to apply them properly. The contingent question of the speaker's intention, even if all speakers are assumed to have a single specified intention, is not relevant in either case. As long as the characterization of the language of morals is undertaken as an empirical inquiry into the intentions, desires, practical purposes for which moral sentences are used it can provide no basis for moral skepticism.

If the noncognitivist is challenged to provide evidence for his hypotheses about moral language or to show that those hypotheses if confirmed would be relevant to the question of moral truth, he can always decline combat simply by making his thesis analytic. Hare, for example, argues as follows: Moral judgments, like other value-judgments, are used for commending. Any sentence used for commending must either be an imperative or entail an imperative. Hence the sentence "Act A is wrong" must entail the imperative "Do not do A" or "Your not doing Act A, please!" If one were to object on common-sense grounds that the second premise was simply false, that there is no grammatical mood which is copyrighted for commending uses, then Hare could reply (and does so) that the sentence "Act A is wrong" is being used in an ethically significant sense only if (and this is by definition) it entails the appropriate imperative.[1] Since imperatives cannot for logical reasons be said to be true or false it would follow that when I say that "I know" that Act A is wrong and providing that I do not merely mean that it is *thought* to be wrong, I must be using the verb "know" in an odd and confusing sense. This argument and the proposal on which it is based are harmless but not very

[1] *The Language of Morals,* pp. 164 ff.

helpful. If, on a non-technical level, declarative sentences may be used for commending, why should we adopt the technical convention which transforms declaratives into commands? Hare suggests that this device will provide a means by which we shall be able to distinguish sentences which are used evaluatively or in an ethically significant sense from those that are not. But this would be true only if we had some independent criterion for distinguishing declaratives which *do* entail imperatives from those which do not. Admittedly this cannot be done in terms of the so-called ethical predicates, and if we return again to function and purpose we are arguing in a circle.

Something of the same difficulty arises for those who wish to make the ceremonial or performatory character of moral pronouncements a matter of definition. The question of how to recognize a performance or a ceremony, especially when these terms are used in an extended and quasi-technical sense, is just as baffling as the question of how to recognize a case of the special sort of entailment prescribed by Hare. In short, it is possible to define moral language in such a way that relative to the definition it is logically improper or misleading to speak of "knowing" or "proving" that an act is right. But we ought surely to require that there be some reason *other* than this for adopting the definitions proposed. As far as I can see, no other reason has been given.

This brings me back to Dr. Johnson and the stone. The fact is that the concept of moral truth (although not the term, which is slightly bookish) is very deeply embedded in our ordinary talking and thinking about moral questions. That an act is right or wrong is something which we quite naturally doubt, assume, believe, try to prove, and occasionally claim to know. This does not *feel* like an extravagant or figurative mode of speech; we do not immediately see the need for the invisible quotation marks. The question is whether the noncognitivists, like Berkeley, have taken account of and thereby forestalled objections based on our simple-minded convictions. It does not seem to me that they have. Compare their account with that of some of the traditional philosophers who have dealt with the same problem. When Plato argues the question of moral knowledge it is in the context of a complete metaphysics. Kant's distinction of pure from practical reason emerges from a radical and highly complex reconstruction of theory of knowledge in general. But contemporary noncognitivists do not concern themselves much with broad epistemological issues. Stevenson, for example, assumes that we know pretty well what is meant by agreement in belief, well enough, at any rate, to see that agreement in attitude is quite different. Hare and Nowell-Smith, in their criticisms of ethical naturalism, take it for granted that if it *were* possible to translate ethical statements into, let us say, psychological statements, then all would be clear sailing. Of course they are not unaware that there are epistemological problems outside of ethics, but they prefer, as if by mutual consent, to suspend inquiry at the more general level and to formulate ethical issues in the language of common sense. There is good precedent for this in Hume. When it comes to the question whether reason or sentiment is the foundation of morals, he does not complicate matters by introducing puzzles about perception or the rationale of induction. He is content to rely on those unsophisticated notions which he elsewhere describes as the products of carelessness and inattention. The role of reason in morals can be discussed only when we turn our attention away from the "academical" paradoxes which obscure the concept of reason in general. Contemporary noncognitivists follow Hume's example and taking as a model the *Inquiry* they adopt a style of exposition which is informal and somewhat belle-lettristic.

This program has one obvious limitation: the robust practical wisdom which restores us to the world of backgammon and sociability is as impatient with moral skepticism as with any other philosophic doubts. The mood in which we know for sure that chairs and tables are real and that the sun will rise tomorrow is the mood in which we know for sure that cruelty and deceit are wrong and that we must fulfill our obligations. This is just to say that one can't claim the advantages of common sense when it comes to scientific knowledge and at the same time claim the advantages of a superior insight when it comes to moral knowledge. To put it another way: if you want to show that it is misleading to say that one knows that an act is right or wrong, then you must provide rules more stringent than those of common sense to govern the use of "knowing."

A noncognitivist might grant this point, which is after all fairly obvious, and yet hold that it is not relevant to his position. He might say this: granting the obvious facts about usage, the philosophically interesting question is whether the analogy between "moral knowledge" and ordinary descriptive knowledge is strong or weak. But no profound epistemological researches are required in order to see that the latter is the case. Knowing that an act is right is knowing in a very different sense from knowing a fact about the world—for instance, that a certain object is yellow. And it is merely to this difference that I wish to call attention.

So far as the example goes, the noncognitivist point is well taken. If there are "different senses" in which one knows, presumably these are connected with the different ways one has of finding out or discovering or proving what is the case. And the procedures appropriate to finding out that something is yellow are clearly different from those appropriate to finding out that an act is right, or, since it is usually in reference to Moore that this example is adduced, to finding out that something is good. Indeed the difference is so obvious that it hardly needs to be mentioned. Only someone like Moore who, according to Keynes, was so unworldly as to be incapable of distinguishing love and beauty from physical objects would even have entertained such an eccentric notion. But from the fact that knowing an act to be right is not at all like knowing an object to be yellow nothing of interest follows. If, to borrow some examples from Baier, we consider such non-moral examples as knowing that a theatre has five hundred seats, knowing that Smith can run faster than Jones, or that a certain man is tall for a pygmy, we find procedures not dissimilar from those employed in showing that an act is right. Here it is not a matter of direct inspection; to establish claims to knowledge it is necessary to invoke criteria (e.g., for speed), standards (e.g., of tallness for pygmies), routines (e.g., counting seats), and there are the usual possibilities of error and the permanent possibility of criticizing and revising standards. But what the noncognitivist must do is to find some characteristic which is peculiar to moral judgments, which is relevant to the validation of cognitive claims, and which cannot be matched among statements which are agreed to be non-ethical in import. So far as I know this has not been done.

There is still the second line of argument advanced by the noncognitivist, and this is the one which follows the lines of Moore's attack on the Naturalistic Fallacy. To know or prove that an act is wrong, it is argued, requires that we have a definition of the predicate "wrong." This definition either will or will not contain related ethical predicates. If it does contain ethical predicates then it will be circular and of no use; if it does not, then it may be used in a proof but the conclusion will be "ethically irrelevant." If, for example, to be wrong is taken as equivalent to "to lead to painful consequences," then an act may be known and proved to be "wrong" by ordinary methods. But such "knowledge" is ethically insignificant. Wrong cannot be defined in "naturalistic" terms and hence there is no set of empirically discoverable characteristics from the occurrence of which we can deduce the wrongness of an act. To every such argument it is always possible to reply: I agree that act A has characteristic C_1 and C_2, but is it really wrong?

Now this argument (which here is much condensed) is partly correct and partly incorrect. Supposing that a definition must pass a substitutability test, it seems probable that no non-circular definition of any ethical predicate can be accepted. What "wrong" means is "what ought not to be done," "what contravenes a moral law," and so forth. It is also clear that anyone who was in doubt about what acts *are* wrong would not be helped in the least by being provided with such a set of equivalents. But it is not the case that a predicate which is incompletely defined cannot function in an argument. Let us agree that the characteristics of rightness or goodness are, as they have often been held to be, supervenient, that is, they are properties which are ascribed to an act or object by virtue of its possession of other properties. A complete definition would consist of a list of all the sufficient conditions and all the necessary conditions under which the ethical predicates would properly apply. There are good and non-mysterious reasons why this is impossible. But all we need for practical purposes is the specification of *some* of the sufficient conditions, that is, the acknowledgment of at least one "right-making characteristic." Once this is granted there can be, in principle, no objection to the sort of argument I have cited. "Act A has characteristics C_1 and C_2 and is therefore wrong."

It must be remarked that a lack of complete definition, if it is a disability, is not peculiar to moral reasoning. Consider the predicate "is a genius." Any definition would be likely to be eccentric or useless, but surely we would agree that if someone, for example, were to write the symphonies of Mozart or to improve on Newton (or Einstein), this would be enough to qualify him. If this seems an unfair analogy because of its evaluative elements, consider the predicates "is a living organism" or "is an artifact."

In summary: The noncognitivists believe that there is something incongruous if not downright wrong about the concept of moral knowledge. I have argued that the burden of proof rests with them and that because of their general commitment to a common-sense position on the question of knowledge in general it is difficult for them to present grounds for discriminating against moral knowledge. Those of their arguments which turn on the characterization of the language of morals are either empirical hypotheses, in which case they do not prejudice the cognitive claims of moral statements, or else definitional, in which case they beg the question at issue and to no apparent purpose. The argument based on the alleged indefinability of ethical predicates is correct with respect to its premises but the conclusion does not follow. Their contention that deductive arguments with moral statements as conclusions are "ethically uninteresting" can be maintained only on the supposition that there are no discoverable characteristics which count as sufficient reasons for saying that an act is wrong. This is a heroic though possible position. Unless they are willing to adopt it or are able to provide better arguments, their scruples about moral knowledge must be regarded as symptoms of false delicacy: their skepticism is not so much a theory as a fashionable mode of speech.

A final note: Moral knowledge, like other knowledge, has practical value; it serves as a guide to action. The relation of moral theory to moral practice is doubtless complex but it is clear that they are in some measure independent. There are people who behave well not mechanically but, as it were, instinctively; and there are those who know what is right and know why it is right but are prevented by weakness of the will, Original Sin, or neurotic disability from doing what is right. "Wisdom" is the term which signifies a conjunction of theoretical and practical excellence. The wise man or virtuous man is the one who knows how to behave, and while this entails it is not entailed by knowing what is right and wrong. What is known in the former sense cannot for logical reasons be supported by evidence or derived from premises. If one believes (as Kant appears to have believed) that the crucial factor in morality is not finding out what is right but rather steeling oneself to do what is recognized as right, then just in this respect one might reasonably urge that moral knowledge is not concerned with establishing cognitive truth. One might argue: "It is all very well to see that Act A, since it has characteristics C_1 and C_2, is wrong, but this is 'ethically uninteresting'; the important thing is to preserve one's conviction in the face of temptation and to actually refrain from doing Act A."

(Compare: "It's easy enough to see that this is a piece of uranium, a bed of poison-ivy; the question is—What are you going to do about it?")

I do not think that the noncognitivists intend to say this, but I think that some considerations of this sort may lie at the bottom of what I take to be the confusion of their arguments.

For Further Reading

Aiken, H. D. *Reason and Conduct: New Bearings in Moral Philosophy.* New York: Knopf, 1962.

Baier, Kurt. *The Moral Point of View,* abr. ed. New York: Random House, 1965 (paperbound).

Blanshard, Brand. *Reason and Goodness.* New York: Macmillan, 1961.

Brandt, R. B. "The Emotive Theory of Ethics," *The Philosophical Review,* 59 (1950), 305–318.

——————. *Ethical Theory.* Englewood Cliffs, N.J.: Prentice-Hall, 1959, Chaps. 7–11.

——————. "The Status of Empirical Assertion Theories in Ethics," *Mind,* 61 (1952), 458–479.

Carter, C. L. (ed.). *Skepticism and Moral Principles.* Evanston, Ill.: New University Press, 1973. Contains Marcus Singer's criticisms of private subjectivism, cultural relativism, and emotivism.

Edel, Abraham. *Science and the Structure of Ethics.* Chicago: University of Chicago Press, 1961 (paperbound).

Edwards, Paul. *The Logic of Moral Discourse.* New York: Free Press, 1955, Chaps. 7–9 (paperbound).

Ewing, A. C. *Second Thoughts in Moral Philosophy.* New York: Macmillan, 1959, Chaps. 1 and 2.

Falk, W. D. "Goading and Guiding," *Mind,* 62 (1953), 145–171.

Feinberg, Joel (ed.). *Moral Concepts.* New York: Oxford University Press, 1970.

Frankena, W. K. "Moral Philosophy at Mid-century," *The Philosophical Review,* 60 (1951), 44–55.

Gewirth, Alan. "Meanings and Criteria in Ethics," *Philosophy,* 38 (1963), 329–345.

Hancock, Roger. "The Refutation of Naturalism in Moore and Hare," *The Journal of Philosophy,* 57 (1960), 326–334.

Hare, R. M. *Applications of Moral Philosophy.* Berkeley: University of California Press, 1972.

——————. *Essays on the Moral Concepts.* Berkeley: University of California Press, 1972.

——————. *Freedom and Reason.* New York: Oxford University Press, 1963 (paperbound).

——————. *Practical Inferences.* Berkeley: University of California Press, 1972.

——————. *The Language of Morals.* New York: Oxford University Press, 1964 (paperbound).

Harman, G. "Moral Relativism Defended," *The Philosophical Review,* 84 (1975), 3–22. A lucid defense of cultural relativism.

Harsanyi, J. C. "Ethics in Terms of Hypothetical Imperatives," *Mind,* 67 (1958), 305–316.

Hudson, W. *Ethical Intuitionism.* New York: Macmillan, 1967. A short historical study of the intuitionist theory.

Kerner, George C. "Approvals, Reasons and Moral Argument," *Mind,* 71 (1962), 474–486.

——————. *The Revolution in Ethical Theory.* Oxford: Clarendon Press, 1966.

Ladd, John (ed.). *Ethical Relativism.* Belmont, Calif.: Wadsworth, 1973.

Mill, John Stuart. *Utilitarianism.* Indianapolis, Ind.: Liberal Arts Press, 1960 (paperbound).

Monro, D. H. *Empiricism and Ethics.* London: Cambridge University Press, 1967. Defends a subjectivist view.

Nielsen, K. "Does Ethical Subjectivism Have a Coherent Form?" *Philosophy and Phenomenological Research,* 35 (1974–1975), 93–99. Argues that it is not clear what it means to say that one is a "subjectivist" or an "objectivist" in ethics.

Nowell-Smith, P. H. *Ethics.* Baltimore, Md.: Penguin Books, 1954.

Perry, R. B. *General Theory of Value.* Cambridge, Mass.: Harvard University Press, 1926.

Prichard, H. A. *Moral Obligation.* New York: Oxford University Press, 1949, Chaps. 1, 2, and 5.

Prior, A. N. *Logic and the Basis of Ethics.* New York: Oxford University Press, 1949.

Raphael, D. Daiches. *Moral Judgment.* New York: Hillary House, 1955, Chaps. 4, 7, and 8.

——————. *The Moral Sense.* New York: Oxford University Press, 1947.

Ross, W. D. *Foundations of Ethics.* New York: Oxford University Press, 1939, Chaps. 2, 3, and 11.

——————. *The Right and the Good.* New York: Oxford Univeristy Press, 1930, Chap. 2.

Sedgwick, Henry. *The Methods of Ethics,* 7th ed., rev. by Constance Jones. Chicago: University of Chicago Press, 1962, Chaps. 3, 8, and 9.

Singer, M. G. *Generalization in Ethics.* New York: Knopf, 1961.

Smart, J. J. C., and Bernard Williams. *Utilitarianism: For and Against.* New York: Cambridge University Press, 1973. A debate between the two authors.

Stevenson, C. L. *Ethics and Language.* New Haven, Conn.: Yale University Press, 1960, Chaps. 1, 2, and 4–6 (paperbound).

Stroll, A. *The Emotive Theory of Ethics.* Berkeley and Los Angeles: University of California Press, 1954.

Swinburne, R. G. "The Objectivity of Morality," *Philosophy,* 51 (1976), 5–20.

Taylor, Paul W. *Normative Discourse.* Englewood Cliffs, N.J.: Prentice-Hall, 1961.

Urmson, J. O. *The Emotive Theory of Ethics.* London: Hutchinson's University Library, 1968.

Veatch, Henry B. *For an Ontology of Morals: A Critique of Contemporary Ethical Theory.* Evanston, Ill.: Northwestern University Press, 1971. From a Thomist background.

Warnock, G. J. *Contemporary Moral Philosophy.* New York: St. Martin's Press, 1967. See also a critical review of Warnock's book by R. M. Hare in *Mind,* 77 (1968), 436–440.

Wellman, Carl. *Challenge and Response: Justification in Ethics.* Carbondale, Ill.: Southern Illinois University Press, 1971.

——————. *The Language of Ethics.* Cambridge, Mass.: Harvard University Press, 1961.

PART XII

Aesthetic Judgment

In this section, we turn our attention to the fine arts, both the visual arts and the performing arts. The visual arts include painting, sculpture, architecture, photography, printmaking—all art forms that attempt to create static (unchanging) objects whose principal value is aesthetic. The performing arts, as the name implies, are those art forms whose end product is a "performance" of some sort, such as music, drama, and dance.

The question that we will focus on is this: Is there, or is there not, an objective basis for asserting that some works of art are better than others? For example, is the statement "The music of Mozart is superior to that of Michael Haydn" (a contemporary of Mozart) capable of being true or false, or is it not? Exactly what are we saying when we say of a work of art that it is good, or fair, or poor?

According to one widely held theory, statements evaluating a work of art are simply expressions of the private preferences or tastes of the individuals making the statements. This is *subjectivism*. "You like Bach, I like the Beatles; you have your tastes and I have mine." According to this theory, statements about aesthetic value cannot be true or false except in the odd sense that someone might dislike a work of art that, for some reason, he or she calls good. There are no qualities objectively present in the work of art that give it aesthetic value: its aesthetic value consists merely in the fact that somebody likes it.

Although this is a commonly expressed theory, it raises some puzzling questions. Is it not possible to argue about the relative merits of various works of art? If so, does this not imply that there are some objective facts to argue about? If not, what exactly are art and music critics writing about in their articles and books? Is there no objective difference *in aesthetic value* between the paintings of Rembrandt and those of the child next door? And if not, why do museums pay millions of dollars for one and not the other?

Such puzzles can be readily solved if one adopts a theory known as *intuitionism*—an objectivist theory. According to this theory, a work of art has aesthetic value to the extent that it embodies beauty. And what is beauty? Intuitionists believe that it is a nonempirical quality that is sometimes present (in varying degrees) in such diverse objects as paintings, symphonies, and sunsets. Disputes about aesthetic value, on this view, are disagreements about the correct answer to an allegedly factual question: Is the quality of beauty present in this object, or is it not? This is what gives point and substance to the writings of the critics. This is what makes reasonable the decision of the directors of a museum to spend millions for a Rembrandt. And this, according to the theory, is why arguments about Bach and the Beatles are different from arguments about the relative merits of chocolate eclairs and peppermint ice cream.

But the objectivist theory gives rise to other puzzles. If beauty is in the object—in the painting, in the music—why can we not *see* it or *hear* it? And if we cannot see it or hear it, how are we supposed to know that it is there? Again, if two people disagree about whether or not a given object is beautiful, how can such a dispute be resolved? Is it not the same, after all, as if they were disagreeing about a matter of taste?

These and other difficulties have led some philosophers to look for a solution to this problem that lies somewhere between subjectivism and intuitionism. One such position that has won a number of adherents in recent years is a theory known as *objective relativism*. According to this theory, while it is the presence or absence of certain empirical qualities in an object that determines whether or not that object has aesthetic value, the tendency of human beings to prefer certain qualities to others (the music of Mozart to a series of random sounds, for example) is a result of the psychological and physiological makeup common to human beings. The qualities that we praise in Mozart—his sprightly melodies, his rhythmic variety, his imaginative harmonies, his fecundity in developing thematic materials, and so on—are objectively present in his music, but we admire these particular qualities, rather than some other qualities, because we are the way we are. Our opinions as to what constitutes beauty are relative to the psychological and physiological makeup of the human species. It is possible, according to this theory, to have poor taste or good taste with respect to the fine arts, but it is not possible to demonstrate conclusively which is which. The music of Bach may *be* objectively superior to that of the Beatles, or vice versa. But it is not possible to prove the superiority of either, since the proposition that such and such qualities are most suitably admired by human beings is not

capable of strict proof. Accordingly, the closest one can come to
establishing the aesthetic value of any work of art is to achieve a
consensus (or at least a majority opinion) among those who are interested
in works of art of this particular kind. Those who share the consensus or
majority view are then said to have "cultivated taste."

52

PLOTINUS (204–270)

The Essence of Beauty

Plotinus has been called "the last great philosopher of antiquity." A student of Plato,
Plotinus attributed the central ideas of his own philosophy to his great predecessor.
His own bent, however, was highly mystical, and he can be described as a philosophical mystic. What emerges from this union of Platonism and mysticism is a highly
original synthesis that was, for many years, more influential than was Platonism itself
(largely because of St. Augustine, who was profoundly influenced by the writings of
Plotinus).

Today, Plotinus would be called an *intuitionist* with respect to aesthetics. According to Plotinus, beautiful things are beautiful by virtue of their participation in beauty.
What, then, is beauty? "What . . . is this something that shows itself in certain material
forms?" It is an eternal and unchanging reality, "something which the Soul names as
from an ancient knowledge and, recognizing, welcomes it, enters into unison with it."
The soul, in short, has a natural affinity for beauty and, thus, is able to recognize beauty
whenever it appears, albeit only partially and imperfectly, in objects. To say "This
object is beautiful" is to judge that beauty is present in this object; and since the soul
knows beauty, such judgments presumably cannot be wrong.

From Plotinus, *The Enneads*, First Ennead, Tractate VI, Sections 1–3, in *The Enneads*, 3rd
ed., trans. Stephen Mackenna (New York: Pantheon Books, 1957), pp. 56–59. Reprinted by
permission of Pantheon Books, a Division of Random House, Inc.

1. Beauty addresses itself chiefly to sight; but there is a beauty for the hearing too, as in certain combinations of words and in all kinds of music, for melodies and cadences are beautiful; and minds that lift themselves above the realm of sense to a higher order are aware of beauty in the conduct of life, in actions, in character, in the pursuits of the intellect; and there is the beauty of the virtues. What loftier beauty there may be, yet, our argument will bring to light.

What, then, is it that gives comeliness to material forms and draws the ear to the sweetness perceived in sounds, and what is the secret of the beauty there is in all that derives from Soul?

Is there some One Principle from which all take their grace, or is there a beauty peculiar to the embodied and another for the bodiless? Finally, one or many, what would such a Principle be?

Consider that some things, material shapes for instance, are gracious not by anything inherent but by something communicated, while others are lovely of themselves, as, for example, Virtue.

The same bodies appear sometimes beautiful, sometimes not; so that there is a good deal between being body and being beautiful.

What, then, is this something that shows itself in certain material forms? This is the natural beginning of our inquiry.

What is it that attracts the eyes of those to whom a beautiful object is presented, and calls them, lures them, towards it, and fills them with joy at the sight? If we possess ourselves of this, we have at once a standpoint for the wider survey.

Almost everyone declares that the symmetry of parts towards each other and towards a whole, with, besides, a certain charm of colour, constitutes the beauty recognized by the eye, that in visible things, as indeed in all else, universally, the beautiful thing is essentially symmetrical, patterned.

But think what this means.

Only a compound can be beautiful, never anything devoid of parts; and only a whole; the several parts will have beauty, not in themselves, but only as working together to give a comely total. Yet beauty in an aggregate demands beauty in details: it cannot be constructed out of ugliness; its law must run throughout.

All the loveliness of colour and even the light of the sun, being devoid of parts and so not beautiful by symmetry, must be ruled out of the realm of beauty. And how comes gold to be a beautiful thing? And lightning by night, and the stars, why are these so fair?

In sounds also the simple must be proscribed, though often in a whole noble composition each several tone is delicious in itself.

Again since the one face, constant in symmetry, appears sometimes fair and sometimes not, can we doubt that beauty is something more than symmetry, that symmetry itself owes its beauty to a remoter principle?

Turn to what is attractive in methods of life or in the expression of thought;

are we to call in symmetry here? What symmetry is to be found in noble conduct, or excellent laws, in any form of mental pursuit?

What symmetry can there be in points of abstract thought?

The symmetry of being accordant with each other? But there may be accordance or entire identity where there is nothing but ugliness: the proposition that honesty is merely a generous artlessness chimes in the most perfect harmony with the proposition that morality means weakness of will; the accordance is complete.

Then again, all the virtues are a beauty of the Soul, a beauty authentic beyond any of these others; but how does symmetry enter here? The Soul, it is true, is not a simple unity, but still its virtue cannot have the symmetry of size or of number: what standard of measurement could preside over the compromise or the coalescence of the Soul's faculties or purposes?

Finally, how by this theory would there be beauty in the Intellectual-Principle, essentially the solitary?

2. Let us, then, go back to the source, and indicate at once the Principle that bestows beauty on material things.

Undoubtedly this Principle exists; it is something that is perceived at the first glance, something which the Soul names as from an ancient knowledge and, recognizing, welcomes it, enters into unison with it.

But let the Soul fall in with the Ugly and at once it shrinks within itself, denies the thing, turns away from it, not accordant, resenting it.

Our interpretation is that the Soul—by the very truth of its nature, by its affiliation to the noblest Existents in the hierarchy of Being—when it sees anything of that kin, or any trace of that kinship, thrills with an immediate delight, takes its own to itself, and thus stirs anew to the sense of its nature and of all its affinity.

But, is there any such likeness between the loveliness of this world and the splendours in the Supreme? Such a likeness in the particulars would make the two orders alike: but what is there in common between beauty here and beauty There?

We hold that all the loveliness of this world comes by communion in Ideal-Form.

All shapelessness whose kind admits of pattern and form, as long as it remains outside of Reason and Idea, is ugly by that very isolation from the Divine-Thought. And this is the Absolute Ugly: an ugly thing is something that has not been entirely mastered by pattern, that is by Reason, the Matter not yielding at all points and in all respects to Ideal-Form.

But where the Ideal-Form has entered, it has grouped and coordinated what from a diversity of parts was to become a unity: it has rallied confusion into co-operation: it has made the sum one harmonious coherence: for the Idea is a unity and what it moulds must come to unity as far as multiplicity may.

And on what has thus been compacted to unity, Beauty enthrones itself, giving itself to the parts as to the sum: when it lights on some natural unity, a thing of like parts, then it gives itself to that whole. Thus, for an illustration, there is the beauty, conferred by craftsmanship, of a house with all its parts, and the beauty which some natural quality may give to a single stone.

This, then, is how the material thing becomes beautiful—by communicating in the thought that flows from the Divine.

3. And the Soul includes a faculty peculiarly addressed to Beauty—one incomparably sure in the appreciation of its own, when Soul entire is enlisted to support its judgement.

Or perhaps the Soul itself acts immediately, affirming the Beautiful where it finds something accordant with the Ideal-Form within itself, using this Idea as a canon of accuracy in its decision.

But what accordance is there between the material and that which antedates all Matter?

On what principle does the architect, when he finds the house standing before him correspondent with his inner ideal of a house, pronounce it beautiful? Is it not that the house before him, the stones apart, is the inner idea stamped upon the mass of exterior matter, the indivisible exhibited in diversity?

So with the perceptive faculty: discerning in certain objects the Ideal-Form which has bound and controlled shapeless matter, opposed in nature to Idea, seeing further stamped upon the common shapes some shape excellent above the common, it gathers into unity what still remains fragmentary, catches it up and carries it within, no longer a thing of parts, and presents it to the Ideal-Principle as something concordant and congenial, a natural friend: the joy here is like that of a good man who discerns in a youth the early signs of a virtue consonant with the achieved perfection within his own soul.

The beauty of colour is also the outcome of a unification: it derives from shape, from the conquest of the darkness inherent in Matter by the pouring-in of light, the unembodied, which is a Rational-Principle and an Ideal-Form.

Hence it is that Fire itself is splendid beyond all material bodies, holding the rank of Ideal-Principle to the other elements, making ever upwards, the subtlest and sprightliest of all bodies, as very near to the unembodied; itself alone admitting no other, all the others penetrated by it: for they take warmth but this is never cold; it has colour primally; they receive the Form of colour from it: hence the splendour of its light, the splendour that belongs to the Idea. And all that has resisted and is but uncertainly held by its light remains outside of beauty, as not having absorbed the plenitude of the Form of colour.

And harmonies unheard in sound create the harmonies we hear and wake the Soul to the consciousness of beauty, showing it the one essence in another kind: for the measures of our sensible music are not arbitrary but are determined by the Principle whose labour is to dominate Matter and bring pattern into being.

Thus far of the beauties of the realm of sense, images and shadow-pictures, fugitives that have entered into Matter—to adorn, and to ravish, where they are seen.

53

GEORGE SANTAYANA (1863–1952)

The Nature of Beauty

Although he was born in Spain and lived for the last forty years of his life in Italy, George Santayana is usually considered an American philosopher because of his long association with Harvard University. He wrote many books, including *The Sense of Beauty* (1896) and *The Life of Reason* (1905–1906). In a four-volume work entitled *The Realms of Being* (1927–1940), he gathers up his various philosophical views into an all-inclusive philosophical system.

Santayana was an articulate spokesman for *subjectivism* in aesthetics. Beauty, he argues, is a particular kind of pleasure that we, nonetheless, regard as a quality of a thing. It is an objectified emotion: the pleasure we experience in perceiving the object is projected onto the object as the cause of that pleasurable sensation.

. . .

7. We have now separated with some care intellectual and moral judgments from the sphere of our subject, and found that we are to deal only with perceptions of value, and with these only when they are positive and immediate. But even with these distinctions the most remarkable characteristic of the sense of beauty remains undefined. All pleasures are intrinsic and positive

From George Santayana, *The Sense of Beauty,* Part I, Sections 7–11 (New York: Charles Scribner's, 1901), pp. 35–52.

values, but all pleasures are not perceptions of beauty. Pleasure is indeed the essence of that perception, but there is evidently in this particular pleasure a complication which is not present in others and which is the basis of the distinction made by consciousness and language between it and the rest. It will be instructive to notice the degrees of this difference.

The bodily pleasures are those least resembling perceptions of beauty. By bodily pleasures we mean, of course, more than pleasures with a bodily seat; for that class would include them all, as well as all forms and elements of consciousness. Aesthetic pleasures have physical conditions, they depend on the activity of the eye and the ear, of the memory and the other ideational functions of the brain. But we do not connect those pleasures with their seats except in physiological studies; the ideas with which æsthetic pleasures are associated are not the ideas of their bodily causes. The pleasures we call physical, and regard as low, on the contrary, are those which call our attention to some part of our own body, and which make no object so conspicuous to us as the organ in which they arise.

There is here, then, a very marked distinction between physical and æsthetic pleasure; the organs of the latter must be transparent, they must not intercept our attention, but carry it directly to some external object. The greater dignity and range of æsthetic pleasure is thus made very intelligible. The soul is glad, as it were, to forget its connexion with the body and to fancy that it can travel over the world with the liberty with which it changes the objects of its thought. The mind passes from China to Peru without any conscious change in the local tensions of the body. This illusion of disembodiment is very exhilarating, while immersion in the flesh and confinement to some organ gives a tone of grossness and selfishness to our consciousness. The generally meaner associations of physical pleasures also help to explain their comparative crudity.

8. The distinction between pleasure and the sense of beauty has sometimes been said to consist in the unselfishness of æsthetic satisfaction. In other pleasures, it is said, we gratify our senses and passions; in the contemplation of beauty we are raised above ourselves, the passions are silenced and we are happy in the recognition of a good that we do not seek to possess. The painter does not look at a spring of water with the eyes of a thirsty man, nor at a beautiful woman with those of a satyr. The difference lies, it is urged, in the impersonality of the enjoyment. But this distinction is one of intensity and delicacy, not of nature, and it seems satisfactory only to the least æsthetic minds.

In the second place, the supposed disinterestedness of æsthetic delights is not truly fundamental. Appreciation of a picture is not identical with the desire to buy it, but it is, or ought to be, closely related and preliminary to that desire. The beauties of nature and of the plastic arts are not consumed by being enjoyed; they retain all the efficacy to impress a second beholder. But this circumstance is accidental, and those æsthetic objects which depend upon change and are exhausted in time, as are all performances, are things the enjoyment of which is an object of rivalry and is coveted as much as any other pleasure. And even plastic beauties can often not be enjoyed except by a few, on account of the necessity of travel or other difficulties of access, and then this æsthetic enjoyment is as selfishly pursued as the rest.

The truth which the theory is trying to state seems rather to be that when we seek æsthetic pleasures we have no further pleasure in mind; that we do not mix up the satisfactions of vanity and proprietorship with the delight of contemplation. This is true, but it is true at bottom of all pursuits and enjoyments. Every real pleasure is in one sense disinterested. It is not sought with ulterior motives, and what fills the mind is no calculation, but the image of an object or event, suffused with emotion.

. . .

9. The supposed disinterestedness of our love of beauty passes into another characteristic of it often regarded as essential,—its universality. The pleasures of the senses have, it is said, no dogmatism in them; that anything gives me pleasure involves no assertion about its capacity to give pleasure to another. But when I judge a thing to be beautiful, my judgment means that the thing is beautiful in itself, or (what is the same thing more critically expressed) that it should seem so to everybody. The claim to universality is, according to this doctrine, the essence of the æsthetic; what makes the perception of beauty a judgment rather than a sensation. All æsthetic precepts would be impossible, and all criticism arbitrary and subjective, unless we admit a paradoxical universality in our judgment, the philosophical implications of which we may then go on to develop. But we are fortunately not required to enter the labyrinth into which this method leads; there is a much simpler and clearer way of studying such questions, which is to challenge and analyze the assertion before us and seek its basis in human nature. Before this is done, we should run the risk of expanding a natural misconception or inaccuracy of thought into an inveterate and pernicious prejudice by making it the centre of an elaborate construction.

That the claim of universality is such a natural inaccuracy will not be hard to show. There is notoriously no great agreement upon æsthetic matters; and such agreement as there is, is based upon similarity of origin, nature, and circumstance among men, a similarity which, where it exists, tends to bring about identity in all judgments and feelings. It is unmeaning to say that what is beautiful to one man *ought* to be beautiful to another. If their senses are the same, their associations and dispositions similar, then the same thing will certainly be beautiful to both. If their natures are different, the form which to one will be entrancing will be to another even invisible, because his classifications and discriminations in perception will be different, and he may see a hideous detached fragment or a shapeless aggregate of things, in what to another is a perfect whole—so entirely are the unities of objects unities of function and use. It is absurd to say that what is invisible to a given being *ought* to seem beautiful to him. Evidently this obligation of recognizing the same qualities is conditioned by the possession of the same faculties. But no two men have exactly the same faculties, nor can things have for any two exactly the same values.

What is loosely expressed by saying that any one ought to see this or that beauty is that he would see it if his disposition, training, or attention were what our ideal demands for him; and our ideal of what any one should be has complex but discoverable sources. We take, for instance, a certain pleasure in having our own judgments supported by those of others; we are intolerant, if not of the existence of a nature different from our own, at least of its expression in words and judgments. We are confirmed or made happy in our doubtful opinions by seeing them accepted universally. We are unable to find the basis of our taste in our own experience and therefore refuse to look for it there. If we were sure of our ground, we should be willing to acquiesce in the naturally different feelings and ways of others, as a man who is conscious of speaking his language with the accent of the capital confesses its arbitrariness with gayety, and is pleased and interested in the variations of it he observes in provincials; but the provincial is always zealous to show that he has reason and ancient authority to justify his oddities. So people who have no sensations, and do not know why they judge, are always trying to show that they judge by universal reason.

Thus the frailty and superficiality of our own judgments cannot brook contradiction. We abhor another man's doubt when we cannot tell him why we ourselves believe. Our ideal of other men tends therefore to include the agreement of their judgments with our own; and although we might acknowledge the fatuity of this demand in regard to natures very different from the human, we may be unreasonable enough to require that all races should admire the same style of architecture, and all ages the same poets.

The great actual unity of human taste within the range of conventional history helps the pretension. But in principle it is untenable. Nothing has less to do with the real merit of a work of imagination than the capacity of all men to appreciate it; the true test is the degree and kind of satisfaction it can give to him who appreciates it most. The symphony would lose nothing if half mankind had always been deaf, as nine-tenths of them actually are to the intricacies of its harmonies; but it would have lost much if no Beethoven had existed. And more: incapacity to appreciate certain types of beauty may be the condition *sine qua non* for the appreciation of another kind; the greatest capacity both for enjoyment and creation is highly specialized and exclusive, and hence the greatest ages of art have often been strangely intolerant.

The invectives of one school against another, perverse as they are philosophically, are artistically often signs of health, because they indicate a vital appre-

ciation of certain kinds of beauty, a love of them that has grown into a jealous
passion. The architects that have pieced out the imperfections of ancient
buildings with their own thoughts, like Charles V. when he raised his massive
palace beside the Alhambra, may be condemned from a certain point of view.
They marred much by their interference; but they showed a splendid confidence in their own intuitions, a proud assertion of their own taste, which is
the greatest evidence of æsthetic sincerity. On the contrary, our own gropings,
eclecticism, and archæology are the symptoms of impotence. If we were less
learned and less just, we might be more efficient. If our appreciation were less
general, it might be more real, and if we trained our imagination into exclusive-
ness, it might attain to character.

10. There is, however, something more in the claim to universality in æsthetic
judgments than the desire to generalize our own opinions. There is the expression of a curious but well-known psychological phenomenon, viz., the transformation of an element of sensation into the quality of a thing. If we say that
other men should see the beauties we see, it is because we think those beauties
are in the object, like its colour, proportion, or size. Our judgment appears to
us merely the perception and discovery of an external existence, of the real
excellence that is without. But this notion is radically absurd and contradic-
tory. Beauty, as we have seen, is a value; it cannot be conceived as an independent existence which affects our senses and which we consequently perceive.
It exists in perception, and cannot exist otherwise. A beauty not perceived is
a pleasure not felt, and a contradiction. But modern philosophy has taught us
to say the same thing of every element of the perceived world; all are sensations; and their grouping into objects imagined to be permanent and external
is the work of certain habits of our intelligence. We should be incapable of
surveying or retaining the diffused experiences of life, unless we organized and
classified them, and out of the chaos of impressions framed the world of
conventional and recognizable objects.

How this is done is explained by the current theories of perception. External
objects usually affect various senses at once, the impressions of which are
thereby associated. Repeated experiences of one object are also associated on
account of their similarity; hence a double tendency to merge and unify into
a single percept, to which a name is attached, the group of those memories and
reactions which in fact had one external thing for their cause. But this percept,
once formed, is clearly different from those particular experiences out of which
it grew. It is permanent, they are variable. They are but partial views and
glimpses of it. The constituted notion therefore comes to be the reality, and
the materials of it merely the appearance. The distinction between substance
and quality, reality and appearance, matter and mind, has no other origin.

The objects thus conceived and distinguished from our ideas of them, are
at first compacted of all the impressions, feelings, and memories, which offer
themselves for association and fall within the vortex of the amalgamating

imagination. Every sensation we get from a thing is originally treated as one of its qualities. Experiment, however, and the practical need of a simpler conception of the structure of objects lead us gradually to reduce the qualities of the object to a minimum, and to regard most perceptions as an effect of those few qualities upon us. These few primary qualities, like extension which we persist in treating as independently real and as the quality of a substance, are those which suffice to explain the order of our experiences. All the rest, like colour, are relegated to the subjective sphere, as merely effects upon our minds, and apparent or secondary qualities of the object.

But this distinction has only a practical justification. Convenience and economy of thought alone determine what combination of our sensations we shall continue to objectify and treat as the cause of the rest. The right and tendency to be objective is equal in all, since they are all prior to the artifice of thought by which we separate the concept from its materials, the thing from our experiences.

The qualities which we now conceive to belong to real objects are for the most part images of sight and touch. One of the first classes of effects to be treated as secondary were naturally pleasures and pains, since it could commonly conduce very little to intelligent and successful action to conceive our pleasures and pains as resident in objects. But emotions are essentially capable of objectification, as well as impressions of sense; and one may well believe that a primitive and inexperienced consciousness would rather people the world with ghosts of its own terrors and passions than with projections of those luminous and mathematical concepts which as yet it could hardly have formed.

This animistic and mythological habit of thought still holds its own at the confines of knowledge, where mechanical explanations are not found. In ourselves, where nearness makes observation difficult, in the intricate chaos of animal and human life, we still appeal to the efficacy of will and ideas, as also in the remote night of cosmic and religious problems. But in all the intermediate realm of vulgar day, where mechanical science has made progress, the inclusion of emotional or passionate elements in the concept of the reality would be now an extravagance. Here our idea of things is composed exclusively of perceptual elements, of the ideas of form and of motion.

The beauty of objects, however, forms an exception to this rule. Beauty is an emotional element, a pleasure of ours, which nevertheless we regard as a quality of things. But we are now prepared to understand the nature of this exception. It is the survival of a tendency originally universal to make every effect of a thing upon us a constituent of its conceived nature. The scientific idea of a thing is a great abstraction from the mass of perceptions and reactions which that thing produces; the æsthetic idea is less abstract, since it retains the emotional reaction, the pleasure of the perception, as an integral part of the conceived thing.

Nor is it hard to find the ground of this survival in the sense of beauty of an objectification of feeling elsewhere extinct. Most of the pleasures which objects cause are easily distinguished and separated from the perception of the object: the object has to be applied to a particular organ, like the palate, or swallowed like wine, or used and operated upon in some way before the pleasure arises. The cohesion is therefore slight between the pleasure and the other associated elements of sense; the pleasure is separated in time from the perception, or it is localized in a different organ, and consequently is at once recognized as an effect and not as a quality of the object. But when the process of perception itself is pleasant, as it may easily be, when the intellectual operation, by which the elements of sense are associated and projected, and the concept of the form and substance of the thing produced, is naturally delightful, then we have a pleasure intimately bound up in the thing, inseparable from its character and constitution, the seat of which in us is the same as the seat of the perception. We naturally fail, under these circumstances, to separate the pleasure from the other objectified feelings. It becomes, like them, a quality of the object, which we distinguish from pleasures not so incorporated in the perception of things, by giving it the name of beauty.

11. We have now reached our definition of beauty, which, in the terms of our successive analysis and narrowing of the conception, is value positive, intrinsic, and objectified. Or, in less technical language, Beauty is pleasure regarded as the quality of a thing.

This definition is intended to sum up a variety of distinctions and identifications which should perhaps be here more explicitly set down. Beauty is a value, that is, it is not a perception of a matter of fact or of a relation: it is an emotion, an affection of our volitional and appreciative nature. An object cannot be beautiful if it can give pleasure to nobody: a beauty to which all men were forever indifferent is a contradiction in terms.

In the second place, this value is positive, it is the sense of the presence of something good, or (in the case of ugliness) of its absence. It is never the perception of a positive evil, it is never a negative value. That we are endowed with the sense of beauty is a pure gain which brings no evil with it. When the ugly ceases to be amusing or merely uninteresting and becomes disgusting, it becomes indeed a positive evil: but a moral and practical, not an æsthetic one. In æsthetics that saying is true—often so disingenuous in ethics—that evil is nothing but the absence of good: for even the tedium and vulgarity of an existence without beauty is not itself ugly so much as lamentable and degrading. The absence of æsthetic goods is a moral evil: the æsthetic evil is merely relative, and means less of æsthetic good than was expected at the place and time. No form in itself gives pain, although some forms give pain by causing a shock of surprise even when they are really beautiful: as if a mother found a fine bull pup in her child's cradle, when her pain would not be æsthetic in its nature.

Further, this pleasure must not be in the consequence of the utility of the object or event, but in its immediate perception; in other words, beauty is an ultimate good, something that gives satisfaction to a natural function, to some fundamental need or capacity of our minds. Beauty is therefore a positive value that is intrinsic; it is a pleasure. These two circumstances sufficiently separate the sphere of æsthetics from that of ethics. Moral values are generally negative, and always remote. Morality has to do with the avoidance of evil and the pursuit of good: æsthetics only with enjoyment.

Finally, the pleasures of sense are distinguished from the perception of beauty, as sensation in general is distinguished from perception; by the objectification of the elements and their appearance as qualities rather of things than of consciousness. The passage from sensation to perception is gradual, and the path may be sometimes retraced: so it is with beauty and the pleasures of sensation. There is no sharp line between them, but it depends upon the degree of objectivity my feeling has attained at the moment whether I say "It pleases me," or "It is beautiful." If I am self-conscious and critical, I shall probably use one phrase; if I am impulsive and susceptible, the other. The more remote, interwoven, and inextricable the pleasure is, the more objective it will appear; and the union of two pleasures often makes one beauty. In Shakespeare's LIVth sonnet are these words:

> O how much more doth beauty beauteous seem
> By that sweet ornament which truth doth give!
> The rose looks fair, but fairer we it deem
> For that sweet odour which doth in it live.
> The canker-blooms have full as deep a dye
> As the perfumed tincture of the roses,
> Hang on such thorns, and play as wantonly
> When summer's breath their maskèd buds discloses.
> But, for their beauty only is their show,
> They live unwooed and unrespected fade;
> Die to themselves. Sweet roses do not so:
> Of their sweet deaths are sweetest odours made.

One added ornament, we see, turns the deep dye, which was but show and mere sensation before, into an element of beauty and reality; and as truth is here the co-operation of perceptions, so beauty is the co-operation of pleasures. If colour, form, and motion are hardly beautiful without the sweetness of the odour, how much more necessary would they be for the sweetness itself to become a beauty! If we had the perfume in a flask, no one would think of calling it beautiful: it would give us too detached and controllable a sensation. There would be no object in which it could be easily incorporated. But let it float from the garden, and it will add another sensuous charm to objects simultaneously recognized, and help to make them beautiful. Thus beauty is constituted by the objectification of pleasure. It is pleasure objectified.

54

MONROE BEARDSLEY (1915– ————)

Can We Dispute About Tastes?

Monroe Beardsley is a contemporary American philosopher who has taught at Yale University, Mt. Holyoke College, and Swarthmore College, and is currently on the faculty at Temple University. Throughout his career, he has been especially interested in aesthetics and has authored both books and articles dealing with aesthetic problems. Among his books are *Aesthetics: Problems in the Philosophy of Criticism* (1958), *Aesthetics from Classical Greece to the Present* (1966), and *The Possibility of Criticism* (1970).

The following essay examines the assertion that we cannot dispute about—that is, cannot have *arguable* disagreements about—matters of taste. If we can have arguable disagreements about art, it would then follow that aesthetic preferences are not just matters of taste. Beardsley claims that we can and do have such disagreements about art; therefore, subjectivism ("aesthetic skepticism") must be mistaken.

Beardsley does not explicitly offer a replacement for the subjectivism that he rejects. He appears to be searching for that elusive middle ground between the transcendental objectivism of Plotinus and the complete subjectivism of Santayana—a position that will *justify* the claim that some people have better taste than others, that some people are *"qualified* readers, listeners, or viewers" whereas others are not. His essay should be read, therefore, as a move toward objective relativism, not as a fully developed formulation of that position.

We are assured by an old and often-quoted maxim, whose authority is not diminished by its being cast in Latin, that there can be no disputing about tastes. The chief use of this maxim is in putting an end to disputes that last a long time and don't appear to be getting anywhere. And for this purpose it is very efficacious, for it has an air of profound finality, and it also seems to provide a democratic compromise of a deadlocked issue. If you can't convince someone that he is wrong, or bring yourself to admit that he is right, you can

From Monroe C. Beardsley, "Can We Dispute About Tastes?" *Swarthmore College Bulletin,* LVI (October 1958), pp. 1–5. Reprinted by permission of the author and the publisher.

always say that neither of you is more wrong than the other, because nobody can be right.

Remarks that serve to close some people's debates, however, are quite often just the remarks to start a new one among philosophers. And this maxim is no exception. It has been given a great deal of thought, some of it very illuminating; yet there is still something to be learned from further reflection upon it. Nor is it of small importance to know, if we can, whether the maxim is true or false, for if it is true we won't waste time in futile discussion, and if it is false we won't waste opportunities for fruitful discussion.

The question whether tastes are disputable is one to be approached with wariness. The first thing is to be clear about what it really means. There are two key words in it that we should pay particular attention to.

The first is the word "taste." The maxim is perhaps most readily and least doubtfully applied to taste in its primary sensory meaning: some people like ripe olives, some green; some people like turnips, others cannot abide them; some people will go long distances for pizza pies, others can hardly choke them down. And there are no disputes about olives: we don't find two schools of thought, the Ripe Olive School and the Green Olive School, publishing quarterly journals or demanding equal time on television—probably because there simply isn't much you can say about the relative merits of these comestibles.

But we apply the word "taste," of course, more broadly. We speak of a person's taste in hats and neckties; we speak of his taste in poetry and painting and music. And it is here that the *non disputandum* maxim is most significantly applied. Some people like Auden and others Swinburne, some enjoy the paintings of Jackson Pollock and others avoid them when they can, some people are panting to hear Shostakovitch's latest symphony and others find no music since Haydn really satisfying. In these cases, unlike the olive case, people are generally not at a loss for words: there is plenty you can say about Shostakovitch, pro or con. They talk, all right; they may praise, deplore, threaten, cajole, wheedle, and scream—but, according to the maxim, they do not really dispute.

This brings us, then, to the second key word. What does it mean to say that we cannot *dispute* about tastes in literature, fine arts, and music, even though we can clearly make known our tastes? It certainly doesn't mean that we cannot disagree, or differ in taste: for obviously we do, and not only we but also the acknowledged or supposed experts in these fields. Consider James Gould Cozzens' novel, *By Love Possessed,* which appeared in August, 1957; consult the critics and reviewers to discover whether it is a good novel. Being a serious and ambitious work by a writer of standing, and also a best seller, it provoked unusually forthright judgments from a number of reviewers and critics—as may be seen in the accompanying quotations. "Masterpiece . . . brilliant . . . distinguished . . . high order . . . mediocre . . . bad;" that just about covers the spectrum of evaluation.

The International Council of the Museum of Modern Art recently took a large collection of American abstract expressionist paintings on tour in Europe. Its reception was reported in *Time.* In Spain some said, "If this is art, what was it that Goya painted?" and others cheered its "furious vitality" and "renovating spirit." In Italy one newspaper remarked, "It is not painting," but "droppings of paint, sprayings, burstings, lumps, squirts, whirls, rubs and marks, erasures, scrawls, doodles and kaleidoscope backgrounds." In Switzerland it was an "artistic event" that spoke for the genius of American art. And of course all these judgments could be found in this country too.

Not a dispute? Well, what is a dispute? Let us take first the plainest case of a disagreement (no matter what it is about): two people who say, " 'Tis so!" and " 'Tain't so!" Let them repeat these words as often as they like, and shout them from the housetops; they still haven't got a dispute going, but merely a contradiction, or perhaps an altercation. But let one person say, " 'Tis so!" and give a *reason* why 'tis so—let him say, "Jones is the best candidate for Senator because he is tactful, honest, and has had much experience in government." And let the other person say, " 'Tain't so!" and give a reason why 'tain't so —"Jones is not the best candidate, because he is too subservient to certain interests, indecisive and wishy-washy in his own views, and has no conception of the United States' international responsibilities." *Then* we have a dispute —that is, a disagreement in which the parties give reasons for their contentions. Of course this is not all there is to it; the dispute has just begun. But we see how it might continue, each side giving further reasons for its own view, and questioning whether the reasons given by the other are true, relevant, and compelling.

It is this kind of thing that counts as a dispute about the possibility of getting to the moon, about American intervention in the Middle East, about a Supreme Court decision, or anything else. And if we can dispute about these things, why not about art?

But here is where the *non disputandum* maxim would draw the line. We do not speak (or not without irony) about people's tastes in Senatorial candidates or missile policies (if the President replied to critics by saying, "Well, your taste is for speeding up the missile program and spending money, but that's not to my taste," we would feel he ought to back up his opinion more than that). Nor do we speak of tastes in international affairs, or laws, or constitutions. And that seems to be because we believe that judgments on these matters can be, and ought to be, based on good reasons—not that they always are, of course. To prefer a democratic to a totalitarian form of government is *not* just a matter of taste, though to like green olives better than ripe olives is a matter of taste, and we don't require the green olive man to rise and give his reasons, or even to *have* reasons. What kind of reasons could he have? "Green olives are better because they are green" would not look like much of a reason to the ripe olive devotee.

The question, then, is whether a preference for Picasso or Monteverdi is more like a preference for green olives or like a preference for a Senatorial candidate: is it *arguable?* can it be *reasoned?*

When we read what critics and reviewers have to say about the things they talk about, we cannot doubt that they do not merely praise or blame, but defend their judgments by giving reasons, or what they claim to be reasons. The judgments of *By Love Possessed,* here quoted out of context, are supplied with arguments, some of them with long arguments dealing in detail with the plot, style, characterization, structure, underlying philosophy, attitudes towards Catholics, Jews, and Negroes, and other aspects of the novel. Collect a number of these reviews together and it certainly *reads* like a dispute. Or here is one person who says, "Mozart's Quintet in E Flat Major for Piano and Winds (K. 452) is a greater piece of music than Beethoven's Quintet in E Flat Major for Piano and Winds (Op. 16) because it has greater melodic invention, subtlety of texture, a more characteristic scoring for the wind instruments, and a more expressive slow movement." And here is his friend, who replies, "The Beethoven quintet is greater because it has richer sonority, greater vigor and vitality, and a more powerful dynamic spirit." There's a dispute, or something that looks very much like one.

But according to the Aesthetic Skeptic—if I may choose this convenient name for the upholder of the "no disputing" doctrine—this is an illusion. The apparent reasons are not genuine reasons, or cannot be compelling reasons, like the ones we find in other fields. For in the last analysis they rest upon sheer liking or disliking, which is not susceptible of rational discussion. The defender of the Mozart Quintet, for example, seems to be trying to prove his point, but what he is actually doing (says the Skeptic) is better put this way: "*If* you like subtle texture and expressiveness in slow movements, *then* you (like me) will prefer the Mozart quintet." But what if his friend cares more for vigor and vitality? Then the so-called "argument" is bound to leave him cold. He can only reply, "*If* you like vigor and vitality, as I do, *then* you would prefer the Beethoven quintet." But this is no longer a dispute; they are talking completely at cross purposes, not even contradicting each other.

The Aesthetic Skeptic would analyze all apparent disputes among critics in these terms: the critic can point out features of the novel, the abstract expressionist painting, the quintet for winds, but when he does this he is taking for granted, what may not be true, that you happen to like these features. You can't, says the Skeptic, argue anybody into liking something he doesn't like, and that's why there's no disputing about tastes; all disputes are in the end useless.

Now this view, which I have here stated in a fairly rough way, can be worked out into a sophisticated and impressive position, and if it is mistaken, as I believe it is, its mistakes are not childish or simple-minded. Consequently, I cannot pretend to give here an adequate treatment of it. But I should like to consider briefly some of the difficulties in Aesthetic Skepticism, as I see it, and point out the possibility of an alternative theory.

The Skeptical theory takes people's likes and dislikes as ultimate and unappealable facts about them; when two people finally get down to saying "I like X" and "I don't like X" (be it the flavor of turnip or subtlety of texture in music), there the discussion has to end, there the dispute vanishes. But though it is true that you can't change a disliking into a liking by arguments, that doesn't imply that you can't change it at all, or that we cannot argue whether or not it *ought* to be changed.

. . . Appreciation isn't something you do if you just decide to. But the fact remains that one person can give reasons to another why he would be better off if he *could* enjoy music or painting that he now abhors, and sometimes the other person can set about indirectly, by study and enlarged experience, to change his own tastes, or, as we say, to improve them. There is not just your taste and mine, but better and worse taste; and this doesn't mean just that I have a taste for my taste, but not yours—I might in fact have a distaste for the limitations of my own taste (though that is a queer way to put it). It is something like a person with deep-rooted prejudices, to which he has been conditioned from an early age; perhaps he cannot quite get rid of them, no matter how he tries, and yet he may acknowledge in them a weakness, a crippling feature of his personality, and he may resolve that he will help his children grow up free from them.

The Skeptic does not allow for the possibility that we might give reasons why a person would be better off if he liked or disliked *By Love Possessed* in the way, and to the degree, that it deserves to be liked or disliked. Sometimes, I think, he really holds that it would not be worth the trouble. After all, what does it matter whether people like green olives or ripe olives? We can obtain both in sufficient supply, and nothing much depends upon it as far as the fate of the world is concerned. That's another reason why we ordinarily don't speak of Senatorial candidates as a matter of taste—unless we want to be disparaging, as when people speak of the President's choice in Secretaries of State, to imply that he has no good reason for his choice. It does matter who is Senator, or Secretary of State—it matters a great deal. But what about music, painting, and literature? Why should it be "alarming," to quote the passage from Dwight Macdonald, if the critics and Book-of-the-Month Club members acclaim a novel that is (in his judgment) unworthy?

Now of course, if we are thinking of our two musical disputants about the relative merits of the two quintets, this is a dispute we may safely leave alone. Both quintets are of such a high order that it perhaps doesn't matter enormously which we decide to rank higher than the other, though there's no harm in trying to do this, if we wish. But the question about *By Love Possessed* is whether it is a "masterpiece" or "bad"; and the question about the paintings is whether they ought to be shown abroad at all. It may not matter so very much whether a person on the whole admires Mozart or Beethoven more, but what if he cannot make up his mind between Mozart and Strauss, or between Beethoven and Shostakovitch?

The fact is that the prevailing level of taste in the general public matters a great deal to me, for it has a great deal to do with determining what I shall have the chance to read, what movies will be filmed, shown, or censored, what music will be played most availably on the radio, what plays will be performed on television. And it has a great deal to do with what composers and painters and poets will do, or whether some of them will do anything at all. But more than that, even: if I am convinced that the kind of experiences that can only be obtained by access to the greatest works is an important ingredient of the richest and most fully-developed human life, then do I not owe it to others to try to put that experience within their reach, or them within its reach? It might be as important to them as good housing, good medical and dental care, or good government.

But here is another point at which the Skeptic feels uneasy. Isn't it undemocratic to go around telling other people that they have crude tastes—wouldn't it be more in keeping with our laissez-faire spirit of tolerance, and less reminiscent of totalitarian absolutism and compulsion, to let others like and enjoy what they like and enjoy? Isn't this their natural right?

There are too many confusions in this point of view to clear them all up briefly. But some of them are worth sorting out. Of course it is a person's right to hear the music he enjoys, provided it doesn't bother other people too much. But it is no invasion of his right, if he is willing to consider the problem, to try to convince him that he should try to like other things that appear to deserve it. When Schroeder makes Lucy uncomfortable because she doesn't appreciate classical music, this puts him one up on her, and in other moods she might retort that it gives her more time to spend pleasurably on trivial pursuits. But Schroeder, by admonishing her, is not denying any of her rights.

The distinction that many Skeptics find it hard to keep in mind is this: I may hold that there *is* a better and a worse in music and novels without at all claiming that *I know for certain* which are which. Those critics and reviewers who pronounced their judgments on *By Love Possessed* are not necessarily dogmatic because they deny that it's all a matter of taste (even though some of them were more positive than they had a right to be). They believe that some true and reasonable judgment of the novel is in principle possible, and that objective critics, given time and discussion, could in principle agree, or come close to agreeing, on it. But they do not have to claim infallibility—people can be mistaken about novels, as they can about anything else. Works of art are complicated. There need be nothing totalitarian about literary criticism, and there is nothing especially democratic in the view that nobody is wrong because there is no good or bad to be wrong about.

It would help us all, I think, to look at the problem of judging works of art in a more direct way. These judgments, as can easily be seen in any random collection of reviews, go off in so many directions that it sometimes seems that the reviewers are talking about different things. We must keep our eye on the object—the painting, the novel, the quintet. Because the composer's love affairs were in a sorry state at the time he was composing, people think that the value of the music must somehow be connected with this circumstance. Because the painter was regarding his model while he painted, people think that the value of the painting must depend on some relation to the way she really looked, or felt. Because the novelist is known to be an anarchist or a conservative, people think that the value of the novel must consist partly in its fidelity to these attitudes. Now, of course, when we approach a work of art, there are many kinds of interest that we can take in it, as well as in its creator. But when we are trying to judge it *as* a work of art, rather than as biography or social criticism or something else, there is a central interest that ought to be kept in view.

A work of art, whatever its species, is an object of some kind—something somebody made. And the question is whether it was worth making, what it is good for, what can be done with it. In this respect it is like a tool. Tools of course are production goods, instrumental to other instruments, whereas paintings and musical compositions and novels are consumption goods, directly instrumental to some sort of experience. And their own peculiar excellence consists, I believe, in their capacity to afford certain valuable kinds and degrees of aesthetic experience. Of course they do not yield this experience to those who cannot understand them, just as a tool is of no use to one who has not the skill to wield it. But we do not talk in the Skeptical way about tools: we do not say that the value of a hammer is all a matter of taste, some people having a taste for hammering nails, some not. No, the value resides in its capability to drive the nail, given a hand and arm with the right skill, and if the need should arise. And this value it would have, though unrealized, even if the skill were temporarily lost.

So with works of art, it seems to me. Their value is what they can do to and for us, if we are capable of having it done. And for those who do not, or not yet, have this capacity, it is not a simple fact that they do not, but a misfortune, and the only question is whether, or to what extent, it can be remedied. It is because this question sometimes has a hopeful answer that we dispute, and must dispute, about tastes. When the political disputant gives his reasons for supporting one Senatorial candidate over another, he cites facts about that candidate that he knows, from past experience, justify the hope of a good performance—the hope that the candidate, once elected, will do what a Senator is supposed to do, well. When the critic gives his reasons for saying that a work of art is good or bad, he is not, as the Skeptic claims, trying to guess whom it will please or displease; he is pointing out those features of the work —its qualities, structure, style, and so on—that are evidence of the work's ability or inability to provide qualified readers, listeners, or viewers, with a deep aesthetic experience.

55

MARCIA CAVELL AUFHAUSER (1931– ———)

Critical Dialogue

Marcia Aufhauser is an American philosopher who has studied at both Stanford University and Harvard University. She is now on the faculty at the State University of New York at Purchase.

Like Beardsley, Aufhauser is searching for that elusive middle position that so many theorists are convinced must be the truth about this matter, but that all find so extremely difficult to define and defend. Aesthetic judgments, she argues, are not subjective (as Santayana held), but are capable of being challenged and defended. In support of this view she attempts to show that it is sometimes possible to specify "the normal observer" with respect to certain types of aesthetic objects, and that such an observer is better qualified to judge the aesthetic qualities of the objects in question than a random collection of observers. Aesthetic judgments are, therefore, according to her view, verifiable to some extent (by reference to the judgments of what should perhaps be called "the *qualified* observer"). She goes on to argue, however, that the purpose of the critic—the person who makes aesthetic judgments—is not so much to prove the validity of his or her perception of the aesthetic object, but to share that perception, to enable other people to perceive (see, hear) the work of art in the same way as the critic perceives it. Aesthetic judgments direct attention to certain features of the object in question, thus provoking a re-examination of the object, which may result in a shared perception.

Though I will be approaching it indirectly, my primary goal in this paper is to deny that aesthetic experience is in some radical sense "subjective" and to defend the position that critical remarks, or aesthetic ascriptions, can be challenged and defended. I will be discussing, then, the community appealed to in the making of such remarks and the nature of that appeal.

First, I want to make out a case for the notion of "the qualified observer" as the *only* subject relevant to the exchange of challenge and defense in

From Marcia Cavell Aufhauser, "Critical Dialogue," *The Journal of Philosophy,* 67 (1970), pp. 339–351. Reprinted by permission of the author and the publisher.

aesthetic contexts. Second, I will argue that not only *can* aesthetic ascriptions be defended, but must be defensible to qualify, in given instances, as aesthetic ascriptions. And, finally, I shall suggest that explicit judgments of value, which have been the concern of aesthetics for so long, are not really at the center— though they typically seem to be—of critical disputes; that, in short, such disputes more generally derive from a disagreement about *what* is seen than about how it is to be valued. If this is so, then understanding the logic of aesthetic judgment is at least largely a matter of understanding the sort of remark with which I am here concerned.

By "critical remarks" or "aesthetic ascriptions" I mean propositions ascribing so-called "aesthetic properties" to an object. Recent attempts to delimit these properties by saying that they are "such that taste or perceptiveness is required in order to apply them"[1] or that they are one sort of property which is not condition-governed[2] are, I believe, in the first case unhelpful and in the second mistaken. So I shall simply say that I have in mind properties like "triteness," "grace," "balance," "harmoniousness," "garishness," and hope that an "etc." is not without suggestiveness. What the relationship is between such ascriptions and explicit evaluations does not concern me here; nor whether or not the ascriptions themselves have some evaluative force (though I think it is clear that they do: to the extent that an image in a poem is trite and is judged to serve no artistic purpose in being so, its triteness would seem to be a good reason for saying that in this respect, at least, the poem fails). Rather, I am concerned with what is required for the making of them, that is, for the making of them to be meaningful in a given context.

What makes for the puzzle here is that aesthetic predicates refer to qualities or aspects of a work—if they are *in* or *of* the work—which can be "directly" experienced. That is, they are not inferred from what we perceive in the object, but are themselves perceived as qualifying the object. Though I may be moved by the fact that Beethoven's Opus 135 was written while the composer was deaf, I cannot *hear* his deafness in the music; whereas I can, presumably, hear its tensions, its grace or lack of grace, all of its many structural, melodic, and rhythmic qualities. To this extent, aesthetic ascriptions resemble descriptions of an object's color. But the latter can be said to be right or wrong, true or false, because we have a clear notion of "the normal observer" and "the normal circumstances of observation" by which to check what color an object appears to be against what it *really* is. And it is just these observers and conditions which seem to be lacking in relation to aesthetic qualities; so we are apparently forced to say that in the last analysis aesthetic ascriptions can only be statements about how the object looks to a particular person. And that as such, they

[1]Frank Sibley, "Aesthetic Concepts," in W. E. Kennick, ed., *Art and Philosophy* (New York: St. Martin's, 1964), p. 351.

[2]Both Frank Sibley and Isabel Hungerland maintain variants of this thesis, the latter in "The Logic of Aesthetic Concepts" in *Proceedings and Addresses of the American Philosophical Association,* XXXVI (October 1963).

are "subjective," *merely* expressions of personal idiosyncrasy or taste; justifiable only "within a coterie" (this last is Hungerland's claim in "The Logic of Aesthetic Concepts").

I. THE NORMAL OBSERVER

But there are many things we say about how things look (sound, feel, etc.) which cannot be verified by "the normal observer" in the usual sense of this term, yet where the properties in question are in no way aesthetic and where the description or ascription is, we feel, as clearly challengeable, falsifiable, and supportable as when we say that an object is red; for example: "That looks like (has the look of) a mediaeval manuscript"; "The dog looks like an Afghan"; "The tumor looks cancerous"; etc. Each of these may be intended as a tentative claim about facts other than "the look" in question, but they may also be claims about how the thing does look. (This is the point behind the frequently made but very misleading claim that "aesthetic vision" has to do, as Vincent Tomas[3] puts it, with the appearance, not the reality of things.) The tumor may truly look cancerous, yet turn out to be benign. The dog may truly look like an Afghan and be a first-class mongrel. But it's fairly obvious, I think, that the person who can sensibly claim that the dog looks like an Afghan must have more than 20/20 vision and an ability to discriminate reds and greens; he must also know about Afghans. Knowledge is required, and it's a knowledge that in fact makes a difference to what one looks for and, hence, perceives. (As Wittgenstein pointed out in *Philosophical Investigations,* the substratum of some experiences is the mastery of a technique.) Inquiring, then, whether or not a person is in a position to make a claim that presupposes knowledge or prior experience is one way of challenging that claim.

What qualifies someone to judge the color of an object is physical normality in certain respects; and most of us are in these respects physically normal. What qualifies someone to judge the look of a tumor is something in addition to good eyesight. Not a mysterious something; just a range of knowledge and experience that in fact many people have not had. In the one case, therefore, the qualified observer is apt to be the observer taken at random: standard and statistical norm coincide; but this is not so in the other.

In sum, 'looks *x* to the normal observer' must in some cases be amended to 'looks *x* to the qualified observer', or modified so as to acknowledge the fact that, normally, seeing the property in question may require more than good eyesight.

What I want to suggest is that "The fugue is tightly knit," "That visual design lacks balance," etc., are very much like "The manuscript looks mediae-

---

[3]In "Aesthetic Vision," in Marvin Levich, ed., *Aesthetics and the Philosophy of Criticism* (New York: Random House, 1963).

val," etc. To the extent that they are statements about how the fugue sounds, the painting looks, etc., it is quite true that the implied audience is not the one with "normal" hearing and vision; but neither is it an audience chosen arbitrarily, or in accordance with the speaker's tastes. Rather, it is an audience that knows what fugues and visual designs are—a matter once again not only of knowing, but of hearing and seeing.

II. ARE AESTHETIC ASCRIPTIONS DEFENSIBLE?

People say things about works of art for different reasons, in different contexts, playing different roles. In saying that a composition is tightly knit or elegant, someone might mean nothing more than that he likes it. But if this were the case, he would not be making, I contend, a genuine critical remark. It would become one, or reveal itself as one, only if it were capable of being defended. Or to put it another way: someone plays the critic's role if, when challenged, he is willing to look for supporting reasons.

In her article, "The Logic of Aesthetic Concepts," Isabel Hungerland contends that "it makes little difference whether we say . . . 'You look elegant' or 'You are elegant,' 'This color scheme looks gay' or 'This color scheme is gay' . . . because in neither case are we committing ourselves to supporting reasons" (*op. cit.,* 25).

I wonder if she would also say: "It makes little difference whether we say 'The composition is in A major' or 'The composition sounds as if it is in A major' "? There are, of course, many instances in which it is truly unclear what key a composition is in, if indeed it is in any key at all. But that's because there are many cases in which it is perfectly clear. Are such remarks about how the music is or about how it sounds? A funny question—because what the music "is" and how it sounds are obviously related; yet they are not identical. A composition might be in the key of A major and yet not sound as if it were, to anyone. Many people are musically well trained enough to be able to identify the key of a piece of music when they see the score, and to tell on hearing it whether it is in a major or a minor key; yet they are unable to identify the key when they hear it played. This might be universally the case. But at the same time, many people *can* hear, sometimes, what key a piece of music is in. And often a composition may sound, to someone who can hear the difference but who has listened carelessly, as if it were in A major, and on a second, more careful hearing, reveal itself as in the related minor, for example.

Hungerland's argument is: (a) that aesthetic ascriptions are, in the broad sense that I have also claimed for them, statements about how an object looks; (b) that since there is no equivalent to "the normal observer" with respect to aesthetic ascriptions, they rather resemble sentences like "The sweater looks red" than "The sweater is red"; and (c) that although for such sentences there are, in Strawson's sense, preconditions for my uttering them, it is not my experience that is being reported; nor is what I say supportable by reference to the experience of others.

But I have argued that there is a perfectly good parallel to "the normal observer" for aesthetic ascribings. And as for (c), I think Hungerland's analysis of what she considers a nonaesthetic analogy is mistaken. There is no usage of "The sweater looks red" for which it is the case both that its looking red to me is not a part of what I assert and that there can be no supporting reasons for my statement. This is an incomplete sentence and expands to a claim about how the object looks to me or would look to others under certain conditions. In either case, it can be challenged and defended, though, in *ordinary* cases, it is true that the only reason I could give for saying that it looks red to me is that it does. But that is partly because it is assumed that I have looked at the sweater and am not color-blind. For if either of these conditions has not been met, my claim is false.

The parallel failures in aesthetic experience are more complicated. If I talk about the visual aspects of a painting, it will also be assumed that I have looked at it. But suppose that I haven't looked at it in the way relevant to perceiving the quality in question—have only peered at a Seurat and, hence, have seen points rather than cones and arcs; haven't noticed the closing in of space in Van Gogh's painting of his room; haven't seen the formal elements in a Cézanne, but only the trees and mountains. In these cases, many claims that I might make about how the painting looks to me would be, if not simply false, certainly open to challenge; for have I, in fact, looked at the painting?

This suggests that not only is there an equivalent to "the normal observer" in relation to works of art, but also to "the normal conditions of observation." Daylight is normally the right condition in which to find out what color an object "really is." But often objects reveal the characteristics in which we are interested only under "abnormal" conditions. In *Sense and Sensibilia,* John Austin asked us to:

> Suppose that there is a species of fish which looks vividly multi-coloured, slightly glowing, perhaps, at a depth of a thousand feet. I ask you what its real color is. So you catch a specimen and lay it out on the deck, making sure the condition of the light is just about normal, and you find that it looks a muddy sort of greyish white. Well, is *that* its real color? It's clear enough at any rate that we don't have to say so (65 and 66).

The "normal" conditions of viewing would not in this case reveal what might be considered the important characteristics. But it doesn't follow that the relevant conditions are abnormal in the sense that they yield an illusory or "merely personal" view of reality. The "right" perceptual viewpoint cannot be stipulated without regard to what is being asked; nor, it is important to note, prior to some knowledge of the object under consideration.

Finally, is it the case that remarks such as "The music sounds tightly knit" and "The music is tightly knit" are interchangeable? Surely not. For one thing, it is difficult to imagine a case in which I would say the first at all; but if I did, it would be to draw attention precisely to a discrepancy between the way the music sounds—in certain passages, played at a certain tempo, listened to with Bach rather than Schubert in mind—and the way it really is, however that would be determined (by looking at the score, perhaps). For another, on a second hearing—just as with my opening example, "It sounds to me as if it's in A major"—I may acknowledge my initial perception to have been mistaken.

And is it the case that the only reason I can give for saying that the music sounds loosely structured is that it does? Structure is, obviously, a function of the relations among a number of possible elements; in the case of music: voices, tonalities, rhythmic patterns, etc. Supporting a remark about its seeming structure would begin with more specific remarks about these elements. My point is not that any such elaboration might be final or conclusive. But only that if I were totally unable to give it, one would ordinarily say that I didn't know what I was talking about. In short, it seems that the one thing a remark like "The Beethoven E flat major piano sonata sounds tightly knit to me" cannot be is a first-person phenomenal report, on the order of "It tastes sweet to me" or "It looks red to me."

If a subjective experience is one describable in terms of myself, the red patch I see when I close my eyes tight, the pain in my left leg, the chill down my spine, the description of an aesthetic experience is at the same time an account of an object.[4] Though of course it need not be. What I see when I look at Van Gogh's *Jacob Wrestling with the Angel* may be a scene from my childhood, and what I hear when I listen to Debussy's *La Mer* may be, simply, last summer's beach. Emma Bovary liked music because it "set her dreaming." We do sometimes use works of art as springboards for associations that have only incidentally to do with the work of art, functioning then as stimulus to response. In this sense, a description of my response need say nothing about the stimulus provoking it. And there can be no sense to asking me how I would justify my reaction. But there is another sense of "response" that has a different logic: here the description will probably take the form of an account of that to which I am responding—for example, in asking me what my response is to someone we have just met, you may expect something from me about how that person made me feel, but you will certainly expect me to say something about how I saw *him;* and you may also, then, ask me to justify that response—which I would probably do by calling your attention to things he had said or done, gestures he had made, etc. In any case, however we answer it, the question of justification is certainly relevant. It is only in this second sense, then, that an account of one's response qualifies at the same time as an aesthetic ascription.

I should perhaps point out that implicit in my argument in this section is a rejection of any hard-and-fast distinction for aesthetic ascribings between

[4] I use this term loosely, leaving open the question of what sorts of "things" can be members in an aesthetic experience.

preconditions and supporting reasons. What is assumed in the making of a remark in one situation may become the first line of defense in another. It depends on who is speaking, on where we are standing, and on whether or not we are on common ground.

III. THE FUNCTION OF CRITICISM

The claim that aesthetic ascriptions are not verifiable is, I hope to have shown, a mistaken claim if it is construed to mean that they are not verifiable to any degree and in any circumstances in which they are challenged. It is, however, a proper reminder that the critic does not so much prove to us the validity of what he says as show it to us, and the condition for this is our being able to understand the words he uses and the conventions to which he refers— 'stretto', 'key', 'voice', 'fugue', 'sonata', 'upbeat', 'downbeat', etc. If we have been reading the first note in a musical composition as its initial pulse, the critic may, in certain clear cases, be able to prove to us that it functions rather as an upbeat. But this task isn't completed until he has shown us the importance of such a difference to the way we hear the music. To do this he may ask us to look more closely at the construction of the entire composition; he may ask us to conduct it or to dance it or to compare it to other compositions.

Suppose we have done all this, and we each seem to see, or hear, what the other sees; but we insist that the initial note really is, or should be played as, a downbeat. At this point, I claim that dialogue *about the music* is at an end. What sense could it make here for one of us to maintain that his is the right interpretation after all (unless this is an appeal to the composer's "intention")? That is, what might be conceived of as a resolution to such a dispute? That we cannot give meaning to the notion of "a resolution" here is related, I believe, to the fact that indeed there is no need of one. There may be a need for me to understand you. But then the focus of our conversation shifts from something presumably shared between us to each other, one consequence of which may be, of course, that we will be able to share the object after all.

I suggested at the beginning that the critic is typically more interested in the question, What do you see? than in the question, How do you defend your evaluation of what you see? He is interested in reformation, but of vision rather than value. Or if this is an unhelpful distinction, what I mean is that he urges us away from standards and the demands of consistency, with which as moralists we must be concerned, but which in our experience of works of art tend toward just what the artist hopes to free us from: rigidity of response. There is not even, so far as I can see, any real counterpart in aesthetics to moral principles. There are, of course, conventions. But these are more like the conventions that define what hospitality is in a given society than like those which rule for or against it.

In general, I suggest that what look like disagreements about the value of a work of art are usually disagreements about what the work of art is—in the broadest sense. Often, in fact, what we are unsure about is just the sort of thing that Sibley, for example, distinguishes from aesthetic ascriptions: whether or not a character in a novel functions as a character, whether or not a passage is a stretto, a fugue is a fugue, a rose is a rose. Of course the catch is that, though we may seem to be seeing the same thing, this may not be the case. So perhaps I should put my thesis in a positive form: so long as there is disagreement about the value of a work of art, one should presume that what is lacking is a shared perception of it, that there remains the possibility of meaningful (i.e., resolvable) dialogue, even though one may not be able to find the right key. (For two people from very different cultures to perceive an event, or a work of art, in the same way, may *in fact* in a given case not be possible. But there is no theoretical impossibility.)

I would also argue, then, that explicit value judgments are not usually the goal of criticism, but its starting point, functioning to provoke re-examination rather than, in the usual sense, defense. I imagine a dialogue, more sophisticated than the following, but for which it may serve as a model:

A. I didn't like that music at all. It was so repetitious.
B. Repetitious? I thought it extraordinarily inventive. What do you mean?
A. Well, just that one silly tune, all the way through, for example.
B. But the whole point was to invent variations on that tune. Didn't you like the third one, where it turned into a waltz? And then the marvelous fifth, where it became the second voice in the Fugue?

Suppose that A acknowledges not having heard the waltz or the fugue. He will be forced to retreat. Which is not to say that B in turn might not be led to reconsider, to rehear, under the tutelage of a more equal opponent.

In ordinary conversation, the answer to "What an exciting play!" may well be, "I found it boring"; to "At least it's honest," "It's a lie"; to "Well, it was certainly skillfully done," "I think it was very sloppy." The ascription—or the remark—functions not so much as a move in a dialogue as in a duel, to which therefore no reasonable conclusion is possible. It is the experience of this kind of exchange that gives rise, I think, to the common belief that aesthetic ascriptions are really remarks not about an object, but about the subject making them; that they are hopelessly "subjective"; that the critic is simply another subject whose personal responses and evaluations have somehow received public sanction.

But there is another kind of exchange whose logic is quite different. One of the antonyms of 'exciting' is 'boring'. But I don't answer your "It's exciting!" in this way unless we are—or I wish us to be—antagonists. When, on the other hand, we think of our relationship as mediated by an object, our exchange goes quite differently:

A. What an exciting play!
B. But it's an imitation of . . . and an inferior one at that.
A. At least it's honest.

B. But the portrayal of . . . is so sentimental.

A. Well, it certainly is skillfully done.

B. But the handling of the dialogue in the third act is out of character.

This is, of course, very sketchy. Each remark could—and in a real conversation would—be countered, expanded, in a variety of ways. Presumably A would not abandon his position so easily. He might respond by saying that B's claim is simply mistaken, or he might argue that, while it would be true if this work were to be construed in one way, it should be construed in another (for example, an event that is improbable in a realistic novel or play and therefore, perhaps, a weakness in the structure, may be improbable and *therefore* an integral part of the structure in an "absurdist" play). The point, however, is that the dialogue proceeds not by the countering of a predicate with its logical contrary, but obliquely, by the providing of ever more specific directions *into the work. There is no end* to the ways in which a play can fail to be exciting, honest, skillful. One can imagine this dialogue continuing, therefore, until someone gets tired or until it becomes clear that one person's reaction is highly idiosyncratic or until, finally, after this kaleidoscopic focusing and assembling of the parts, both people are satisfied that they are seeing pretty much the same thing.

The logic of the above conversation is such, then, that it comes to an end not with victory or defeat, but with a shared perception of the object at hand. Not, of course, that this is always, or often, attained. And it is almost certainly and nontrivially true that no two people ever see a work of art or experience an event in exactly the same ways. But communication often breaks down long before this ultimate limit is reached; for a sharing of an aesthetic experience requires many things: equal sensitivity to the medium, similar training in and experience with the medium, patience, intelligence, imagination, and often conversation itself.

If critical remarks, aesthetic ascriptions, are ever "objective," they must be intersubjectively verifiable. But I have been suggesting that this leaves open the questions: Which subjects? Under what conditions? And furthermore, *When?* What the critic says is tested not by how the object looks *now* to the observer qualified to see what he is asked to see, but by how it *will* look when he has followed the critic's directions. The critic is certainly appealing to a community—a community, however, not achieved, but in the making. The critic's experience of the work of art may *in fact* be shared by no one. I take it that this is something of what Arnold Isenberg had in mind when he claimed, in "Critical Communication"[5] that "it is a function of criticism *to bring about* communication at the level of the senses" (my emphasis).

This difference between construing aesthetic ascriptions like 'It's exciting,' '. . . honest,' 'well-constructed,' as answerable by their logical contraries, on

---

[5] *Philosophical Review*, LXIII, 4 (July 1949):330–334; reprinted in Levich, ed., *op. cit.,* p. 549.

the one hand, and by a greater specificity in the direction indicated, on the other, provides a clue to an analysis of the so-called "criteria of value" for works of art; for example, those proposed by Monroe Beardsley: Unity, Complexity, and Intensity. The troubles with trying to establish any such criteria of value are well known and legion. For one, whether or not a work *is* unified is just as open to conflicts of opinion as whether or not it's good. For another, unless one construes 'unity' so broadly as to render it useless, it is questionable whether every work we consider to be valuable we also consider to be unified. So it seems we must choose between construing an ascription of unity as unverifiable, and regarding it as verifiable but having little to do with the aesthetic experience and what makes it valuable.

The dilemma results, however, from taking: (a) "The work has unity" as a report, confirmed on finding the quality of unity in the work, disconfirmed if it is absent; (b) the conversation in which such a remark functions as an argument; and (c) the relationship between "The work has unity" and "The work is good" as that between premise and conclusion, or reason and verdict. Working backwards, suppose we construe (c) "The work is good" not as the conclusion to an argument, but, as I have suggested, as a very general directive to re-experience the work, to look at it again; (b) the conversation not as an argument *about* the work, but an investigation of it, a joint voyage into it (it is as if there were here a dialogue with three members: the work of art is not so much spoken *about,* as spoken *to,* addressed); and finally (a) unity, for example, not as a quality residing in some sense in the work of art, but as a vantage point from which to view it; that is, as indicating one of a great number of possible questions to put to it. Knowing which questions are indicated in any given case already requires knowing, or learning something about, this particular work of art; which is why trying to define 'unity', construed as a property, leads us to think that it is hopelessly ambiguous. Considering the unity in a work of art means considering the relationship of its parts to one another. I am unable to follow the instructions if, for example, I don't even know what to consider, to begin with, as the parts. The structural elements of a baroque fugue are not the same as those of a romantic symphony. And if I listen for the same elements and relations I am apt to make a muddle of one, if not both. In short, there are not so much criteria of value, as there are kinds of questions to be asked.

In conclusion: that we are not all equally qualified to talk about works of art; and that our various qualifications may make crucial differences to what we perceive, and hence, one would think, to how we feel, in the largest sense, about works of art, seems clear. It is even clear that, contrary to the arguments of Sibley and Hungerland, there are necessary conditions, and even occasionally sufficient conditions, for some aesthetic concepts. For example, it is a necessary condition for a painting to be "garish" that it not be monochromatically black, white, or pastel; it is a sufficient condition for a piece of music to be "well-constructed" that it be a fugue obeying the rules of counterpoint in Piston's *Elementary Harmony*. How, then, have philosophers been led to deny the obvious? It's a question we often ask ourselves about philosophy in general, but it is particularly important, I think, in aesthetics, and I can only make a couple of suggestions here:

A. Responding to a work of art is not a matter of identifying it correctly as a four-part fugue, etc. But it follows neither: (a) that hearing it as a musical structure composed of voices in certain relations to one another is irrelevant to how I respond to it; nor (b) that learning about fugues, which involves learning to hear notes *as* voices, for one thing, is irrelevant to how I will eventually respond to it. Responding to a work of art which is a four-part fugue and which does make certain harmonic modulations, etc., is at its best—that is, most attentive, most responsive, least "subjective"—a matter of hearing those voices and those changes—though of course one may not be able to put a name to them. And this hearing inevitably involves certain responses in terms of feeling. Though it's not so much, I think, that the hearing produces the feeling, as that sometimes ways of hearing and seeing are themselves ways of feeling. (I have been talking about what is required in the way of skill and prior experience for the justification, or justifiability, of a critical remark. But equally important—though a subject for another paper—is what is required in the way of feeling for the claim to have had "an aesthetic response" to be legitimate. I would say that unless one feels something like remorse—some species of pain —one cannot claim "to know" that he has wronged another. And something comparable is undoubtedly true of the claim—to put it very generally—to have "understood" a work of art.)

B. We identify the work of art with the work of genius; and genius is, in our mythology, mad, rule-defying, transcendent, unpredictable. It breaks all precedents. And isn't that just to say that there can be no conditions that the work of genius must satisfy? But it doesn't spring full-grown from its author's head. It is new and original in relation to a past; and what it transcends is the past as actual, taken as marking the limits of the possible. Any competent music student can write a "tightly-knit" fugue. There is no guarantee, and little hope, that it will also be inventive. But that's another matter. The difference between art and craft, genius and talent, may be enormous, but it's not categorical. Or if it is, the relation between the categories is that between originality and convention: originality "breaks" from convention in expanding it, playing with it, taking it somewhere new. The task of criticism is in part to reveal the old in the new and the new in the old, to trace the bridge between them. Which way it looks in any given case depends on what we have missed, or are likely to.

A final note: there is, I think, no class of judgment that can be set apart as requiring discrimination and sensitivity. It may require perceptiveness to notice that a corner of the scarf is protruding from the magician's sleeve; that two lines are really the same length after all; even, depending on the weather and one's mood, that the sun is shining. Whether or not, and to what degree, perceptiveness is required is not a function of the predicate itself, but of the situation and the person perceiving. Noticing that the rhyming words of a poem form a significant sentence probably requires a little greater attentiveness than usual from most people and none at all from a Yeats. But even this depends on the particular poem.

Nor is there any class of judgment that can be set apart as eliciting or presupposing feeling. It is of the essence of art to challenge old ways of thinking and perceiving, and, as Dewey reminded us in *Art as Experience,* this is by nature a disruptive, sometimes even a painful, process. Art is more likely, therefore, to push us to the limits of awareness and to make more demands on us in all ways than other sorts of experience. It is also, therefore, more likely to force us to talking about what we see in new ways. But speaking metaphorically, as it were, is neither a matter of mere self-expression nor of pretending, but of seeing connections to which our previous concerns did not call attention. The community to which the work of art addresses itself may, then, in fact be very small. It is the critic's task to make it larger.

For Further Reading

Berenson, Bernard. *Aesthetics and History.* New York: Pantheon Books, 1948. See "Conclusion" for an astonishing statement of the relativist position.

Bosanquet, Bernard. *Three Lectures on Aesthetics.* London: Macmillan, 1915. Includes an interesting discussion of an alleged distinction between "easy" beauty and "difficult" beauty.

Dewey, John. *Art as Experience.* New York: Capricorn Books, 1934. See especially Chap. 13, "Criticism and Perception."

Diderot, Denis. "The Beautiful," In K. Aschenbrenner and A. Isenberg (eds.). *Aesthetic Theories: Studies in The Philosophy of Art.* Englewood Cliffs, N.J.: Prentice-Hall, 1965, pp. 129–147. Includes an overview of the aesthetic theories of many writers from Plato to Francis Hutcheson.

Ducasse, C. J. *Philosophy of Art.* New York: Dial Press, 1929. Chap. 15, "Standards of Criticism," gives a subjectivist account of aesthetic value.

Heyl, Bernard. *New Bearings in Esthetic and Art Criticism.* New Haven, Conn.: Yale University Press, 1943, pp. 125–155. A relativist account.

————. "Relativism Again," *Journal of Aesthetics and Art Criticism,* 5 (1946), 54–61. A further elaboration and defense of the relativist position.

Hume, David. *Of the Standard of Taste and Other Essays,* ed. by J. W. Lenz, Indianapolis, Ind.: Bobbs-Merrill, 1965. A famous statement of relativism by a philosopher best known for his writings on other subjects (notably, epistemology).

Hutcheson, Francis. *An Inquiry into the Origins of Our Ideas of Beauty and Virtues,* 1725. An early examination of many of the issues still being discussed by writers on aesthetics.

Jeffrey, Francis. "Essay on Beauty," in K. Aschenbrenner and A. Isenberg (eds.). *Aesthetic Theories: Studies in the Philosophy of Art.* Englewood Cliffs, N.J.: Prentice-Hall, 1965, pp. 277–294. A widely read statement of the subjectivist theory.

Joad, C. E. M. *Matter, Life and Value.* London: Oxford University Press, 1929, pp. 266–283. An intuitionist account that owes much to Plato.

Kant, Immanuel. *The Critique of Judgment,* 1790. An analysis of the beautiful and the sublime. For patient readers only!

Lewis, C. I. *An Analysis of Knowledge and Valuation.* La Salle, Ill.: Open Court Publishing Co., 1946. See Chap. 15, "The Esthetic Judgment." An objectivist view.

Moore, G. E. "The Ideal," in *Principia Ethica.* New York: Cambridge University Press, 1959 (paperbound). A famous and lucid statement of the objectivist view.

Ogden, C. K., I. A. Richards, and J. Wood. *The Foundations of Aesthetics.* London: G. Allen & Unwin, 1922. Includes a discussion of no less than sixteen definitions of beauty.

Osborne, Harold. *Aesthetics and Criticism.* New York: Philosophical Library, 1955. See Chap. 11, which is concerned with the role of the critic.

Pepper, Stephen C. *The Work of Art.* Bloomington: Indiana University Press, 1955. See Chap. 2, "Can a Judgment of Beauty Be True?" The author argues that it can.

Plato. *Greater Hippias.* Many editions. A light-hearted but inconclusive dialogue that seeks an answer to the question, What is beauty?

Santayana, George. *Reason in Art.* New York: Scribner's, 1905. See especially Chap. 10, "The Criterion of Taste," pp. 191–215.

Vivas, Eliseo. "The Objective Basis of Criticism," in *Creation and Discovery.* New York: Noonday Press, 1955, pp. 191–206. Defends a nonintuitionist form of objectivism.

Weitz, Morris. *Philosophy of the Arts.* Cambridge, Mass.: Harvard University Press, 1950, pp. 191–204. A critique of subjectivism from the perspective of what the author calls the "organic" theory.

PART XIII

World Views

Philosophy, as we have said, has two principal tasks, one critical and the other constructive (see above, pp. 1–2). The critical task is to question truth claims, to ask the question "Is it really so?" The constructive task is to figure out "how it all hangs together," to construct an all-inclusive picture of reality in which every element of knowledge and experience finds its proper place.

The challenge to philosophy on its critical side is to make sure that only true propositions get established as part of what is accepted as the truth. This task is as important as it is difficult—important because undetected errors lead to further errors, difficult because the errors most likely to be made usually have the support of both tradition and common sense. It is hard to convince people whose everyday experience teaches them otherwise that the earth really is round rather than flat, that the earth goes around the sun rather than the sun around the earth, that material objects are not in reality the static unchanging entities that they appear to be, that the authority of government may not rest on self-evident truths, or that the status of value judgments is such that one's pronouncements in ethics and aesthetics do not warrant the dogmatism that frequently accompanies such pronouncements in everyday life. For critical philosophy, the unpardonable sin is to assent to a falsehood. To avoid this sin, critical philosophy insists on questioning everything that is put forward as the truth—even the most obvious deliverances of common sense. We have encountered philosophy of this kind in the preceding parts of this anthology.

The challenge to philosophy on its constructive side is to "put it all together" in a way that does justice to all the facts. If the philosopher qua critical philosopher is a professional skeptic, the philosopher qua constructive philosopher is a professional believer, espousing some "picture of the whole," some *world view* that is held to be true. Moreover, the philosopher is as passionate in presenting and defending this world view as in attacking those theories that contradict it.

A correct world view—a picture of the whole of reality that is adequate to all the known facts as well as to all additional facts that shall become known in the future—is, then, the ultimate goal of all philosophy. Such a world view must have the following characteristics: (1) it must provide a plausible explanation of some facts, that is, there must be some evidence supporting it, (2) there must be no evidence that decisively counts against it, that is, none that cannot be plausibly accounted for within the world view, and (3) it must be internally consistent, that is, it must not contradict itself. Any time a world view is advocated, it is implicitly claimed that it meets these three conditions.

The most fundamental and all-embracing problem in philosophy, therefore, is the problem of world views. Which all-inclusive picture of the whole of reality is most adequate to the facts? This problem, which has been lurking in the background in many of the preceding discussions, will now be addressed directly.

56

AUGUSTINE OF HIPPO (354–430)

The Earthly and the Heavenly Cities

St. Augustine, as one would expect, advocates the world view of *ethical theism*. The main elements of this world view are well known: God exists and is the Creator of everything else that exists; His will reigns supreme in all things; the first man and woman were created good, but, through their sin, human nature became corrupted,

From Augustine of Hippo, *The City of God,* Book XIV, Chapters 1 and 28; Book XIX, Chapters 13 and 17, in *Nicene and Post-Nicene Fathers of the Christian Church,* ed. P. Schaff (New York: Charles Scribner's Sons, 1907), pp. 263, 282–283, 409–410, and 412–413.

and this corruption ("original sin") has been passed on to all their descendants; God, in His mercy, has seen fit to save some from this corruption; they, the elect, are in this life intermingled with those who remain in their corruption, but in the end will enjoy eternal salvation whereas the others will suffer eternal punishment. Few have expressed these beliefs so eloquently, however, as has the great Bishop of Hippo.

In the selection that follows, St. Augustine contrasts the "city of God" (the elect) with the "city of this world" (everybody else). As he develops this theme, however, he states or alludes to many of the principal beliefs that comprise his world view. (See p. 144 for a biographical note on St. Augustine.)

THAT THE DISOBEDIENCE OF THE FIRST MAN WOULD HAVE PLUNGED ALL MEN INTO THE ENDLESS MISERY OF THE SECOND DEATH, HAD NOT THE GRACE OF GOD RESCUED MANY.

We have already stated in the preceding books that God, desiring not only that the human race might be able by their similarity of nature to associate with one another, but also that they might be bound together in harmony and peace by the ties of relationship, was pleased to derive all men from one individual, and created man with such a nature that the members of the race should not have died, had not the two first (of whom the one was created out of nothing, and the other out of him) merited this by their disobedience; for by them so great a sin was committed, that by it the human nature was altered for the worse, and was transmitted also to their posterity, liable to sin and subject to death. And the kingdom of death so reigned over men, that the deserved penalty of sin would have hurled all headlong even into the second death, of which there is no end, had not the undeserved grace of God saved some therefrom. And thus it has come to pass, that though there are very many and great nations all over the earth, whose rites and customs, speech, arms, and dress, are distinguished by marked differences, yet there are no more than two kinds of human society, which we may justly call two cities, according to the language of our Scriptures. The one consists of those who wish to live after the flesh, the other of those who wish to live after the spirit; and when they severally achieve what they wish, they live in peace, each after their kind.

.   .   .

OF THE NATURE OF THE TWO CITIES, THE EARTHLY AND THE HEAVENLY.

Accordingly, two cities have been formed by two loves: the earthly by the love of self, even to the contempt of God; the heavenly by the love of God, even to the contempt of self. The former, in a word, glories in itself, the latter in the Lord. For the one seeks glory from men; but the greatest glory of the other is God, the witness of conscience. The one lifts up its head in its own glory; the other says to its God, "Thou art my glory, and the lifter up of mine head."[1] In the one, the princes and the nations it subdues are ruled by the love of ruling; in the other, the princes and the subjects serve one another in love, the latter obeying, while the former take thought for all. The one delights in its own strength, represented in the persons of its rulers; the other says to its God, "I will love Thee, O Lord, my strength."[2] And therefore the wise men of the one city, living according to man, have sought for profit to their own bodies or souls, or both, and those who have known God "glorified Him not as God, neither were thankful, but became vain in their imaginations, and their foolish heart was darkened; professing themselves to be wise,"—that is, glorying in their own wisdom, and being possessed by pride,—"they became fools, and changed the glory of the incorruptible God into an image made like to corruptible man, and to birds, and four-footed beasts, and creeping things." For they were either leaders or followers of the people in adoring images, "and worshipped and served the creature more than the Creator, who is blessed for ever."[3] But in the other city there is no human wisdom, but only godliness, which offers due worship to the true God, and looks for its reward in the society of the saints, of holy angels as well as holy men, "that God may be all in all."[4]

OF THE UNIVERSAL PEACE WHICH THE LAW OF NATURE PRESERVES THROUGH ALL DISTURBANCES, AND BY WHICH EVERY ONE REACHES HIS DESERT IN A WAY REGULATED BY THE JUST JUDGE.

The peace of the body then consists in the duly proportioned arrangement of its parts. The peace of the irrational soul is the harmonious repose of the appetites, and that of the rational soul the harmony of knowledge and action. The peace of body and soul is the well-ordered and harmonious life and health of the living creature. Peace between man and God is the well-ordered obedience of faith to eternal law. Peace between man and man is well-ordered concord. Domestic peace is the well-ordered concord between those of the family who rule and those who obey. Civil peace is a similar concord among the citizens. The peace of the celestial city is the perfectly ordered and harmonious enjoyment of God, and of one another in God. The peace of all things

[1] Ps. iii.3.
[2] Ps. xviii.1.
[3] Rom. i. 21–25.
[4] 1 Cor. xv. 28.

is the tranquillity of order. Order is the distribution which allots things equal and unequal, each to its own place. And hence, though the miserable, in so far as they are such, do certainly not enjoy peace, but are severed from that tranquillity of order in which there is no disturbance, nevertheless, inasmuch as they are deservedly and justly miserable, they are by their very misery connected with order. They are not, indeed, conjoined with the blessed, but they are disjoined from them by the law of order. And though they are disquieted, their circumstances are notwithstanding adjusted to them, and consequently they have some tranquillity of order, and therefore some peace. But they are wretched because, although not wholly miserable, they are not in that place where any mixture of misery is impossible. They would, however, be more wretched if they had not that peace which arises from being in harmony with the natural order of things. When they suffer, their peace is in so far disturbed; but their peace continues in so far as they do not suffer, and in so far as their nature continues to exist. As, then, there may be life without pain, while there cannot be pain without some kind of life, so there may be peace without war, but there cannot be war without some kind of peace, because war supposes the existence of some natures to wage it, and these natures cannot exist without peace of one kind or other.

And therefore there is a nature in which evil does not or even cannot exist; but there cannot be a nature in which there is no good. Hence not even the nature of the devil himself is evil, in so far as it is nature, but it was made evil by being perverted. Thus he did not abide in the truth,[5] but could not escape the judgment of the Truth; he did not abide in the tranquillity of order, but did not therefore escape the power of the Ordainer. The good imparted by God to his nature did not screen him from the justice of God by which order was preserved in his punishment; neither did God punish the good which He had created, but the evil which the devil had committed. God did not take back all He had imparted to his nature, but something He took and something He left, that there might remain enough to be sensible of the loss of what was taken. And this very sensibility to pain is evidence of the good which has been taken away and the good which has been left. For, were nothing good left, there could be no pain on account of the good which had been lost. For he who sins is still worse if he rejoices in his loss of righteousness. But he who is in pain, if he derives no benefit from it, mourns at least the loss of health. And as righteousness and health are both good things, and as the loss of any good thing is matter of grief, not of joy,—if, at least, there is no compensation, as spiritual righteousness may compensate for the loss of bodily health,—certainly it is more suitable for a wicked man to grieve in punishment than to rejoice in his fault. As, then, the joy of a sinner who has abandoned what is good is evidence of a bad will, so his grief for the good he has lost when he is punished is evidence of a good nature. For he who laments the peace his

[5]John viii. 44.

nature has lost is stirred to do so by some relics of peace which make his nature friendly to itself. And it is very just that in the final punishment the wicked and godless should in anguish bewail the loss of the natural advantages they enjoyed, and should perceive that they were most justly taken from them by that God whose benign liberality they had despised. God, then, the most wise Creator and most just Ordainer of all natures, who placed the human race upon earth as its greatest ornament, imparted to men some good things adapted to this life, to wit, temporal peace, such as we can enjoy in this life from health and safety and human fellowship, and all things needful for the preservation and recovery of this peace, such as the objects which are accommodated to our outward senses, light, night, the air, and waters suitable for us, and everything the body requires to sustain, shelter, heal, or beautify it: and all under this most equitable condition, that every man who made a good use of these advantages suited to the peace of this mortal condition, should receive ampler and better blessings, namely, the peace of immortality, accompanied by glory and honor in an endless life made fit for the enjoyment of God and of one another in God; but that he who used the present blessings badly should both lose them and should not receive the others.

.   .   .

WHAT PRODUCES PEACE, AND WHAT DISCORD, BETWEEN THE HEAVENLY AND EARTHLY CITIES.

But the families which do not live by faith seek their peace in the earthly advantages of this life; while the families which live by faith look for those eternal blessings which are promised, and use as pilgrims such advantages of time and of earth as do not fascinate and divert them from God, but rather aid them to endure with greater ease, and to keep down the number of those burdens of the corruptible body which weigh upon the soul. Thus the things necessary for this mortal life are used by both kinds of men and families alike, but each has its own peculiar and widely different aim in using them. The earthly city, which does not live by faith, seeks an earthly peace, and the end it proposes, in the well-ordered concord of civic obedience and rule, is the combination of men's wills to attain the things which are helpful to this life. The heavenly city, or rather the part of it which sojourns on earth and lives by faith, makes use of this peace only because it must, until this mortal condition which necessitates it shall pass away. Consequently, so long as it lives like a captive and a stranger in the earthly city, though it has already received the promise of redemption, and the gift of the Spirit as the earnest of it, it makes no scruple to obey the laws of the earthly city, whereby the things necessary for the maintenance of this mortal life are administered; and thus, as this life is common to both cities, so there is a harmony between them in regard to what belongs to it. But, as the earthly city has had some philosophers whose doctrine is condemned by the divine teaching, and who, being deceived either by their own conjectures or by demons, supposed that many gods must be invited to take an interest in human affairs, and assigned to each a separate function and a separate department,—to one the body, to another the soul; and in the body itself, to one the head, to another the neck, and each of the other members to one of the gods; and in like manner, in the soul, to one god the natural capacity was assigned, to another education, to another anger, to another lust; and so the various affairs of life were assigned,—cattle to one, corn to another, wine to another, oil to another, the woods to another, money to another, navigation to another, wars and victories to another, marriages to another, births and fecundity to another, and other things to other gods: and as the celestial city, on the other hand, knew that one God only was to be worshipped, and that to Him alone was due that service which the Greeks call λατρεία, and which can be given only to a god, it has come to pass that the two cities could not have common laws of religion, and that the heavenly city has been compelled in this matter to dissent, and to become obnoxious to those who think differently, and to stand the brunt of their anger and hatred and persecutions, except in so far as the minds of their enemies have been alarmed by the multitude of the Christians and quelled by the manifest protection of God accorded to them. This heavenly city, then, while it sojourns on earth, calls citizens out of all nations, and gathers together a society of pilgrims of all languages, not scrupling about diversities in the manners, laws, and institutions whereby earthly peace is secured and maintained, but recognizing that, however various these are, they all tend to one and the same end of earthly peace. It therefore is so far from rescinding and abolishing these diversities, that it even preserves and adopts them, so long only as no hindrance to the worship of the one supreme and true God is thus introduced. Even the heavenly city, therefore, while in its state of pilgrimage, avails itself of the peace of earth, and, so far as it can without injuring faith and godliness, desires and maintains a common agreement among men regarding the acquisition of the necessaries of life, and makes this earthly peace bear upon the peace of heaven; for this alone can be truly called and esteemed the peace of the reasonable creatures, consisting as it does in the perfectly ordered and harmonious enjoyment of God and of one another in God. When we shall have reached that peace, this mortal life shall give place to one that is eternal, and our body shall be no more this animal body which by its corruption weighs down the soul, but a spiritual body feeling no want, and in all its members subjected to the will. In its pilgrim state the heavenly city possesses this peace by faith; and by this faith it lives righteously when it refers to the attainment of that peace every good action towards God and man; for the life of the city is a social life.

57

ERNEST NAGEL (1901– ————)

Naturalism Reconsidered

A distinguished American philosopher, Ernest Nagel was, for many years, John Dewey
Professor of Philosophy at Columbia University. He has primarily worked in the areas
of logic and philosophy of science. Among his many books are *An Introduction to
Logic and Scientific Method* (coauthor, 1934), *Principles of the Theory of Probability*
(1939), *Logic without Metaphysics* (1956), and *The Structure of Science* (1961).

The selection that follows constitutes an exceptionally clear and compact statement
of the principal tenets of the world view of *naturalism.* Nagel presents two main
theses: (1) the materialist thesis: the primary and most ultimate entities in the universe
are material entities (matter), and (2) the pluralist thesis: plurality is an ultimate fact
about the universe, not a mere appearance behind which lies some hidden unity. He
then develops a view of human nature and human existence consistent with these
views.

. . .

The discharge of the important obligation which is mine this evening, seems
to me an appropriate occasion for stating as simply and as succinctly as I can
the substance of those intellectual commitments I like to call "naturalism."
The label itself is of no importance, but I use it partly because of its historical
associations, and partly because it is a reminder that the doctrines for which
it is a name are neither new nor untried. With Santayana, I prefer not to accept
in philosophic debate what I do not believe when I am not arguing; and
naturalism as I construe it merely formulates what centuries of human experience have repeatedly confirmed. At any rate, naturalism seems to me a sound
generalized account of the world encountered in practice and in critical reflection, and a just perspective upon the human scene. I wish to state briefly and
hence with little supporting argument what I take to be its major tenets, and
to defend it against some recent criticisms.

From Ernest Nagel, "Naturalism Reconsidered," *Proceedings of the American Philosophical
Association,* 28 (1954–1955), pp. 5–7, 17. Reprinted by permission of the author and publisher.

Claims to knowledge cannot ultimately be divorced from an evaluation of the intellectual methods used to support those claims. It is nevertheless unfortunate that in recent years naturalists in philosophy have so frequently permitted their allegiance to a dependable method of inquiry to obscure their substantive views on things in general. For it is the inclusive intellectual image of nature and man which naturalism supplies that sets it off from other comprehensive philosophies. In my conception of it, at any rate, naturalism embraces a generalized account of the cosmic scheme and of man's place in it, as well as a logic of inquiry.

I hasten to add, however, that naturalism does not offer a theory of nature in the sense that Newtonian mechanics, for example, provides a theory of motion. Naturalism does not, like the latter, specify a set of substantive principles with the help of which the detailed course of concrete happenings can be explained or understood. Moreover, the principles affirmed by naturalism are not proposed as competitors or underpinnings for any of the special theories which the positive sciences assert. Nor, finally, does naturalism offer its general view of nature and man as the product of some special philosophical mode of knowing. The account of things proposed by naturalism is a distillation from knowledge acquired in the usual way in daily encounters with the world or in specialized scientific inquiry. Naturalism articulates features of the world which, because they have become so obvious, are rarely mentioned in discussions of special subject-matter, but which distinguish our actual world from other conceivable worlds. The major affirmations of naturalism are accordingly meager in content; but the principles affirmed are nevertheless effective guides in responsible criticism and evaluation.

Two theses seem to me central to naturalism as I conceive it. The first is the existential and causal primacy of organized matter in the executive order of nature. This is the assumption that the occurrence of events, qualities and processes, and the characteristic behaviors of various individuals, are contingent on the organization of spatiotemporally located bodies, whose internal structures and external relations determine and limit the appearance and disappearance of everything that happens. That this is so, is one of the best-tested conclusions of experience. We are frequently ignorant of the special conditions under which things come into being or pass away; but we have also found repeatedly that when we look closely, we eventually ascertain at least the approximate and gross conditions under which events occur, and we discover that those conditions invariably consist of some more or less complex organization of material substances. Naturalism does not maintain that only what is material exists, since many things noted in experience, for example, modes of action, relations of meaning, dreams, joys, plans, aspirations, are not as such material bodies or organizations of material bodies. What naturalism does assert as a truth about nature is that though *forms* of behavior or *functions* of material systems are indefeasibly parts of nature, forms and functions are not themselves agents in their own realization or in the realization of anything else. In the conception of nature's processes which naturalism affirms, there is no place for the operation of disembodied forces, no place for an immaterial spirit directing the course of events, no place for the survival of personality after the corruption of the body which exhibits it.

The second major contention of naturalism is that the manifest plurality and variety of things, of their qualities and their functions, are an irreducible feature of the cosmos, not a deceptive appearance cloaking some more homogeneous "ultimate reality" or transempirical substance, and that the sequential orders in which events occur or the manifold relations of dependence in which things exist are *contingent* connections, not the embodiments of a fixed and unified pattern of logically necessary links. The existential primacy of organized matter does not make illusory either the relatively permanent or the comparatively transient characters and forms which special configurations of bodies may possess. In particular, although the continued existence of the human scene is precarious and is dependent on a balance of forces that doubtless will not endure indefinitely, and even though its distinctive traits are not pervasive throughout space, it is nonetheless as much a part of the "ultimate" furniture of the world, and is as genuine a sample of what "really" exists, as are atoms and stars. There undoubtedly occur integrated systems of bodies, such as biological organisms, which have the capacity because of their material organization to maintain themselves and the direction of their characteristic activities. But there is no positive evidence, and much negative evidence, for the supposition that all existential structures are teleological systems in this sense, or for the view that whatever occurs is a phase in a unitary, teleologically organized, and all-inclusive process or system. Modern physical cosmology does indeed supply some evidence for definite patterns of evolutionary development of stars, galactic systems, and even of the entire physical universe; and it is quite possible that the stage of cosmic evolution reached at any given time causally limits the types of things which can occur during that period. On the other hand, the patterns of change investigated in physical cosmogony are not patterns that are exhaustive of everything that happens; and nothing in these current physical speculations requires the conclusion that changes in one star or galaxy are related by inherent necessity to every action of biological organisms in some remote planet. Even admittedly teleological systems contain parts and processes which are causally irrelevant to some of the activities maintained by those systems; and the causal dependencies known to hold between the parts of any system, teleological or not, have never been successfully established as forms of logically necessary relations. In brief, if naturalism is true, irreducible variety and logical contingency are fundamental traits of the world we actually inhabit. The orders and connections of things are all accessible to rational inquiry; but these orders and connections are not all derivable by deductive methods from any set of premises that deductive reason can certify.

It is in this framework of general ideas that naturalism envisages the career and destiny of man. Naturalism views the emergence and the continuance of human society as dependent on physical and physiological conditions that have not always obtained, and that will not permanently endure. But it does not in consequence regard man and his works as intrusions into nature, any more than it construes as intrusions the presence of heavenly bodies or of terrestrial protozoa. The stars are no more foreign to the cosmos than are men, even if the conditions for the existence of both stars and men are realized only occasionally or only in a few regions. Indeed, the conception of human life as a war with nature, as a struggle with an implacable foe that has doomed man to extinction, is but an inverted theology, with a malicious Devil in the seat of Omnipotence. It is a conception that is immodest as well as anthropomorphic in the importance it imputes to man in the scheme of things.

On the other hand, the affirmation that nature is man's "home" as much as it is the "home" of anything else, and the denial that cosmic forces are *intent* on destroying the human scene, do not warrant the interpretation that every sector of nature is explicable in terms of traits known to characterize only human individuals and human actions. Man undoubtedly possesses characteristics which are shared by everything that exists; but he also manifests traits and capacities that appear to be distinctive of him. Is anything gained but confusion when all forms of dependence between things, whether animate or inanimate, and all types of behaviors they display, are subsumed under distinctions that have an identifiable content only in reference to the human psyche? Measured by the illumination they bring, there is nothing to differentiate the thesis that human traits are nothing but the properties of bodies which can be formulated exclusively in the language of current physical theory, from the view that every change and every mode of operation, in whatever sector of the cosmos it may be encountered, is simply an illustration of some category pertinent to the description of human behavior.

Indeed, even some professed naturalists sometimes appear to promote the confusion when they make a fetish of continuity. Naturalists usually stress the emergence of novel forms in physical and biological evolution, thereby emphasizing the fact that human traits are not identical with the traits from which they emerge. Nevertheless, some distinguished contemporary naturalists also insist, occasionally with overtones of anxiety, that there is a "continuity" between the typically human on the one hand, and the physical and biological on the other. But is man's foothold in the scheme of things really made more secure by showing that his distinctive traits are in some sense "continuous" with features pervasive in nature, and would man's place in nature be less secure if such continuity did not obtain? The actual evidence for a continuity of development is conclusive in some instances of human traits, however it may be in others. But I sometimes suspect that the cardinal importance philosophers assign to the alleged universality of such continuity is a lingering survival of that ancient conception, according to which things are intelligible only when seen as teleological systems producing definite ends, so that nature itself is properly understood only when construed as the habitat of human society. In any event, a naturalism that is not provincial in its outlook will not accept the

intellectual incorporation of man into nature at the price of reading into all
the processes of the cosmos the passions, the strivings, the defeats and the
glories of human life, and then exhibiting man as the most adequate, because
most representative, expression of nature's inherent constitution. No, a mature
naturalism seeks to understand what man is, not in terms of a discovered or
postulated continuity between what is distinctive of him and what is pervasive
in all things. Without denying that even the most distinctive human traits are
dependent on things which are non-human, a mature naturalism attempts to
assess man's nature in the light of *his* actions and achievements, *his* aspirations
and capacities, *his* limitations and tragic failures, and *his* splendid works of
ingenuity and imagination.

Human nature and history, in short, are *human* nature and history, not the
history and nature of anything else, however much knowledge of other things
contributes to a just appraisal of what man is. In particular, the adequacy of
proposed ideals for human life must be judged, not in terms of their causes and
origins, but in reference to how the pursuit and possible realization of ideals
contribute to the organization and release of *human* energies. Men are animated by many springs of action, no one of which is intrinsically good or evil;
and a moral ideal is the imagined satisfaction of some complex of impulses,
desires, and needs. When ideals are handled responsibly, they therefore function as hypotheses for achieving a balanced exercise of human powers. Moral
ideals are not self-certifying, any more than are the theories of the physical
sciences; and evidence drawn from experienced satisfactions is required to
validate them, however difficult may be the process of sifting and weighing the
available data. Moral problems arise from a conflict of specific impulses and
interests. They cannot, however, be effectively resolved by invoking standards
derived from the study of non-human nature, or of what is allegedly beyond
nature. If moral problems can be resolved at all, they can be resolved only in
the light of specific human capacities, historical circumstances and acquired
skills, and the opportunities (revealed by an imagination disciplined by knowledge) for altering the physical and social environment and for redirecting
habitual behaviors. Moreover, since human virtues are in part the products of
the society in which human powers are matured, a naturalistic moral theory
is at the same time a critique of civilization, that is, a critique of the institutions
that channel human energies, so as to exhibit the possibilities and limitations
of various forms and arrangements of society for bringing enduring satisfactions to individual human careers.

These are the central tenets of what I take to be philosophical naturalism.
They are tenets which are supported by compelling empirical evidence, rather
than dicta based on dogmatic preference. In my view of it, naturalism does not
dismiss every other differing conception of the scheme of things as logically
impossible; and it does not rule out all alternatives to itself on a priori grounds.
It is possible, I think, to conceive without logical inconsistency a world in
which disembodied forces are dynamic agents, or in which whatever happens

is a manifestation of an unfolding logical pattern. In such possible worlds it would be an error to be a naturalist. But philosophy is not identical with pure mathematics, and its ultimate concern is with the actual world, even though philosophy must take cognizance of the fact that the actual world contains creatures who can envisage possible worlds and who employ different logical procedures for deciding which hypothetical world is the actual one. It is partly for this reason that contemporary naturalists devote so much attention to methods of evaluating evidence. When naturalists give their allegiance to the method of intelligence commonly designated as the method of modern empirical science, they do so because that method appears to be the most assured way of achieving reliable knowledge.

As judged by that method, the evidence in my opinion is at present conclusive for the truth of naturalism, and it is tempting to suppose that no one familiar with the evidence can fail to acknowledge that philosophy. Indeed, some commentators there are who assert that all philosophies are at bottom only expressions in different idioms of the same conceptions about the nature of things, so that the strife of philosophic systems is mainly a conflict over essentially linguistic matters. Yet many thinkers for whom I have a profound respect explicitly reject naturalism, and their espousal of contrary views seems to me incompatible with the irenic claim that we really are in agreement on fundamentals.

Although I do not have the time this evening to consider systematically the criticisms currently made of naturalism, I do wish to examine briefly two repeatedly voiced objections which, if valid, would in my opinion seriously jeopardize the integrity and adequacy of naturalism as a philosophy. Stated summarily, the first objection is that in relying exclusively on the logico-empirical method of modern science for establishing cognitive claims, naturalists are in effect stacking the cards in their own favor, since thereby all alternative philosophies are antecedently disqualified. It is maintained, for example, that naturalism rejects any hypothesis about trans-empirical causes or time-transcending spiritual substances as factors in the order of things, not because such hypotheses are actually shown to be false, but simply because the logic of proof adopted dismisses as irrelevant any evidence which might establish them.

This criticism does not seem to me to have merit: the logico-empirical method of evaluating cognitive claims to which naturalists subscribe does not eliminate by fiat any hypothesis about existence for which evidence can be procured, that is, evidence that in the last resort can be obtained through sensory or introspective observation. Thus, anyone who asserts a hypothesis postulating a trans-empirical ground for all existence, presumably seeks to understand in terms of that ground the actual occurrences in nature, and to account thereby for what actually happens as distinct from what is merely imagined to happen. There must therefore be some connection between the postulated character of the hypothetical trans-empirical ground, and the empirically observable traits in the world around us; for otherwise the hypothesis is otiose, and not relevant to the spatio-temporal processes of nature. This does not mean, as some critics of naturalism suppose the latter to maintain, that the hypothetical trans-empirical ground must be characterized exclusively in terms of the observable properties of the world, any more than that the sub-microscopic particles and processes which current physical theory postulates must be logical constructions out of the observable traits of macroscopic objects. But it does mean that unless the hypothesis implies, even if only by a circuitous route, some statements about empirical data, it is not adequate to the task for which it is proposed. If naturalists reject hypotheses about trans-empirical substances, they do not do so arbitrarily. They reject such hypotheses either because their relevance to the going concerns of nature is not established, or because, though their relevance is not in question, the actual evidence does not support them.

Nor does naturalism dismiss as unimportant and without consideration experiences such as of the holy, of divine illumination, or of mystical ecstasy, experiences which are of the greatest moment in the lives of many men, and which are often taken to signify the presence and operation of some purely spiritual reality. Such experiences have dimensions of meaning for those who have undergone them, that are admittedly not on par with the import of more common experiences like those of physical hunger, general well-being, or feelings of remorse and guilt. Yet such experiences are nonetheless events among other events; and though they may be evidence for something, their sheer occurrence does not certify *what* they are evidence for, any more than the sheer occurrence of dreams, hopes, and delusions authenticates the actual existence of their ostensible objects. In particular, whether the experience labelled as an experience of divine illumination is evidence for the existence of a divinity, is a question to be settled by inquiry, not by dogmatic affirmations or denials. When naturalists refuse to acknowledge, merely on the strength of such experiences, the operation or presence of a divine power, they do so not because their commitment to a logical method prevents them from treating it seriously, but because independent inquiry fails to confirm it. Knowledge is knowledge, and cannot without confusion be identified with intuitive insight or with the vivid immediacy of profoundly moving experiences. Claims to knowledge must be capable of being tested; and the testing must be conducted by eventual reference to such evidence as counts in the responsible conduct of everyday affairs as well as of systematic inquiry in the sciences. Naturalists are therefore not engaged in question-begging when, through the use of the logic of scientific intelligence, they judge non-naturalistic accounts of the order of things to be unfounded.

There is, however, a further objection to naturalism, to the effect that in committing itself to the logic of scientific proof, it is quite analogous to religious belief in resting on unsupported and indemonstrable faith. For that logic allegedly involves assumptions like the uniformity of nature or similar principles which transcend experience, cannot be justified empirically, and yet provide the premises that constitute the ultimate warrant for the conclusions of empirical inquiry. But if naturalism is thus based on unprovable articles of faith, on what cogent grounds can it reject a different conception of the true order of governance of events which rests on a different faith?

I cannot here deal adequately with the complex issues raised by this objection. Its point is not satisfactorily turned by claiming, as some have done, that instead of being articles of faith, the alleged indemonstrable postulates of scientific method are simply rules of the scientific game which *define* what in that game is to be understood by the words "knowledge" and "evidence." As I see it, however, the objection has force only for those whose ideal of reason is demonstration, and who therefore refuse to dignify anything as genuine knowledge unless it is demonstrable from self-luminous and self-evident premises. But if, as I also think, that ideal is not universally appropriate, and if, furthermore, a *wholesale* justification for knowledge and its methods is an unreasonable demand and a misplaced effort, the objection appears as quite pointless. The warrant for a proposition about some specific inter-relations of events does not derive from a faith in the uniformity of nature or in other principles with a cosmic scope. The warrant derives exclusively from the specific evidence available for that proposition, and from the contingent historical fact that the special ways employed in obtaining and appraising the evidence have been generally effective in yielding reliable knowledge. Subsequent inquiry may show that we were mistaken in accepting a proposition on the evidence available earlier; and further inquiry may also reveal that a given inductive policy, despite a record of successful past performance, requires correction if not total rejection. Fortunately, however, we are not always mistaken in accepting various propositions or in employing certain inductive policies, even though we are unable to demonstrate that we shall never fall into error. Accordingly, though many of our hopes for the stability of beliefs in the face of fresh experience may turn out to be baseless, and though no guarantees can be given that our most assured claims to knowledge may not eventually need revision, in adopting scientific method as the instrument for evaluating claims to knowledge, naturalists are not subscribing to an indemonstrable faith.

The bitter years of cataclysmic wars and social upheavals through which our generation has been passing have also witnessed a general decline of earlier hopes in the possibilities of modern science for achieving a liberal and humane civilization. Indeed, as is well known, many men have become convinced that the progress and spread of science, and the consequent secularization of society, are the prime sources of our present ills; and a not inconsiderable number of thinkers have made widely popular various revived forms of older religious and irrationalistic philosophies as guides to human salvation. Moreover, since naturalists have not abandoned their firm adherence to the method of scientific intelligence, naturalism has been repeatedly charged with insensitivity toward

spiritual values, with a shallow optimism toward science as an instrument for
ennobling the human estate, and with a philistine blindness toward the ineradi-
cable miseries of human existence. I want to conclude with a few brief comments on these allegations.

It is almost painful to have to make a point of the elementary fact that
whatever may happen to be the range of special interests and sensibilities of
individual naturalists, there is no incompatibility, whether logical or psychological, between maintaining that warranted knowledge is secured only
through the use of a definite logical method, and recognizing that the world
can be experienced in many other ways than by knowing it. It is a matter of
record that outstanding exponents of naturalism, in our own time as well as
in the past, have exhibited an unequaled and tender sensitivity to the esthetic
and moral dimensions of human experience; and they have been not only
movingly eloquent celebrants of the role of moral idealism and of intellectual
and esthetic contemplation in human life, but also vigorous defenders of the
distinctive character of these values against facile attempts to reduce them to
something else.

It seems to me singularly inept, moreover, to indict naturalism as a philosophy without a sense for the tragic aspects of life. For unlike many world-views,
naturalism offers no cosmic consolation for the unmerited defeats and undeserved sufferings which all men experience in one form or another. It has
never sought to conceal its view of human destiny as an episode between two
oblivions. To be sure, naturalism is not a philosophy of despair. For one facet
in its radical pluralism is the truth that a human good is nonetheless a good,
despite its transitory existence. There doubtless are foolish optimists among
those professing naturalism, though naturalism has no monopoly in this respect, and it is from other quarters that one usually receives glad tidings of a
universal nostrum. But in any event, neither the pluralism so central to naturalism, nor its cultivation of scientific reason, is compatible with any dogmatic
assumption to the effect that men can be liberated from *all* the sorrows and
evils to which they are now heirs, through the eventual advances of science
and the institution of appropriate physical and social innovations. Indeed, why
suppose that a philosophy which is wedded to the use of the sober logic of
scientific intelligence, should thereby be committed to the dogma that there are
no irremediable evils? On the contrary, human reason is potent only against
evils that are *remediable*. At the same time, since it is impossible to decide
responsibly, *antecedent* to inquiry, *which* of the many human ills can be
mitigated if not eradicated by extending the operations of scientific reason into
human affairs, naturalism is not a philosophy of *general* renunciation, even
though it recognizes that it is the better part of wisdom to be equally resigned
to what, in the light of available evidence, cannot be avoided. Human reason
is not an omnipotent instrument for the achievement of human goods; but it
is the only instrument we do possess, and it is not a contemptible one. Although naturalism is acutely sensitive to the actual limitations of rational

effort, those limitations do not warrant a romantic philosophy of general despair, and they do not blind naturalism to the possibilities implicit in the exercise of disciplined reason for realizing human excellence.

58

PAUL TILLICH (1886–1965)

Realism and Faith

Paul Tillich was a German philosopher-theologian who left Nazi Germany and came to the United States just prior to the outbreak of World War II. He remained here for the rest of his life and, in his later years, lectured to large audiences all over the country. In addition, he held teaching positions at Union Theological Seminary, Harvard University, and the University of Chicago. He was immensely influential during his lifetime, both as a teacher and as an author. His writings in English include *The Protestant Era* (1948), *The Courage To Be* (1952), *The Religious Situation* (1956), *Dynamics of Faith* (1957), and a three-volume work entitled *Systematic Theology* (1951–1963).

Tillich perceived himself as a "mediating" philosopher-theologian. He was equally at home in theology and philosophy, in the church and the secular world, and his self-assigned task was to facilitate communication between the two. For Tillich, every "either-or" problem was a challenge to find some higher truth in which the apparent impasse between the two could be overcome.

The selection that follows is a case in point. Tillich, although he does not use the phrase "world view," contrasts the world views of theism ("faith") and naturalism ("realism"). He distinguishes several forms of each, then attempts to formulate an alternative view that includes elements of both. He calls this view *self-transcending realism.*

Reprinted from *The Protestant Era,* by Paul Tillich, by permission of The University of Chicago Press. Copyright © 1948 and 1957 by The University of Chicago.

Self-transcending realism is a universal attitude toward reality. It is neither a merely theoretical view of the world nor a practical discipline for life; it lies underneath the cleavage between theory and practice. Nor is it a special religion or a special philosophy. But it is a basic attitude in every realm of life, expressing itself in the shaping of every realm.

Self-transcending realism combines two elements, the emphasis on the real and the transcending power of faith. There seems to be no wider gap than that between a realistic and a belief-ful attitude. Faith transcends every conceivable reality; realism questions every transcending of the real, calling it utopian or romantic. Such a tension is hard to stand, and it is not surprising that the human mind always tries to evade it. Evasion is possible in two ways—in the way of a realism without self-transcendence or in the way of a self-transcendence which is not realistic. For the latter I want to use the word "idealism," for the former the word "self-limiting realism." Neither of these attitudes is necessarily irreligious. Positivism, pragmatism, empiricism—the different forms of realism which refuse self-transcendence—may accept religion as a realm beside the philosophical and scientific interpretation of reality, or they may connect the two realms in terms of a theology of immanent experience (the former more an English, the latter more an American, type). Idealism, on the other hand, in its different forms, such as metaphysical, epistemological, moral idealism (the first a classical German, the second a universal bourgeois, the third an Anglo-Saxon type) is essentially religious but in such a way that genuine religion must be critical of it. Faith is an ecstatic transcending of reality in the power of that which cannot be derived from the whole of reality and cannot be approached by ways which belong to the whole of reality. Idealism does not see the gap between the unconditional and the conditioned which no ontological or ethical self-elevation can bridge. Therefore it must be judged from a prophetic and Protestant point of view as religious arrogance and from the point of view of a self-limiting realism as metaphysical arrogance. In this double attack, from the side of faith and from the side of realism, idealism breaks down, historically and systematically, practically and theoretically. It is the glory of idealism that it tries to unite an autonomous interpretation of reality with a religious transcending of reality. Idealism is always on the way to "theonomy." Most of the theological, philosophical, and political critics of idealism have not even understood its problems. Their feeling of superiority over idealism is based on their ignorance about the depth of its questions and answers. The limitation and tragedy of idealism lie in the fact that it idealizes the real instead of transcending it in the power of the transcendent, i.e., in faith. Hence we are led to the result that faith and realism, just because of their radical tension, belong together. For faith implies an absolute tension and cannot be united with any attitude in which the tension is weakened. Idealism relativizes, self-limiting realism denies, but self-transcending realism accepts the tension.

.   .   .

The question now arises: What is the relation of historical realism to what we have called "self-transcending realism"? Historical realism strives to grasp the power of reality or the really real in a concrete historical situation. But the really real is not reached until the unconditioned ground of everything real, or the unconditioned power in every power of being, is reached. Historical realism remains on a comparatively unrealistic level if it does not grasp that depth of reality in which its divine foundation and meaning become visible. Everything before this point has preliminary, conditioned reality. Therefore, historical realism has truth to the degree that it reaches the ultimate ground and meaning of a historical situation and, through it, of being as such.

But it is the character of the unconditional that it cannot be grasped; its power includes its unapproachable mystery. If we try to grasp it, it is no longer the unconditional that we have in our hands—even if it has the highest religious or ontological names. Idealism is the philosophy that makes this mistake. It confuses the world of essences and values and their unity with the unconditionally real. It fails to transcend this sphere of pure reason, a sphere that can be transcended only by accepting that which is "before reason," the *Unvordenkliche,* as Schelling has called it ("that before which thinking cannot penetrate"), the originally given, the ground and abyss of everything that is. There was a feeling for this limit in all Greek philosophy. Indeed, pure idealism is not Greek, because the ancient mind could not overcome the belief in the eternally resisting matter, the negative, restricting power of which excludes an unconditional divine power. Genuine idealism is possible only on Christian soil, on the basis of the idea of creation which affirms the essential goodness and unity of the world. Perfect systems like those of the great idealists presuppose the Christian victory over the remnants of religious dualism in Greek thought. But they arise only because the other Christian idea is disregarded, the gap between God and man through finitude and sin.

In this respect positivism is more Christian than idealism. It accepts the limited and fragmentary character of the human situation and tries to remain in the sphere of the conditioned. It shows more humility than idealism in taking the given as it is and rejecting romantic or utopian syntheses which have no reality. But positivism does not see the problem of self-transcendence. It restricts itself to the immanence, not because of the unapproachable mystery of the transcendent, but because of its unwillingness to trespass the limits of the empirically given. Positivism is realism without self-transcendence or faith.

Self-transcending realism is the religious depth of historical realism; therefore, it is opposed to mystical and technological realism. Mysticism is not aware of the unapproachable nature of the divine ground of reality (including the "soul"). It tries to reach the unconditional in conditioned steps, in degrees of elevation to the highest. Mystical self-transcendence is a continuous approximation to the ultimate; it does not realize the infinite gap between the finite and the infinite; it does not realize the paradoxical character of faith and of a realism which is united with faith. This does not mean that mystical realism excludes faith. In every mystical experience an act of self-transcendence or faith is implicit. The complete union with the ultimate is, according to all mystics, a gift to be received and not a perfection to be achieved. Therefore, it is a mistake when Protestant theologians, from Ritschl to Barth, establish an absolute contrast between mysticism and faith. It is true, however, that mysticism tries to transcend faith in the experience of mystical union and that it disregards the historical situation and its power and depth. This is different in a self-transcending, historical realism which experiences the ultimate in and through a concrete historical situation and denies any degrees of approximation to it, knowing that it is always, at the same time, unconditionally near and unconditionally far.

Technological realism is even less capable of becoming self-transcendent. It separates realism and faith. In later Ritschlianism, faith became the means of elevating the ethical personality above nature to moral independence, leaving nature to technical control. The technological interpretation of nature, its complete subjection to human purposes, was accepted but not transcended. And domineering personality used faith as a means for maintaining this position of independence and control. This theology expresses very well the difficulty of combining faith with technological realism. Although the faith of which, for instance, a man like William Hermann speaks, is in itself warm, powerful, and passionate, its function in the context of a technological interpretation of reality is the creation of the personality of the victorious *bourgeoisie*. In English positivism no attempt is made to unite faith and realism. "Faith" is the conventional or serious acceptance of the creeds and institutions of the church. And realism is the technological attitude to nature and society. But there is no union between this kind of faith and this kind of realism. They are two worlds, connected only by a powerful social and intellectual conformism.

Self-transcending realism is based on the consciousness of the "here and now." The ultimate power of being, the ground of reality, appears in a special moment, in a concrete situation, revealing the infinite depth and the eternal significance of the present. But this is possible only in terms of a paradox, i.e., by faith, for, in itself, the present is neither infinite nor eternal. The more it is seen in the light of the ultimate power, the more it appears as questionable and void of lasting significance. So the power of a thing is, at the same time, affirmed and negated when it becomes transparent for the ground of its power, the ultimately real. It is as in a thunderstorm at night, when the lightning throws a blinding clarity over all things, leaving them in complete darkness the next moment. When reality is seen in this way with the eye of a self-transcending realism, it has become something new. Its ground has become visible in an "ecstatic" experience, called "faith." It is no longer merely self-subsistent as it seemed to be before; it has become transparent or, as we could say, "theonomous." This, of course, is not an event in nature, although—as always in spiritual matters—words and pictures have to be used which are taken from the spatial sphere. But it is the whole of the personality, including its conscious center, its freedom and responsibility, which is grasped by the ultimate power that is the ground also of every personal being. We are grasped, in the experience of faith, by the unapproachably holy which is the ground of our being and breaks into our existence and which judges us and heals us. This is "crisis" and "grace" at the same time. Crisis in the theological sense is as much a matter of faith as grace is. To describe the crisis as something immanent, open for everybody at any time, and grace as something transcendent, closed to everybody and to be accepted only by a personal decision, is bad theology. Neither crisis nor grace is in our reach, neither grace nor crisis is beyond a possible experience. The present situation is always full of "critical" elements, of forces of disintegration and self-destruction. But it becomes "crisis" in the religious sense, i.e., judgment, only in unity with the experience of grace. In this way historical realism becomes self-transcendent; historical and self-transcending realism are united.

.   .   .

Self-transcending realism requires the criticism of all forms of supranaturalism —supra-naturalism in the sense of a theology that imagines a supra-natural world beside or above the natural one, a world in which the unconditional finds a local habitation, thus making God a transcendent object, the creation an act at the beginning of time, the consummation a future state of things. To criticize such a conditioning of the unconditional, even if it leads to atheistic consequences, is more religious, because it is more aware of the unconditional character of the divine, than a theism that bans God into the supra-natural realm. The man of today, who feels separated by a gulf from the theistic believer, often knows more about the "ultimate" than the self-assured Christian who thinks that through his faith he has God in his possession, at least intellectually. A Christian who unites his supra-naturalistic belief with the continuous denial of his historical situation (and the historical situation of many others for whom he is responsible) is rejected by the principles of a self-transcendent realism that is always also historical realism. . . .

59

JEAN PAUL SARTRE (1905–1980)

Existentialist Humanism

Jean Paul Sartre is undoubtedly the best known and most widely read of the twentieth-century existentialist philosophers. He has written voluminously in many genres: novels, plays, and essays, as well as philosophical treatises. Many of the principal themes of his philosophy are worked out systematically in his book *Being and Nothingness.*

Sartre is presented here as a representative of a *humanist* world view. The thesis of this essay is that atheistic existentialism is a form of humanism. Human beings, in Sartre's view, are not children of God (theism), nor can they be understood simply in terms of matter and its laws (naturalism). Human beings are essentially consciousnesses—nonmaterial entities—and are totally free. They are nothing until they choose what they shall be. This is the meaning of Sartre's statement that, in human beings, "existence precedes essence." Each of us, so to speak, creates humanity—decides what humanity ought to be—by choosing what we ourselves shall be. Thus, as a corollary of our total freedom, we are also totally responsible.

Most of the people who use this word (existentialism) would be quite confounded if asked to define it. For now that it has become fashionable, one readily declares that a certain painter or musician is "existentialist." A columnist in *Clartes* signs himself, "The Existentialist." Indeed, the word today has been used so broadly and extensively that it no longer means anything at all. It seems that, for lack of any new avant-garde doctrine, such as surrealism, those who are eager for scandal and commotion have addressed themselves to this philosophy, which in most respects holds no appeal for them. In reality this is the least scandalous and most austere of all doctrines; it is intended strictly for technicians and philosophers. It can, however, be easily defined.

The complications arise from the fact that there are two types of existentialists. In one group are the Christians, among whom I would include Jaspers

From Jean Paul Sartre, *L'Existentialisme est un Humanisme,* originally published by Les Editions Nagel. Translated for this volume by Carol Halverson.

and Gabriel Marcel, who are Catholic.* The other group is composed of existentialist atheists, among whom one must place Heidegger, the French existentialists, and myself. The two groups have in common simply the fact that they assert that *existence* precedes *essence;* or, in other words, that one must begin with the subjective. Precisely what do we mean by this?

When one considers a manufactured product—such as a book or a paper-knife, for example—this object has been made by a craftsman who has drawn his inspiration from a concept. He has referred equally to the concept of a paper-knife, and to a pre-existing production technique which is part of that concept and is, essentially, a formula. Thus, the paper-knife is both an object which is produced in a certain manner, and, at the same time, one which has a definite utility, for one cannot suppose that a man would produce a paper-knife without knowing its purpose. We say, then, that for the paper-knife, its essence—that is to say, the collection of formulas and qualities that allow it to be produced and defined—precedes its existence. And thus, the presence of this paper-knife or of that book is determined in my sight. We have here, then, a technical view of the world, in which we can say that production precedes existence.

When we conceive of a creator God, this God is usually compared to a superior craftsman. Whatever doctrine we are considering, whether it be like that of Descartes or of Leibniz, we always accept that the will more or less follows from the understanding, or at least accompanies it, and that God, when he creates, knows exactly what he is creating. Thus the concept of Man in the mind of God is comparable to the concept of the paper-knife in the mind of the manufacturer. God makes Man according to a certain procedure and conception, exactly as the artisan produces a paper-knife according to a specific design and production technique. Consequently, the individual man is a realization of a certain concept in the divine understanding.

In the philosophical atheism of the eighteenth century, the notion of God was suppressed, but not, even then, the idea that essence precedes existence. We continue to encounter a little of this idea everywhere; we find it in Diderot, in Voltaire, and even in Kant. Man is the possessor of a human nature; this human nature, which is the human concept, is found in all men, meaning that each man is a particular example of the universal concept, Man. According to Kant, this universality extends so far that the man of the woods, the man of nature, and bourgeois man are all subject to the same definition and possess the same basic qualities. Thus, here again the essence of Man precedes this historical existence which we encounter in nature.

Atheistic existentialism, of which I am a representative, is more coherent. It holds that if God does not exist, there is at least some being whose existence precedes its essence—a being which exists before it can be defined by any concept—and that this being is Man or, as Heidegger calls it, the human

*Sartre is in error in classifying Jaspers as a Catholic [Ed.].

reality. What is meant here by "existence precedes essence"? We mean that Man first exists, encounters himself, appears in the world, and then defines himself afterwards. If Man as the existentialist conceives of him is not definable, it is because he is nothing at first. He will not be anything until later, and then he will be such as he makes himself to be. Thus, there is no human nature, since there is no God to conceive of it. Man simply is. Yet he is not only such as he conceives of himself, but such as he wills himself to be and as he sees himself after existence. Man is as he wants to be after this rush toward existence; he is nothing besides what he makes of himself. Such is the first principle of existentialism. And such, also, is what is called "subjectivity," for which our critics constantly reproach us. Yet what do we mean to say by this, if not that man has a greater dignity than a stone or a table. For we mean that a man first exists—that is to say, that man is first of all something which propels itself towards a future, and which is conscious of doing so. Man is primarily a project which lives its life subjectively, instead of being a moss, a mold, or a cauliflower. Nothing exists prior to this project, nothing intelligible hovers in the skies and, from the very beginning, man is and will be only that which he determines himself to be. For what we ordinarily understand by willing or wanting is actually a conscious decision made, for the most part, after we have become what we are. I can exercise my will to join a certain party, to write a book, or to get married, yet all of these will be nothing other than the manifestation of choices more original and spontaneous than that which is usually called the will. However, if existence really precedes essence, man is truly responsible for what he is.

Thus, the primary task of existentialism is to place each man entirely in possession of his being and to cause the full responsibility for his existence to fall upon himself. And, when we say that Man is responsible for himself, we mean that he is responsible not only for himself as an individual, but for all mankind.

There are two senses of the word "subjectivity," and our adversaries play upon both of these. Subjectivity refers on the one hand to the ability of the individual subject to choose for itself and, on the other hand, to the inability of Man to transcend human subjectivity. It is this second sense which is fundamental to existentialism. When we say that Man chooses for himself, we do indeed mean that each one of us defines himself; however, we also mean that, in choosing oneself, one makes a choice for all men. Indeed, no action we take, in creating ourselves as we wish to be, can avoid creating at the same time an image of Man as we believe he should be. To choose to be this or that is to simultaneously affirm the value of our choice, for we can never choose the worst. That which we select is always the best, and nothing can be good for us without being so for everyone. Furthermore, if existence precedes essence and we will to exist at the same time that we fashion our image, that image is then valid for everyone and for the entire epoch in which we live. Thus our responsibility is greater than we would have supposed, for it involves the whole of humanity.

If, for example, I am a worker, I might choose to join a Christian trade-union rather than to become a Communist. And if, by that choice, I mean to indicate that resignation is fundamentally the proper attitude for Man and that the kingdom of Man is not on earth, my decision involves not only myself, but all mankind. I choose resignation for everyone, thus involving humanity as a whole in my decision. Or if, taking a more personal example, I elect to marry and have children, even if this decision proceeds solely from my situation, from my own passion or desire, I thereby commit not only myself, but all of humanity, to the practice of monogamy. Thus I am responsible for myself and for all men, and I create a certain image of man as I choose him to be. In defining myself, I define man.

For Further Reading

Boyce Gibson, A. *Theism and Empiricism.* London: SCM Press, 1970.

Britton, Karl. *Philosophy and the Meaning of Life.* Cambridge, Eng.: Cambridge University Press, 1969.

Edman, Irwin. *Four Ways of Philosophy.* New York: Henry Holt, 1947.

Ewing, A. C. *Value and Reality: The Philosophical Case for Theism.* New York: Humanities Press, 1973.

Feigl, Herbert. "Logical Empiricism," in Dagobert D. Runes (ed.). *Twentieth Century Philosophy.* New York: Philosophical Library, 1943. Reviews several philosophical problems from the point of view of a contemporary naturalist.

Flew, Antony. *God and Philosophy.* London: Hutchinson, 1966. Detailed critique of arguments for theism.

Hick, John. *God and the Universe of Faiths: Essays in the Philosophy of Religion.* New York: St. Martin's Press, 1974.

Krikorian, Yervant H. (ed). *Naturalism and the Human Spirit.* New York: Columbia University Press, 1944.

Kurtz, Paul. *The Fullness of Life.* New York: Horizon Press, 1974. A humanist reflects on the good life.

Lamprecht, S. P. *The Metaphysics of Naturalism.* New York: Appleton-Century-Crofts, 1967.

Maritain, Jacques. *Existence and the Existent,* trans. by Lewis Galantiere and Gerald B. Phelan. Garden City, N.Y.: Image Books, 1956 (paperbound). See Chap. 5, "Ecce in Pace." Representative of what might be called a "Christian humanist" point of view.

Mitchell, E. *The Justification of Religious Belief.* London: Macmillan, 1973.

Montague, W. P. *The Chances of Surviving Death.* Cambridge, Mass.: Harvard University Press, 1934.

Niebuhr, Reinhold. *Beyond Tragedy.* New York: Scribner's, 1937. A collection of essays by a modern theist.

Otto, M. C. *The Human Enterprise.* New York: Appleton-Century-Crofts, 1940.

Pepper, Stephen C. *World Hypotheses.* Berkeley and Los Angeles: University of California Press, 1942. For patient readers only!

Russell, Bertrand. "A Free Man's Worship," in *Mysticism and Logic.* New York: Norton, 1929, pp. 46–58. A famous delineation of the naturalist position.

Sorley, W. R. *Moral Values and the Idea of God,* 3rd ed. New York: Macmillan, 1924. See especially Chaps. 18 and 19 for an interesting discussion of some of the problems implicit in the theistic view.

Stace, W. T. "Man Against Darkness." First published in the September 1948 issue of *The Atlantic Monthly* and in several anthologies since that time. A rather despairing account of the naturalist position.

Whitehead, Alfred North. *Process and Reality.* New York: Harper & Row, 1960 (originally published in 1929). See Part I, Chap. 1, "Speculative Philosophy."

PART XIV

Philosophies of Life

A philosophy of life is a set of convictions about how life ought to be lived in view of what one takes to be the most fundamental truths about humanity and its place in the scheme of things. It is the sum of the practical wisdom that one derives from one's world view. It is the part of philosophy that one takes along when one leaves the classroom or the study and enters the arena of life.

A philosophy of life contains three essential elements: an opinion concerning humanity's place in the universe, a view concerning the meaning of life, and some basis for deciding how to spend one's time, that is, a value system. Let us look briefly at these three elements.

One's view concerning humanity's place in the universe marks the point where one's philosophy of life is most closely joined to one's world view. Are human beings the favorite creatures of a loving God, or are they the accidental products of a mindless evolutionary process? Or are they, perhaps, something different from both of these? The answer depends on one's world view. If one holds a theistic world view, the "favorite creature" view of human beings is highly plausible. If one holds the world view of naturalism, the "accidental product of evolution" view is clearly to be preferred. And if one holds the world view of transcendentalism or of humanism, still other views of human beings follow.

There is a second fundamental question that a philosophy of life must answer: Does human life have any meaning, and if so what is it? This, as we shall see, is a difficult question, one that the readings will help to clarify. Let us note here, however, that one answer is that life has no meaning, that nothing is inherently worth living for. This is *nihilism,* and an important question for adherents of the world view of naturalism is whether nihilism can be avoided. If not, they must consider whether or how nihilism can be incorporated into an acceptable philosophy of life. The principal alternatives to nihilism are (1) the theory of *cosmic purpose,* that is, the view that human life finds meaning through participation in the divine purpose, (2) the theory of *immanent purpose,* that is, the view that transcendent values worthy of our allegiance emerge from time to time in the course of our daily life, and (3) the theory of *temporal purpose,* that is, the theory that we create the meanings that we find in the activities and goals to which we give ourselves. While nihilism is most closely related to naturalism, the natural affinities of the other three theories are theism (cosmic purpose), transcendentalism (immanent purpose), and humanism (temporal purpose).

Finally, on what basis shall we decide what to do with our life? This is the third question that a philosophy of life must answer. As long as we live, we have to do something with our time. What shall it be? Shall we pursue pleasure? knowledge? wealth? piety? oblivion? We answer these questions with our lives—by the way we spend our time—and our answer implies a system of values, a ranking of this above that, a preferring of this activity to that. The values implicit in our actions, the values in terms of which we choose to do this rather than that, are an essential and important part of our philosophy of life.

A complete description of a philosophy of life, then, would speak to all three questions. In actuality, however, writings rarely contain a complete and systematic exposition of a philosophy of life. Rather, fragments of a philosophy of life are interwoven with discussions of other matters. Nor is it only professional philosophers who create such fragments: they are to be found in the sacred writings of all religions, in poetry and novels and plays, in editorials and interviews and letters to the editor. Wherever human beings think about the mystery of human existence and the questions that emerge from reflecting upon that mystery, there will be created some fragments of a philosophy of life. To assemble such fragments into a coherent whole—to develop one's own philosophy of life—is the task of a lifetime.

60

BLAISE PASCAL (1623–1662)

Thoughts on Nature, Man, and God

Blaise Pascal had intended to gather up his fragmentary thoughts, jotted down at various times throughout his life, into a sustained defense of Christianity. Fortunately, he did not do so—and the result is that we have his random thoughts on a variety of topics just as they occurred to him. Upon reading them, one cannot avoid the feeling that they would have lost their freshness and charm had they been forced into the framework of an apologetic treatise.

It is futile to attempt to summarize Pascal's philosophy of life. He was a theist—a believer in cosmic purpose—but one whose theistic beliefs were the product of a long struggle with doubt and uncertainty. He agonized over humanity's ambiguous position in the universe, found hope in the human capacity for thought, and, in the end, endorsed the conventional Christian virtues. (See p. 134 for a biographical note on Blaise Pascal.)

(72)

Let man then contemplate nature as a whole in its grand and full majesty. Let him avert his eyes from the base objects of his environment, and look upon the brilliant light placed like an eternal lamp to illuminate the universe. Let the earth appear to him as a point in comparison with the vast circle which this star describes, and let him be amazed at the fact that this vast circle itself is but a very fragile point compared to that encompassed by the stars revolving in the firmament. But if our vision fails us here, let our imagination continue; it will sooner grow weary of conception than will nature tire of supplying it. The entire visible world is but an imperceptible speck in the ample bosom of nature; no idea approaches it. In vain we inflate our conceptions beyond imaginable space; we produce only atoms in comparison with the reality of things. It is an infinite sphere whose center is everywhere, whose circumference

From Blaise Pascal, *Pensées,* fragments 72, 146, 172, 199, 205, 208–210, 347, and 549 (Brunschvieg numbering system). Translated for this volume by Carol Halverson.

nowhere. In a word, it is the greatest perceptible manifestation of the omnipotence of God that our imagination loses itself in that thought.

Let man, returning to himself, consider what he is in comparison with all that exists; let him regard himself as wandering in an obscure province of nature. And from this small dungeon in which he finds himself lodged, I mean the universe, let him learn to assess the earth, the kingdoms, the cities and himself at their true value.

What is man in the infinite?

But to present to him another marvel equally astonishing, let him investigate the most delicate of the things he knows. Let us present to him a mite, with its small body made of parts incomparably smaller—of veins in its legs, of blood in its veins, of humours in the blood, of drops in its humours, of vapors in these drops. Dividing again these last things, let him exhaust his forces in contemplation, and let the last object at which he can arrive now be the subject of our discourse.

He will think perhaps that this is the extremity of minuteness in nature. I would let him see therein a new abyss; I would paint for him not only the visible universe, but the immensity of nature of which one can conceive in the confines of this abridged atom. Let him see therein an infinity of universes, each with its firmament, its planets, its earth, in the same proportion as in the visible world; on each earth animals, and finally mites, in which he will again find that which the first contained. And he will find again in the others the same thing without end and without rest. Let him lose himself, then, in these marvels, as amazing in their minuteness as were the others in their vastness. For who will not wonder that our body, which not long ago was not imperceptible in a universe which was itself imperceptible in the bosom of the whole, is now a colossus, a world or, rather, an everything with respect to the nothingness which one cannot reach.

Whoever so considers himself will certainly frighten himself; and in observing himself as he is, in the body which nature gave him, suspended between these two abysses of infinity and nothingness, he will tremble in view of these marvels. And I believe that, his curiosity changing to admiration, he will become more disposed to contemplate them in silence rather than to investigate them with presumption. For indeed, what is man in nature? A nothing in comparison with the infinite, an everything in comparison with nothingness. A mean between nothing and everything, infinitely removed from comprehending the extremes. The end of things and their beginning are, for him, invincibly hidden within an impenetrable secret. He is equally incapable of seeing the nothingness from which he was formed and the infinity in which he is engulfed.

What else can he do, then, but to comprehend the appearance of the middle of things, in the eternal despair of understanding neither their beginning nor their ending? All things are brought forth from nothingness and are carried toward infinity. Who will follow these amazing steps? The Author of these marvels understands them. No one else can do so.

In failing to contemplate nature, men have foolishly been inclined to investigate nature, as if they bore some proportion to her. It is a strange thing that they have wanted to understand the origins of things, and from there to arrive at knowledge of the whole, by a presumption as infinite as their object. For without a doubt this design cannot be formed without a presumption or without a capacity as infinite as nature.

When one is educated he understands that, nature having graven her image and that of her Author on all things, they almost all possess her double infinity: it is thus that we see that all sciences are infinite in the scope of their research. For who doubts that geometry, for example, has an infinite infinity of propositions to resolve. They are also infinite in the multitude and the fastidiousness of their principles. For who does not see that those which are proposed as the ultimates cannot support themselves, and that they are based upon others which, having still others for support, can never allow finality.

But we describe some as ultimate for reason, just as with material things we call that point indivisible after which our senses can no longer perceive it, however infinitely divisible it may be by its nature.

Of these two infinities in science, that of greatness is the more perceptible, and this is why a few persons have claimed to know all things. "I will speak of everything," said Democritus. But infinity in smallness is much less visible. Philosophers have more often claimed to have arrived at it, yet it is there where all have stumbled. This has resulted in such ordinary titles as *The Principles of Things, The Principles of Philosophy,* and others similar to them, equally ostentatious in fact, although less so in appearance than another which startles the eyes: De omni scibili.*

One naturally believes oneself more capable of arriving at the center of things than of embracing their circumference, and the scope of the visible world obviously surpasses us. But since it is we who surpass the small things, we believe ourselves more capable of grasping them; however, it requires no less capacity to arrive at nothingness than at the whole; each is infinity. And it seems to me that he who would understand the ultimate principles of things could also come to grasp infinity. One depends upon the other, and one follows from the other. These extremes meet and reunite by the force of their distance, and find each other ultimately in God, and in God alone.

Let us know, then, our capacity: we are something, and we are not everything. That which we are conceals from our knowledge the original principles which are born of nothingness. And the paucity of what we are hides from our vision the infinite. Our intelligence holds the same position in the order of intelligible things which our body holds in the expanse of nature.

Limited in all ways, this state which represents the mean between two extremes can be found in all of our qualities. Our senses perceive no extremes. Too much sound deafens us, too much light blinds us, too great or too small a distance impairs our vision. Too lengthy or too brief a discourse is obscure,

*"About Everything Knowable" [Ed.].

too much truth shocks us. I know of those who can not understand that zero minus four leaves zero. The first principles are too self-evident for us. Too much pleasure makes us uncomfortable, too much harmony in music displeases us, and too much kindness irritates us. We want to have the means to overpay our debt. We feel neither extreme heat nor extreme cold; excessive qualities are our enemies and are not perceptible; we no longer feel them, we endure them. Too much youth and too much age impede the mind, like too much or too little education. Indeed, extreme things are for us as if they did not exist at all, and we are not within their consideration; they escape us, or we them.

This is our true state. This is what renders us incapable of certain knowledge and absolute ignorance. We sail within a vast sphere, always uncertain and floating, pushed from one end to the other. Whichever limit we ponder, cling to and affirm, it wavers and leaves us; it slips past us and flees in an eternal flight. Nothing stops for us: this is the state which is natural for us and, nevertheless, is most contrary to our inclinations. We burn with desire to find a firm position, an ultimately constant base upon which to build a tower which will rise to infinity, but our entire foundation cracks, and the earth opens to the abysses.

(146)

Man is obviously made to think. This is his whole dignity and merit, and his sole duty is to think as he ought. Now, the order of thought is to begin with oneself and one's Author and one's end.

Now, of what does the world think? Never of this! But of dancing, of playing the lute, of singing, of composing verses, of chasing the ring, etc., of fighting, of making oneself king, without thinking of what it means to be a king and to be a man.

(172)

We are never content with the present. We anticipate the future as too slow in coming, as if to hasten its course; or we recall the past to retard its too swift flight. How imprudent that we wander in the times which are no longer ours and never think of the only ones which do belong to us; how fruitless that we muse on those which are no more, and let the only ones which do subsist escape without reflection. For the ordinary present offends us. We hide it from our vision because it troubles us, and if it is pleasant to us, we regret seeing it slip away. We try to hold on to it by the future and think about arranging things which are not in our power for a time which we have no certainty of reaching.

Let each one examine his thoughts; he will find them all occupied with either the past or the future. We hardly ever think of the present, and if we do think of it, it is only to acquire a light with which to prepare for the future. The present is never our end. The past and the present are our means, only the future is our end. Thus we never live, we only hope to live; and, continually preparing to be happy, it is inevitable that we never will be so.

(199)

Let one imagine a number of men in chains, and all condemned to death, of which several each day are slaughtered in the sight of the others. Those who remain see their own fate in that of their peers and, watching each other with sadness and without hope, await their turn. This is an image of the condition of man.

(205)

When I consider the short duration of my life, engulfed by the eternity preceding and following it, the small space that I fill, and similarly that I see, overwhelmed by the infinite immensity of spaces of which I am ignorant and which are unaware of me, I am frightened and amazed at being here rather than there: for there is no reason why here rather than there, why now rather than then. Who has put me here? By whose order and guidance have this place and this time been destined for me?

(208)

Why is my knowledge limited? My size? My lifetime to one hundred years rather than to one thousand? What reason did nature have for giving me such and for choosing this environment rather than another in the infinity from which there is no more reason to choose one rather than another, none being more alluring than the others?

(209)

Art thou less a slave for being loved and flattered by thy master? Thou art indeed blessed, slave, thy master flatters thee. He will beat thee soon.

(210)

The last act is tragic, however pleasant the rest of the play has been. In the end, some earth is thrown upon one's head, and that is all forever.

(347)

Man is but a reed, the weakest thing in nature; but he is a thinking reed. It is unnecessary for the entire world to arm itself to crush him; a vapor, a drop of water is sufficient to kill him. But if the universe destroys him, man will still be more noble than that which has killed him; for he will know of his death and of the advantage which the universe has over him. The universe knows nothing of this.

All our dignity consists, then, in thought. It is through this that we must lift ourselves up, and not through space and time which we do not know how to fill.

Let us struggle, then, to think well. Such is the principle of morality.

(550)

I love poverty because He loved it. I love goods because they afford me the means of assisting the poor. I remain faithful to everyone. I do not give back evil to those who wrong me, but I wish for them a condition like mine, where one receives neither evil nor good from men. I try to be righteous, truthful, sincere, and loyal to all men. And I have a tender heart for those with whom God has closely united me. And whether I am alone or in the view of men, I keep all my actions in the view of God, who must judge them and to whom I have consecrated them all.

These are my sentiments. And all the days of my life I bless my Redeemer, who has given them to me and who, from a man full of weakness, misery, lust, pride and ambition, has made a man free from all these evils by the power of His grace, to which all the glory is due, since I have in myself only misery and error.

61

FRIEDRICH NIETZSCHE (1844–1900)

The Advent of Nihilism

Fredrich Nietzsche is one of the towering figures of the late nineteenth century, an original and seminal thinker whose writings were virtually unknown during most of his own lifetime, but whose influence in the present century has been enormous. The son of a Protestant minister, he became a passionate critic of Christianity, which he characterized as a "slave morality." He sought a new basis for ethics and civilization in what he regarded as the most basic of human drives: the will to power. The most recent German edition of his collected works runs to twenty-three volumes, most of which have not yet been translated into English. Among his best-known writings are *The Birth of Tragedy* (1872), *The Gay Science* (1882–1887), *Thus Spake Zarathustra* (1883–1892), and *The Will to Power* (posthumous).

Nietzsche is presented here as a prophet of nihilism. His first astonishing pronouncement is that "God is dead." People apparently do not yet realize it, Nietzsche says, but the truth is that we no longer believe in God—not really. People go on about their lives as if nothing has changed, but, in fact, the very foundation upon which Western civilization has been built—belief in God—has crumbled.

Nietzsche's second message is the unqualified prediction that the next period in Western civilization will be characterized by nihilism, which, he claims, is an inevitability. With the death of God, we have lost our belief in the significance of the temporal process. We have also lost the sense of an ultimate unity within apparent diversity. Most serious of all, we have lost our belief in a permanent reality separate from and somehow underlying this world of change or, as philosophers often express it, a world of true being behind this world of becoming. Nihilism is the void that remains when the concepts of purpose, unity, and being have lost their power—and that, Nietzsche argues, is what has happened to the Western world.

From Friedrich Nietzsche, *The Gay Science* and *The Will to Power*, translated for this volume by David Nichols.

THE DEATH OF GOD

The mad man. Have you not heard of that mad man who lighted a lantern in the bright morning, ran to the market and cried unceasingly, "I am looking for God! I am looking for God!" Since there were many standing around there who did not believe in God, he stirred up a great laughter. "Has he gotten lost then?" said one. "Has he lost his way as a child?" said another. "Or is he keeping himself hidden? Is he afraid of us? Has he shipped out, emigrated?" —thus they cried out and laughed in confusion. The mad man sprang into their midst and penetrated them with his gaze. "Where is God?" he shouted. "I will tell you! *We have killed him*—you and I! We are all his murderers! But how have we done this? How were we able to drink up the sea? Who gave us the sponge to wipe away the whole horizon? What did we do when we unchained this world from its sun? Where does it revolve now? Where are we going? Away from all suns? Are we not plunging incessantly? And backwards, sideways, forward, in every direction? Is there still an up and a down? Are we not wandering through an endless night? Does not empty space breathe upon us? Has it not become colder? Does not night and more night come perpetually? Must not lanterns be lighted in the morning? Do we still hear nothing of the sound of the grave diggers who are burying God? Do we still smell nothing of the divine decay? Gods also decay! God is dead! God remains dead! And we have killed him! How shall we comfort ourselves, the murderers of all murderers? The holiest and most powerful thing which the world possessed until now has bled to death under our knives. Who will wipe off this blood from us? With what water could we cleanse ourselves? What ceremonies of atonement, what holy games will we have to invent? Is not the greatness of this deed too great for us? Must we not ourselves become gods, only to seem worthy of it? There never was a greater deed—and on account of this deed, whoever will be born after us will belong to a higher history than all history until now!" Here the mad man became silent and looked again at his audience: they also became silent and looked at him, astonished. Finally he threw his lantern on the ground so that it shattered and went out. "I came too soon," he said then. "I have still not come at the right time. This monstrous event is still underway and wandering—it has still not penetrated the ears of the people. Lightning and thunder require time, the light of the stars requires time, and deeds require time, even after they are done, in order to be seen and heard. This deed is still as distant from them as the farthest stars—*and yet they have done this very thing!*" They still tell how the mad man broke into various churches on the same day and there began to sing his *requiem aeternum deo.* Led out and taken to task, he replied only: "What are these churches, then, but the tombs and monuments of God?"

THE RISE OF NIHILISM

1. Great things require that one keep silent before them or speak grandly: grandly, that is to say cynically and with innocence.

2. What I am explaining is the history of the next two centuries. I am describing what is coming, what no longer can come differently: *the rise of nihilism.* This history can already be told: for necessity itself is at work here. This future speaks already in a hundred signs, this destiny announces itself everywhere; for this music of the future all ears are tuned. Our whole European culture is moving for a long time with the torture of anticipation which grows from decade to decade, as loosed toward a catastrophe: restless, violent, headlong: as a current which seeks *the end,* which no longer contemplates, which is afraid of contemplating.

3. The one who speaks here has, on the other hand, done nothing so far but *contemplate:* as a philosopher and recluse by instinct, who found his benefit on the opposite side, on the outside, in patience, in delay, in holding back; as a tempter to hazard . . . who has already lost himself once in every labyrinth of the future; a bird of prophecy who *looks back* when he tells what will come; as the first perfected nihilist of Europe, who, however, already experienced nihilism to the limit in himself—who has it *behind himself, under himself, outside himself.*

4. For one should not be mistaken concerning the meaning of the title with which this future-gospel is begun: "The Will to Power." An attempt at reevaluation of all values—with this formula a *reaction* is expressed, with the intention of a principle and proposition; a movement which in some future will set loose that perfected nihilism; which, however, *presupposes* it, logically and psychologically, which can come absolutely only *on it* and *out of it.* For why is the rise of nihilism now *inevitable?* It is because of the values we have had until now, which draw their final consequence in it; because nihilism is the logic, thought out to its end, of our great values and ideals,—because we must first experience nihilism in order that what was the *value* of these "values" may come after it . . . We need, at some time or another, *new values* . . .

THE DECLINE OF COSMOLOGICAL VALUES

Nihilism as a *psychological condition* must be entered into when we have sought a "meaning" in all events which is not in them: so that the seeker finally loses courage. Nihilism is then the becoming-conscious of the long *waste* of

strength, the torment of "in vain," the uncertainty, the lack of opportunity
somehow to recover, of some occasion to set one's mind at rest—the self-
shame, as though one has all too long *deceived* oneself. That meaning could
have been: the "fullfillment" of a highest moral canon in all events, the moral
world-order; or the increase of love and harmony in the interaction of living
things; or the advance on a general state of good fortune; or the attack itself
on a general condition of nothingness—a purpose is still a meaning. What all
these kinds of conceptions have in common is that a *something* should be
attained through the process itself: and now one comprehends that with the
becoming *nothing* is achieved, *nothing* attained. . . . Thus the disappointment
concerning the alleged *purpose* of *becoming* as the origin of nihilism: be it in
regard to a completely fixed purpose, be it, in general, the insight into the
insufficiency of all purpose-hypotheses up to now, which affect the whole
"development" (—man *no longer* contributor, let alone the middle-point of
becoming).

Nihilism as a psychological condition commences, secondly, when one has
established a *unity*, a *systematizing*, an *organization* in all events and under
all events: so that the thirsty soul revels in the conception of unity, of a highest
form of command and government (—if it is the soul of a logician, then
absolute consistency and material dialectic are sufficient to reconcile everything). A kind of unity, some form of "monism": and in consequence of this
belief, man, in the deep feeling of a connection and dependence on a unity
which is endlessly considered by him, a mode of divinity . . . "the benefit of
the universal demands the surrender of the particular" . . . but look, there *is*
no such universal! Fundamentally, man has lost belief in his values, whenever
a valuable unity does not operate through it: that is, he has conceived such a
unity *in order to be able to believe in his values*.

Nihilism as a psychological condition has still a *third* and *last* form. Given
these two *insights*, that with becoming nothing should be achieved and that
beneath all becoming there is no great unity in control in which the particular
may be fully submerged as in a principle of highest value: so a *way out* remains
open, to condemn this whole world of becoming as a deception and to discover
a world which lies on the other side, a *true* world. As soon as man gets behind
it, as only psychological necessity has built this world and as he has absolutely
no right to it, so begins the last form of nihilism, which comprises the *disbelief
in a metaphysical world,*—which forbids itself the belief in a *true* world. From
this standpoint one admits the reality of becoming as *sole* reality, and forbids
oneself every kind of underhanded means and false godliness—*but does not
suffer this world, which one yet does not wish to disavow*. . .

What has happened, fundamentally? The feeling of worthlessness was
achieved when one considered that neither with the concept *"purpose,"* nor
with the concept *"unity,"* nor with the concept *"truth"* may the unitary
character of existence be interpreted. Nothing is achieved or arrived at this
way; it misses the over-reaching unity in the multiplicity of events: the charac-

ter of existence is not "true," it is *false* . . . , one simply no longer has a reason to convince onself of a *true* world . . . in short, the categories "purpose," "unity," "being," with which we instilled a value in the world, are again *removed* from us—and now the world appears *worthless* . . .

62

ALBERT CAMUS (1913–1960)

The Myth of Sisyphus

Albert Camus was a French writer whose novels and plays are usually classified as "existentialist" literature. His writings, which earned him a Nobel prize for literature in 1957, include *The Stranger* (1942), *The Plague* (1947), *Man in Revolt* (1951), and *The Fall* (1957).

"The Myth of Sisyphus" is a short essay in which Camus examines "the absurd hero," the person condemned to endless, meaningless toil. It is a haunting picture that Camus paints, and it becomes even more so when we realize that Sisyphus is a symbol for all mankind: *all* human effort, according to Camus, is equally devoid of meaning. Is life worth living, then, in such a nihilistic world? Yes, replies Camus, for human beings are *conscious* of their fate, and, by this consciousness, they rise above it.

The gods had condemned Sisyphus to ceaselessly rolling a rock to the top of a mountain, whence the stone would fall back of its own weight. They had thought with some reason that there is no more dreadful punishment than futile and hopeless labor.

If one believes Homer, Sisyphus was the wisest and most prudent of mortals.

According to another tradition, however, he was disposed to practice the profession of highwayman. I see no contradiction in this. Opinions differ as to the reasons why he became the futile laborer of the underworld. To begin with, he is accused of a certain levity in regard to the gods. He stole their secrets. Ægina, the daughter of Æsopus, was carried off by Jupiter. The father was shocked by that disappearance and complained to Sisyphus. He, who knew of the abduction, offered to tell about it on condition that Æsopus would give water to the citadel of Corinth. To the celestial thunderbolts he preferred the benediction of water. He was punished for this in the underworld. Homer tells us also that Sisyphus had put Death in chains. Pluto could not endure the sight of his deserted, silent empire. He dispatched the god of war, who liberated Death from the hands of her conqueror.

It is said also that Sisyphus, being near to death, rashly wanted to test his wife's love. He ordered her to cast his unburied body into the middle of the public square. Sisyphus woke up in the underworld. And there, annoyed by an obedience so contrary to human love, he obtained from Pluto permission to return to earth in order to chastise his wife. But when he had seen again the face of this world, enjoyed water and sun, warm stones and the sea, he no longer wanted to go back to the infernal darkness. Recalls, signs of anger, warnings were of no avail. Many years more he lived facing the curve of the gulf, the sparkling sea, and the smiles of earth. A decree of the gods was necessary. Mercury came and seized the impudent man by the collar and, snatching him from his joys, led him forcibly back to the underworld, where his rock was ready for him.

You have already grasped that Sisyphus is the absurd hero. He *is,* as much through his passions as through his torture. His scorn of the gods, his hatred of death, and his passion for life won him that unspeakable penalty in which the whole being is exerted toward accomplishing nothing. This is the price that must be paid for the passions of this earth. Nothing is told us about Sisyphus in the underworld. Myths are made for the imagination to breathe life into them. As for this myth, one sees merely the whole effort of a body straining to raise the huge stone, to roll it and push it up a slope a hundred times over; one sees the face screwed up, the cheek tight against the stone, the shoulder bracing the clay-covered mass, the foot wedging it, the fresh start with arms outstretched, the wholly human security of two earth-clotted hands. At the very end of his long effort measured by skyless space and time without depth, the purpose is achieved. Then Sisyphus watches the stone rush down in a few moments toward that lower world whence he will have to push it up again toward the summit. He goes back down to the plain.

It is during that return, that pause, that Sisyphus interests me. A face that toils so close to stones is already stone itself! I see that man going back down with a heavy yet measured step toward the torment of which he will never know the end. That hour like a breathing-space which returns as surely as his suffering, that is the hour of consciousness. At each of those moments when he leaves the heights and gradually sinks toward the lairs of the gods, he is superior to his fate. He is stronger than his rock.

If this myth is tragic, that is because its hero is conscious. Where would his torture be, indeed, if at every step the hope of succeeding upheld him? The workman of today works every day in his life at the same tasks, and this fate is no less absurd. But it is tragic only at the rare moments when it becomes conscious. Sisyphus, proletarian of the gods, powerless and rebellious, knows the whole extent of his wretched condition: it is what he thinks of during his descent. The lucidity that was to constitute his torture at the same time crowns his victory. There is no fate that cannot be surmounted by scorn.

If the descent is thus sometimes performed in sorrow, it can also take place in joy. This word is not too much. Again I fancy Sisyphus returning toward his rock, and the sorrow was in the beginning. When the images of earth cling too tightly to memory, when the call of happiness becomes too insistent, it happens that melancholy rises in man's heart: this is the rock's victory, this is the rock itself. The boundless grief is too heavy to bear. These are our nights of Gethsemane. But crushing truths perish from being acknowledged. Thus, Œdipus at the outset obeys fate without knowing it. But from the moment he knows, his tragedy begins. Yet at the same moment, blind and desperate, he realizes that the only bond linking him to the world is the cool hand of a girl. Then a tremendous remark rings out: "Despite so many ordeals, my advanced age and the nobility of my soul make me conclude that all is well." Sophocles' Œdipus, like Dostoevsky's Kirilov, thus gives the recipe for the absurd victory. Ancient wisdom confirms modern heroism.

One does not discover the absurd without being tempted to write a manual of happiness. "What! by such narrow ways—?" There is but one world, however. Happiness and the absurd are two sons of the same earth. They are inseparable. It would be a mistake to say that happiness necessarily springs from the absurd discovery. It happens as well that the feeling of the absurd springs from happiness. "I conclude that all is well," says Œdipus, and that remark is sacred. It echoes in the wild and limited universe of man. It teaches that all is not, has not been, exhausted. It drives out of this world a god who had come into it with dissatisfaction and a preference for futile sufferings. It makes of fate a human matter, which must be settled among men.

All Sisyphus' silent joy is contained therein. His fate belongs to him. His rock is his thing. Likewise, the absurd man, when he contemplates his torment, silences all the idols. In the universe suddenly restored to its silence, the myriad wondering little voices of the earth rise up. Unconscious, secret calls, invitations from all the faces, they are the necessary reverse and price of victory. There is no sun without shadow, and it is essential to know the night. The absurd man says yes and his effort will henceforth be unceasing. If there is a personal fate, there is no higher destiny, or at least there is but one which he concludes is inevitable and despicable. For the rest, he knows himself to be the master of his days. At that subtle moment when man glances backward over his life, Sisyphus returning toward his rock, in that slight pivoting he contemplates that series of unrelated actions which becomes his fate, created by him, combined under his memory's eye and soon sealed by his death. Thus, convinced of the wholly human origin of all that is human, a blind man eager to see who knows that the night has no end, he is still on the go. The rock is still rolling.

I leave Sisyphus at the foot of the mountain! One always finds one's burden again. But Sisyphus teaches the higher fidelity that negates the gods and raises rocks. He too concludes that all is well. This universe henceforth without a master seems to him neither sterile nor futile. Each atom of that stone, each mineral flake of that night-filled mountain, in itself forms a world. The struggle itself toward the heights is enough to fill a man's heart. One must imagine Sisyphus happy.

63

THOMAS NAGEL (1937– ————)

The Absurd

Thomas Nagel was born in Yugoslavia and educated at Cornell University, Oxford University, and Harvard University, and is currently professor of philosophy at Princeton University. He is the author of *The Possibility of Altruism* (1970).

Why do the smallness of human beings in relation to the universe, or the shortness of human life, or the apparent futility (in the long run) of human toil, seem to support the conclusion that life is absurd? It is this question that Nagel addresses in the following selection. The reasons that are usually given to show that life is absurd, he argues, really do not hold up. If life is absurd, it is not at all obvious that it would be less so if we were larger, or lived longer, or if some of the "purposes" for which we live were events occurring after our demise. Why, then, do we persist in thinking, or

From Thomas Nagel, "The Absurd," *Journal of Philosophy,* 68, no. 20 (October 21, 1971), pp. 716–727. Reprinted by permission of the author and publisher.

perhaps only feeling, that smallness, brevity, and the like make life absurd? Nagel suggests that the answer lies in a clearer understanding of a certain kind of absurdity that is implicit in the human situation.

Most people feel on occasion that life is absurd, and some feel it vividly and continually. Yet the reasons usually offered in defense of this conviction are patently inadequate: they *could* not really explain why life is absurd. Why then do they provide a natural expression for the sense that it is?

I

Consider some examples. It is often remarked that nothing we do now will matter in a million years. But if that is true, then by the same token, nothing that will be the case in a million years matters now. In particular, it does not matter now that in a million years nothing we do now will matter. Moreover, even if what we did now *were* going to matter in a million years, how could that keep our present concerns from being absurd? If their mattering now is not enough to accomplish that, how would it help if they mattered a million years from now?

Whether what we do now will matter in a million years could make the crucial difference only if its mattering in a million years depended on its mattering, period. But then to deny that whatever happens now will matter in a million years is to beg the question against its mattering, period; for in that sense one cannot know that it will not matter in a million years whether (for example) someone now is happy or miserable, without knowing that it does not matter, period.

What we say to convey the absurdity of our lives often has to do with space or time: we are tiny specks in the infinite vastness of the universe; our lives are mere instants even on a geological time scale, let alone a cosmic one; we will all be dead any minute. But of course none of these evident facts can be what *makes* life absurd, if it is absurd. For suppose we lived forever; would not a life that is absurd if it lasts seventy years be infinitely absurd if it lasted through eternity? And if our lives are absurd given our present size, why would they be any less absurd if we filled the universe (either because we were larger or because the universe was smaller)? Reflection on our minuteness and brevity appears to be intimately connected with the sense that life is meaningless; but it is not clear what the connection is.

Another inadequate argument is that because we are going to die, all chains of justification must leave off in mid-air: one studies and works to earn money to pay for clothing, housing, entertainment, food, to sustain oneself from year to year, perhaps to support a family and pursue a career—but to what final end? All of it is an elaborate journey leading nowhere. (One will also have some effect on other people's lives, but that simply reproduces the problem, for they will die too.)

There are several replies to this argument. First, life does not consist of a sequence of activities each of which has as its purpose some later member of the sequence. Chains of justification come repeatedly to an end within life, and whether the process as a whole can be justified has no bearing on the finality of these end-points. No further justification is needed to make it reasonable to take aspirin for a headache, attend an exhibit on the work of a painter one admires, or stop a child from putting his hand on a hot stove. No larger context or further purpose is needed to prevent these acts from being pointless.

Even if someone wished to supply a further justification for pursuing all the things in life that are commonly regarded as self-justifying, that justification would have to end somewhere too. If *nothing* can justify unless it is justified in terms of something outside itself, which is also justified, then an infinite regress results, and no chain of justification can be complete. Moreover, if a finite chain of reasons cannot justify anything, what could be accomplished by an infinite chain, each link of which must be justified by something outside itself?

Since justifications must come to an end somewhere, nothing is gained by denying that they end where they appear to, within life—or by trying to subsume the multiple, often trivial ordinary justifications of action under a single, controlling life scheme. We can be satisfied more easily than that. In fact, through its misrepresentation of the process of justification, the argument makes a vacuous demand. It insists that the reasons available within life are incomplete, but suggests thereby that all reasons that come to an end are incomplete. This makes it impossible to supply any reasons at all.

The standard arguments for absurdity appear therefore to fail as arguments. Yet I believe they attempt to express something that is difficult to state, but fundamentally correct.

II

In ordinary life a situation is absurd when it includes a conspicuous discrepancy between pretension or aspiration and reality: someone gives a complicated speech in support of a motion that has already been passed; a notorious criminal is made president of a major philanthropic foundation; you declare your love over the telephone to a recorded announcement; as you are being knighted, your pants fall down.

When a person finds himself in an absurd situation, he will usually attempt to change it, by modifying his aspirations, or by trying to bring reality into better accord with them, or by removing himself from the situation entirely. We are not always willing or able to extricate ourselves from a position whose absurdity has become clear to us. Nevertheless, it is usually possible to imagine some change that would remove the absurdity—whether or not we can or will implement it. The sense that life as a whole is absurd arises when we perceive, perhaps dimly, an inflated pretension or aspiration which is inseparable from the continuation of human life and which makes its absurdity inescapable, short of escape from life itself.

Many people's lives are absurd, temporarily or permanently, for conventional reasons having to do with their particular ambitions, circumstances, and personal relations. If there is a philosophical sense of absurdity, however, it must arise from the perception of something universal—some respect in which pretension and reality inevitably clash for us all. This condition is supplied, I shall argue, by the collision between the seriousness with which we take our lives and the perpetual possibility of regarding everything about which we are serious as arbitrary, or open to doubt.

We cannot live human lives without energy and attention, nor without making choices which show that we take some things more seriously than others. Yet we have always available a point of view outside the particular form of our lives, from which the seriousness appears gratuitous. These two inescapable viewpoints collide in us, and that is what makes life absurd. It is absurd because we ignore the doubts that we know cannot be settled, continuing to live with nearly undiminished seriousness in spite of them.

This analysis requires defense in two respects: first as regards the unavoidability of seriousness; second as regards the inescapability of doubt.

We take ourselves seriously whether we lead serious lives or not and whether we are concerned primarily with fame, pleasure, virtue, luxury, triumph, beauty, justice, knowledge, salvation, or mere survival. If we take other people seriously and devote ourselves to them, that only multiplies the problem. Human life is full of effort, plans, calculation, success and failure: we *pursue* our lives, with varying degrees of sloth and energy.

It would be different if we could not step back and reflect on the process, but were merely led from impulse to impulse without self-consciousness. But human beings do not act solely on impulse. They are prudent, they reflect, they weigh consequences, they ask whether what they are doing is worth while. Not only are their lives full of particular choices that hang together in larger activities with temporal structure: they also decide in the broadest terms what to pursue and what to avoid, what the priorities among their various aims should be, and what kind of people they want to be or become. Some men are faced with such choices by the large decisions they make from time to time; some merely by reflection on the course their lives are taking as the product of countless small decisions. They decide whom to marry, what profession to follow, whether to join the Country Club, or the Resistance; or they may just wonder why they go on being salesmen or academics or taxi drivers, and then stop thinking about it after a certain period of inconclusive reflection.

Although they may be motivated from act to act by those immediate needs with which life presents them, they allow the process to continue by adhering to the general system of habits and the form of life in which such motives have their place—or perhaps only by clinging to life itself. They spend enormous quantities of energy, risk, and calculation on the details. Think of how an ordinary individual sweats over his appearance, his health, his sex life, his emotional honesty, his social utility, his self-knowledge, the quality of his ties with family, colleagues, and friends, how well he does his job, whether he understands the world and what is going on in it. Leading a human life is a full-time occupation, to which everyone devotes decades of intense concern.

This fact is so obvious that it is hard to find it extraordinary and important. Each of us lives his own life—lives with himself twenty-four hours a day. What else is he supposed to do—live someone else's life? Yet humans have the special capacity to step back and survey themselves, and the lives to which they are committed, with that detached amazement which comes from watching an ant struggle up a heap of sand. Without developing the illusion that they are able to escape from their highly specific and idiosyncratic position, they can view it *sub specie aeternitatis*—and the view is at once sobering and comical.

The crucial backward step is not taken by asking for still another justification in the chain, and failing to get it. The objections to that line of attack have already been stated; justifications come to an end. But this is precisely what provides universal doubt with its object. We step back to find that the whole system of justification and criticism, which controls our choices and supports our claims to rationality, rests on responses and habits that we never question, that we should not know how to defend without circularity, and to which we shall continue to adhere even after they are called into question.

The things we do or want without reasons, and without requiring reasons —the things that define what is a reason for us and what is not—are the starting points of our skepticism. We see ourselves from outside, and all the contingency and specificity of our aims and pursuits become clear. Yet when we take this view and recognize what we do as arbitrary, it does not disengage us from life, and there lies our absurdity: not in the fact that such an external view can be taken of us, but in the fact that we ourselves can take it, without ceasing to be the persons whose ultimate concerns are so coolly regarded.

III

One may try to escape the position by seeking broader ultimate concerns, from which it is impossible to step back—the idea being that absurdity results because what we take seriously is something small and insignificant and individual. Those seeking to supply their lives with meaning usually envision a role or function in something larger than themselves. They therefore seek fulfillment in service to society, the state, the revolution, the progress of history, the advance of science, or religion and the glory of God.

But a role in some larger enterprise cannot confer significance unless that enterprise is itself significant. And its significance must come back to what we can understand, or it will not even appear to give us what we are seeking. If we learned that we were being raised to provide food for other creatures fond of human flesh, who planned to turn us into cutlets before we got too stringy —even if we learned that the human race had been developed by animal breeders precisely for this purpose—that would still not give our lives meaning, for two reasons. First, we would still be in the dark as to the significance of the lives of those other beings; second, although we might acknowledge that this culinary role would make our lives meaningful to them, it is not clear how it would make them meaningful to us.

Admittedly, the usual form of service to a higher being is different from this. One is supposed to behold and partake of the glory of God, for example, in a way in which chickens do not share in the glory of coq au vin. The same is true of service to a state, a movement, or a revolution. People can come to feel, when they are part of something bigger, that it is part of them too. They worry less about what is peculiar to themselves, but identify enough with the larger enterprise to find their role in it fulfilling.

However, any such larger purpose can be put in doubt in the same way that the aims of an individual life can be, and for the same reasons. It is as legitimate to find ultimate justification there as to find it earlier, among the details of individual life. But this does not alter the fact that justifications come to an end when we are content to have them end—when we do not find it necessary to look any further. If we can step back from the purposes of individual life and doubt their point, we can step back also from the progress of human history, or of science, or the success of a society, or the kingdom, power, and glory of God,[1] and put all these things into question in the same way. What seems to us to confer meaning, justification, significance, does so in virtue of the fact that we need no more reasons after a certain point.

What makes doubt inescapable with regard to the limited aims of individual life also makes it inescapable with regard to any larger purpose that encourages the sense that life is meaningful. Once the fundamental doubt has begun, it cannot be laid to rest.

Camus maintains in *The Myth of Sisyphus* that the absurd arises because the world fails to meet our demands for meaning. This suggests that the world might satisfy those demands if it were different. But now we can see that this is not the case. There does not appear to be any conceivable world (containing us) about which unsettlable doubts could not arise. Consequently the absurdity of our situation derives not from a collision between our expectations and the world, but from a collision within ourselves.

[1] Cf. Robert Nozick, "Teleology," *Mosaic,* XII, 1 (Spring 1971):27/8.

IV

It may be objected that the standpoint from which these doubts are supposed to be felt does not exist—that if we take the recommended backward step we will land on thin air, without any basis for judgment about the natural responses we are supposed to be surveying. If we retain our usual standards of what is important, then questions about the significance of what we are doing with our lives will be answerable in the usual way. But if we do not, then those questions can mean nothing to us, since there is no longer any content to the idea of what matters, and hence no content to the idea that nothing does.

But this objection misconceives the nature of the backward step. It is not supposed to give us an understanding of what is *really* important, so that we see by contrast that our lives are insignificant. We never, in the course of these reflections, abandon the ordinary standards that guide our lives. We merely observe them in operation, and recognize that if they are called into question we can justify them only by reference to themselves, uselessly. We adhere to them because of the way we are put together; what seems to us important or serious or valuable would not seem so if we were differently constituted.

In ordinary life, to be sure, we do not judge a situation absurd unless we have in mind some standards of seriousness, significance, or harmony with which the absurd can be contrasted. This contrast is not implied by the philosophical judgment of absurdity, and that might be thought to make the concept unsuitable for the expression of such judgments. This is not so, however, for the philosophical judgment depends on another contrast which makes it a natural extension from more ordinary cases. It departs from them only in contrasting the pretensions of life with a larger context in which *no* standards can be discovered, rather than with a context from which alternative, overriding standards may be applied.

V

In this respect, as in others, philosophical perception of the absurd resembles epistemological skepticism. In both cases the final, philosophical doubt is not contrasted with any unchallenged certainties, though it is arrived at by extrapolation from examples of doubt within the system of evidence or justification, where a contrast with other certainties *is* implied. In both cases our limitedness joins with a capacity to transcend those limitations in thought (thus seeing them as limitations, and as inescapable).

Skepticism begins when we include ourselves in the world about which we claim knowledge. We notice that certain types of evidence convince us, that we are content to allow justifications of belief to come to an end at certain points, that we feel we know many things even without knowing or having grounds for believing the denial of others which, if true, would make what we claim to know false.

For example, I know that I am looking at a piece of paper, although I have no adequate grounds to claim I know that I am not dreaming; and if I am dreaming then I am not looking at a piece of paper. Here an ordinary conception of how appearance may diverge from reality is employed to show that we take our world largely for granted; the certainty that we are not dreaming cannot be justified except circularly, in terms of those very appearances which are being put in doubt. It is somewhat far-fetched to suggest I may be dreaming; but the possibility is only illustrative. It reveals that our claims to knowledge depend on our not feeling it necessary to exclude certain incompatible alternatives, and the dreaming possibility or the total-hallucination possibility are just representatives for limitless possibilities most of which we cannot even conceive.[2]

Once we have taken the backward step to an abstract view of our whole system of beliefs, evidence, and justification, and seen that it works only, despite its pretensions, by taking the world largely for granted, we are *not* in a position to contrast all these appearances with an alternative reality. We cannot shed our ordinary responses, and if we could it would leave us with no means of conceiving a reality of any kind.

It is the same in the practical domain. We do not step outside our lives to a new vantage point from which we see what is really, objectively significant. We continue to take life largely for granted while seeing that all our decisions and certainties are possible only because there is a great deal we do not bother to rule out.

Both epistemological skepticism and a sense of the absurd can be reached via initial doubts posed within systems of evidence and justification that we accept, and can be stated without violence to our ordinary concepts. We can ask not only why we should believe there is a floor under us, but also why we should believe the evidence of our senses at all—and at some point the framable questions will have outlasted the answers. Similarly, we can ask not only why we should take aspirin, but why we should take trouble over our own comfort at all. The fact that we shall take the aspirin without waiting for an answer to this last question does not show that it is an unreal question. We shall also continue to believe there is a floor under us without waiting for an answer to the other question. In both cases it is this unsupported natural confidence that generates skeptical doubts; so it cannot be used to settle them.

Philosophical skepticism does not cause us to abandon our ordinary beliefs, but it lends them a peculiar flavor. After acknowledging that their truth is

---

[2] I am aware that skepticism about the external world is widely thought to have been refuted, but I have remained convinced of its irrefutability since being exposed at Berkeley to Thompson Clarke's largely unpublished ideas on the subject.

incompatible with possibilities that we have no grounds for believing do not obtain—apart from grounds in those very beliefs which we have called into question—we return to our familiar convictions with a certain irony and resignation. Unable to abandon the natural responses on which they depend, we take them back, like a spouse who has run off with someone else and then decided to return; but we regard them differently (not that the new attitude is necessarily inferior to the old, in either case).

The same situation obtains after we have put in question the seriousness with which we take our lives and human life in general and have looked at ourselves without presuppositions. We then return to our lives, as we must, but our seriousness is laced with irony. Not that irony enables us to escape the absurd. It is useless to mutter: "Life is meaningless; life is meaningless . . . " as an accompaniment to everything we do. In continuing to live and work and strive, we take ourselves seriously in action no matter what we say.

What sustains us, in belief as in action, is not reason or justification, but something more basic than these—for we go on in the same way even after we are convinced that the reasons have given out.[3] If we tried to rely entirely on reason, and pressed it hard, our lives and beliefs would collapse—a form of madness that may actually occur if the inertial force of taking the world and life for granted is somehow lost. If we lose our grip on that, reason will not give it back to us.

VI

In viewing ourselves from a perspective broader than we can occupy in the flesh, we become spectators of our own lives. We cannot do very much as pure spectators of our own lives, so we continue to lead them, and devote ourselves to what we are able at the same time to view as no more than a curiosity, like the ritual of an alien religion.

This explains why the sense of absurdity finds its natural expression in those bad arguments with which the discussion began. Reference to our small size and short lifespan and to the fact that all of mankind will eventually vanish without a trace are metaphors for the backward step which permits us to regard ourselves from without and to find the particular form of our lives

[3] As Hume says in a famous passage of the *Treatise:* "Most fortunately it happens, that since reason is incapable of dispelling these clouds, nature herself suffices to that purpose, and cures me of this philosophical melancholy and delirium, either by relaxing this bent of mind, or by some avocation, and lively impression of my senses, which obliterate all these chimeras. I dine, I play a game of backgammon, I converse, and am merry with my friends; and when after three or four hours' amusement, I would return to these speculations, they appear so cold, and strain'd, and ridiculous, that I cannot find it in my heart to enter into them any farther" (Book 1, Part 4, Section 7; Selby-Bigge, p. 269).

curious and slightly surprising. By feigning a nebula's-eye view, we illustrate the capacity to see ourselves without presuppositions, as arbitrary, idiosyncratic, highly specific occupants of the world, one of countless possible forms of life.

Before turning to the question whether the absurdity of our lives is something to be regretted and if possible escaped, let me consider what would have to be given up in order to avoid it.

Why is the life of a mouse not absurd? The orbit of the moon is not absurd either, but that involves no strivings or aims at all. A mouse, however, has to work to stay alive. Yet he is not absurd, because he lacks the capacities for self-consciousness and self-transcendence that would enable him to see that he is only a mouse. If that *did* happen, his life would become absurd, since self-awareness would not make him cease to be a mouse and would not enable him to rise above his mousely strivings. Bringing his new-found self-consciousness with him, he would have to return to his meagre yet frantic life, full of doubts that he was unable to answer, but also full of purposes that he was unable to abandon.

Given that the transcendental step is natural to us humans, can we avoid absurdity by refusing to take that step and remaining entirely within our sublunar lives? Well, we cannot refuse consciously, for to do that we would have to be aware of the viewpoint we were refusing to adopt. The only way to avoid the relevant self-consciousness would be either never to attain it or to forget it—neither of which can be achieved by the will.

On the other hand, it is possible to expend effort on an attempt to destroy the other component of the absurd—abandoning one's earthly, individual, human life in order to identify as completely as possible with that universal viewpoint from which human life seems arbitrary and trivial. (This appears to be the ideal of certain Oriental religions.) If one succeeds, then one will not have to drag the superior awareness through a strenuous mundane life, and absurdity will be diminished.

However, insofar as this self-etiolation is the result of effort, will-power, asceticism, and so forth, it requires that one take oneself seriously as an individual—that one be willing to take considerable trouble to avoid being creaturely and absurd. Thus one may undermine the aim of unworldliness by pursuing it too vigorously. Still, if someone simply allowed his individual, animal nature to drift and respond to impulse, without making the pursuit of its needs a central conscious aim, then he might, at considerable dissociative cost, achieve a life that was less absurd than most. It would not be a meaningful life either, of course; but it would not involve the engagement of a transcendent awareness in the assiduous pursuit of mundane goals. And that is the main condition of absurdity—the dragooning of an unconvinced transcendent consciousness into the service of an immanent, limited enterprise like a human life.

The final escape is suicide; but before adopting any hasty solutions, it would be wise to consider carefully whether the absurdity of our existence truly presents us with a *problem,* to which some solution must be found—a way of dealing with prima facie disaster. That is certainly the attitude with which Camus approaches the issue, and it gains support from the fact that we are all eager to escape from absurd situations on a smaller scale.

Camus—not on uniformly good grounds—rejects suicide and the other solutions he regards as escapist. What he recommends is defiance or scorn. We can salvage our dignity, he appears to believe, by shaking a fist at the world which is deaf to our pleas, and continuing to live in spite of it. This will not make our lives un-absurd, but it will lend them a certain nobility.[4]

This seems to me romantic and slightly self-pitying. Our absurdity warrants neither that much distress nor that much defiance. At the risk of falling into romanticism by a different route, I would argue that absurdity is one of the most human things about us: a manifestation of our most advanced and interesting characteristics. Like skepticism in epistemology, it is possible only because we possess a certain kind of insight—the capacity to transcend ourselves in thought.

If a sense of the absurd is a way of perceiving our true situation (even though the situation is not absurd until the perception arises), then what reason can we have to resent or escape it? Like the capacity for epistemological skepticism, it results from the ability to understand our human limitations. It need not be a matter for agony unless we make it so. Nor need it evoke a defiant contempt of fate that allows us to feel brave or proud. Such dramatics, even if carried on in private, betray a failure to appreciate the cosmic unimportance of the situation. If *sub specie aeternitalis* there is no reason to believe that anything matters, then that doesn't matter either, and we can approach our absurd lives with irony instead of heroism or despair.

---

[4]"Sisyphus, proletarian of the gods, powerless and rebellious, knows the whole extent of his wretched condition: it is what he thinks of during his descent. The lucidity that was to constitute his torture at the same time crowns his victory. There is no fate that cannot be surmounted by scorn" (*The Myth of Sisyphus,* Vintage edition, p. 190).

64

RICHARD TAYLOR (1919– ————)

The Meaning of Life

Richard Taylor is professor of philosophy at the University of Rochester. He previously taught at Brown University and Columbia University, and has been a guest professor at several American universities. He is the author of *Metaphysics* (1963), *Action and Purpose* (1965), *Good and Evil* (1970), *Freedom, Anarchy and the Law* (1973), and *With Heart and Mind* (1973). He is also associate editor of *American Philosophical Quarterly*.

Taylor attempts in this essay to clarify the questions, What would have to be the case in order for human life to be meaningful, and is it possible for human life to have such meaning? Our lives, he argues, are similar to that of Sisyphus: "We toil after goals . . . of transitory significance, and, having gained one of them, we immediately set forth for the next, . . . with this next one being essentially more of the same." Can such lives be "meaningful," and if so what kind of meaning can they have? Taylor's answer is that they can be meaningful, and that this meaning results from "the fact that we are deeply interested in what we find ourselves doing." Although this is a "strange meaningfulness," it is the only kind of meaning possible for us—and it is sufficient.

The question whether life has any meaning is difficult to interpret, and the more one concentrates his critical faculty on it the more it seems to elude him, or to evaporate as an intelligible question. One wants to turn it aside, as a source of embarrassment, as something that, if it cannot be abolished, should at least be decently covered. And yet I think any reflective person recognizes that the question it raises is important, and that it ought to have a significant answer.

If the idea of meaningfulness is difficult to grasp in this context, so that we are unsure what sort of thing would amount to answering the question, the idea of meaninglessness is perhaps less so. If, then, we can bring before our minds a clear image of meaningless existence, then perhaps we can take a step toward coping with our original question by seeing to what extent our lives, as we actually find them, resemble that image, and draw such lessons as we are able to from the comparison.

MEANINGLESS EXISTENCE

A perfect image of meaninglessness, of the kind we are seeking, is found in the ancient myth of Sisyphus. Sisyphus, it will be remembered, betrayed divine secrets to mortals, and for this he was condemned by the gods to roll a stone to the top of a hill, the stone then immediately to roll back down, again to be pushed to the top by Sisyphus, to roll down once more, and so on again and again, *forever*. Now in this we have the picture of meaningless, pointless toil, of a meaningless existence that is absolutely *never* redeemed. It is not even redeemed by a death that, if it were to accomplish nothing more, would at least bring this idiotic cycle to a close. If we were invited to imagine Sisyphus struggling for awhile and accomplishing nothing, perhaps eventually falling from exhaustion, so that we might suppose him then eventually turning to something having some sort of promise, then the meaninglessness of that chapter of his life would not be so stark. It would be a dark and dreadful dream, from which he eventually awakens to sunlight and reality. But he does not awaken, for there is nothing for him to awaken to. His repetitive toil is his life and reality, and it goes on forever, and it is without any meaning whatever. Nothing ever comes of what he is doing, except simply, more of the same. Not by one step, nor by a thousand, nor by ten thousand does he even expiate by the smallest token the sin against the gods that led him into this fate. Nothing comes of it, nothing at all.

This ancient myth has always enchanted men, for countless meanings can be read into it. Some of the ancients apparently thought it symbolized the perpetual rising and setting of the sun, and others the repetitious crashing of the waves upon the shore. Probably the commonest interpretation is that it symbolizes man's eternal struggle and unquenchable spirit, his determination always to try once more in the face of overwhelming discouragement. This interpretation is further supported by that version of the myth according to which Sisyphus was commanded to roll the stone *over* the hill, so that it would finally roll down the other side, but was never quite able to make it.

I am not concerned with rendering or defending any interpretation of this myth, however. I have cited it only for the one element it does unmistakably contain, namely, that of a repetitious, cyclic activity that never comes to anything. We could contrive other images of this that would serve just as well, and no myth-makers are needed to supply the materials of it. Thus, we can imagine two persons transporting a stone—or even a precious gem, it does not matter—back and forth, relay style. One carries it to a near or distant point where it is received by the other; it is returned to its starting point, there to be recovered by the first, and the process is repeated over and over. Except in this relay nothing counts as winning, and nothing brings the contest to any close, each step only leads to a repetition of itself. Or we can imagine two groups of prisoners, one of them engaged in digging a prodigious hole in the ground that is no sooner finished than it is filled in again by the other group, the latter then digging a new hole that is at once filled in by the first group, and so on and on endlessly.

Now what stands out in all such pictures as oppressive and dejecting is not that the beings who enact these roles suffer any torture or pain, for it need not be assumed that they do. Nor is it that their labors are great, for they are no greater than the labors commonly undertaken by most men most of the time. According to the original myth, the stone is so large that Sisyphus never quite gets it to the top and must groan under every step, so that his enormous labor is all for nought. But this is not what appalls. It is not that his great struggle comes to nothing, but that his existence itself is without meaning. Even if we suppose, for example, that the stone is but a pebble that can be carried effortlessly, or that the holes dug by the prisoners are but small ones, not the slightest meaning is introduced into their lives. The stone that Sisyphus moves to the top of the hill, whether we think of it as large or small, still rolls back every time, and the process is repeated forever. Nothing comes of it, and the work is simply pointless. That is the element of the myth that I wish to capture.

Again, it is not the fact that the labors of Sisyphus continue forever that deprives them of meaning. It is, rather, the implication of this: that they come to nothing. The image would not be changed by our supposing him to push a different stone up every time, each to roll down again. But if we supposed that these stones, instead of rolling back to their places as if they had never been moved, were assembled at the top of the hill and there incorporated, say, in a beautiful and enduring temple, then the aspect of meaninglessness would disappear. His labor would then have a point, something would come of them all, and although one could perhaps still say it was not worth it, one could not say that the life of Sisyphus was devoid of meaning altogether. Meaningfulness would at least have made an appearance, and we could see what it was.

That point will need remembering. But in the meantime, let us note another way in which the image of meaninglessness can be altered by making only a very slight change. Let us suppose that the gods, while condemning Sisyphus to the fate just described, at the same time, as an afterthought, waxed perversely merciful by implanting in him a strange and irrational impulse; namely, a compulsive impulse to roll stones. We may if we like, to make this more graphic, suppose they accomplish this by implanting in him some substance that has this effect on his character and drives. I call this perverse, because from our point of view there is clearly no reason why anyone should have a persistent and insatiable desire to do something so pointless as that. Nevertheless, suppose that is Sisyphus' condition. He has but one obsession, which is to roll stones, and it is an obsession that is only for the moment appeased by his rolling them—he no sooner gets a stone rolled to the top of the hill than he is restless to roll up another.

Now it can be seen why this little afterthought of the gods, which I called perverse, was also in fact merciful. For they have by this device managed to give Sisyphus precisely what he wants—by making him want precisely what they inflict on him. However it may appear to us, Sisyphus' fate does not appear to him as a condemnation, but the very reverse. His one desire in life is to roll stones, and he is absolutely guaranteed its endless fulfillment. Where otherwise he might profoundly have wished surcease, and even welcomed the quiet of death to release him from endless boredom and meaninglessness, his life is now filled with mission and meaning, and he seems to himself to have been given an entry to heaven. Nor need he even fear death, for the gods have promised him an endless opportunity to indulge his single purpose, without concern or frustration. He will be able to roll stones *forever*.

What we need to mark most carefully at this point is that the picture with which we began has not really been changed in the least by adding this supposition. Exactly the same things happen as before. The only change is in Sisyphus' view of them. The picture before was the image of meaningless activity and existence. It was created precisely to be an image of that. It has not lost that meaninglessness, it has now gained not the least shred of meaningfulness. The stones still roll back as before, each phase of Sisyphus' life still exactly resembles all the others, the task is never completed, nothing comes of it, no temple ever begins to rise, and all this cycle of the same pointless thing over and over goes on forever in this picture as in the other. The *only* thing that has happened is this: Sisyphus has been reconciled to it, and indeed more, he has been led to embrace it. Not, however, by reason or persuasion, but by nothing more rational than the potency of a new substance in his veins.

THE MEANINGLESSNESS OF LIFE

I believe the foregoing provides a fairly clear content to the idea of meaninglessness and, through it, some hint of what meaningfulness, in this sense, might be. Meaninglessness is essentially endless pointlessness, and meaningfulness is therefore the opposite. Activity, and even long, drawn-out and repetitive activity, has a meaning if it has some significant culmination, some more or less lasting end that can be considered to have been the direction and purpose of the activity. But the descriptions so far also provide something else; namely, the suggestion of how an existence that is objectively meaningless, in this sense, can nevertheless acquire a meaning for him whose existence it is.

Now let us ask: Which of these pictures does life in fact resemble? And let us not begin with our own lives, for here both our prejudices and wishes are great, but with the life in general that we share with the rest of creation. We shall find, I think, that it all has a certain pattern, and that this pattern is by now easily recognized.

We can begin anywhere, only saving human existence for our last consideration. We can, for example, begin with any animal. It does not matter where we begin, because the result is going to be exactly the same.

Thus, for example, there are caves in New Zealand, deep and dark, whose floors are quiet pools and whose walls and ceilings are covered with soft light. As one gazes in wonder in the stillness of these caves it seems that the Creator has reproduced there in microcosm the heavens themselves, until one scarcely remembers the enclosing presence of the walls. As one looks more closely, however, the scene is explained. Each dot of light identifies an ugly worm, whose luminous tail is meant to attract insects from the surrounding darkness. As from time to time one of these insects draws near it becomes entangled in a sticky thread lowered by the worm, and is eaten. This goes on month after month, the blind worm lying there in the barren stillness waiting to entrap an occasional bit of nourishment that will only sustain it to another bit of nourishment until. . . . Until what? What great thing awaits all this long and repetitious effort and makes it worthwhile? Really nothing. The larva just transforms itself finally to a tiny winged adult that lacks even mouth parts to feed and lives only a day or two. These adults, as soon as they have mated and laid eggs, are themselves caught in the threads and are devoured by the cannibalist worms, often without having ventured into the day, the only point to their existence having now been fulfilled. This has been going on for millions of years, and to no end other than that the same meaningless cycle may continue for another millions of years.

All living things present essentially the same spectacle. The larva of a certain cicada burrows in the darkness of the earth for seventeen years, through season after season, to emerge finally into the daylight for a brief flight, lay its eggs, and die—this all to repeat itself during the next seventeen years, and so on to eternity. We have already noted, in another connection, the struggles of fish, made only that others may do the same after them and that this cycle, having no other point than itself, may never cease. Some birds span an entire side of the globe each year and then return, only to insure that others may follow the same incredibly long path again and again. One is led to wonder what the point of it all is, with what great triumph this ceaseless effort, repeating itself through millions of years, might finally culminate, and why it should go on and on for so long, accomplishing nothing, getting nowhere. But then one realizes that there is no point to it at all, that it really culminates in nothing, that each of these cycles, so filled with toil, is to be followed only by more of the same. The point of any living thing's life is, evidently, nothing but life itself.

This life of the world thus presents itself to our eyes as a vast machine, feeding on itself, running on and on forever to nothing. And we are part of that life. To be sure, we are not just the same, but the differences are not so

great as we like to think; many are merely invented, and none really cancels
the kind of meaninglessness that we found in Sisyphus and that we find all
around, wherever anything lives. We are conscious of our activity. Our goals,
whether in any significant sense we choose them or not, are things of which
we are at least partly aware and can therefore in some sense appraise. More
significantly, perhaps, men have a history, as other animals do not, such that
each generation does not precisely resemble all those before. Still, if we can in
imagination disengage our wills from our lives and disregard the deep interest
each man has in his own existence, we shall find that they do not so little
resemble the existence of Sisyphus. We toil after goals, most of them—indeed
every single one of them—of transitory significance and, having gained one of
them, we immediately set forth for the next, as if that one had never been, with
this next one being essentially more of the same. Look at a busy street any day,
and observe the throng going hither and thither. To what? Some office or shop,
where the same things will be done today as were done yesterday, and are done
now so they may be repeated tomorrow. And if we think that, unlike Sisyphus,
these labors do have a point, that they culminate in something lasting and,
independently of our own deep interests in them, very worthwhile, then we
simply have not considered the thing closely enough. Most such effort is
directed only to the establishment and perpetuation of home and family; that
is, to the begetting of others who will follow in our steps to do more of the
same. Each man's life thus resembles one of Sisyphus' climbs to the summit
of his hill, and each day of it one of his steps; the difference is that whereas
Sisyphus himself returns to push the stone up again, we leave this to our
children. We at one point imagined that the labor of Sisyphus finally culminated in the creation of a temple, but for this to make any difference it had
to be a temple that would at least endure, adding beauty to the world for the
remainder of time. Our achievements, even though they are often beautiful, are
mostly bubbles; and those that do last, like the sand-swept pyramids, soon
become mere curiosities while around them the rest of mankind continues its
perpetual toting of rocks, only to see them roll down. Nations are built upon
the bones of their founders and pioneers, but only to decay and crumble before
long, their rubble then becoming the foundation for others directed to exactly
the same fate. The picture of Sisyphus is the picture of existence of the individual man, great or unknown, of nations, of the race of men, and of the very life
of the world.

On a country road one sometimes comes upon the ruined hulks of a house
and once extensive buildings, all in collapse and spread over with weeds. A
curious eye can in imagination reconstruct from what is left a once warm and
thriving life, filled with purpose. There was the hearth, where a family once
talked, sang, and made plans; there were the rooms, where people loved, and
babes were born to a rejoicing mother; there are the musty remains of a sofa,
infested with bugs, once bought at a dear price to enhance an ever-growing
comfort, beauty, and warmth. Every small piece of junk fills the mind with

what once, not long ago, was utterly real, with children's voices, plans made, and enterprises embarked upon. That is how these stones of Sisyphus were rolled up, and that is how they became incorporated into a beautiful temple, and that temple is what now lies before you. Meanwhile other buildings, institutions, nations, and civilizations spring up all around, only to share the same fate before long. And if the question "What for?" is now asked, the answer is clear: so that just this may go on forever.

The two pictures—of Sisyphus and of our own lives, if we look at them from a distance—are in outline the same and convey to the mind the same image. It is not surprising, then, that men invent ways of denying it, their religions proclaiming a heaven that does not crumble, their hymnals and prayer books declaring a significance to life of which our eyes provide no hint whatever.[1] Even our philosophies portray some permanent and lasting good at which all may aim, from the changeless forms invented by Plato to the beatific vision of St. Thomas and the ideals of permanence contrived by the moderns. When these fail to convince, then earthly ideals such as universal justice and brotherhood are conjured up to take their places and give meaning to man's seemingly endless pilgrimage, some final state that will be ushered in when the last obstacle is removed and the last stone pushed to the hilltop. No one believes, of course, that any such state will be final, or even wants it to be in case it means that human existence would then cease to be a struggle; but in the meantime such ideas serve a very real need.

THE MEANING OF LIFE

We noted that Sisyphus' existence would have meaning if there were some point to his labors, if his efforts ever culminated in something that was not just an occasion for fresh labors of the same kind. But that is precisely the meaning it lacks. And human existence resembles his in that respect. Men do achieve things—they scale their towers and raise their stones to their hilltops—but every such accomplishment fades, providing only an occasion for renewed labors of the same kind.

But here we need to note something else that has been mentioned, but its significance not explored, and that is the state of mind and feeling with which such labors are undertaken. We noted that if Sisyphus had a keen and unappeasable desire to be doing just what he found himself doing, then, although his life would in no way be changed, it would nevertheless have a meaning for him.

---

[1]A popular Christian hymn, sung often at funerals and typical of many hymns, expresses this thought:

> Swift to its close ebbs out life's little day;
> Earth's joys grow dim, its glories pass away;
> Change and decay in all around I see;
> O thou who changest not, abide with me.

It would be an irrational one, no doubt, because the desire itself would be only the product of the substance in his veins, and not any that reason could discover, but a meaning nevertheless.

And would it not, in fact, be a meaning incomparably better than the other? For let us examine again the first kind of meaning it could have. Let us suppose that, without having any interest in rolling stones, as such, and finding this, in fact, a galling toil, Sisyphus did nevertheless have a deep interest in raising a temple, one that would be beautiful and lasting. And let us suppose he succeeded in this, that after ages of dreadful toil, all directed at this final result, he did at last complete his temple, such that now he could say his work was done, and he could rest and forever enjoy the result. Now what? What picture now presents itself to our minds? It is precisely the picture of infinite boredom! Of Sisyphus doing nothing ever again, but contemplating what he has already wrought and can no longer add anything to, and contemplating it for an eternity! Now in this picture we have a meaning for Sisyphus' existence, a point for his prodigious labor, because we have put it there; yet, at the same time, that which is really worthwhile seems to have slipped away entirely. Where before we were presented with the nightmare of eternal and pointless activity, we are now confronted with the hell of its eternal absence.

Our second picture, then, wherein we imagined Sisyphus to have had inflicted on him the irrational desire to be doing just what he found himself doing, should not have been dismissed so abruptly. The meaning that picture lacked was no meaning that he or anyone could crave, and the strange meaning it had was perhaps just what we were seeking.

At this point, then, we can reintroduce what has been until now, it is hoped, resolutely pushed aside in an effort to view our lives and human existence with objectivity; namely, our own wills, our deep interest in what we find ourselves doing. If we do this we find that our lives do indeed still resemble that of Sisyphus, but that the meaningfulness they thus lack is precisely the meaningfulness of infinite boredom. At the same time, the strange meaningfulness they possess is that of the inner compulsion to be doing just what we were put here to do, and to go on doing it forever. This is the nearest we may hope to get to heaven, but the redeeming side of that fact is that we do thereby avoid a genuine hell.

If the builders of a great and flourishing ancient civilization could somehow return now to see archaeologists unearthing the trivial remnants of what they had once accomplished with such effort—see the fragments of pots and vases, a few broken statues, and such tokens of another age and greatness—they could indeed ask themselves what the point of it all was, if this is all it finally came to. Yet, it did not seem so to them then, for it was just the building, and not what was finally built, that gave their life meaning. Similarly, if the builders of the ruined home and farm that I described a short while ago could be brought back to see what is left, they would have the same feelings. What we construct in our imaginations as we look over these decayed and rusting pieces would reconstruct itself in their very memories, and certainly with unspeakable sadness. The piece of a sled at our feet would revive in them a warm Christmas. And what rich memories would there be in the broken crib? And the weed-covered remains of a fence would reproduce the scene of a great herd of livestock, so laboriously built up over so many years. What was it all worth, if this is the final result? Yet, again, it did not seem so to them through those many years of struggle and toil, and they did not imagine they were building a Gibraltar. The things to which they bent their backs day after day, realizing one by one their ephemeral plans, were precisely the things in which their wills were deeply involved, precisely the things in which their interests lay, and there was no need then to ask questions. There is no more need of them now —the day was sufficient to itself, and so was the life.

This is surely the way to look at all of life—at one's own life, and each day and moment it contains; of the life of a nation; of the species; of the life of the world; and of everything that breathes. Even the glow worms I described, whose cycles of existence over the millions of years seem so pointless when looked at by us, will seem entirely different to us if we can somehow try to view their existence from within. Their endless activity, which gets nowhere, is just what it is their will to pursue. This is its whole justification and meaning. Nor would it be any salvation to the birds who span the globe every year, back and forth, to have a home made for them in a cage with plenty of food and protection, so that they would not have to migrate any more. It would be their condemnation, for it is the doing that counts for them, and not what they hope to win by it. Flying these prodigious distances, never ending, is what it is in their veins to do, exactly as it was in Sisyphus' veins to roll stones, without end, after the gods had waxed merciful and implanted this in him.

A human being no sooner draws his first breath than he responds to the will that is in him to live. He no more asks whether it will be worthwhile, or whether anything of significance will come of it, than the worms and the birds. The point of his living is simply to be living, in the manner that it is his nature to be living. He goes through his life building his castles, each of these beginning to fade into time as the next is begun; yet, it would be no salvation to rest from all this. It would be a condemnation, and one that would in no way be redeemed were he able to gaze upon the things he has done, even if these were beautiful and absolutely permanent, as they never are. What counts is that one should be able to begin a new task, a new castle, a new bubble. It counts only because it is there to be done and he has the will to do it. The same will be the life of his children, and of theirs; and if the philosopher is apt to see in this a pattern similar to the unending cycles of the existence of Sisyphus, and to despair, then it is indeed because the meaning and point he is seeking is not there—but mercifully so. The meaning of life is from within us, it is not bestowed from without, and it far exceeds in both its beauty and permanence any heaven of which men have ever dreamed or yearned for.

For Further Reading

Bambrough, Renford. *Reason, Truth and God.* New York: Barnes & Noble, 1969.
Includes an exhortation to philosophers to concern themselves with philosophies of life.
————. *Wisdom: Twelve Essays.* Totowa, N.J.: Rowman & Littlefield, 1974.

Capps, Walter H., and Donald E. Capps (eds.). *The Religious Personality.* Belmont,
Calif.: Wadsworth, 1970 (paperbound). Centers on the ways religion may orient the
personality.

Fried, C. *An Anatomy of Values: Problems of Personal and Social Choice.* Cambridge,
Mass.: Harvard University Press, 1970.

Friedman, Maurice. *The Hidden Human Image.* New York: Dell, 1974 (paperbound). Wide-ranging discussion of the condition of contemporary human existence.

Hoffer, Eric. *Reflections on the Human Condition.* New York: Harper & Row, 1973.
A longshoreman's comments.

Joske, W. D. "Philosophy and the Meaning of Life," *Australasian Journal of Philosophy,* 52 (1974), 93–104. Argues that philosophy is relevant to determining whether, and
in what sense, life is or is not meaningful.

Kaufmann, Walter. *Without Guilt and Justice: From Decidophobia to Autonomy.*
New York: Peter H. Weyden, 1973. Argues for an emphasis on human creative autonomy.

Margolis, Joseph. *Negativities: The Limits of Life.* Columbus, Ohio: Charles E.
Merrill, 1975. Discusses death, illness, inequality, and related topics.

Mayeroff, Milton. *On Caring.* New York: Harper & Row, 1971. An analysis of what
it means to be human.

Nielsen, Kai. *Ethics Without God.* Buffalo, N.Y.: Prometheus Books, 1973 (paperbound).

Pepper, Stephen C. *The Sources of Value.* Berkeley: University of California Press,
1970.

Peters, Richard S. *Reason and Compassion.* London: Routledge & Kegan Paul, 1973.

Rosen, S. *Nihilism: A Philosophical Essay.* New Haven, Conn.: Yale University
Press, 1969. A defense of a rationally ordered life.

Schacht, Richard. *Alienation.* Garden City, N.Y.: Doubleday, 1971 (paperbound).
A history of the concept.

Thielicke, Helmut. *Nihilism: Its Origin and Nature—With a Christian Answer,* trans.
by John W. Doberstein. New York: Schocken Books, 1969. A sympathetic but critical
study.

Weiss, Paul, and John Weiss. *Right and Wrong: A Philosophical Dialogue Between
Father and Son.* Carbondale, Ill.: Southern Illinois University Press, 1974 (paperbound).

White, F. C. "The Meaning of Life," *Australasian Journal of Philosophy,* 53 (1975),
pp. 148–150. A critique of Joske's argument (see above).

INDEX

ABOUT THE AUTHOR

WILLIAM H. HALVERSON is Associate Dean of University College and Adjunct Professor of Philosophy at The Ohio State University. He holds degrees from Augsburg College (B.A., 1951), Augsburg Seminary (B.Th., 1955), Princeton Seminary (Th.M., 1957), and Princeton University (M.A., 1959; Ph.D., 1961). He has contributed articles to *Mind, The Pacific Philosophy Forum,* and *The Journal of Religion,* and is the author of the widely used text *A Concise Introduction to Philosophy,* which is currently in its fourth edition (New York: Random House, 1981).